EMILY HOBHO

Boer War letters

Yours ever affect^ly

Emily Hobhouse

EMILY HOBHOUSE

Boer War letters

Edited by
RYKIE VAN REENEN

HUMAN & ROUSSEAU
Cape Town   Pretoria   Johannesburg

Publication of this book
at a reasonable price was made possible
by a generous contribution from
the Gencor group

Frontispiece: Portrait by Antoon van Welie, London, 1903.
(War Museum, Bloemfontein).

Copyright © 1984
All rights reserved
First edition 1984
Second edition, second impression 2000
First published in 1984 by
Human & Rousseau (Pty) Ltd.
Design Centre, 179 Loop Street, Cape Town
Typography by Etienne van Duyker
Typeset in 10 on 12 pt. Baskerville
Printed and bound by NBD,
Drukkery Street, Goodwood, Western Cape

ISBN 0 7981 3928 5

CONTENTS

(Illustrations appear between pp. 122 and
123. Sources on p. 546)

Editor's note

At the request of her friend Mrs. Isabella Steyn, wife of the President of the Orange Free State, Emily Hobhouse during the last years of her life wrote "a little memoir of my connection with South Africa". These chapters of a draft autobiography are among the Hobhouse papers in the Steyn collection in the state archives in Bloemfontein. For reasons explained in the preface (pp. 7-9) they are written in the form of a long letter to Mrs. Steyn.

The memoir is fleshed out with contemporary letters and there is a considerable overlap between the letters and the memoir. Since the letters by themselves constitute an almost continuous journal and have all the vividness of on-the-spot reporting, they have been published here free of later comment. Where, however, the memoir of a quarter of a century later adds fresh detail or salient comment, these are added as a follow-on to the relevant letter and are designated thus: *a*), *b*) etc. Numerals in the text refer to the Notes on pp. 435–540. Each group of letters (and in one instance a brief diary) is preceded by a narrative passage from the memoir providing the necessary bridge in time. The introduction to the group entitled *Work in England* has also, where the rough draft of the memoir calls for it, drawn on E. H.'s narrative in the relevant chapter of *The Brunt of the War*.

However, in the section on the Boer home industries the procedure described above could not be followed. E. H. had had her journal letters to family and friends typed for the record, but "alas!" she writes, "I never saw them again." Fortunately, a lively if condensed diary has been preserved, covering the period January to April 1905, which marks the start of the Boer home industries adventure. The story is then taken further by the memoir narrative. Relevant extracts from other contemporary material by E. H. are added at the end of the narrative. Thus, some extant letters to her aunt and brother among her papers in the Steyn collection reflect her spirited interest in South African politics and personalities of this post-war period, as well as her own saddening mood of these years. Her letters to Lady Charlotte Graham Toler, chairman of the Boer home industries committee, focus too exclusively on the industries to be of lasting general interest in their entirety but do provide telling details on the day-to-day running of the schools. Extracts from these have therefore also been incorporated.

Contemporary comment from E. H.'s fellow-workers Margaret Clark and Marion Rowntree which they made available to the editor, appears in the Notes.

1

As a postscript to E. H.'s account of her South African years a final group of letters has been added which does not form part of the original draft autobiography. These have been drawn mainly from the Smuts papers in the state archives, Pretoria, and the Steyn collection in the state archives, Bloemfontein. They are letters about her disrupted visit to South Africa in 1913 to unveil, at President Steyn's request, the women's memorial at Bloemfontein. Her *Vrouwen-Dag* speech shows a broader perspective on the war and the new challenges she envisaged for the women of a future South Africa. It has not lost its relevance.

Some of E. H.'s scattered observations to Mrs. Steyn on writing for the record have been collected from the memoir and are here published as a preface.

Apart from general notes, a separate section has been added on family and friends mentioned in the text. This attempts to give not only the biographical details but to reflect, as far as possible by means of contemporary comment and quotation, a somewhat fuller picture of these people as E. H. knew them.

The manuscript of the memoir is palpably a first draft, as E. H. says in her covering note. It was typed partly by E. H. herself (at times in bed, during her last winter, with the typewriter propped on her knees) and partly by others. Obvious typing errors overlooked by E. H. have been corrected, as have been evident misspellings of Afrikaans surnames and place names, e.g. Oswegan for (van) Aswegen, Kronstadt for Kroonstad; but the sometimes rather eliptical syntax of her hurried letters and her cavalier treatment of military rank, which preserve the flavour of the original, have generally been left unaltered, and little attempt has been made to impose conformity on her lavish, if erratic use of capitals in true Victorian fashion. The notes, however, follow the present trend to capitalize as sparingly as possible. Editorial additions and deletions are marked with square brackets, those of E. H. herself with round brackets and dots. In the letters she copied into her memoir E. H. sometimes gives the opening address and final greetings, sometimes not.

Annotation has been immensely facilitated by recent contemporary source publications, which are gratefully listed among the references on pp. 541–6.

Before and during the preparation of this book personal conversations and interviews were fortunately still possible with several people who knew E. H. and her circle of friends personally and could make their memory vividly real. Among them were Mr. Oliver Hobhouse, Mrs. Margaret Gillett (Clark), Mrs. Marion Wilkinson (Rowntree) and Dr. G. P. Gooch in England, and, in South Africa, Mrs. Steyn, Advocate Gladys Steyn, Dr. Petronella van Heerden, Miss Constance Cloete, Miss Winifred de Villiers (daughter of Mr. "Charlie Avignon" de Villiers), Miss Maynie Fleck, Mrs. May Murray Parker (daughter of Dr. and Mrs. Chas. Murray), Mrs. Hannah Osborn (Rood), Mrs. Jocelyn Purcell (daughter-in-law of Dr. and Mrs. F. W. Purcell), Mrs. Carrol Williamson (daughter of Mr. and Mrs. Charles Molteno, niece of Miss Betty Molteno and pupil of Miss Alice M. Greene) and Mrs. Jacoba von Moltke (Boshoff) who had been in the Aliwal North concentration camp. My indebtedness to them is particularly great.

The team effort to collect photographic material of which in the end only a fraction could be used, has involved, among others, Karel Schoeman, who also drew the present publishers' attention to E. H.'s still unpublished draft autobiography; the always helpful and cheerful personnel of the state archives in Bloemfontein, Pretoria and Cape Town; the photographic division of the Pretoria municipality; the cultural and historical museum in Boom Street, Pretoria; the Africana museum in Johannesburg; the national war museum in Bloemfontein (especially the chairman of its board, Professor M. C. E. van Schoor, and its research officer, Miss Elria Wessels); the national museum in Bloemfontein (notably Mrs. Martie Venter), as well as many other persons such as Mrs. Jocelyn Purcell, Mrs. Carrol Williamson, Mr. Edward Molteno who made available material from the estate of Miss Kathleen Murray, Mrs. Cato Meaker (born Sauer), Mr. Gustav Opperman of the Independent Film Centre, Dr. D. J. J. van Velden and Miss Ilse Pellissier, principal of the Oranje Girls' High School in Bloemfontein, the late Mr. Oliver Hobhouse and Mr. Paul Hobhouse of Hadspen in Somersetshire who, with the trojan help of Judith Wurtzel, saw to it that "Aunt Mary" and "Uncle Arthur" got here in time.

The book has been fortunate in the Human & Rousseau editorial team who handled it: Miss Karin Fischer-Buder who had the unenviable labour of subediting, Mr. Etienne van Duyker, whose sympathetic layout work transformed a monstrous manuscript into elegance, and Miss Petra Pieterse, in charge of nonfiction, whose initial may well have stood for Patience.

Finally there remains one whose wish – well, command – not to be thanked in public places leaves a major debt here unacknowledged.

Wynberg-Yzerfontein
April 1984

Outline of Emily Hobhouse's life

1860 E. H. is born (9 April) to Reginald Hobhouse, rector of St. Ive in Cornwall, and Caroline Salusbury, born Trelawny. She is the fifth of their six surviving children.

1864 E. H.'s youngest brother Leonard is born (8 September).

1876 Her one term at school is terminated by ill health.

1880 Her mother dies after a long, painful illness.

1889 Her sister Maude marries, and she is left alone in the rectory with an ailing father.

1895 Her father dies (27 January) and she leaves St. Ive. Interested in Cornish miners who have emigrated to America she proceeds to Minnesota and does interdenominational church and social welfare work in the rough mining community of Virginia.

1896 With the prospect of marriage to J. C. Jackson, a Virginia business man and mayor at the time, she goes to Mexico and buys a ranch there.

1897 She visits in England and returns to Mexico, accompanied by her cousin.

1898 Her engagement finally broken off and her money largely lost in a speculative venture, she returns to England. She works in the Women's Industrial Committee becoming familiar with methods of investigating need on a large scale. She does research on the history of British children under the factory system prior to the Factory Act, and writes a novel on the subject which, however, she shortly afterwards destroys.

1899 The Anglo-Boer war breaks out (11 October), the South African Conciliation Committee is formed (1 November) and E. H. becomes honorary secretary of its women's branch.

1900 She initiates and organizes the big women's protest meeting against the war in the Queen's Hall, London (13 June). Reports of farm burnings start reaching England and she feels called to succour the destitute Boer women (September). Obtaining government consent for a non-political, non-sectarian South African women and children distress fund, she collects some £300 for the fund, and leaves for South Africa (December).

1901 In Cape Town she learns of the existence of "refugee" camps, obtains permission from Kitchener to visit such camps at and south of Bloemfontein and leaves for the war zone with a train truck of clothing, bedding and footstuffs. On

4

26 January she pays her first visit to the Bloemfontein camp and in the next three months visits other camps in the Orange River and Cape colonies. Appalled by the camps situation she sails for England (7 May) to put the matter before the British government and public. The government, upon her suggestion, makes certain concessions to improve the camps. It also appoints a ladies' committee to investigate the camps but neither includes E. H. in it nor allows her to go back to the camps on her own because of the "sympathy" she is accused of showing the Boer women. She nevertheless again leaves for South Africa (October) with the purpose, she explains, of visiting British refugees in the coastal towns. When her ship, the R.M.S. *Avondale*, anchors in Table Bay she is not allowed to land and is later forcibly transferred to the troop-ship *Roslin Castle* and deported under martial law.

1902 She retires to the south of France to recuperate and to work on her first Boer War book, *The Brunt of the War and where it fell*, which is published later in the same year. The peace of Vereeniging is signed (31 May) and E. H. returns to England, starting a "furnishing fund" (into which she also pays her royalties) for destitute Boer families returning to burnt-out farms.

1903 She returns to South Africa to investigate post-war conditions in the former republics. She visits the ruined districts in the Orange River and Transvaal colonies. Aghast at the "repatriation muddle", the compensation situation and the starvation she meets, she takes steps in South Africa and England which to an important extent alleviate the situation.

1904 Back in England, she takes up a plan, conceived on her visit in 1903, of starting Boer home industries as a measure of rehabilitation and reconciliation. With this aim in view she studies lace-making and spinning and weaving in Europe and Ireland. The death of her uncle, Lord Hobhouse, leaves her torn between her desire to stay with her aged and bereaved aunt and her commitment to get the industries started.

1905 Encouraged by her aunt she sails for South Africa, taking two helpers with her. The first spinning and weaving school gets under way at Philippolis (13 March) and a second at Langlaagte (August). Meanwhile her aunt's death in May leaves her without any family responsibilities in England.

1906 She builds a cottage for herself in the Johannesburg suburb Bellevue, from where she intends supervising both schools. In April she visits England to consult with her committee on the future of the schools.

1907 Industrial education is taken over by the newly granted responsible government of the Transvaal. The Johannesburg school moves to Pretoria and E. H. follows suit. She is appointed adviser to the board managing public funds for the schools. She then arranges with the new responsible government in the Orange River Colony to take over the schools of that colony as well.

1908 Finding her post as adviser to the board a sinecure, she resigns (August). Shortly before she leaves South Africa (October) the Pretoria homecraft coun-

5

cil, in recognition of her services to the industries, presents her with a portrait of herself by Hugo Naude. She takes a young Boer girl, Johanna Rood, with her to Europe to study lace-making (thus equipped, Miss Rood starts the first lace-making school at Koppies in 1909). For reasons of health and climate E. H. now lives mainly in Italy, with regular visits to England.

1913 Invited by President Steyn to unveil the women's memorial at Bloemfontein she is prevented by the condition of her heart from getting beyond Beaufort West but her speech for the occasion is read and distributed at the ceremony (16 December).

1914 World War I breaks out and E. H. is involved in the international women's movement for peace and works at its secretariat in Amsterdam for three months. She concerns herself with the plight of Belgian and other refugees and prisoners-of-war. She also makes a controversial attempt to mediate personally between Great Britain and Germany, going on a secret mission to Germany to interview the minister of foreign affairs, Von Jagow, in Berlin.

1919 After the war she throws herself into the work of alleviating starvation in Europe and is involved in the Swiss Relief fund, the Russian Babies' fund (which she chairs) and eventually the comprehensive Save the Children fund to which South Africa, at her request, contributes substantially.

1921 A South African fund started by Mrs. Steyn enables E. H. to buy a house at St. Ives on the Cornwall coast. With, at last, a home of her own she starts collecting and sorting her letters with a view to an autobiography and a memoir of her South African work as requested by Mrs. Steyn.

1923 She moves to London, to be nearer her friends and events of the day. Her translation from "the Taal" of the diary of Mrs. Alida M. Badenhorst is published as *Tant' Alie of Transvaal, her diary (1880–1903)*. She also works on her translation of her collection of other Boer women's war reminiscences which, as a pioneer source document on civilian suffering in war, is published after her death: *War without Glamour* (1927).

1924 An Afrikaans translation of her *The Brunt of the War* is published: *Die Smarte van die oorlog en wie dit gely het.*

1925 She rents a bungalow at Chichester on the Sussex coast for the winter and, all but bed-ridden and with inadequate domestic help, continues work on her memoir.

1926 She goes for a visit to the Isle of Wight but, taken seriously ill, returns to London by ambulance and dies (8 June) of what in her death certificate is described as pleurisy, cardiac degeneration and some internal form of cancer. There is a burial service at St. Mary Abbot's church in Kensington. Her ashes, however, are placed in a niche at the women's memorial at Bloemfontein (26 October).

"It was a great occasion and we buried her like a princess," Smuts writes to her nephew and executor, Oliver Hobhouse.

Preface

To Mrs. Steyn

I draw rather largely, dear Friend, upon my old letters because rereading them I see that they constitute a running comment upon my comings and goings – almost a journal. A real journal I never could attain to. I think I am temperamentally incompetent. Over and over again I have bought a fat MS book and begun a journal, but none of them get beyond three or four pages. I regret it now and would too gladly find some daily account of my work. For such writing, however, it has seemed a necessity in my case to have the human factor – I could only write as if *to* someone. Consequently I wrote very fully and regularly[1] to my Aunt or Brother, though naturally in too careless or familiar a manner to admit of wholesale quotations.

This curious feeling of wanting some sympathetic person to whom to speak with the pen persists, and you see an instance in this memoir which I felt I could *not* write except in the form of a letter to yourself. Possibly this is the result of a solitary life. The greater part of mine has been spent in silence, without mental or spiritual companionship, often without even the relief of a servant to speak to. The human desire for interchange of speech is strong, and was, I think, the force which inspired my constant letters. My pen was my tongue. To sit down and talk to *myself* in a *diary* was only to accentuate solitariness, and I invariably shrank from the effort.

The letters faithfully depict feelings that then existed, exaggerated and vehement as they may now seem. A generation has passed and Time has done in your country, too, the wonders it always does do. We can, I believe, look on this picture as one whose face is turned to the wall.

There are odd holes in memory or, at any rate, in mine. I wonder if everyone has the experience that small, even trivial, incidents attach themselves while events ardently desired and immensely cared about have vanished and no effort will recall them. Since writing these pages for you I have frequently paused, struck by the peculiarities of memory. It happens that I have beside me a pile of letters and whenever I have written an account which I remember "quite clearly", as we say, I turn to these for verification. You would be surprised how often I have convicted myself of inaccuracy. So, for the sake of exactness, I have written little beyond whaᵗ is verified in these contemporary letters. They, too, may err, but at least they record impressions and opinions accepted and acted upon at the moment.

As to memory, I now realise the danger suggested by Schopenhauer:

"Memory always idealizes and sometimes almost transfigures the attitude we have taken up at any period of the past." He ascribes this to "the inability to remember all the fleeting influences which disturbed us on any given occasion. Memory is, in this respect, like the lens of a camera obscura: it contracts everything within its range, and so produces a much finer picture than the actual landscape affords."

I give this quotation upon memory in general though it does not all apply to the case in point, but because it does to memoirs as a whole. It seems worth the digression, for I want you to bear it in mind, lest in reading what from the very nature of the thing is a condensing of incidents I have been connected with, you should carry away a better impression than is true. Affectionate and just I know you will be and I ask no more. The danger has haunted me all along in writing these recollections. It is instinctive and almost unconscious to try and make the best of oneself. It is like putting on one's best clothes to appear in company.

Schopenhauer does not explain, however, why unimportant incidents so often stay in mind while others of far more influence in one's life vanish completely. There may be different reasons but it has happened so often in my life that I have given the matter careful observation and convinced myself that it is a matter of health. If one has heart trouble and a consequently imperfect circulation, the brain is often insufficiently nourished. When an event is of special interest, emotional excitement still further impedes the action of heart and circulation; the brain is empty, lacks vigour and receptive power, and memory has no record. It is worth dwelling upon this item because it will make you better understand one of the trials of my sort of illness which has naturally increased as circulation has become more impeded. It causes many misunderstandings. If people ask me questions or tell me anything when I am standing up, I am unable to answer or to remember. It has become a habit now to lie down before listening to anything of importance. When on my feet I have no power of retaining what is said to me.

As I read over the old letters and papers of sixty years, the first thing that strikes me is the many mistakes I have made – the frequent misjudgement of men and things. Viewing it all in the light of riper experience I see in a flash how much better I could have acted, or written, or spoken. Is this, I wonder, a universal experience? Waller must have felt this when he wrote:[2]

> "The soul's dark cottage, battered and decayed,
> Lets in new light through chinks that time has made.
> Stronger by weakness, wiser men become
> As they draw near to their eternal home."

Secondly, I am struck how *pain passes*, whether physical, mental or spiritual. Gashes may be left, but they *do* heal. One can read with surprise the burning words written under pressure of some torture through which one has passed.

And thirdly, how often I have been misunderstood – almost entirely from my lack of ability to explain myself, through lack of ready words, or through lack of courage.

. . . I like Maeterlinck's thought: "The dead live again every time we remember them."[3] If this is true, perhaps the best of me, dear Friend, will come to life every time you recall me to your mind. It is a solace to feel that, as I pen these words to you.

The camps
1899 – 1901

Introduction

The spring of 1899 was very beautiful and we spent it at Crowsley Park in Oxfordshire not far from Shiplake on the Thames. It was lent to my Uncle by Colonel Baskerville. I shall never forget the beauty of the garden nor the song of the nightingales there – contrast after influenza in my chambers! I took long walks with my Uncle and little Meg, his dog, and long drives with my Aunt.

This beloved pair formed indeed the very background and foundation of my life for very many years. They were full of character, of wide knowledge and experience and, childless themselves, beloved by a large circle of nephews and nieces of two generations. In their own old-fashioned way they were immensely hospitable. With Aunt Mary one could talk at times on ordinary topics such as household affairs and even clothes, but much as I loved them I never found it easy to talk to them very confidentially. The conversation at their table was always on a lofty plane no matter what the subject introduced, and at no other table have I since met with such well-informed and interesting people, and it is one of the things I have missed most since they left us.

Those weeks were full of peace and loveliness, but it was calm before long years of storm. Already the clouds were gathering. Milner's[1] dispatches from South Africa filled many wise men with apprehension. I well remember one dispatch from sir Alfred which I read out at the breakfast table at that time. "That means war in my opinion," said Lord Hobhouse, who was much disturbed by it. To my inexperience it seemed incredible, but he was right and the clouds darkened as the summer advanced.

Lord Hobhouse never labelled himself a pacifist but he certainly was one in the best possible sense. He was always against the arbitrament of war, never failed to recognise errors on both sides, saw always points where peace could be maintained by methods of reason, and never shrank from a general exposure of the underlying causes of wars – greed, desire of territory, commercial advantages, and so forth. His judicial position in the Privy Council made public expression of his views on any existing wars impossible, but privately they were well known. The following sentences from a short article on Patriotism, written by request of an advanced London Journal, indicate his line of thought. The little article was one of a series which the Editor was publishing from the pens of leading public men:

13

"If you can make people see that a nation does not become great by increasing the number of its subjects without regard to quality or proximity; that extension of dominion by military force brings weakness and not strength; that peace cannot be had except by scrupulous observance of justice and moderation towards the weak as well as the strong; that to insist on having our own way means war; that patriotism is the readiness of man to sacrifice himself for his country and not his readiness to exalt his country at the expense of others; that the truest and bravest patriots are those who dare to warn their countrymen when hurrying in ignorance or passion to do wrong; that to support one's country in ill-doing is as selfish as to support his family or friends or Party in ill-doing; that precisely the same moral laws and sanctions apply to nations as to the individuals who compose them, . . . that to do as one would be done by is the golden rule for all, whether acting in multitudes or singly; that to admit an error and to make reparation for a wrong is just as wise for a nation as for a man; that large armaments are a serious danger to the nation that creates them; that those who take away the liberty of others are on the highway to lose their own; that free thought and speech are, with occasional friction and inconvenience, the very life-blood of mankind without which they dwindle into insignificance . . . if these maxims are made more acceptable by your agency, you may when your work is done lie down to rest with the assurance that it is good."

South Africa filled the public mind throughout the summer as the long negotiations dragged on. Lady Hobhouse was fully in accord with the aims of the South African Conciliation Committee[2] which started its campaign of education that autumn. I had joined this excellent body, being most kindly invited to do so by its President, Mr. Leonard Courtney, and acquaintances there met became the friends of many years. "The keynote of the committee", wrote Mr. Courtney, "is Conciliation, and it aims at keeping before the public the necessity of people of Dutch and English extraction living together in South Africa and living in friendly relations, if there is to be any peace." We were exhorted to press the truth as we saw it with zeal and courage but without temper or exaggeration.[3] By means of this committee facts were received from the best and most reliable South African sources and disseminated throughout the country by ardent workers, and many were the meetings at which we spoke. It was by this means that I first came into contact with South Africa, her history and her affairs, and, free from that period, I gave myself whole-heartedly to the cause, gradually dropping or delegating to others work I had previously been doing.[4]

Just before we assembled at Charlton House near Bristol in August, my Uncle and Aunt celebrated their golden wedding, going for this purpose alone to the coast at Devonshire where, fifty years before, their first honeymoon had been spent. They entertained a great deal that year, young and old, rich and poor, and many of the arrangements fell to my share. Nevertheless, as Charlton House is but a few miles from Bristol I was able to do something towards building up the Conciliation Committee in that town.

We were hardly back in London before the storm broke. There had been days of growing tension. I well remember the crucial moment when coming through Trafalgar Square I saw the Ultimatum placarded and knew the last hope was gone. War was declared October the 11th, 1899. It sounded the death knell of tens of thousands of people completely innocent of its cause and it bore within it seeds of things worse than death for England.

From this moment it was difficult to concentrate the mind on anything but the war. Few except those who had been absorbing the facts presented by the Conciliation Committee in London and Manchester were prepared for the struggle that ensued.

I was then living in a flat in Chelsea where I had greater liberty for the work of sending out pamphlets, speaking at meetings and attending them. I had there too, near at hand,[5] the helpful guidance of Mr. Courtney, always willing to help the politically ignorant. He was so wonderfully easy of approach, so lenient towards inexperience, so wise in pointing out the best way that few of my generation ever left his house without feeling mentally enlightened and morally strengthened.

Hitherto my work in the Women's Industrial Committee had done much to open my eyes to need on a large scale, together with methods of investigation; it had also impelled me to a long course of reading in the British Museum where I studied amongst other things the history of our children under the factory system prior to the passing of the Factory Acts. In this way I learned much of the dire results of overcrowding and of underfeeding and suchlike ills in their effects upon child life. Indeed, I had employed much of that year in writing a story dealing with the children of that day and this book was completed on the eve of the outbreak of war. I then tied it up and never looked at it again except to burn. It was not for others to read but for my own education. That was abundantly clear. It was but another of the curious preparations which I underwent for the work that was coming . . .

In December a large audience gathered in the long dining-room in Bruton Street to hear Mr. Frederic Harrison[6] lecture on the history of English dealings with the Cape. This meeting was at the instigation of Mr. George Lefevre and Mr. Arthur Elliot and the invitations were issued by them . . .

War fever did indeed permeate the country in a most alarming – and as the months advanced, most increasing – way. Few of that generation had ever seen such exhibitions of national passion. I had seen something similar . . . as recorded earlier, in the United States of America, when during the trouble with Cuba,[7] war passion seized the people and patriotism shewed itself in wearing flags and suchlike puerilities. Little did I think I should ever see English people similarly roused. I had thought it was just due to American excitability. Since those far-off days we have all had too much opportunity for studying war-fever in all its stages and degrees, from mere puerilities and credulities down to the extremest exhibitions of inhumanity and cruelties. From the close of 1899 onward, truth and reason were obscured and every difficulty faced those (and they were but few) who kept cool heads. This excitability, fanned by the Press and the Pulpit, culminated on what was known as Mafeking night (18 May)[8] when the populace poured into the streets of London and in mad exultation over the taking and relief of that tiny village indulged in all kinds of license and buffoonery. A leading feature of the proceedings was the tickling with feathers; numbers armed themselves with peacock feathers for that purpose, insolently tickling the faces of passers-by, and obliging self-respecting citizens to remain within doors. Indeed, the feather-tickling scourge continued for some time to annoy the public but one trusts is now as dead as the verb "to Mafeking"[9] which, as descriptive of any form of mad and undue excitement, threatened at one time to find a permanent place in the language. But this is somewhat of a digression.

Meetings of the South African Conciliation Committee or S.A.C.C. as it was familiarly known, were usually held in private houses and it was after one of these at the Courtneys' house in December 1899 that a holiday in Switzerland was mooted. It had been a year of hard work and many of us needed change. Thither, therefore, the Courtneys went for Christmas and my brother and I followed with other friends, joining them at Caux.

I look back on it as one of the few real holidays of my life. The exhilarating air, the beauty of the Swiss mountains, the companionship of interesting and sympathetic friends combined with the real if childish enjoyment of the winter sports in the snow, formed material for a few weeks of what would have been perfect mental rest had not the war cast its shadow over all . . . It was memorable as the last time of feeling young. We drew our toboggans up the hill, then, sitting down on them, slid over the snow like lightning; we then dragged them up the hill again, patiently continuing this simple but healthy exercise till dusk. I remember how I laughed on arrival at the station to see the staid and dignified Mr. Courtney drawing his toboggan by a string, but found I had to follow suit and was soon racing him down a precipitous hill round abrupt corners, and doing it in $2\frac{1}{2}$ to his 3 minutes.

We had barely three weeks, and were in London again by mid-January [. . .] We returned to a year of singularly hard work – against collar all the way. A very great support, however, for all on the side of sanity, was the appearance in January of a London edition of the *Manchester Guardian*. Previously, for daily organ, we had been reduced to the small but plucky efforts of the *Morning Leader*. Many were the meetings one spoke at in town and country. Pre-war work which I had still on hand had perforce to be dropped or delegated as the war increased in ferocity and the larger subject filled the mind's horizon. A woman's branch of the South African Committee was formed of which I became Honorary Secretary and this entailed much work.

Wintry weather had put both my Aunt and Uncle on the sicklist and in addition a young Indian medical student who shared my flat was laid up with a painful disease of the eyes requiring much care. "So," I wrote to my brother on 2 February, "my hands are full but I stole time last night for the debate and heard Chamberlain questioned and his honour assailed.[10] I thought he looked cowed, miserable and unlike his jaunty self. And I heard Sir Edward Grey, so slim and boyish-looking, stand in front of the long line of grey-headed ministers and scold them as if they were schoolboys, himself with all the solemnity of a schoolmaster . . . We had such a meeting at the Queen's Hall for Frederic Harrison – you would have warmed your soul at the fire of his eloquence."

During those days a Liberal conference was preparing for 14 February which I greatly wished my Brother would attend. The divided party needed leadership. I wrote to my Brother:

"I believe Mr. Courtney is dying to be there, but he told me to be discreet and say nothing. What a pity you won't all 'kiss and be friends'. You really all *must* keep coming together and consulting till you find who is the 'coming man' amongst you. If you don't, it will be Sir Edward Grey and Imperialism. If I were a man I'd stir Heaven and Earth rather than let it be him. You are all so hopeless. I wish I were an M.P. I could hardly help speaking through the grating last Thursday."

My Brother, however, did not see his way to leave Manchester, and on the 17th I wrote him as follows:

"I was very sorry when I got to the Liberal conference not to find you there. It would have done you good. For over two hours we were lapped in the luxury of absolute unanimity of feeling; Liberals to right of you, Liberals to left of you, Liberals in front of you volleyed and thundered. It gave a nice warm feeling, with no cold Conservative draught anywhere. Mr. Cronwright-Schreiner[11] at one elbow, Mr. Farrer with his cosmopolitan sympathies at the other and *Punch's* 'Vagrant' in the Chair. Nevertheless, I have one thing against that Liberal conference in that they were so far luke-warm, so far *bad* Liberals, that *they did not invite a single woman* to share their deliberations. Is not this to cut off their best arm, their most ardent support, their most enthusiastic workers and relegate them to a lower place? Had it not been that a few women under Miss Bryce thought of giving the delegates tea and so for very shame were allowed in, even the 9 of us who were there would have demanded admittance in vain! How long is man to be approached through his stomach and through that only?"

My work was interrupted by the necessity of taking my Indian friend to Italy, and thither my Uncle very kindly sent us for her recovery. For the first time in my life I did not feel anxious to go abroad; but I could not refuse and we visited Venice and Rome, returning before the end of April.

During these weeks Miss E. D. Bradby – always a tower of strength in this cause – kindly took my place on the women's branch and continued to organize our methods of work, drawing-room meetings, discussion groups and instruction classes . . . My Aunt helped our branch by giving a drawing-room meeting at which Mr. Cronwright-Schreiner spoke. He had also spoken at the Liberal conference with excellent effect. His visit to England had done much to keep us in touch with Colonial opinion, and many other South African families that came and went brought vivid accounts of the intensity of feeling in the Cape Colony and the unsettling effects that would follow annexation. This feeling was by no means confined to the Dutch; it was shared by many of English name, including the Editor of the *South African News*.[12]

Studying old documents and papers is to realize once again the passion of indignation felt by a considerable section of our country at the threat of annexation. Many who had taken the war lightly or even willingly as far as to give the Boers a beating, paused before the injustice of annexation. "Self-determination" was not in fashion with our Statesmen then. We longed to protest, and it occurred to me that women, at least, might make a public protest without rousing undue criticism.

The idea came to me at a small dinner-party given by Mr. Courtney's sister, Mrs. Oliver, at her house in Collingham Gardens. The dinner was of a private nature, only old Miss Williams and myself beside the Courtneys and our hosts. The coming annexation was discussed and deplored and when the obstacles to a general protest were dealt with and felt to be overwhelming, I, as Honorary Secretary of the Women's Branch of the South African Conciliation Committee, proposed that we, the women, should hold a meeting of protest. To my great joy, but considerable surprise, Mr. Courtney agreed in principle to the proposal [. . .] Thus backed, I carried the idea to our next women's committee and urged it there with success.

A date, 13 June 1900, was fixed, and, resolving to do it on a large scale as a demonstration of real importance, the Queen's Hall was secured. From that moment my flat in Chelsea became organizing Headquarters and with the devoted help of Miss Anna Griffin we began on 1 May the arduous work of preparation. We formed, of course, branches throughout London with excellent workers but even so, six weeks is scant time for filling the Queen's Hall with women only and all the drawbacks of an unpopular subject in time of war.

There was an immense opposition to contend with and the conciliation attitude to be always maintained. The great bulk of the correspondence fell on Miss Griffin and we laboured from 8 a.m. to – often – 11 p.m. for those six weeks. The result

18

was a magnificent assemblage of women, representative not only of London but of the entire country, for it was attended by delegates of the Women's Liberal Foundation which was holding its meetings at the time . . .

I write to you rather fully about this meeting because I know full well how sore a trial it has been to you and your People to lose your independence as a result of that War, and I feel it may be an alleviation after all these many years to know that a large section of the English People worked hard in protest against it. True, we hardly perhaps realized at that time how very deeply it would pierce your hearts, and our protest was more largely due to our proud desire for England's Honour and our horror lest her Rectitude be marred by an unjust act . . .

Our poet William Watson, the passionate lover of a lofty-minded England, embodied our view in the sonnet he wrote for our meeting at the special request of Mrs. Courtney. He wrote:

"Yet being brave, being women, you will speak
The thought that must be spoken without fear.
The voice of chivalry is faint; the note
Of patriotism is well-nigh overborne.
For what is patriotism but noble care
For our own country's Honour in men's eyes."[13]

Madame San Carolo's vigorous recitation of this poem brought out the full weight of his thought and thus added a fine touch to the meeting.

Free admission to the hall was decided on by the committee but only for bearers of tickets supplied by me. There was need for this caution in those days. Besides, it was to be a purely women's meeting and as a matter of fact *no* men were present, except, it was said, the organ blower! I recall with amusement Mr. Courtney's keen wish to be present and how he begged me for a ticket, but there was the strict prohibition of men and, besides, Mrs. Courtney was nervous and did not wish him to be present fearing lest there should be disturbances. For those were turbulent days. We had great fun over this little plot, for plot it was, as he was determined to be there and continued to beg me secretly for a ticket. I was adamant as regards allowing him into the hall, but on his solemn promise that he would come no further than the corridor and be content to listen behind the curtain, I eventually gave way. I well remember catching sight of the fine dome of his head against the red *portière* just as I was making my own speech and how nervous it made me.

Below are the resolutions passed with, I believe, only one dissentient, and that feeble voice was, by some accounts, the cry of a baby!

"Resolution I
That this meeting of women brought together from all parts of the United Kingdom condemns the unhappy war now raging in South Africa as mainly due to the

bad policy of the Government, a policy which has already cost in killed, wounded and missing over 20 000 of our bravest soldiers, and the expenditure of millions of money drawn from the savings and toil of our People, while to the two small States with whom we are at war, it is bringing utter ruin and desolation.

"Resolution II
That this meeting protests against the attempts to silence, by disorder and violence, all freedom of speech, or criticism of Government policy.

"Resolution III
That this meeting protests against any settlement which involves the extinction by force of two republics whose inhabitants, allied to us by blood and religion, cling as passionately to their separate nationality and flag as we in this country do to ours.

"Resolution IV
That this meeting desires to express its sympathy with the women of the Transvaal and Orange Free State, and begs them to remember that thousands of English women are filled with profound sorrow at the thought of their sufferings, and with deep regret for the action of their own Government.[14]
"God Save the Queen."

I was not amongst the list of distinguished women who were the published speakers,[15] but when it was finally resolved to append the fourth resolution it fell to me to propose it. It chimed with my feelings and formed the keynote of my life and thoughts for years to come. And now, in my old age, the tables are turned and the women of the two former republics think with sympathy of me in my weakness and constantly, by work and deed, show me that they never forget.

Amongst the many sins and iniquities which were at that time attributed to our Boer enemies was that of ingratitude. We must all testify as we know and I can only say that the overflowing gratitude shewn to me by the mass of the Boer People, thousands of whom have never even seen me, must be almost, if not quite, unique. It would be almost impossible to sum up the instances. Apart from the touching presentation of a little house in which they wished me to end my days in comfort and to the gift of which many thousands contributed,[16] even now, a quarter of a century after my work for them, every year brings me a birthday gift in the form of a box of their delicious farm products sent me in rotation by one after another of the little country towns of the Free State. I call this my Wonder Box[17] and truly, it has all the character and charm of a fairy gift. Indeed, it is one of the leading characteristics of a Boer that he never forgets a kind deed or a kindly word. But this is a digression.

[. . .] This vast meeting [. . .] was an undoubted success. Many had criticised it on the score of its uselessness for practical results. I had put this point before Mr.

Courtney who replied that even when nothing practical could result it was always well to register calm, combined *protest* against injustice. It is, I feel, also well that the two former republics should know, as a matter of history, that we women did do so. When it was over we all felt the relief of people who have given due vent to their feelings.

The Jingo Press, of course, excelled itself in virulence and inaccuracy and made it almost impossible to give Truth even a bare chance. There was one paper we used to nickname the *Daily Liar*. I had always kept as far as possible apart from journals of this type but one day its representative was sent to interview me. Being Sunday, my maid was absent and opening the door myself, I was caught. He was admitted before I knew his errand. The incident, which has implanted in me a lifelong contempt for press opinion, comes back to me as I read an old letter to my Brother describing the scene:

"I have been so amused, I must tell you. I have just been interviewed by the *Daily Liar*. To my surprise I found him a human being – more – he had a heart – more still – he confessed to being a very strong pro-Boer and said (though I must not publish it) that in his opinion most of the journalists were. 'But what can we do,' he said, 'we have to write as we are told, to get our daily bread'. I lectured him and told him to temper the *Daily Liar*. He said if anything nasty was put in about us it would be the sub-editor, not him. He said the reason for the virulence was because it was a forced thing – not what they really felt – but they were paid to put that side forward and had to, or lose their livelihood, like lawyers defending a bad case, he said. (He forgot that in the trial the lawyer on the other side has equal chance of putting forward his facts.) He went away promising me to temper his share of the paper. It was funny to have the *Daily Liar* confessing its sins to me and baring its inmost heart."

It was shortly after this, early in July, that I went down to Liskeard with Mr. Lloyd George to speak at a meeting. Liskeard is in Cornwall, about four miles from my old home.[18] The meeting, under the auspices of the Women's Branch of the S.A.C.C., was organized locally mainly by the Quakers in the vicinity. Mr. Quiller-Couch (now Sir Arthur), the distinguished Cornish author, was the Chairman. We needed one with tact and patience and he had both, but even he could not cope with the planned and prepared rowdyism which disgraced Liskeard that day. Not one of us was allowed really to deliver a speech. Some never uttered a word. The hall was crowded and round about the platform were thronging friends from my childhood, people who had walked in from St. Ive to see and hear me once more. Their tears fell as the mob of roughs howled us down. These finally stormed the platform, hurling forms and chairs at our heads.

Mr. Lloyd George spoke no syllable, he who could so have charmed! I can see him now, facing the storm, erect, courageous but stern and absolutely mute. We

21

stood our ground for an hour till indeed it was no longer prudent; then finally, as the missiles flew, there was no alternative but to retreat into the green-room at the back of the platform. There the organizing committee received us with streaming eyes and shamed apologies for their town. They hurried us across the open parade to our hotel. And it was as well. The bad feeling was especially directed against Mr. Lloyd George and I admired his cool courage throughout the evening. We were told that all sorts of wild tales had been deliberately circulated to work up feeling against him. How little they dreamed, those passion-blinded people of Liskeard, that the man they would not hear would one day lead the country! I find among my papers the little account of his expenses to Cornwall. He wrote:

"I very much regret that the committee could get so little for their money, but I am sure you will admit that that was no fault of mine! Better luck next time."

Mr. Quiller-Couch summed up the essence of the affair in a very dignified letter to the *Western Morning News* which proved unanswerable.

Liskeard was the stronghold of Mr. Courtney's constituency[19] and the hope that this meeting might do good to his political chances was thus quenched; it probably did harm; at any rate, another candidate was selected and the Seat lost.

For me this meeting and several others at which I spoke during the summer were followed by a storm of abuse from relatives and acquaintances, some of whom even attacked me in the press. I lost the majority of the friends of my girlhood and it was a great loss. There was a divergence of principle at that time which broke many a bond, and taking up the work publicly I could not escape a painful severance of old ties. Some compensation there has been in the closeness of many new friendships then formed, yet these later ones lack some precious qualities that seem to belong only to the ties made in youth.

In her quiet room in Bruton Street my old Aunt awaited with unfailing sympathy and interest the result of the Cornish meeting. She was disappointed. She felt so keenly the folly and disgrace of these exhibitions of passion and rowdyism. In those days she had been led to parody Rudyard Kipling's fine *Recessional*[20] in these terms:

"For we, with Empire drunk, let loose
Wild tongues to shout, base pens to write,
Slanders and lies and boast to use
That stir the blood, that rouse the fight.
God of all men – condemn us not.
We have forgot, we have forgot.

"For heathen hearts that put their trust
In heaps of gold, in hosts of men,

22

To friends untrue, to foes unjust,
In quest of England's seeming gain;
For ruthless deed, for vengeful word
Have mercy on our People, Lord."
etc.

The executive of the S.A.C.C. maintained continued correspondence with our fellow-subjects, the leaders of thought and action in the Cape Colony, as well as with well-known South Africans who visited England on and off during that year.

As you will recollect, feeling in the Cape Colony had found its first deep expression in the People's Congress at Graaff-Reinet, 31 May of that year. This representative gathering, under the impression, largely correct, that the English People were misinformed or ignorant of the real state of affairs and feelings at the Cape, decided to send delegates to England.[21] To use their own words, "These delegates shall go as from us, the People, to the People of Great Britain and Ireland . . . to tell the simple truth as they know it concerning the real facts of the South African situation." More sensible a plan could not have been proposed, only it should have been done a year sooner.

As is known, this great congress was followed by some twenty others throughout the Colony, and while these were passing similar resolutions the deputation from Graaff-Reinet took ship and reached London in the second week of July. They were joined on arrival by the Rev. Moorrees of the Paarl. We welcomed them most heartily, hoping, if they could get a hearing, their message, delivered with such pathetic simplicity, might reach the hearts if not the heads of England.

I well remember how lost these good men seemed in our big London in the midst of the gay and crowded season, coming from the space and solitude of their land; and though, too, coming from a warmer climate, how incapable of standing the oppressive heat of a London July!

Professor De Vos was the leader of the deputation and his saintly bearing and old-world dignity made a deep impression. He resembled some prophet of old. My Aunt had a large drawing-room meeting to meet and listen to them. It was a lovely day and very hot. The afternoon wore on and the delegates did not appear. The guests were arriving and the packed room growing oppressive. Anxiety grew, so, asking someone to fill the gap by an improvised address, I hastily hailed a hansom and dashed across London to find the delinquents. They were in their boarding-house having quite forgotten the day, hour and place! I bundled Professor De Vos into the cab and entreating the others to follow as soon as they had changed their coats, which they pleaded hard to do, I drove the one I had caught at fullest speed back to Bruton Street where the guests awaited him. Alas! we had no rapid taxis in those days. He, fortunately, was able to fill the time till his colleagues appeared. Few will forget his impressive words and prophetic mien. Unperturbed by the unseemly hurry to which I had subjected him, he delivered the message entrusted to him by his compatriots with calm dignity, speaking with closed eyes and folded hands as though in prayer. He seemed to have stepped out of the Old Testament into our garish modern life.

But the People of Great Britain, as a whole, did not want or welcome messengers from the People of their colony of the Cape. Though much trouble was taken to prepare meetings for them, few were the places and few the people who would lend them an ear. Manchester and one or two other towns gave them a fair reception, but these could not atone for the general indifference.

Wherever he was seen and heard Professor De Vos made a deep impression and Mr. Moorrees did valiant work with an eloquence which was as rich and moving in English as in Dutch. During the summer he spoke in the West of England and while I was with my Aunt and Uncle in their country retreat in Somersetshire Mr. Moorrees spent a night or two with us. Much work and correspondence fell to my share in preparing these meetings for him. I find amongst my papers lists of the people to whom I wrote and who were moved to help make the meetings a success.

But the Deputation was in great difficulties. First, they were confronted with the great disappointment, too manifest on all sides, of the indifference of the English population to the feelings of Cape Colonials, and their lack of desire even to listen to facts. Secondly, they were sheep without a shepherd, not being provided with a competent Organizing Secretary to arrange their programme throughout England, to see that preparatory work was done in each centre to ensure a good meeting and arouse interest; also to make certain of their trains and hospitable reception. Everything needed to be arranged for them and there was no one authorized to do it nor any fund to meet the expenses.

In Oxford I succeeded, with the help of Mr. Charles Murray, in arousing interest, and we found support from Dr. Estlin Carpenter, Sir William Markley, Professor Steadman Addis and others, with the result that Mr. Moorrees was enabled to speak at a crowded meeting, his eloquence creating a deep effect. Later I did the same for him at Bristol. His visits and awakening eloquence should have been followed up by the official delegation, but it seemed impossible to fix them. August had come – the worst month in the year for public work or meetings – and the Deputation, much discouraged and disillusioned, began to speak of departure.[22]

Their mission was by no means useless. If it failed to instruct the country at large, it at least enlarged the view and strengthened the hands of those who were on the side of Protest and striving to spread the truth.

From Charlton House I could and did bicycle in and out of Bristol and there help to work up the S.A.C.C. For holiday-making was spoilt that year. There could be no freedom of mind for enjoyment with that terrible war going on and each morning's news of battles, farm burnings and devastation cast a shadow over the usual picnics and pleasures. Guests came and went and the peace of the old house and its beautiful garden and parkland offered a permanent contrast to the

24

mental picture of storm and misery in South Africa. These things were stirring within me.

You know we were all called pro-Boers. It was purely a nickname and never seemed to fit though for convenience we adopted it ourselves. We were pro-Englanders. From the first I, and indeed all whom I knew, had been concerned primarily about our *own* country and whether or not she was acting upon the highest principles of Justice and Humanity. We had thought comparatively little of the Boer side. But now, as the months advanced and every post brought news of the effects of English policy and actions upon an innocent population of women and children, when one saw the concrete results of our policy upon human life, I was filled with indignation and a passionate desire to show concrete sympathy to these unfortunates by taking them material relief to soften their suffering.

Mr. Morley[23] had made his great speech at Oxford in June, and his strong, clear words had been a clarion call and gave a lead to us poor toilers for the higher ideals as well as a sense of support in our daily task of confronting those who condemned or despised us. He expressed so entirely the case as it presented itself to my mind that I will quote a few sentences. It was a noble utterance and strengthened the party for peace. He said:

> ". . . When you are told that the war was made necessary by the Boer Ulti-matum don't believe any such thing. . . Our relations with the Transvaal from the Raid to the war were clumsy and provocative and the objects of the war, putting those objects at their highest, were not worth all the waste of treasure and the hideous sacrifice of life and the kindling of abominable passions . . . and I will assert to the end, be the end what it may, that none of the alleged wrongs of the *Uitlanders* nor all the wrongs put together, were worth the desolation of a single British or a single Boer home."

That was just what I felt – not worth the desolation of British or Boer homes . . . yet daily British homes were darkened by death and Boer homes by destruction and desolation. My work on the Conciliation Committee had enabled me to follow the story in closest detail. Farm-burning, which had begun spasmodically in January 1900, became as the spring advanced Lord Roberts's settled policy. For a similar policy he had earned a reputation in Afghanistan,[24] a protest in remonstrance to that policy bears the signature of Mr. Joseph Chamberlain. Lord Hobhouse had signed it also. Those had been Mr. Chamberlain's Radical days. My Uncle had not changed his coat.

As now this destructive policy proceeded, soldiers' letters[25] in the Press con-stantly described the horrible scenes which, to their honour, they for the most part evidently found most distressing. Thus the constantly renewed picture of women and children homeless, desperate and distressed, formed and fixed itself in my mind and never once left me. It became my abiding thought. The thought deepened to torture and by a kind of second-sight such as had often visited me in my life the whole became a vision of vivid reality wherein I saw myself amongst the sufferers bearing relief. I never doubted then that I should go and that, be the obstacles what they might, they would be surmounted. Perhaps you, dear practical Mrs. Steyn, will laugh at my confession of second-sight, but you asked me to tell you all that brought me to my work for your People and so I tell you exactly how it came about.

Recently, in reading one of George Eliot's works, I came upon this passage, which offers some explanation. She wrote:

> "Second-sight is a flag over disputed ground. But it is a matter of knowledge that there are persons whose yearnings, conceptions – nay, travelled conclusions – continually take the form of images which have a foreshadowing power: the deed they would do starts up before them in complete shape, making a co-ercive type; the event they hunger for or dread rises into vision with a seed-like growth, feeding itself fast on unnumbered expressions. They are not always the less capable of the argumentative process nor less sane than the commonplace calculators of the market; sometimes it may be that their natures have manifold openings . . . where there may be a greater and more miscellaneous inrush than through a narrow portal."

Anyhow, explain it as you will, it was a curious and most solemn feeling that possessed me and, nurtured in the quiet of the country, it grew into a definite plan when I returned to the solitude of my Chelsea flat.

No one as yet knew of my intention nor excercised any influence upon me. I thought out my plan. Evidently the first step was to secure a fund for relief. Already in September I had been sounding prominent people with that in my mind and I find under the date 20 September the following letter from the Rev. S. E. Gladstone and clearly recall the help it gave me. He wrote:

> "It is most dreadful, most painful and so hard to see any remedy such as often follows grievous injustice. However, I do feel that every individual protest to what has been done, and is being done, has its weight and at least some little comfort to the injured parties. But the great grief is for Britain's Name and Fame. May God bless you and others for your brave and resolute struggle for Justice to the weak. We all know in our several degrees what it costs us personally."

Money had been coming in to me privately and from many parts of the country people had been writing to ask me to whom they could send contributions. Encouraged by this and the view of many other prominent men and women, I felt the time had come to start a public fund for the distressed women and children. To

26

do this I must enlist the support of our leader, Mr. Courtney. Immediately, therefore, on my return to London I sought him out.

Armed with encouraging letters I recall going in one morning to consult Mr. Courtney. I rise early and the day was well advanced for me but he and Mrs. Courtney had not yet risen from table. They were very kind. He let me expound my ideas to him and my desire to open a public fund for the burnt-out women and children. He demurred at first. I can see it all so clearly now. He rose from his chair and paced the room as he so often did when considering a matter; then went and stood before the window looking out into their charming little garden where the autumn tints were already glowing in the sunshine and, tapping on the window pane, one by one he put before me the objections to such a scheme:

There was too little information.
Who would distribute such a Fund?
What could we hope to collect? At most perhaps £10 000.
What use could such a small sum be?
Would the Military allow such a Fund? And so forth.

All these objections I had fully anticipated and was prepared with answers more or less good for them all. It ended by my securing a consent, if somewhat constrained and dubious, to bless such a movement. That, for the moment, was all I wanted. And I came away with a hopeful feeling that in like manner all the walls of Jericho would fall.

And then I set earnestly to work. My Aunt and Uncle were in full sympathy and my Aunt willing to be one of a committee. She did more. She at once offered to put the fund on the right basis by obtaining official sanction and guarantees for distribution. Before me lie copies of her letters to Lord Lansdowne and Mr. Chamberlain and their replies which express general sympathy with the object of the fund and a promise to communicate with Sir Alfred Milner about it.

The Government made, of course, certain quite natural reservations with regard to distribution lest supplies should be so placed as to leak through to men in arms against us. Their cordial consent was a great help in the furtherance of our movement. For my main object in forming this philanthropic committee was to secure, if possible, adherents of all shades of opinion. The name chosen was The South African Women and Children Distress Fund. Its character was clearly described as "purely benevolent, non-political, non-sectarian, national." And its object "to feed, clothe, shelter and rescue women and children, Boer, British or others who had been rendered destitute and homeless by the destruction of property, deportation, or other incidents of the military operations."

It is incorrect to think as is unfortunately stated on page 232 of the *Life of Lord Courtney* by Dr. G. P. Gooch, that this committee grew out of the "Women Workers of the S.A.C.C.". It had a *wholly* different foundation; it was non-political and was

27

composed of men as well as women. People of every shade of opinion were invited to join it and many did so. Others refused. I have before me the letters of such representative leading men as the Rev. Hugh Price-Hughes, the Rev. A. H. Stanton, Canon (now Bishop) Gore and Lord Northbrook, all of whom refused to subscribe their names to this fund; while on the other hand Sir Edward Fry, Canon Barnett, the Master of Balliol, Herbert Spencer, the Bishop of Nottingham, the Marchioness of Ripon, Mrs. Bryce (now Lady Bryce), Lady Rendel, Mrs. Humphrey Ward and many others willingly gave their names and support. Sir Thomas Acland became Chairman, Lady Farrer Honorary Treasurer and Mr. C. A. Maurice its very helpful Honorary Secretary. The working committee was a strong one and contained only one or two of those who had previously belonged to the "Women Workers". Notably among these was Miss Bradby[26] whose organizing powers and common sense were a great contribution.

The formation of the Distress Fund occupied my whole time from October. It entailed endless correspondence and many interviews, explaining to people the need of the Fund, its purely benevolent character and the desire to have on the Executive people of all views – a truly national body. To each influential person was sent a copy of the agenda outlining the proposed committee . . .

It was quite an education, interviewing influential people to explain these aims and, I regret to say, modified adversely my too idealistic view of human nature. The chilling attitude of some accounted most saintly, the lack of imagination in others whose known gifts presupposed imagination, the fear of those with big reputations lest those should be marred – all left an indelible impression on my mind. Of those I interviewed the memory of Canon Scott-Holland[27] stands out – his large friendliness and sympathy.

Working on at the preliminaries, and seeing the Distress Fund taking real shape, and finding that money was being sent me privately with many an anxious enquiry as to who would convey relief, I realized the time had come to break my own intention to my relations, and thus form a point towards which to direct effort.

Though independent and free and living at that time alone in my Chelsea flat, I yet did not feel justified in pursuing my long-nourished plan without the full acquiescence of my kind Aunt and Uncle. To obtain that was the hardest part of the enterprise. This cannot be realized by girls of the present day; to understand all that is to turn back to the ideas of the 19th century, already so antiquated. I always plead my own cause badly and was nervous in proportion of the intensity of my feeling. I was armed with numerous letters from the Cape, all inexpressibly sad, and with many from English sources asking how funds could be sent. I merely hinted at the depth of determination which for months had been growing in me and the certainty I felt that the difficulties ahead, which I did not underrate, could be overcome. My Aunt and Uncle were interested but dubious. But I persevered and in the end succeeded in eliciting a qualified assent. They expressed it in a formula which I felt was tantamount to a sanction: "We do not wish to withhold

28

our acquiescence if you feel it right to go, but we do not ourselves believe strongly enough in the plan to give you any material help." This, however, I had not expected or wished, for well I knew that if one undertakes a mission under compulsion of some inward force which cannot be conveyed to others and which merely rests on one's own faith for achievement, one must be prepared to carry it through without the help of others, at least as far as material things go.

It had been part of my plan to save up for the journey, so I at once replied that I neither expected nor even wished for help of that nature, I only desired approbation. Also that I believed my money would hold out with care.

I broke it also to my Brother who wisely urged me to consider the points against my project. I find my reply to him:

> *First, disease.* This had already choked off the B's [Boers] who are liable to enteric. For me Life has no attractions, Death a good many; so the argument has no weight.
>
> *Second, calumny.* I get that in England and am by long use too tough to mind it any more.
>
> *Third, it is too soon; better later.* This I do not agree with. Destitution, starvation, etc. do not wait for opportune political moments, and all who *come* from there say "go and go at once". And I told him of the many Colonials who were in full accord.

Mrs. Murray[28] had already left for the Cape but I had written, asking her to let me know the views of leading Cape women.

South Africans whom I consulted were in keen sympathy with my plan of going to South Africa, amongst them Mr. J. H. Hofmeyr and Professor De Vos.[29] I wrote to my Brother:

> "I had a long talk with Professor De Vos on the eve of his sailing and told him about it. I can't forget how the light broke over his sad face. Even if we did not go beyond the Cape Colony, he said, it would do more to heal the breaches and bridge the chasms than anything else could do. A few people like us (not just the snobs that crowd out here) have it in their power, he considers, to even prevent a rising in the Colony by soothing their feelings. He did not mean public speaking or taking political part in things."

I worked hard to let my flat and on 29 November was able to announce success to Mrs Charles Murray. I wrote:

> "I feel such an absolute confidence in the Dutch (Boers) that I am sure I could pass from one to another amongst perfect strangers without a tremor. It is such a strange relief after the long tension to go where one's sympathies

29

have been for so long. I could not rest for the feeling I *must go* – it's like some strong call. And so I can't but believe that some good to those women deprived of everything but their fine spirit may come through my puny efforts."

I took a second-class ticket on an "intermediate" to economize as far as possible and stayed in England only long enough to be present at the first meeting of the Distress Fund Committee where provisional officers were elected. As a nest-egg I was able to hand the Committee the £300 I had collected privately and this sum they banked in Cape Town so that I found it there on arrival; and it paid for the first truck-load of food and clothing which I took with me to Bloemfontein.

I sailed on 7 December, going quite alone and travelling second class. By a coincidence Mr. and Mrs. Joshua Rowntree[30] who had first arranged another date were sailing by the same ship, but they were travelling first class, and had no connection with me, being, I believe, bound on a Quaker mission. I was glad for my Aunt's sake to be able to assure her the Rowntrees were on the same boat, but the statement that I went with them is inaccurate. The second-class deck was crowded to discomfort. It contrasted with the first class, which had only four passengers, namely the two Rowntrees and their nephew and Mr. Tarr, who years later in Philippolis gave much help to the home industries.

It was my first experience of the tropics and the voyage seemed and was very long. I remember the beauty of the day at the Canaries and the relief from the crowd of passengers, the sunshine and the glory of the scarlet hibiscus. The rest of the time I spent reading books upon South Africa and above all in trying to learn as much Boer Dutch as possible. The lessons I had had in London were a great help. It was difficult to learn because there was no certainty in the spelling. Now I understand your Authorities have recently altered the spelling and it is to be fixed by their agreement. Certainly that will make it easier for present-day learners, but I find it too hard to acquire yet another form of spelling. Your language always attracted me, dear Mrs. Steyn, it seemed to me such a perfect vehicle for all primitive and delightful things. What humour it can convey, what tenderness, what poetic feeling! How suited to intimate family life![31]

It is slowly, since that war, that efforts have been concentrated upon stabilizing grammar and spelling. And a literature in the language of the People is being built up and yearly added to. So did Dante do much to fix Italian, and our early English writers also – and now I hear you have a committee at work translating the Bible – which will do more, I suppose, than anything to fix the language. It is such a relief to the People to be able to write as they *speak*. It has given a fresh impetus to literary expression, full of promise for the future.

Looking back, I think, as I have often thought, how delightful were all those people who joined in forming the humanitarian committee and what a privilege it had been to be brought into contact with them. Mrs. (now Lady) Byles had given me immense help, drawing sympathizers from her large circle of friends, the Bradbys, Mr. C. E. Maurice, Mr. Frederick Pethick-Lawrence, Mrs. (now Lady) Courtney, Mr. Nevinson, Mr. Trotter and many others. Many have already gone on before, some have been estranged by recent events from their former views, others still remain unchanged, ready as then to champion noble but unpopular causes and to help the innocent in distress, of whatever nationality. Some few, I think, you met in England in after years, but I wish you could have known them all intimately for I well know how you would have appreciated them. To have worked so long with people so far above myself in knowledge and attainments I have always held to have been one of the great privileges of my life.

You see how it came about. Deeply I had felt the call. Passionately I resented the injustice of English policy. Whole-heartedly I offered myself for relief to the distressed. Carefully, step by step, I prepared the way. Sternly I economized and saved. Greatly I felt the wrench and anxiety for my aged relatives. But never did the vision fade of these desolate women and children, nor the certainty that I must go to them.

After six months of steady, persistent preparation I broke away from the circle of kind friends to face the uncertainties of war-time in a strange country.

Letters

1. TO LEONARD HOBHOUSE

Kenilworth, Cape Town

30 December – 1 January 1901

I must write something by this mail, but it will be rather vague and muddly for I am rather like a sponge continually sopping up new ideas and impressions, and am reduced to a state of mental indigestion, having had no time to think it over and sort it all out. The beauty of the scenery impresses one all the time, and makes the background for everything together with brilliant weather, light bracing air and gorgeous flowers.

The day of my arrival was a very full one – we came to anchor in Table Bay at 4 a.m. and shortly after that hour I was nearly knocked down by (the overpowering magnificence of) Table Mountain with its attendant Devil's Peak and Lion's Head, seen by sunrise. They are magnificent – but what pleases me still more are the Blue-Berg Mountains,[1] a long range with jagged peaks which came as a surprise for I had never heard of them.

By 5 p.m. I was eating figs and apricots on a stoep and nursing an African *miercat*[2] as if I had known it always. The interval was spent in landing myself and the Rowntrees and trying to fit them into rooms – a very hard business, for every hotel was choked. The docks are too full for the ships to get in, so we had to come off in tugs. They came over, very kindly, in an electric launch to fetch me, but my impatience to leave the ship was such that I *would* start in the first tug with the third class and so passed the launch on the water; which, finding I had left the ship, hurried back after me again. At last the Rowntrees came and we stuck to them till they were housed and then came out here which is much cooler than town and within easy reach by train or tram. After 2½ days I succeeded in getting my luggage, having lost all at the docks.

The first realisation of war comes on landing. The congested docks piled with forage, etc., – the long lines of military trucks in the streets of Cape Town – the swarms of Khaki people everywhere, sprinkled thick – the pavement crowded with idle people – prices of everything very high.

My welcome has been very warm. Everyone seems to know me.[3] Mrs. Murray is a dear, but far from strong. Though all are as nice as can be I think I like best of all hitherto Mrs. Sauer.[4] Both he and she seem people of very solid worth, so perfectly unaffected and high-minded; and she has a good deal of charm of manner. She was a Miss Cloete of the well-known Constantia family. The Harry Curreys, Sauers, Charles Moltenos and Merrimans have asked me to stay with them and I go on

Thursday to the Merrimans at their farm near Stellenbosch. There are many people there whom I am told I must see. In fact they are all anxious to keep me here till I have seen and known all of them, and seen such women as here and there have strayed down from the Republics.

Whether I can get up there or not, who can tell! Since we sailed so much has altered for the worse that it will be very difficult. The general feeling and indeed certainty is that news is held back continually and it makes people restive.

2. TO LADY HOBHOUSE

Kenilworth, Cape Town
31 December 1900

My hand shakes with heat so I find it difficult to write, though I am seated on a cool shady stoep with a south-east breeze blowing which is supposed to keep us all alive and fresh. There is so much to say I hardly know where to begin. As to my chance of getting north, it is far worse than when I left England, but I do not despair . . . All the best heads here from Sir Henry de Villiers[1] downwards think, and I think myself, that my best plan is to go straight to Sir Alfred Milner with your note and tell him what I want to do. Meantime there is much for me to learn here. Already I have countless impressions but no opinions to offer yet, it is early days for that.

I have had such a very warm welcome not only from the Murrays, but from numbers of other people; they seem to know my name quite well and I am invited to stay at five or six different houses provided I have the time. On Thursday I am going for a few days to the Merrimans at their home, a farm near Stellenbosch; there are women near that town who have been deported and she will give me much information . . .

As for the scenery it is lovely; far more beautiful than I had been led to expect. Kenilworth is some miles from Cape Town but is joined on by a train and a tram. It is one of a series of residential districts which wind round Table Mountain and look across a flat to a very lovely range of mountains, the Blauwberg. Table Mountain with the Lion's Head and Devil's Peak form a beautiful group, often pure cobalt in colour though so close by, and coming in as background to every picture.

We anchored last Thursday at 4 a.m., so had our first view of this imposing mass by sunrise. The ship could not get into dock owing to the congested condition of things; and we had to be landed in tugs and lighters and in consequence lost every shred of luggage for two days. A friend came to fetch me in an electric launch, but I was so heartily tired of the ship that I had gone off in the first tug and so passed it on my way. However, that was soon put right and later when the Rowntrees landed too we spent a long time helping them to find rooms. All the hotels are so crowded. It was well for me that I had house room ready and waiting for me by the kindness of Mrs. Murray.

Mr. Schultz,[2] who has all along been Secretary of the committees here, tells me

33

his latest news from Johannesburg, speaks of 4 000 women and children in some sort of camp prisons there[a] ... A good deal is learnt from officers who come up to the Cape. One told a friend of mine this week that he himself helped in the burning of 600 farms, hating and loathing it. He said that it was nonsense to talk of guerilla warfare, it was guerilla only in method, but quite properly organised and in his opinion nearly 20 000 men still in the field.

Mr. Schultz has succeeded in getting one truck of clothing through to Bloemfontein but it is fraught with difficulty. As to the address for our cases of English goods, Mr. Adrian van der Byl, who is at the head of the Customs, most kindly consents to give his name as consignee.[3] I have seen Mrs. Roos[4] today and Mrs. Steytler and got full particulars of their relief committees. I am told there are 57 boy prisoners at Green Point Prison-of-war Camp, from 17 down to 9 years. The committee tried to get these freed to send them to school but only succeeded with one. He was eight years old.

From the memoir

a) I saw during that week many poor harassed women who had been deported from the Republics after seeing their homes destroyed. It seemed almost impossible to credit the sad tales they had to tell, but the main features of these were again and again repeated by women from wholly different parts. Yet until I went north and heard similar stories from scores and hundreds of destitute women I hardly grasped the fullness of the truth.

The main fact learnt was that in many places large camps were now forming where women and children were crowded, but that these families at the Cape had been sent down previously when, rendered homeless, there was nowhere else to place them. These camps one soon heard spoken of as Refugee camps, a misnomer which had slender connection in line with the facts and which, persistently used, gave rise to grave misunderstanding.

Terrible anxiety existed with regard to these camps, but there was no clear knowledge of their condition. In England we had heard nothing of the formation of such camps.

As the people interned in them were in many cases near relatives of the residents of Cape Colony, this knowing nothing and fearing everything amounted to agony.

More than ever I felt I must get to them, cost what it might.

3. TO LEONARD HOBHOUSE

Schoongezicht
6 January 1901

It is frightfully hard to find time to write when I have to go from place to place talking to people, besides being agreeable and not too shut up in the house in which

34

I may be staying. The endless tales I am told are most confusing and to keep them clear at all I have to write down every woman's conversation when she is gone. The things I am told are humiliating and heart-rending in the extreme, and the effort to listen to it all sympathetically for a few hours exhausts one more than I had deemed possible. Perhaps in due time I shall grow hardened to it.

I called at Government House with my introduction,[1] but unfortunately hit upon mail day, a very busy one. So the Secretary told me I should be communicated with and an appointment made. I was asked the subject on which I desired an interview and replied "the condition of women and children", upon which the Secretary remarked it was not likely that Sir Alfred would see me on *that* topic. Then I had to come here, two hours from Cape Town, leaving word with a friend to wire me the day and hour of His Excellency's appointment and I would come at once. Unfortunately, I have missed this first chance, for a kind invitation was sent me to lunch at Government House yesterday, the very day the invitation was received and the notice being so short I received the telegram too late. However, I will write a letter of apology and explanation and deliver the same in person to-morrow morning and try for a talk without lunch, which I should much prefer, and so make a clean breast of all I want to do. Miss Hauptfleisch[2] writes from Port Elizabeth that a telegram has been received there from the Princess of Wales enquiring into the matter, so I trust public opinion is beginning to bear fruit and will back me up. But recollect the camp at Port Elizabeth is the best of all so far as we can learn. It is very small, is the only one easy of access and to which it has been possible to convey substantial help. There are so many others.

I feel a little nervous about my coming interview with Milner, so much depends upon it. But Miss Ellie Cronjé's[3] face was an inspiration and if I could have gone straight from her to him I could have spoken out. I saw her and her mother yesterday at Wellington where I went to spend the day. As Mr. Morley has espoused her cause I think I shall venture to send him an account of my interview with her in case he should think fit to publish it . . . So I must not write it to you also as time presses. But she is charming. I was proud to be able to speak a few sentences in Dutch to her mother.

I lunched with Dr. Andrew Murray, the well-known minister and pioneer of education.[4] His daughter was there and told me the story of her deportation from Bethlehem[5] and of the fortnight she had spent in the women's camp at Pietermaritzburg. Dr. Andrew Murray was very full of a portion of his school he is now building to be called Uppingham House in memory of Edward Thring of whom he is an enthusiastic admirer.[6] When I told him he was related to my Father, he was overjoyed and said his respect for me was doubled!

I have seen also Miss Neethling, two of whose sisters married two Hertzogs of the Free State. One is the Mrs. Judge Hertzog whose so-called attempt to escape excited comment at home recently. The story is not exactly true. Her baby, a prisoner-of-war aged 17 months, was very ill, and she was almost distraught. There are no barriers to that camp, only sentries posted about, and Mrs. Hertzog was wandering almost demented not knowing where she was going when a sentry with a bayonet stopped her and turned her back.[7] That was all. Miss Neethling, the sister, went from here to see if she could help these married sisters, but could not get them out. However, as the baby was so ill she applied for leave to get him out and after going from one authority to another it was thought the British Empire would not suffer much if a permit was given for his release though without his mother. As her husband is defending his country still, *she* must remain in prison. The baby is a pathetic-looking child in reality, not a bit like this smiling likeness I enclose; he cried at the sight of me but after a while I won him round with an orange-coloured flower and he let me kiss him. The little Hertzog boy that died was this baby's cousin. He was eight years old and had measles on him at Jagersfontein and two doctors had said he was too ill to travel. I will not dwell on his story for the details have already been sent to England; but he died a few days after reaching the camp.

Here in the Colony we feel martial law may creep further south any day, it is very near now. Some people are discharging their coloured servants so that they may not be exposed to the chance of the false information such people are tempted to give.

This call to arms[8] is a mad step, calculated to excite ill feeling. However, they say it is mostly riff-raff and unemployed who have enrolled themselves. When you see these people quiet and composed, more concerned with their fruit-growing and the price of strawberries and apricots than anything else, you feel how absurd it is to dream of rising amongst them and laugh at the Maxims now hoisted over Cape Town and the precautions of sending the Boer prisoners out to the Bay in ships. They are so terrified.

The Merrimans are charming and this old Dutch farm away under the mountains is lovely.[9] Given a field of grass and it would be perfect. Mr. Merriman . . . is trying hard "not to lose by his farm", as he puts it, and is up at 5.30 daily gathering apricots and superintending his work-folk . . .

I return to Cape Town to-morrow and go on the 11th to the Harry Curreys, subject of course to what may pass at His Excellency's.

. . . We have complained in England that people here do not send their names with their stories. I see the reason now. They dare not. In almost every case the woman has some relative who would be injured by it – a man on parole would be put back in prison – a prisoner now in the Colony would be sent to Ceylon – a farm would be burnt; goods confiscated – or perhaps the chance of getting a relative out of prison destroyed. This last is the case of the Englishwoman just down from Potchefstroom whose husband the Dutch Consul is trying to release.[10]

Kenilworth
8 January 1901

I have just come back from Cape Town and from lunching at Government House. It is such a relief that this meeting is over and I think I may say it was on the whole a satisfactory interview and thanks to your introduction so pleasant. I admit that I was in a "blue funk"[a)] for twenty-four hours beforehand, not that I was afraid of His Excellency, but afraid I should not plead my cause at all adequately. There were eight gentlemen at lunch[b)] and only me. Afterwards Sir Alfred took me alone to the drawing-room and we sat together on the sofa and went at it hammer and tongs for an hour. He admitted the farm-burning was a mistake (how mild to put it like that)[1] and he said he thought something should certainly be done to ameliorate the condition of the women and children, about whom he was evidently uneasy, for with his own eyes he had seen some truck-loads of women when he came down the line, and it had occurred to him that it was rather terrible. Finally, after I had told him many details (and I did not mince matters) and told him how uneasy the English conscience was growing and how desperately sore the Afrikanders felt and how for the Honour of England we ought to mend matters in the camps, then finally he said he would do all in his power to forward my going the round of the camps as representative of the English movement and with me a Dutch lady – whoever I and the people here like to choose as representative of South Africa. Then I said I must be allowed to take two trucks with me, one with clothing and one with provisions, and this too he conceded, but – there is a "but" and here it comes: he must refer it to Kitchener.[2] He said he could do no more than recommend and urge Kitchener to allow us to go, if only on the practical ground that these camps must be properly organised for they are likely to have to exist not weeks but months and possibly run into years. In a few days he will let me have Kitchener's reply, and meanwhile we are to settle on the Dutch woman (probably Mrs. Roos) and I want him to throw me in a third party in the shape of Ellie Cronjé who begged and implored me to take her and whose knowledge of the country would be invaluable.

I cannot tell you anything like all that passed. I implored him to offer terms – I told him a little kindness might lead the Dutch Boers anywhere. I described to him the attitude and spirit of all the deported women I had met and asked him how he thought he was going to govern thousands of Joans of Arc.[3] We parted very good friends . . . He struck me as amiable and weak, clear-headed and narrow. Everyone says he has no heart, but I think I hit on the atrophied remains of one. It might be developed if he had not, as he says he has, made up his mind to back up the Military in everything.

Now I wait on Kitchener,[4] and if he refuses, must attack again. Sir Alfred enquired kindly for Henry[5] and asked to be remembered to you. Now the chances are that

Kitchener, though a woman-hater, may welcome *two* women because of the difficulty (he has created for himself) of dealing with *thousands*.

A soldier, fresh from Johannesburg, gave me a horrible description of the camp there. He, a rough man, was broken-hearted over it. Johannesburg has about four thousand in this camp. I know already of at least 11 camps and there are more. I can't tell the exact numbers in these camps but they are large and growing.

I promised Sir Alfred to say nothing while negotiations are going on. If it is arranged for me to go he will gladly have it put in the papers. I feel so relieved, but still, I may be doomed to be snuffed out by Kitchener.

. . . I had such a happy time with the Merrimans at their farm near the mountains, where they rise at 5.30 daily to grow and pack fruit . . . We think, so far as we can see, that the best people to form a committee here to distribute funds and command confidence at home would be the Rev. Andrew Murray of Wellington, Sir Henry de Villiers and Sir Bisset Berry.[6] Of these Dr. Murray has consented and the other two will be approached . . . The distribution shall be placed in the hands of persons deputed by the committee and shall not run counter to the requirements of the Local, Civil, and Military Authorities. I gave the circular to Sir Alfred who approved.

The good folk at home who withdraw support because of the military cause are very foolish. We *must* work beside them even if not through them. As I told Sir Alfred I should give with my own hands but did not wish to cross the Military; and he was quite reasonable and amenable. Let those people only come here and see what it is to have martial law upon your heels as we have and Maxims pointing at you and khaki everywhere, and they would realise that you must submit to the powers that be – but if the Authorities (as he agrees to do) will put it into our hands to organize, what more can you expect under the circumstances?

I don't suppose I shall get north before next mail so I may write again and report progress.

I have only a few minutes to write this. In great haste, –

Your loving E. H.

From the memoir

a) I was weighed down with anxiety at the thought of that interview. I was well-nigh sick with terror lest I should prove incompetent for the ordeal. And as was (and is) usual with me in moments of mental or emotional strain my heart beat so violently I could hardly breathe. If I failed in my presentment of the cause, the scheme for which I had toiled for months would fall to the ground and countless lives be lost that might be saved. I went alone in the train from Kenilworth to Cape Town, unable to bear even companionship. I had in my pocket the mail letters which had just arrived, amongst them one from Kate Courtney.[7] In the hope of relieving the torture of mind I read this and was rewarded at the end by finding a

38

rare and very special thing, viz. a few words from the blind Mr. Courtney – written in his own hand – he could hardly guide a pen. It was just this:

"I add two words, Be prudent, be calm.
    affectionately yours,
    Leonard Courtney."

Coming from him, himself – at such an agitated moment – the simple words were both a sedative and a tonic. There seemed a background of support and I always felt that more than any outside thing his message helped me through that longed-for but most difficult interview.

b) I had set my heart on seeing Sir Alfred alone and was alarmed at finding myself in a luncheon party of eight men, not one of whom I knew. And there was no other woman. I sat next Milner, it is true, but felt choked in that to me unusual atmosphere of militarism and unable to speak of what I had so much at heart when seven strangers were listening. They must have thought me, too, a strange animal and an awful bore. Sir Alfred began the subject, but I cut him short saying that I could not discuss it at luncheon and imploring him to give me a few minutes afterwards. He pleaded press of work; I pleaded this was part of the work and of great importance and at last he promised me fifteen minutes, *not more*. In the end, when withdrawn and deep in the subject, I was with him for over an hour. I found him very willing to concede my special requests, viz. that a Dutch lady should go with me, and I put forward the name of the well-known Minister's wife, Mrs. Roos. He approved her, but said all must be referred to Kitchener. It was wonderful how, as we sat on the low couch in the coolness and quiet of that spacious room, with its windows opening upon the green sward and grand old oaks of the garden, my nervousness passed away and I was able to converse freely. This return of calm was undoubtedly due in large measure to Sir Alfred's singular charm and sympathetic manner so calculated to put one at ease. He spoke very openly and I left at last with a great load off my heart and the certainty that he would do all that he could. And he did.

I came out of that cool and calming room into the blazing Cape afternoon feeling as if wings were attached to my feet and made my way hastily back to Kenilworth.

5. TO LEONARD HOBHOUSE

Cape Town
12–16 January 1901

Yesterday at Mrs. Sauer's I met several Transvaal and Free State women, amongst them Mrs. Van der Merwe and her sister . . . Their brother is Mr. Blignaut of

39

Bloemfontein, a well-known man there. They are unhappy because one of the Blue-Books contained an untruth about him which they consider should be exposed and denied. I have not seen the Blue-Book in question so cannot vouch for what is said there, but they tell me it is alleged that Mr. Blignaut at the beginning of the war enticed a young Colonial up, to fight against the British. Now this they assert is wholly untrue, and rests merely upon the fact that his own son (Free State-born) *would* go and fight.

Mr. Blignaut thought this boy, a lad of fourteen, too young to go on Commando and, just before the war broke out, in spite of the boy's protestations he brought him down and placed him in school in the Colony at Wium School, a private one near Wellington. The boy wrote and begged his father to let him come back and telegraphed for money for the journey; but Mr. Blignaut remained firm. So one day, a few weeks after the outbreak of war, the lad ran away from school, sold his bicycle and with the money went home and joined the Commando. He had been fighting ever since; but that boy is the "Colonial" said to have been enticed away . . .

I met also two Miss Burgers, daughters of the former President of that name . . . and Miss Juta. Two of these young girls were among the voluntary band of nurses who tended the Boer forces and afterwards nursed in Pretoria. One of them nursed the British officer Captain or Colonel Haigh who was lying at death's door with enteric. She said: "I was determined if nursing would do it he should live; and he did." She had taken the Red Cross oath of the Geneva Convention and that is to them a reality and it tied their tongues so that they would speak no syllable against the English in any way. Only one complaint they made. Recently, since Kitchener's reign began, they had prepared in Pretoria an ambulance to go out to the Boer lines, but when complete he refused to let it pass, and that, they say, is contrary to the Geneva Convention . . . All talk freely to me but never for a moment allowing themselves to forget I am English or saying anything that could hurt my feelings. They value sympathy so much and jump greedily at all I tell them of our feelings at home because, they say: "That sounds like the England we knew and believed in" . . . The women are the most controlled and the most determined. The more you see and talk to them the more you see that annexation is an impossibility unless accompanied by years of unrest and bloodshed and material ruin.

This is the sort of thing I was told. A burgher surrendered and went home to his wife.

"Are you wounded?" she said.
"No."
"Are you ill?"
"No."
"Then go away at once and don't come near me again till you return with the freedom of your country."

40

And the woman rules the roost in the land! . . .

I was never among such a desperately "loyal" set of people as many of the Colonials here. It is quite pathetic. They have been evidently brought up to idealize and to idolize England. They had her on a pedestal and simply worshipped. Now the fall seems all the greater . . .[a]

Milner has *himself* written fully to Kitchener instead of wiring (as the wires are so blocked) about my request. If I really go I feel pretty sure Mrs. Roos will go with me – also I want to take Ellie Cronjé who pleaded hard to be allowed to go.

It has been amusing this week, for without knowing it I have been talking away quite openly to women who turned out to be of the Loyal Ladies' League.[1] My attitude seemed a revelation to them and they ended by begging to be taken with me. I got them to see in the end how unfair their title was because it intimated that everyone else was disloyal.

We are having some very hot days which make it almost impossible to concentrate one's mind even on a letter. I am staying with the Harry Curreys[2] this week and that is delightful. The hospitality shown me everywhere is wonderful.

From the memoir

a) I was struck, for instance by the intense devotion to England, a devotion which had received a severe blow. This feeling differed entirely from our own natural love for our country which allows us to see her faults without abating our devotion. The Cape people had seen England through a veil of idealism which had small relation to the reality. The Tory Government's war policy had torn asunder this veil with disastrous results. The effects were deep. Something lifelong had snapped within them – their bearings were lost.

Lively anxiety about their friends in the North added to their troubled state of mind. Hardly a family was there which had not blood relations settled in the Republics; it was a hard lot to see war of a harsh and cruel nature made upon their own kith and kin by the mother-country they had so passionately admired, and yet remain neutral in word and deed as they were required to do.

They did, however, almost universally achieve this degree of neutrality: to control their sentiments also was beyong the power of the majority. From the very first, Cape homes had given shelter to women and children homeless or deported and this they would have gladly done on a wide scale as the misery increased. Official refusal (or more precisely military refusal) to permit this sensible plan merely intensified bitterness while adding to the overcrowding and suffering in the camps.

Thus, I soon found that beneath the calm exterior of the Cape Colonists whom I met, there were deep currents of bitterness which came to the surface in moments of roused emotion and which vitiated judgment, producing an unreasoning atti-

41

tude. Thus, difficulties and misunderstandings arose, comprehensible enough considering the provocation endured.

One felt very great sympathy with them.

6. TO LADY HOBHOUSE

Cape Town
15 January 1901

... This week I am staying with the Harry Curreys ... their house is all amongst pine trees like Bournemouth but with the big mountains close behind. The grapes are just ripening and peaches, apricots and other fruits abound. The flowers and flowering shrubs are legion.

16 January. I was lunching with the De Villiers yesterday and Lady De Villiers and I discussed your letter. She is quite willing to give her name.[1] In fact so is the Chief Justice, but they think one name is enough and he has been so unwell of late that she is anxious to keep him out of everything new as far as possible.[2] We all think a committee of three on this side quite enough, so now you have two of them, viz. Lady De Villiers and Dr. Andrew Murray. The third, Sir Bisset Berry, the Speaker, I have approached by letter, but as he is now some way off at a country town it may yet be some days before I hear from him. In fact, as likely as not, his letter may be censored.

After lunch we all went to visit Boer wounded prisoners in the Wynberg Camp. They have a weekly permit and they got a special one for me from Colonel Heyman. On hearing my name he asked who I was because he is related to Sir Charles Hobhouse. This may be very helpful to me because he is Chief (now Colonel Trotter has gone home) in regard to dealing out passes. Some people have dreadful trouble about their passes. You can't get even to Stellenbosch without one now.[3]

There is partial relief in the De Villiers household, for though Lord Roberts would do nothing, yet Kitchener, after a special appeal from the Chief Justice, has released Mr. Cloete, their daughter's husband.[4] He is in Ceylon and is to be allowed to go to England where she will join him. It is a great joy to them but not specially magnanimous as there was nothing in the world against him. He was a Transvaal burgher, but had been so against fighting the English (being Colonial-born) that he had never borne arms and only served as a despatch rider. When our troops occupied Pretoria they took possession of his house and after ransacking everything, found in a drawer of his dressing-room a letter from a Colonial (quite a stranger to him) asking his opinion about sending up a few Colonial sympathizers to the Transvaal. Mr. Cloete had answered this letter, strongly condemning such an idea, but the Authorities did not investigate the matter further nor would they listen, but whipped him off to Ceylon. Kitchener, they say, has done a few kind things, which gives me some hope for my own bit of work. At any rate all agree that

42

he seems and acts more as a man than Lord Roberts whose popularity seems to me chiefly a newspaper one.

The Boer prisoners were most interesting to me. One of them had only been brought down yesterday. He was under Hertzog in the invading Commando and was wounded at Colesberg. He was so patient. His face will haunt me a long time. It was nice to hear the Chief Justice talking to them. They report that their fellows still in the field are hopeful.

I am going down to the docks to see the Merrimans off to-morrow.[5] We shall not feel quite happy till they are off. He might be prevented somehow. As it is he has not dared to go back to Stellenbosch to pack his things, lest a pass to come up again be refused.[6] Men will not sit beside him in public places – and poor Mrs. Merriman's nerves have been much tried. They do deserve some English sympathy for he has made a fine stand and needs a little encouragement. The pity is that he is rather too bitter; still, that is not surprising.

7. TO LEONARD HOBHOUSE

Cape Town

20–22 January 1901

I send two letters . . . one is an account of the experience of Miss Murray, a daughter of the well-known Dr. Andrew Murray of Wellington. When she told me of the story it was very interesting. Her account of the firing on Mrs Van der Merwe's farm which she witnessed[1] is of value because it is the same incident for describing which the Editor of *Ons Land* has been arrested.[2] The other is written by an Englishwoman who married a Hollander and lived at Potchefstroom where her husband was a manager of railways. He never bore arms and had been for three months laid up with an accident met with on the line, when he was arrested and is at Green Point. She is now trying to procure his release[3]. . . .

This week has been such a rush . . . After what seemed a long waiting, Kitchener's answer came[4] and the Governor sent it to me with a letter from himself.[a)] I at once went up to Government House to talk it over with him and he kindly vouchsafed me another interview and he said he would do his best to secure me a comfortable journey. Then he offered his Secretary to work out the details for me and we two saw the Military Head of the Lines, Colonel Cowie, and the Head of Permits (Major Moseley Leigh, I think).

My truck[5] is to start to-morrow night the 21st and I follow on Tuesday the 22nd. So far, so good. But alas. Kitchener only vouchsafes half of what I asked and which Milner himself "urged and recommended". He forbids the Dutch companion or anyone but me and will not at present allow me further north than Bloemfontein . . .

I believe the camps at Johannesburg and Potchefstroom defy description – the soldiers who came down are aghast at them . . . But I thought it was wiser to accept such permission as was vouchsafed and work on from that rather than fly into a pet and say I must have all or nothing. This is what the more violent folk here advise but I can't see it in that light. I think, considering the state of the country, to be allowed within the war areas at all is a considerable concession. And much needs doing at Bloemfontein and at Kimberley and at camps south of Bloemfontein – notably Norvals Pont. Milner recommends me to visit them from that base. I explained to him that it would not satisfy me unless I got to Johannesburg and he replied that he thought Lord Kitchener was fairly well disposed towards the plan and that if I wrote to him direct from Bloemfontein no doubt he would let me proceed. Anyhow, now I can make a beginning. Of course Port Elizabeth is now after much pressure fairly well organised and Pietermaritzburg not so bad either – but farther north . . . ! ! !

I hope it will be thought I have decided rightly in going thus far, but it is a great disappointment about Mrs. Roos and will double my difficulties. You would have smiled at the sentence in Lord Kitchener's telegram in which he spoke of "the women whom the Boers are keeping out of their homes". Delicious self-deception . . .

All to-morrow I shall be packing my truck, 12 tons – 6 of food and 6 of clothing. Prices of food here are horribly high so a hundred pounds does not go very far I find, but I buy wholesale of course. The difficulty is to know where to draw the line between what the Military ought themselves to give the women and what the donors of the Fund would wish added to that. Till I have actually been in a camp it is difficult to judge how many necessaries they should be allowed to lack, pending the rightful but tardy provision of such necessaries by the Authorities.

I hope the Committee will remit quickly what funds they have and will set about getting more. It will be horrible to be up there with empty hands, which would be the case in a very few weeks . . .

You must realise that we are kept on very short commons here as regards news of any kind and what we know is chiefly learnt from stray people, Officers and others who come down from the veld. Martial law is almost here too – everyone has to give up their arms of all kinds and they are digging trenches on the flats just below us. Four large guns are mounted behind Mr. Van der Byl's[6] house Roodebloem, encircled with barbed wire, while a lot of tents are pitched upon his property.

At the Paarl you are forbidden to bicycle after 7 p.m. and bicycles may not be bought or sold any more than horses. Further, inhabitants must be indoors at 9.30 and lights out at 10.30 – yet no Boers are anywhere near.

. . . I hope some day Nora[7] will see this country. She would revel in the flowers and the mountains – the hedges are mostly of blue plumbago and pomegranates and the wild flowers upon the hills are brilliant. The colours on the hills themselves are best of all. The last four days we have had rain, or as that is too mild a way to put it, I should say waterspouts. Never has such weather been known at midsummer or at least not, they say, since the year the slaves were emancipated.[8] Dozens of waterfalls have been coming down Table Mountain and the Devil's Peak. I am watching two or three of them as I sit writing this on the stoep.

Last Thursday we went down to say goodbye to the Merrimans – so relieved that he got off without detention, but he dared not return to Stellenbosch to pack his clothes.

From the memoir

a) It was a great relief and I felt truly grateful to Sir Alfred for the trouble he had taken and the goodwill he had shown me. The two limitations in Kitchener's message were disappointing, but it was a case in which half a loaf is better than no bread and I did not hesitate to accept it thankfully. Sir Alfred, too, strongly advised it, hinting that later on I could again apply to the Commander-in-chief. His refusal to allow a Dutch lady to accompany me was at the moment more baffling. I had so desired and counted on Mrs. Roos to enable me to face the difficulties of the country, climate and language and I had built upon Sir Alfred's own willingness to arrange it. The Cape Dutch, too, had set their hearts upon it and took the prohibition badly. Some indeed really stirred up bad feeling, accusing me of "keeping in with Milner" and wishing to keep everything in my own hands, and also blaming the Governor himself. I was unable to make the matter clear, having been specially asked by Sir Alfred to say nothing about Kitchener's mention of the Dutch lady and having promised him to be silent upon the subject.

8. TO LADY HOBHOUSE

Cape Town
20 January 1901

These are but a few lines to say I am really off to Bloemfontein on Tuesday and hope to begin dispensing food and clothes before long. From that base I can hope to work Edenburg, Kroonstad, Norvals Pont and other camps. There are numbers of them.

21 January. All day I have been loading my big truck. I have taken a great quantity of foodstuffs and all the clothing which had come from our English sources. The food came to nearly £200 . . .[1] It was such a pity not to have been able to cram the great truck full, as I have been allowed it carriage-free, and I want to make myself a big base of supplies in Bloemfontein and work up to Johannesburg from there as soon as I can wheedle Lord Kitchener into giving me a further permit.

The state of Johannesburg Camp is a scandal. My host has just returned from Kimberley and up-country and describes the British Army – sick, weary, worn, spiritless, fit for nothing. The Boers have seldom had a better chance than they have at this moment. For instance, they were simply *let* through into the Colony by a man who had 15 miles of frontier to guard, but who had neither the wit nor the energy left to put patrols on that piece of line. I wish you could hear the accounts from eyewitnesses of some of the engagements lately fought.

After Nooitgedacht[2] the other day 7 000 Boers raised another Memorial – each man brought a stone, put his mark on it, and solemnly swore to fight for independence till death.

I think if you could see these people you would see their spirit is wholly unquenchable, while the spirit of our soldiers is gone out like a candle.

I have been meeting Mr. Fichardt, a charming young man, educated in England of course and lately Mayor of Bloemfontein. He was wounded and taken prisoner soon after Paardeberg,[3] he was one of the 1 200 who rode out and escaped from Cronje's laager through 40 000 British troops. He is here on parole. His family are people of position in Bloemfontein and he has asked his mother to put me up when I get there on Friday. They housed both Milner and Kruger with their attendants at the memorable Conference.[4] A year ago he was superior in command to De Wet. He gave me thrilling accounts of the early battles.

The more I see and hear the more cruel I think it is to our men to let the war go on. They are so tired and ill. They know they will never catch De Wet and frankly say so.

How grieved everyone here is about the Queen's illness[5]; all wish she would express the dying wish that the war should end and that could be made an excuse for giving it up.

9. TO LADY HOBHOUSE

Bloemfontein
26 January 1901

A line which will probable be read by the Censors, just to say I am here and am well and hard, very hard at work – no time to write now as fully as I should like. I can only send a line hoping the Boers, the Censors, Martial Law and all other impediments will let it catch the mail at Cape Town because I know you will be anxious to have some tidings.

I am preparing a really long account of things for next week if possible. Meantime, do get them to remit the Fund to Cape Town and hurry up with clothing, which is greatly needed.

I have a family of nearly 2 000 here,[1] leave alone other places.

Heat, mosquitoes and extreme fatigue prevent more – I am so busy I can only write scraps this week. But I have much to tell – so much, my pen won't go quickly enough.

I do hope you are both keeping well. I am, in spite of the heat, etc., and people are so very kind.

Bloemfontein
26 January 1901

The splendid truck given me at Cape Town, a large double one, was capable of holding 12 ton. Colonel Cowie had sent word I was to have the largest they had available ... My humiliation was that I was not able to fill it. £200 worth of food, groceries, etc. barely filled half, and all the clothing I could muster left much space in the other half. And it was such an opportunity missed for it travelled up gratis. It left Cape Town the day before I did and was hitched on to my train at De Aar and so arrived when I did.

The first thing I did next day was to go down to the goods station, claim the truck and arrange for its unloading. Mr. Arthur Fichardt, the son of my hostess here, has most kindly put a row of vacant rooms at my disposal and this morning I have spent arranging all my stores – unpacking and sorting them. It is very hot work. I think the essence of delightful work is when you quite forget you have a body, but here the heat keeps you in constant recollection that you are still in the flesh, and it is a great hinderance.

I did not have a bad journey from Cape Town, though it was rather a lonely one.[a] Going through the Karoo it was very hot and the second day there were horrible dust-storms varied by thunderstorms. The sand penetrated through the closed windows and doors, filled eyes and ears, turned my hair red, and covered everything like a table-cloth. As far as extent and sweep and sky go the Karoo is delightful, but it is a vast solitude and in many parts the very plants grow two or three yards apart as if they abhorred society. But from Colesberg on it was a desolate outlook. The land seemed dead and silent, absolutely without life as far as eye could reach, only carcasses of horses, mules, and cattle with a sort of mute anguish in their look, and bleached bones, and refuse of many kinds. I was reminded of Verestchagin's[1] pictures – only there the snow hid much ghastliness. I saw a few burnt farms – but those unburnt seemed still and lifeless also, and no work is going on in the fields. Really, the line the whole way up is a string of Tommies – and these always crowded to the carriage windows to beg for newspapers or anything, they said, to pass the time. I gave them all, and all my novels. They said they were so tired of it and so longing to get home.

The disappointment of the journey was that no Boer Commando swooped down and captured our train! It would have enlivened the journey and been immensely interesting ...

I arrived at Bloemfontein,[b] the only woman, and began to learn from that moment what it is to be dominated by the Military. All the railway officials sink into nobodies and soldiers rule the station. You can't stir without their sanction. The whole town is full of soldiers – and the little hotels and the post office and a great ring of camps all round and picquets continually demanding your pass. It is a

47

perfect terror, and I feel inclined to kick all day long. The inhabitants are weary of it all, and heart and hope is gone out of them. Business is at a standstill.

I slept at the inn the first night and the next day, early, Mrs. Fichardt[2] sent her carriage for me and (when I reached her house) told me how much she would like to welcome me to her house but in view of the extraordinary and unlooked-for things done under martial law, for the sake of her sons here she did not dare receive me unless General Pretyman[3] gave written permission which should ensure them protection.

I went to see him, and he greeted me very warmly saying he and Mrs. Pretyman had meant to ask me to stay at Government House but typhoid had broken out and they were overrun by doctors and nurses. But he gave me a general invitation to meals whenever I like. He had known Aunt Eliza and Aunt Catty at Bournemouth in old days (I have constant reason to bless my relations) and I well remember going with Aunt Eliza to see some Pretymans and being frightfully shy of the soldier. I had hoped a link might be found in this way and so it proved. However, this time I did not feel any shyness, finding only a harassed and worried Military Governor conscious of gigantic blunders committed and with a problem before him he doesn't know how to solve. The more one talks to these men in power the more one feels they are hopelessly on the wrong track. The character of the people to be dealt with and the moral aspects of the question are wholly disregarded and they try madly to bring about their will by force and force alone. They'll never succeed.

General Pretyman nearly jumped out of his skin when I said I wanted to stay with Mrs. Fichardt, provided no ill should react upon her sons. "Oh, but," he said, "she is very bitter." "Just so," I replied, "but my visit may have a softening effect upon her." This was a new idea to him and he admitted there was something in it and I stood over him while he wrote me a permit, stating his approval. Rather against the grain, but nevertheless he did it.

So I am in this large cool comfortable house,[4] receiving great kindness, all unknown as I am. My lines have fallen in pleasant places,[5] but in this country and amongst this hospitable people that seems almost inevitable. Poor Mrs. Fichardt is very sad; she lost her husband six months ago in the midst of the war and her two girls[6], one of whom is an invalid, are at Cape Town and not allowed to return to her – not even since their father's death – and the invalid is pining for home. I shall beg General Pretyman to let them come back, but it may rest with still higher powers. Such an act would do more to allay the poor woman's bitter feelings than anything else could do.

But I must pass on to tell you about the women's camp which after all is the central point of interest. General Pretyman gave me his blessing over it and a permanent pass and introduced me to Captain Nelson who, until recently, has been in charge of it. The Authorities are at their wits' end and have no more idea how to cope with the one difficulty of providing clothes for the people than the man in the moon. Crass male ignorance, stupidity, helplessness and muddling. I rub as much salt into the sore places of their minds as I possibly can, because it is so good for them; but I can't help melting a little when they are very humble and confess that the whole thing is a grievous and gigantic blunder and presents an almost insoluble problem, and they don't know *how* to face it.

I explained that I was not going to do what the Military *ought* to do, but really, when looked into, what they are able to do is *so* little that I feel that donors would wish that the suffering of the women and above all the tiny children should be the chief thing taken into account. Major Cray[7] now in charge not only of this camp but of every one in the once Free State told me how he was curtailed – no money, no trucks in sufficient quantity – no power to do what he would like to have done. He begs me to go to all the camps – the wild demand for clothing at places like Rhenoster drives him to despair and he and I together are going to concoct a letter to Kitchener to obtain leave for me to go up north. I hope he will.

The camp is about two miles from this town, dumped down on the southern slope of a kopje right out on the bare brown veld. Not the vestige of a tree in any direction, nor shade of any description. It was about four o'clock of a scorching afternoon when I set foot in the camp and I can't tell you what I felt like, so I won't try.

I began by finding a woman[8] whose sister I had met in Cape Town. It is such a puzzle to find your way in a village of bell-tents with no street or names or numbers. There are nearly 2 000 people in this one camp of which some few are men – they call them "hands-up men" – and over 900 children. Imagine the heat inside the tents and the suffocation! We sat on their khaki blankets rolled up inside Mrs. Botha's tent and the sun blazed through the single canvas and the flies lay thick and black on everything – no chair, no table, nor any room for such, only a deal box standing on its end served as a wee pantry. In this tent lived Mrs. Botha, five children (three quite grown up) and a little Kaffir servant girl. Many tents have more occupants.

Mrs. Pienaar came in and Mrs. Raal, Mrs. Roux and others and they told me their stories and we cried together and even laughed together and chatted bad Dutch and bad English all the afternoon. Wet nights, the water streams down through the canvas and comes flowing in (as it knows how to in this country) under the flap of the tent and wets their blankets as they lie on the ground. While we sat there a snake came in. They said it was a night adder and very poisonous. So they all ran out to make room and I attacked the creature with my parasol. (Afterwards I was told it was a puff-adder.) I could not bear to think the thing should be at large in a community mostly sleeping on the ground. After a struggle I wounded it and then a man came with a mallet and finished it off.

Mrs. Pienaar is so brave and calm. She has six children, ranging in age from fifteen down to two years *and she does not know where one of them is.* She was taken right away from them. Her husband is in detention of some kind in Bloemfontein but not allowed to see her. She expects her confinement in about three weeks, yet has to lie on the bare hard ground till she is stiff and sore and she has had nothing to sit on for over two months but must squat on a rolled-up blanket. I felt quite sure you would like her to have a mattress and I asked her if she would accept one. She did so gratefully and I did not rest yesterday till I had got one out to her though it had to go right under the eyes of the picquet who constantly refuses to let things pass. All her baby linen was in readiness at her home, but all is lost. This is but one case, quite ordinary, amongst hundreds and hundreds.

The women are wonderful: they cry very little and never complain. The very magnitude of their sufferings, indignities, loss and anxiety seems to lift them beyond tears, and these people, who have had comfortable, even luxurious homes, just set themselves to quiet endurance and to make the best of their bare and terrible lot. Only when it cuts afresh at them through their children do their feelings flash out. Mrs. Meintjes, for instance, she has six children in camp all ill, two in the hospital with typhoid and four sick in the tent. She also expects her confinement soon. Her husband is in Ceylon. She has means and would gladly provide for herself either in town or in the Colony where she has relatives or by going back to her farm. It was not burnt, only the furniture was destroyed. Yet there she has to stay, watching her children droop and sicken. For their sakes she did plead with tears that she might go and fend for herself.

It is such a wholesale cruelty and one of which England must be ashamed. It never can be wiped out of the memories of people here. And it presses hardest on the children. They droop in the terrible heat and with the insufficient, unsuitable food.

Whatever you do, whatever the Military Authorities may do – and Major Cray, I believe, is doing his best with very limited means – it is all only a miserable patch upon a very great wrong; whatever you do is only temporary alleviation and can only touch a very few. The whole system is a mistake and has placed thousands physically unfit in conditions of life which they have not strength to endure. In front of them is blank ruin – and whole families are severed and scattered they don't know where.

Will you try somehow to make the British Public understand the position and force it to ask itself what is going to be done with these people? There must be already full 50 000 of them and I should not wonder if there were not more. Some few have means, but most are ruined and have not a present penny. In one of two ways the British Public must support them; either by taxation through the Military or else through voluntary charity. If they want to save their purses (you see I appeal to low motives) let a fuss be made in Parliament to allow those who can maintain themselves to go to friends in the Colony, where they would be received with open arms. That would be some relief. Then, if only the English People would try to exercise a little imagination – picture the whole miserable scene and answer how long such a cruelty is to be tolerated. Should not this hideous wrong patiently

50

endured by these women act as a lever powerful enough to make the Government offer some terms to Steyn, Botha and De Wet, and not insult them by merely sending as envoys[9] burghers whom they can only regard as traitors to their country? Dear Aunt Mary, couldn't you write such a letter about it to *The Times* as should make people listen and believe and understand – which would touch their conscience? Is England afraid of losing her prestige? Well, that's gone already in this country, but maybe some of it might yet be won back by an act of mercy, however late. To keep these camps going *is murder to the children.*

Of course, by judicious management they could be improved. First and foremost I mean to ask for a *matron* speaking both Dutch and English for every camp – besides the officer in charge. She would keep an eye on the morals of the camp – most necessary here with the soldiery all round – and the women could come to her with their wants.

Next, a *mortuary tent* (I learn there is one now, but the dead don't get taken there quickly from the tents.) It is horrible that the corpses should lie in the hot tents with eight or ten living beings. A little Kaffir corpse was laid outside in the cooking sun just wrapped in a blanket, and the stench, I am told, was horrible. Close by were two tents full of measles.

Then, more *water.* For seven or eight persons two buckets for washing, cooking and drinking are not enough.

Next, *soap.* Think of the heat, the dust-storms, etc. and no soap in the rations; evidently because the military supply was short.

Then some sort of *school* for the children – and so on.

But do what you will, you can't undo the *thing itself* which is odious.

Today is Sunday and all the morning your unregenerate and unsabbatarian niece has been toiling and moiling over the bales of clothes, unpacking, sorting and putting up in bundles. We were so glad of such *odd* things . . . such as little boys' braces. I found some baby-linen for Mrs. Pienaar. I do not think, tell Mrs. Chitty,[10] that there is a single superfluous article. But what a family to clothe! How I wish I had Barbara Bradby with her clear methods of investigation to help me . . .

As to the rations:[11] At first they sometimes had potatoes – seven potatoes for seven people – but that is now impossible. Soap also has been unobtainable and none given in the rations. Some people have money and may add to the above by purchasing certain things at some little retail shops allowed in the camps which charge exorbitant prices; for instance 6d. for a reel of cotton! But they are naturally terribly afraid of parting with their money, feeling it is all they will have to begin life again, for everyone's income has stopped, nothing is coming in. It is indeed a dreary prospect. Some few of those who had cash in hand buried it out in their farms for safety and now cannot, of course, reach it.

30 January. So far I have found no one going down who would take this to Cape Town. Also, just as I was getting on with Major Cray he was taken ill – gastric –

51

and now we have no Head. I had a long talk again today with General Pretyman; he is nearly crazy, but gets leave to-morrow as Major Goold-Adams[12] succeeds him. He asked me my opinion and I told him those women should be sent home and the sooner the better. All say if released, they would make a living somehow, and shelter beneath the ruined home would be as good as these rotten tents. I should send them off by degrees, not wholesale. He evidently thinks this wisest but is powerless in that way. It would be hard enough even so, but countless children's lives would be saved thereby.

Meanwhile I have written to Cape Town for more nurses but doubt whether they are obtainable. If not – could the Committee send any from England (not Army nurses)? If so, Authorities would give a bell-tent, rations and 5/- a day. Rather rough of course. But prevention is better than cure. We have much typhoid and are dreading a great outbreak, so I am directing my energies to getting water of the Modder River boiled. As well swallow typhoid germs whole as drink that water. Yet they cannot boil it all; for first, fuel is very scarce. That which is supplied weekly would not cook a meal a day and they have to search the bare kopjes for a supply. There is hardly a bit to be had. Secondly, they have no utensil to hold the water when boiled. I propose therefore to give each tent another pail or crock and issue a proclamation that all drinking water must be boiled. It will cost nearly £50 to do this . . . But the Governor gave orders I was to be obeyed and it should be paid from the Treasury. He also appointed a temporary Head – a certain Captain Hume – who is to drive me out this afternoon with orders from the Governor to do what I tell him. And I can hardly make up my mind where to begin. Soap, I think. All the tents I have been in are exquisitely neat and clean except two; and they were ordinary. And such limitations! . . .

On Saturday I hope to start for Norvals Pont and other places. I have been running round all day and at over 90° Fahr. I enclose a packet of "cases" taken at random through the camp which might appeal to the conscience of the country to let these innocent people go free. It is so pathetic. They think I have come from England with magic powers to let them free and it is dreadful to explain there is no chance of that. Nothing but famine lies before us if they may not go and cultivate at least a little for themselves. England must feed the whole country shortly, that even the Military admit, but they lightly say: "Never mind, only another Mansion House Fund."[13]

31 January. Captain Hume, Dr. Pern and I sat in council yesterday, and the Doctor supported me loyally. I suggested a big railway boiler to boil every drop of water before it is served out. This will economize fuel and be cheaper in the end, besides ensuring the end desired, for many could not be trusted to boil their own.

Next, forage for the cows. We have just secured fifty and only get four buckets from the poor starved things. Next, small boilers to boil the milk. A wash-house with water laid on from the town. A matron to superintend everything, and SOAP.

True, I was given *carte blanche* to order what I thought necessary and I shall see how much of what I ask is given. We have sent to Cape Town for nurses and medical appliances.

It appears these camps are to be run with Civil money though by Military order – and each wants to shift the onus onto the other. But this I will say – I do think they all want to make matters as sanitary as possible; but nothing done in that way can undo the thing itself and the best must be bad. The chief officials strongly disapprove the policy but men like Captain Hume and that grade of official cannot see the cruelty to women and children and think any means justified that would end the war. Now they are angry because they find it did not end the war.

Their line generally is to speak of "refugee" camps and make out the people are glad of their protection. It is absolutely false. They are compelled to come and are wholly prisoners. In fact, I consider we are all more or less prisoners in Bloemfontein. We cannot move without passes. Everything is censored – spies abound – barbed wire and picquets surround the town – newspapers nearly all prohibited – we have no news and know nothing but vaguest rumours. Nevertheless, with all this rigour, General De Wet knows everything that goes on, in which case, I asked him [Hume], what was the use of wearing out the patience and ruining the business of the inhabitants by this deadening Martial Law? It is only making the people more determined and more bitter. If De Wet gets the news he wants anyhow, just as well relax the rigour.

Everything is getting short in the town because no business house is allowed to get supplies; shops grow emptier and prices higher daily.

The women's camp is already one-third of the population of Bloemfontein itself, and there is also a large camp of Natives (Kaffirs) – about 500 – to be looked after.[14] A ring of soldiers' camps extends all round the town so all put together it's a large population to feed and water, with diminishing supplies, and unusual drought. The dry weather, though making scarcity of fodder, may be a blessing in disguise, for a great outbreak of typhoid is expected with the rains. Already there is plenty of it.

The Hospital Commission[15] created great amusement here. Weeks beforehand it was known the Commissioners were coming, and there was great painting of the red roses white. Pits were dug and large quantities of things buried, and bonfires made to burn up all that was unsightly – and as they (the Commissioners) arrived at the healthy time of the year, everything was in good order for their inspection . . . But they have been K.C.B'd, have not they?

Occasionally I see poor Mrs. Steyn walking about, always followed by a soldier with a bayonet, and whatever house she goes into he stands outside. As they no longer recognize Steyn as President one wonders why thus torment his wife. She is very dignified and takes the line of never even seeing the soldier who guards her. I am to meet her to-morrow.

53

Today I returned Bishop Webb's[16] call. He is a dear old man. He knew my Father in Cornwall and of course Uncle Edmund's[17] name was familiar to him. He was sent out here again last September to "conciliate". He calls once a week on Mrs. Fichardt[18] for this purpose, to tell her it is wrong to sympathize with her people. He gave me a pamphlet which he had written many years ago on the settlement of South Africa. In his opinion all would settle down if it were not for Olive Schreiner,[19] Mr. Merriman, the Bond and all Colonial agitators. In fact if you turned all the other side out of the country, I suppose.

He said one of his Sisters of Mercy had visited the camp some time ago and reported that all that was needed was a little cotton and a little soap. They were happy and well off otherwise.

Then I went straight to my camp and just in one little corner this is what I found. Nurse Kennedy[20] underfed and overworked, just sinking onto her bed, hardly able to hold herself up after coping with some thirty typhoid and other patients with only the untrained help of two Boer girls – cooking as well as nursing to do herself. Next I was called to see a woman panting in the heat just sickening for her confinement. Fortunately I had a nightdress in my bundle to give her and two tiny baby-gowns. Next tent, a little six months' baby gasping its life out on its mother's knee. The doctor had given it powder in the morning but it had taken nothing since. Two or three others drooping and sick in that tent. Next, a child recovering from measles sent back from the hospital before it could walk, stretched on the ground white and wan, three or four others lying about. Next, a girl of 24 lay dying on a stretcher. Her father, a big gentle Boer, kneeling beside her while in the next tent his wife was watching a child of six also dying and one of about five also drooping. Already this couple had lost three children in the hospital and so would not let those go, though I begged hard to take them out of the hot tent. "We must watch these ourselves", they said. Captain Hume had mounted guard over me – he thinks I am too sympathetic – but I sent him flying to get some brandy and get some down the girl's throat. But for the most part you must stand and look on helpless to *do* anything, because there is nothing to do anything with. Then a man came up and said "Sister," (they call me Sister) "come and see my child, sick for nearly three months". It was a dear little chap of four and nothing left of him except his great brown eyes and white teeth from which the lips were drawn back too thin to close. His body was emaciated.

"Captain Hume," I said, "you shall look." And I made him come in and shewed him the complete child-skeleton. Then at last he did say it was awful to see the children suffering so. The little fellow had craved for fresh milk, but of course, there had been none until the last few days and now our fifty cows only give four buckets, so you can imagine what feed there is for them. I sent Captain Hume for some of this and then made them lay the child outside on a pillow to get the breeze that comes up at sunset.

I can't describe what it is to see these children lying about in a state of collapse –

54

it's just exactly like faded flowers thrown away.[21] And one hates to stand and look on at such misery and be able to do almost nothing.

Today, 1 February, Mr. Grosskopf[22] came to see me. He is really a German from Berlin and that fact has saved him from the fate of too many. He holds a service for them in the camp every Thursday morning. He has throughout taken a firm bold line and has bravely told the Authorities that they are making the terrible mistake of appointing officials quite unfit for the posts. Men of low character or boys like Captain Hitchcock (only 23 and made Provost Marshal over the whole district) – ignorant and hot-headed and, worse still, making a habit of listening to false information. In this way things go here from bad to worse and all the good respectable well-established citizens of the town are terrorized and feel quite unable to find any link with the Military or their hangers-on.

Just imagine, that Adriaan Hofmeyr[23] is here, and was out at the camp today haranguing the people. Captain Hume spoke to me of him in glowing terms and was surprised when I told him he was a man I should refuse to meet – a disgraced character from the Colony, and who carried no weight with the Dutch who all knew his history. Now that man has gone on to Norvals Pont.

Mr. Grosskopf tells me 55 deaths have taken place in the camp during the last six or seven weeks . . . the normal death rate amongst the farms is very low.

Mr. Grosskopf ministered to that poor man Pienaar[24] who was hanged for shooting a soldier. He, Mr. Grosskopf, did plead so hard with the Authorities to postpone the execution till all the men who could give evidence could be got at. But they would not. There was really no evidence against him and Mr. Grosskopf does not doubt his innocence. He died quite quietly and content in his mind. They said his execution would have a good effect.

It is almost impossible to describe the moral atmosphere of this town. It affects me so that I am beginning to feel paralyzed and intimidated. I do not know how to put the feeling into words – like being in continual disgrace or banishment or imprisonment. Some days I think I must cut and run – escape on foot if a pass is refused, but escape somehow. The feeling is intolerable. To watch all these Englishmen taking this horrible line and doing these awful things, and if you are thought to be taking a different view, to be watched all the afternoon by a man like Captain Hume – it's insufferable. Oh, how I wanted to box his ears! I never realized it would be so hard. I only thought of physical hardships but they are nothing to this terror.

I have made it a rule to talk politics to no one under a Governor or a General. They at least respect my views and even ask my opinion, and I feel no harm can come of speaking to them boldly, but talk to these ignorant, narrow, heartless subordinates I will not – nor would it be safe.

I had rather a scene at the camp this morning with Captain Hume, the doctor and Mr. Macarty, the new Head of the camp. These men are watching me narrowly; they are insufferable and utterly devoid of feelings. If they allow that the rest of the world has feelings, they won't admit that Boers have. In the end I flung out at the doctor alone and bid him tell Captain Hume that I would never be spoken to again in such a way; that I would take orders from no one but the High Commissioner or Lord Kitchener in the camps. I had nothing to do with subordinate officers and if he interfered with me in any way I would report it to Sir Alfred Milner. And on the next occasion I shall repeat this to his face. I refuse to be under such men in any degree though I am quite willing to work with them so long as that does not mean an utter disregard of all natural and human feelings. I have no language strong enough to tell you what I think of the type of man placed in positions here which involve the well-being of hundreds of people – narrow, conceited and heartless. It is pitiable.

It is difficult to say how I dread my next plunge into the unknown at Norvals Pont, etc. . . . I am a real coward over it but it must be done. Just the way these subordinates look at you is enough, as if you were a fool, an idiot and a traitor combined. One fine day my tongue will get the better of me and I shall burst out very sharply. I am beginning to realize all the Dutch have felt all this time, but their way is to endure silently and I don't think they ever relieve themselves by a torrent of language. I can't in a letter make you understand a bit what it is like when your whole sense of justice and right is offended at every turn. This letter is all written in bits and scraps as I find time and I fear may not present any clear picture to you of things here. As to when it will be sent, I can say nothing for of course the Censor would not pass it and I have to wait a trustworthy hand to send it down by.

There has been a little stir among the troops this week for Commandos are all round us and De Wet passed only 15 miles off between us and Sanna's Post last night going south with 4 000 men. They have sent off 7 000 men to catch him by train and say they will have him this time. But it seems they were quite misinformed of his route – because they believed he was going the other side of Thaba 'Nchu. We also heard Lord Kitchener is sweeping the country with 100 000 men, starting from the North, laying waste everything as he goes. But we trust nothing we hear.

Today I had a long quiet talk with Mrs. Steyn – a handsome woman, dignified and self-controlled. She gave me a long and interesting account of her experiences – her surrender and her re-arrival in Bloemfontein.[25] I think she felt most her father's arrest and imprisonment – and her young and pretty sister brought from Philippolis in a cattle-truck and driven through the streets of Bloemfontein on foot in front of a soldier right out to the prisoners' camp.[26] The indignities to which they have been subjected are so great.

Now at last I must close this long-winded rigmarole; disjointed as it is, it may yet be of some interest to you. As I am starting for the South of the State to-morrow, I must leave this parcel to go by the first bearer to Cape Town and thence home . . .

Do not worry about me at all. I am perfectly well in body, only desperate in

56

mind, and I understand now how wise it was in Bible days to send people out two by two when there was something difficult to be done.[27] . . .

From the memoir

a) My kind Cape friends provided me with a box of foods such as should more or less withstand the heat and a kettle lamp for making tea and cocoa, and a few of them saw me off the evening of the 22nd.

It was a glorious moonlight night. Their kindness had been unceasing and I felt I had in them a solid background in case of need. But as the train moved off towards the strange hot war-stricken North with its accumulations of misery and bloodshed, I must own that my heart sank a little and I faced the unknown with great trepidation, in spite of the feeling that the deep desire of months which had laid so urgent a call upon me, was indeed finding accomplishment.

Young women of this generation could not, I think, credit the state of miserable cowardice in which I found myself when the train moved off – my friends were left behind and I had to face alone not only the strange country and strange language but the unknown and terrible strangeness of war . . .

It was a solitary journey. I was the only woman on the train and indeed I did not see another woman till my arrival in Bloemfontein.

It was wonderful to see the totally new world which greeted me at dawn and to watch the sun rise for the first time over the silent Karoo. The train was very slow and stopped about a good deal for meals as there was no food on the carriage. These station meals were very unappetizing and as they were thronged by British officers it was always difficult for a mere woman, middle-aged, and somewhat dowdy at that, to squeeze in. When there was time a relay was arranged which gave me chance of getting something. Oftener I fell back on my own supplies, which of course after the first day naturally failed in variety; the butter particularly, in spite of damp cloths and tin, soon ran away. But my great stand-by was a large tin of apricot jam – I recall it with gratitude for that tin served me through all my tedious journeys for months, moistening the inferior bread I could get here and there. For days, even weeks together, bread and apricot jam was my only food three times a day with a cup of cocoa. It got me through and that was the chief thing, but with the result that for many years to come I could not bear the sight, much less the taste, of apricot – such is it to have too much of a good thing!

b) Bloemfontein Station, crowded with men, chiefly soldiers, appalled me, as I found myself still the solitary female – and it needed much showing of papers to get through. I had also difficulty in getting a room in the little hotel which I had been told was the best in the town and at the sight of the people thronging there, my hopes fastened upon the welcome which Mr. Fichardt had assured me would await me at his mother's house.

57

Stormberg Station

7 (or 9) February 1901

A line from this junction where I am halting *en route* from Aliwal North back to Bloemfontein. The fact is, journeys in South Africa at present are mostly made up of halts. Such a waste of time and always spent in the society of Tommies of every grade.

I am more satisfied with affairs at Aliwal North (as they concern my work) than I could have anticipated and so also, in less degree, at Norvals Pont.[a] Now, therefore, I am hurrying back to Bloemfontein as quick as may be, having much to do there, and I live in hopes of getting further north where I am much needed. The distances are so huge. I cannot stay now to write details but I hope this may reach you about the time of my long letter, and so temper the sadness of that.

I have been travelling chiefly in the guard's vans of goods-trains this week, which leaves one more dead than alive – and to add to the difficulties of travel the ladies' waiting-rooms are all either locked up or made into offices and given up to the soldiery. Then you are put on a siding and left there for hours and hours and woe betide you if your lunch basket is empty! Coming from Springfontein I sat bolt upright for 15 hours in a guard's van shunting all night long, with only some boiled milk in a bottle for company. But the sunrise on the veld near Bethulie made me forgive it all. One night I was laid up in the train at Jagersfontein in a fortified siding – in fact De Wet has made it a little difficult this week to get about . . .

An old Basuto woman told me this week her heart was very sore for the Queen and questioned me much about the new King and his wife, whom she deemed most important of the two.

It is rather curious writing these vague sort of letters with nothing in them.

From the memoir

a) Shocked by the suffering and condition of Bloemfontein Camp and by the too evident lack of means and material to improve them – added to the fact that on high authority it was announced that more and more convoys of women and children were coming until the entire country population were swept up and interned – brought feelings of almost complete hopelessness. My own little fund was not calculated to provide such primal necessities as a water supply, tents, fuel and such things of huge cost. Yet without those things detailed relief was hardly more than a mockery. I had to think of the other camps (of which, I learnt, there were about 40) towards which I had also responsibility. I thought I ought to visit some of these and find out if their condition was similar or if Bloemfontein alone was in such distress and would need the greater help. It would also be easier when the total population of the camp was established to calculate the provision required in tents, huts, water, etc. It was useless expense to lay on $\frac{1}{2}$-inch water pipes to supply a camp of 2 000 if in a fortnight's time a 1-inch pipe would be needed for 4 000–6 000. Yet that is what happened.

I determined therefore to inform myself by a visit to the other camps while helping them by the gift of some cases of clothing, etc.

12. TO LADY HOBHOUSE

Begun at Naauwpoort Station
10 February 1901
(The Land of Nod)

... I wrote a few lines yesterday from Stormberg Station, and now should like to begin a more detailed account of Norvals Pont and Aliwal North Camps. It has been an exciting week because I had picked on the same days as De Wet had done for careering up and down this line.[1] At the best of times travelling is bad enough in this hot, dry, thirsty land, but add to that military control of everything, absence or partial disappearance of ordinary officials, permits and passes of endless kinds, the danger of travelling at night – the line occasionally torn up or a train burnt and the route blocked by countless strings of troop-trains and supply-trains all having to pass each other at sidings as the line is single – and you have some idea of the patience required.

One very hot day our eyes were refreshed by continual mirages presenting delicious views of cool stretches of water and imaginary cliffs. Sometimes I have slept in the train at sidings, sometimes at ghastly so-called hotels. A German Lutheran missionary has shown me much hospitality,[2] and guards have been most kind in admitting me to their vans. Everything being in military hands it is all dirty and uncared-for.

I had great fears as to what I might find in the camp at Norvals Pont knowing there was no town to draw upon for supplies or help of any kind. But I am glad to be able to report that it is far superior to the camp at Bloemfontein. It was first organised by a Lieutenant Wynne and now Captain Du Plat Taylor is Commandant. The spot chosen is a slope surrounded by hills and about a mile from the station. From the Captain's tent there is a pretty stretch of the Orange River visible and far off the blue square-topped hill which marks Bethulie. The general character of the hills is similar to this – Table Mountains constantly recurring all through the land.

The population of this camp is about 1 500, and it is well laid out in rows and streets – with numbers so that you can find your way about. There are only a few marquees and those are put in a row on one side to accommodate the true Refugees ... generally a very inferior type of underbred English, very pleased with themselves and very scornful of the country and the people as a whole. As these people are quite in a minority it is wholly absurd to call the camps by their name, "Refugee"; and even they cannot be said to have come quite of their own free will

– they were told their particular town was to be emptied out and they would starve if they did not come. So the British public has to maintain all these thousands of people.

The people I call prisoners-of-war occupy the centre and great bulk of the camp and beyond a broad space on the other side are pitched the tents of the single people who have surrendered or taken oaths or suchlike. Between the hours of 6 p.m. and 8 a.m. this part of the camp is prohibited from passing to the other side, and the soldiery have no tents, either, in the precincts of the camp. I must get this plan adopted in Bloemfontein.

Instead of drinking the waters of the Orange they use the river only for bathing and Captain Taylor had pipes laid on to a farm where a spring gives 14 000 galls. per hour, and this pure water is brought into the camp.[a]

Much to my delight I found there was much less overcrowding in Norvals Pont and that each tent was supplied with a low wooden bed, one or more mattresses, a bench, table utensils. Consequently the whole aspect of the people was different. The rations also were slightly better.

There was no violent outbreak of sickness though I understand that all the cases nursed in the hospital had died. This I attribute, and so did the people, to bad nursing. They have no trained nurse. I hope one may soon be procured.

The heat was very great. Captain Taylor told me himself that his large cool breezy marquee was usually 104° Fahr. and he believes the bell-tents with single canvas rise to 110° Fahr. The doctor said he could not use his clinical thermometer in them as it would not go down at all. I get greatly exhausted after sitting in these tents talking to the people a whole day, especially as there are six or seven in the tent, and others from outside come and throng round the narrow opening excluding any possible breath of air.

Captain Taylor had employed the men in the camp to make a tennis court[3] and this was just completed – sports of some kind are needed for exercise and to give something to do: the idle life is so demoralizing.

Sir Alfred Milner . . . is sending round the Education Commissioner[4] to arrange about schools . . . In Norvals Pont two large marquees are set apart and mistresses duly certificated are available from the camp population. Now the need of clothing for the children is very great.

Captain Taylor had been so unhappy about the clothelessness that he had ordered £150 worth and had given it out, but had received a reprimand for his extravagance. So I undertook to forward some and chose some women in the camp to store and distribute it where most needed.

I found two nice Miss Boshoffs[5] . . . These girls are ladies of good position and education. They have been singled out for exceedingly good treatment by the English – extras like jam and biscuits given to them and English papers supplied, etc. They have a bell-tent to themselves lined with thick green baize, two beds and all as neat and comfortable as can be.

60

They know where the Boer ammunition is stored and many secrets which the British would fain find out, so they laugh over the jam and biscuits, the officers' daily visits, etc. as all effort to worm from them their information. So they say plainly: "Though you hang us we will not tell you," and they are respected the more, though the jam, etc., is falling off. One of them took me a long walk to see the bathing place . . .

As we sat having tea at the door of the officers' tent, we could see horsemen sweeping across the plain about three miles off in a cloud of dust, and so near are the Boers that Major Legh thought it was a Commando.

The death rate is not nearly so high in this camp – less overcrowding and better water. I felt a great deal relieved and finding the Commandant at the station a vague sort of person with very little red tapeism, I seized the opportunity to squeeze a pass out of him to get on to Aliwal North. It was an awful journey as I have elsewhere told you, but still I did get there. If I were shaped like a truck and ran on wheels I should be much better suited for my present work. Major Legh had thought me an impostor when I first reached Norvals Pont and no wonder. I had been travelling two days and though it was late in the day had had no opportunity to wash and was so fagged I could hardly drag myself the length of the platform to get my letters of introduction out of my trunk. I explained this and then he laughed at my plight and said he would believe me, but that did not suit me so I fetched the letters and then he would not look at them.

A commercial traveller next befriended me by turning out of his room to let me have it on condition he might leave half his things in it. It was an appalling room; you had to stand in it with your skirts drawn round you – and to add to the misery a sandstorm came on and the heat was the most excessive I have felt out here. My tongue felt as if it were tied into a knot. After much worry I got two black ladies to come and wash the place out, and then I made a ring with insect powder and lay down in the centre of it. It was a very ghastly night and though not amusing at the time, I feel very much amused now in thinking of my absurd hunger, thirst, fatigue, dirt, loneliness and general misery.

I stayed as short a time as I could in this lovely lodge and then made off for Aliwal North . . . After endless difficulties I succeeded in getting there, and a dear little town it is. Unfortunately, as I had come unexpectedly, I had left my introduction to people there behind and could hardly tell where to begin. So after reporting myself I went to the Post Office and finding a fascinating young clerk got him to write me down a list of the chief inhabitants. So I managed to pick out the right ones to call upon, beginning with the Mayor and working down to the Medical Officer. They had formed a town committee to deal with the camp and have done their work really well.

Poor little Aliwal with only 800 inhabitants had in four weeks to receive and provide for a population of over two thousand – nearly three times its own number. And it does them credit for it is far away beyond the other camps – but then, they have a most helpful Commandant in Major Apthorpe[6] who could not speak highly enough of the people, their patience, good conduct and uncomplainingness under their privations and losses . . .

His camp can barely be called a prison, he has no soldiers or sentries and everyone is free to walk into the town or to receive visits from the people in the town without passes. The towns of Smithfield, Rouxville and Zastron are all there and so far only two deaths have taken place. Everything is beautifully arranged and provided for. He gives two tents to large families and offers sailcloth to any who care to put up wooden framework to make extra rooms. He encourages them to come and state their needs. The rations here are better – compressed vegetables are given and 1 lb. of potatoes twice a week. And potatoes are 6d. a pound, or eight times as dear as in London.

I found there a young woman, a complete cripple from hips downwards and therefore quite unfit for tent life, but anxious to earn her own living as she could do so by sewing in a town. He was perfectly willing she should go, if she knew where and how, and I am trying to get this arranged in Aliwal North.

Clothing for children is much needed, especially now the schools are opening, and I chose some women to receive and distribute the goods. The great lack has been soap. In neither camp has any been supplied, and those without money have been unable to wash clothes or persons properly. This seems to have been due to a careless order from Headquarters with regard to the rations, and men don't think of these things unless it is suggested to them, they simply say: "How dirty these people are!"

The fact is, I believe, the military supply is very short. I bought soap in the town and sent it into the camp for immediate needs, also material for the women to make up for themselves. Many have brought their sewing-machines when they saved nothing else.

13 February. From Bloemfontein. I have only just today found hasty opportunity to send my first long letter down to Cape Town (employing the Education Commissioner for the purpose) . . . I wish this could have followed with it, but I had no time to arrange. This letter being about better camps would mitigate somewhat the badness of Bloemfontein Camp. I hope to hold up the others as patterns so as to make them bring this one up to the mark . . . However, *soap* is promised at last in Bloemfontein and the brick ovens for boiling the water are complete; but the three little hospitals are full of typhoid and many sick lie in the tent.

General Pretyman has left and is succeeded by Goold-Adams . . . I must feel my way. His reign seems to have begun with greater stringency. For instance on Saturday the market place was suddenly surrounded by soldiery and everybody seized and their passes demanded. Numbers who were merely passing or attending to business had left their passes at home, or had not got the right kind of pass and these were fined or imprisoned. It's a regular terror, these passes. For instance, Dr.

Bidwell,[7] an Englishman I know, has to have four different kinds of passes and then lives in continual dread of arrest.

Mrs. Simpson, an Englishwoman, has just been arrested and deported. She has a good house just outside the town and is accused of signalling to the Boers by night. No Jingo, even, for a moment believes this to be true, but it is supposed the Military have need of her house.

A few nights ago, the Provost Marshall (an office we all learn to dread) surrounded with soldiers the house of a Mrs. Du Toit, whose husband, a minister of the Church, is deported, and who is now earning her living by keeping a boarding-house. He and his Lieutenant entered the house and without knocking or any kind of warning, walked into every room in the house at 10.30 p.m. and searched them. The inmates, many of whom were Jingoes, were furious. It was stated afterwards that De Wet was supposed to be in hiding in the town in woman's clothes !!!

. . . From all accounts the mass of the Boer prisoners are determined never to live under British rule and now this camp system with all that led up to it has consolidated the feelings of the women into one strong desire to retain at all costs the independence of their country . . . Not that, as far as I can discover, they hate the English at all. The English hate the Dutch and take every opportunity of shewing it and of saying so, but the Dutch women, though aghast at the barbarities committed by what they believed to be a civilized nation, bear no hatred and are quite prepared to be friendly with any English individually, though determined not to have their rule. This is quite clear everywhere.

In Aliwal North it was quite disgusting, the fulsome kind of spurious loyalty displayed. It protruded itself everywhere and grated horribly. One had to be constantly disssociating oneself from it. Major Apthorpe quite agreed with me it was unbearable – the manners and language and attitude of this class of English – and we could not wonder that the Dutch feel offended by it.

In this Land of Nod I fall asleep between the sentences as I write them and waking up can't remember what I wrote on the last page. This terrible affliction of which I am much ashamed is the cause of the disjointed character of my letters. Now and then I have to give in, lie down and sleep soundly, then start again. It is a matter for congratulation that I have no reputation to lose, because if I had I should certainly lose it. I begin to have a fellow-feeling for the foolishness of our various Generals. I get up about 5 a.m., however, so the day is fairly long and you must not believe me too lazy.

I wonder if the Committee at home will think me wrong or right in proposing to spend some of the Fund in the education of some of the highest-class girls in the camp. The thing is this: Dr. Andrew Murray's daughter, Miss Murray, was Head of the Dames Institute here. It is a large place where the elite of the country girls were always educated. Of course, everything was upset or destroyed there, but now Miss Murray has been asked by Government to come back and try to begin work again, under certain conditions which she did not deem too hard. But she has,

63

of course, no boarding pupils though she may get some day ones. Those who would be her scholars are scattered far and wide or in camps – and no money forthcoming.

I suggest taking some girls out of the camp here and paying their schooling for – say – six months; say £25 for six months – tuition, board and lodging inclusive. As I am not sure you will approve (please ask the executive)[b], I will only begin with four girls. The mothers cannot bear to see their girls month after month idle in these camps. The life tends to be very demoralizing and this camp in particular is quite bad for young girls. We all feel that. I can rig them out with clothes from my stores. You must tell the Fund Committee I have been very economical of the money so far, because I found that by pressure and representations the Military could be squeezed into doing much more, I thought I would begin by using influence rather than money.

Now I am beginning to find out the best ways of spending the money . . . [e.g.] to provide, if procurable, materials for both men and women to work at for their own use for sale and for occupation. A man said if only he had some leather he could keep his family in shoes and cobble those of others for a few pence. To-morrow I shall try and purchase the material but you must recollect everything here is scarce and I may have to go to Cape Town. Today I found a man making jolly little baskets most cleverly just out of bushes from the kopje. The Dutch are so very full of resource and so clever. Then, too, they can make their own soap with fat and soda and though after three weeks' nagging I have now got the Government permit to supply soap in the rations, yet we may find it cheaper to supply the materials and employ a few women to make the necessary supply for the camp. At last, too, the tanks have come and now we shall be able to begin boiling all the water before giving it out and I hope this may lessen the fever.

The throat complaints are, the Doctor says, owing entirely to the bad smells resulting from the bad sanitary arrangements.[8] This I have begged him to have altered at once and was able to quote the superior plans of Aliwal North. He promised to carry out the improvements, not being a bad little man at all; but he is only an Army doctor and has no experience of women and children and their complaints, so he is a square man in a round hole. A poor girl died last night. He had had her wrapped up in wet sheets at a wrong time – it went to her head; she was raving mad awhile and gradually sank.

Last night we had tremendous rain. I was walking back from the camp watching the lightning which has a way of standing still here, bolt upright, like a bar against the inky sky. Fortunately Mrs. Steyn, who was driving home with her trooper behind her, caught sight of me in the distance and wheeled round to pick me up. She is allowed to drive to a certain distance. To-morrow I am to spend the afternoon with her, there is so much she wants to hear and to tell. She says my coming has been the first ray of joy since she was brought back a prisoner. It is hard to see how. Mrs. Steyn speaks so gratefully of young Lieutenant Hole. He was her first gaoler and so very kind and good to her and regardful of her feelings. He writes to her now, signing himself "Your Affectionate Enemy". She is a very winning woman.

On Friday I am invited formally by the Ladies' Loyal Guild to meet the members . . . I have accepted . . . I have offered them a short address on my work and its objects.

Tonight, coming from camp, I got stuck in a bog. The rain has been tremendous and, not knowing the look of the ground, I carefully stepped where it looked driest and so sank to my knees in solid black mud. It was too comical; and there I stuck till a cart came by with someone in it I knew and pulled me out.

I can't describe how good and kind Mrs. Fichardt is to me. The comfort of her house really makes it possible for me to do much more than I could otherwise manage, and her carriage is constantly at my disposal. Tonight I am going to write to Sir Alfred Milner to ask if he will let her girls come back; she pines for them so.

I am finishing off this letter in haste because Mrs. Pretyman is going down to Cape Town and I have a hope she may take the packet of papers for me. Censorship is very strict. Mrs. P. is going to England and you must be prepared to hear her say that the women's camp is a wonderful place – everyone happy and cheerful – and the healthiest spot in Bloemfontein. She walked through it once without eyes or sympathy and has never enquired into the death rate or the need of soap or anything else.

I want to get to Kroonstad. There are 4 000 there and the Government is at last beginning to see it must clothe as well as feed. A young Lieutenant has been wildly running round the town buying flannelette and thought he had done marvels by sending 50 yards to a huge northern camp. The feminine part of the community is much amused and I mean to make it my text in calling on Colonel Goold-Adams to-morrow.

Don't be surprised if at any time you don't hear from me.

I really think the Military conscience is aroused about these camps and they (the Military Authorities) only need some direction and suggestions to really try and make them fairly liveable. At the best they are horrid and the people sad and weary, but so very good.

A little incident will shew you the feeling. A few days since, Adriaan Hofmeyr went out to harangue the camp. This week they sent out Piet de Wet,[9] brother of the General, to address the women and ask them to induce their husbands to surrender. A large concourse assembled. When he had finished he looked markedly at a prominent women – a Mrs. Botha – a nice good creature, asking her support. Mrs. Botha returned the look, solemnly shook her head and moved off to her own tent followed by a string of all the women, till the wretched orator found himself alone on the platform.

I have been very interested in a little baby born this week in a wee tent, so poverty stricken. The mother asked me to name the child with a name suitable to the times – I suggested "Dolores" or what I thought would be better still, "Hope". But the sad, sick mother could see no hope and chose "Dolores" for her little child.

Tell Mrs. Chitty and Dorothy Bradby the clothes are lovely and so useful and appreciated. But the Dutch in Holland have more ideas than our workers for they have sewn letters of sympathy inside the legs of combinations and the sleeves of sundry undergarments; and these have caused great interest in the camp.

I do wish some half dozen Sir Edward Frys could come out here and teach a little law and justice. It is sickening.

Yours affectionately, E. H.

P.S. Just come from a long interview with Goold-Adams who is agreeable, energetic, and very desirous of making the camps what they should be. He felt with me that this one is *not* what it should be. He is open and kind-hearted but evidently not a man of any particular mental power. He is trying to carry on a Government with no money and seems a little perplexed, but the faith of all of them in Alfred the Great and his policy is implicit and they don't look beyond.

From the memoir

a) I tried to get the same method adopted in Bloemfontein but was told the cost was prohibitive.

b) Not having witnessed as I had the demoralizing side of camp life (quite apart from its physical effect on the girls) the Committee were not in sympathy with my plan of rescuing some girls by placing them in schools, though the four already so placed could continue. No doubt they were in a sense just; I had conceived the idea when, confronted with the mass for whom *nothing* effective could be done failing the provision of prime necessities by the Government, it seemed wiser to save and arm for the future at least a few. So it was only four and never more. That the money was not thrown away I have had frequent assurance and curiously only a short time ago (now nearly a quarter of a century after), a letter reached me from one of the four:

Writing from Boshof, Eunice van Schalkwyk says:

> "Seeing your address in a little magazine . . . I am going to let nothing deter me from writing to you.
>
> "I am Eunice Ferreira, one of the girls you sent to school in Bloemfontein from the camp there. Afterwards I obtained a Government bursary and continued my studies in the Eunice High School and later on qualified for teacher. I taught for several years and have been married now for nine years.
>
> "I have always wanted to write to you, to thank you personally for what

you did for me and also for my people at the camp at Bloemfontein. It was through you I was able to go to school and consequently stood the chance of getting a bursary. So you see I have practically to thank you for my education, and believe me, my dear Miss Hobhouse, I have always and ever will appreciate your kindness with a very thankful heart. You live in the heart of the South African women and we will pass it on as an inheritance to our children.

"Of course we have never really been out of touch with you. Through Mrs. Steyn we often hear about you, and sometime she places parts of your letters in our magazines; so you see you are amongst us still in spite of your personal absence.

"My mother, Mrs. Theo Ferreira, was visiting here last month and she said if I did write to you I must give you her very best love. She still has flower and vegetable seeds which you gave her. We so often speak of you when we are together . . ."

13. TO MRS. CHARLES MURRAY

Bloemfontein
12 February 1901

I was truly glad for the letters you forwarded which I received today on my return from my little tour. It has been a hard ten days physically, but with a good deal to gladden me. I fear I am a terrible bother to you about forwarding letters, but you are so very kind and it is such a help . . .

I gather from Mr. Rowntree's letter that you could not rightly have understood my letter about the nurses.[a] It was not a "suggestion" but a "demand", and an urgent one, for trained nurses. Untrained we can get, but we need trained, and I wrote with the full sanction of Major Cray to see if one, two, or three could be procured from Cape Town or, failing that, from England.

Pay: 5/– a day, rations and a tent.

Remember, this is just to do the one work of coping with enteric, dysentery and other ills and has nothing to do with the general work for which I have plenty of sympathizers, and interpreters galore.

Perhaps I had better run down to Cape Town myself and hunt some up . . . Send me full particulars of any you can hear of. I will submit them to the Authorities here and get passes arranged for them. Our one trained nurse is very weary and if she breaks down, where should we be? We have three little hospitals full in the camp and many sick in the tent.

There is no responsibility resting on you – merely, we must have nurses and I thought you and Dr. Murray would be sure to know if there were any in or about Cape Town.

I have much to tell you, both bad and good.

a) The question of nurses touched on in this letter was of supreme importance – it had been acute. [...] Before any could be found a regulation had been made that only women chosen and passed by Dr. J. Waterston[1] should be allowed. That of course meant the employment of Johannesburg refugees – in themselves by a large percentage very undesirable people and seldom trained to any such work. In addition, for the most part, bitterly opposed to the Boers. Major Goold-Adams asked me to interview and advise upon these women, which I did, feeling Dr. J. Waterston's choice had been most injudicious – the events proved it to be so. One drank and another was discovered to have been a forger, etc. They disappeared, though what the Military did with them is unknown to me.

14. TO LEONARD HOBHOUSE

Bloemfontein
18–22 February 1901

I suppose I must in duty bound write to someone though I have become such a doormouse I would a great deal rather go to sleep.

Our camp is getting slowly better and more towards the level of Aliwal and Norvals Pont. Today my whole mind has been bent upon mattresses. Colonel Goold-Adams is quite concerned about them and Sunday afternoon he rode out to the camp and we had another chat. Finally (as he says for love or money he can get no mattresses) we agreed that we would procure material and stuffing – get camp women to make them and pay them for their work. This will be best, for then they can earn a little. It is all so difficult because material of all descriptions is getting as short as made goods. So in a few weeks I trust each tent will have a single mattress and the inmates be able to take turns in getting a comfortable night. Besides this I am promised a larger supply of tents so that there may be less overcrowding. At present it averages six to a small tent, which of course means nine or ten in many cases. The cubic capacity is under 500 cubic feet – considerably; so even for six persons imagine the atmosphere at night.

I have such splendid helpers in Mrs. Blignaut,[1] Miss Fleck[2] and Mrs. Krause[3], three ladies of the town . . . Mrs. Blignaut is President Steyn's sister . . . She and Miss Fleck toil like slaves and take the bulk of the clothing off my hands, so that I can devote the whole of my attention to "squeezing the Authorities"!

Captain Hume is reduced to a state of abject deference, continually asking what my wishes are and how they can best be carried out. You see I had told Goold-Adams what I thought of him and he said he must appoint him Commandant from lack of other men, but he would give him a good talking to. He did so with excellent results and yesterday he asked me if the Captain was doing better. I was able to report that he had shewn more vigour and interest.

Now Colonel Goold-Adams has sent to ask me to an interview to give my opinion where to plant out the nurses just had up from Cape Town. Four have come. I don't approve of these nurses because they are British Refugees from these States and not, I think, the right kind of person to put in any way over the people in the camps. However, they may do their work well – we shall see.[4] But it is Hobson's choice; nurses are so scarce. I had written to my friends at Cape Town, begging them to find some fully trained nurses who spoke both Dutch and English and they reply that there are none. The Army won't give us nurses because the camps are now *supposed* to be civilian, so we must make the best we can of these half-trained women. They will have no jurisdiction, of course, beyond the precincts of the hospitals.

At my interview today I hope to broach again the subject of ministers. Births, deaths, and even marriages occur, for Lord Kitchener himself can't stop the course of nature and they do need their own Dutch ministers! I enjoyed asking him (Goold-Adams) about it the other day because it tied him into such knots of perplexity. Understand that since his arrival Civil Government is *supposed* to have begun and the camps in particular are *supposed* to be run on civil lines. The Deputy Administrator, as he is called, wears civilian clothes and it certainly is good to see someone out of khaki. Moreover, if any civilian wears khaki he will be arrested. So we play at pretending the war is over and we are developing the civil life of the community. It is such a curious position – hollow and rotten to the heart's core – to have made all over the State large uncomfortable communities of people whom you call Refugees and say you are protecting, but who call themselves prisoners-of-war, compulsorily detained and detesting your protection. The whole object, of course, is to enable Chamberlain to say in Parliament that the country is settled and Civil Administration begun. It's a farce.

A few days since, Mr. Blignaut, who served the Free State Government many years,[5] was sent for and asked if he would take office. He replied: "No, not as long as the war is going on – when peace is declared, I will." So about the ministers the same difficulty comes up. They can't say the country is settling and developing, etc. without the Church doing its part and they dare not risk the influence the Dutch ministers are supposed to have over the feelings of their people.

I gather from the little English news, well censored, that is allowed to filter through, that you people at home think the war is over – or if not you, personally, yet the majority. And those who don't think that, are weary and try to make-believe it is over by pushing war telegrams into obscure corners of the paper. It is childish to pretend like that. There never was such a mistake. The war is not over and we here can see no glimmer of hope that it ever will be over unless a miracle completely reverses the policy which directs it.

It rouses strong anger in us that people at home can so lightly put aside, just because they are weary and uninterested, a great matter which is causing the misery, ruin and death of thousands. They were mad for war news while it was the rage; they ought to have it thrust down their throats whether they will or not, now that it nauseates. I wish all Jingoes would come out here and have a good course of martial law. That's the best cure I know of for the military spirit. A homeophathic cure perhaps, but a very thorough one.

It's one thing to admire marching regiments, it's quite another matter to be dominated and ruled by those regiments. They seize and monopolize every public office – the best private houses fall to their share. You cannot stir in or out of town without their leave – nor live in the town unless they permit it. They say what newspapers shall be read and what news may be given in the favoured journals; they read your letters before you get them and as many as they choose of what you write before they are despatched. You can't ride a bicycle without leave, nor be out after 9 p.m.; in many places lights must be out at 8.30, and to bed you must go. In fact your life is hemmed and hedged in by military rules and you can't realise what that means till you come and see what an imprisonment it truly is.

Some few kick against it, as it goes on, month in, month out, with a sort of impotent fury; others relapse into dull, dogged sulks. Of course it kills energy and enterprize – trade stands still, people are heartless and hopeless, only asking "how long?". But those who are suffering most keenly and who have lost most, either of their children by death or their possession by fire and sword, such as the recon-centrated women in the camps, have the most conspicious patience and never express a wish that their men should be the ones to give way. It must be fought out now, they think, to the bitter end. Something might have been effected in the way of settlement had proper emissaries been employed, but another error was made in sending as Peach Envoys[6] men whom the Burghers[6] could only look upon as traitors to their country. Since then the Rev. Adriaan Hofmeyr has again been deputed to go round the country and talk to a People who know his past and cannot respect him or trust him.

Sometimes it seems to me that Steyn and De Wet are Juarez and Porfirio Diaz[7] over again. There, too, the French held the capital, Mexico City, also the chief towns, and Juarez was driven from place to place, and later Diaz had only a hand-ful of patriots compared with the great French Army; but his skill and mobility won the day and history may repeat itself . . . However, when you read all this a month hence, the war *may* be over – De Wet captured, Kitchener triumphant . . .

I am planning to go to Kimberley next week and take Springfontein again *en route*. Fever has broken out there badly. It will be a hideous journey right down to De Aar and up again and De Wet may be on the war-path. Today I have heard that Kitchener has had a narrow escape of capture. The Boers heard he was on the war-path sweeping down to De Aar, so they laid a trap to catch his little armoured train; but it so happened an empty train was in front of him containing nothing but a cannon: so they took that and Kitchener, just behind, found out they had mis-taken the train in time to escape by rushing back.

After the elaborate preparation I witnessed last week – the loaded troop-trains, the truck-loads of Cape-carts, waggons, artillery, men, horses and mules; the noise and excitement and scurry and delay and paraphernalia – De Wet was not caught this time! I felt sure he was safe as I sat for hours (waiting for my train) watching the manifold preparations. Why on earth don't they try his methods of fighting? However, the trip after him was not fruitless for they captured Steyn's gold sleeve-links,[8] and these are now bandied about amongst the officers in the town. It is nice to have something to shew after a big movement of troops round the country!

Today I have been addressing the Loyal Ladies' League who call themselves a non-political organization . . . I gave them an account of my work and I suggested to them to take up the work of looking after the Native camps which have been formed and where I gather there is much sickness and destitution.

I am sorry that I cannot give at all a good account of the War Office nurses. Everywhere it is the same story – their giddiness, inattention to duty, slovenly work and flirtations. Only today two nurses of widely different experience have each told me they feel ashamed of their uniform, and all agree that the majority came out only to get what fun they could out of life. Theatres and riding parties are their delight and the Tommies tell me they loathe the very sight of them. Now Kitchener has ordered that their riding is to be prohibited and it serves them right, for they have abused their privileges and disgraced the career which Florence Nightingale had made and ennobled. Of course there are a few splendid exceptions: I speak of the general tone of the mass. (In one hospital here the milk for the entire establishment is *kept* on the window-sill of the *enteric ward*.)

22 February. I have not much to add today because I was laid up yesterday and took a day off in bed – nothing really amiss, but I needed a rest. In the morning word came that the two Miss Bothas had been let out of camp and allowed at my request to go to Miss Murray's school[9] and I had to go and see that they were clothed and shod. Poor girls! They said it had been such a treat to sleep in a bed once more after four months in camp on the ground. One of them who had a slight tendency to deafness has now become, I fear, permanently deaf in both ears; she caught such chills from the draught and damp coming under the tent. Consequences such as this which don't appear in the death-rate or anywhere else will be very common results of this camp system.

I do wish someone would come out and take up the question of the Native camps. From odd bits I hear it would seem to be much needed and I dare not spare a moment to look into the question. It is true I asked the Loyal Ladies here to investigate the matter, but though they said they would I could see that they were not the right kind of person to be of any use and they were quite sure beforehand that there was neither sickness, suffering or death amongst those people. I hear there is much of all three.

An old man called Rensburg was arrested in our camp yesterday. Even the Sergeant-Major was very angry about it. It appears that a disagreeable and gos-

71

siping woman Refugee went to the Commandant and stated that she had heard the old man say: "Perhaps the Boers will be in Bloemfontein again some day." So he was arrested and sent into town to prison. Many say the old man never said it, but if he did – why, it's only what crowds think and say almost daily . . .

I heard last night that De Wet had taken the mail-train so I fear for my letters, but there is no certainty if it was an up or down train.

Oh! *Do* write strong articles and wake people up to stop this wretched state of things in a better way than by sending more men, or by continual repression of all the best and strongest and wisest folk in the country. It's a problem I am always trying to work out. How long can you by force go on repressing thought, speech, feeling before it bubbles up and boils over? Perhaps a good while with this quiet sort of people, but what a fizz there will be some day. Far better lift the lid now a little and let steam gradually work off – that's the only chance, if chance there be.

Are the Liberals going to be worth anything this session? If only they knew how sore, depressed, worried and well-nigh hopeless the Heads of things out here are, for really they don't know how to act. They say *every single thing has turned out different* to what they expected, and really they are puzzled and humiliated.

It would surely strengthen the hands of critics at home to press harder and harder and not be so weak-kneed. Make them hammer away to send proper envoys to Steyn and De Wet, etc. and not to bother about the invasion of the Colony: we are invading their country all the time.

I simply long to escape from the horrid atmosphere of this Orange [River] Colony (under martial law) . . . I wonder how you all are; you have not exactly showered letters upon me . . .

Tell Nora all the clothing is a godsend here – nothing is superfluous. Small boys have a wondrous gift for wearing out their clothes and now autumn has come I hardly know how we shall get them all clothed fast enough. Whatever one does is such a drop in this ocean of misery.

Yours, E. H.

P.S. I could wish the Marlborough masters[10] had given that Captain Hume a more effective education and a good many more lickings!!

15. TO MRS. CHARLES MURRAY

Bloemfontein

24 February 1901

Your letter of the 17th reached me last night. The trains have been slow this week.

I am glad you have heard of some nurses you deem suitable, but since I wrote to you Colonel Goold-Adams tells me that a rule has been made that all nurses sent up to this country *must be passed by Dr. Jane Waterston,*[1] but I fancy she would be glad enough to hear of some who really have qualifications. So the first step would be to go to her, I suppose . . .

With regard to Aliwal North, you are not correct in thinking it wholly of Refugees. They are in every camp quite the minority . . .

I have kept very well so far and do not feel so fagged now the more autumnal weather is setting in. I often think of you all and long with a thirsty longing to jump into a train for Cape Town . . .

16. TO MRS. CHARLES MURRAY

Bloemfontein
25 February 1901

Forgive such frequent letters, but I am anxious the enclosed [No enclosure] should be read by you and should reach Mr. Schultz so that you may be prepared to forward clothing, etc. should either Sir Alfred Milner or the Military Authorities send word that a truck is ready.

I am very anxious to make a base of supplies here. Today I have been talking to a gentleman (civilian) just made Superintendent of Kroonstad Camp[1] and agreed with him to bring more clothes as soon as I can procure more. We have given away nearly all I brought up, here and at Norvals Pont, and I hope to take the remainder to Springfontein this week. I am going to Kimberley for a bit – please address to me there . . . It will be a difficult journey.

So grateful for all your letters and so anxious and sorry about the plague.[1] Do boil your water always.

17. CORRESPONDENT NOT IDENTIFIED

Bloemfontein
25 February 1901

Unfortunately that wonderful paper, the *Bloemfontein Post*, has got hold of me[a] and is employed in holding me up to ridicule,[1] so since I have been thus made public they have begun censoring my letters, which is most annoying. Do be careful what you write to me. They opened Kate Courtney's letter today. How grieved I am to hear of her new worry about Mr. Courtney – this affection of the heart sounds rather serious and she says will put an end to much, if not all, public speaking. If he and Mr. Morley both get shelved through illness alas! for South Africa. It will have to work out its own salvation, I think . . .

I have refreshed my jaded soul with the *Speaker* today. It is nice to find these things are still being written and that some people are still battling, for here it is hard to believe it . . . I am working at trying to get some of the people released, and sent either to friends or to their homes *if on the railway line*. Two mails now I have heard nothing from Aunt Mary, which makes me very anxious, but De Wet has taken one or two trains and my letters may have fallen to his share.

27 February. This week and today is the anniversary of Paardeberg and Cronjé's surrender. I fully believe the Authorities had meant to make De Wet surrender this week and they had made vast preparations. From De Aar to Norvals Pont the land bristled with Colonels and Generals. But again they have failed and we hear De Wet has broken his barriers and escaped – whither we know not. It is a great trial that he has chosen that spot for his operations because it makes one's work almost impossible. For several days we were cut off from all postal communications with Cape Town but now the trains do get through, slow and late, but all civilians are turned out at Norvals Pont and allowed to go no further. As there is no sort of accommodation there, this is pleasant! . . .

I have just been seeing off a German woman from the camp who has a permit to go back to Germany. She tells me she will have to go via East London, thence by sea to Cape Town – the line is more or less open that way . . .

I have now got a permit for Kimberley with leave to break the journey at different camps – but what's the use? The highest Authorities may issue it, but when you get to the station they refuse to issue a ticket. I found the Widow Minnaar there today with her four children. She was released from camp and given a permit to go to her people at the Paarl. Arrived at the station she was refused a ticket beyond Norvals Pont. Such a scene with her and the officials all yesterday and it began again today! So I begged her to go that far and wait the first opportunity to get on. Poor thing! She went about wailing: "Shall I have British protection?" till we couldn't help laughing. She is frightened out of her wits and thinks it best to keep on asking for "British protection", till all the officers are perfectly tired of "protecting" her. I say, serve them right for uprooting her from her home and casting her adrift. They only say: "What a tiresome woman, we can't have her here, planted at the station."

A Mr. Webb was here last night. He is a Rand Refugee, and an old friend of Mrs. Fichardt. He has just been appointed civilian Head of Kroonstad Camp and came to talk matters over with me. He says he means to be very kind to the people and I think he is most kindly disposed, but evidently has no sort of idea how to organize. But the plan is to try and get posts for the various Johannesburg Refugees now living at the coast towns, weary and hard up as they are. It was very amusing to hear this man give his views on the British Army and above all on the officers; their laziness, incompetence, and love of amusement. He is afraid his temper is too short to work under Martial Law – it *is* a fearful drain on one's patience.

This army, it is thought, will never catch De Wet; there is too much riding and shooting and picnicking and polo and golf-playing for war to have much place. Possibly a small fresh army with some fight in it, and before they fall into the habits here, might ride after him and catch him. But all those Tommies asleep upon the line and all the badly kept offices! Oh, dear!, it's dreadful. Still, I have a fellow-feeling for the sleepy and think anyone who keeps awake in this country deserves a V.C. But as Mr. Webb says, the officers *might* behave like gentlemen. I assure you I

74

do not exaggerate when I say that we all feel the same about it and when any given officer does behave in a gentlemanly way it is remarked on as a matter of surprise. So you see we are not in love with the Imperial Army!

I am beginning to think a good deal about the future and my best plan of procedure. The demand for clothing is so huge that it is hopeless to think that the private charity of England and Colonial working-parties combined can effectively cope with more than a very small portion of it. The Government recognize that they must provide necessary clothes and I think we all agree that having brought these people into this position it is their duty to do so. Yesterday Captain Trollope, now Chief Superintendent of camps throughout the Colony, asked me right out if I would pay for all the clothes they provide and I refused most decidedly.[b] You see they (the Government) are very hard up.[c] It is of course a question for the English folk to decide how long they like to go on making and sending clothes. There is no doubt they are immensely appreciated; besides, they are most *made up*, which the Government clothing won't be. But if I am not here to distribute them or at least to choose and form a suitable and reliable group of women to do so, the things would all be lumped together by the Superintendent and the knowledge that they are the gift of sympathizers entirely lost.

So far five camps have been and are open to me – but several more remain in this State and very large and important ones in the Transvaal. I may by luck get to Kroonstad, etc. but Lord Kitchener has twice distinctly refused me permission to go further north. I have written again to him and perhaps by the time I return from Kimberley the reply may have come. Supposing it is an unswerving negative as I half fear it will be, I am wondering what will be my best plan. Possibly to arrange (as I am doing) a set of people in each place to receive clothing and comforts sent, and to keep in touch with the Committee in Cape town, and – for myself – to come home to give what information I can upon the general situation . . .

Any amount of money *could* of course be spent in making the people more comfortable, especially now that they are getting to the end of such small sums as they had with them, and much might be spent in getting girls and boys to the *good* schools; but the largest sums will be needed as and when they are allowed to leave and go back to begin life again. If I knew how much money was likely to come together I should better know how to lay it out to the best advantage. For instance I should not hesitate to provide one mattress for every tent in Bloemfontein Camp. I have waited and waited for the Military yet nothing is done, though I got all the estimates for them myself. I reckon if forage were given me for stuffing, it would yet cost £87 to give each tent a *small* mattress *made by themselves*; and a small low bedstead for each would cost as much again. Now I still hope the Government will keep their promise and provide these necessaries and then I can give little extras; for the autumn nights have come and it is cold after the heat of the day. Soon it will be very cold . . .

I think I shall decide this: to go to Kimberley next week taking the southern camps *en route* and spend some time there. On my return to have a final "see" into things here and, if allowed, go further north. Should Kitchener prove obdurate, then go down to Cape Town and explain the situation to people interested there before going home. But I entertain a hope that in three weeks' time travelling may be easier than at present, though it is a slender hope.

Considering that in England you know really far more than we do of what is going on *all* over this country you will best be able to judge if the time has come to carry out what we proposed at home, viz. L.B.B.'s[2] visit to be a sequel to mine. I think she could stand the work in the winter, which all tell me is really a perfect season, but I feel glad she was not here to attempt work in the heat. Then arises the question – would she be allowed to come up? Would Milner, Kitchener and Co. pass her? There perhaps you at home can judge best for you may see some end to the war which truly we do not. My name, as you see by enclosed, has now been incorporated in the new rules just drawn up by Captain Trollope for this Colony and that gives me a certain position,[3] but perhaps they would substitute her name for mine. It is difficult writing of plans so long beforehand. You will not read this for a month at least, and she, if she comes, could not be here without the lapse of another month and the future is so dark and vague.

I ought to be starting home about the second week in May. I aim, of course, at staying up north the last moment possible, but when I leave this hospitable house which has been my Headquarters, it will mean a very rough life and I do not know how long my strength will hold out. Probably I shall beg to be allowed to go myself into the camp at Norvals Pont as a "paying Refugee"!!!. . .

The four girls selected for the institute are: Hetty Botha, Lizzie Botha, Engela van Rooyen, Eunice Ferreira, aged 14 to 18 years. The day after her arrival Eunice developed typhoid and we must send her to the Volks Hospital and select another girl in her place. Mrs Botha, mother of the above girls, is my great help and stand-by in the camp. She was née Stegmann, of an old Cape family. Her husband was Landdrost of Philippolis and she has of course lost everything. But she has set a splendid example in the camp of what you may call common sense, and besides allows us to make her tent a regular depot for bundles of clothing, comforts, etc. of all kinds. She does hours of untiring interpreting for me personally. I have failed to get as matron the woman I wanted, and so I have definitely engaged Mrs. Botha to give five hours a day to go round the tents and look after the sick and emaciated babies and the women who are ill but unable to go to the hospital either because that is full or because of so many small children they cannot leave. I have offered her one pound a week to do this and I feel it is money well laid out. So many of the more ignorant *bywoners*[4] are puzzled by the doctor and the Captain and all the officials and need a link through a kind sensible woman like Mrs. Botha. To her, now almost penniless, the money will be an immense boon. She is also doing a great deal of voluntary work, such as undertaking 200 families for the clothing com-

76

mittee (no sinecure) and cooking and tending a dear old prisoner named Pio who is in a consumption and came up from Green Point war prison because the sea air was killing him.

You know we have three tin hospitals – each containing sixteen beds, always full – for men, women, and children, also two or three marquees for other cases. Sister Kennedy had done splendid work in her domain battling against incessant difficulties. She is the daughter of a clergyman close to Salcombe, and has been out here nursing sixteen months, but she is not a War Office nurse. So she has worked in this camp since its formation for the 5/- a day and rations of a civilian – without the field allowance or colonial allowance of an Army nurse. When I tell you we have had some 70 cases of typhoid besides an epidemic of measles, pneumonia, tonsilitis and other cases you will realize what the strain on her has been. In addition, she has had the worry of nothing ready to her hand – the very hospitals only built by degrees through it all. And to crown the work, she has had the task of training Boer girls to work under her. Until lately she has had to get meals how and when she can. She is very small and delicate but full of pluck. Now, she can speak very highly of the Boer girls saying they are making great progress and developing into good nurses – far superior to the terrible type of women (semi-qualified Johannesburg Refugees) sent up to help us from the Cape.

One of these, who *seemed* to promise well, we sent to Kroonstad and she has just returned from there because she drinks, so we have been given her here to keep a close eye upon her. Another horrible woman has been sent us also, who, I am told, forged her papers and has come only to secure food and lodging. These are the nurses selected for us by Dr. Jane Waterston of Cape Town under Government House.

I am sending some camp photographs.[5] There is a photographer there, amongst other professions. The people are rigged out in "their only clothes" and have the bundles of bush which they go to cut on the kopje in the morning. Of the Geldenhuys family the mother and two children have since had typhoid and two of the other children a horrid affection of the eyes to which many have been subject.

The Authorities have put up five rows of corrugated iron rooms (I cannot call them houses), two rows of single rooms back to back – ten in a row, twenty in a building. And each of these rooms contains a family. One hundred families are thus accommodated. The iron partitions don't run to the roof nor does the outside wall by several inches; so noise, draught, infection can play through the entire structure. Some prefer them because they have floors. I hear £2 000 has been expended on the erection of these bare miserable rooms apart from all the other expenses of the camp. It is, you see, a costly business upon which Kitchener has embarked, and even at such a cost hardly the barest necessaries can be provided and no comforts.

It is so strange to think that every tent contains a family and every family is in trouble: loss behind, poverty in front, sickness, privation and death in the present.[d]

But they are very good and say they have agreed to be cheerful and make the best of it all.

Poor Mrs. Fichardt, the officers are most terribly hard upon her. She had a weekly pass to drive every Tuesday to their farm Brandkop, where her husband is buried, and now they have taken it away from her; and Miss Smith, the old English governess who lives with her, had also a pass to drive on Wednesdays for some air and that, too, has been cancelled, and all for no reason whatever. Young Mrs. Arthur Fichardt was driving one day with her pass, when the picket stopped her, saying he had orders to arrest everyone of the name of Fichardt, and she was taken to the Police Court. This family is constantly annoyed, it is dreadful for them and such bad policy on the part of the British, for they are of the leading families and *were* wholly English in their sympathies and education. You can hardly understand what it is like.

Forgive a dull letter. I have been packing clothes for Springfontein besides walking in from the camp in the heat of the day and I am tired.

Yours, E. H.

P.S. It seems to me that two people ought to come out if the Fund grows large enough to be of real use in re-establishing the people when the camps disband. The area is immense and the number to be dealt with so huge.

From the memoir

a) I had accepted these ladies' invitation only on the promise that the gathering should be entirely a private one. It was difficult to find the time and strength, but I did not wish to seem discourteous by refusing. On the other hand I wished to avoid all publicity. I was therefore very naturally surprised and indignant when a notice of my visit to them appeared in the Press, together with a garbled version of my remarks.

b) I made answer that I could not make myself responsible for the clothing of the entire Free State camp population without consulting my Committee, and knowing the numbers involved. They had increased and he [Captain Trollope] had told me that they might further increase almost indefinitely. Seeing here an opportunity for a bargain and continued friendly co-operation, I wrote, proposing to undertake to supply the clothing needs of the *women* and *children* (not men) of those camps I had been allowed to visit, on the understanding that *two* English ladies should immediately come as my successors . . . This proposal received no definite reply, Captain Trollope [later] wrote to ask me if I would provide the £100 necessary to turn an iron family-shed into a children's hospital . . . I had to reply that it was the Government's duty to provide these buildings – my Fund was intended for such comforts as could not be expected from that source.

c) Captain Trollope ... too, was kind and interested in his work, but powerless in the face of limited means. The line from the Cape was single and had to bring supplies for the towns of the two Republics, the entire Army, and now the ever-increasing population of the camps. Before the devastation of the farms – about 30 000 were burnt – this population was self-supporting and the stock and flour and foodstuffs they possessed were recklessly destroyed. There appeared to have been no effort to preserve these precious supplies either for the Army or for the owners, or the general body of consumers.

The resulting shortage affected also the towns; for the newly-founded camps of homeless families it was acute. The fact was plain that what did not exist could not be given; the question for *me* was how far there might be super-Army supplies which could by pressure be drawn upon. Failing this, the power to insist on supplies and the money to provide them could only come from England. Conversations with the Authorities made this clear to my mind, and I felt my little funds useless for more than alleviation.

My letter gives some notion of the difficulties under which the Authorities had to cope with this state of affairs, difficulties for which one always made full allowance – the wrong lay behind: a policy had been adopted but not thought out or provided for by any organization such as was necessary to ensure its proper furtherance. The Hague Convention[6] to which Great Britain was a signatory adopts the clearly stated principle that it is a duty to maintain/provide for prisoners-of-war. Women and children were now made prisoners-of-war, but no provision had been made.

d) For the number of deaths which were increasing daily more forced attention – at first I had hardly realized their significance. I began to compare a parish I had known at home of 2,000 people where a funeral was an event and usually of an old person. Here some 20 to 25 were carried away *daily*. Captain Trollope remarked on it too, and when I asked him what a normal death-rate was, shewed himself disturbed. The full realization of the position dawned upon me – it was a death-rate such as has never been known except in the times of the great plagues. To produce such a tale of deaths practically everyone was below par – the majority sick, and the dying on all sides. The whole talk was of death – who died yesterday, who lay dying today, who would be dead to-morrow.

They accused me of talking politics whereas we could only talk of sickness and death; they objected to "shewing sympathy" but that was needed in every act and word.

It was all kept very quiet; after a while the corpses were carried away at dawn, and instead of passing through the town approached the cemetery another way. Many were buried in one grave. The little canvas tents covered their tragedy, and the little tin hospitals – but there was a man who kept a list of the deaths, and only those who kept in close touch with the people themselves and with the vital statistics of the camp knew what was passing. For some cannot read what is graven on the human countenance.

Years later I read in *I Promessi Sposi* Manzoni's vivid acount of the plague in Milan, and felt the similarity. Pepy's[7] account of the 1665 plague in London gives also some idea, but is written too much from the outside.

It was astounding that Englishwomen, Quakers and others, could move about in other camps where a similar death-rate was registered and yet by their reported words and deeds shew satisfaction. Probably their minds were very full of religious services and meetings[8] and they had not had previous experience of working among people on a large scale.

To live in a community with a death-rate of anything from 200 to 300 per 1 000 is an experience foreign to English and most people of the present date, and a walk through the alleys of a neatly laid-out camp does not bring enlightenment.

Dancing, amusements [are] necessary to some temperaments.

18 TO LADY HOBHOUSE

Springfontein
4 March 1901

I am again in this queer little spot – the highest place, they say, in the Free State. And I am again taken in by the Rev. Sandrock, a poor but most hospitable German Lutheran missionary. They give me a room and the best of everything they have (which is not much at the best of times, poor souls, and now their living is very sparse). But I enjoy seeing how they live and they are charming in their simple way and truly generous. I brought them down a big box of groceries from Bloemfontein to help on a bit. Everything here is so scarce, many necessaries unobtainable.

The day before I left Bloemfontein there was a sound as of Sir Alfred Milner in the air and when I got to the station there was his saloon and he ensconced therein, eating a good breakfast. His train moved on north, so it is supposed he is at last gone up; but no one really knows, they say, what his intentions may be.

I am very sorry to leave Mrs. Fichardt's house; she has been so very kind to me . . . I have left a small committee to work in the camp and watch the interests of the people there and I am anxious to visit Kimberley and other camps. My difficulty is that in spite of my permit I am not allowed to travel below Norvals Pont, and one has to go down to De Aar and up again to reach Kimberley.

Meantime I have several days' work here. It is a comparatively small and recent camp, but the people are poorer and more utterly destitute than any I have yet seen. This was largely because there was no adjacent town from which supplies could filter in.

The Commandant, Major Gostling, is really a kind man willing to help both the people and me as far as possible, but his limitations (and mine) through lack of material are woeful. Fortunately I brought three cases of clothing with me, but it is a drop in the ocean of their needs.

All day I have sat on a farmhouse stoep and had each family in succession brought to me from the tents, fitting each in turn with clothes as far as possible, just to cover their nakedness. Each woman tells me her story[1] – a story which, from its similarity to all which have gone before it, grows monotonous. But it is always interesting to note the various ways in which the great common trouble is met by diverse characters. Some are scared, some paralyzed and unable to realize their loss; some are dissolved in tears; some, mute and dry-eyed, seem only to be able to think of the blank, penniless future; some are glowing with pride at being prisoners for their country's sake.

A few barely-clothed women had made petticoats out of the rough brown blankets (so-called khaki blankets); one had on a man's trousers; nearly all the children have nothing left but a worn print frock, with nothing beneath it, and shoes and socks long since worn away. Shoes we must leave – it is hopeless – until we can procure rolls of sole-leather and uppers, lasts and sprigs, and then the men can make *veldschoone*[2], a kind of simple rough shoe.

I clothed about 15 families today or about 60 persons and hope to do the same to-morrow and I may collect some old clothes from the few residents here to help us along. In despair I went to the one village shop, but it is long since cleared out and I came away empty save for some packets of needles. I had been giving some materials for women to make their own boy's clothing, but we are stopped by the utter famine of cotton or thread. Scissors are handed round from tent to tent, thimbles are very few.[3]

Everything here is so scarce that the sight of my rough deal packing-cases created quite a sensation – not for what was *inside* but for the actual wood. They are destined to make low bedsteads, tables, etc. and a few bits for firing.

Mattresses I fear are out of the question here on account of the lack of material; but we thought low bedsteads might be made if a little wood could be found and strips of sacking nailed across. This would lift them off the ground for the winter. Perhaps we shall manage a few.

The crying need in this camp is fuel – wood there is none – a little coal is served out, but so little that many days the people cannot cook at all, and their rations are raw meat and meal and coffee, so each of these needs fire. If you could peep at Springfontein you would at once realize the hopelessness of getting any fuel – a bare veld, covered with sparse short grass, ringed by barest kopjes – stony and without even grass. Except at the farm where I sat to give out the clothes there are no trees, and those have been grown with greatest pains. So there is nothing to burn.

I thought Lord Kitchener was considered such a great organizer, but is it good organizing to have so little forethought and make so little preparation that thousands of people find themselves dumped down in strange places where there is *nothing* ready for their reception – in hundreds of cases not even a canvas covering?

Lord Kitchener is in my black books; I have had three denials from him to go further than Bloemfontein, so I am engaged in planning how to go for him a fourth time. If only I could catch him in the flesh I feel sure I could wheedle him round but nobody ever knows where he is. I had a friendly note from Sir A. Milner today and think the best plan will be to set him at Kitchener. Now that he has gone north he ought to have power enough to order my movements. Only today an urgent appeal reaches me from Kroonstad for clothing and things for the hospital . . .I must *send* to them if I cannot go.

Tonight, to my joy, I have just had my English letters – dated 3 February, arrived 5 March – I am so glad you and Uncle Arthur keep well in spite of cold and snow; it sounds so odd to hear of all that in this brilliant weather. I feel glad the Fund Committee is working away harmoniously and I think as people know more about it and grow bolder it will increase largely. Many women to whom I have given nothing nor even offered to, and who neither ask or wish for charity, express deepest gratitude for the bare tidings that any English people *feel* for them. They are very sore at heart and are really helped by the knowledge that we understand at all the aspect of affairs as it appears to them. They are so tired of being told by officers that they are Refugees under the "kind and beneficent protection of the British". In most cases there was no pretence that there was treachery, or ammunition concealed, or food given, or nothing – it was just that an order was given to empty the country.

When one sees these ragged women standing up in groups in their bare tents, one grows a little indignant at our soldiers who meantime are occupied in making small fortunes to themselves by the sale of goods looted from these people's homes. Tommies have often come to this house offering to sell things of this sort – mats, chairs, women's brooches, etc. – and at the station quite a trade has been driven in sewing-machines.

Some people, newcomers, have furnished their rooms quite cheaply with goods bought thus from the soldiers. One woman told me today that a waggon-load of her goods was brought away by the soldiers and followed their convoy. She begged hard for a favourite chair of hers but was refused.

Major Gostling tells me today the war is practically over. Good hearing, if true. But I take his information with a grain of salt because only this morning he told me news had come De Wet was caught and this evening he was obliged to contradict the statement. But, undoubtedly, he, De Wet, has had a narrow escape this time. Such thousands went after him and they were all cock-sure of success. He and Steyn swam the flooded river[4] and now he is at large not far from here. Yesterday I saw a company of Australian Bushmen go out to catch him, and as they were *riding* and had not more than two or three vehicles behind them, it did seem more likely they would succeed. (I hear four of the enemy's waggons were captured.) Meanwhile all those thousands of troops, mules, horses, waggons, Cape-carts, artillery and stores are moving up the line again and blocking mails and everything. It's wearisome to watch them. One can't help feeling what many say: how much better they would get on without the line at all.

One afternoon a poor young Tommy came to the door of this house to buy eggs. He was from Somersetshire, near Taunton, and "zo Zomerzet" in his talk that I had to go out to interpret. Poor boy! He was very sorry for himself and longing for home. *Never, never, never* would he go to war again – he had had a "sickener". He thought De Wet had "taught our Generals a thing or two" and made them "move round a bit". He was just out from hospital and an attack of slow-fever and was jealous of the C.I.V.'s[5] going home so soon. I gave him my pot of Rowntree's cocoa which he said would be a great treat. He had had to sleep in six inches of water and all his rations were swamped, and those of his companions.

I just want to say while it is in my mind that the blouses sent from England and supposed to be full-grown are only useful *here* for girls of 12 to 14 or so. *Much* too small for the well-developed Boer maiden who is really a fine creature. Could any *out-out* women's sizes be procured? And for camp life dark colours are best; it's hard to keep clean and soap is a luxury – water not super-abundant. You would realize the scarcity and poverty a little had you seen me doling out needles and pins by twos and threes and dividing reels of cotton and bits of rag for patching. A few combs I brought up from Cape Town were caught at with joy.

There is very little time here for letter-writing as I'm busy in camp all day and then we all have to be in bed and lights out by 8.30 p.m.

It's rather nice living with the sun in this sort of way.

With regard to the vexed question of differing nationalities, is it generally known and realized at home that there are many large *Native* (coloured) camps dotted about? In my opinion these need looking into badly. I understand the death-rate in the one at Bloemfontein to be very high and so also in other places – but I cannot possibly pay any attention to them myself. Why shouldn't the Society of Friends send someone if the War goes on, or the Aboriginees Protection? In *my* camps there are many kinds (of nationalities) ... They are all suffering alike and it is not always possible to pick out the pure Boer and leave those mixed or intermarried. Often there are little Kaffir servant girls whipped up and carried off with their mistresses, and those too need clothing. Decency demands that all should be provided and though it is the business of the Government which has either burnt or left behind their own clothes, yet that Government is so slow and so uncertain and so poverty-stricken that it is on the cards the camp will be disbanded before it provides material! ...

Though the camps are called "Refugee", there are in reality a very few of these people ... It is easy to tell them because they are put in the best marquees and have time given them to bring furniture and clothes. Very few, if any of them, are in want.

I am finishing this letter in the train drawn up nowhere – waiting for nothing as far as we can ascertain. We are likely to spend the night in it, for just now travelling at night is dangerous and we are so belated there is no chance of Norvals Pont tonight. The Boers are close all round. De Wet has escaped again. Troops are going up and down in every direction – one moment to the East, another to the West, then South, then to the North, and De Wet and Fourie, who is down here now, dash about across the jealously guarded line and harry and worry. He knows every inch of the country and it seems to me they never go inland (from the line) really to seek him amongst his hills. It is now past six o' clock and growing dark with a thunderstorm raging, so it may go badly with us tonight if we don't get into Priors Siding or Donkerpoort and be guarded . . .

I feel quite content to leave my poor camp folk here in the care of Captain Gostling: He is a really kind man[6] . . . To the people his manner is tactful and excellent . . .

Now we are moving on already in the dark, so goodnight and goodbye for the time.

Yours ever, E. H.

P.S. It's extraordinary how pleased all the Military are with the *extreme* kindness we British have shown in putting these women into camps! It shows how topsy-turvy their minds are.

19. TO LEONARD HOBHOUSE

Norvals Pont

8 March 1901

This time I am really located in a women's camp – but, I am rather sorry to say, under the most *comfortable* circumstances, at least as far as outward things are concerned. That is because the Commandant has put me into a large marquee belonging to a Miss Fischer, a Refugee had up from Cape Town to be teacher of the newly formed school. Her companionship is such a trial and such an impossibility under the circumstances, I must flee to-morrow. She is rabid, foolish, narrow, discontented, and one wonders why the Authorities persist in sending up people who hate and loathe the Boers, think themselves so vastly superior and complain all day long . . . So I keep my mouth shut tight and my temper as well as I can. However, this camp won't be troubled with her long for she means to leave, though she has a big marquee to herself, a kitchen-tent, and two servants. At one time she was put on the ordinary camp rations and then there was a fuss; she couldn't possibly live on that – yet many women as good as she is are bound to do so. The Cape Town Refugee nurse here is the same. She is a good sort and doing her work well, but the rations given in camp disgust and, she says, starve her.

I felt glad they should know what these captured women put up with month after month.

Our train was kept by nightfall at Priors last night and we only came on at five o'clock this morning. The Captain had sent a cart for me and I drove straight up. The first person I saw was my former friend Miss Boshoff, who wanted to warn me that the two Refugees just mentioned, viz. the nurse and the teacher, had agreed together to set a trap for me. By feigning pro-Boerism they hoped to draw me out and make me say things which could be reported to the Commandant. So I talk of everything from wild flowers to American spelling and keep off the Boers and politics.

This camp is now supposed to be civil, not military, and one good result of that is that the sentries are withdrawn and in the afternoon the people may walk to the river or up the valley and cut wood or gather flowers. I walked down to the Orange River with the Boshoffs and Miss Pyper. We found a number of very pretty wild flowers, small and delicate, names all unknown to me. Since the rain many have sprung up. Miss Boshoff tell a humorous tale that in this last effort to catch De Wet he himself heliographed to the British Generals: "De Wet nearly surrounded. Send one column more." And they did!

One portion of this camp is fenced off new for men prisoners-of-war, and recently about 60 were brought in, captured at Fauresmith. These bring good news of De Wet's men and horses from their point of view – very different from the lamentable accounts of his condition with which we have been favoured. Not long ago six men went out from here to join him – last night, being what they called a Boers' night, namely dark and wet, two more escaped but though they got beyond Donkerpoort were caught and I saw them brought in early this morning.

I think it will interest you to know that neither Miss Boshoff nor Mrs. Steyn believe for a moment in the shooting of Wessels (Peace Envoy). They admit the death of Morgendaal is possible because he has acted treacherously before and had been strongly warned; but they think Wessels is sent with other prisoners to their stronghold behind Senekal.[1]

The story rests only on Native evidence and Wessels is likely to turn up alive, like MacLachlan and other murdered men.[2]

There has been a lot of petty tyranny here under Captain Taylor. For instance, at my last visit I found three girls living in a tent at the top of the camp with a table, a bench and a bed. Today I found them in the very last tent at the bottom near the Kaffir tents, denuded of their furniture. The reason simply this: They were heard one evening to sing the Free State anthem as they sat at the door of their tent and so were punished. This sort of thing increases their national feeling and determination to be Free Staters always.

To-morrow I make my effort to get to Kimberley and I fancy I have some chance of procuring a ticket, for De Wet is thought to be going eastwards again and the line will be unmolested.

10 March. R.S.O.'s office. I have already sat here four hours in this office of the

Railway Staff Officer, and it appears likely I may spend the night in it. I feel some right to it because it was once in better days the ladies' waiting-room. I had no difficulty in getting my ticket for Kimberley but was expressly told it must be at my own risk. The Boers are very near. I was wakened this morning in camp by the roar of a cannon and heard afterwards that there was a fight just across the line at Spitskop. But no one will tell one anything about it. I suppose they are all under orders to be as secretive as possible.

I was rather upset by a nasty encounter with the doctor today. He was very insulting but he is an insufferable cad and I pretty plainly told him so, also that I brooked no criticism, interference or impertinent questions from subordinate officers like himself. It was a real scene. I had to mount a very high horse and believe I had the best of it. This man has lived six years in Jagersfontein and is of the kind who cannot open their mouths without using invectives against the Boers – going out of their way to do so. It has become a sort of habit I think, and makes one hot all over and ashamed of the name of English. Clear the whole crew out of the land and things might settle down. I cannot make you understand the insults these people manage to throw into their very look at you if they suspect you of the least sympathy with a Boer woman. It is almost impossible to stand it, and it makes the work a great strain.

Don't you think it is very mean and unworthy of our officers to try and get recruits for their Army from the Boer prisoners in these camps? They come and wheedle and now have succeeded in enticing about 28 from Norvals Pont. It's horrible. I know one weak-natured man who went has still two brothers on Commando. Of course of these 28 several go with the intention of at once running away to join Commandos again, others simply to escape the *ennui* of the camp; but in any case it disgusts me to think they should be asked to fight their own countrymen. One man came and told me he had just been enticed but had angrily refused. He, like many of the others, had taken the oath of neutrality, and that is how the English here respect the oath they have themselves imposed. I long to escape from this network of lies and horrors.

I wish you could impress on the English public that one can't speak generally about these camps or the condition of the women therein. One is very different from another. I mention this because there is likely to be any amount of assertion and contradiction on this subject. You will probably hear the northern camps condemned and southern ones praised; whereas all are different and the amount of discomfort depends upon various matters:

First: the style of Commandant.
Secondly: natural conditions (proximity of wood and water).
Thirdly: distance from a base store.
Fourthly: presence of public opinion.
Fifthly: date of commencement.

86

The earlier camps of course had opportunities of getting many necessaries which are no longer obtainable.

It is now 9.30 p.m. and no train. I can't imagine where to go or what to do for the night – and yet be on the spot for the train at dawn. The floor of this office is all that presents itself to my mind, but if leave is refused I don't know where to go!

10 or 11 March. Naauwpoort. We have been shunting here for the last two hours, so I might as well write a few lines as do nothing. Some Tommies on the platform are busy packing their kit. They amuse me. One man looking on says: "One would think you were going to start a dry-goods store!"

Another picked out a silver candlestick, much bent with packing, saying, "Look at the curios!" It was an odd conglomeration they had spread out, looted I suppose from the denuded and deported women.

Today it has been so cold I have to stand in the sun to warm myself.

I don't think Roberts will be as popular with soldiers after this war as before. Many seem to criticize him and to feel that he was cruelly and unnecessarily hard upon his men in that (so-called) brilliant march which was the death of so many soldiers.[3] A very superior man of the Grenadier Guards told me terrible stories of that march which he went through himself. In one bit of it from Klipsdrift to some place I forget, more men died than in any battle. He was telling me, this man was, that Lord Roberts had been mobbed in London recently. Is that true, I wonder? It evidently gave the man considerable satisfaction. He described, too, how Lord Roberts came one day and made the men a speech and as he left the field, not a man cheered; perfect silence.

I was in luck's way last night at Norvals Pont Station. About 10 o'clock they told me finally no train would come in. So I asked if they were going to close the R.S.O.'s office, and learnt it would be open all night. There was no resource but to ask to sit there too, and was told I could.

Afterwards I went out for a turn in the air and to my surprise was followed by the R.S.O. himself, who very shyly, awkwardly and gruffly asked if I would care to have his bed for the night. He said he had a van. So he took me away to a siding where an old guard's van stood by the soldiers' camp and lo! he had made of it a bed- and dressing-room. Then he marched off with his pyjamas and left me in possession. I was so undone by this unusual and unlooked-for bit of kindness that when he was gone I collapsed into a fit of hysterical weeping ... It had been rather a trying day with opposition and contempt in the very atmosphere, after which a bit of kindness unnerves. Then I examined my van and found a bath ready set with water; and a mattress and khaki blankets – no sheets. But it was a lovely night. Shades of Oliver![4] – how he would have enjoyed it – a night in a van! I felt he would have appreciated it even more fully, if that were possible, than I did. I don't know the man's rank in the Army; his name is Bates, which doesn't imply much; but I have canonized him in my mind and he is St. Bates of the Cheshires. Perhaps

Manchester is responsible for him, for all his things were stamped "Manchester" and he was reading the *Evening Courier*.

Altogether, I am inclined to thinking that office is pro-Boerish; one of St. Bates's papers had a cartoon about De Wet and beneath it he had written in Spanish his criticism thinking perhaps that no one would understand it; but I could.[5] Then his junior officer, who was markedly civil to me (when no one was looking) held a vigorous argument alone against some men who urged every possible vengeance against De Wet. He maintained De Wet, if he had shot the Burgher Envoys, had done only what the British Army would have done to officers who were traitors.

Well, the end of it was that some time next day the train came sauntering in and after waiting an hour or two for nothing and nobody we sallied forth and in the end of time reached De Aar.

At De Aar I found a gallant Major also bound for Kimberley, so we threw in our lot together with a determination to get through somehow. We slept in the station that night with a lullaby of shunting "goods", but were turned out at 4 p.m. by the cruel guard, as he said he was starting for Cape Town. Three hours after that, the train was still motionless, and we both wanted to sjambok that guard! The temptation to get into all trains going to Cape Town is very great; we all feel it. When I see a carriage with "Cape Town" on it I have to look the other way – it's so hard to resist. The Major said the same. He owned also to a terrible craving for a fried sole; the longing for it quite haunted him. He has been 18 months up in the Transvaal and recently has been employed in "sweeping the country". Rather a nice man – pity he was not used for something better.

After running round the station for three hours trying to get information which no one possessed we finally got into a guard's van with an armoured truck in attendance and jolted away to Kimberley. It was a melancholy journey; for one thing I was feeling very unwell and had to pretend I wasn't. Then our line took us by the battlefields – the new historic scenes of the disasters: Belmont, Modder River, Magersfontein[6] came in succession and we could see the ridge towards which the Highlanders advanced and the long, long trench where the Boers lay and shot down the Black Watch. It's all so quiet now, the plain and the hills – nothing to mark the spot but the trenches and the groups of graves.

And now I'm in Kimberley enjoying the comparative luxury of the Queen's Hotel! It seems a much larger town than Bloemfontein which from outside always looks as if you might easily cover it with a saucer. This is straggling and untidy and has offshoots like Beaconsfield, and the mine heaps sticking up here and there. These are not so picturesque as our Cornish mine heaps – being all of the dingy blue-grey stuff in which the diamonds are found.

It was very hard to know where to begin in this town as I could get no map and none of my various introductions have addresses. It seemed best to begin by visiting the German Lutheran ministers. They are a splendid set of men and always so kind. This answered well, and by their help I got handed on from one person to another and have all my threads ready to begin work to-morrow.

Today I wrote to Sir Alfred Milner telling him Kitchener's reply to me and putting the matter finally in his hands. If he can do nothing to facilitate my further movements then I shall send him a sort of Ultimatum and retire from the scene. I am afraid he has not any power really. Kitchener is the stronger man.

One thing more I must say and that is I saw a whole train-load of Baden-Powell's Police[7] and sorrow filled my heart for the unhappy people who are to be policed by them – why, they looked as if they needed police for themselves. Where on earth was such a low, rough, almost criminal-looking crew raked together? And such lads! Poor South Africa! Will no nice English people ever come out here?

An idea occurs to me which, as you are fond of experiments on children, would be useful. Couldn't you and your household try living for – say – a month on the rations given here in the camps? I want to find out whether it is the small amount of food the children suffer from so much, or its monotony or the other abnormal conditions under which they live. It would be easy housekeeping for Nora and nice small bills at the end of the month.

> Coarse meal: 1 lb a head daily
> Meat (with bone): $\frac{1}{2}$ lb. a head daily
> Coffee: 1 oz. a head daily
> Sugar: 2 oz a head daily
> Salt: $\frac{1}{2}$ oz. a head daily

You must promise faithfully to abjure every other meat and drink – only adding for the children one-twelfth part of a tin of condensed milk a day. I should like to be able to prove it is the diet which hurts so. You could stop it if you were all taken ill.

13 March. All day I have been in the camp, fortunately only 20 minutes' walk from my hotel. First I called on Major Wright, the Commandant. He is an old resident – a Colonial Volunteer and a coarse, lazy, indifferent old man. He often does not go near the camp for days together and no wonder I found it in such a neglected condition. It practically runs itself. (N.B. He holds too many other posts.) He has made his own son Corporal of the camp.

The camp is the smallest in area that I have seen – the tents too close together and the whole enclosed in an eight-foot-high barbed-wire fencing which is supposed to be impregnable and cost £500! Sentries at the gate and walking inside. No nurse; an empty unfurnished marquee (which might be a hospital); overcrowded tents, measles and whooping cough rife; camp dirty and smelling; an Army doctor who seems to know nothing of children's ailments; fuel almost none; general laxity in the management.

I fell in with a delightful woman in Mrs. Snyman, née Visser, of the Free State. I need not tell her story because she is going to write it down.[8] She is a handsome, vigorous and able woman and has travelled in England and Europe. Her father was Director of a bank and very wealthy. He owned the farm at Jagersfontein where the diamonds were found and which he sold to the company. Many and many an English person out here for health has stayed at their farm and been nursed to strength by her mother. She has been my guide and interpreter today; her husband is helping me too.

Commandant Louw's wife is here with six children. It is so sad about her baby. Her whole story is a long one and sad, one I must write separately. But about the baby I must just tell you. It is so typical of subordinate military callousness and carelessness.

Lord Methuen came to her house with his column to sweep her away. The Louws have a large farm, a good house and are well-to-do people. Mrs. Louw is a delicate-looking gentle woman with a white skin and beautiful scarlet lips so seldom seen out of books. Her baby was only 17 days old when Methuen came, and she was very weak. She could not nurse the child and so it, like all her children, was being brought up on donkey's milk. This she explained to Lord Methuen who gave special commands that wherever Mrs. Louw went that donkey was to go – even to Vryburg and Kimberley. Well, by degrees, she arrived in Kimberley and the donkey came also to the town. But once she was in the camp that donkey disappeared. They either couldn't or wouldn't produce it. The baby failed and pined. They tried everything – cow's milk, condensed milk, foods – all no good. It was a splendid child and it dwindled to skin and bone. In vain they begged Major Wright to send the donkey.

At last the new Superintendent who is sent from the Orange River Colony arrived. Mrs. Snyman and others appealed to him and shewed him the dying child. *At once* he produced that donkey. But it was too late; the baby had got so weak it was past recovery. We tried what we could but today it died. It was only 3 months old but a sweet little thing. Mrs. Louw is much respected and there is much sympathy felt for her. It was still alive this morning when I called. In the afternoon they beckoned me in to see the tiny thing laid out – with a white flower in its wee hand – "a murdered innocent". And an hour or two afterwards another child died.

I am going to buy Mrs. Louw some mourning. Don't think that foolish or extravagant. You would not if you knew how much these people think of a bit of black and it seemed to me the best way of shewing some sympathy. I hate mourning myself, but the Boers are like our Cornish folk in the importance they ascribe to black clothes; so I understand their feeling exactly. Cornishwomen would spend their last shilling on a piece of crape. So Mrs. Louw's mourning will be a present from England.

I wonder how Lady Roberts or Lady Methuen would like Botha to swoop down upon them, burn their houses and their clothes; and carry them off to Hampstead

Heath where their children would die of exposure in tents. I wonder what they would do.

A terrible evil just now is the dew. It is so heavy and comes right through the single canvas of the tents, wetting everything. The night I slept at Norvals Pont I found this out for myself. Even in a marquee with *double* canvas all my clothes were damp through and these people have to put on their things saturated day after day. All the mornings the roadways are filled with the blankets and odds and ends regularly turned out to dry in the sun.

The doctor told me today he highly disapproved of tents for young children and expects a high mortality before June. I hope before that a civil doctor will be appointed as those who are from the Free State are to be put under a separate civilian Superintendent. Isn't it ridiculous to split the camp in that way? They urge economy, won't give soap or mattresses, then go and pay *two* Superintendents and *two* doctors and so forth and £500 for a barbed-wire fence, which anybody determined to escape could easily cut through.

Mrs. Snyman who has lived much among the Natives tells me they firmly believe in the ultimate triumph of the Dutch. There are certain little bones they wear, with which they make forecasts of the future and which they believe in like the Bible. These have told them that a *very* dark hour will come to the Dutch but after that they will prevail. So, she says, that is their fixed opinion and though they will meantime bow to the English, getting much money thereby, their opinion is unshaken.

Mrs. Snyman knows several Chiefs. The Native is paid by the English to bring information which they, the English, *believe.* They go and volunteer information to the Boers which the Dutch only *half* believe – that is to say, they never act unreservedly upon it but simply take extra precautions. For instance, a Kaffir acting as scullion to Methuen's kitchen orderly, heard his force was to attack the Boers at a certain time and place next day. All night he ran, and reaching the Boer Commander told him this and by dawn was back in his kitchen. Well, the Boer did not altogether believe him, but, on the chance of truth, made ready for attack and sent his scouts wider. When Methuen arrived there was no surprise.

I thought, too, that we English were pledged not to arm Natives. This is constantly done. I have myself constantly seen stray ones with arms, and Mrs. Snyman said their party was brought to Vryburg Station by a large number of armed Blacks. She calculated about 300. In some parts they make Police of them. The women brought from Ficksburg to Bloemfontein were brought part way by Kaffirs. This hurts them almost more than anything.

I have just heard that Methuen has arrived near here with a huge convoy and that Pretyman has gone out to meet him. They say he has brought a large number of women and we fear they will be dumped down here pending the formation of a fresh camp at Warrenton. And we have not a tent to put them in. One wonders when this sweeping business[9] is over how much further Lord Kitchener will find himself. Further behind than ever, I think. As Miss Boshoff pointed out to Captain

91

Taylor, the Orange River Colony is the khaki-coloured railway line, Bloemfontein and Kroonstad: the Free State stretches wide on every side.

The women tell me the sentries are all very sorry for them. They pity them with tears in their eyes and one said: "Believe me, we have to suffer too, for we are not allowed to write home to our wives and families." Is that because they have been writing descriptions of all this of which the authorities disapprove? I must try and find out.

You must not think I pick out bad cases to send home. I never pick out at all. The tents are entered at random and I note what they say and often leave a camp without having seen people who have had the worst experiences.

There is an active and kind-hearted committee here in Kimberley of Afrikanders which has done good work. It was formed by Mrs. Hurdus[10] before she left and bears the terrible name of South African Mothers' Christian Union. But like our own it is non-sectarian and works on our lines. It will be the body to correspond with in future and I think of leaving a grant of money in its hands for future use. Two of these Christian Mothers have been driving me round Kimberley and De Beers all the afternoon to call on various "cases". Amongst others the Rev. Wilcox, Dutch Pastor of Vryburg, on bail with half a dozen absurd charges against him.

15 March. Today I got Mrs. Louw's clothes (all hers were burnt) and took them up. Another child had died in the night and I found all three little corpses being photographed for the absent fathers to see some day. Two little wee white coffins at the gate and a third wanted. I was glad to see them, for at Springfontein a young woman had to be buried in a *sack* and it hurt their feelings woefully.

These women in this camp are by far the bitterest and most antagonistic I have met. Not to me – far from it – but towards the English *policy* and about what they have suffered. Their attitude is most determined. I wonder how far this is owing to the worse conditions prevailing in this camp. I should like to pick you out half a dozen of these high-spirited girls and send home to talk to English Cabinet Ministers. You couldn't beat them in argument – or anything else. The Misses Boshoff, Earle, Van Niekerk, Viljoen, (who nursed two of our officers back to life), Horak, Rabie, Betty Olivier, etc. They are fine creatures, nearly all good-looking and brimful of patriotic fervour. Mrs. Snyman is one of them and still handsome. How angry she was at Vryburg when the troops came early to the parsonage where she was. They were but just out of bed and her husband gone to the bathroom, when an officer burst into her room and threw himself on her bed. She was dressing. In vain she said she was a lady and wished to dress in private. He only replied he was too tired to look at her and lay still on the bed. (His name was Carruthers and he was with Methuen.)

16 March. Today I called on General Pretyman. First to get special authority *re*

this camp, and second a pass back to Bloemfontein. I found him looking very ill and tired and horribly cross. I always notice they are dreadfully testy whenever they hear of deaths in the camp, and the news of the three little deaths yesterday had reached him. Their way out of it is to abuse the Dutch as a whole, and these mothers in particular, as brutal, heartless, ignorant people who deliberately murder their children with foolish remedies.[a)] I answered him that the doctor provided was a young military doctor, quite unversed in children's complaints and unsuited for the post; and I thought the mothers knew much better than he did. Their homely remedies don't kill them on the farms; it's lying on damp ground during and after measles. So we fought a battle over that.

With regard to my pass back to Bloemfontein I find myself in a trap. *There* they told me that Pretyman could give me the pass back, but *here* he says he has no right further than De Aar. But he can give to Cape Town. So I am in a fix. My only plan (unless Milner and Kitchener improve) is to go down to Cape Town and get General Walker to send me up to Bloemfontein again.

Two things make this desirable. First, the collection of another truck-full of clothes; secondly, the chance of a talk with Mr. Rowntree before he leaves for England. He tells me too that two lady Friends[11] are coming out, and it would be well to meet them. So about Lady-day[12] I may flit south, and a few days' sympathetic companionship there will be refreshing. If, however, Milner sends to me the permits I want for the North, this Cape Town plan may not be carried into execution. I don't mean to be beaten without a good fight.

Major Wright called on me today and caved in a good deal. Quite another tone to that previously adopted. He seems quite willing to work with me now, taking a leaf out of Mr. Schutte's book who was so conciliatory.

They have been giving me presents up in the camp today – I wish they would not – and oh! the sweet treacle-like coffee I have to drink is really a trial; but it is the only thing they have to offer and I have not the heart to refuse.

Today bought and presented some clothes and combs and soap and towels to the women who tried to run away. They are of course in disgrace, and I felt so sorry for them that I felt the best thing was to make them a little happier in camp. In each case they are mothers separated from and desparately anxious about their children. I told them in their place I should also have tried to escape though I am quite sure I should have failed and I don't think it would have been wise – and I counselled them not to try again. I fancy they were a wee bit softened and soothed and won't try to escape any more but wait and try to get news of their children. It struck me the children may be in Methuen's last sweepings now at Warrenton.

18 March. Today I called on the Commandant of Kimberley by his request – Captain Forbes Taylor – and I found a man of sense. Such a treat. He began by saying, "Don't let us call these camps 'Refugee' because they are not. They [the people] were deported, compelled", etc. – I was delighted: The very first Military

man who would acknowledge that palpable fact. He willingly promised me more tents, and said I could do nothing till they were put up and the people thinned out a little. We had a jolly talk and I hope a useful one. It appears they are forming a camp at Warrenton and I shall have to go up there.

Today I have met in committee the plucky little body of women who have tried to meet and succour the distress in the camp and out of it. They work on the same lines as we do – non-sectarian and non-political. Of course they are mainly people of quite small means – for all the wealthy are De Beers people[13] in some shape or form and all afraid (except one or two in absolute secrecy) to aid any fund to help Boers! It's wonderful what these kind people have done with their very limited means. I shall leave a grant of money with them to use for extras when I have squeezed all I can out of the Authorities.

The proceedings at committee began by reading in St. Luke about the Good Samaritan and then Mrs. Wagner engaged in prayer, during which it transpired that I was the Good Samaritan, which came upon me rather as a shock, for I had not thought of myself in that capacity. Then I addressed them for half an hour and we conferred, and finally closed with prayer again which consisted of thanksgiving for poor unfortunate me! But one gets hardened to everything, even to being publicly prayed over!

They are dear, good old souls, immensely amused to hear of J. B. Robinson[14] figuring as a magnate in London – "and his father the veriest old drunkard". By the way, one of J. B. R.'s brothers was in this camp; I fancy he is gone now – escaped I think.

After the meeting I called on an old Mrs. Joubert. Her husband, Commandant-General[15] Joubert, aged 77, is more on parole. He never took up arms, and is here simply because a married son of 47, for whose actions he is in no way responsible, is fighting. Their stock is all taken – it is hard on the old couple. Her first husband was Mr. De Villiers, uncle of Sir Henry de Villiers. She is a nice old lady. They were in camp first and then allowed to live in town at their own expense. This they can't much longer do, having little cash (though every comfort at their farm near Boshof) and shortly, she says, they must apply for rations. I feel I ought to give them some help. It's so hard on old people and to know their doors and windows are all smashed and nothing to go home to.

18 March 1901 (continued). The day before the relief of Kimberley a waggon-load of women and children went to visit the Boer laager at Alexanderfontein. Nearing the spot it was found that the English had occupied it. At twenty yards' distance the English fired on the waggon-load. Commandant Fourie, who was with them, was killed on the spot, his eldest daughter shot through the arm which was broken and has kept her in hospital many months; a little sister of four years was shot through the shoulder. Miss Fourie feels no animosity towards the English, but forgives and loves them. They were so near they could hear the soldiers talking.

Near Beaufort West. Only imagine, I am on my way to Cape Town, envied by no end of people. For four reasons. First, I heard the Rowntrees were sailing the 27th and I think it important to see him as well as the ladies who are coming out to continue *his* work. Secondly, I want to see the new Governor about getting Warrenton and Mafeking Camps put under civil authority – I have agreed with General Pretyman to attempt this. Thirdly, I want to see about getting a truck-load of clothes. Fourthly, I was caught in a trap in Kimberley and could not get a permit back to Bloemfontein from Pretyman. I shall have to get round General Forestier-Walker[16] at Cape Town.

But before going to Bloemfontein I want to go back and finish my visit to Kimberley and see Warrenton and Mafeking. At present the Warrenton people are massed in the church and school.

So now I am in the Karoo and have brought this letter up to date and must close it.

From the memoir

I had myself as a girl studied Culpepper[17] deeply – often followed his receipts curious as they are – and made simple remedies also as found in an old receipt book belonging to my Grandmother, Lady Trelawny.

In my Father's parish there was no doctor and none nearer than $4\frac{1}{2}$ miles – a long distance in those days. So the villagers were wont to look to the Rectory for cures and my Mother had had much skill in her day, and I carried it on. The people would tell us of the remedies they also employed. Never did I hear of any ill produced by their cures which ran on the same lines as those of which the Boer women were accused.

Two accusations were prominent: One, that they painted their children with green paint and the other – carried by Mr. Brodrick into the House of Commons – that they fed them on raw carrots.

The green paint turned out to be an ointment made of eucalyptus leaves, doubtless very soothing. Raw carrots were shewn to be much used in various countries, the inside grated and mixed with sugar and either restored to the carrot or put in a muslin bag and given the child to suck. Since I became a vegetarian I often eat raw carrots grated or mixed and find it excellent food. You will remember also in *Tant' Alie*[18] how her little boy, Wessel, pining away, got hold of some raw carrots and ate the whole basket in the pantry. She tells us how from that moment the child improved. Certainly the number of children who were given carrots must have been few, for vegetables were in most camps unobtainable. I only wish more raw carrots could have been eaten – many children, like little Wessel, might have been saved.

As to baths, the same stupid superficiality of criticism prevailed. There are at present in the so-considered highly civilized city of London many thousands more people who do not take baths than the entire population of the Concentration Camps – indeed of the two Boer Republics – and for the very same reason: because they have none. In the Borough of Kensington alone we have housing and water and sanitary conditions which make a clean people well-nigh impossible and throughout London and other large cities our criticism can most usefully be turned.

During the war people whose utensils had all been destroyed could not, unprovided with other means, take a bath – moreover, towels and soap did not exist. Except during the weeks in and out that I was the guest of Mrs. Fichardt I do not remember having a bath. Even water was often difficult.

Once only, I recollect, in Miss Fischer's marquee in Norvals Pont Camp I had a bath, which stands out as the most refreshing of a lifetime. It was a hole dug in the hard dry ground, the depth of a flat bath; over this was thrown a waterproof sheet, and a bucket of cold water poured in. It was a perfect refreshment but obviously quite impossible for dwellers in bell-tents. Of course dirty people are to be found in every country, but in the camps there were but few.

There is nothing to be surprised at in the story Mrs. Fawcett thinks it worth while to publish[19] of a girl in Orange River Camp who when asked how long it was since she had had a bath replied about two years. The war had been going on nearly two years and all that time it was not easy – usually impossible. Such superficial criticisms make one impatient.

After this Pharisaical posture it is refreshing to read the Duke of Wellington's boast that he had never had a bath in his life; and of his rebukes to a servant in Lord Westmoreland's house who prepared him one, to the effect that he was not a "feather-bed soldier".

20. TO LADY HOBHOUSE

Kimberley
14 March 1901

I hope you have not been pestered with too many letters from me, all scrappy and disjointed as I had time to jot things down. Anyhow, this is only a short note to say where I am and that I expect to stay ten days or so and by the 25th hope to be able to arrange further movements.

There is a great deal to do here and I am hard at work all day. Fortunately the climate is superb if a little hot at midday. I have only the evening for writing and writing my notes out takes much time each day.

Spring will be upon you when you get this . . .

Don't believe much that you read in the papers.

Kenilworth,[1] Cape Town

26 March 1901

You will be surprised that I am down here again, but I ran down for a few days . . . to engineer a few important matters.[2] I hope to be off again on Monday the 1st.

It has been a great treat after the strain of the last two months to come south and mix with the sympathetic people here. Today I have addressed a gathering of Afrikanders,[a] and spent an hour and a half describing the camps to them.

It took me three days to come down from Kimberley and I nursed sick Tommies[b] on the way and botanized with sound ones.

I doubt if during my next tour I shall be able to write anything but scraps because of new regulations forbidding private delivery of letters or sending such by rail or road by private hand – under penalties – so I am baulked. Be careful how you write to me and expect nothing of interest from me. The autumn weather here is perfect.

Katrina Fourie[3] I took down with me.

From the memoir

a) I remember an assemblage of the Cape workers at the house of Mrs. Koopmans where I told them what I had heard and seen and described the camps.

Mrs. Koopmans has so long since left us that young people of today can know little of that remarkable woman. She was a striking personality, a real *grand dame* in manner and bearing. She was gifted as a conversationalist and, devoted to her country and people, was smitten to the heart by the war against her own flesh and blood. Her last years were devoted to the mitigation of their suffering. It is difficult to say exactly in what her influence lay, but it was very real and I think safe to say that no one who met Mrs. Koopmans-De Wet ever forgot her. I have several charming letters from her.

In her house, therefore – now a beautiful museum – I met the Cape workers for the camps and was able to describe to them the exact conditions. The silence was profound, and I never forgot the tears when it became clear to them that the vast majority slept on the bare earth. They had at least pictured to themselves nice wooden floors – but with very few exeptions and then much, much later, after the reforms, the people lay on the ground.

b) Many and long were the hours our train lingered on the Karoo. It was full of sick Tommies whom I nursed and cooked for and they taught me to draw boiling water from the engine to make tea and cocoa – a valuable hint in that dry and thirsty land. Often we wandered on the surrounding veld watching the wild cats, botanizing, gathering gum-arabic and finding ice-plants and other fascinating things such as grow in those parts while the train stood still we knew not why.

97

Cape Town
31 March 1901

I must leave a few lines behind me to go by this mail because once up north again I shall find myself pen-bound indeed. I have just sent off two truck-loads of clothing, etc. and follow them to-morrow after being medically examined. Travelling gets more and more difficult.

I am going back to Kimberley first to finish my work there. I have been trying to get the camp put under civil authority there as elsewhere. I have found Sir Walter Hely-Hutchinson[a] whom I had to interview here very pleasant and tractable (to my wishes) but not a genius nor likely to set the Thames on fire.

General Forestier-Walker[1] also helped me and he is really charming.

Don't be anxious if you hear but little.

From the memoir

a) I had one or two long and particularly interesting interviews with the new Governor, Sir Walter Hely-Hutchinson. Kimberley and the last group of camps I had visited being in Cape Colony, the Cape Governor had a certain priority of jurisdiction, and General Pretyman, worried and tired in Kimberley, much desired to shift all responsibility. Several questions connected with the control and joint management[1] of these camps he begged me to lay personally before Sir Walter. This I did and was surprised to find he was unaware even of the existence of these camps at Kimberley, Warrenton and Mafeking, and was greatly interested in all I told him. He promised to look into it and to his more active sensible initiative I believe Kimberley owed the great improvement of the camp that was well advanced before Miss Monkhouse got there in July and the Ladies' Committee in August.

He and Major Deane, Military Secretary, and General Forestier-Walker were al very kind and helpful in regard to my return passes and the transport of my goods. I secured from them a permit for Mafeking to save further trouble in Kimberley and also made sure of my pass back to Bloemfontein.

Sir Walter Hely-Hutchinson received me with every courtesy and showed deep interest in all I told him. In fact in all my experience I found in all high officials both civil and military more than mere courtesy – I found kindness and even sympathy. This was in most cases a contrast to their public attitudes and actions, which, later on, I realized was dictated by their *policy*, not their *heart*. Discourtesy and opposition were common enough amongst subordinates of both services but I seldom took notice of that so long as I felt behind me the confidence of the Authorities.

23. FROM E. H.'s DIARY [*started in view of stricter censorship*]

Kimberley
Good Friday
5 April 1901

I got back to Kimberley after ten days in Cape Town. It was a long journey lasting from Monday evening to Friday afternoon. My only solace was that because we halted a night at Orange River Station I was able to enquire into the size and needs of the tiny camp there. I was taken to it by the Intelligence Officer, a dreadful-looking creature who eyed me askance until he found how very English my Dutch was and then he left me to myself – only remarking he did not know I was fresh from England, he was afraid I belonged to the "Stellenbosch clique". I held my peace and just talked to the people, finding only a few families – 24 children in all and five or six women. Two are "expecting" and begged for baby clothes. I am going to make up a bundle for each.

I find it rather hard to buckle to work again after the comparative dissipation of ten days in Cape Town – though I was *very* busy there too. I had many interviews from the Governor downwards and spent no small portion of my time in the goods yard. Today also I began the day with an hour or so in the goods yard at Kimberley, finally securing the help of old Mr. Hendrikz to unload and deliver the goods.

After that was put *en train* I found a bundle awaiting me, mostly censored, some doubly censored. After devouring these I sallied forth to see General Pretyman and the new Commandant, Colonel Park of the Imperial Yeomanry. The General was out and I only saw the stupid Lord Acheson to whom I will not state my business. Colonel Park is a sad come-down after Forbes-Taylor and it's no use expecting much help from him.

7 April. Easter Day. I forgot to say that in our train last week coming up we carried two truck-loads of armed Natives so it's a delusion to imagine they are never armed. They are widely used as scouts and intimidate the people terribly.

After church today I saw Colonel Park again and found him in somewhat chastened mood. Anyhow, he agreed I should telegraph to Cape Town for a nurse for the camp and allowed that things were in a muddle, that Lord Kitchener grabbed everything up his line and no tents could be got, and no sailcloth and there was a hitch about the whole thing and nothing could be done and 600 more people were coming in and no tents for them.

Over and over again one sees it is the things our money *cannot* get that are needed really to lighten the sufferings and prevent the sickness of these prisoners.

Kimberley
Easter Eve
6 April 1901

I arrived here last evening after a long journey from Cape Town about which you should hear in another letter. I find here yours of 22 February and 1 March awaiting me and feel very grateful for the same. They have followed me round. Also Mr. Courtney's of 15 March containing the first intimation of the arrival of my first general letter. Very glad it reached you safely after many vicissitudes.

Matters here are very unsatisfactory but I cannot dilate on them in this. I hope, all being well, to run up to Warrenton and Mafeking this week. I was much pleased with the letter from the *Daily News* but now there are far more than 10 000 people in the O.R.C. and [Cape] Colony camps, leave alone Transvaal camps, which are huge. More are swept in daily. I have just heard that a 1 000 more have come in to Springfontein where they had not tents for 500.

An urgent appeal reaches me to come at once to Kroonstad where sickness abounds and they have no shoes, etc. I shall fly round to Bloemfontein in about ten days and thence to Kroonstad if Kitchener will relent.

Please don't worry about me. I hope to pay my way in spite of first-class fares – and having hundreds and thousands of wardrobes on my mind, I feel exempt from looking after my own!

It is quite a mistake to think that I am not working in fullest co-operation with the Cape Colony Dutch, for I am.

25. TO LADY HOBHOUSE

Mafeking
9 April 1901

I arrived here this afternoon after a long and singularly tedious journey. I felt obliged to come, having learned that there were about 800 women in this camp besides those at Warrenton *en route*. I felt uneasy, for I could learn no details at all about the people here except that the camp was four miles out of the town.

At Warrenton there *were* only about 310, pushed into the church and school as tents were well-nigh unattainable, but *now*, only yesterday, many hundreds more have been brought in there; in fact, the whole town of Hoopstad.

Did you know or does anyone realize that this town has been besieged for the last eight months (ever since last August) and was only relieved about a week since?

A young Captain got into my compartment at Warrenton and travelled with me all day. He told me all about it. Since August they had been beleaguered and knew absolutely nothing of the outside world. The siege of Kimberley was nothing to it, he said. He was a nice young fellow – told me his name and regiment – but his coat was in rags and tatters, and his breeches, he confessed, he had got off someone else. He did not know Lord Roberts had gone home – knew nothing in fact; the death of the Queen was the only news the besieging Boers had allowed to pass into the town.

He only got into Warrenton that morning with a great convoy and he was dead tired. He had swept in the stock and the women and children, burnt all food and clothes behind him and allowed the Natives to loot the Boer houses as money is too short to pay them in a better way. He was very sick of it all and agreed it was a war of extermination. Every animal that lagged or did not keep up with the convoy had its throat cut and was left behind.

And there, in a great mass by the railway line, I saw all his sweepings,[a] thousands of animals of many kinds, carts and waggons, soldiers and horses, crowds of human beings both black and white. And I happen to know there is not a tent at Warrenton to put them into!

This young Captain had heard nothing of his people for eight months nor they of him. He was very tired so slept for hours and then I made him some tea and would have mended his rags but they were too far gone. He said his men when on duty always had to extemporize kilts out of blankets to maintain decency.

I mean to visit Warrenton on my way back if all is well. I do grudge the time spent on the mere journeying – it makes a large hole in my few remaining weeks. The air here is lovely, so light and pure. Mafeking is a queer little village and the country round is all flat or gently undulating with a few sparsely growing low bushes, chiefly mimosa. One wonders how it was successfully besieged.

I am too tired to write tonight – the journey was extra fatiguing because I travelled second class, not from choice but from necessity. I took a first-class ticket and booked my seat the preceding day but though I arrived an hour before the train went, I failed to get a seat – the officers crowd in and always get the best seats so that an unfortunate female had no chance. First class here is about equal now to third class at home so that anything below is very dirty, smelly and disagreeable.

At Kimberley I stayed at the Queen's Hotel – not altogether bad. Easter Monday I breakfasted about 6 a.m. to catch the train and the housekeeper came and waited upon me. She couldn't help asking me if I was any relation of Bishop Hobhouse, whom she used to see at Botley. She was so interested to learn I knew the place and the Jenkyns'. She enquired particularly for Mrs. Pilkington and said her own maiden name was Houghton and her father worked for Uncle Henry Jenkyns. The consequence was I had a very nice loaf of bread to take with me wrapped in clean paper and feel I owed it to my cousins.

In the same hotel I happened on Mr. White who is organizing the school in Kimberley Camp. He, too, wanted to know if Uncle Edmund was related to me, also Hadspen[1] generally. He was at school at Bruton and had helped to cheer when Henry Hobhouse was first returned to Parliament. A nice young man who, earlier, had fought with Brabant's Horse, but left it and finds tuition more to his taste.

101

My writing is very bad and scrawling but, truth to say, it is always done under difficulties. Not since I have been in Africa have I had the enjoyment of a writing-table!

10 April. Mafeking. Today I have been out in the camp the whole day. I had to take a Cape-cart and drive out for it is full six miles – a lonely, lonely spot. Mafeking itself feels like the end of the world and the camp seems like driving six miles into space.

There are 800 or 900 people and it is the oldest of all the camps I have visited – in fact, nearly a year old. They were very glad to see me. The hospital nurse said it would put new life and courage into her. She was feeling so downhearted about it all.

I found some very nice people whose relations I had made friends with in Bloem-fontein Camp and also in Kimberley. It is quite interesting sorting out the people and telling them where their relations are. I am at present hunting for the mother of two little boys aged about six and seven who were swept up by a different convoy. The Mafeking Camp folk were very surprised to hear English women cared a rap about them or their sufferings – but they *did* know that a few Members in the House of Commons spoke up for them. It has done them a lot of good that real sympathy is felt for them at home and so I am glad I fought my way here, if it is only for that reason.

The camp was specially interesting to me as the first I have seen under Trans-vaal rule.[2] For rations and fuel it is far the best I have seen, but as usual no soap. The Superintendent is a Scotchman . . . The rations are better than any other camp (known to me) through a fortunate accident – too long a story to dilate upon in this short letter. They are badly off in blankets, many having none. Also soap and candles and clothes and in having *no one* to visit them or care for them from the outside. For miles round no habitation can be seen, and Mafeking folk are too bitter to do anything to help them.

11 April. Today I took to the camp large bundles of stuff as suitable as Mafeking can supply – the choice is not large. I formed a clothing committee of seven women and in the afternoon we met and I showed them how to organize their work for the camp. They are very pleased and are going to meet every Thursday, besides divi-ding the camp into sections and making a house-to-house (tent-to-tent) visitation. All the seven women are themselves in need of clothes and they have all had their houses burnt, one by Kaffirs and the rest by British troops.

Amongst them were the Hartmanns (in whose tent we met). I had met their relations in Bloemfontein and found all the family first-rate people. Old Mr. Hart-mann is a dear old Boer, with a long white beard and bright dark eyes. He was keeping his 69th birthday and managed to be cheery and even mirthful in spite of the consciousness that late in life he was without house, stock or money. The

Military had given him *one* of his own cows and that had died in camp. He was immensely amused at our meeting of *women*, for he said he had never seen such a thing in his life and he kept popping in and out just to see how we managed and what we talked about.

One old lady I saw was very interesting, a real character, a Mrs. Coetzee. She was very broken-hearted, more so than anyone I met. She harangued me on the subject of her feelings and experiences the best part of an hour in really eloquent Dutch and [with] much solemnity. She described, with the extraordinary unself-consciousness which characterizes them all, the whole history of Lord Methuen's visit and actions – and how she had thrown herself flat on the stoep and implored him to trample on her and kill her. And she showed me the clothes she had brought with her, and there was nothing for herself but her white "*dood-kleere*", viz. her dead-clothes. I fancy she thought that would be all she would want in camp. It was rather a Job-like scene. She sat in her bare, baking tent, a circle of friends round her, an intensely religious woman, trying to understand God's dealings with her and her people in letting *everything* be taken – and she ended at last with a solemn thanksgiving to *Onze Heer* that the Engish people cared even to send someone just to *look* at their misery. Altogether the old woman was a striking figure and very pathetic.

13 April. Kimberley. I have just returned. At Warrenton I found about 150 people left, the rest were being sent on. At the station were two train-loads full of them, quite half in open coal-trucks – all piled up and wedged in with such goods as they had been able to bring. They were tired and hot. I went and spoke to several of them and found in a truck the parents (Du Toit) of the little boys I mentioned earlier. There were 240 packed in and they followed us and our armoured train. On arriving here I saw Mr. Schutte, the Superintendent, who was at hand to meet the arrivals. He told me that after begging, borrowing and buying he had scraped together 25 tents for 240 people. So there will be more overcrowding!

I ran up to one of the committee women to see if anything could be done in the way of getting them a meal after their journey, but nothing had been known of their coming and late Saturday night we could not tell where to turn to procure either fuel or kettles etc. to supply such an inrush of people.

From the memoir

a) I think that bad as the camp at Mafeking was and terrible as the death-rate continued to be – in so much that 500 died in the few weeks between the first and second visit of the Ladies' Commission and the Superintendent was dismissed – yet the appalling tragedy of it all came home to me in the sight I witnessed at and near Warrenton both going and returning.

Those truck-loads of women and children unsheltered and unfed, bereft of home,

103

bearing the vivid recollection of their possessions in the flames; and that mass of the "sweepings" of a wide military "drive" – flocks and herds of frightened animals bellowing and baaing for food and drink, tangled up with waggons and vehicles of all sorts and a dense crowd of human beings – combined to give a picture of war in all its destructiveness, cruelty, stupidity and nakedness such as not even the misery of the camps (with their external appearance of order) could do.

26. TO LEONARD HOBHOUSE

Kimberley
15 April 1901

I have been up in Mafeking for a week and found a whole budget awaiting my return. Very many thanks for snubbing the *Daily News* for me. I saw the paper in Cape Town and was furious. What is the use of printing gossipy nonsense like that part relating to me, which could serve no useful purpose? However, I exonerate Mr. Rowntree, feeling he had no idea it would be printed. I suppose Mr. Ellis did it, thinking initials would hide everything. Of course in Cape Town every initial was as clear as daylight. I fancy the people there were not best pleased either and I feel as if I shall be quite ashamed to face H. E.[1] again.

A *meercat*, tell Oliver, is smaller than a cat and has short forepaws and a quaint way of sitting upright to warm itself in the sun. It has a sharp nose and black eyes and chuckles with pleasure when you cuddle it. They tame easily and are sweet . . .

I am writing just these few lines before leaving this on Friday and plunging again into the outer darkness of the O.R.C. All is censored there and I am conscious of being well watched.

I hope my more recent letters may have had some interest for you. I am frightfully tired tonight, having had a hard day and hosts of letters to answer.

I was much distressed in the tent of two women, sisters, whose children are wasting to emaciation. We have at last got a new doctor – civilian – and who speaks Dutch, so I hope we shall move on a bit and he will help me find out the cause of the emaciation. Thanks be! From 9 April every Army doctor was withdrawn from the camps and civilians substituted! A good riddance of bad rubbish (I expect they keep the good ones for the Army).

Seven children died here the few days I was at Cape Town and two since my return; besides Mrs. Van der Walt whom they carted about from pillar to post *with the measles on her* till she died. Mrs Scholtz has been taken to the Hospital in town. She is very ill from a kick in the stomach from a drunken soldier – something internal. He was punished, I believe, but that does not cure her.

16 April. I have had such a to-do today about a nurse and interviews quite endless. Amongst others Sister Henrietta of St. Michael's Home here. Of all the rude women she is about the rudest I have ever met. What ever is it takes the English out

104

here? I think the air gets into their heads and turns them upside-down. And I only called to ask her if she could help me about a nurse for the camp hospital. You would never believe what she said. Such stories I could tell today, but my mind and pen are too tired.

All this afternoon I was kept in Mrs. Louw's tent by a downpour of rain. Half the tent floor (bare ground) was a pool of water which the Kaffir boy was vainly trying to bale out. Two pails caught the pourings from the tent door. All round and above it dripped, making pools on the bedding and on the mats and us as we sat huddled up – two Kaffirs, five children, Mrs. Louw and myself – in the steaming atmosphere until I began to turn sick as I generally do in the tents. When it rains in the night, as often, it drips on them all night and makes little pools on their beds. No wonder children sicken and die. The cloth of the tents seems very thin and poor.

Poor Mrs. Earle. I had a long talk with her today. I had heard she had been "punished" and I went to hear the facts from her own lips. It appears that very often meat is bad, maggotty. But lately she was served, three days running, with meat crawling with *worms* – worms nearly half an inch long that wriggled about the plate.

One of our committee saw it herself. So Mrs. Earle took it back to the Superintendent and they were very angry and said she should go without. So for sixteen days she and the eight people in her tent were kept without any meat except on Wednesdays and Sundays. It was cruel. The neighbours fed her with bits. At last some of the committee complained to the Town Commandant who came up and stopped it, saying the Superintendent had no right to punish in that way. So she has food now but he wreaks his vengeance on her by not allowing her a pass outside the fence – and all because her husband is a Commandant and she won't ask him to surrender.

It was so pretty to hear her youngest girl, aged five, a sweet and very lively child, stand up in front of me and sing one of their national songs – in English too. The refrain ran:

"We will show the English Queen
We can die for land, and mean
To keep the Independence of Transvaal."

The child gave it out with such spirit.

I think I won't write any more and yet there is so much to say . . . I ought to turn up the end of June if all is well and war, pestilence, famine and shipwreck all survived . . . The English clothes sent are lovely . . . I shall have many tearful farewells here to-morrow and then off to my old haunts at Bloemfontein which camp has since doubled! I think L. B. B. should come and take up this set of camps in the Cape Colony. It is one person's work.

105

Kimberley

17 April 1901

To-morrow I leave[a) for Bloemfontein and thence make my final effort to get north. Urgent demands come from Irene and elsewhere, but Milner may not care to urge it on Kitchener, and in the O.R.C. you can't move a step without his authority. I [think] an Englishwoman, say Barbara Bradby, should come out and take charge of the row of camps on this line, all in Cape Colony – or British Bechuana Land – Orange River, Dronfield, Kimberley, Warrenton, Fourteen Streams, Vryburg, Mafeking. There are people at all these places.

I fancy there would be no difficulty in getting permission for these. The O.R.C. is different and the Transvaal harder again.

One more try I must make to see the northern camps and to answer in person the appeal from Kroonstad – and, failing that permission, go home.

From the memoir

a) I left Kimberley about 18–19 April, taking with me some clothing to leave at Orange River Camp as I passed. By August (when first returns were supplied) it had a population of 1 507 with a death-rate of 56 per 1 000, which rate by October had swelled to 440 per 1 000.

The journey was tedious and now autumn had come the nights were cold in the train. There stands out in my mind a bare spot where the eye swept the horizon in vain for even a tree and no human creature was in sight, where I talked with a Tommy almost mad with the aching solitude around him. He poured out his feelings: (accustomed to town life) he found himself in this – to him – torturing silence. He said he had been out for months and had never yet seen an enemy but felt going out of his mind with loneliness and lack of employment. I gave him my novel to read – it was a Dickens – and such papers as I had and suggested collecting the strange flowers and insects, or tilling the ground, and we crawled away and left him on the silent veld. What is it Kipling wrote on these boys?

"Few, forgotten and lonely
    Where the white car-windows shine,
No, not combatants only,
    Details guarding the line.

"Out of the darkness we reach
    For a handful of week-old papers
And a mouthful of human speech . . ."

Bloemfontein

22 April 1901

Here I am again in Bloemfontein. I arrived yesterday, taking two and a half days from Kimberley. Mrs. Fichardt has taken me in again with the warmest welcome and greatest sweetness though I fear she has already suffered from having done so. Her pass allowing her to drive once a week to their farm at Brandkop has been taken away and enquiries at the Intelligence Office elicited the information that one of her sins was that "she had harboured Miss Hobhouse". But nothing daunted she is harbouring me again.

The air is very pleasant here now in this autumn weather and the gardens are green after the rains and full of chrysanthemums. A little spring is oddly mixed up with the autumn such as lilacs and violets.

My camp work grows so fast and so rapidly that I feel it is almost impossible to cope with it. Here there are now 4 000 or double the number I left six weeks ago. At Springfontein I left a manageable little camp of 500, now it has swelled to 3 000 and as we passed yesterday morning there was a train-load in the station of 600 more. It was pitiable to see them massed into the train, many of them in open trucks. It was bitterly cold and I was wrapped in your thick grey shawl; all night there had been a truly torrential downpour of rain and water stood everywhere upon the ground. On the saturated ground they were trying to dry themselves and their goods.

Some women were pushing their way to the platform to try and buy food for their children. The soldiers would not permit this; I expostulated; the men said they were sorry for them, but they had to obey orders. It was Sunday morning and Springfontein's one small shop closed, and I knew the Refreshment Room was the only place where food was available. Just then little Clara Sandrock[1] ran up from the Mission Station with a can of hot coffee for me. I had waved to them from the train as it passed the house and had seen the old clergyman run in and warn his wife that I was passing. So Clara and I ran down the platform to the cluster of women and gave them the coffee and I took them all the food I had in the train with me. Fortunately I had just bought a two-penny loaf (for 1/-) and I had some tinned meat. A nice-looking woman with a very white face spoke to us – said they had been travelling two days and no food given and the children were crying with hunger. I gave Clara Sandrock some money and told her to buy all the food she could in the station and take it down to them, and to devote the day to it, leaving alone church. The girl promised and I had just time to jump into my train. I would have stayed myself and seen to it but my permit was not stamped to break the journey so I could not do so. I know Clara will do her best; she is only 15 but very womanly.

As there was not a shelter of any kind at Springfontein I heard the whole lot were to be sent on to Bethulie, for now a camp is forming there. It is endless and hopeless.

I have just heard from a man who met the same train-load at Edenburg that four children died on the journey.

If only the camps had remained the size they were even six weeks ago, I saw some chance of getting them well in hand, organizing and dealing with the distress. But this sudden influx of hundreds and thousands has upset everything and reduced us all to a state bordering on despair. I feel paralyzed in face of it. I feel money is of little avail, and there are moments when I feel it would be wisest to stop trying and hasten home to state plain facts and beg that a stop may be put to it all.

Yesterday I lunched with Colonel Goold-Adams and he was, as always, very agreeable. But he tells me that more and more are coming in. A new sweeping movement has begun, resulting in hundreds and thousands of these unfortunate people either crowding into already crowded camps or else being dumped down to form a new one where nothing is at hand to shelter them. Colonel Adams says, what can he do? The General wires: "Expect 500 or 1 000 at such a place" – and he has nothing to send there to provide for them. He being wholly out of tents, has sent to Port Elizabeth and had 30 shelters made of sorts, and there they lie, he can't even get them sent up. And I told him I wasn't surprised for I don't believe all his power as a Deputy Administrator (and that is not much) would get things sent up unless he went and stood in the goods yards himself and saw the trucks packed as I found necessary at Cape Town or I should never have got a garment north.

About food too – the Superintendent of a camp is getting in rations for such and such a number and suddenly 500 more mouths are thrust in upon him and things won't go round. Last Saturday 400 families were without meat in Bloemfontein Camp for that day and Sunday. This would not matter if there was an alternative but there is only the ordinary supply of coarse bread to fall back upon, with black coffee and sugar. No wonder sickness abounds. Since I left here six weeks ago there have been 62 deaths in camp and the doctor himself is down with enteric.

Two of the Boer girls we had trained as nurses and who were doing good work are dead too. One of them, Poppy Naudé, was a universal favourite. She did not know where her mother was. Her father was in Norvals Pont and there had been some talk of my taking her to join him; but in the end she thought she was doing useful work where she was, earning 2/- a day, and she had better stay and nurse the people in Bloemfontein Camp. And I come back to find her dead! The doctor, the nurse and all had said: "We can't spare Poppy".

But in spite of the death-toll I think your friend has saved and strengthened many children. Mrs. Botha I engaged, you will recollect, to go the rounds daily amongst the sick babies and children and they calculate she has saved about 100 by that care. A few drops of brandy, maizena, Mellins and, where possible, fresh milk.

The Government clothing about which they made so much noise has hitherto come to nothing. I formed, as agreed, the committees; the camps were divided into sections, the minimum required was noted down and the total requisitioned for. There it has come to a full stop. Now Goold-Adams says the Superintendent must certify that not one of the applicants has anybody in the camp who could rightly maintain her; amongst so many to find that out is well-nigh impossible. The Superintendent hesitates and the whole thing hangs fire. Thus had it not been for our clothing, things would have been bad indeed.

Colonel Goold-Adams is going to try to get me up to Kroonstad where no help has been given. I see Mrs. Maxwell, wife of the Governor-General of Pretoria, Major General Maxwell,[2] is appealing to the United States for clothing for Irene Camp. She is an American. I think of writing to her and getting into touch with her.[a]

From the memoir

a) I lost no time in writing to Lady Maxwell, but she had already left Pretoria. General Maxwell, however, wrote to me to explain her silence; but by that time I also had left South Africa and his letter followed me to England. He admitted the need and suggested distributions of clothing through the Military Directory Superintendent.

Colonel Goold-Adams also failed to procure me a permit for Kroonstad, and a telegram from Sir Alfred Milner dated 23 April in reply to my final appeal was final.

It was quite plain to me that nothing could be done for the reform of the camps except from England and by the will of the English People.

I asked for my pass to Cape Town. My private affairs also necessitated my return – for the great expenses had mostly emptied my private purse, and only enough remained for the return journey. It was only afterwards that the letter came containing a gift from my Aunt and Uncle; they were now fully convinced of the urgency of my work and prepared to re-inforce my slender resources.[3]

29. TO LADY HOBHOUSE

Bloemfontein
28 April 1901

I have just received three of yours together (29 March, 4 and 5 April) for which very many thanks indeed. I am sorry you have had another lay-up in bed on account of your throat as well as your knee. You seem to have had horrid cold biting weather (which I am glad to have missed) and which is, I fear, the cause of your bad throat.

You write about the pros and cons of my home-coming.

It has been difficult to see my way plain. When I wrote the letters you have now answered, in the back of my mind I thought as you and Leonard and Lady Farrer all seem to, viz. that for the world's sake I ought to remain. But things change and I am of the opinion, and so are all my friends, that I should go home. The reasons for

109

this I cannot dwell upon here and now. The post is just off which may catch this week's boat, so I must defer a fuller letter.

I am, and I believe rightly, applying for my pass[a] to Cape Town and shall try for a passage in the boat of 15 or 22 May.

A cable would stop me there if considered most necessary.

I think the fact that Sir Alfred Milner is going home will make it as easy to get fresh permits for (myself) or B. Bradby in England as here. Probably also the War Office would have to be approached.

Unfortunately I am feeling rather done though it only shews itself in loss of voice. But that is important as I have to talk a good deal.

Forgive this scrap.[b] I will write more lucidly when I have more time.

Hope you will enjoy beautiful Crowsley.

P.S. The needle-book arrived safe. Please thank Smith.[c]

From the memoir

a) My pass was delivered to me and I paid my farewell visit to the camp – I went there daily. I told the people I hoped to be able to help them far more by going away than by staying for I believed the English people, if they knew about it, would insist on their relief.

I wrote to Mrs. Murray to secure me a berth and on 1 May I left Bloemfontein.

b) This short note was one of those innocuous letters written with a special eye to the Censor. It was well I did so for my Aunt received it "opened by the Censor".

c) This was a little gift from my Aunt's old maid [Smith] for the camp at Spring-fontein on hearing of the lack there of all such necessaries. [Letter 18]

30. TO LADY HOBHOUSE

Railway
1 May 1901

I seize the opportunity while the train stops to write a letter to you about the difficult question of my successor, and my own decision to go home or stay here.

I received yesterday Mr. Lawrence's cablegram saying a successor would start in May, and as I am unable to cable myself from these regions I have asked them to cable from Cape Town for me as follows to L.B.B.[1]:

"Sanction improbable. Wait letters".

Well, this is the letter intended to explain the cable. But when I begin to explain I find it difficult not knowing how far it is prudent to do so. Perhaps I had better write quite shortly just this: I must myself go home, of that I feel pretty sure, and many, able to form sound opinions, advise me to do so.

I am afraid that *very* innocent paragraph in the *Daily News* mentioning the *very* innocent meeting in your house practically sealed my fate; and also that of my successor. If sanction is to be obtained it must be procured in London from H. E. and the War Office. On this side I have tried in every way but since that moment have failed. I pin my faith, or at least my hopes, to interviewing the beforementioned at home. You see matters changed almost immediately after my last letter to you.

I am told that steamers are so full that berths are hard to find and though I am trying to secure one for 15 May or following week success is doubtful.[a] I have left links wherever I have been so that whatever betide, our gifts and help can be continued.

From the memoir

a) Hardly expecting to secure a berth before 15 May at the earliest I had planned fresh visits to Springfontein, Aliwal, Bethulie and Norvals Pont.

I broke my journey at Springfontein. There, to my horror, still massed on the railway siding, I found the same unfortunate people whom I had seen when passing north 10 days previously – their conditions beggars description; the picture photographed on my mind can never fade.

Afterwards, in the train, I wrote my Aunt the full description of what I had seen and this letter – a long one – was posted on my arrival in Cape Town. It went in the end by the same mail as myself and was safely received, but to my great sorrow it has utterly disappeared. My letters were handed about, and several shorter ones were lost; but I particularly regretted the disappearance of this long and full account.

Again I was the guest of the Sandrocks, but every moment was spent with the people. The camp had swelled to some 3 000 and the cold was bitter in that high altitude. Still, Mr. Gostling was a fairly competent Superintendent and made things go as far as they could. There was, at least, external order and cleanliness.

For the moment the greater need lay with the poor abandoned families on the railway over whom, in the prevailing red-tapeism, the Camp Superintendent had no control.

The women there clung to me. One said: "There is an old lady and her husband here, aged aunt and uncle to Paul Kruger. She has no skirt. They were in the Great Trek (of 1836) – Van der Walts." I found the old couple near 90 years of age, and, slipping off my underskirt, put it on the old woman. In those days we wore sensible clothes and an underskirt was a long full garment, making ample covering. The old lady was so pleased. They sketched in outline the vicissitudes of their life. And now in their last days had come this shattering blow – their home destroyed, and

111

they carried they knew not whither. Where their fate lay was plain enough and within two weeks they found a grave in Bethulie Camp. He was, I am told, the first to be buried there. Brave and dignified old people, they faced their final uprooting as "the will of the Lord".

They belonged to a type fast disappearing if not already vanished from the plains and uplands of South Africa. You, dear Mrs. Steyn, must have known many such. I wonder if you too will be fearing, as you look over the country, that present-day life fails to produce such strong self-reliance and simple dignity.

The people massed there had no tents. Some crept under the railway trucks while some had begged bits of sailcloth from Tommies and sticking two or three sticks in the ground threw the canvas over, thus making a rude shelter in which, however, one could seldom stand upright.

To such a shelter I was called to see a sick baby. The mother sat on her little trunk with the child across her knee. She had nothing to give it and the child was sinking fast. I thought a few drops of brandy might save it, but tho' I had money there was none to be had. I thought of the Superintendent of the camp – a mile off – and sent a hasty message to ask him to let me have some for a sick child, but the reply was that his supplies were only for his camp. There was nothing to be done and we watched the child draw its last breath in reverent silence.

The mother neither moved nor wept. It was her only child. Dry-eyed but deathly white, she sat there motionless looking not at the child but far, far away into depths of grief beyond all tears. A friend stood behind her who called upon Heaven to witness this tragedy and others crouching on the ground around her wept freely.

The scene made an indelible impression upon me. The leading elements in the great tragedy working itself out in your country seemed to have gathered under that old bit of sailcloth whose tattered sides hardly kept off sun, wind or rain.

"Tragedy," says George Eliot, "must represent irreparable collision between the individual and the general. It is the *individual* with whom we sympathise, and the *general* of which we recognize the irresistible power."

Years after, when Mr. Van Wouw[2] came to Rome to carry out the monument, a work which President Steyn so finely inaugurated, I described to him this scene as it seemed to me to hold in itself the centre and core of the tragedy: broken-hearted womanhood, perishing childhood. Mr. Van Wouw as you know reproduced the scene in bronze. Had he seen it with his own eyes, the child would have borne more directly the aspect of emaciation and death.

I spent till dusk in the camp, finding myself rather superfluously accompanied in my rounds by Mr. Gostling, and I looked forward to the quiet walk back to the Sandrocks' house under the stars. To my surprise he insisted upon walking with me in spite of my assurances that I was quite able to go alone as usual. During this walk as during the day his one object seemed to be to draw me into talking politics. He talked nothing else, while my efforts were to introduce other topics – the vege-

112

tation, prices, the stars, and so forth. It was a trying ordeal, this setting a snare for me, so exhausted as I was. He further tried to extract some remark as to the Sandrocks' views, but I shied away. The train was due at midday so I had yet another morning in the camp. Again he stuck to me, again walked with me to the Sandrocks', and leaving, assured me he should come to take me and my bag to the station at one o'clock. I assured him the Sandrocks would see to that. He was set upon it. So I started early, the Sandrocks kindly carrying my bag, and hoped the train would be there. Alas! it was not and Mr. Gostling hurried after me and never left me till, three hours late, it was signalled.

Can you believe it, but the *whole* of that time he talked politics, returning to it again and again as I as often changed the subject. In vain I told him I wanted to read and rest, in vain suggested that I did not like to take up his time from the camp. There he stuck like a leech, till at 4 o'clock, just before the train appeared, he drew from me some general remark as to there existing different opinions upon Milner's policy. Then it was clear. He had got what he wanted and greatly elated he left me, not staying even though the train was in sight to hand in my bags. In a few hours I should be out of that country, I knew, and free once more to speak. Under his cruel pressure that sense of coming freedom broke out in one very innocent general remark. It found its way to Milner.

Mr. Gostling died later on in the camp. He was better than some Superintendents, having a sense of law and order, but he was narrow and hard and lent himself to the dirty work of an *agent-provocateur*.

I halted at Norvals Pont, finding changes had taken place there and my kind friend Major Bates and all vanished. It was hinted that they were "*stellenbosched*", I do not know.

I had a final talk with Mr. Cole-Bowen, who spoke of the great need of a building especially for the old folk during the coming winter. He calculated £50 would cover the costs; later he wrote kindly saying the old people were cheering up at the thought of a roof again.

Norvals Pont of course had a fine water supply irrespective of the rivers, but also it had been fortunate in its three Superintendents, all of whom had been excellent in their different ways. Mr. H. Dahms in his account of Bethulie Camp, which is inserted in *Die Smarte van die Oorlog*,[3] describes the coming of Mr. Cole-Bowen to that camp and his energetic and wise remodelling of the place.

It was I think on this last occasion that I found myself at night stranded. I had left the camp early and returned to the station, the train being one about four. It did not come, we waited on till dark. It was then announced there would be no train that night, and not till next morning.

I had nowhere to go, the few little houses and shanties were packed. As before the Military possessed the whole station and the friendly elements were gone.

Tired as I was, there was no alternative but to climb the long road to the camp.

Carry my handbag I could *not*, and begged leave to put it in the R.S.O. Imagine my distress on reaching to crossroads leading to the camp to find a picket of soldiers stationed there, who called me to halt. Fortunately I knew the sign and the counter-sign but they demanded my pass. Alas! all my papers I had left in my bag at the station. In vain I told them so and explained the position; they were, quite rightly, firm.

I was too exhausted to return to the station to find my bag, and probably the office would have been closed. If I could not pass into the camp, lying quiet below in the moonlight, I must ask leave to stay all night with them. There was no alternative. Underfed and exhausted, my legs would carry me no more. I hated having to persuade them against regulations, but I had to do so and at last they gave in and I crept by moonlight through the camp, thinking it best to go to the Miss Boshoff's tent and beg for shelter. Lights were out and all was silent; rather alarmed they untied the flap of their tent and most kindly sheltered me that night. The train was expected at seven, so very early they roused me and I thanked the sleepy soldiers as I hurried past.

I was in time and with soldiers all the way for company reached Cape Town the early morning of the 5th. I was indescribably dirty and unkempt. Washing had been almost impossible for days even for face and hands and hair and clothes were permeated with red dust.

News was brought me that the ships were all full, the only available berth being an upper one in a first-class cabin on the *Saxon*. This was to leave in two days and was to carry Sir Alfred Milner to England. I was beset with uncertainty. Should I do more good by remaining at Cape Town? I felt *not*. There was but an hour to decide lest the berth be lost. I took it and sailed on 7 May. [. . .]

31. TO MRS. CHARLES MURRAY

R.M.S. Saxon
17 May 1901

May I send you a few lines from Madeira to account for myself thus far? Shaky lines I fear, for this is about as throbbing a ship as they make them!

I am so grateful to you and Mrs. Henry Cloete for introducing me to the Pot-gieters,[1] for he is by far the nicest man on board. But what a family to travel with! A host, an army! He made me welcome to their table, which is good practice in Dutch for me. As for the mass of the passengers, it is hard to know how so many German Jews were raked together. What a noise and what a crowd! Also 180 children on board with obstreperous spirits.

For peace and quiet about a dozen of us retire to the seclusion of the upper deck where also on a little raised dais sits H. E. alone in his Glory.

He has told the Captain he does not wish to mingle with anyone nor speak to any lady. However, he came and spoke to me as soon as waves and wind allowed and I

114

plunged into my subject. We were fighting through when a cruel and noisy wind-lass cut us short. So I shall wait a few days and then bring him to boot – probably choosing a moment after the heat of the equator and before the roll of the Bay,[2] because I find the sea is no respecter of persons and even Excellencies succumb!

I find Mrs. Nicol of Natal a perfect cabin companion. Indeed she would be more fitly called Mrs. Angel from Heaven! But we live in dread of 41 extras to be taken on in Madeira lest one should fall to our share.

It *is* true that the Rev. Hofmeyr[3] is on board – but never shows. Never comes to meals. He gives out he is summoned home by the Colonial-Secretary and is of H. E.'s party. This Mr. Walrond (Private Secretary to H. E.) strenuously denies and threatens to expose the statement publicly in the smoking-room. He says beyond his teaching Sir Alfred Dutch, they never had anything to do with him. Something odd somewhere! What a coarse, repulsive-looking man he is!

This is a dull letter, but equatorial temperature is not conducive to literary effort, or so I find. This must not go, however, without carrying one more word of gratitude to you for your unceasing kindness which so reduced my difficulties of every kind and got me through.

I shall always regret the *meercat*.

32. TO MRS. CHARLES MURRAY

R.M.S. Saxon, Southampton
22–24 May 1901

With frozen hands brought about by our northern climes I must try and make my pen tell you of our safe arrival here.

We hear we are to be bothered to death and our patience sorely tried by the King threatening to meet Sir Alfred!!!! To be hindered by Royalties at the end of a tedious journey is indeed an added vexation! We should easily have been in on Thursday but have orders to slow down to Friday noon. So tiresome!

I have had a long talk with H. E.[a)] As I thought, the Bloemfontein spies had told him all sorts of things, such as that I was causing discontent in the camps, talked politics, and so forth.

We argued it out and I told him I left because I would not work where I was suspected and that if I went again it must be with the clear understanding that I must be above suspicion. He acknowledged the justice of this and said (graciously enough) that if he allowed anyone to go again he would prefer *me*, but as yet he had not made up his mind – must consult Colonial Office and so forth and hear names of alternative ladies. And on the other hand I said I was not sure of being able to go again either because of my own or my Aunt's plans. Thus it rests that we are to write to each other after arriving in England.

The last week he has much come down from his high horse and talks to the four ladies who haunt the higher deck, viz. Miss F., Mrs. Gildea, a German lady and myself. Of course through Mr. Walrond the ship soon learnt my history and so I find myself much shunned – which I am bound to say does not affect me in the smallest degree. Only too glad to be left in peace. [. . .]

From the memoir

a) To me the most important part of the voyage was the chance offered of a talk with Sir Alfred Milner.[1]

It was somewhat difficult to find a convenient and quiet moment, but as we left Madeira the time did come. The bulk of the people were still below, watching the receding cliffs, and I found myself alone with Sir Alfred on the upper deck. We went rather fully into the matter then. One or two points have always remained in my mind. One of small importance related to my own conduct. He stated that some sixty-four reports of me had been sent to him.

Certain as I was that spies dogged my steps and *agents-provocateurs* like Mr. Gostling had endeavoured to draw me, I was astounded at this number. What an army of informers to pay!

I assured him that I had kept to my undertaking to avoid politics or any political influence and told him of the Gostling incident. I told him I had understood he trusted me and was astounded that he was having me watched, because that was *not trust*. I pointed out the low class of people that were willing to be informers. I think on the whole he believed me. [. . .]

Long after, I came across the following passage from Macrobius:

> "A Roman knight after unfair censure by Augustus Caesar said: 'Caesar, when you make inquiries about honourable men, see that you employ honourable men to make those inquiries'."

I, too, would willingly have had my work and my words enquired into by honourable men.

There were two Alfred Milners – there was the charming, sympathetic, gracious and cultivated man, whose abilities and culture found rather a desert in South Africa, and whose really liberal leanings were in contrast to the military men surrounding him, and there was the politician who had given his word to carry out the ideas of the English statesmen and felt bound in honour to do so. The clash must have given him many dolorous moments of extreme agony.

Was it the other Milner that was allowing the Private Secretary Mr. Walrond to say publicly that it was useless for me to learn *Taal* from Mr. Potgieter because I should *not* be allowed to go out again?

Life is a curious jumble, dear Mrs. Steyn, of good and evil, of best and second-best – but then, we cannot forget that we have lived to see Milner stand out in recent days for saner measures and more pacific policies than those around him.[2]

116

The other point that issued from our talk was of deeper importance because it gave me an insight into the fatal and futile policy which lay behind the war, devastation, and the camps.

We landed on 24 May and Sir Alfred Milner received a peerage.[3]

Work in England

1901

Introduction

We landed on 24 May – cold as May can often be with us. The voyage had not rested me; voyages do not – and if you have voyaged in the *Saxon* you will know she has a horrid trick of vibrating more than most. So it was soothing to get ashore, and as my Aunt and Uncle were in the country I soon found myself in all the beauty of the Oxfordshire house in which they were spending Whitsuntide.

I had, of course, missed news from home for at least two months past, so had much to learn. Some letters followed me about but never reached me till months later and of course when it was known I was sailing it had been useless to write. It was therefore only after arrival that I learnt fully of the responsibility and anxiety my friends had felt, wishing to make use of the information I had sent in order to elicit sympathy and funds, but deterred by fear lest the Authorities should object and in consequence debar my further work. The Committee of the Distress Fund considered everything very carefully, and as I now, 25 years later, read for the first time all the correspondence which passed, I marvel at the wise counsels both of my Aunt and my Brother and their thoughtfulness in allowing no publicity which could affect my position (Mr. Ellis' publication of portions of Mr. Rowntree's letter had been a mistake.)[1]

I know, however, that part of my letters were – through Lady Harcourt – shewn to Brodrick and Balfour[2] who both felt the subject needed enquiry. It was probably from that time that amelioration began in the camps as far as canvas and iron accommodation went, water and fuel supply. Improved sanitation and more hospitals and nurses so changed the appearance of the camps in the four months that elapsed between my visit and that of the Ladies' Commission,[3] life in them was a different thing from that which I had witnessed. Food was, however, not increased till the Ladies' Commission insisted in their interview with Kitchener and the death-rate did not abate till after the extra food was distributed.

[Meanwhile on return to England] I felt the need for the joint advice of our inner circle. My Brother kindly came down from Manchester, but Mr. Courtney was away for Whitsuntide and plans must be made without him. I was anxious to take no public step until I had heard from Lord Milner who had promised on the *Saxon* to write very soon. I felt that the Whitsuntide recess might delay him too. On the other hand a month had already passed since I left the camps and the work was of a nature and gravity that brooked no delay. My Uncle and my Brother

121

talked it all round and it was agreed that my right course was to seek an interview with the War Minister, Mr. Brodrick. It was felt that Lord Milner could not disapprove of such an obvious duty.

I find a rough draft of my note to Mr. Brodrick amongst my papers:

> "Dear Sir,
> I have just returned from several months' work in the women's camps in South Africa. I am, of course, responsible in the first place to the committee whose funds I have been administering and do not know if they will publish my report or otherwise. In view, however, of the courtesy which has been shewn me by the Government, I think that if you desire it, you should have the information beforehand in case publicity is given to my statements. Should this appear desirable to you I will wait upon you wherever you decide."

I received a courteous welcome by return, appointing me to wait upon the Minister at the War Office on Tuesday, 4 June.

My Brother, with his never-failing helpfulness, drew up with me a list of the points upon which I should dwell with the Minister. Introductions were also given me and appointments made with various leading men, Sir Henry Campbell-Bannerman and others. I spent a night with the Courtneys while my Aunt made her move back to London and then I retired to my Chelsea flat convenient for serious work.

Having heard nothing from Lord Milner, I ventured, on 7 June, after the Whitsuntide, to write and ask him if he could now send me the promised letter. His reply dated 27 June expressed regret at the delay in writing and merely said that as now the matter had been laid before the Government it was better that they should answer my suggestions direct. It appeared as if he were annoyed that I had carried the matter to the Minister of State. If this was so, I am sorry, but in view of the need for instant action I had no right to delay. Anyhow, it shewed me that the affair must now be considered under the Home Government only and, though sorry that the personal link with Lord Milner should be broken, I did feel it a step forward that the Cabinet as a whole should take *so grave* a matter in hand.

The position was somewhat complex, and cause and effect intertwined. It was obvious, as Lord Hobhouse had always asserted, that the Government was one that would yield only to fear, viz. fear of public opinion. Mr. Brodrick, in private a kindly man, was not a Minister of any power, nor one with imagination enough to grasp the scope and gravity of the situation. He did, I believe, his best, but his best was not good enough for the occasion. It became necessary to publish the facts and this was done by circulating in both Houses a pamphlet containing extracts from my letters.[4]

Instantly, the sentiment of the country was aroused and had it been allowed its

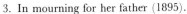

1. Emily (left) with her sister Maud. "Wherever I am, I shall always be Missis," her Valentine card read.

2. E. H. with her "pet nephew" Oliver on the Rectory lawn at St Ive.

3. In mourning for her father (1895).

4. Character, elegance, class.

5. On the threshold of her work in South Africa.

6. The ostrich-feather portrait.

7. With her fiancé, J. C. Jackson (left), her brother, Leonard, and his wife, Nora.

8. In the garden of Warren House at St Ives on the Cornish coast, South Africa's gift to E. H. On the table, a jar of canned fruit from one of her annual Free State "Wonder Boxes".

9. The woman whose capacity for sympathy was her "crime".

10. Throughout her life a great letter-writer.

11. A larger than life-size oil by Hugo Naudé, in memory of her work with the Boer home industries.

12. Portrait (1923) by E. S. J. Reva, in the Oranje Girls' High School in Bloemfontein.

13. Bust by prof. A. Molinor of Leipzig, commemorating her work for a starving Europe after the First World War.

14. Possibly the last portrait of E. H. before her death in July 1926.

15. E.H. in old age.

CHIEF CORRESPONDENTS

16. Mrs. Isabella (Tibbie) Steyn.

17. Lady Hobhouse – "Aunt Mary".

18. Leonard Hobhouse.

19. Mrs. Chas. Murray.

FRIENDS AND HOSTESSES

20. Mrs. Mary Sauer.

21. Olive Schreiner.

22. Mrs. Anna Purcell.

23. Mrs. Caroline Fichardt.

24. Miss E. M. (Betty) Molteno and Miss Alice Greene.

25. Lord Hobhouse – "Uncle Arthur".

26. Mr. Leonard Courtney.

27. General J. C. Smuts ("Oom Jannie") with his son Japie (1905).

28. Mr. Jacob de Villiers (1907).

29. Mr. J. W. Sauer at the front door of Uitkijk, Stellenbosch.

THE CONCENTRATION CAMPS

30. Boer families conveyed to the camps in open cattle trucks.

31. A farmhouse in flames, its inhabitants destitute.

32. Boer women and children move to camp, carrying what they may.

33. Sir Alfred Milner –
the farm-burning
was a "mistake", he
admitted to E. H.

35. Springfontein camp.

34. Camp orphans.

36. Camp women washing, available soap eked out.

37. Waiting to be taken to camp.

38. Visitors at Harrismith camp baffled by the huge needs of its inhabitants.

39. With firewood at a premium, small boys chop wood to keep the cooking-fires going.

40. President and Mrs. Steyn with General Christiaan de Wet (centre), at the Zastron Street house in Bloemfontein where Mrs. Steyn lived during the war.

VISIT TO THE
RUINED DISTRICTS

41. The mule cart in which E. H. set off from Bloemfontein.

42. Leaving from Kaya Lami in Church Street – Mr. Enslin, E.H. and (backs to the camera) probably Mr. Arthur Fichardt who arranged the trip and his mother, Mrs. Caroline Fichardt, with house servants.

43. E. H. waves and they're off – Mr. Enslin holding the reins, Jacob the whip.

44. E. H. with shawls and hand baggage for the trip.

45. After the peace – their country's independence lost, their home ruined, their stock destroyed. Despair and boredom.

46. A returning family makes a fresh start on the empty veld. A least, a few goats to milk.

APPRECIATION

47 and 48. Pretoria reception for Miss Hobhouse (1903). Third from the left, General Smuts; next to E. H., General Beyers.

49. E. H. showered with roses. Scene at Pretoria station.

BOER HOME INDUSTRIES

50. Cambridge graduate Margaret Clark (centre, back) among the Boer girls she taught spinning and weaving at Philippolis.

51. Visiting the school at Langlaagte: President Steyn talks to Con Cloete from the Cape, who came to keep house for E. H.

52. At the dyeing vats – expert Mr. Milroy demonstrating.

53. The draughty stable of the Orphanage at Langlaagte where the first Transvaal school was started.

54. Boer Generals whom E.H. entertained at her Chelsea flat after the War – De Wet, De la Rey, Botha. What a problem there was to find cigars!

55. Anton van Wouw's original maquette for the main group of the Women's Memorial.

56. The eventual centre group of the Women's Memorial at Bloemfontein – reconstruction of a war-time scene at Springfontein station which E. H. described to the sculptor.

AAN ONZE
HELDINNEN
EN LIEVE KINDEREN
"UW WIL GESCHIEDE"

true expression, not only would the camps then and there have been adequately reformed, but very possibly the war would also have dwindled in popularity and been ended. Wishing to take advantage of the wave of sentiment, my Committee hired the Queen's Hall arranging that I should speak. The Bishop of Hereford promised to take the Chair, and the hall was secured and the tickets sold when – imagine! – the Authorities got behind the scenes and pulled the wires so that the lessor of the hall broke his contract. He still owes us for the expenses we incurred. Some of the Distress Fund then wished as a body to sue him for breach of contract and probably this would have been done, but Lord Ripon[5] objected as he did not desire Lady Ripon to be involved in a law suit. As you know, the Deacons of Westminister Chapel which was offered me instead, behaved in a similar fashion so that the meeting which would have meant so much for your People never took place.

Before me as I write lies a letter from the Chief Constable of York, suggesting that there would be disturbance if I held my meeting there and that "the results would be serious". Pure nonsense! In Manchester the same effort was made to prevent the meeting, but the Chief Constable refused to give in and the meeting, the largest I held, was crowded and quiet and enthusiastic.

Such matters, contemptibly small in themselves, would not be worth mentioning were it not that it was continued throughout the country. For it shewed the determination on the part of the Government to prevent my appeal to national sentiment, and this opposition was accompanied by a whisper to the Chamberlain Press to vilify me – which it did, I believe, quite successfully do. I never read that Press, but now and then picked up a paper in a railway carriage during my many journeys and got a glimpse of the sort of thing that was said. I also experienced much rudeness and ostracism in London drawing-rooms. You see I have survived to tell the tale. Lived also to sum up Governments as poor things more careful of their own prestige than of justice and right. And always, when the conduct of war is in question, devoid of conscience. That is, I think, one of the worst features of war – far worse than death or bodily pains or material destruction – the rotting away/ jeopardy of Justice, Truth and Humanity.

To me the great disappointment was that I was prevented from adequately keeping my word to the Boer women, viz. that I would tell the English People of their sufferings, and I could not prove my assurances to them that our People, if they knew, would set things right. Something, however, was accomplished, for considerable reforms were set going in the camps . . .

[As to telling the English People] the first time I spoke was in private at Aunt Mary's house to a large assembly of people, mostly ladies. This was on 10 June. I remember telling them how hard I found it to speak to people well-dressed and well-fed like themselves, of those whom I had left in squalor and hunger. I was very nervous, but at least they were interested and several, including Mrs. Humphrey Ward,[6] came and questioned me about it when I had finished. Directly after, she

123

began to organize another fund for the camps, but a passing illness delayed her when, finding the ladies of the Victoria League were also stirring in the matter, she wrote me that she was merging with them.[7]

It would weary you to tell of all the meetings I spoke at during those summer months. It was hard work, more so than I could have imagined. I so well remember Lord Ripon warning me it would be so. He had had experience of stumping the country and he said: "It's not the travelling or the actual speaking that so fatigues, it's the social part. But," he added, "a woman can always plead a headache!"

I found he was right. Strength was drained by private talk and the necessary civilities to a daily changing circle of hospitable but quite unknown hosts. My Uncle was so good, he gave me money to travel first class. Consequently I could write and rest and think in the trains, and arrived fresh.

The meetings themselves were a joy. Though the larger halls were made impossible by Governmental action, and the large audiences whose sympathies were first deterred by being told I was a rebel, traitor and such other libellous terms a foolish Press delights in, halls there always were and crowded at that, and the relief was good of thus unburdening my message.

I was appalled by the ignorance I met. Few seemed to grasp the difference between the Transvaal and the O.R.C., the Cape Colony and Natal. I was vastly amused when, after one meeting (I think Birmingham), a young man came up to the platform armed with Olive Schreiner's *Story of an African Farm*. He was obsessed with the powerful portrayal of Tant' Sannie – certainly a very unattractive character – and his argument was that Boer women being like that, their extermination was desirable!! I kept my temper and first took the line of informing him that Olive Schreiner's book dealt with the Cape Colony, not with the two Republics, and that Tant' Sannie was a British subject. This line failed to impress because of the predominant geographical ignorance, so I suggested that though Dickens had drawn Sairey Gamp[8] it did not follow that all Englishwomen resembled that undesirable person. He reluctantly acknowledged this and departed. But Olive Schreiner would have been amused had she known how often Tant' Sannie confronted me that year!

He was followed by an elderly man who drew a letter from his pocket which he said he had written denouncing me and all my works to *The Birmingham Post*. Then, hearing that I was to speak that night, he judged it prudent to refrain from posting it till he had heard what I had to say. "And now," he said, "having heard you, it will not be posted."

The subject made people easily interested, but I did not speak well. One has to learn as one goes along. At Manchester my Brother heard me speak and told me I gave too much detail. After that I think I improved. There was such a lack of imagination that I had thought by detail to drive home a complete picture. My meetings were crowded into June and July because I so greatly hoped to be allowed to return to the camps but, as you know, Mr. Brodrick knocked that on the head.[9]

124

With Mr. Brodrick I had, of course, no further dealings. I had done all that was possible through him only. As the death-rate increased[10] throughout those months and the Ladies' Commission[11] was acting rather leisurely, I wrote him the open letter[12] which appeared in *The Times*. I wrote it in a white heat of feeling consequent upon the last issue of the death-rate of those months.

Let us give Mr. Brodrick his due. Good, but unequal to the position, he had done something to reform the camps. Many improvements had been made – enough to present them in a very different light to Mrs. Fawcett's Committee when it entered them four months after I had left. But the evils were too deep and too widespread for mild treatment. The sterner but stronger control of Mr. Chamberlain was needed, and when, as immediately afterwards, he took the matter into his own competent hands, reforms were quickly effected and the death-rate fell.[13]

[Of meetings with other leading men] two stand out with special clearness, viz. those with Mr. Morley and (what had probably more far-reaching consequences) with Sir Henry Campbell-Bannerman. Both were so marvellously receptive, it just made you talk, and both in their several ways had the gift, by a word here and there, of keeping one close to the most important lines of the subject. Kindly as Mr. Brodrick listened, he was devoid of that gift. It reminded me of singing in a hall with good accoustics which just seems to take your voice and sing for you, as contrasted with a badly constructed room which makes every note an effort. As I was desperately shy this help was much needed. I find among my papers an account of the interview (with Sir Henry) [. . .]:

> "Of all whom I saw at that time, deeply interested as they were, he alone – greatly occupied as he was – seemed to have the leisure and the determination to hear and understand everything. Indeed he gave me so much scope that I was enabled to pour out to him more fully than to anyone else I met the detailed horror of those camps. For nearly two hours he listened with rapt attention, now and then putting a question to elucidate a point. As I dwelt upon the wholesale burning of farms and villages, the deportations, the desperate condition of a burnt-out population brought in by hundreds in convoys, the people deprived of clothes, bedding, utensils and necessities, the semi-starvation in the camps, the fever-stricken children lying sick unto death upon the bare earth, the disease-laden atmosphere, the appalling mortality, the attitude of the sub-officials and the disastrous effect of all this upon the Colonial mind, he was deeply moved and now and then murmured *sotto voce* 'methods of barbarism'. He was right. His words, criticized or resented by many who were (and indeed are) unaware of the circumstances, seemed to me, who had witnessed those methods and their results, most fitting."

125

According to the writer of his obituary in the *Manchester Guardian*, which chimes with my own recollection, Sir Henry spoke that evening at the Holborn Restaurant:

> "Sir Henry had been listening that morning for some hours to the terrible tale of woe brought from South Africa by Miss Hobhouse. He was evidently suffering from strong suppressed emotion [. . .] for suddenly he raised his voice and broke out into that passionate passage of denunciation in which he described the war in South Africa as being conducted in 'methods of barbarism'. It was the only time I saw him completely moved out of himself. What moved him was the passion of humanity."

126

Letters

33. TO MRS. MURRAY

Crowsley Park, Henley-on-Thames
29 May 1901

Till Saturday I am in this delicious world of green and spring flowers, and songs of countless birds, but for two days I have been in town working my tongue so hard that that unruly member is rebellious and exhausted. Everybody wants to know everything and I am breathless with incessant talking.

All yesterday morning I was *tête-à-tête* with John Morley and he was delightful. He said I made Boer feeling more real to him in five minutes than two years of newspapers. My Brother has been with him all this morning and this afternoon I took Mr. Potgieter to convey to Mr. Morley the ideas of the Progressive burghers. He is one of these.

Mr. Molteno[1] came to see me last night and several others to discuss my best line of action. I am quite overcome by the responsibility resting upon me and by the importance attached to every word I speak. My letters, too, are regarded as strong documents and are to be printed in some form[2] as soon as I can break from the Authorities. But first I am to appeal to them and give them their chance. Editors are after me and interviewers and people clamouring for meetings and I am vainly trying to keep my head cool and my facts clear and distinct.

I think Morley is strengthening, we have tried to put him into stays.[3]

England looks green and lovely beyond words – like one big garden – but such a toy-like beauty after that of your country.

Miss Monkhouse and Miss Mellor left on the 25th, so I only saw the former for a few minutes. I tried, but in vain, to postpone their going.[a] They must have Dutch lessons in Cape Town; it is essential. My little Dutch was invaluable.

From the memoir

a) I thought their departure a mistake considering the uncertainty of the position, and as a matter of fact they wasted many weeks in Cape Town awaiting permission to go to Kimberley, during which interval great changes had been made in that camp though its condition was still bad enough when the Ladies' Commission visited it in August. Mrs. Murray, with her great hospitality, took them in all those weeks.[4]

34. TO LEONARD HOBHOUSE

21 Rossetti Mansions
4 June 1901

I have just seen Brodrick[a] and come away with a strong impression of his gentlemanly incompetence – slippery but pleasant, mediocre and agreeable; ready to listen, ready also to drift. Standpoint: How good we are, how right we have been.

Did not feel I got my claws into him *anywhere*. Brought in almost all our points and brought him quite up to date[1] by letters fresh from the camps last night. Mrs. Van Breda has escaped again (from Kimberley Camp), this time successfully.[2]

He asked me to write fully my suggestions[3] for ameliorating matters and will discuss with Colonial Office and Milner.

Meantime I am pressed to speak at the Queen's Hall.[4] What an opportunity!

Poor Brodrick! When I ended by telling him I should be obliged to make public his refusal to let me go again, he turned white as a sheet!

From the memoir

a) It was my first interview with a Secretary of State and I felt very nervous, but after a few minutes that passed away, and the time flew as he expressed ignorance and interest. It was nearly 2 p.m. when he glanced at the clock. I took it as a hint and rose. He had been most willing to listen, perhaps what appalled me was finding a Minister in such ignorance of what was being done under his rule.

He asked for my suggestions which I had tabulated previously and which I handed in at the War Office the same afternoon. I had pleaded hard; the vision of the camps and suffering women was vivid and I felt myself the mediator between them and the Powers of England.

My belief – always instilled into the women – that their suffering would never be tolerated by the English People if they were but known, carried me through this interview and the fact that my suggestions were called for continued to uphold my view. Alas! I had not reckoned with the Cabinet as a whole; with hard anger at the delay of Victory; with the expense which seemed vast even to a Government; with accepted policy; with dull imaginations . . .

35. TO MRS. CHARLES MURRAY

21, Rossetti Mansions, Chelsea
21 June 1901

Only a line to tell you I am sending you my report and am in the throes of preparing for my big speech on the 24th.[1]

Thanks many for your letter telling me of Miss Hogg[2] and I now hear by cable that Mrs. Rendel Harris[3] has got leave to go up . . . I am working up everyone all I can.

128

I saw Mrs. Louis Botha in London and on her authority, straight from her husband, can contradict the story that either French or Buller were ever on parole or prisoners. Botha laughed at the idea that he would have let them off if he had caught them! Please tell Mrs. Koopmans this.

36. TO MRS. CHARLES MURRAY

29 Frederick Road, Edgbaston

11 July 1901

One little line to thank you for your letter and to say I will do my best to see Miss Wessels, etc.[1] She has seen Miss Bradby and others, but unfortunately I am always on the move now; my life seems to have become like a kaleidoscope – daily a different town, a different audience and a different circle.

The Government has made me various concessions,[a][2] but they are furious with me, I am told, and regard me as a thorn in their side.

Keep perfectly quiet the good news that Miss Hogg has got her permit for Volksrust and Mrs. Rendel Harris has wired for money from Johannesburg. She finds great want there. So far so good, but much more remains to be done. I must work on, bringing pressure on the Authorities here.

I speak *here*, in Birmingham, tonight. Have had some splendid meetings but still have to be very careful in my presentment of the subject.

I have seen Mrs. Anderson.[3] And Barbara Bradby is now turned Hammond[4] and we all assisted at the wedding which was truly original.

The great heat makes my hand shaky.

If you see Mr. Merriman tell him that the meeting at which he did *not* speak[5] almost ruined my work – made it far more difficult, and Adriaan Hofmeyr and Mrs. Stuart[6] have done their worst!

Yours, E. H.

P.S. Brodrick has just refused my request to go (to the camps) again. But I shall not give up. Perhaps questions in the House of Commons will bring him round.[7]

From the memoir

a) It was a long wait of over three weeks for the formal answer which reached me on 28 June . . . The concessions allowing the departure from the camps of women who had friends to take them in gave me profound relief and though I feared that clause "unless there is some military objection", yet I hoped it might bring relief to many.

Mrs. [Kate] Courtney wrote to my Brother:

"It is a great triumph, the Government really accepting your sister's suggestions, though their friends will probably continue to abuse her and us as traitors."

37. TO LEONARD HOBHOUSE

Darlington
20 July 1901

Last night I was not allowed a hearing.[1] A large audience of quiet, thoughtful people had gathered and sat patiently waiting and we on the platform sat and patiently faced them while 12 or 15 organized roughs sat in a group and howled and sang for one and a half hours. The policy of non-resistance prevailed in this Quaker town so they were not interfered with. We simply sat and they (the audience) sat – perfect order prevailed. Mrs. Backhouse and Lady Dale were not allowed to speak and of course I never even stood up. So Lady Dale said she would have a meeting next morning in her own home and I have just finished addressing a large audience at 10 a.m.

[added on 24 July]
. . . There was something extraordinarily impressive that night in the silent platform facing the silent massed hall – for one and a half hours. We sat out the time the speeches would have taken if delivered. In the midst of this order and silence, this serious purpose and repose, a tiny group of noisy roughs, empty and aimless. There was something symbolic about it, and in one way it was the most wonderful and impressive of all my meetings . . . It was a feature . . . that at most places the majority of the audience filed past the platform to shake hands with me.

38. TO MRS. CHARLES MURRAY

Manchester
15 August 1901

I have been sorry not to have heard from you for the last two weeks, but can well understand how busy you have been. I had so looked forward to hearing from you of some women being *actually released* in consequence of the concession.[a)1] Please let me know at once the first case you hear of – for instance the two for whom you have applied and Mrs. Hertzog at Port Elizabeth.[b)] Many others I have in mind. Remember I shall write to you every week without fail, so you will know.

I am very tired today for I spoke at Rochdale last night and shall at Oldham tonight and Sheffield on Sunday. So excuse a short dull scrap.

I was cheered this week by receiving news straight from Bloemfontein. I account for it by the fact that there is a new Censor there apparently.

Remember me to all you see whom I know, not forgetting the *meercat* who is I

130

hope well and not tied up any longer! Any scraps of news sent are most gratefully received. I hope to have an article in the September *Nineteenth Century*.[c]

From the memoir

a) Cabled to the Cape, this concession encouraged many to apply for release of relatives but few indeed were successful.

b) One case in particular impressed me greatly, viz. that of Mrs. Hertzog, wife of General J. B. M. Hertzog. Parted from her only child [pp. 35–36] she endured the horrid monotony of Port Elizabeth Camp for two years and the danger and disease of Merebank Camp for many months.

What should we think if enemies were to imprison the wives of our leading Generals? If Lady Methuen or Lady Maxwell were to be thus treated?

Her father, Mr. C. M. Neethling, acting on the concession, applied for his two daughters' release and this is the answer he got: ". . . the G.O.C. regrets that in the present state of affairs in the Colony he cannot yet sanction their removal to Stellenbosch."

Strange, is it not, as we look back, to note the turn of Time's wheel. As I write that delicate baby boy reared by his grandparents is now a student at Oxford, while Mrs. Hertzog is taking the leading place as wife of the Prime Minister of the Union.

For many, however, things have not turned out so well and health was wrecked and lives lost that might have been saved by the application of even that one concession, had it been given in practice as well as in principle.

c) Mr. Jas. Knowles, Editor of *The Nineteenth Century and After*, accepted an article from me on the camps[2] on the condition that I would refrain from further correspondence, and I was glad of the offer. I cancelled one or two letters to *The Times*. (It [had been] an added labour to reply to some of my critics who wrote to *The Times* though I rather doubt if it was wise to do so. The writers mostly knew nothing of the subject.)

39. TO MRS. CHARLES MURRAY

21 Rossetti Mansions, Chelsea

29 August 1901

I was at Portsmouth last Sunday and had a very good meeting there, quite winning over both papers, Jingo Liberal and Conservative, to take an interest in my subject. Certainly, bits of vegetable marrow, etc. were thrown at me, but the cheering was greatly in the ascendant and quite deafening.

I was to have been at Bath to-morrow, but my Cousin Violet's sudden death made me cancel this pro tem.

131

So this week is given up to fighting *The Times* and other newspapers and to endless arrears of correspondence. I am trying to find and send two more (women) who will act like your two recent guests and fight patiently till they win.[1]

We read with avidity all the news we can get of you all, and yesterday's tidings of what has happened to one we had so recently with us in England depressed and saddened us on all sides.[2] I simply sat down and cried. I was lunching with Canon and Mrs. Barnett who were also full of sympathy.

I am so grateful for all your letters. They help to keep me in touch with all that is happening to people in whom I feel so deep an interest.

How is Dr. Murray? My respects to him. It is refreshing to think of him pursuing the even tenor of his healing way, and at intervals bringing delicious melody into the life of the house.

Our sunny days are already closing in and soon all will be at work in London again. My love to your neighbour at Cumnor, please. And I shall end with a riddle to amuse you!

Why is a woman like a telegraph?

Because her intelligence is always in advance of the male (mail).

Isn't this true? Will Dr. Murray believe it?

Obliged to fill up with nonsense because sound sense can't be written.

40. TO MRS. CHARLES MURRAY

Charlton House, Portbury, Bristol
5 September 1901

We have all been much interested in your account of your interview with the Commission – and Mrs. De Villiers also wrote me an account substantially the same.[1] It is only what we feared, and I think we must just ignore them and simply go on working and get kindly women amongst them (in the camps). I am urging our Committee to send out two more without delay who shall persist till they succeed. If you have any news of your late guests, let us know – we have none.

We are disappointed at the sudden (to us) return of Mrs. Rendel Harris. I believe she lands today. Our Committee had sent her a large sum, besides what her own people had sent, and we had no idea she was not going to stay and administer it in person. Did you see her on her return? I want to see her very much but I fear I shall have no chance.

I had a nice long letter from Mrs. Philip Botha by last mail. What a comfort that she is at last housed. Miss Bradby wrote that they wanted to send her anything that she specially needed. I think I asked you to see that she had clothing from our bales; but they wonderd if there was any special need she had; if you or Miss Molteno could find out.

Do let me know how the Joint Committee you declined to join gets along. Your letters are a great pleasure.

P.S. I suppose you have seen Sir Neville Chamberlain's letters.[2] He is a Field-Marshall.

Arrest and deportation
1901

Introduction

A few quiet days at Charlton House were most soothing after the *Sturm und Drang* of these varied months. Great was the love and sympathy awaiting me there. But it could not be for long. I was whirled round and round continually, needing to return to London for interviews.

While North, Lady Ripon invited me to spend a few days with them at Studley Royal and much I enjoyed that repose, the beauty of Fountain Abbey and above all the advantage of long quiet talks with Lord Ripon.

It was after very full discussions with him that I decided to return to the Cape Colony – not of course to the camps, which had been prohibited, but to continue another branch of the work about which letters from the Cape were continually arriving.[1] This was the condition of the deportees, of whom many were in the coast towns: Durban, East London, Port Elizabeth and Cape Town itself. They were in sore need of help. In addition, I had been urged both from Africa and England to take up the cause of the British Refugees and I was very ready to investigate their need, though many *on the spot* had assured me further help was not required.

Lord Ripon was fully in accord with this outline of work, but Lord Ripon knew geography and did not conclude, as so many did, that going to South Africa necessarily meant going to the camps. Lady Ripon, too, kindly furnished me with a letter to Lady Hely-Hutchinson. Consequently I made preparations to start early in October.

Having definitely decided upon my journey and having found acquiescence in it from a number of my best advisers, I cut short my visit to Studley Royal and hurried to London for final arrangements. Being much out of health I longed for the rest of the voyage and for the sunshine of the Cape. But it seemed prudent to take a companion and I did so in the shape of a young and capable nurse, Miss Phillips, whose skill would later, I felt sure, be of utmost value in the shortage of nurses throughout the country. She had been recommended to me by Mrs. Barnett when I discussed the matter with her and Canon Barnett at Bristol.

We sailed on the *Avondale Castle*, an intermediate slow vessel, on 5 October. We had a terrible storm in the Bay, the Captain telling me it was my fault and that I was the Jonah! That was his little joke, with a spice in it. But we were fairly good friends. It was a dreary voyage and, far from resting me, made me very unwell. Doubtless I was suffering from the strenuous work of the past year. The only intellectual companionship was that of Miss Steedman on her way to become Principal of Bloemfontein School for Girls.

I had been very much in the limelight and, needing rest and quiet, had taken pains to keep my journey unknown and to this end had secured the promise of the Union Castle Company to omit my name from the passenger list. I was therefore the more surprised that my movements were known and arrangements had been made to arrest me. Not till much later did I learn that a busybody journalist had got wind of it and published the fact in a London paper. His woeful ignorance of what is possible under martial law made him believe and publish that I was going back to the *camps*. As already stated the Government had definitely refused permission and I should never have dreamed of anything so undignified as attempting to go behind that prohibition even had it been possible, which, with martial law in control throughout the interior, it certainly was not. Since the European War people have a rather closer comprehension of what martial law means.

Inaccurate journalists are mischievous people, and I have suffered much at their hands one time and another.

Letters

41. TO LEONARD HOBHOUSE

S.S. Avondale Castle, Table Bay
29 October 1901

There seems much to tell of feelings and experiences if not of facts since our arrival here on Sunday, the 27th. We dropped anchor as the clock struck 4 p.m., and we were all dressed and ready to go ashore, ready with the readiness of those who had been 22 days at sea, grinding along with an asthmatic engine against strong currents and head winds. The tropics were very cold and we were all wrapped up to the tips of our noses. I never felt well all the way.

The only person of interest to me on board was Miss Steedman, late of Manchester School, going out to take the Principalship of Bloemfontein Dames Institute from which Miss Murray was deposed. Of her more anon.

All was calm and lovely as we glided into the Bay and our spirits were at boiling point. Of course we had to wait for pratique, but when the steam tug came out alongside of us I saw with horror the khaki in it and knew at once the worst had come.

They boarded us and the Officer sat in the smoking-room and proceeded to examine every single individual of the 450 passengers. Our spirits sank. No possibility of going ashore that night and sorrowfully we unpacked again. Presently it came to my turn, and then the Officer, one Lieutenant Lingham, when he had digested my name, informed me that he would prefer taking me at the very end of all. From this I augured no good, but I bowed and withdrew, still expecting only a more detailed and searching examination.

It was a long business. Not till the dinner bell rang did he come to me and say he wished to speak to me. Crowds of people were everywhere and there was no square inch of quietness. I took him to the Captain's cabin, for I had an instinctive turning to the Captain at that moment as the only man to stand by me. He welcomed us in and was himself withdrawing when the Officer stopped him saying that the matter concerned him also. He, Lingham, then turned to me and informed me I was placed under arrest, that I should not be allowed to land in South Africa *anywhere*, and that I was to hold no communication with anyone on shore by word or letter. I drew up and asked him from whom he had received such an order, and he replied from Colonel Cooper, Military Commander of Cape Town. I further asked from whom did the Colonel receive such instructions, and he replied he could say no more. Then he turned to the Captain, who looked horridly miserable, for we are very good friends, and said I was placed in his charge and he would be held

139

responsible for me. He was to see I did not leave the ship nor hold communication with anyone.

Next he gave me the alternative of returning home by the *Carisbrooke* on the Wednesday or of remaining where I was. I replied that to return by the *Carisbrooke* was out of the question for I felt quite wholly unfit for another long voyage. I then asked if he would take letters for me to the Commandant and the Governor, etc. and this he agreed to, promising to call for them when he came to finish the ship in the morning.

Altogether I kept my head fairly well, but I was so taken aback that I could hardly at the moment think what it was best to do. Then I had to keep up and walk down to dinner calm and unconcerned, though through the Purser the news had flashed through the ship in a second. However, I was just able to chatter merrily all dinner-time, and then after I went and poured myself out to Miss Steedman. She was intensely astonished and angry and truly sympathized – a good type, of the average English view that we are all right and everything is going pretty well, this was her first lesson in the sort of things really being done in South Africa, and she was horrified. We had made great friends and though she had before embarking had the usual newspaper view of me, she had been quite turned round to see and understand me as I am.

With her help I wrote four letters – to Milner, Kitchener, Hely-Hutchinson and Colonel Cooper. I will try to send you copies of these and the replies as I receive them.[1] She agreed with me that it was my duty to stay and fight the point and that it would never do to turn round and meekly obey them by going home.

All night I lay awake shuddering from head to foot with the effects of the shock, for oddly enough it was a shock and unexpected in that form. Then I began to see my way and brace myself to the battle.

I shall be very polite, very dignified, but in every way I possibly can a thorn in the flesh to them. I see already many ways of being a thorn. For instance, *they* don't want it much talked of in Cape Town and I mean that it shall be. We are to move into dock as soon as the gale subsides and I shall at once demand a guard; partly because it is extremely disagreeable for Captain Brown to be my goaler, and partly that the guard is their witness that I keep the rules laid down. Most of all because I understand they don't want to do it because of making it conspicuous. I know soldiers hate guarding women. I also mean to refuse to return to England until such time as I myself feel willing and able, unless of course they send me under force of arms. I shall not move a limb in that direction. If the *Avondale* unloads immediately she will be able to continue her voyage in ten days' time and then they must find another prison for me.

I have already petitioned all the Authorities for a *land* prison; rocking out here in the cold is awful and I cannot sleep.

It would be too ludicrous if it were not for the great tragedy of which it is one little outcome. Anyhow I think they will find me a bore, polite but a bore, before we have done. I felt happier when I had made up my mind what course to steer. The Captain who, though by no means a political sympathizer, likes me personally, is acting most courteously in a trying position. He is very angry and thinks it a great cheek of them to have used his ship as a prison and himself as a goaler.

Remember, of all this story you can publish just whatever you like, and the more widely the better, I should think. I am hoping to send the packet home by the officers of this ship to be posted in England. Nurse[2] says they will do it, for one immediate result of the affair has been that everyone who avoided or disapproved of me before has now turned round in my favour.

The first day of my imprisonment seemed very long. It was exasperating to see all the others land and to stay out tossing oneself in the south-easter. So I began to sketch and did two little oils of Table Mountain and the Lion's Head. I could not read. Today we were to have gone into dock, but the gale was too strong, so I managed another sketch – a big panorama scene of the whole group of mountains. The wind was terrific, but I pinned my paper on to the deck itself and did it lying down. The Captain calls me "Napoleon in St. Helena".

I bethought me today of other cases of imprisonment in our family, but so far can only think of Hugh Hobhouse of Bristol, imprisoned for Quakerism about 1660, and of course old Bishop Trelawny.[3] I wonder if 20 000 Englishmen "will know the reason why" about poor me! So today finding Macaulay in the library I read up the whole story of his little difference with the Government, hoping to get some wrinkles [sic] for my own guidance. And I found one at least. Those seven good Bishops refused to pay for their keep in the Tower and I shall refuse to pay my keep on board this ship. It is 10/- a day. Here I see another way of being a bore. Also if they send me home, Government must pay my passage. I find that it is the rule of the Company in cases of undesirables who may not land. And so has ended my second day.

I forgot to say that I asked if Nurse might land and Lingham replied: "Probably, but she must be searched." Captain and I both laughed so at this, that he looked very silly. Nurse is of course much put about, but though wishing to remain with me and "tend" me she has decided to remain in the Colony if I go home. This being so I do not like to injure her prospects by keeping her with me, and so having permission I shall send her ashore with a letter of introduction to Lady Hely-Hutchinson and she will also take Lady Ripon's letter to Lady H.-H. What I wish is that she should join forces with little Miss Aldis[4] and that they should push their way together to the camps. The *Kinfauns Castle*, on which vessel I believe she is, lies now alongside of us unable also to get into dock. How I felt for the poor girl when I saw the steam tug meet her and that Khaki Lingham board her. I wonder if they will let her land. I have told Nurse to get into touch with her through Rev. Dewdney Drew.[5]

I shall miss Nurse very much. She will be a great stand-by. No more tonight. I am too weak in the hand to wield the pen any longer. I hope I may sleep tonight, but if you could only hear the wind; it is like great guns going off. This[a)] must close.

With love, E. Hobhouse.

From the memoir

a) This letter, after all, was putting the best face on it. The shock to my whole system was far greater than I myself knew. To find martial law at the Cape could be no great surprise, for it had been long talked of, so long indeed that I had perhaps ceased to expect it. It was disagreeable and would make one's work difficult but no more. The shock was to find oneself – a law-abiding, free Englishwoman – arrested and imprisoned. Brought up as we were in strict obedience to law and enjoying freedom as the breath of life, this illegality stunned me. No warrant for my arrest was produced and no reason assigned. In vain I asked for the reason. A quarter of a century has passed but none has ever been given – the explanation being that there was none to give.[6]

You, who know how invalided I now am, will well understand how upsetting it must be to turn back in mind to that distressfull time. I have been carefully reading old letters and accounts of eyewitnesses and have lived again through the successive days of that trial, facing once more the solid power of the *Force* that confronted me – Force to face which I had nothing to bring but my English heritage of freedom and liberty, together with my innocence of any infraction of legal or even military regulations. The shock was so sudden and astounding, and to this day I feel its effects physically, while mentally it could not fail to change my outlook upon life and henceforth I reckon the boasted English liberty and justice at its real value. From the first I realized the full import of the incident as one of public concern, and saw that every word and act of mine must be careful and justifiable, for a principle was at stake which had wide application. Without adviser and having no precedent, guide I had none but my common sense. Others with greater experience might have acted better. I knew only one way, viz. passive resistance to acquiescence in an injustice. Had a charge been made against me so that I could have defended myself it would have been easier. [. . .]

In 1901 the Civil Courts were sitting in Cape Town, but in vain I begged to be tried by them.

42. TO THE COMMITTEE OF THE DISTRESS FUND[1]

[. . .]

I wrote as follows to Colonel Cooper:

To the Commandant, Cape Town

Dear Sir,

Lieutenant Lingham kindly undertakes to be the bearer of this note.

It was a matter of immense surprise to me when that officer brought me your message forbidding me to land or hold communication with friends ashore, and stating that I was to be made a prisoner on board the ship. He had no reason to offer me for this communication, and be did not even wish to hear what my reasons were for visiting South Africa.

I therefore deem it wisest and due to myself to approach you direct in order to gain some information concerning the matter.

I could understand the rigour of martial law being applied to me if I had in the past taken or even now intended to take political part of any kind. But this I have never done. Both in South Africa and in England my words and work have been purely and consistently philanthropic in character. I have left politics severely alone.

My intentions in revisiting South Africa were simply to carry on this philanthropic work amongst all classes of sufferers of all nationalities in the various coast towns where, when I left England, no martial law existed. I have been urged from end to end of England to ascertain the exact needs of the British refugees of whom so much has been heard, and I have come here simply for that purpose, being in a position to obtain considerable sums for them in England when I have been able to satisfy myself of the extent and nature of their needs.

If we are to believe the outcries of the papers, much needs doing in that direction. Still, if for any reason the Government objects to such useful and necessary work I am of course willing to forego it; but what objection can be offered to my living quietly in Cape Town for a while where I have many old friends?

I have been out of health, and, shrinking from the cold of an English winter, came to this warm climate. I do not feel equal to the strain of an immediate return voyage which you offer me, nor the alternative of remaining a prisoner on board the *Avondale Castle*.

I am enclosing a letter which I earnestly ask you to convey to the Governor, also one to Lord Milner and one to Lord Kitchener.

I must further appeal to you on behalf of my nurse, a young woman who came as my attendant and masseuse. She intended living with me while nursing the needy sick under direction, and hoped eventually to settle in the country. Will you allow her to land, and be the bearer for me of a letter from Lady Ripon to Lady Hely-Hutchinson, also one from myself to that lady?

In any case, I trust you will in the just exercise of your office give full attention to this letter. It cannot but seem to me that the summary arrest of an Englishwoman bound on works of charity, without warrant of any kind or stated offence, is a proceeding which requires explanation.

I am, Sir, yours faithfully,

E. Hobhouse

I wrote also to Lord Milner and Lord Kitchener in similar strain, intimating that I could not believe they were cognizant of my arrest. And I appealed to Sir Walter Hely-Hutchinson,[2] as England's representative in Cape Colony, to protect me. I asked Colonel Cooper also to read and forward a letter to a lady friend.

Next day the following reply was received from Colonel Cooper:

The Castle, Cape Town
28 October 1901

Madam,

I am in receipt of your letter of this date and regret it is not in my power to allow you to land in South Africa.

The letters you enclose will be forwarded as requested to the High Commissioner, the Commander-in-Chief, the Governor, and Mrs. Charles Murray.

There is no objection to your nurse landing.

I am, Madam, your obedient servant,

H. Cooper
Colonel Commandant.

The passengers for Cape Town all landed that day (Monday) and on the Captain returning from shore in the evening I discussed the situation with him. He informed me he had orders to take the ship into dock next morning, and we agreed that in that case difficulties would arise, and I ought to have in writing the regulations imposed on me. He also wished me to give him my word to adhere to them, and at first I was willing, but after reflection I refused, feeling it was not right he should be my goaler; the Authorities ought to provide a guard. I therefore wrote the following letter to Colonel Cooper:

Avondale Castle,
28 October 1901

To the Commandant, Cape Town

Sir,

I have to thank you for your kindness in giving prompt reply to my letter, and am obliged to you for forwarding my enclosures. My nurse, with your permission, will land to-morrow, and take the letters (Lady Ripon's and mine) to Lady Hely-Hutchinson.

I feel it my duty to ask you to let me have in writing exactly the regulations to

144

which you wish me to conform whilst a prisoner on this vessel. Word of mouth is vague at the best, and as we are moving into dock to-morrow, I can foresee many occasions may rise where it will be difficult to guide myself without written instructions. As we move early I should be obliged to receive these at once.

Moreover, I conceive that it would be wiser to appoint a regular guard to see that I do not pass the limits of these regulations. May I ask you to send one for that purpose? A guard will be not only a satisfaction to your mind but he will be a witness also to my adhesion to your regulations, until such time as you see fit to intern me in a land prison.

I am, Sir, yours faithfully.

E. Hobhouse

P.S. Do you allow me to communicate with a washerwoman, or is uncleanliness part of the régime to which I must submit?[3] A bath here is also impossible. [. . .]

Wednesday [30 October] we moved into dock and I was grateful to find that a few of my friends had bravely demanded permits to see me, and had succeeded. Evidently because the officials thought I should leave that evening by the *Carisbrooke Castle*. This, I felt and told them, was impossible.

A letter was brought me from the Governor:

Government House, Cape Town
28 October 1901

Dear Miss Hobhouse

Your letter of yesterday was delivered to me this afternoon. I presume that you have been detained on board the *Avondale Castle* under the powers conferred on the Military Authorities by martial law, and I will therefore lay your complaint before the General. In the meanwhile I may assure you that the care of the British refugees is in safe hands, and that you need have no anxiety on that account.

Yours faithfully,
Walter Hely-Hutchinson

At four o'clock Colonel Cooper asked to see me. The interview was short.

He said, "I am sorry, Miss Hobhouse, to make your acquaintance under these circumstances."

I said: "I am sorry, too."

There was silence awhile, then Colonel Cooper asked if I did not think it best to leave on the *Carisbrooke* that afternoon.

I replied as before that I felt unequal to it and needed rest; that no reason had been given me for my detention, and I knew of none which could warrant a proceeding so arbitrary on the part of the Authorities.

He inquired what then were my plans. I answered they had been to land and, after rest, do my work in the town, but now my plans appeared to be somewhat in his hands; that I should naturally prefer the alternative of remaining on the *Avondale*, where I knew the ship's crew, to being sent on board any other vessel in the Bay, until answers had come from Lords Milner and Kitchener, who I hoped were unaware of my arrest.

If it would enhance the honour or add to the safety of England that I should be imprisoned I was willing, but I begged it might be a land prison. Until justice could be obtained any cell and any fare would do on land.

Colonel Cooper remarked on the unpleasantness of a ship unloading in dock, noise, dirt, and smells prevailing. I assured him it was not my wish to remain in it, but, disagreeable as it was, anything was preferable to another immediate voyage.

I further said it was incredible to me that English officers or Englishmen could insist on imposing on me a long sea voyage immediately following on a previous long voyage. I had not felt well since leaving England, was overdone when I embarked, my arrest had been a great shock, and I shrank from further strain; I considered that both in reason and justice I was entitled to rest if not to freedom.

The same evening Lieutenant Lingham came, mainly in reply to my letter demanding a guard rather than the gaolership of the Captain. He seemed to have some objection to this, and wished me to give my parole that I would not escape. I said it appeared to me a disagreeable and unfair position for Captain Brown, who was my personal friend, and that I could not understand interfering with people's liberty, detaining them in prison, and yet not taking the trouble to guard them. Giving my parole not to escape was tantamount to keeping myself in prison, and why should I do that? I was detained at their wish, not at my own. He said parole was a usual thing, and I answered I believed that was so only in quite different cases, for I understood people were let out of prison on parole, not detained thereby. Further, he was asking for a thing which by their own actions the Authorities deemed worthless. I had told them repeatedly I had come on no political errand, that such work as I should do would be philantropic merely and open to supervision. If, therefore, they refused to believe me or trust my word on shore, how could they trust my word afloat, the value being the same on land or sea. Mr. Lingham appeared to have no answer to this argument, but pressed for parole, though sorry to trouble me.

I assured him I attached no blame to him, regarding him merely as mouthpiece of a tyranny and injustice higher than himself. I inquired what alternative he proposed failing my parole, but this he refused to reveal beforehand.

Dreading therefore being forcibly placed on a strange ship out at sea I resolved to compromise by agreeing to give my parole until I received answers from Lords Milner and Kitchener, and then I must reconsider my position. The interview was protracted, but Mr. Lingham expressed himself satisfied with this, and departed.

I do not wish to dwell on my personal discomfort or suffering, but it is perhaps necessary to state that the shock and strain of the past three days on the top of a trying voyage and previous hard work now naturally resulted in collapse. This amounted to loss of power, muscular and nervous, so that physical and mental exertion became impossible for a time. It is the way in which reaction after undue strain shows itself in me.

It would have been far easier, and in some respects pleasanter, for me to yield to their importunities, but I felt that a principle of public importance was at stake, and that I ought to suffer personal discomfort rather than acquiesce in its violation.[a]

In spite of my parole a detective was left, who watched me closely, so next day I asked for his withdrawal.

Thursday the 31st was spent in continual interviews with officials which would be tedious to relate in detail. As I had been unable to sleep or eat they were sufficiently harassing to me.

A young officer was sent with a paper stating that a berth had been assigned to me on the *Roslin Castle*, and it would be necessary to embark that day. I was too unwell to read the paper. Later Mr. Lingham arrived and said a great deal which I was too weak to follow, and he read aloud something, the contents of which I did not grasp, but which he explained to be a telegram from the Commander-in-Chief, who, in agreement with the High Commissioner, ordered my immediate deportation. The officer told me the meaning of it, and I said "I am not strong enough to entertain the idea." This he demanded in writing, and I roused myself to scrawl a pencil note to Colonel Cooper, saying I was sorry I could not face the proposed voyage.

I must have dozed a little when he left, for when I next opened my eyes a lady was beside me, who had kindly sought leave to see me again, on the ground of trying to arrange for a laundress. (I may add that this was never done, and the return voyage of twenty-four days was undergone without that necessity). Her presence was a comfort, though from physical weakness I could not talk to her.[b]

Later Mr. Lingham returned saying the orders must be carried out. My reply was necessarily the same, and that if left in peace to recover strength, I might be fit to take the mail the following week, if still compelled. He said he should then be obliged to use force. I answered, "I cannot help what you do; that is your affair; I can only judge what is right for myself to do. Why not take me on shore and hang me? Why torment me so?"

He pleaded his orders. I replied that I believe the whole British public would exonerate him if he refused to carry out such orders as forcing a sick, overwrought woman to take a long voyage without even a few days for rest.

A card was brought me with the name Lieutenant-Colonel Williamson, R.A.M.C., which I returned, saying I was too unwell to see a stranger. In a few minutes the owner thrust himself upon me, saying he was Medical Officer, and had orders to examine me.[4] In vain I refused examination by a stranger, saying I had asked to see my friend and medical man in Cape Town.[5] He would not go, and at length for very weariness I submitted to a superficial examination. He said I had not heart disease, which I knew before.

Under martial law the stewardesses were ordered to pack my clothes, and the Chief Officer was told to get my trunks from the hold. He rightly insisted on written orders before doing this.

Throughout I maintained the same attitude, that I did not feel able to go, that this made it more unjust I should go, but that I would do my best to be well enough for the mail should respite not come, and I would let Lord Kitchener know as soon as I felt fit. I said repeatedly I still had faith enough in English men and English officers to believe that they would not force a sick woman on a long journey against her will, and that I should retain that faith as long as possible.

Finally Dr. Williamson brought two Army nurses, Sisters MacKillan and Nicholson, to take me by force.

The Chief Officer of the ship was present at my request, besides the military men, and I spoke quietly to the women asking them to lay no violent hands upon me. They answered they were under military orders, and this I said I understood, but I put before them that the laws of humanity and nature are, or should be, higher than military laws, and appealed to them not to mar their sacred office as nurses by molesting a sick woman. I had appealed in vain to the men, but hoped I should not appeal in vain to my own sex.

Both Sisters turned, and silently left the room, and I thanked them as they went. They behaved like true Englishwomen. I was left alone.

It must have been an hour later, about 7 p.m., when Dr. Williamson returned, followed by two soldiers. He approached, and, touching me on the shoulder, said: "Will you yield to technico?" I said: "I don't know what you mean." He explained: "Will you yield of your own free will, otherwise there are the soldiers." I could only say, "Sir, I cannot and will not give other reply than what I have said from the beginning. My refusal was based on principle, and principles do not alter in a day; nor can they be frightened out of me by force. I am weak and ill, unfit to take this voyage. It is not a right thing in any case, and especially unreasonable to ask it without giving me previous rest. I will not go one step voluntarily towards the *Roslin Castle*. I beg you to leave me."

"Madam," he said, "do you wish to be taken like a lunatic?"

"Sir," I replied, "the lunacy is on your side and with those whose commands you obey. If you have any manhood in you, you will go and leave me alone."

He signed to the soldiers to come forward. They looked at me and hesitated a moment, and I took the opportunity of appealing to them to afford me the same respect as they would like shown to their own wives and mothers in similar condition. One man turned and was making for the door when Dr. Williamson, fearful of losing his last chance, urged the other forward, and reluctantly they did their work.

My shawl was wound round me, confining my arms, and I was forced on to the deck where several soldiers were waiting. They carried me away through the ship and on the dock where a carriage was in readiness.

I spoke a few words to the men who bore me, otherwise there was silence. The stars were brilliant, and the fresh night air revived me a little.

At the dock where the *Roslin* lay I was asked to board her voluntarily, but I refused as a matter of principle. Even had I possessed the strength to do so I would not move one step towards the vessel. My whole strength was centred in the resolution to refuse acquiescence in the injustice of the order, and for the time it deprived me of power in other ways.

Orderlies were summoned who carried me, as before, to a cabin, where I lay till placed under charge of Colonel Clowes, officer in command of the transport, whom I begged to release me or appeal to Colonel Cooper to do so. He spoke kindly, and said he would see Colonel Cooper in the morning.

Next morning the medical man I had wished to see succeeded with difficulty in getting a permit, not, however, until too late; when he arrived the vessel was gliding from the quay.[6]

The voyage took twenty-four days, and my weak condition at starting made it one of great suffering for me, lightened only by the devotion of my nurse; there was no stewardess on board.

My nurse, Miss Phillips, altered her plans and most unselfishly refused to leave me, judging me unfit to be left to strangers.[c]

From the memoir

a) Ill as I was – prostrate from shock – every power of mind and body was concentrated on the effort to stand firm in the non-acquiescence which I believed my duty, and for the sake of the sufferers whose champion I had become. My prostration indeed made it easier to refuse an immediate return journey for which I knew myself totally unfit. My great comfort in that unequal contest – which could only end in the momentary triumph of Injustice and Force – was the exquisite sympathy and affection poured out to me by my group of Cape Town friends, some of whom succeeded in overcoming official prohibition and in coming to visit me, bearing fruit and flowers. Without their sustaining help I think I should never have got through. Another source of help was the beauty of the Bay and the majesty of Table Mountain which provided a feeling of strength and security in this uncertainty of things, both physical and moral, while the ship rocked in the south-easterly gale and the principles in which one had been nourished tottered to their fall.

b) Miss Molteno sat in silence near me the whole day, her mere presence the greatest solace.

149

c) The South African Press had (under censorship) given almost no news of my arrest, and I had been forbidden to communicate with the shore. Hence it was at first quite impossible for me to send word to England. But on the third day, when the ship came into dock and one or two of my friends had courageously secured permission to see me, Alice Greene most kindly promised to try and send a cable in cypher, and this she did with the one word "Deported". My friends could not understand why I myself was silent. They had never lived under martial law. Miss Greene dared not risk more than one word, lest the cable should not get through. Further, I wrote to Lord Hobhouse and Lord Ripon, trusting that, as peers, their letters would not be interefered with, and these I managed to get posted by the kindness of a ship's officer to catch the outgoing mail. I had not been prohibited from communicating with England, but the cencorship was so strict that I dared not write plainly, only allusively; consequently these letters, which reached England on 18 November, were perhaps more puzzling than enlightening.

"It is a relief", wrote Lord Ripon on 5 November, "to find that it is deportation, not imprisonment. The deportation will not hurt Miss Hobhouse and may do the cause good."

And on the 7th:

> "I cannot help being anxious to know whether you have any further information about Miss Hobhouse. If she had been actually deported from Cape Town I should have thought that even in South Africa the newspaper correspondents would have got hold of the fact and found some means of transmitting it to their journals in this country. I am therefore puzzled to know what to think. Do, please, let me know if you receive any further information."

43. TO SIR WALTER HELY-HUTCHINSON[1]

Table Bay
1 November 1901

I am obliged to you for your note, and am sorry that you could lift no finger to help an Englishwoman brutally treated.

I shall make the whole affair very widely known in England that people may realize the sort of thing being done in their name.

One blushes for the name and honour of England.

I am glad to have in writing from you a statement so authoritative as to the welfare of British refugees. It seems a pity, if what you say is true, that some official statement of the kind has not all these past months been made in *The Times* to allay the anxieties in the public mind. I will gladly quote you.

Excuse a pencil scrawl but I am weak and exhausted.

It seems to me if I were a governor without power enough to protect one sick

Englishwoman from torment and brutality I would resign from a post so useless.

I have the honour to be,

Yours in bitter shame for England.

E. Hobhouse

44. TO LORD KITCHENER

Roslin Castle

1 November 1901

Your brutality has triumphed over my weakness and sickness.

You have forgotten so to be a patriot as not to forget that you are a gentleman.

I hope that in future you will exercise greater width of judgement in the exercise of your high office. To carry out orders such as these is a degradation both to the office and the manhood of your soldiers. I feel ashamed to own you as a fellow-countryman.

Emily Hobhouse

45. TO SIR ALFRED MILNER[a][1]

Roslin Castle

1 November 1901

Your brutal orders have been carried out and thus I hope you will be satisfied.

Your narrow incompetency to see the real issues of this great struggle is leading you to such acts as this and many others, staining your own name and the reputation of England.

I liked you first and would have helped you. But now I see you more clearly as you really are and can believe it is true what a man once said to me: that you have "the soul of a spy". Perhaps that is necessary in a despot. At least you should try, in the words of Burke, so to be a patriot that you do not forget you are, or ought to be, a gentleman.

You have lost us the heart of a fine people; beware lest that is but the prelude to the loss of their country also.

Emily Hobhouse

From the memoir

a) Through those trying days I had kept calm and patient and had addressed carefully drawn-up letters to all the Authorities I had to deal with, but when it was all over and my final urgent request (at least not to be sent back till I had had a week's rest on shore) refused, my anger blazed out and I wrote just as I felt to the two men who alone were responsible in South Africa, Lords Kitchener and Milner. Perhaps I was wrong to have done so because no good could have come from it at

151

that eleventh hour, but my feminine desire to speak my mind was strong. So, moved by force to the *Roslin Castle*, my first act was to write to Lord Kitchener [. . .] To Lord Milner I wrote in similar strain but perhaps sharper. For though from Kitchener little sense of freedom was to be expected, yet from Milner one had hoped for more. And I had liked him, had been loyal to him, and, feeling the good qualities he possessed, was in greater measure disappointed. And all that people were wont to say of him in that bitter time rushed back on me. Yet now long after one doubts if the unconstitutional act was really under his control; with martial law reigning Kitchener must have been paramount. And during recent years Milner has done good work and retrieved his name; and so in his case I feel rather sorry that in my helpless anger I wrote so sharply.[2] The other letter I do not regret.

46. TO MRS. CHARLES MURRAY

Roslin Castle

4 November – 7 November 1901

10–14 November

Today for the first time I feel able to take a pencil in hand and try to call my scattered thoughts together. My body has been so absurdly powerless. It seemed to have stopped working, like an unwound watch. My pulse is very low and weak and my temperature still below normal. I suppose it was all brought on by the shock to my nervous system and a week or so in prison on land or stationary in dock would have given me space to pull myself together and prepare to return alone in a proper boat. As it is, I could not have done without Nurse. I was quite helpless, but it is hard on her to have taken her back all this long way and will cost me a good sum to send her out again which of course I was bound to promise. She has been very loyal.

It is a hideously uncomfortable ship.[a] We are aft, just over the throbbing propeller, moreover the rolling is abnormal. They call her the "Rolling Castle", a very suitable name. There are no stewardesses and the bedroom steward is also deck and dining-room steward rolled into one. You can therefore imagine the service. After the *Avondale* the food is horrible and for days I could not touch it. We were both made sick by a horrible smell which we have now found out to be rotting onions. Worst of all, the ship is all under the Military, so the Captain and officers are not in evidence as in ordinary vessels and there is no one to speak to.

The Colonel commanding the vessel means to be very kind and enquires for me daily, but naturally I feel no relish for British officers now and shrink from their approach. Nurse and I feel as if we dare not face the long three weeks before us – we are to touch at St. Vincent, which makes it longer than need be.

It was so splendid of Dr. Murray to have procured the permit and found his way down to the ship, and it was hard that he was too late. He would have got me off I know and have made them give me leave to rest and get well and return by the next mail. It is horrible being a prisoner all the way home! [. . .]

For clothes we don't know what to do. Nurse is trying to make herself some today. She has been wonderfully brave and good and so loyal to me. And so patient, for they lost her big trunk for her. She looks forward to rejoining her bicycle some day and will repay you what it may have cost to pass through Customs and take to Kenilworth.

I am writing to the Standard to tell them to place £355 to your credit; the odd five pound is to pay you for all I owe in various ways – cables, doctor and a week's compensation for rooms. If I have sent too little, please let me know. The other £50 I will send straight to Miss Steedman who will deliver it as I appoint. Will you, please, when received send a receipt for the £350 that I may hand over to the donor, and some day a rough sketch of how it is disbursed? And will you tell Mrs. M. that you have it all right?

I have not been able to sleep much since coming to this ship, and all the events of those weary days would go round and round in my head. But I do not think if I had it to go through again that I should act differently. It seemed to me then, and does still, a matter of principle to withstand such tyranny and injustice and the degradation of martial law to a mere instrument of that tyranny, injustice and torture. I would have gone, quietly enough, to any prison on land or sea and put up with any amount of supervision or have quietly gone to be hanged, but so insensate an order as the one carried out by brute force against a sick woman, who was willing to prepare for the journey in a few days – it seemed to me a first duty to withstand, in justice to myself, to Nurse, and to all concerned, the honour of England included! The men hurt me a good deal, their hands are so rough and strong, and I am much bruised. Moreover I strained my side on the *Avondale* in a storm and the rolling of this vessel brought the pain on again. So far I have not felt equal to going to the saloon.

I have just a few shillings left with which to cable to my Uncle from St. Vincent and ask them to meet me with money and help. For I suppose even *this* voyage of 22 days *must* end some time, though at present it seems interminable. I shan't feel well till I am on land again, so there is nothing for it but patience.

I had looked forward so much to a quiet, warm, restful month at Cape Town and then going on to Port Elizabeth and East London and Durban, to find out and relieve the distressed. I know the names of several in those towns on the verge of starvation, and I had been specially written to from East London to come and help the British refugees there and had replied, promising to do so. Well, as you truly say, I have done all I can do and must rest on that; and you must all be certain that I will still do what is possible in England to help the distressed.

Please tell Miss Stegmann and Mrs. Philip Botha that their fruit and bottled peaches have been my *only* diet all these seven days and are only just finished. I could not eat anything else. The flowers, too, keep fresh and are our only solace in a

153

weary voyage. How good you all were to me! I shall never forget it; and the thought makes me glad I came in spite of all. Shall we ever meet again? I doubt it now.

P.S. My love and gratitude to your kind sister for her unfailing patience and sympathy that trying day.

Spend some of the money upon putting Mrs. Botha's little boy and perhaps Mrs. V.'s to learn something if you can. It would be a solid piece of good.

The smells are horrible. Fancy 7 000 men always smoking. I can get no square inch safe from tobacco anywhere and it makes me sick, this coarse tobacco.

10 November. It may be we shall be unable to post this at St. Vincent,[b)] and then it will be long before you receive it.

14 November. The trials of this voyage grow worse. The vibration of a propeller always out of water is on my nerves and I have to strive against constant hysteria. I cannot write much, so will you let all my kind friends know how we fared and how much I thank them all and I would write to all in due time but think it might be wiser not to do so till the world comes to its senses.

From the memoir

a) It was a truly horrible return voyage. To begin with it was a troop-ship and 8 100 men were on board. The dirt and disorder were indescribable, and the *smell* sickening. It overpowered me to faintness when I was carried in and laid on my bunk. We heard later that it had carried a cargo of rotten onions. The Captain was not master, he told me, in his own ship. Military rule was there too, and of a kind that did not know the importance of cleanliness on a vessel. There were only two women on board – officers' wives – and they never spoke to me. Never did a ship roll so terribly. Recovery seemed impossible and the only respite the few hours' rest at St. Vincent. Nurse Phillips was my only comfort.

The cold was dreadful as we came north, for we had no winter clothes with us. We had gone to pass a summer at the Cape and were now plunged unexpectedly into winter. This was a slight realization in my own person of what tens of thousands of your countrywomen endured and still were enduring, torn by military force from home, belongings and comforts to meet exposure unprepared.

b) A cable awaited me at St. Vincent, perhaps the sweetest I ever received. For the value of a message is relative to the condition of the recipient. It was just one word from my Aunt of welcome to her home, but it was the first sign from England that the news of this military tyranny was known. My Cape Town friends had tried to cable, but we had no certainty that the Censors had let it through.

154

You can imagine too how grateful I was when at last we reached Southampton to find those kindest friends, the Courtneys and Miss Bradby. They had come down from London to meet me. It was a wonderful act of kindness on the part of an old man like Mr. Courtney. But indeed all my friends had been full of kindness, and most tenderly apprehensive for my welfare. They had been waiting three weeks in anxiety and suspense getting no news of what was happening. Not knowing therefore in what condition I might be, or if even free to land in the ordinary way, they had consulted as to whether a solicitor should meet me, or, as the Courtneys urged, some well-known man like himself – and he offered to go. In the end it was so decided, and thankful indeed I was to see him come on board. Besides the obvious advantage, it was a protection from the crowd of pressmen and would-be interviewers, and the three made an escort for me and Nurse, taking us through the crowd to a quiet hotel room where we could rest and talk till the train started. I was so weak – 48 days on board ship – worn out, nerve-racked, still prostrate from the shock, exhausted too from inability to eat the bad ship food in that condition, I could not give them a very lucid account. Few understood how greatly my health had suffered from a shock of which to this day I feel the effects.

Perhaps only now, as I read over their old letters, do I fully realize the anxiety felt in England on my account, not only – as would be natural – by my Brother and Uncle, but by others with whom I had worked or who had known me. And their perturbation was – as I wished it to be – as much a matter of anxiety for the public honour (right) as for my welfare, which was indeed quite a secondary interest.

47. TO MRS. CHARLES MURRAY

15 Bruton Street

4 December 1901

I suppose this is the Christmas mail and must take my warmest love to all my Cape Town friends. I wish I could get out and buy presents for you all, but I am too weak still to do anything but the actually necessary. So my love and best wishes for a free and *un*-imprisoned, if not a peaceful and happy, Christmas must find its way to you all alone.

It is noon but almost midnight and I am writing by the light of a dim lamp and thinking of what I have lost this month in your bright sun, clear air and lovely scenes. I had laid such plans for solitary days – with my paint-box on the slopes of Table Mountain – and had further determined on a collection of wild flowers ... This recent proclamation will, however, keep out many persons undesirable like myself, but it will, I fear, preclude Nurse's return till the war is over, and when will that be? She is taking a maternity course at the New Hospital before her return and is much obliged to you for befriending her bicycle. Her trunk has not turned up yet. I half hope the *Avondale* may have found it and bring it back this week.

I have received your long letter of detailed evidence which may be of great use. Your sister's has not yet appeared, but I hope it will or at all events she has kept a copy.[1] I am very anxious to see her account. My own statement has been published this morning and I will try to send you some of the pamphlets.[a] A more detailed statement is in the lawyer's hand. We (that is my Uncle, Lord Hobhouse) have put the case in Sir George Lewis's[2] hands, and he is desirous of my bringing an action against Kitchener, Milner, Cooper and Lingham "for having imprisoned and assaulted her under the circumstances before stated, and we have therefore to enquire whether you will give instructions to the Solicitor to the War Office to appear on behalf of these three officers and Lord Milner in the action which Miss Hobhouse proposes to bring".

This he has sent to Brodrick and of course *he* will do nothing,[3] but it will clear the ground for further action.

People are much excited about it but for myself I am still suffering so much from the shock that I feel callous – only dimly conscious that my carcass is thrown into the public arena and all legal and political carrion crows will tear and rend and devour me.

They say anyhow that if I lose my case it will necessitate the redefinition of English law, and that is necessary and useful.

I, being only a female, and not deeply interested in an abstruse legal point, feel *much* more strongly the personal-outrage side of the question – first, having a strange doctor forced upon me; second, not being allowed a week's rest *if even in prison* before being forced on a voyage for which I was unfit. That appeals most strongly to me and would, I think, to the mass of unlearned folk. Our difficulty is to find a defendant as they are all in South Africa, except Colonel Clowes, and he was only technically guilty as a gaoler of a prison to whom a prisoner is consigned.[4]

Did I tell you, there were only two ladies on board (besides Army nurses who were not ladies at all), and these two never uttered a syllable to me the whole 24 days.

The voyage was a nightmare and the whole of the events crowded into those five days in the Bay have gone and still go round and round in my brain in weary succession – the shock stamped itself so upon me.

I am beset with requests to speak at public meetings but cannot yet do so – perhaps after Christmas I may begin again.

I enjoyed a visit from Mrs. J. Molteno on Sunday; she looks much better.

Mr. Courtney dropped in yesterday. He too has wonderfully improved in health and has made two speeches this week. I heard the peroration at Oxford was unusually fine.

Yesterday I had tea at the Hammonds amidst their wedding-present-furnished flat and met the MacKails (who do the second-hand clothing for the Committee), the *Morning Leader* Editor, and others. They are all very sympathetic but all look at me rather as some strange animal who has been through an unusual experience, and for myself I must say I feel very much now as if I belonged to "No Man's Land". That feeling may wear off.

Tell Mrs. Philip Botha that I hear the money for the schooling of the girls has safely reached Bloemfontein, so that is arranged till March ends I suppose. By that time, where shall we be? . . .

From the memoir

a) On my return my Uncle advised me to see no one but quietly to write down the exact sequence of events while fresh in my mind. Being very prostrate I found this very hard. But I did it in the form of a letter to my Committee, and after submission to him and to Lord Ripon, Frederic Harrison and others, it was communicated to the entire Press with a covering letter written by my Uncle himself.

48. TO MRS. CHARLES MURRAY

15 Bruton Street

12 December 1901

What a good letter-writer you are. You make me ashamed of the horrid scraps I have written you hitherto, but ill-health has been greatly my reason, combined with the really crushing correspondence of London. Every hour fresh letters come pouring in.

We had a long Committee [meeting] today lasting two hours and were delighted at the return amongst us of Mrs. Bryce. She only landed last night after her trip to the West Indies and she is a host in herself. We are just publishing a financial statement for the subscribers.

I have just heard that the sum of money I told you was to be transferred to you, by a stupid mistake of the donor never left the Standard Bank of *London*, so now I have to give fresh directions about it and there may be some delay before you get it, perhaps a week after this letter arrives. I am so sorry . . . Turning to another subject, I have read carefully the letters you enclosed about our Delegate and her supplies and it has been put before the Work Committee who will write both to you and her on the subject. I feel very much for you about it, but can assure you we are just as much puzzled by the letters addressed straight to our Secretary. The other lady does not communicate with us officially but her letters to her mother are more intelligible. The Friends are exactly in the same position with regard to their helpers. We can but grope our way along in the dark, doing the best we can. And I feel sure *some* good will be done though not all we could and should do if less hampered.

For my own self I can assure you that I am mending slowly. It was almost as if I had been knocked into the grave and am only coming back to life slowly and painfully – my full nerve-life of consciousness and powers, I mean. Aunt Mary provides beef-tea in the morning and hot milk at night and her own doctor is giving me a very strong tonic, also a sedative to get my sleep back again. So my hollows are filling up and there is already much more of me than when I landed. Just yet he won't let me do any public speaking though requests pour in. He says it will take time to pull round, in fact he rather implies that I am not so young as I was – a fact most strikingly apparent to all! However, if I live at all, I mean to be young for some time longer yet, and so I refuse to be put on the shelf!

I shall probably go up to my Brother for Christmas and then pay a few visits to our friends the Joshua Rowntrees and others. Fancy, just a year ago I was arriving (at the Cape) for the first time and received that warm welcome from you, and fell in love with your lovely scenery. I cannot believe it is barely a year; it seems more like ten for all I have seen and done and all the varied experiences I have passed through – all I have lost and all I have found in that period.

I have been very deeply touched by a poem which has appeared this week in the *New Age*, which has entered so much and so truly into my feelings and aims on those sad days. It is dated "Cape Town, November 6", and much I wonder who is the writer.[1] If you know, tell him or her how grateful I am for the appreciation shewn in it, though expressed in language more flattering than I deserve. Various English minor poets have addressed me, but not one who understood as this Afrikander does. But how can the people here understand? They do not *know*, even the most sympathetic.

Give my love to your sister and say how much I want to thank her properly, and that I hope she kept a copy of her statement of that day's story, for the one sent never reached me . . .

Miss Hobhouse
Arrested and deported under martial law, November 1901

The Terror reigns! Our lips are dumb:
   The Terror reigns! Our hands are tied:
Yet hither did a woman come
   Across two oceans wide.

She came to pierce the mist and gloom
   That hang above this fated land,
To face the Terror, fight the Doom,
   Or meet it hand in hand.

She could not rest. Those "faded flowers"[2]
   Moaned ever, "Wherefore didst thou stay?"
Those Camps of death where Horror lowers,
   All summoned her away.

O Englishwoman, tall and fair,
  O Englishwoman, calm and brave,
Within the breach thou standest there
  Those innocents to save!

Thou standest there with outstretched arms,
  Like some Madonna, strong to bless,
To soothe their childish wild alarms,
  And comfort their distress.

Thou seem'st to say, in accents low,
  "If on these babes ye mean to tread,
"Then ye must o'er *my* body go,
  "And trample on *my* head.

"I stand here for old England's Right:
  "I stand here for old England's Fame,
"For what to me is England's Might
  "Without her old good name?

"If at these babes ye dare to strike,
  "Ye strike at England's heart as well;
"Then hang and starve us all alike,
  "Complete your deeds of Hell!

"A thousand times I'd give my blood,
  "Pouring it out in glad free tide,
"If we might stand where once we stood,
  "and face the world with pride.

"Alas! Alas! the wish is vain.
  "A thousand thousand lives in one
"Could ne'er buy back our peace again,
  "Nor undo what we've done.

"We stand condemned. The load of debt
  "We've piled so high before the Throne
"By blood alone can now be met –
  "Shall I not give my own?"

She came. She stood in fiery scorn,
  She faced the Terror, fair and free.

159

"Thou evil thing, of meanness born,
  Wilt take these babes from me?"

She faced the Terror free and fair –
  Our Englishwoman, strong and brave . . .
It leapt upon her from its lair,
  When there was none to save.

And there she fought it, hour by hour,
  Standing within the breach alone:
Fought it with all her woman's power,
  Till the long day was done.

Now o'er her body they have passed,
  And trampled on her heart as well.
The fort she held they've won at last,
  And garrisoned for Hell!

She brought us hope, she brought us light,
  She brought us help in either hand.
She's gone, and Darkness, black as night,
  Now settles on the land.

Yet on that sea which darkly rolls,
  And parts for ever shore from shore,
She, star-like, shines, and in our souls
  She lives for evermore.

Visit to the
ruined districts
1903

___

Introduction

It had been arranged for me to go abroad, my health having never recovered itself, and I was in need of sun and silence. But not idleness. I took all my papers with me and started off alone to a very perfect and quite solitary spot on Lake Annecy.[1]

Twenty years has robbed many a place of its charm; bungalows, villas, rows of lodging houses, charabancs and motor cars have brought endless trippers and vulgarized lovely scenery in the most "civilised countries", so I should fear to visit Tallories again, wishing rather to keep the memory of what was than be distressed by the change these rushing years may have wrought even in that secluded spot.

In April 1902 I was the only "tripper" there, and during my stay in the old Convent Inn[2] I spoke to no one during the eight weeks of my visit except the French peasants busied in their work. So restful it was. The beauty and peace of the place was indescribable . . . – "there is no sound but the echo of my own footsteps and the lapping of the lake against the garden wall . . . I have everything lovely outside from snow-capped mountains to flower carpets and walks innumerable", I wrote to my Brother.

I had crossed to Antwerp and stayed in Brussels *en route*. There I saw Mrs. Louis Botha and had a long talk with her.[3] I found her much refreshed and rejuvenated by her long stay and looking very pretty. So different from the harassed war look she had worn when passing through London. She was, however, in great grief over the last news from her country. This was of an attack by Kaffirs on a small group of Boers and the murder of many. Her distress was very great. Later she wrote that 56 men had been killed, that 3 000 Kaffirs had encompassed the little band and not one escaped. Before the war the Vryheid Kaffirs one and all hadn't a gun to shew between them.[4] Who armed them?

Your old friend of Bloemfontein, Abraham Fischer, the delegate, came to call on me and talked long. He had not much hope of peace about which negotiations were then going on. [. . .]

13 May 1925: Today as I dwell in thought on those past years and turn over the documents and letters which tell the tale again, today comes in tidings of Lord Milner's death.[5] It was told me through the wireless set in this quiet room, told as things are told by broadcasters in what often seems a curiously intimate way, as if

163

told for your ear alone. I felt as if I wanted to say back that I was sorry, very sorry. For as a man it was impossible to help liking Milner; his charm was irresistible and I had liked him very much. Twenty-five years soften all dislikes, especially those of only a public nature, and though my arrest and deportation *must* never be forgiven because it was an offence against English rights and freedom, yet I myself had sought him out and met him during the Great War in 1917 as one of the few of our statesmen who then took the wiser view. We met then in the friendly spirit of those with the same object at heart.

One after another they pass, all the actors on your South African scene, and you and I, dear Friend, will soon quit the stage. Chamberlain, Kitchener, General Buller, Judge Mackarness and many others mentioned in my story. On your side the loss of your own great comes first by De la Rey's tragic death, followed by Botha, De Wet, Beyers and Abraham Fischer, and at the Cape Lord De Villiers, Olive Schreiner and her brothers, Charles Molteno and Mr. Merriman's devoted wife. And now Milner, who seemed so much the centre of it all, has made his final exit.

I shall now go over what I have written and be able perhaps to write more openly of his words and deeds.

This at least I have always believed, that however terrible may have been the acts resulting from the policy he had agreed to adopt and felt bound to pursue, as a *man* he was not callous, as some thought, but he suffered. I saw that.

A great help to me, while I was at Talloires, was the Geneva lady, Madame Degli Asinelli, who, though I had at that time never met her, most kindly offered to copy letters, etc., do secretarial work generally.[6] This was the lady who in 1905–1906 gave such devoted assistance to the industries. She met me in Geneva and we spent a few hours together.

I was working quietly at Talloires when the news came that the negotiations Mr. Fischer had not thought likely to succeed had indeed brought peace at Vereeniging.

I was sitting beside the lake that lovely June morning when I opened my papers 23 years ago, just such a day of beauty as this first of June on which I am now writing. Till that moment which brought the news of its end, I had hardly realized the strain which the war had been. The sudden release from that tension seemed too much and I remember how I sat there by the waterside and cried my heart out. It's the blessing of being a woman that one can cry. It's the best relief nature has to give and relieves in joy as much as in sorrow. This peace news was mingled. On our side there was all joy – just that it was over, and not another life need be sacrificed – but I could not forget how bitterly the brave women in the camps would feel its terms and the crushing of hopes that had borne them up through loss and pain. For them it contained sorrow . . .

164

When, shortly after, my rest at Talloires was ended, I returned via Holland and put up at The Hague for a few days. While there, the Prime Minister, Dr. Kuyper, called upon me, and I was later entertained by his daughters. Dr. Kuyper told me full details of his efforts on behalf of peace. I have no authority to speak of these in detail, but he had worked assiduously by the help of a mutual friend, through Lord Lansdowne, and though twice all had dropped and seemed hopeless, yet the final terms agreed upon were practically the same as those which he had been forwarding. Dr. Kuyper appeared to have no doubt that his efforts had been largely instrumental in bringing peace. Mr. Kestell's vivid account of the negotiations in his book seems to prove the truth of this view.[7]

I hurried home to meet many whom I wanted to see from the Cape. As I need not remind you, amongst those that summer were you yourself with the prostrate President, and you will remember how he was trans-shipped at Southampton into the Dutch boat which Mr. Kröller[8] so kindly sent over for the purpose . . . and thus by his forethought President Steyn was saved the physical and mental strain which landing in England must have entailed.

My impulse had been to run down to Southampton and meet you. No other woman in England knew you and I felt sure you would feel very strange and lonely and in need of a woman's help. So I arranged to go, but was prevented by hearing that Mr. Fischer, who had come over to London, had expressly stated that your wish was to be *quite* private and see no one. It was distressing afterwards to hear that you had looked forward to seeing me and were greatly disappointed. So you passed on with your invalid to the Continent and began that long nursing which repaid you so richly by many years of his companionship.

I had certainly *not* expected to see the President, knowing his serious condition, and was much touched when three weeks later Mr. Fischer wrote me from his bedside at Villa Nuova, Scheveningen:

"Even the best of patients sometimes disobey doctor's orders, and on one of the few occasions when President Steyn has done so – by speaking when he has been ordered to keep absolutely quiet – he wished me to remember to tell you, when we met, how deeply grateful he felt to you for what you had done for our suffering women and children. 'Tell her Afrikanders can never repay her but they will never forget her.' He would have said more but I stopped him."

A few weeks later the three Generals arrived – Botha, De Wet and De la Rey. A friend of mine, Miss Molteno, happened to be arriving by the same ship, and in company with her sister Mrs. Murray – already in London – I went to Southampton to meet her.

The vessel was expected early, so we went the afternoon before and were kindly allowed to sleep on one of the Union Castle ships lying in the docks. We were

165

naturally very anxious to see the famous Generals too, as indeed were more important people, for we heard that Mr. Chamberlain, Lord Roberts and Lord Kitchener were in a vessel which lay alongside in the dock, partly, no doubt, to see the trio and partly for the naval review.

I wrote to my Aunt:

"We, Mrs. Murray and I, went out in the Company's tug to meet the *Saxon*; it was a lovely sight as the great vessel slowly emerged from the silvery morning haze and towered above us in our little tug. I was thus the first English person to welcome them to English soil as they stood at the top of the gangway with their staff to receive us, while hundreds of Khakies, who crowded the ship, looked on. They are a striking trio. Each is so different from the other. Botha is a kingly person with very courtly manners and commanding air; De la Rey a patriarch, very gentle and quiet; De Wet is impressive. His face is enigmatical but stamped with the responsibility and the sorrow of the war . . . I felt they were not merely great soldiers but great men. They are very simple and direct, and their dignity astonished and to some extent rebuked. To me they were perfectly sweet.

"They gave 'Joe' a five minutes' visit on his ship and annoyed him by resolutely refusing to attend the review, and then came back and we all went up to town together in a saloon carriage. I sat between Botha and De Wet with De la Rey opposite, and there were Mrs. De la Rey and the chaplain and staff; and Miss Molteno, Mrs. Murray and myself were the only people with them.

"It is very different meeting these men to meeting the womenfolk. These make you understand the ruin of their land and people and what it means to the *men* of the country to have seen the women so treated. The women themselves would turn off their troubles with an 'I don't care' or an occasional joke; not so the men. It has created in them a feeling stronger than any I was ever brought in contact with. I had a long talk with them again on Sunday when they came back from their visit to the King."

To my Brother I wrote:

"Their line of work is not yet decided; it depends largely on the outcome of their interview with 'Joe'. But of one thing I am sure: they will maintain a very dignified attitude and do the work they decided upon in a thorough but very sober way. Fêting, starring, etc. are far from their thoughts. You cannot make people understand too clearly that they are here as a *solemn duty*, in the interests of their broken and ruined people, and the fair and just carrying out of the peace terms. The state of their country and their women is ever present to them . . . Not all the women put together have made me

166

realize what the farm-burning, etc. was to them, as these three men have made me feel it. Their indignation is very strong.

"Their surrender, it appears, unnecessary from a military point of view, was a fine act of self-sacrifice to save the lives and honour of their women. They are not conquered and they shew it. Colonel Kekewich said: 'They are not a conquered people; it would have taken another two years to conquer them.' They told me Milner turned white as a sheet when they handed to him the manifesto which embodied their reasons for accepting the terms offered, and he read what those reasons were (printed in full in *Through Shot and Flame* by J. D. Kestell).

"They, the Generals, seem *wholly* ignorant of English politics and affairs. Mr. Courtney seems a shadow to them and they vaguely class together Mr. Morley and Mr. Stead! . . . They ought, I think, to talk their English programme over with someone not in official political life who knows all the ropes, or is it best for them to take their own simple direct way of going to work oblivious of English parties and complexities?

"On board De Wet wrote ten hours a day at his war history.[9] His face is an enigma."

Few in England realized the compelling object of the Generals' hurried voyage to Europe. Ten thousand persons were destitute and needed instant relief, besides the widows and orphans who would shortly issue from the camps, and the sick and wounded. This mission was entrusted to them at Vereeniging, and, as you will recollect, is plainly stated in the farewell message to their people printed at Cape Town the day before they sailed.

Arrived in England they lost no time in setting to work. They first sought an interview with Mr. Joseph Chamberlain wishing to find out what further relief could be obtained from the Government. From all accounts the interview was not a very pleasant one. Anyhow, after pressing their point, Mr. Chamberlain replied: "We had better not enter into discussion in detail upon points of that kind," and after some remarks upon British generosity he concluded: "We have done all that we can afford to do, and I think that it would be undesirable that the Generals should press us any further in the matter either now or in writing."

Taking this as final the Generals had no resource but to issue their Appeal to the civilized world. It ran:

"We were deputed by our representatives to proceed to England in order, in the first place, to make an appeal to our new Government to alleviate the awful distress which exists, etc. . . . As we have not, up to the present, succeeded in inducing the British Government to grant further assistance to our people . . . no other course is open to us but to apply to the peoples of Europe and America, etc., etc. In this great distress we turn to the world, . . ."

167

The Generals made the tactical mistake of going to the Continent and issuing this appeal from Holland, a mistake which alienated much sympathy as England was very sore with Continental criticism at that time. It was natural enough that the Generals should be quite unaware of this, but Mr. Chamberlain's letter to General Botha shortly after shewed that he took exception to their appeal, and he nullified its effect by adding:

> "On the general question of your Appeal . . . I desire to say that the Colonial Government is making itself *entirely responsible* for the maintenance of all destitute orphans, etc., etc. . . . and suitable provision is also being made for widows."

To this General Botha could but recall what passed at their interview on 5 September. He replied:

> "Had we at that time received the assurance that the Government would undertake full responsibility for the maintenance of widows, orphans and destitute our Appeal would never have been issued in its present form."

As reported in *The Times* Mr. Chamberlain repeated his promise of responsibility in the House of Commons, and Botha at once wrote to express his gratification. He added: "Meanwhile the needs of the sufferers are pressing."

Ah! dear Mrs. Steyn, those paper promises, how easy they are to make, how often disappointing in the result. I felt little confidence myself, and when I come to tell you of what I found in 1903 you will see that my doubts were justified.

The instinct of the Generals was right: they knew that at all costs they must try to re-instate the ruined white population, at best a long and slow labour, and that it must be done before heart and hope were lost. The fact that there was a great delay and that it was never properly done has been one of the main contributary causes to your vastly increased problem of "poor whites". The destitute crowded into the towns forming slum quarters foreign to your country.

Shortly after their arrival I invited each of the Generals to supper at my flat. One after another they came on three separate evenings. I felt very uncertain of my powers of entertaining them with my small knowledge of Afrikaans. And I felt sure they would want to smoke and (odd as it may seem now), I felt very helpless to supply that need. Finally I asked a man friend to buy me three large fat cigars, which he did, but to my surprise (and joy) each of the three refused to smoke Perhaps I offered the wrong thing. Anyhow, it was my first and last attempt to buy tobacco in any form.

At quiet moments like these one could sometimes get De Wet to talk, and he and I soon reached the friendliest terms. In large gatherings he seemed miserable, and the constant need of an interpreter made it impossible for people to appreciate the force and humour of his words; their pathos too. Once, on 31 October, he kindly came to a gathering in my Aunt's house in Bruton Street, actually reminding her it was just the anniversary of my arrest, but it was evidently an effort, though he was very kind in going at my special request. In London he reminded one always of a lion in a mesh. He needed the whole expanse of the veld about him, and chafed at the lion-hunters who all wanted a glimpse of the redoubtable General.

The three Generals came and went between the Continent and London. While at Horrex's I recollect the Dutch artist Van Welie[10] came over and stayed there, painting the whole group. His portrait of Mrs. Louis Botha hangs now in the Pretoria museum. His crayon studies were full of character. The artist was anxious to paint me too, and the crayons he did were admirable. The oil portrait he had not time to finish. I do not know what became of any of these productions, but some of them he exhibited years later in London, and amongst them, to my annoyance, the crude unfinished portrait of myself.

Botha and De la Rey spoke for their fund at several places and on one occasion at a large private gathering of devoted workers in Mrs. Bradby's house. I recollect it well because Botha called me aside to tell me he had just received by cable the sad news of the death of one of his dearest brothers, and the effort to attend this meeting was very great. I admired so much the complete way in which he put this fresh private grief behind him and took the leading part with his accustomed grace that evening. No one guessed that he had come straight there after the shock of this sad news.

The Rev. Dewdney Drew, impressed by much he had himself seen in the Free State, had come to England in the spring of 1902 to give information. Returning to the Cape in the early summer he thence wrote me what General Hertzog had told him regarding the position which led the Boers to accept the terms offered at Vereeniging. He wrote:

> "Judge Hertzog gave me facts relative to the condition of women and children in De la Rey's and Botha's Commandos. There were ten thousand women and children who, the Judge says, were denied admission into the camps, though we went on destroying their homes and foodstuffs. Their condition it was, together with the wholesale arming of the Natives, which necessitated the surrender, and not any military compulsion."

This report substantiated that of the other Generals and made evident the danger there had been of more such tragedies as the murders by the Vryheid Kaffirs which as I mentioned had so deeply distressed Mrs. Botha. It was, however, humiliating to know (what various telegrams had hinted) that as soon as our efforts had brought about a healthy and decent condition in the camps, Kitchener refused to bring in families he continued to make homeless.

169

Herein lay proof (if proof were needed) that the camps did not spring from humanitarian feeling as was the fashion to aver, but were in truth what *The Times'* Special Correspondent asserted, conceived as a *"scheme which was designed to bring pressure upon the Boers in the field"*.

After the tension of the two years and eight months' war one was sensible of a feeling of collapse. Much of it fades from my mind after my return from the Continent. There was the Coronation – I remember some one gave me a ticket for a seat on the grand stand flanking St. Margaret's Church where I had a fine view of Parliament Square and the crowd, always itself the most thrilling thing at these public events. Conveyances were few that day, so I walked from Chelsea, going by the river, and found the streets quiet. One never sees much of the Chief Actors on these occasions, and the only figure remaining in my mind was that of Kitchener on horseback keeping order or something of the kind in the open space below. He seemed quite unable to manage his horse; the animal would only walk sideways or backwards. It was very funny and undignified.

During our usual holiday in Somersetshire my Uncle kindly helped me about the final issue of my book, in correcting the proofs of which I was busy.[11] There were opinions for and against its publication, but the balance were in favour and certainly I should never have had another opportunity. I gathered my Brother thought it badly put together from a literary point of view, but I was only a novice unversed in the art of presentment. All I wanted was to put down the facts as plainly and simply as I could. And I am quite sure it wasn't the inferior literary merit that made the Authorities suppress it,[12] but those very plain facts. It brought me many appreciative letters, though from its very nature it could only be what my Aunt called it: "a very painful book".

In the course of a congratulatory letter Professor Sully wrote:

> "It seems to me to be a matter of first importance that English men and women should know in this way, from the lips of the victims, what a war of conquest waged by a Christian nation really means. I know not of any earlier record of the kind. It is sad to reflect that my ignorance may be explained by the circumstance that England has never before set herself to conquer and crush a Christian people capable of speaking out and of letting the world know of its long agony."

In this Professor Sully expressed my own views; it was the same feeling which so many years after has made me go to the trouble and expense of translating the diary of *Tant' Alie of Transvaal*.[13]

In the autumn I was in Edinburgh where I delivered the inaugural address to the Young Scots' Society, and was the guest of Mr. and Mrs. Thomas Shaw (now Lord Dunfermline). This made the *Scotsman* shew its teeth as usual but my skin was

170

getting tough and I had a valiant champion in Mr. Hector Macpherson. After this visit we settled down for the winter.

Very unsettling letters were in the meantime constantly arriving from South Africa picturing the troubles of the people, who, gradually returning to their farms and villages, were confronted with ashes and blackened walls. These letters were written by ministers and their wives to relatives at the Cape, who forwarded them to me. They were simple statements of fact, in no sense begging letters. This unconscious simplicity rendered them the more effective and graphic.

Another witness to the state of things was Mrs. Dickenson, the Australian, whose letters are freely quoted in *The Brunt of the War*. Her husband, a doctor in Bethulie Camp, had lost his life there and soon after peace she returned to put up a stone to his memory. She travelled widely over the late Republics and wrote: "some of the people sent back to their farms are absolutely starving".

Later in October she wrote:

> "There are three doctors and one Assistant Superintendent all dead within two months in Bethulie, and in the camp burying-ground lie 1 500 bodies, mostly women and children who died during the latter part of 1901 and the earlier months of this year. After these plain facts who can dare to say that your statements were exaggerated?
>
> "The work of repatriation is slowly progressing. Compensation claims do not seem to meet with any attention, and there is a great deal of poverty and distress amongst people formerly in excellent circumstances. It has been an interesting experience for me going right through the country as I have done. The people are leaving the camps daily, but still there are two thousand at Bloemfontein, almost as many as Springfontein, and 2 500 here at Bethulie. There is very little sickness in the camps now, shewing how much was preventible. Everything now is of course in a thoroughly sanitary state. I should hardly recognize Bethulie Camp again with the wide spaces between the tents and the orderly way everything is arranged. Any globetrotter coming out now would be impressed by all this."

Many such letters deepened my wish to help the brave women I had known. Mr. Chamberlain went himself to visit South Africa during the winter[14] and it is said he learnt many valuable lessons there. As with him the desire was strong in me to visit the country and see it in time of peace, or at least to follow the families to their ruined homes and see what Fate had in store for them there. I tried to make their difficult position known by a series of articles in the *Manchester Guardian*, but the really effective appeals are those written from the spot.

My own knowledge of the country and its conditions left no doubt in my mind that the help no longer wanted in the camps was now terribly needed in ruined homes. It was not so easy to convey this fact to others whose experience of a

171

devastated country was nil. I felt very strongly the call to go and broke the fact to my Aunt who admitted she had suspected the idea was growing in me and who was as usual sympathetic and helpful though her own wish was to keep me beside her. My dear old Aunt was, I think, the only relative who ever really *wanted* me after my Father's death. At the time I thought it my duty to follow up this work which I had begun, but looking back I often wonder if perhaps I ought to have devoted myself unreservedly to her old age. She had everything the world has to offer except a daughter. You, dear Friend, know full well the blessing of daughters. It is only recently, in my solitary old age, with no young relative, that I have fully understood her craving for younger companionship and help.

I was still feeling ill and in need of a holiday, and as my Brother also wanted change we made a little party of four, he and his wife and Dorothy Bradby and myself, and went to Paris for a few weeks. There I met and was entertained by M. Paul Loyson, the poet and dramatist. He was the son of the well-known Père Hyacinthe, and expressed unlimited admiration of my public work. He dedicated his play *L'Évangile du Sang* to me[15] and wrote most laudatory letters.

All this, however, did not prevent him in 1915 from attacking me in an open letter simply because I had written one of a series of leaflets calling on the Women of Europe to try their best to bring pacific influences to bear in their respective countries. M. Loyson had been a leading Pacifist, but like many other such he became a prominent Jingo. I first noticed this approaching change in him in 1912 when passing through Paris. He came to see me on that occasion and described to me the ever-growing military feeling in France. He said war-like feeling was being encouraged officially and their pacifist party was powerless against it. He described the growing tendency to militarize all public assemblies and events – soldiers, processions, bands, etc. and almost invariably such gatherings ended with the *Marseillaise*, and often the shout of "à Berlin, à Berlin!". He was so sure of the tendency of all this that he ended by declaring he thought it would be best to let war come, allow this feeling to find full vent, and so exhaust itself. – False reasoning indeed!!

But in far-off 1903 Paul Loyson was still Pacifist and took me to a banquet where French Pacifists had gathered to celebrate Washington's birthday and to present M. Passay, their eminent President, with his bust. I sat beside M. d'Estournelles de Constant, the well-known Internationalist, and was unexpectedly required to speak. I did it very lamely being nervous of a clever French audience, but the French were good-natured and *La Fronde* reported kindly next morning. It said:

> *"Pour nous le plus vif intérêt de ce banquet était la présence de Miss Hobhouse . . . Puissions-nous voir souvent des femmes donner comme elle l'exemple de la solidarité internationale."*

Those words pleased me, dear Mrs. Steyn, and I quote them because they embody what all my life I have longed to advance so far as one poor body may: international solidarity – or to put it more comprehensively – to emphasize the essential unity of mankind.

Thus, you see, the grounds of my Pacifism lie deep and can never be moved by the passing policies of my own or other nations, such as induce them suddenly to think they must fight another people or perish. Mixed wrong and right there always is on *both* sides, and only misery comes of fighting about it. Fighting kills off the best in a nation. Victory is of no value because it is then won by Might instead of Right – whereas if the dispute were submitted to arbitration Right has a chance of gaining the victory. I believe this the only way to guard Civilization, and the views of both sides will obtain consideration.

Forgive this digression.

My puny efforts to collect for South Africa the funds for houses and furniture, seeds and tools, and all that is wanted to resume life came to almost nothing, baulked, as was the Generals' Appeal, by Mr. Chamberlain's ample promises, reiterated and underlined as they were by people and press. The stream of charity was dried up. Moreover the tendency was to say the war being over it was better to forget – that being easy enough for the majority in England, who had not been near war of suffered materially. I embodied the letters from the O.R.C. describing the ruin in the farms and villages in an article for Canon Scott-Holland's paper,[16] but he blue-pencilled it so vigorously that its urgency was lost. He feared "lest it should lacerate wounds beginning to heal". That wounds on the other side were far deeper and in greater need of healing did not seem to occur to him.

I devoted to this little fund the royalties that came to me from *The Brunt of the War*, absurdly little because, as I have elsewhere told you, the book was suppressed in every way possible. It only brought me between £30 and £40 – not enough to furnish one house! I do not know what the Generals' Appeal brought from other countries, but from England very little. Before leaving they published (1 December) their subscriptions which amounted to about £26 000. Of this, £20 000 was the gift of Mr. Phipps and, I believe, ear-marked for widows.[17]

Therefore, on our return from Paris, I determined to prepare for the voyage.

Mr. and Mrs. J. Ramsay MacDonald had been in South Africa during the autumn of 1902 and journeyed through large sections of the two former Republics. On his return Mr. MacDonald published *What I saw in South Africa*. Mr. Chamberlain had been there part of the same time and must – in spite of careful guiding – have seen much of what Mr. MacDonald saw. His chapter on "Repatriation and Compensation" foreshadowed all that I afterwards found, and he dwells upon the incompetence of the personnel and on the fact that the payment of £1 a day to the members of all these boards while sitting made, with other expenses, a large hole in the elusive £3 000 000. Mr. MacDonald's book should be reprinted in South Africa as a valuable contribution to her history, for it gives an astonishingly lucid and careful picture of the state of affairs in the two new colonies immediately after

173

the war. If his book had been widely circulated at the Cape when issued, the facts which I exposed later in the year would have received less stupid criticism. The intervening months had brought drought, failure of harvest, semi-starvation of the poor and despair born of vain waiting for help.

I left England at the end of April in the *Carisbrooke Castle* and reached Cape Town on 12 May.

The coming months proved perhaps the most exhausting of my life physically, emotionally and mentally.

174

Letters

Carisbrooke Castle
6 May 1903

The wind continues to head of us, making a horrid vibration, though at the same time keeping us cool. This makes writing a difficulty and I can only manage one letter *per diem* and that but shakily. It has been very hot and I feel warmed through. The water all round us was 85 degrees, so you can imagine what *we* were. Now, since we have crossed the line, it grows daily fresher. As far as material comforts go this is the best voyage I have made. I have a good cabin and get much attention and good service. As I kept my name out of the list I made several friends before my identity was discovered. The discovery alienated most. But I was pleased to have retained the friendship of Mr. and Mrs. D. of Edinburgh, very nice, earnest, middle-class, well-to-do Scotch folk, at whose width of mind I wonder, knowing they must be nourished upon the *Scotsman*.

With these good folk I went ashore at Madeira and we went up the inclined railway to a garden of Eden on the hill, leaving picturesque Funchal beneath our feet. Al fresco we breakfasted, with camellias in full bloom and rows of arum lilies. All the way up the steep line the barefoot children ran and pelted the passengers with flowers, each garden we passed through contributing its quota. After breakfast we walked about and saw gorges and flowers, etc. and then came down the hill quicker than we went up, in the basket sleighs or toboggans which, however, you do not guide yourself but are kept straight by a Portuguese on either side with a rope. These baskets are rather narrow for two full-grown Englishwomen, and Mrs. D. is not slim, so we were crammed in and down we went over the slippery paving stones, while Mr. D. and the gentlemen escorting us followed in another behind. I do not know how we reached the bottom or avoided crashing into the roofs of Funchal or the water of the harbour. Mr. Payne, who built the railway, took us to see his garden, and then we came away laden with fruit, flowers and wicker chairs to join our ship again. After four days' illness it did us all good.

A few days after Mrs. D. suddenly asked me my name, while I had been thinking she knew it! However, it is evident she never heard of me, being wrapped up in her home circle, and our relations continue amicable. I have, however, made a conquest of the Chief Engineer who confessed that when he heard of my arrest he had said: "Serve her right". I asked him what his train of reasoning had been, and he replied: "None, I simply believed the newspapers.[a] But now," he said, "as soon as I saw your face I knew you were genuine."!!!

175

Don't you think I might wear a card with the words "I am genuine"?

My chief friend on board is a gentleman who is scientific. We had talked for ten days before he said that he had only just found out that I was *the* Miss Hobhouse, and we had a little talk about it in which he said he did not at all approve of the Government or the war. Then he brought his autograph book and made me put my name next to Lord Shaftesbury's[1] under the heading "Philanthropists". I play his accompaniments and in the evenings he gives me lectures on the stars, astronomy being one of his subjects . . .

The sea has been dull this voyage and excepting a veritable flotilla of nautiluses (or should I say nautili?) we have seen nothing. These were in such masses as to turn the water pink and have the effect of beds of garden flowers . . .

From the memoir

a) You must bear in mind that people who read the Chamberlain press, and these are the majority, imagined I was a person to be boycotted and ostracised, and on hearing my name were wont to turn the cold shoulder. This insolence, against which of course I had no weapon, created difficult situations for many years. It has also many amusing incidents.

50 TO LEONARD HOBHOUSE

Cape Town

13 May 1903

I am still in a dream and not fully able to say what I feel about anything. It was a lovely morning when we arrived, the moon setting on one side and the sun rising on the other, and the great mountain trio rising gigantic out of the early mist. Even the dirty docks looked like fairyland. Mrs. Murray[1] and Mrs. De Villiers,[2] Mr. Schultz[3] and Mr. Van der Horst[4] came to meet me very early and most glad I was to see them,[a)] but for over an hour we could only look at each other from afar because of these regulations about the new Immigration Bill,[5] and all the examination which the whole ship had to go through on that account, and none might land till that was over. I began to get nervous, but it was all right in the end, and I was brought up here to Mrs. De Villiers' pleasant house[6] in the Gardens. It is high up under the shadow of Table Mountain and beyond the heat and noise of the town. They say it is winter and call it cold, but to me it is full summer and a great camellia bush in full rose-coloured bloom stands outside my window to witness to the warmth. My friends had been very good and kept my arrival perfectly quiet, so it only crept out gently, yet all that day Dutch ladies toiled up the hill in succession and I sat on the stoep and received and talked to them.

It was rather fun at the Custom House. Mrs. Murray helped me through and w both had a good laugh over the officials there. Instead of devoting themselves to

176

the inspection of my boxes they wanted to inspect me myself, and were divided in mind between surprise that I wasn't the sort they expected and curiosity and suspicion. One man followed me about for some time, always trying to get exactly in front of my face. At last he succeeded in squaring himself just in face of me, and fixing his eyes on mine, as if he could read the inmost secrets of my soul, said imploringly, "Miss Hobhouse, tell me, tell me the real truth – *have* you got any firearms?" We burst out laughing in his face and offered the keys.

Another man was entering my items and when he came to my name he could not get on. He simply stood and stared till I was quite hot. At last he gasped out: "Beg pardon, but *are* you the original Miss Hobhouse? Sorry to ask, but you see I've read your book."[7] As he would not get on with his work I was obliged to admit my identity, but rather timidly, not knowing how he would take it. To my surprise he lifted his cap and served me bare-headed till I left the Customs.

Afterwards I went to my bank and enquired if there were any letters and papers for Miss Hobhouse. The bank clerk looked at me and said in a tone of ineffable disgust: "Miss Hobhouse! You don't mean to say that Miss Hobhouse is coming to South Africa again?" and he looked quite evil with concentrated Jingoism as he said it. So I made him a little bow and said: "I *am* Miss Hobhouse." Complete collapse of the clerk! You see I happened to have on a tidy dress and was looking quite neat and not a bit like the type he expected. Next time I went it was not necessary to give my name; he served me promptly and with marked docility.

Later. It would be quite impossible to tell all the stories I have had poured into me since my arrival. They are most interesting but I cannot recollect one half of them. Just a steady flow of stories and anecdotes, and they come all mixed up with household tales. Lord Milner and the washing, Chamberlain and cook worries, martial law and dairy work, all in a tangle – the two main subjects which occupy all feminine minds.

Tired when I started I have been very unwell since landing. Partly in conse-quence of this I have accepted the Charles Moltenos' invitation to spend next week with them in their new house on the Cape Flats which is very quiet.[8]

To *me* my most interesting visitor was Mrs. Van Breda.[9] Do you remember her name? She was the woman who, separated from her children, twice ran away from Kimberley Camp, the second time with success. I last saw her sitting in bitter misery and abject poverty on the dusty ground of a wretched tent, glad to accept a cotton blouse from me. I could hardly recognise the handsome, well-dressed woman, gloved and bonneted, who called on me last night. It appears she belongs to a Cape family and has come to visit relatives and collect money (not for the poor but for their church at Petrusburg which had all its fittings destroyed). But she did not come to beg of me of course, only to pour out her subsequent story and her gratitude.

It appears that after her second flight she reached her deserted home safely, walking all night in the mountains until she met Boers who helped her on her way. Finally she found her baby with her husband and the other children at the parents' farm and there they lived three months in peace. Then the whole family was swept up again and taken to Bloemfontein Camp, which of course was much worse. The man was sent to Bermuda and she with the baby of 21 months put into the town gaol of Bloemfontein as punishment for escaping from Kimberley. She was kept there eight days, food only being given once in 24 hours. The baby got so sick that at last they were released, but too late to save the child which died shortly after.

On two subsequent occasions she was put in gaol while in Bloemfontein Camp for complaining in company with others that the meat was quite uneatable. On the second of these she was within two weeks of her confinement and felt so unable to go that she refused to get into the cart. A small orderly was sent to put her by force into the vehicle, but she easily brushed him aside. Then a big burgher police and the Superintendent and the small orderly all seized her and lifted her in, and to prison she went. Fortunately in a few days the prison doctor said it was not fit for her and she was released. Her baby was born on Kruger's birthday to her joy, and was triumphantly named Paul Marthinus de Wet after the two Presidents.[10] She says her experiences alone would fill a volume and she kissed me with much affection and will put me up at Petrusburg.

I had also a long visit from Miss Haupt, formerly the schoolmistress at Philippolis, where she supported her mother of 85, her sister and a niece. *All* were deported to Springfontein Camp where the old lady was very ill. Miss Haupt now earns a living by working as Secretary for Mr. Schultz. Recently she put in her claim for compensation, all her goods being destroyed as well as her position lost. The reply was she must make her claim in person at Philippolis. She begged that it might be accepted through an agent with power of attorney, for she could not afford either the time or the money to go. She was, however, ordered to do so and had a week's journey and £10 cost to get there. Since then her claim has been sent round from one board to another, but so far she can get no money. I recommend her to nag away and not give up. She reports that various other people known to her were also summoned to make claim in person, having come costly journeys, but on arrival found the Claims Office had left and their journeys in vain . . .

I went at the first opportunity to visit Mrs. P. J. Botha, my friend from Bloemfontein Camp, and had a hearty welcome. I found her in a quaint old house in a lovely part of Rondebosch where she is bravely trying to earn a living for her family by keeping a boarding-house. It is uphill work but with health she may succeed. Her husband, an ex-Landdrost, has just begun to receive a small monthly pension from the O.R.C. Government. I gather ex-officials are receiving something according to the number of years they served under the old regime.

I am quite unable to return all the calls but I did go to see dear old Mrs. Koopmans-De Wet and found her in the last state of aggravation. It appears Milner (or his subordinate) is worrying her to fits because he won't let her give

away 250 cases of clothing by private hand to whom she chooses, but say,
shall go through the official hand of the Repatriation Board and so (she fears,
National Scouts.[11] No one here seems to know what really is going on up the
country, though all are sure there is much suppression of facts.

Yesterday I returned Mr. J. H. Hofmeyr's[12] call, for he lives in a beautiful old
house[13] close to the De Villiers' and said he was always at home Sundays. "Onze
Jan", I mean.

He shewed me his bookful of telegrams which passed between him and Steyn
and Kruger before the outbreak of war, which shew his efforts to maintain peace;
and he told me about "Joe's" visit to Cape Town[14] and how he began by sending to
him to say that he ("Joe") would not ask for £10 000 000 but did he think the
Dutch would give £5 000 000? Mr. Hofmeyr soon disabused his mind on that
point. When asked to do something to help matters on, Mr. Hofmeyr said anything
he might do would be entirely ruined if Visser[15] were executed at Kimberley (you
recollect the case), and he won his reprieve, for he shewed me the Governor's letter
saying that "in order not to hamper his efforts", etc. he consented to spare Visser.
Then he got the amnesty such as it is out of "Joe". I spoke to him of the two
Nieuwoudts[16] still in prison and likely to remain there now Van den Berg[17] is
acquitted, and Mr. Hofmeyr promised to write to Chamberlain about them this
mail.

Tonight there was a gathering to meet me . . . It was all so very nice and yet they
are without a cook!! Nearly all the ladies present said they were cookless; it is one
of the effects of the war – the complete demoralization of the coloured servants. I
asked which they thought the greatest trial – a bad cook or a bad High Commissioner, and all declared a bad High Commissioner was the worst evil and they
would willingly sacrifice the best of cooks (if they had them) if by so doing they
could get rid of the High Commissioner.

From the memoir

a) You can well imagine, dear Mrs. Steyn, that I could not enter the waters of the
Cape Town docks again without much emotion, and it was most thoughtful of my
Cape friends to come and meet me.

51. TO LADY HOBHOUSE

[Cape Town]
22 May 1903

I am feeling a great deal better this week, finding my land legs and becoming
acclimatized. Thus I hope to apply for my permits early in next week and prepare
for my jouney . . . I am staying now in the beautiful home of the Charles Moltenos[1],
a very quiet spot on the Cape Flats, within easy reach of town by train.

Ir. Dewdney-Drew called on me here. He is feeling the political
keenly, is giving himself largely to journalistic work, and will pro-
emfontein to be Editor of *The Friend*[2] which the Liberals there have
: the Eckstein Press!![3]

52. TO LEONARD HOBHOUSE

[Wynberg House], Cape Town
25 May 1903

I have had long talks with the Chief Justice, in whose house I now find myself,[a]
about the situation generally and "Joe's" visit. All seem fairly content with the
way things are gradually working out in *this* Colony. "Joe" told Sir Henry that a
week here in Cape Town had caused a great alteration in his mind and views,
especially in the question of the rebellion. Also the 300 men composing the Afrikander deputation made a profound impression upon him; they were physically
and mentally a very fine set, and "Joe" gave great satisfaction by markedly polite
manners to them, shaking hands with everyone, etc. All agree that if the loyalists
would be *as* conciliatory as the Colonial Secretary,[1] harmony might return, but
they go on rubbing in loyalty at every turn.

To me it seems that the bitterness against England is far deeper and more intense
than on my previous visit, the sense of injustice has gone in so deep that it can never
be effaced; in fact so much is this the case that now and then it makes me feel hot
and uncomfortable to hear what is said; they speak out in front of me as if I were
one of themselves . . .

They know nothing here of what is going on up-country, and on many points
know far fewer facts than we English . . . But books are not easily come by; my
book,[2] MacDonald's book,[3] Kestell's book,[4] *Songs of the Veld*[5] and others – all seem
under silent prohibition. The first consignments got in, but they are quietly squashed
now, though if any bookseller chose to bring the matter into Court probably the
prohibition would be removed, as was the case with Van Edelingen's *History of the
War*.[6] But no one will take that step, so the bulk of the population neither see nor
hear of such books. Olive Schreiner wrote me a very nice letter about mine. She
appreciates fully the difficulties of my position in writing it and says she does not
think it could, considering those, have been better done. This is kind of her but I do
not agree . . .

Lady De Villiers took me for a wonderfully lovely drive yesterday to Groot
Constantia, famous for its wine. It is the old family place of the Cloetes' and is a fine
specimen of the old Dutch style of house with thatched roof and white gables. The
oak avenues about it are very fine, and in one of these the great alfresco luncheon
was given to Chamberlain. The most beautiful thing is the view from the stoep,
which is of almost unrivalled beauty, across a richly cultivated plain with woods
and fields to the sea and the cliffs of False Bay and beyond the sea the grand range

of mountains around Stellenbosch. On the other side rose Table Mountain and its attendant peaks, and over all the rich autumn colouring, the vines golden as bracken is at home.

Today I have been to town to get my permit, and meeting young Mr. Van Zyl in the road got him to go into office with me. I had to fill in a form asking all kinds of questions and seeing I was English the official was most hearty, said there was no difficulty – I could go everywhere. Presently he read my paper attentively and it began to dawn upon him who I was – his manner changed at once and he hummed and hawed and raised difficulties and said I must come again to-morrow and meanwhile he would see. From this I imagine my name must be on some list for special consideration or reference to His Excellency and so I await my verdict tomorrow.

The weather has been very wet and rather cold and I have been prevented from getting about as I should wish . . . I have a great number of invitations[b] to stay with people, more than I can possibly accept . . . Now I want to hurry on not to miss the cold weather at Pretoria and in the North Transvaal, and work southwards as the weather grows warmer.

From the memoir

a) While there, Captain V. came to lunch and entertained us with many stories of the war. The more humorous ones I should spoil in the telling, but I found the following characteristic: Captain V. told us he had captured a young girl of eighteen, a Miss J. (I will suppress her name). He had come across a small body of Boers, and in a cart with them, also armed with a rifle, was this pretty girl. He went up to her and touching his hat said he was sorry to have to molest her, but it would be necessary to send her to Springfontein Camp where he felt sure she would be very comfortable. "That," she replied, "I feel sure I shall *not*, for I have lived there already four months and escaped, finding it unbearable."

The Commandant of the Boers told Captain V. that the girl had such spirit and courage, more so than any of his men, that he had found it necessary to place her in a cart and order her to keep in the rear.

She was sent by Captain V. to the camp. After peace he visited the family now re-united, whom he found sheltering in an outhouse on their farm. The mother thanked him for capturing the girl about whom she had been extremely anxious. He gave the girl a Queen's medal, thinking she deserved it!!

b) Miss Emmie Murray had asked me to visit her Home for Girls in Wynberg and I see[7] that the last day of the month was spent with her there. Her information, as noted down, is serious, but cannot here be repeated.[8] The daughter of the Rev. Andrew Murray, she had worked a good deal with the Salvation Army. If someone would write a book on the effect of war on public morality her experiences should find a place.

Cape Town
28 May 1903

If the servant difficulty is felt a little in England be assured that it cannot bear comparison with the woes experienced by housewives in and around Cape Town. Every household feels the pressure more or less. This scarcity of servants is largely brought about by the war, for coloured men received then such high wages that their womenfolk no longer care to earn their own living, and for works of many kinds the Military are still employing large numbers of these men and at a high figure . . . Thus in despair many ladies have tried the women sent out under the Emigration Scheme[1] and stories about these girls fill all feminine conversations.[a] One rather amusing story was that of a good soul who took ship and came out here at her own expenses and went into service with some friends of mine. She said she came because Mr. Chamberlain had said there were so many and such good chances of matrimony and this country. As time passed and the lovers did not appear she waxed wrath with Mr. Chamberlain and began to abuse him roundly for having misled her. She was 55!

Of those sent out under the Emigration Scheme the only successful or, rather, partially successful instance I have yet been able to hear of is the parlourmaid in the house I am now in. She is Scotch and has had a rough training, but has, says my hostess, a whole regiment of suitors from the neighbouring camps. "That girl is in love, that girl is in love," sighs the poor mistress at every meal, as plates or something else are forgotten continually, and no doubt "Joe's" promised land of matrimony will be entered in a few months . . .

It appears that being led away during the long voyage, ere anyone can come and meet the vessel, they have generally vanished, each with a lover, and often have to be hunted up in low inns and restaurants of the town, sometimes with a policeman to make them understand that they are under contract to some lady or other and *must* come. Frequently they make light of these contracts and say they have others for themselves. A family had two of them, but after a few days' service they were found to have escaped early one morning through the larder window.

Cape Town rings with stories of this kind and it seems a shame that people at home should be asked to subscribe, as is being done, to send girls out in batches to almost certain ruin.

From the memoir

a) It had been very interesting to me to see this reverse side of the Emigration Scheme for young women after all we had heard and read about it at home. It had been officially pushed and supported by many who knew nothing of the country and conditions, and its rash imprudence had distressed us.

Cape Town
5 June 1903

I am all ready packed for my journey and will begin my mail letter to fill up the time. The skies have not been shining upon me and today when I had a lot of odds and ends to do it has rained heavily. Cape Town in rain is truly awful, as owing to the steepness of the streets one is always walking in streams. Moreover, when the rain is very bad as at present, they have a horrid practice of stopping the tram cars. They say it is because the streams cover the rails and wash stones into the ruts and it becomes dangerous, but it seems a little hard upon a soaked public.

The rain today was also unfortunate because it was the opening of Parliament and the Chief Justice gave me a ticket to attend the ceremony. They give plenty of space and air to ladies here, and for the Opening the floor of the House is given up to ladies besides the gallery, while the members of both Houses and the Foreign Consuls are put on side benches on either hand. So one could see and hear and breathe – all impossible in the House of Commons. The Governor wore a uniform and a cocked hat which he kept on and read his speech sitting. It was a very dull speech full of nothing, but he read it very well and clearly, so that we could hear. When the short ceremony was over we went to the House of Assembly to see the new members sworn in, among whom was our old friend Cronwright-Schreiner. I really felt Time was bringing things round a bit when I saw him taking his seat after being so reviled, and saw Mr. Malan with some of his prison sadness still hanging over him,[1] sitting with Mr. Harry Currey and other friends. Just opposite, too, was the other late prisoner, Mr. Cartwright,[2] reporting diligently. Then there were Mr. Merriman and Mr. Sauer, sitting together cracking jokes as usual and looking equal to any amount of fighting.

We lunched after it was over with the Sauers and Mr. Merriman in the restaurant of the House, and I enjoyed that. There came to lunch with us Mr. Pretorius, a member of the Upper House.[3] There was such a babel of tongues in the room that I did not at first catch his name, but I was very much struck by his face and manner. He looked like a man who had been through something very terrible and it was stamped upon his face. It was a merry lunch but he never smiled, and every time I looked at him I felt as if it were heartless to laugh and joke as we were doing. Afterwards I heard that he had been one of those to suffer much under martial law – a most respected member of the Upper House – and was among those compelled to attend and witness the execution of young Marais. I believe Marais was a personal friend of his; in any case the scene affected him terribly and he cried out involuntarily: "Oh God, I call Thee to witness they are murdering this man!" This angered the Commandant and in consequence he was deported and endured much humiliation – one of the most loyal men, the backbone of this country.

Last night several people came to see me, amongst them Mr. Theron,[4] Leader of the Bond, an alert elderly man with very bright eyes. Also M. who had met me in

Edinburgh when one of the Young Scots. He has come here to live and hopes to start a Young South Africans, which is needed. He had been first to Natal, and coming back he found on the ship four Intelligence men, spies. One of these, after plentiful whisky, told him they had been sent to the political meetings at Grahamstown, etc. to mark what farmers came and what they said amongst themselves, and get information; if necessary they would arrest about one in five so as to keep them in their place! The espionage, he affirmed, was to be kept up another twelve months. They were keeping an eye on Mr. Sauer who was on that vessel. This man was a draper's assistant from London who had joined the Volunteers.

Mr. Louw, Field Cornet of Johannesburg, who delivered the keys to Lord Roberts,[5] also called with his son. He remained in Johannesburg after the Occupation, doing his business until after the camp there was formed. Then when he tried to ameliorate things and pleaded with the Military for food and shelter for the women and children, he was deported as an undesirable, and coming to Europe, held meetings to collect funds for them. On this account he is refused a permit to return to his house and after endless applications, all in vain, has settled down, a permanent malcontent, in Cape Town.

His son, young Louw, stayed on in Johannesburg doing business and looking after two sisters. He tells stirring stories too long to write, and he confirms the rumours we used to hear of how freely the Boers used to come in and out of the town. He used to walk about quite freely with Danie Theron, De Wet's famous scout, who would even stay two or three days together openly in one of the big hotels. Of course the Military were more or less aware of this and made spasmodic but always fruitless efforts to catch them. One day when he was walking with Danie Theron, a cordon was suddenly drawn round the centre of the town and everyone caught in the net was searched. Even the Imperial officers and the Commanding Colonel himself were searched. Theron was dressed in the uniform of a British Captain, but thought now his time was come. Asked his name he replied, "Captain Scott", etc. – "But he was shot a week ago," was the reply. "So I have just heard," said Theron, "but it was a false report. Here are my passes."

He had the whole outfit of the dead man and so got off once more. Five shillings to a poor starved Tommy would always get him into Johannesburg, but when in uniform he did not trouble to bribe, but just walked in.

Did I tell you the sequel to the bank clerk story? I found a marked change in the manner of the bank clerks towards me (Cape banks are not like ours, there are so many walking about and many errands done there). Then the Manager sent for me, and was extremely agreeable, and it transpired that one of my hostesses (very wrongly, I think) had told him the story of the man's rudeness, and he wished to apologize and begged I would point out the culprit, for, said he, "Banks should have no politics". He said he had already been right through the bank trying to find out and had given a piece of his mind about it. Failing to hit on the individual he hoped I would tell him. This I refused, not wishing to get the man into trouble,

184

and said I had only repeated it as a joke, otherwise the incident was quite beneath my notice. I never thought it would come to his ears. He did his best to make me tell but I wouldn't, and now it is lovely to see how they run to serve me in the bank, and the insolent man himself is evidently grateful because I would not name him, so the war-paint and feathers of his Jingoism are much tarnished and if he is not a pro-Boer he certainly is a pro-Hobhouse.

This small incident makes me hope that though I may have trouble with sub-ordinates I shall be decently treated by their superiors.

I had an interesting talk with Mr. Theron, Chairman of the Bond. He told me Chamberlain sent for him for a private interview, and told him he wanted three things: £10 000 000 from the Cape Colony for the war expenses; a contribution to the Navy; and a conciliatory movement on the part of the Dutch.

Mr. Theron waited patiently till "Joe" had said his say and given all his reasons, and then said if he would allow perfectly plain open speaking he would put the case before him as it appears to the South African party. And, taking him back to the Jameson Raid, he traced for him the whole story of the Dutch attitude and their continual protests and deputations right up to date, and then said: "Now, can you repeat your request for £10 millions from us?"

"No," said "Joe", "I cannot."

And from that moment he dropped it and never metioned it or the Navy idea to anyone else.

The conciliatory letter to the Dutch[6] he got out of J. H. Hofmeyr who in return secured the life of Visser and the amnesty. With regard to that same letter of his Mr. Hofmeyr is much vexed because he printed and circulated about 3 000 copies and sent to as many heads of things as he thought advisable. But the Government on its own hook printed about 100 000 and spread broadcast doing much harm, for coming from that source it had another effect.

Mr. Hofmeyr, Onze Jan as they call him, is most agreeable and insisted on seeing me off last night. In fact I had quite a bodyguard to conduct me to the train and wish me good speed, among them Mr. Schultz, Mr. Van Zyl, Mr. Van den Horst, Professor Fremantle[7] (cousin of Mr. Brodrick) and others. There was a concert that night for the Boer Funds at which I was specially asked to be present, so I went for half an hour and Onze Jan escorted me thence to the station.

55. TO LADY HOBHOUSE

Beaufort West
6 and 7 June 1902

I had a pleasant journey to Beaufort West where I am now writing, and found the Karoo as attractive to me as ever. War signs about here have mostly disappeared, only some barbed wire left and stone fire-places with bits of pipes for chimneys, relics of Tommy.

185

Quite a little party had gathered at Beaufort Station to meet me. Olive Schreiner,[a] Miss Molteno, Rev. Van der Merwe, Dr. and Mrs. Neethling, Mr. and Mrs. Kriel and Miss Theron (sister of the famed Boer Scout) and Mrs. van Heerden, aunt of General Malan, etc.

If you could have heard the conversation at our tea on the stoep, you would realize a little what the feeling is towards England in this country.[b] It is the same as at Cape Town, only far, far more so. Here where Martial Law worked its wicked will, and the best families of the town have seen one or other of their members in the prison classed with Kaffirs, working as convicts in the streets, denied chairs, knives, forks and such necessaries, even if supplied by their relatives; where the Rev. John Murray[1] was sentenced in the public square and had his hat knocked off by a common soldier, where countless such acts of insult and oppression have taken place, more than I can possibly record – here one is made aware of the full vials of their great, but suppressed wrath. The cord of love that bound them to England is snapped, only now and again bits of the old feeling come out in the form of excuses for the old Queen for whom they still entertain a tender feeling.

I have been taken tonight to see a very old dame, Tant Sara Pienaar, called "the mother of Beaufort", and from this wonderful old lady, with her feet in the grave and her head as clear as day, I heard the undiluted Colonial view of the war, the Peace, the great personages connected therewith, and the future. There was a large mixture of the Old Testament of course, and England was artistically likened to Nebuchadnezzar. Most of all was she hurt because the Military had stopped the church services along the line. "The English," she scornfully remarked, "do not even know there is a God."

Nevertheless, at leaving she threw her arms round my neck and kissed me repeatedly, not willing to let me go . . .

The result of the Van den Berg trial and his subsequent acquittal has taken away the last remnant of belief in English justice; and there seems to be no appeal because it is a criminal case. The Military know full well that it was a miscarriage of justice, and some of the officers say the punishment of the five men, three by death and two by imprisonment, was the darkest deed of the war.[2] It appears that Huddlestone, the Intelligence officer who egged Van den Berg on to forgery, is kept under lock and key by the Military who fear he will turn round and inform against them.

The two Nieuwoudts, who have served two years and four months as convicts, are now come out; they are perfectly quiet and calm with that terrible calm which has settled down upon the people and which is so unnatural and dreadful . . . The Peace fell like a great blow that nearly killed them, but the women pray that all the children born to them now may be boys, for in sixteen years such will be of burgher age. They think it is the hand of God that most babies born since the Peace have been boys.

But no words of mine can portray the attitude of mind towards England. Every

186

atom of respect and love has vanished; it is a deep disdain both for the policy and the methods by which that policy has been carried out.

A spy sits at the table with us in this boarding-house.

I suppose you understand that though Van den Berg was acquitted (to save the Military reputation) yet Pienaar, who was incriminated by his story, was set at liberty last week. It was all nicely arranged so that the innocent men should no longer suffer and on the other hand the Military will not be disgraced. From the Chief Justice downwards everyone is disgusted, but I don't suppose anyone in England cares a rap about a trial with which this whole country rings. The feeling was dramatically shewn at Pienaar's trial. The statement of his case had taken some days. At its close Olive Schreiner turned round to shake hands with him, but at that moment his old father and mother came up and kissed him, and the ice thus broken there was a sudden stampede of every woman and girl in the Court and with the cry "Ach! maar hij is een waare rebel," they all flocked round and kissed him, the Magistrate quite powerless to prevent this sudden onslaught upon the prisoner.

The gaols are so dear to the people now, full of associations of their best and closest friends and relations, and mothers tell their children when they grow up they must never marry anyone whose father hasn't been in prison.

I am a guest in a boarding-house here and my host was himself thrown into prison without charge. He comes and entertains us at meals when also we are waited upon by a wee Bushman boy who is very quaint, with wee crisp curls and a flat nose, quite a different type from Kaffirs. We cannot talk at meals of public matters because of the spy.

It seems like Italy here and day and night are equally beautiful.

From the memoir

a) Nothing of the actual journey north remains in my mind except the break at Beaufort West where I was to stay a few days and meet a group of high-souled women – Olive Schreiner, Miss Molteno, Miss Greene and their friends.

It was memorable to me if only as my first meeting in the flesh with Olive Schreiner – a meeting which developed into a friendship lasting so many years. I remember our walks together in the little town. Lifted suddenly from the coast to the pure air of the sunlit Karoo, the town and its dryness presented a healthful dryness to the winter rains of Cape Town. The altitude which tried me so greatly ten years later was stimulating at that date. We sat and basked in the dry sunny air and I listened and marvelled as Olive poured out her thoughts and feelings with an eloquence and power I have never heard equalled by any other woman. Hers was a magnificent spirit pathetically confined in a frail body. When she left us in 1920 it was as if a light had gone out in South Africa. Yet an after-glow remains in the light of which we lesser folk may toil. Since her death many criticisms of her life and

187

work have circulated – all true in parts but all strangely erring. Few understood the enigmatic character of her genius. Perhaps it was not understandable. English critics have attempted to compress her into the European mould and judge her so, forgetting she was South African-born and bred and belonged to the vast spaces and simple life of the veld, and was subject to its strange influences. South Africans, I think, try to judge her by their standards alone, forgetting that her mind and spirit had burst all frontiers and racial bonds and embraced the world.

It is hard for my unskilled pen to find words to describe your South African Olive. One gained breadth and grandeur from her. She gave me the illimitable feeling of the veld. She gathered Time and Space into herself and absorbed them.

People who never knew her, or but superficially, ask what token exists of her claim to genius beyond the brilliant novel of a girl[3] and a few allegories.[4] It is difficult to reply; hers was a wayward genius, and clogged, too, in its outflow by two life-long limitations – frail health and poverty. Olive thought deeply – for days together I have found her wrapt in silence. At such periods she would not respond. On these occasions she withdrew into herself and was mentally occupied in bringing to the bar of her own lofty judgment things seen and heard. Such spells of silence were followed by the necessity of speech when relief only came by the outpouring of her thoughts. It was curious to note that she seemed unaware that much of what she said was common knowledge – it all came pouring out interspersed with gems of thought which flashed light amid the commonplace like diamonds in a dust heap. To gather these jewels one gladly waited at her feet. Others with scant patience or no time would leave her thinking she was an overestimaged woman.

Her powerful imagination, lacking its normal outlet in the continued writing of novel or romance, preyed upon common life and one soon found she mixed imagination with fact until it was not clear which was which. Thus one learnt not to rely on her statements of facts, her dates or her figures – though there never was a truer person. Whatever she said or did was true to the core and teaching of Truth itself, though often inexact in statement of detail. She was a lofty soul from whom one sought inspiration, certainly not one whose statements of detail one would accept. Matters of fact related by her might and often did differ every day according to the working of her imagination or her relations to the person she was talking to. All this took me time to discover. But at last I did understand. Olive Schreiner resembled the sun from which one draws all-embracing light, heat and inspiration.[5]

Such was the woman I now met and whose talk dazzled my slow mind. At the moment her heart was torn with the sad case of those Hanover men falsely accused and condemned for wrecking a train at Taaibosch, though Commandant W. Malan had publicly stated he had himself done it as an act of war. The young Marquis de Kersausan, a Frenchman who had served with Malan, also bore witness to the truth of this and had written to me to that effect. But Olive could not forget that two of the innocent men, the Nieuwoudts, were still in prison[6]; the men for whose release I had begged Mr. Hofmeyr to plead. The sense of injustice crushed her.

b) You will of course, dear Mrs. Steyn, understand that feeling in the Cape Colony was *very* different to that in your country. Much regret as the Free Staters shewed at the attitude and policy of England, there was a complete lack of the bitterness of those who, like the Cape Colonists, were *British* subjects and faced with the impossible duty of being loyal to a country to which they had not long been annexed and which was fighting against and exterminating their kith and kin. They felt blood was thicker than any duty to a former conqueror – hence many a rebel. A harder position could hardly be found and one which needed the gentlest handling – instead, the harsh measures adopted drove more and more young men to side with the struggling Republicans. Such rebels – as the incident at Pienaar's trial shews – were adored by the girls. It was a really wonderful tribute to English rule as a whole that rebellion did not become universal, in spite of the cruelties, executions, imprisonments, deportations and restrictions of all kinds instigated by the Military Authorities under martial law. I doubt if any section of the South African people suffered such moral and spiritual agony as did the Dutch of the northern parts of Cape Colony. For the people of the Republics the issue was at least straight.

Those who kept to the rigid letter of the law, and they were the majority, could not change their *feeling*, and for the mere suspicion of this they were sternly dealt with though no charge was brought against them. It could not be, since they had committed no offence. One was thankful to do what one could to soften their wounded feelings and shew sympathy in the unusual trial which had been theirs.

56. TO LADY HOBHOUSE
Beaufort West
[Undated]

After closing my last letter to you I went with Mr. Van der Merwe, the D. R. clergyman,[a] to see the orphanage. The Beaufort West people (who only number 6 000 *including* coloured people) have undertaken 32 orphans on their own account. These are mostly from the O.R.C. Camps . . . I suppose this is only the first of many orphanages[1] I am likely to see and if all are as bright and cheerful and homelike it will be well for the children. They have a large cheerful house just outside the town, and the children, half of whom are boys and half girls, attend the town schools. Their clothes were clean and good, all given as a labour of love by Beaufort ladies, for they had arrived with only upper garments.

The children, girls especially, seemed to me a very superior set, but it is probable that those of best family will be taken into private families ere long, indeed already they have invitations for the holidays. There are funds in hand for twelve months guaranteed by the congregation, and clothing also. So I felt it needed no help from us and Mr. Van der Merwe agreed that the help should be kept for the North.

I liked the orphanage because it did not seem a bit like an institution. There was a great plant of maidenhair fern upon which my eyes rested with pleasure, being the only spot of green in or round Beaufort for scores of miles. "We have had such a beautiful garden," said the minister, taking me into a large enclosure of what I should have supposed was a turnpike road if I had not been told it was a garden. "And we shall supply our own vegetables," he went on, "if it rains."

But it has *not* rained for eighteen months and there was neither leaf nor blade to be seen. This drought is very terrible over a large part of the Colony and some days trains could not run for want of water. All is parched. The farmers, already impoverished by martial law and uncompensated claims, are losing their stock by the thousand, dying of drought. Long water famines in this district have generally been weathered by the help of the great Beaufort Dam, but the Military wasted it so seriously letting the water run as if it were England, that they emptied it and it lies nearly dry.

The people, however, see the Hand of God in this drought because, unable to feed the cattle themselves, they are driving them up by thousands to those parts of the Free State where rains have fallen and so, they say, a source of income is thus found for their ruined kinsmen who could not otherwise get upon their legs. Milner, they say, wants the ruined people to remain impoverished and suppressed, but God wills it otherwise.

I have very thoroughly enjoyed meeting Olive Schreiner. She is full of life and spirits, a tremendous talker in spite of her asthma. She understands her people down to the ground and all the spirit of all the Boer women seems to be condensed and concentrated in her. She says my book is the only one on the war which she has cared for and all the people I have met here call it their "sweet drop".[2] Every house is gradually getting one, a permanent possession, part of their experience, to place with the family Bible and Hymn Book on the shelf . . .

The Beaufort people gave me a very kindly send-off. One sent hard-boiled eggs, and one sandwiches, another a tin of cakes and another a bottle of milk. Olive gave me oranges and Worcester raisins, and an old gentleman sent his carriage and pair to take me to the station, if I would "honour it by sitting in it".

Mrs. S., who gave me the eggs, had a lovely pair of horses which her husband had given her for a wedding present. She was very proud of them, they were worth £120. She had just refused £95 for them when they were commandeered and sent to the front. The officer chose to value the pair at £31 and gave her a receipt for only that. When the receipt was sent in, a cheque for only £15 was received, and that they leave lying at the bank too disgusted to cash it.

For many months she was rationed on her farm, all their stores of food being called in. It was 29 miles to fetch the rations, with the horses all taken and only enough given for a week at a time. But better off than some she had a donkey to

190

come in with, which took the whole day. Getting the permit and waiting hours at the Office took another day, and the third day was spent in getting home – a three days' business to fetch a week's food. Enough to vex a saint! I asked her if she did not bury or hide anything when the food was called in, and she confessed to hiding some meal and sugar and coffee. For as she said she knew better than the Military the difficulty of getting 29 miles and back every week with no horses and a family to be fed. Anything might happen. So she took a large packing case and nailed art muslin round it and placed it in her bedroom as a toilet table, and inside put three big bags of meal. One day a column passed and the officers wanted to wash and dress, so they had to go into her bedroom and in terror she waited while they combed and shaved at her toilet table, but actually they never lifted the art muslin nor found the bags of meal . . .

As I left Beaufort I felt that I had perhaps served a useful end as a safety valve.

From the memoir

a) I was interested to lunch with the Rev. Van der Merwe whom I had last seen in Norvals Pont Camp. After I left that camp he went also, to Springfontein and Bloemfontein Camps. He told me Goold-Adams and other authorities constantly asked him how to stop the people dying. He replied: "Food." He thought the work of the Ladies Commission very superficial. They seldom went into the tents.

It was at Beaufort that I met Ds. Neethling of Lydenburg[2] who was with the Commandos to the end. He told me when his medicines were gone Kitchener refused him permission to fetch more from *their own stores* sent up from Delagoa Bay. He dwelt upon the good health of the women and children who stayed out on the veld. He knew of no deaths amongst them. This confirms what I heard from nearly all the districts – the danger to women arose only locally where Kaffirs were armed and on the loose and at the *very last* from the lack of clothing in the North and East Transvaal. Ds. Neethling, like many, had been against the peace that was made. He said the Red Cross rules were broken on all sides.

57. TO LADY HOBHOUSE

Bloemfontein
10 June 1903

Nearing Springfontein early today I waved out of the window to the German Mission Station where my old host and hostess[1] lived. Then, as the train stopped there for breakfast, I ran down to the house for all I was worth, had a talk with the family, a hot cup of coffee, and tore back in time to catch the train. The whole camp was gone, Mr. Sandrock said, but he spoke most gloomily of the state of the country and people. He knew of no case in which compensation had been received.

His own claim for £1 600, largely the Mission property, had been sent in but disallowed.

I enquired into the work of the local Repatriation Board[2] and he said it was now shut up and gone. It had consisted of twelve men who had received £1 a day, but he knew of no single case in which it had helped the people. The farmers could not come in for lack of transport, and he himself could not get out to them for the same reason.

From Germany he had received much help, £100 for the orphanage at Bethulie, of which he was Vice-President, and after I left in 1901 much clothing was sent from Germany for the camp. He begs me to return and go through the districts here.

I but just caught the train and as we passed the site of the camp I saw nothing was left of that big canvas town but the rows of white stones marking the streets and squares and a few sod huts. Across the line on the slope of the opposite hill was the big graveyard where something like 1 000 lie, Mr. Sandrock himself having buried 650 of the number.

It was a great relief to leave parchment-coloured Beaufort and enter the (comparatively) green O.R.C. Just a film of verdure in a few places, but with great plains biscuit-coloured. The cold – it is very cold, and I began to repent having chosen the winter. Mercifully I brought my fur cape, but I can't see how the people bore this peculiar cold in the camps. The south wind is cutting.

I received a very warm welcome from the Fichardt family[a] and am installed in my old room with every luxury. Judge Hertzog came down to see me at once and with Charlie Fichardt and Mr. Daniels, all in the legal line, we had a long and detailed discussion. I asked them to tell me what had become of the £3 000 000,[3] and they said they hoped I had brought it, for nothing had been seen of it here! Four thousand of it was embezzled here and £1 200 at Boshof, £1 700 at Kroonstad, rumours of the same at other centres, and there are the salaries of the committees; they know of nothing else to show for it, but all look forward to the account of its expenditure with curiosity.

Strings of compensation claims pass through the hands of these men, but very rarely is one attended to, and then he is lucky if he gets a small portion. Generally these claims go round from board to board and end up here in Bloemfontein again where they stick hopelessly.

With military receipts the trouble is the same; they cannot get them paid or only in small proportions. You remember Chamberlain's speech in which he said all must be paid in full, a British officer's word good as a bank-note, etc.[4] Well, that did for the British Public and the outer world, but *here* made not the slightest difference. Many instances are forthcoming of these receipts being handed in after that speech and receiving the same reply: "They can't expect to be paid *in full*."

This is the case with English folk and Jingoes as well. Boer military receipts are equally ignored.

The three million being a "*free gift*" as stated in the Peace terms is a joke. Except some scanty rations to widows and orphans I can hear of no "gift". Security is demanded for every atom of help.

As to the proposed Government Loan on easy terms, that is so hedged about with regulations as to be worthless. These are the opinions and experiences of these three men before-mentioned who deal with the matter daily; it coincides with Rev. Sandrock's statement and with what the old Boer in the train poured out to me during our journey. If the people could have but the half or the quarter of their claims paid they might at least live, and if, as the old Boer said, the Government wants to make the people satisfied, that is the only way. A starving population cannot feel pleased.

My mind is set upon a speedy trip into the country districts, but ways and means are hard to find. Horses and mules and carts are all scarce and costly. Yet a farmer by name Enslin,[5] lately from Ceylon prison, is likely to take me. He is of course ruined and, unable to do anything on his farm, he thought of trying to earn a living by trading. So he filled a cart with food and drove into the country districts to sell to the people who could not come to town. He has returned with his goods unsold, because though the people are well-nigh starving, subsisting in parts upon berries etc., they had no money to buy of him. Miserable at the poverty he witnessed and his own failure, he told Arthur Fichardt he had best go to Parys and try to start market gardening.

Mr. Fichardt at once suggested that he should first drive me on the same round as he went, for he knows the man well and has perfect trust in him as an escort. For sympathy's sake and because it is me, he agrees (after consultation with his wife, for no Boer acts without consent of Mrs. Boer) to postpone his departure to Parys and to take me round. He provides a wagonette, namely a vehicle large enough to take food to the people as well as our own supplies and bed, four mules, a Kaffir, forage, and his own time and services thrown in.

I expect it will be a ten days' tour, and costly, so it is plain my country tours must cease unless I can hit on a district where I can be handed on from one to another. That is the usual method and what they all *wish* to do, but in these days they lack the carts and horses and are themselves mostly stationary in consequence. And yet it is the country districts to which I *must* get and where such great destitution prevails. I have fully considered all other modes of locomotion, but for one reason or another all are impossible. Bicycles, horseback, walking, post carts, etc. I shall work on as far as my means will allow, which of course won't be long.

My plan is, after my return from this tour, to rest here a day and then run over to Thaba'Nchu by rail where General Brand[6] will drive me to Tweespruit Relief Camp to visit Miss Monkhouse[7] and her work there. I had written from England asking Mrs. Blignaut to write to Miss Monkhouse about sending dried vegetables, etc. for the people, and Mrs. Blignaut tells me today that she did so at once but received *no reply* from Miss Monkhouse. Rumour says the wages have been raised from 4/6 to 7/- in the Relief Camps and if this proves to be fact it is probably the result of your sending the letter to Chamberlain.

Mr. and Mrs. Fischer lunched here today and he corroborates all that I have written and much more about the Government dealings with Repatriation. He attributes much of the failure to the absolute incompetency of the men composing the boards, men who have no idea of making a methodical plan to work upon for the whole country, thus avoiding uneven administration, and who cannot even keep accounts. In this office during the trial of the embezzler it was found that the cash book had not been made up for three weeks, no entries of the daily items. I wish I could explain the whole position more lucidly and wish some of these men would themselves write fully to English friends, but I find here the same feeling as in the Colony: silence is best, to tell England things is like dropping water into the ocean – no one heeds. Leave England on one side to go blundering on in her ignorance, sit and laugh at the mistakes her administrators are making, get what fun out of it that is possible, nothing can be worse than it has been, and people who have no more to lose and have suffered everything can afford to laugh. Every mistake made makes it better for them, throws more and more English residents into their ranks and brings the day nearer when it will clearly be seen they must govern their own country.

To speak now or call attention might spoil all. Let the Jingoes and the Uit-landers do the complaining for them. So they sit silent and grin with amusement. That is their attitude roughly put, and the humor they see in the situation keeps them alive and going. The stories are so funny I laugh all day, and have laughed more since I reached South Africa than I have for two years at home. And certainly it relieves the tension of all the misery past and present. Knowing, as I do, that England is comfortably feeling that the Boers have now realized their mistake and are rejoicing in the Peace and the Flag and the good Rule and forgetting the camps and singing "God Save the King", and is also thinking how generous a conqueror she has been with her millions, it is too curious to find how different the attitude here really is and that the Boers, silent to the outer world, are shaking their sides with laughter at England, her complacency and her mistakes! So they let her go her own way and out of these mistakes will come their opportunity. For one thing they know perfectly well: they are not conquered.

They don't mind what they do just to live while they bide their time. One big farmer is driving a cab in Bloemfontein. Why not, he says; in a drought, that is more lucrative. Another says: "Don't pity me, pity the porcupine. The English-man turns me out of my house, I turn the Kaffir out, the Kaffir turns out the porcupine, let the pity go to the porcupine."

The story of the meeting of the Boer deputation with Chamberlain is too funny. Of course the accounts we read were wholly inaccurate and Chamberlain had a hot four hours with them. It is too long to describe now.[8] They argue that it is useless to send the true account to England, for it won't be believed. Why trouble

194

what the English think? To an English person it is, as you can imagine, very humiliating to see the utter disdain in which we are held, but I think we deserve it, and to me personally they are all so good and they appreciate so highly all our efforts that I cannot feel offended.

Today Mrs. Hertzog came to see me, still suffering from her long camp life, the effects of which she never expects will leave her. Gentle and uncomplaining and quiet. Merebank Camp where her last seven months were spent was horrible indeed, she gave me sad details.

None of the leading Boers invited to attend Chamberlain's banquet would accept. De Wet refused to meet socially the man who had publicly called him a liar; Mr. Fichardt said he was a Liberal in politics and had no interest in meeting a Conservative; Hertzog said he could not break bread with those who had exposed his wife to such terrible indignities and sufferings and separated her for two years from her only child.[b] In this way all replied and none went.

I must not go on writing this gossip, for it is late, but it may serve to make you understand the Boer mind, their anger with Chamberlain's rudeness, their disgust with the present administration, and their determination to prepare quietly to govern themselves.

I might write sheets about the new Legislative Council[9] and the farce it is, and the disdainful amusement it causes, but have no time, for I must prepare for my journey which I hope will afford material for my next letter home and be of more solid interest than this one.

Dorothy Bradby will like to know that I found about six bales of clothing, etc. lying in Cape Town, and Mr. Schultz has agreed to consign three of these to me *here* and three at Pretoria. He felt so ignorant of the state of the country that he was still retaining our money and now hopes to make it over to me when I shall have reported to him. £100 we agreed to give to Frankfort. The Rev. Thom from that heap of ruins came down to Cape Town and said charity had never reached them and told me that out of 800 houses in his village and district four remained. We told him on what lines we wished the money spent and he agreed that it was wise to do so.

P.S. The Rev. Thom was *very* quiet and afraid to *write* as he *felt* in the papers. Privately he told me much. While he was in Ceylon his wife and eight children were turned out of the parsonage. One of his girls was in bed with typhoid fever but was turned out and sent off with the rest in a cart while the house was burnt literally over their heads.

From the memoir

a) How vividly I remember my arrival in Bloemfontein and the warm welcome at Kaya Lami and Mrs. Fichardt's charming hospitality! Now it was a cheerful

195

household, for the beloved and longed-for daughters had returned from the Cape and there was laughter and music and much to hear and to tell. Two years had indeed worked wonders in that home and we little dreamed of the fresh sorrow so soon to follow.

As regards public affairs there was little to cheer. I found myself at once plunged into the reparation muddle.

b) After unearthing this bygone letter it is strange to turn to the papers and read of the cordial reception being given to the Prince of Wales under Hertzog's administration and to learn from your letter, dear Mrs. Steyn, of Mrs. Hertzog entertaining the Prince at tea in Groote Schuur, and of your own presence on the occasion.

58. TO LADY HOBHOUSE

Bultfontein Farm
12 June 1903

I am writing this in the bedroom of a Boer, and if being kindly treated makes you comfortable, then I am comfortable. It would be also impossible for any English person to be critical under the circumstances, for these well-to-do folk, the Rheeders, have been ruined by the war and I am in a burnt farm, where one half of the family is living in the waggon house and the other in the patched-up back rooms of the burnt and roofless house.

Mrs. Rheeder has given me her own bed and turned her children out of the room and she cannot do more. The ceiling is made of reeds, the floor covered with sacks and little goat-skin mats, and there are a few articles of furniture such as they have been able to scrape together since the peace. Not a penny of compensation has been received and the question, I notice, always raises an incredulous smile. In fact except two months' rations fetched eighteen miles from Bloemfontein weekly and the offered loan of oxen for ploughing after someone else had used them (which made it too late), no help whatever has been received. Even the Jingoes say in Bloemfontein: "The word 'compensation' has lost its charms."

We all had our meal together at 6.30. It consisted of coffee, bread, biltong, and confiture of some fruit which they eat with the bread and biltong. That was all. (This fare was of course luxury compared with that possible for the majority.) The man behaved and did the honours exactly like a gentleman, which in mind and manners he certainly is. His wife speaks good English and kept herself alive in Bloemfontein Camp 23 months by dressmaking.

My escort, Mr. Enslin, has been provided with a mattress on the floor of the adjoining room. He and I and Jacob, the Kaffir boy, started from Bloemfontein today at 10 a.m. Our four mules brought us along fairly well and we got here shortly before sunset, just time enough for me to make this rapid sketch of the farm.

We outspanned for lunch near a dam halfway across an endless veld, and though there was thick ice when we started, I was baked and scorched all day.

One of the women here was "out on the veld" all the war, and in consequence there is a group of pretty, healthy children, the youngest aged three, having been born in the war out on the hills.

To-morrow by 8 o'clock we are to be up and away.

It is a great jump from the luxury of the Fichardt's house, with fires, electric light and hot-water bottles, to the barrenness of this devastated place where I write by the light of the cart lantern with my feet upon my rolled-up bed.

I omitted to tell you that yesterday afternoon, before I left Bloemfontein, I spent with Mr. and Mrs. Fischer upon their farm, or estate if you like to call it so. It is so much easier to understand people in their own surroundings and Mrs. Fischer is a personage in her own domain, proud of her gardening and her plans for beautifying the place.

The house is built on the top of a kopje and is surrounded by orange trees hung thick with fruit, gold and green; paths and steps run down the sides of the hill to various avenues of gums and firs in the dale below and other little kopjes ornament the ground. Over the dam hung the willow trees still clothed in autumn gold. The farm is seventeen miles in circumference but the central position is so commanding, the air so clear, that you can see it all at once, and oddly enough it does not look large – in fact you look far beyond it some seventy miles towards Boshof, eighty towards Hoopstad, forty towards Brandfort, and so on. Size and distance are so deceptive here. The vegetable garden full of fruit trees – orange, lemon, loquat, almond, apricot and many others – seemed about four acres, but is in reality nearly seventeen acres and so on. Of course all the destruction wrought by the Military who occupied the farm was pointed out to me, and in the house itself only three rooms are now temporarily furnished, all Mrs. Fischer's furniture and silver having disappeared. And thereby hangs a tale which is both amusing and painful but too long to write. Some of his silver Mr. Fischer found in Government House where it was being used, and Mrs. Fischer's carriage came back from the same place. As to the rest of his silver – let us cast a veil. I learnt a great deal during my afternoon with them – of sweet veld and sour veld and all sorts of things that ought to be learnt in this country.

13 June. Strijker's Farm. We got here at 5 p.m. today. I got up early as agreed, for we were to start at 8 a.m., but alas! in the night the mules had stampeded and there was nothing to be seen of them. It took Mr. Enslin and the Kaffir hours to find them, so I occupied the time by sketching another ruined farm across the river. At 11 o'clock we got off and now after two days of driving, I feel myself dried up by sun and air, just like a piece of biltong.

We rested at noon at the Steenekamps' farm, where was the same story of no Government help – claims sent in but not a penny received; the people living in patched-up rooms at the back of the house; no oxen to plough with and another season lost. If they could but get £100 apiece *now*, it would be better than the full claims a year hence. But will they ever get anything? I begin to doubt it and so does Mr. Strijker, Field Cornet, of this farm, and so does everyone.

It is very difficult to write with a row of Boer children watching me.

For lunch we outspanned at the Aswegens' farm, and there found great poverty. They had not even coffee, and it is dreadful to a Boer to have no coffee to offer to a guest. I gave them some I am taking round with me and some rice. Ten days' rations (with an account) when they left the camp, but not another penny of help from Government have they had. No cows. Some hens which cannot lay for want of food. They live on goats' milk, hares and birds which they trap, and springbok which they shoot. You may ask how do they shoot without guns? Well, the answer shews what use may be made of the Constabulary – the only use I have yet heard that body of men to be. When they come to a farm with their guns this Boer says: "Lend me your gun and five or six cartridges and I will shew you how to shoot springbok and give you one."

Thus he gets his supply and keeps the official in good-humour.

The springbok are coming back again after the war and I saw crowds today racing across the veld. It is nice to see the veld being re-peopled with something living.

14 June. Boshof. I wrote the above at Strijker's farm, but the sun set, leaving me suddenly in the dark and I had to stop. There was more hospitality and kindness than anything else at the Strijkers', but I had a bedroom given me, while the entire family, parents and six children, squeezed themselves I don't know where. It was all quite clean.

I am afraid I hurt Strijker's feelings somewhat by bringing in my own *pad kos*[1] instead of eating his, but I was tired and hungry and *could* not. And when he learnt I intended to continue my trek on Sunday instead of staying over with him I fell low myself and brought the English people lower still!

Poor Strijker! such a handsome, sad-looking man, a real God-fearing Boer. The Peace was to him a bitter wrong on the part of his own people, a distrust in God which is like a sin to him. Satisfied, he says, he is not and can never be. "Give me," he said, "my Land, my Capital, my President, and take from me everything else and I will be satisfied. Never unless."

He thinks it is God's will to try them a little longer before giving them back their country. He is not a wealthy farmer, but a man whose character makes him of some influence and importance. In common with the other Boers far from the towns, he can get no Kaffir labour, for the Military have spoilt them with high wages and they will live near the towns to have a good time. We all sat round the table for family prayers, when he read to us in Dutch and prayed a long extempore prayer and all sang.

198

This morning early, about 5.30 a.m., I was awakened by more Dutch prayers in the *eet-kamer* (eating-room), and the rise and fall of the hymn singing. Just after the sun had risen we inspanned, and snatching what breakfast I could we departed in a biting wind, wrapped in fur rugs and cloaks.

I forgot to say that yesterday we called at Mrs. Venter's to breathe the mules as we passed. I went in and talked to the woman who was ill in bed. She told me how during the war she was standing on her stoep talking to Mrs. Willman, a neighbour, whose child of two was in her arms. Three English soldiers shot at them and a bullet went through the child's head, killing it on the spot. Another grazed her dress and passed in at the door. When the men came up and saw the dead child they said it was shot by the armed Kaffirs who were, however, much farther off, and young Venter, who also told me about it, said he watched the affair from the kopje near and saw the white men shoot.

We drove for two hours and then stopped to breathe at Piet Nel's of Palmietfontein. The house, which was burnt to the ground, is a large one, and Nel, having a good deal of money, has been able to rebuild it, and has made it very habitable. But he has lost heavily. He is an old man and the day they were captured was a bloody one and stands out in their memory. Hearing a column was near they prepared to flee to the hills close by and hide. The women were in an open cart and Nel was in front with the waggon of goods. The soldiers fired at the women in the cart and shot Christine Nel, a girl of fifteen, through the head. Nevertheless, though the girl was dying, the house was fired, the outhouses destroyed, 28 horses killed and between 4 000 and 5 000 sheep slaughtered in the kraals. The bleached bones are there still to tell the tale. They took me to the sheep kraal to see them – masses of white skulls and countless bones strewed thick over the wide kraal and piled in heaps upon the veld outside. All the bales of wool burnt too. They were all taken on towards Kimberley, the wounded girl dying on the way and she was buried at the next farm. In Kimberley Camp they were fifteen months. Another child died in the camp. Miss Nel spoke of Miss Mellor, our representative there, as very kind. This family has had no Repatriation help, has received nothing for claims, and could not get even the loan of a waggon from the board to bring out material for building from Boshof.

They were very polite and served us with coffee,[a] and so we left the Nels' farm and their bones behind us. But bones are never quite left behind – bleached bones lie everywhere, in groups or singly; the poor animals have been slaughtered beside every road.

We outspanned for lunch and built a fire at Quaggafontein where I visited the Groenewalds. Both of these (a young well-educated couple) spoke English well; the wife had been in Bloemfontein Camp with her two children who were always sick there and have never really recovered from it. They look white and ill now, utterly different from those hardy children I had recently seen who were always on the veld. The man returned from prison to find he had nothing but his wife and two children, but grateful to find them alive. He is now a tenant farmer at a rental of £36 a year and is living on almost nothing. Claims, as usual, sent in, but nothing paid.

He said some excitement was caused this week by the fact that 25 men in Boshof District had been compensated. But they were *all* hands-uppers supposed to be under the special protection of the British, and now they all seem to think it would be just as well not to have been thus protected. Coetzee, who lived close at hand, had claimed £250, and had been handed a cheque for £15, but as he had been given a month's rations on leaving camp, £6.15s was demanded back in payment for that, so £8.5s was his compensation. And he had surrendered under Lord Roberts' first proclamation! Ah! it makes them full of bitter mirth.

Another man, Mr. Schrinder of Kaalplaas, whom I saw later in the day, also under our protection, deported, sent to prison, brought back, sent to a camp, his wife also in a camp, his house burnt, etc. claimed for £1 450 and received £48! How they laugh!

Neither is the compensation equally doled out, for another claiming £96, and another claiming £50 both got £14. All these things are noted in their book. The *wilde Boer* in his own heart feels the three million pounds of the Vereeniging terms will never come his way.

Can't anything be done in Parliament to ensure a juster and quicker distribution of the promised help? Cannot at any rate pressure be put to get the payment of the military receipts for which Chamberlain has given his word? Money *now* is so needed. Already a second seed-time has passed and sowing cannot be done. Yet help should come to enable the sowing of mealies[2] and potatoes in the autumn months (the spring here).

They are wonderfully brave and plucky, and the Groenewalds' house was so exquisitely clean and fresh, all they could borrow having been spent on doors, windows, roof, etc.

We trekked on, and by and by, after losing our way, halted a few minutes at Kaalfontein. Here we went into the house and coffee was brought.

Mrs. Van Niekerk, a former widow, lived there and had a military receipt for £70 unpaid. It was for a cart and horses which they took, and Thorneycroft gave the receipt. She was in Brandfort Camp at the time. This is another instance to add to those already sent. Unfortunately, as I learnt in Bloemfontein, they purposely lose these receipts at the Office after the Boer has sent them in and get out of payment in that mean way. So now the lawyers are advising people always to insist upon a *receipt* for their receipt, so as to have proof.

Can't the Liberal members get these paid? This widow in question is not so much in want of money as are many, but she had *no* relative fighting and ought to be repaid. Since peace just lately she has married again and is now Mrs. Rheeder.

Directed by these people we went on, and after an hour or so saw a tree. It stood against the sky and beneath it was a bell-tent and beside it a broken house. So we got out to find water for the mules and three young men issued from the tent. To my surprise two were called Lotz, whose sister I have often corresponded with, and the third, Mr. Jacobs, late under the Free State Education Department. They said the place was called Enkelboom (one tree), and they were overjoyed to see me drop as from the skies upon them. They said it was 14 June, the anniversary of the day their Commando laid down its arms, and they were keeping it very sadly and only solacing themselves by reading my book, when lo! I suddenly appeared! They were very nice, gentlemanly fellows, and belong to an important family here. But not believing in Government loans or Repatriation Boards at all, they determined to club together and go their own way. Borrowing from other sources through a law agent they bought sheep in the Colony, are tending them themselves, and proudly showed me 450 lambs of this season. They are young, unmarried and full of vigour.

But I must finish, as this will catch the mail tonight.

From the memoir

a) Please remember that when coffee is mentioned it seldom means that berry. Many curious things masqueraded under that name. The coffee used ran at that time from 6d to 9d per lb.!

59. TO LADY HOBHOUSE

Boshof Parsonage
15 June 1903

My last letter broke off suddenly because my host told me it could catch the English mail if then sent. I had not finished telling you about my journey here. I passed a widow, *Mev.* Uys, with four children, quite without means and young. Mr. Lotz said she much needed help, so I gave her one pound of coffee and of rice, packets of which I had in my cart. Rations have been given, I find, to some of the very poor up to 31 May, but they have been told there will be no more. How does this square with Mr. Chamberlain's promise to Botha that we would look after widows and orphans, etc.? And to my horror I find these rations are far worse than those in the Concentration Camps, viz. meal and bully beef *only* – no coffee or sugar or milk, *nothing* but the two articles.

I saw widows here today who have subsisted months on only these two articles. One who has five children told me that for the month her rations were half a bag of meal and forty-eight tins of bully beef! Her plan was occasionally to sell a tin and buy, instead, a little coffee or sugar. I gave her some rice and coffee, but she is quite below par, evidently from lack of food.

The clergyman and I have been round together seeing some of the worst cases, and we have made plans for trying to put some of these upon their legs. Their

201

houses were scrupulously clean and neat. The little town has about 600 inhabitants, and all of these are impoverished, many destitute. About one-third of the town consists of ruined houses – doors, windows, etc. gone, some houses wholly razed to the ground, trees cut and fences broken. Many are living in one room of a house for which a window could be obtained while the other windows have sacks nailed over them. All this ruin gives a dismal appearance to an otherwise pretty little town.

I drove in just as the bells were going for evening service and the afterglow was throwing a charm over everything. So the parson and his wife who welcomed me had to hurry off to church, leaving me in possession of the house, and I was glad of rest and quiet.

When I looked in the glass I laughed aloud for my trek had so altered me I did not know myself. I am like the raw springbok biltong which is to be seen hanging in strings outside some farmhouse walls, and my hair is electrified and blazes when I comb it![a)]

We all agreed that mules are impossibly slow and tedious and will be a great waste of time, so I have dismissed my nice escort and his team, Ceylon, Bermuda, and the others (called after prisons), and from from here to Hoopstad I am to be handed on from farm to farm with relays of horses prepared in advance for me, Boer fashion. My arrival at Hoopstad has been wired and I shall find a welcome awaiting me.

I have learnt a great deal in this trek and would not have missed it, hard though it has been. It would have done Mr. Chamberlain good, and our roads ran parallel but his further south in a better district. This route, the Boers say, has not yet been disinfected!

I have left money with Mr. Bosman to help four cases – Mr. and Mrs. Britz and four children; I had known these in Kimberley Camp. He broke his leg in St. Helena. They are living in a bell-tent, but he bravely set to work to build himself a house; when he got to the roof he could not manage it owing to his lame leg. So to get the house finished and his family properly sheltered I have given him £10, and very pleased they are.

Mr. and Mrs. Jacobs: both in bed with pneumonia. She lost her health (or her chest, as she puts it) in Kimberley, he in India. Four children, saw both in bed, and their house. Relays of Christian Endeavourers are nursing them.

Widow Van der Merwe: lost two children and her health in Bloemfontein Camp. Five children left. A sewing-machine, but no means, no house; thinks she could see her way with poultry. Gave £8, five to buy poultry and set up, and £3 to cover rent of a room if procurable for six months. No clothes.

Widow Britz: four children; lost her health in Kimberley Camp; not had a penny for four years except £3.15.0 Rev. Bosman gave her. Two years in camp, one year here on rations of *only* meal and tinned beef. Quite destitute and can think of nothing whereby to earn a living but sewing. No one in Boshof well enough off to employ these widows. Decided to give her a sewing-machine and six months' rent and a little to buy extras, so below par.

I dare not give much here as the cases of distress are so much more numerous elsewhere, and even more acute.

Mr. Marais, the lawyer here, who has all the people's cases in hand and is called "the father of the district", drove me out this afternoon to various burnt farms, a group belonging to the Bosman brothers and Mr. Neethling's farm. They have fixed up a room or two for dwelling purposes in each case, and walk sadly in and out of their ruins and wonder when and how they can rebuild. We covered 25 miles in the afternoon, besides paying three long visits.

Mrs. Bosman is a splendid woman. She was in Kimberley Camp. She regaled me with sweet coffee and candied water melon, which is delicious. She has a "peace" baby which they tease her by calling "Kitchener". There is quite a crop of "peace" babies, I find, and in this district where most families lived in the veld and kopjes and eluded the troops, not only are they the picture of health, but there is also a whole set of "war" babies born while flying before the columns.

Mr. Bosman had that morning received the official refusal of his military receipts, which he presented me with and which I enclose. There are hundreds and hundreds of them all over the country sent in since Chamberlain's speech. Every day I meet fresh cases. The farmers feel they have been fooled at every turn, and the dissatisfaction grows deeper daily. They have been asked to send in the receipts they had from the Military, and at first they never doubted they would receive full payment. Soon it was found payment was not forthcoming. Then came Chamberlain's speech, saying military receipts should be paid, and with renewed ardour they were sent in. But to no purpose.

I have not yet *met* a single instance in which a man has received payment of his receipts from our Military, but I have *heard* of a few cases in which a small proportion of the money due has been paid, namely a widow who had £30 for two horses, and the case of a farmer Smidt. General Bruce Hamilton gave Mrs. Smidt a receipt for her whole flock and herds, a large number, and insisted on sending them to a military grazing camp, where he assured her they would be under British protection. After peace Smidt was told he should be paid in Bloemfontein. Arrived there he was sent to Hoopstad. Hoopstad said it had no money; and at last after endless waiting he is told only eight oxen remain, and is sent a cheque for £12.8.0 for the eight – oxen being worth in this part £25 apiece *at least*.

This is but one instance amongst hundreds. Every kind of excuse is made. In Chamberlain's speech I recollect no reservation being made but a simple statement that the receipts given by the British officers were to be paid. But it is not being done. What I want to know is whether such a receipt becomes void for any action committed by the receiver subsequent to the business transaction. Whether a man took up arms again after Roberts' Proclamation, or whether he didn't, is equally used as a reason for non-payment. The only ones that seem to have a

203

chance are those who *voluntarily* came into the camps as refugees and became mostly National Scouts. I am sending, probably under another cover, a few instances of cases where the receipts are disallowed. It is now twelve months since peace that they have waited and if only these monies could be paid (which are nothing like so large as the compensation claims) they would have something to help them besides *feeling* more satisfied. Now they feel the whole thing is *British* and that means unjust, dishonest, grasping and oppressive. I ought to say that many receipts taken to the Office are there conveniently lost, so that now lawyers advise demanding a receipt for the receipt.

Boer receipts. They have also been instructed to send in these and the English Government would make itself responsible. Nothing has so far come of it, and now it is said that yet another Special Commission is to sit on these receipts.

Compensation claims. This is a sore subject indeed, and the word compensation should never have been used. The whole thing has raised false hopes which are now dying away in bitterness. Why ask them to set down all their losses and get a lawyer's help and travel miles to and fro at great expense only to find their claims disallowed, or, at least, to receive only a modicum which is laughable! On the other hand, the losses are so great and the total amounts figure out so high, in spite of each item being valued below par, that it is impossible to suppose any sum of money could meet it. All feel it would have been far better to pay the receipts and let the further loss lie forgotten rather than have raised hopes for nothing. But large sums have been flowing into the hands of the worst men of each district – the National Scouts and members of the Repatriation Board, and so forth.

Here is an instance, the story of which is ringing from the Vet to the Orange.

Mr. Franz Marais was schoolmaster at Bultfontein. He was taken to Brandfort Concentration Camp, and after peace went to live on a farm at Paardeberg. His claim was sent in. His former home being Bultfontein, a letter was sent there saying he must come to Hoopstad to receive his claim. The letter was forwarded to Paardeberg, seventeen hours' trek from Hoopstad. It cost him £12 to get there and £2.2.0 forage for his mules while in this town. He waited three days, when he was told that after all the cheque had been sent to Bultfontein. He went on to Bult-fontein and found his cheque had been forwarded to Paardeberg. He got back at last and found a cheque for 1/9. They had paid only for some eggs, and summoned him seventeen hours' trek at a cost of £14 and more before he got home, and I hear he refuses to cash this cheque but will keep it as a token and memento of British justice and British red-tapeism.

This is literally true and it does not stand alone. Over and over again men are summoned to town from huge distances at great cost to give evidence about their claims, and arrive to find the offices shut and the board away on holiday or unable to see them. It would weary you to tell all the instances one hears. And then a sum is given which does not equal the expense of travel.[b] Over this wide country at every little speck dotted about, which means a farm house or its remains, there sits a man laughing bitterly and brooding over his wrongs, yearning for his President and his Free State law. What are they to do? So they ask. We must submit, says the very old man in the chimney corner. We must fight again to a finish, says the middle-aged burgher whose rifle is his only mode of expression. We must *say* what we think and organize and protest, says the young burgher, and the land will yet be ours. This is what I gather from countless stories and interviews.

I had a three hours' drive with Commandant Du Plessis, a singularly intelligent and thoughtful young man, who fought to the end. He thinks the dissatisfaction so great and the present situation so serious that he said he hardly liked to express himself about it, but he turns with relief to the idea of giving vent to their thoughts and feelings by political organization.

In so many small ways their lot might be made easier. For instance, the springbok have come back in their hundreds and are leaping and bounding over the veld. This animal is meat, clothes and furniture to the Boer, but he has no rifle to shoot them with. Mr. Marais pointed this out to Goold-Adams and suggested that farmers should all be allowed rifles of *different kinds* and then no danger could accrue, and the Governor agreed it was a good idea, but he did nothing. It is dreadful to see food at their doors and not to be able to get it.

Hoopstad. I reached here last night. Leaving Boshof as the sun rose I crossed the Vet River drift into Hoopstad just as the sun sank, about seventy miles' drive. I came fast, over no sort of roads, with relays arranged in advance, and only five minutes' pause to change the cart and horses here and there. It seems a case of drive, drive, forever drive here, and I hope I shall hold out, but the jolting tires one so that at last you fall asleep over the endless tales that every one wants to tell. I think I shall have to be very strict and put a limit, say twenty stories a day; and then there is the strain of hearing lots of them in Dutch.

This town is also one-third destroyed, and the church a good deal, and the corner stone taken out. The minister and his wife, who have given me a sweet welcome, had lost everything.[c] A burgher in the town had carved out the word "Welcome" in wood and put it on red silk and with a light behind it made thus an ornament over the front door to greet me.

I am too tired to write more. The person who most deserves help is what we should call the tenant farmer who has no land to offer in security and who stands penniless and stripped bare today. The lowest class *bijwoner* I think we must leave to the people of the place.

P.S. It will be rather amusing, but horses are so scarce that I have to pursue my journey to-morrow in company with a Jingo Africander member of the Repatriation Board. I stop at Bultfontein, five hours from here. I hope I shan't see so many bones. I'm weary of bones. The country is a sort of Ezekiel's valley.[1] Thousands of sheep on one side and hundreds on the other – skulls and bones white as snow,

205

and horses, horses, all along the way. They remind me of Tom Pearse's old mare "ghashly white" in our West-country ballad *Old Uncle Tom Cobbleigh and all*.[2]

From the memoir

a) The three days' trek had been most tiring and my face was sore and painful I knew not why. Having had no mirror for three days I was wholly unaware that the dry wind, together with sun, had turned me scarlet, and the skin of my face hung in ribbons. I was a complete *Rooinek!*[3] It was a warning, dear Friend, never to face your climate again without emollients. I realized that the shelter and protection of a kapje[4] was the perfect head-gear for your winter. It is sad to learn from recent arrivals from your parts that the kapje, so picturesque, becoming and protective, is no more to be seen. I cannot picture the Boer girl without it, and hope that common sense will restore it to use.

b) During this trek it became abundantly plain to me that the only wise plan for the Boer, whether *wilde* Boer, hands-upper, National Scout or Roberts' man, was to set aside all thought of "free gift", compensation, or military receipts, and face life trusting to his own arm and such help as Cape relatives might offer. The delay and despair were injuring their prospects more than any money from the Government could put right. I determined to advise all to forget it, and forge ahead as chance offered.

c) Being deeply impressed with the need of the people in and around Hoopstad I suggested to the mininster that he and the leading farmers should themselves make known their condition in a letter to the Lieutenant-Governor. They, of course, felt nervous under the Coercion Act.[5] I assured them it was not possible that harm could follow such an innocent step and I drafted for them the following appeal.

Keeping a copy of the appeal I suggested its use in other bad districts also.

> "TO HIS HONOUR THE LIEUTENANT-GOVERNOR
> "Your Honour,
> "Knowing your kindness and desire for the welfare of the people, we, the undersigned inhabitants of the vicinity of . . . venture to approach you in our great need.
> "Your Honour will be aware that the crops of last summer failed, and in consequence there was great scarcity of food. Following upon this has come an unprecedented drought. People are without money and without food, besides other necessaries of life. Full six months must elapse before another harvest can be reaped. At this serious juncture of affairs the Repatriation Boards last June closed their food supply unless cash was paid for such food. The people who need the food have not any cash at all. Scores of families

206

are without meal or meat, coffee, rice or any grocery. At this time there are no vegetables, and unless seed can be given there will be none when the season comes. People exist today on mealies alone and many eat only once in the day of those. Mealies are dear and they cannot afford much longer to continue even this nourishment. Between eighty and ninety families in Reitz Church District alone are in deep distress, an equal number in Lindley District, besides Frankfort and other parts. In addition the Kaffir population of these districts is in a similar condition, and has neither money nor food.

"We have collected money from friends in the Colony and had assistance from England and elsewhere, but though this has helped the people over the past months, such funds cannot continue and the outlook is deplorable.

"In view of the distress thus slightly indicated, we beg your Honour to re-open the supply of food and to continue it for six months till the reaping of the corn harvest.

"Considering the ruined condition of the country and the houseless and penniless state of those concerned, we would humbly submit that the food supplied to be of service *must be free*, and not considered a debt laid on the shoulders of the recipients – a debt which they can see no hope for years to come of redeeming. Rather than incur such debt many would prefer the utmost privation. Freely given their gratitude will be deep, hope will revive and they will have a chance of helping to restore the country to its former prosperous condition.

"We would further beg Your Honour that in order to ensure that all those in distress should be relieved and none overlooked, equal powers be given to the ministers of every district in concert with the Resident Magistrate to draw up a list of families, white and black, to be supplied.

"Trusting our appeal will receive the speedy and favourable response due to its urgent nature and in view of the acute suffering now endured,

"We have the honour to remain,

"Your obedient servants,

"etc., etc., etc."

60. TO LADY HOBHOUSE

Bultfontein
18 June 1901

One of these little towns is much like another, so I half fear if I write to you about every one you will weary of my letters. I set off today with Mr. Bridger, and we drove across an endless waste of sand from 9 a.m. to 4.30 p.m. Just an hour we stayed for lunch and water at a farm and I walked about to stretch my legs after the narrowness of a Cape-cart.

There was a row of aloes at some distance, so I went to look at them, there being nothing else. But when I looked over the hedge I saw it was a kraal and full of bones. I tried to count the skulls but they ran into too many hundreds; the little goat skulls with their horns looked disdainful, but the sheep gazed at me reproachfully through their hollow eyes. Beside the hedge was the black ruin of the house. Some way off was the new house rapidly put up of corrugated iron, costing £300, borrowed from the Repatriation Board, and inside were ten women with their tale of so many left dead in the camp.

Mr. Bridger, who keeps a store in Hoopstad, is very sad about the prospects of the farmers. He says there is almost no cash in the country and the hope of compensation has kept many a man waiting about to see what he will get to begin upon rather than mortage his land. It has done great harm.

He, Mr. Bridger, has known the people so long and lived amongst them all his life, and now men formerly rich come to borrow from him £2 or £3, as they are penniless. Yesterday a once well-to-do farmer *walked* forty miles into Hoopstad to see if he could buy some cattle, and unable to afford a bed he slept on the veld in one blanket. He must tramp back again as he came.

The Repatriation Boards are broken up, but in most centres certain stores of food remain over. This is often, as in Hoopstad, bad and rotten. The people have notice that no more will be given out, but I learn that the food left is consigned to the Magistrate who *may* use it for needy folk at his discretion. The worst is he seems always to be too busy to look into it, and the Dutch Reformed clergy are afraid to stir in the matter. I have begged them to try and work in with the magistrates. Unfortunately there is considerable cleavage and great timidity on account of the Peace Ordinance (Coercion Act).[1] Mr. Bridger said they could have done much better work on the repatriation if they had not been hampered by a continual succession of changing orders, if they could have been left to their own common sense. The Government Loan, he remarked, was practically useless, it was hedged with impossible rules.

Some great capitalist who would loan money on easy terms – say six per cent – is what this poor country needs. Hasn't Mr. Carnegie finished with libraries yet?[2] Business men say that money loaned up to half the value of the farms is a safe and good investment, and a good many Cape colonists with means have so invested. (The Chief Justice told me he had.) But it needs more than can be got from there. The average Boer is safe and honest in payment of his interest.

The hospitality of the D.R. ministers and of all is very great . . . Mr. and Mrs. Dönges, with whom I have just been staying, had every stick of furniture destroyed, besides every kind of worry, and have begun again with odds and ends of gifts from Cape Colony friends.

The minister here is in the same plight, but he is single so it doesn't matter much. He took me to see some of his poor. When I say *here* I mean Bultfontein, a place which had nothing but sunrises and sunsets to make one desire it. These are very beautiful. I was housed most sweetly by the store-keeper of English blood – a quiet, neutral man, who was repaid by the entire destruction of his furniture and stores – and yet is still quiet, though with his eyes wide open in surprise at his country's deeds.

They celebrated my coming by a kind of choir practice in the room adjoining mine, where a large circle of men and women sang hymns. I was faint with hunger and fatigue. It was *very* difficult to get horses to leave Bultfontein, and when at last promised, one fell sick, so then two mules replaced one pair. That arranged, harness could not be found, but the minister, who seems everywhere both a pope and a factotum, scoured the village and at last harness was promised by an "English Afrikander". Later this person discovered that the harness was for *my* use, and then he refused to loan it, as I had "done good to the Boers". So it was late before some less political harness was found, and we started. On our way we saw some sad cases. One was Jan de Wet, who with his family was housed in a stable that had no window and he lay ill with rheumatic fever. The trifle he had been able to earn as *bijwoner* was thus stopped. The stable where neither air nor sun could enter struck so dank and cold that I *could not* stay in it, and he lay there with that pain. I begged them to take him out and lay him in the sunshine which is so reviving.

Two children had died in the camp and the eldest daughter lost her health there completely, and now they are starving in their stable which was beautifully clean and neat and well arranged. Fortunately I had some food, which to him would rank as delicious, in my basket, and that I left with him, and I left some money with the minister to feed him while ill, etc. The Committee will understand that I never give the *money* but always leave it with the minister with written agreement how and for whom it is to be spent. The outlook in this man's case was particularly sad – and yet there are so many like it.

I was particularly sorry for Mrs. Cornelius Prinsloo who is first cousin of President Steyn. Such a fine good woman and with a number of children. Their house, a stone one, had been just completed before the war and is now a roofless ruin and they crowded into a stable. She and her children fled always, so they are healthy, but now so evidently underfed, she said they were literally without a penny and had to get food on credit from the shops. (This custom is growing and is pressing hard on the store-keepers.) She also confessed to being *very* short off for clothes and that was plain to see. I sent her material today. They have sown a little corn and just need to be helped and fed over the next few months till September brings the lambs and the crops will bring some return.

There are hundreds in just their case and most nobly and bravely they are struggling; living on meal and what they can trap on the veld. But I will not weary you with more cases now.

209

Brandfort

[Undated]

My team of combined horses and mules got me here through the dust by sunset, where the De Bruyns, whom I had met in London, were awaiting me. I wrote lately of the cost of travel, but as I told you I sent back my first cart and mules from Boshof as too slow, and since then I have been sent about by arrangement between the clergy and the farmers, consequently free, *for they would never take payment*. If this continues I shall get on all right, but though it is the custom I do not quite like it. The farmers always do what the D. R. ministers tell them; but at this juncture it is a great tax on them, the horses are scarce and poor, and forage a fabulous price. I insisted on paying the forage of this last drive, but *no more would they take*. If this habit continues in other places I shall get through very cheaply, but I do not want to count upon it.

The De Bruyns took me out today, calling. I was much interested in the Van Graans, two brothers on different farms. They are first-class superior farmers, who had been wealthy and their wives the best sort of Boer women. One of them was clad in a complete corduroy suit from England, of which he is very proud, and Mrs. De Bruyn had given them curtains to divide their stable into rooms. On his great farm he has now only sixteen sheep and these he bought cheap from a friend because they had scab which, by careful doctoring, he has cured. There are seven little mouths to be fed. He got seed potatoes from Repatriation for a promissory note, but the drought killed them. His brother lent him oxen to plough with, so he put in a little seed, but till it is ripe he has *nothing* to live upon. His beautiful house is in ruins, his blue gums all but two cut down, his fruit trees chopped.

But how he laughed, and how his brother laughed! There is getting to be something quite terrible to me in this laugh of the Boers which meets me everywhere. It is not all humour, nor all bitter, though partly both; it is more like the laughter of despair. We sit in a row by these stable walls and discuss every project possible and impossible, and then we laugh. Now and again the tears come into the men's eyes, but never into the women's except when they speak of children lost in the camps.

I would like to get this man a milch cow, but about here that is not procurable, so shall try for a few goats that the children may have milk and some for market and then their angora wool is so valuable.

I thought of giving a bag of meal to another man as he refuses to buy on credit and must be helped till the winter is over. His was a big house close to the old Concentration Camp, where his wife was put, while not a hundred yards away she saw her beautiful house demolished and every stone carted away while she might not save so much as a cushion or a blanket.

I passed across the site of the camp and was angry to see piles of the tents just lying on the ground in heaps exposed to sun and air, and rotting, yet I hear when the people ask for these they are told they cannot have them *without paying for them*.

This afternoon I visited the orphanage. Twenty-three children, six total orphans, twelve motherless, five fatherless. Mrs. Du Toit, the matron, was very sad, for *all* her own children had died in camp. They are struggling along, but food is such a price that it is hard to make ends meet. Government gives no help except that they attend school free and have their books provided. They are short of clothes now, but I think Bloemfontein Work Party will undertake this in future. Their food seemed so bare that I bought them some jam and some cheese. They are now waiting anxiously for a bale of Miss Bradby's clothes to reach them.

I hear of another orphanage just being started in the Colony, at Oudtshoorn, and I think we may be sure these children will be cared for. I am much more troubled about the children of the best kind of farmer, where the parents are still alive but too impoverished to pay for the schooling which is needed, and whose homes are too far away from any village to make use of the Government schools.

Another class which troubles me is that of the poorer-class *bijwoners'* daughters, big strong girls with nothing to do and eating their parents' heads off, and whom in England we should at once send to service. But service never enters their heads – that is Kaffir work. Yet the Kaffirs are so tiresome and the whole country is crying out for good servants, and here are just the girls for it. But they won't. They have but two ways whereby to earn their living – sewing and teaching. If near a town they will also *iron*, but they will not wash. That is Kaffir work.

These people I wholly refuse to help, because I am sure their old customs *must* be altered owing to the great upheaval the country has undergone, and pressure of circumstances must drive them to take service. When everyone wants to take in sewing and no one wants to put it out, it doesn't pay. I have begged the ministers' wives to use their influence to inculcate this idea into the girls' minds and some of them are willing, others again say they could not bring themselves to do it. In consequence (as they all agree) these *bijwoner* families are sinking to a condition below respectable Kaffirs. You must recollect, however, that there are two *distinct* classes of *bijwoners*, and the other class, though possessing no land, is often as well off and superior as the farmers are, and in possession of large flocks and herds, etc.; so when I speak of a *bijwoner* you must not always picture a wretched family.

I leave this class entirely on one side. Only the minister and his wife can deal with it, but I should like to see a school of domestic economy and training started for them in Cape Colony or somewhere.[a] I suppose I shall see the great mass of them in the Relief Camp, where I hope to be next week visiting Miss Monkhouse, etc.

Sunday, 21 June. Today is the shortest day and it might well be 21 December as at home. It is snowing hard and the people are struggling to church through the wind and wet. To have moisture of any kind is to me so delightful that I care not what form it takes. I walked over to the camp graveyard yesterday, and the

211

dryness of the veld seemed to scorch my feet. It was very hot in the midday sun and I tried to sketch the melancholy spot.

Mr. De Bruyn tells me the church offertories have never before been anything like so large as they have been since the war and the people so poor! There is a great recrudescence of church feeling, largely owing, I think, to the fact that the church is the one thing left of the old life, and so they cling passionately to it, and the minister has more power than ever. I wonder if any priesthood ever had such complete power over a people while at the same time being on terms of perfect equality with all their people. Undoubtedly their political influence is very great and no wonder the Government hates them.

Another curious thing is the abnormal number of marriages since the war. The widows and widowers won't remain lonely much longer, I think. In a country like this men *must* have wives, and if women won't take service they *must* have husbands. Mr. De Bruyn has in normal times about twenty couples in a year to marry, but now in the last two months he has married thirty-eight pairs. Mr. Bosman called one hundred banns the other day at one time and I hear the same story everywhere.

To-morrow I return to Bloemfontein, having learnt much on my first tour. I have been through the *best* districts, and now I must go gradually down to worse and worse misery and ruin. At least so I am told. I shall soon see. The money given me by the Committee won't last much longer; three-fourths is gone or promised already. Just *now* money is needed and could save many from being pressed by starvation into the Relief Camps. Two sets left Bultfontein for the Tweespruit Camp the morning of the day I arrived. Had I been two days earlier I might have saved them and found means to set them going. A few shillings here and there is *no good*, except in cases where a man has crops in the ground or some stock saved, then £1.15.0 for a bag of meal may keep him till the return comes. In the other cases it takes pounds to put a family on its legs with a few goats or sheep or something.

b) I left Brandfort early, driven to the station by old Mr. Erwee.[b)] He was one of the nine men in Brandfort who night by night were forced to stand, unarmed, beside the English sentries on the railway bridge as a protection to these sentries – on the same principle as that on which my host, the Rev. De Bruyn, had to ride upon the engines of the train. Of substantial build, Mr. Erwee is broad enough to protect at least two Tommies while presenting a good target for his countrymen.

Before I left, Katrina Fourie,[1] the girl to whom the Committee gave a year's schooling because our troops shot her through the arm (you will remember the case) came to see me. She was much improved and spoke very pretty English. Now she is able to earn her living by teaching and help support her widowed mother and family . . .

She brought with her the girl she is teaching to speak English – a Miss Els – who is known as a heroine in these parts. For she led the great meat riots in Brandfort

Camp and was sent to Bloemfontein Gaol for doing so. She is now eighteen and strikingly beautiful – flashing eyes and dazzling complexion. When she organized the riots, heading the procession herself with Free State banners aloft, she was but sixteen. When brought out of gaol to be tried she would only remark that she would do exactly the same thing again under similar circumstances. So back to gaol she was sent. A lovely vision – quite a model for a Joan of Arc – and I was sorry not to have seen more of her. She is living in a stable . . .

From the memoir

a) It has been most satisfactory, dear Mrs. Steyn, to learn from you that in recent years such a school of domestic training has been started and does prepare girls for useful domestic lives. But again and again as I dwell on the past one sees how that war ruin increased the number of "Poor Whites" and added immensely to your problem. Work is the only solution, but how much I wish it could be work on the land or in country districts and not of a kind that crowds people into the large towns and tends to the creation of slums. Avoid our bad European methods and mistakes if you can.

b) Fortunately the train could help me back to Bloemfontein from Brandfort and later to Thaba'Nchu to pay my visit to Miss Monkhouse, now in charge, as I believed, of the Relief Camp at Tweespruit. Today I learn the motor car is universal in South Africa, so all my difficulties about locomotion must sound to you prehistoric. You are fast overcoming both time and space. I wonder if the Cape-cart is ever seen now outside a museum. Anyhow, this generation of Free Staters will not be able to enter into the fatigues, slowness and difficulties encountered in my treks.

A day in Bloemfontein was very restful and my kind hostess gave me full directions how to keep the skin on my face in meeting your winter, cold winds and terrible dryness. She was full of interest in all I had to tell, and despatched me next morning to the train with Kaya Lami munificence of personal fodder.

62. TO LADY HOBHOUSE

Thaba'Nchu
[Undated]

The train starts early for Thaba'Nchu but though it starts it does not move much, and three and a half hours were wasted over these few miles. We passed the water-works where the big convoy was captured,[1] and there we had to sign a paper that the rest of the journey was taken at our own risk.

General Brand, son of the late President, met me at the station, but he thought it

213

too late to go on to Tweespruit today and so I have unwillingly had to idle an afternoon at Thaba'Nchu.[a] The place is chiefly filled with Natives, and the few whites are not in want. No ruined houses as the place was "occupied".

From the memoir

a) I remember, however, the pleasant surprise of a call from the English clergyman. His must have been a lonely life and he impressed me as longing to speak to some one fresh from England as a change. He presumed I was going to Tweespruit Camp where he frequently went, for he knew Miss Monkhouse and considered her in his parish – indeed he was trying to get her to teach the girls in camp the Church Catechism in Dutch.

The next morning General Brand drove me to Tweespruit, where I found Miss Monkhouse in a spacious marquee hung all round with birds' nests which she had collected. You will remember that this lady had been engaged and sent out by our London Committee for work as a nurse in the Concentration Camps. Matters had not gone very smoothly and finally she took service under the Government. Our Committee had, however, continued to supply her with clothes for the people and was still doing so, and they were anxious for some insight into the distribution of the gift and the further need. Miss Monkhouse assured me she found no need and indeed had quite a store not distributed. I reported the circumstances to the Committee, arranging that these much-needed clothes should in future be sent to other centres where they could reach the people.

As a camp, Tweespruit had nothing to complain of. Its hygiene was good. The Authorities had learnt something about camps by that time. But the tendency of these Relief Camps – whatever temporary use they may have afforded – was submersive and bad. For they were the very antithesis to repatriation, in fact they retarded it. They perpetuated many of the evils inherent in the Concentration Camp system and fostered the growth of a "Poor White" population uprooted from the soil. Though undoubtedly affording a slender help in a few individual cases, these cases could have been still better helped on their farms with the money spent on the camp expenditure.

63. TO LADY HOBHOUSE

[Kaya Lami, Bloemfontein]
[Undated]

I am in hot water. A letter from the Acting Lieutenant-Governor because I went to call on Miss Monkhouse without his permission. Such a surprise! Because I had thought everything and everybody was free now and never dreamed a permit was necessary, as indeed I do not believe that it is ... Somehow these men have got into the Martial Law attitude of mind, and they *cannot* get out of it, and treat people as if

214

they were pawns. He has issued orders not to admit me into Relief Camps, somewhat premature because I do not want to go. I had already made up my mind that my next useful work lay *outside*, among the isolated farms and the far-off ruined villages and *not* in the camps . . . I do not hear that any other person has had to get a permit to visit that camp which to all appearance is open as any village, and I believe my offence was simply that I was driven there by General Brand. They seem *desperately* afraid of all the Generals and of their influence . . . If it had not been for General Brand's good nature and his good ponies I should not have been able to get there at all. Anyhow if trouble comes out of this business I will cable . . . though I do not in the least know what they *would* arrest me for unless it be pure hatred arising from bad consciences![a]

From the memoir

a) From this letter to my Aunt you will see how heavy was the impression of the Coercion Act then in force and how, in my case, a burnt child dreads the fire. It was only 1½ years after my illegal arrest.

Tweespruit Camp was free, like a village, for people to come and go, and I was, in fact, under the impression that Miss Monkhouse was the principal authority there. The English clergyman had taken it for granted that I was going there, and neither he nor anyone else spoke of a permit being necessary, and as a matter of fact it was not. General Brand was most good-natured in driving me there, so you can imagine our astonishment when after driving into the open camp we were accosted and I must say attacked with extreme insolence by a man whose name I do not know but who said he was its Superintendent. What curious people do get put in positions of authority in war-time! The incident would not be worth recording (we had a perfect right to visit Miss Monkhouse) except that it resulted, on my return to Bloemfontein, in a letter[1] from Mr. H. J. Wilson, who was Acting Lieutenant-Governor in the absence of Colonel Goold-Adams.

Ah! dear Mrs. Steyn, what a thing it is to be "clothed in a little brief authority"! One must exercise it to enjoy it to the full. And Mr. H. J. Wilson had the satisfaction of announcing that he had issued directions to refuse me entrance to any of the Relief Camps in future, oblivious of the fact that I had neither desire nor intention of visiting them. He actually affirmed that it was usual to ask permission of the owner of a farm, whether private or governmental, before entering it!!! He recalled "the courtesy which you have hitherto shown in your relations with this Government" as a reason for addressing myself to him before "engaging in any enterprise". He forgot that the courtesy always shewn by me to those in authority had not been returned and my *only reason* for entering Tweespruit was to call on Miss Monkhouse, which anyone was free to do.

(I was, of course, delighted with this spontaneous testimony to my "courtesy".)

As time went on I found the Authorities were nervous at the influence of the Boer

215

Generals. Yet it was thirteen months after peace and the entire country was disarmed! It was the custom to drop the "General" and speak of Mr. Botha, Mr. Jan Smuts, Mr. Brand, Mr. Hertzog, and so on. Well, we have lived to see how futile was this effort, for in succession these men have become the leaders not only of their own country but of all South Africa.

64. TO LADY HOBHOUSE

De Wet's Farm[1]

1 July 1903

I am actually staying with De Wet,[1] having arrived at the uncompromising hour of 2.45 a.m. Only one train in the day stops at Koppies Station, and that, when it is not late, at 1 a.m. But it usually *is* late. It was a fine night but the new moon had turned upon its back and sunk into the veld before we left Kroonstad, so there were only the stars to tell me when I had got to the siding and to light us on our drive across the country. Two young De Wets came to meet me and I felt quite certain they would be able to see in the dark, which indeed they could. The eldest speaks very fair English, having been educated at Grey College before the war . . . We slunk into the house as quietly as we could and very glad of a warm bed after the cold drive. I was indeed glad I had collected countless wraps including a sheepskin rug recently presented. I am shocked to see how thin General De Wet has become, only a shadow of what he was in London. This is partly owing to hard work, he says, but also to a bad finger which for seven months has caused him acute pain. He ran a needle into it and part of the knuckle bone has worked out. Now it is better, and he is riding about his farm on the white horse[2] which carried him all through the war. This white horse was captured once, having had a lame leg at the time, but it wisely ran away and came back to its master. When the war ended this horse and his rifle were all the moveable possessions he had in the world.

He found his wife in Vredefort Camp, three hours distant (18 miles), and brought them here and he told me that then he himself climbed the little kopje above the homestead and sat down to look for the first time at the heap of ruins spread beneath. Houses, outhouses, kraals, wiped out; fruit trees cut down – not any tree left; a desert all round. Of all the money he had spent upon the place only the great dam remained.

He told me as he sat there on the kopje wondering where and how to begin came an English officer from the neighbouring camp and by way of a cheerful remark cried out: "Hullo, De Wet, how do you think your farm looks?"

"Pretty well," replied De Wet, "seeing it has been at the mercy of men who make war on women and children."

And the officer mounted his horses and rode off without another word.

Like all the other burghers De Wet is laughing. If he did not, he says, he should die. It makes him great fun. I do regret not being quick enough to catch all the

Dutch proverbs which spice his conversation, nor the humour which runs through all the family talk – they speak so quickly.

Mrs. De Wet is a second Mrs. Poyser[3] and goes about the house flinging out the same sort of stinging remarks, with the English Government and the English soldiers as never-failing targets for her wit . . . If you can picture Mrs. Poyser's anger and indignation if the French, say, had burnt all she had in the world with the exception of her sewing-machine and the endless material she would have found for her wit at their expense, then you have Mrs. De Wet to a nicety. Down to the smallest De Wet, whose brown eyes barely come above the table, every child of hers is carefully instructed never to forget the camps nor their sufferings therein. Mrs. De Wet is a character but has none of her husband's charm or power. He is quite delightful in his own house, though here as elsewhere seldom to be found. In the evening one can catch him at last for a talk, but not for long, as at 8.30 p.m. we all go to bed. I think he is having a very hard pull this year, the only help he has had was the comparatively small sum he got for his book and a royalty of 6d on each volume which has not yet been paid him. It was all he had to begin life upon again. Owing to the fact (first learnt in Cape Town) that *none* of Mrs. Koopman's letters reached him, and others on the same innocent topic were kept back two months, the building I despatched to him last year[4] has only *just* arrived, and instead of being able to shelter his family in December they had to wait till March and then get into this half-finished house . . .

Early in the morning there is coffee and about 9 o'clock they have breakfast of broiled mutton and bread and butter. At 1.30 more broiled mutton with boiled rice, potatoes and bread. Nothing to eat in the afternoon and about 7 p.m. a bowl of mealie pap eaten with hot milk . . . Vegetables and fruit are now unobtainable and there is nothing upon the farm. I do not think they could afford to buy anything but meal, and of course kill their own sheep.

Things will be better when the sheep-shearing comes and money comes in for the wool. De Wet is also selling some hay which, in this upside-down land, they seem to make in the winter. Anyhow, he is independent and in another twelve months may prosper again as the result of very hard work. But, as he says, hope is about all he has now.

He looks less oppressed with responsibility than when I saw him in London and hopes eagerly for the fall of "Joe" over this tariff question,[5] though he dare not dwell on it too firmly. The one question they all ask shows the one burning desire of their hearts: "Will a Liberal Government give us back our independence?"

It is hard to have to say I do not think there are any Liberals strong enough to do so, now Gladstone is gone . . . It is an unspoken deep hope.

The recall of Milner, says De Wet, won't do any good, for he is helping the Boer cause so ably by the anger he is creating in his own followers, so if a Liberal Ministry does recall him it won't have much practical though it may have some moral effect . . .

217

De Wet has glorious dams, the largest I have seen, about 1 700 yards long in a semi-circle. It looks blue and refreshing.

Yesterday while I was writing a Constabulary man came to the door. I wondered if he had been sent to arrest me! But he had only called to remind De Wet he must buy a gun licence to-morrow, which he already knew. They have to find errands for these men and they also like to keep an eye on De Wet. He is spending very calm and simple days, going from Chamberlain to his sheep and from his sheep back to Chamberlain, devouring all the papers but not believing any of them. They are thirsty for their independence, and not even Representative Government will satisfy them. That may be a step, but De Wet says he does not believe in half-measures. He and Mrs. De Wet send their greetings to all the English friends, whose sympathy they value. There are many little De Wets and tonight they took out ping-pong and proceeded to play on the long table. They play very well. My favourite is Betty, aged eight.

I am just finishing this before my midnight start to catch the 1 a.m. train. I shall reach Heidelberg to-morrow, having promised De Wet to attend Botha's great *Volks Vergadering*.[6] At first I refused, but I was strongly urged to go as men from all over will be there and they want to see me and I them, and so hear of each different district. The same day Milner is holding his Inter-Colonial Council[7] at Johannesburg, a thing no Boer takes any notice of – the really important gathering, the voice of the masses, will be at Heidelberg. The cleavage is complete. Each goes its own way, regardless of the other, or it would be truer to say socially regardless; politically each keeps a sharp eye on the other.

The Free Staters are very angry at Milner's pooling of the railroads.[8] Hitherto their railway has been a great source of revenue, and now part of it will go to pay the war costs, they think. This I repeat to you like a parrot, not understanding financial matters, nor exactly what it means. Their idea is that not until every step has been taken to which they most object will Representative Government be given.

65. TO LEONARD HOBHOUSE

De Wet's farm
[Undated]

Here is another refused and partly lost receipt.[1] To lose the receipts and claims seems part of the game.

Coming here I met Mr. Van Graan at Bloemfontein Station who said they had been summoned about their claim. It costs about 9/- return from Brandfort and they can barely buy bread. Time, too, is precious. It takes three days and the expenses in town. The satisfaction he got was to hear that the claim was lost and he had better come again on the 24th of next month. Hope deferred maketh the heart sick. He spoke with the deepest thanks of the bag of meal I had sent him through the Minister.

Botha tells me he has lately written to you[2] so I suppose you know more than I yet do about the Transvaal. He has arranged a great *Volks Vergadering* or People's Gathering at Heidelberg, and he has urged me to come, as numbers want to meet me who will not otherwise have the chance. So I have promised to go if it is kept entirely private. I think it will be a very interesting sight. Many of the rank and file in the Orange River Colony long for some such outlet. They did hold a protest meeting of farmers in Bloemfontein in regard to the Military Manoeuvres Bill,[3] but that was passed after all. "The Ayes have it", which is the refrain in the Legislative Council, is a joke in Bloemfontein, almost proverbial. De Wet, with whom I am now staying, thinks it quite useless to meet or protest. The time it takes they cannot, at this juncture, spare from their farms, and as to going to meet Milner on any deputation, he himself, if given the choice, would prefer to meet, I won't say who!!! Of the 52 Free Staters at the meeting with Chamberlain I am told not *one* would shake hands with Milner.

There is no doubt in my mind that my arch-offence was not in visiting Tweespruit but in allowing myself to be driven there by General Brand. In their eyes that made it a *political* drive and a *political* visit.

66. TO LADY HOBHOUSE

Pretoria
4 July 1903

This has been a full week and leaves me suffering from mental indigestion. I am with the Van Veldens[1] and as they live in a nice quiet house at the far end of Pretoria I can be alone a little while. Seeing so many people, and all full of past and present trouble, is very tiring. Everyone in this country has a story, and everyone wants to tell that story and wants to tell it to me . . . As soon as they are introduced they begin, and it would be a great disappointment if they were not listened to. When the stories are, as often, in Dutch, the strain becomes very great.

It was a wonderfully interesting day at Heidelberg where Botha held his first great meeting. At first I decided not to go, but both De Wet and Botha urged it strongly, for the burghers were looking forward to see me and for many it would be the only chance. I felt too that I should get much information and learn how best to get about the country. So I went.

It was cold leaving De Wet's farm at midnight, and I had a long wait for the train under the stars. It came at 1.30 a.m. and for Heidelberg I had to get out at Germiston at 6 o'clock. Here I found no waiting-room or anything hot to be got, so I took the first train on to Heidelberg. At every station we took up Boers and on all sides across the veld I could see them collecting, specks of dust trending towards Heidelberg.

219

I sometimes amuse myself by talking to Boers who do not know who I am, but simply recognize that I am English. In this way I learn their attitude towards the average English person – studied civility, combined with icy indifference – showing they have not the slightest desire to continue the conversation; there is a gulf between. Then, if I reveal my identity, they change all over, and beam with kindness and overflow with confidences and become delightful.

It shows me that the average "Brit" and the National Scouts have a chilly though civil reception. Indeed the Scouts, it is said, are growing miserable from a kind of melancholia. One committed suicide in the Free State a few days ago and many are thought to be tending that way. They say they are forsaken by God and man, life is hateful to them and they wish they could undo the past. A few have confessed such things to the *predikants* and been received again as penitents. There has been no excommunication,[2] as alleged, on the part of the Church, but the ministers and all feel that the Scouts are guilty of a crime against their country and must repent before they can again mix with their fellow-men. Thus they are treated rather like lepers and received into no house, and in this land where houses have hitherto been open to every passer-by it is a great change for a man to find himself refused admittance. They are feeling themselves outcasts . . .

Heidelberg is a really pretty little town nestling among hills, and with a good share of trees. The Boers were swarming into the station to meet Botha, expecting him by the train next after mine, but he had been too 'cute to trust himself to the trains of the day and had arrived the preceding night. His wisdom was justified, for General Smuts and Van Velden and others bearing important papers for the meeting were "accidentally" detained three hours *en route* and arrived when all was over.

It was by their train that Botha was expected to come, and as careful enquiries could discover no sort of accident on the line as alleged, they all feel sure the train was purposely delayed. This is too much of a piece with the kind of things done here to elicit the least surprise; to elude these tactics on the part of the Authorities taxes the *slim*ness of the Boers, and they laugh at it as part of Milner's game. It was very bad taste if it *was* done of malice prepense, for Botha had written to Milner telling him openly that he had called the meeting and hoped to have a succession of them. So there was no secret about it. But as he was already in the town all was well, and, mounted on a very fine horse, he joined the Boers at the station and headed this strange procession to the market square. Six or eight Generals rode beside him and his staff, and as many as had horses followed riding, others crowded into carts, spiders and buggies of every description, many walking and a few cycling.

The Boers are undemonstrative and there was perfect silence as they plodded on through the red dust, but you felt they were one and all in desperate earnest and their welcome to Botha the more real because of its voicelessness. Poor, hungry-looking, shabby – they had come from far and near, many tramping from thirty to

220

fifty miles to be present, others again clubbing together to get a cart, or one lending harness, another an animal, and so helping each other.

I had never seen a mass of Boer *men* before and certainly was deeply struck by this strange procession of impoverished men – their seriousness, their silence, their orderliness, their perfect good humour, and their deep sense of the importance of the occasion. Some of the ladies of the town accompanied this procession in carriages, and I was with Mrs. General Viljoen and Mrs. Broers (daughter of our old friend Professor De Vos).

So with a thick veil of red dust over us all we reached the market square, at the higher end of which stands the really pretty stone church with a long broad flight of steps leading up to it. At the top of these steps Botha stood, the address of welcome was read and he replied, speaking in Dutch, loud and clear, to the patched and shabby crowd surging round. On the outskirts stood little groups of the Constabulary, looking wonderingly on at the people who took not the slightest notice of them. Three hundred extra soldiers had been sent to Heidelberg for the occasion; too funny when you think what a quiet set of men was gathered together, no pushing even as in a London crowd.

As the hall engaged for the meeting was quite too small, we went to a garden, the whole crowd walking to it without scrimmage or fuss. There, under the trees, tables were set for platforms, and the burghers who could not get near enough climbed into the trees and hung upon the branches like swarms of bees.

Botha spoke on various points:

First: The amnesty promised by Kitchener not yet fully accomplished.[3]
Second: The education and language question.[4]
Third: The money supposed by Chamberlain to be in Europe.[5]
Fourth: The thirty-five millions saddled on the Transvaal.[6]
Fifth: The labour question.[7]

Resolutions were passed and for three hours I listened to Dutch speeches on these topics. Once or twice there was a laugh, but on the whole the affair was intensely quiet and almost solemn, like a church service.

When it was over, Botha told the throng that they were all invited to a garden party where he was going to introduce them to me. And then they cheered almost like Englishmen.

So we walked away like a huge family party to another garden where in less time than it takes to write it the Boers, though there was *no* grass in the place, sat down, in number about two thousand. Sandwiches were handed to them, and coffee. It was great fun, but I had to sit at a table with the Generals. I had been very unwell and giddy all day – I think it was partly the altitude – and by this time I was feeling very ill indeed.

Then they said the orphans had arrived and the garden party was going to begin. Out of the medley a square suddenly formed, on one side of which the orphans were drawn up in a phalanx, eight in a row. Opposite to these sat the eight Generals, with me at the top. On another side stood the Rev. Louw, the minister, with his workers, and in the middle was a little tree wreathed about with pink tissue paper. Ill and dizzy I wondered what was going to happen next, when eight small orphans stepped shyly across the square and pinned eight minute bouquets on the eight Generals' breasts. They were tiny children and it was a pretty ceremony. Botha rose and spoke to the children and told them about their fathers who had fallen. I thought it must be all over when two more orphans, the minutest of all, walked up to me and gave me a basket of flowers. Botha then introduced me to the people. Those two thousand men cheered as I stood up beside Botha and clung to the little tree for support. Everything was swaying round me. Then Mr. Louw said he was going to address me and someone would interpret his remarks. Wishing to shorten the ceremony lest I should faint, I said quietly to Mr. Louw: "Ek kan verstaan, danke", not thinking anyone would hear. But the crowd caught the words and screamed and cheered with delight.[a]

Mr. Louw's words were touching and unforgetable. I thanked them all in a few words which the *Transvaal Leader* has twisted into nonsense.[8] The little tree again came handy to steady and help me through. It was all ended with the Doxology and a long prayer, and then when I ought to have spoken separately to the burghers I had to decamp and have a couple of hours in bed. But only a couple, for I was invited to a dinner-party[b] and it began early. Our hosts were the Bezuidenhouts, a family whose beautiful home is in ashes, so they are living in a town house *pro tem.* Mrs. Bezuidenhout, smiling and dignified, had been one of the inmates of Merebank Camp sent there because her husband would not surrender on 15 September 1901 (in accordance with Kitchener's Proclamation). I think all the ladies present had been in camp.

It was a delightful gathering and I enjoyed it very much, getting talk with Mr. Louw, Botha, General Viljoen, Commandant Alberts, Pretorius and others, with whose names the war has made us familiar. I made plans for my future treks. The number of invitations I get would take a twelvemonth to get through.

Coming away next morning was also interesting, because a number gathered at the station to see us off, several coming from far to see me, "because they were mentioned in my book". Botha and several others conducted me straight to Pretoria and we got dreadfully snapshotted at Heidelberg Station.

When the train drew up who should jump out of it but the Charles Ashbees of Chelsea memory, as astonished to see me as I to see them. They are rushing round South Africa in a month.

When we reached Pretoria I found to my surprise not only the Van Veldens but a whole host of ladies to meet me – all very smart while I was in my shabbiest travelling clothes, as usual, and peppered red with dust.[c]

It was a great hand-shaking business and the orphans brought a bouquet of violets and roses. The Rev. Bosman honoured me by coming, and indeed it was the élite of old Pretoria that turned out to welcome me. Between them and the new élite a cleavage exists, and so far I see no way of bridging it.

These ladies are preparing a garden party whereat everyone can have a chance of meeting me. They asked the Government to be allowed to hold this in the Burghers' Park. It was refused, but they were told they could have had it if they had not said it was for a party in *my* honour.

I am now busy arranging my Transvaal treks to the North, South, and East. I hope it will be the warmest first[9] for without my fur cloak, lost at this station in the bustle of arrival, I cannot face the cold of the High Veld. I must find means to get meal out to the distant solitary farms. They have no Relief Camps in the Transvaal but instead Settlements, five or six in number. Apparently these have the same object in view, viz. to submerge the people, for they get into the clutches of the syndicate or whoever runs them and cannot get out till the uttermost farthing is paid.

From the memoir

a) The incident came back to my mind when recently I read of the pleasure occasioned at the Cape by the Prince[10] saying his few words in Afrikaans. You love the foreigner to recognize your language above all things. In that you are like other people.

b) I remember thinking a Boer dinner-party offered many good hints. The size of the table did not limit the number of the guests but all were asked likely to make the party pleasant. This turns out usefully where servants are few or bad, for the guests who can't sit down wait upon those who do, and afterwards relays fill the table. Moreover, men smoked before dinner instead of after, so that they could come and be agreeable to the ladies when the meal was over instead of breaking the party in two as in England. Smoking only began again quite at the end when it was time to come away. Whereas in England, as I expect you know, it has now to be endured even sitting round the table at dessert, and no matter how sick and ill this horrible habit makes you feel, there is *no escape* and it has to be endured.

c) It was in fact during this visit that I heard with amusement that people said: "We can't think what the Boers can see in Miss Hobhouse, she can't even dress !!!"

67. TO LEONARD HOBHOUSE

Pretoria
6 July 1903

I hear many things which would interest you, but I forget a great deal, and hardly find time to write the rest. However, you are all so taken up about other matters in

England now that I sometimes wonder if there is much use in writing information about South Africa.

I hope you received safely Botha's letter for publication,[1] his hope being that you would receive and make it public just at the time that he said the *same* things at his meeting at Heidelberg.[a)] I feel a little sorry for Botha. Of course he has Smuts' counsel and support here, but otherwise he seems so left alone to bear the burden of his people. De la Rey has retired to his Lichtenburg district and is unget-at-able, and De Wet to his farm and the O.R.C., and Botha, who would gladly have gone and attended to his private affairs, cannot do so but just must stay here in Pretoria. Numbers of men come into the town and always want to see him, and he has on his mind not only the widows and orphans but the deaf and dumb, and all in need.

It is he who is plodding on about the promised amnesty for the rebels (about fifty Colonials he tells me still in Europe unable to return home)[2], and every section of the Boer community looks to him for leading and advice. He is perplexed now about the families of the men (nearly 800) who will not sign the declaration and are kept in India. Their wives too have begged them, but all in vain, and numbers of these families are destitute, and what to do for them no one knows. Botha thinks the Government is bound to support them. Charity has helped them, but that cannot continue. Fortunately some of the irreconcilables are unmarried men like Charlie Theron, who has vowed he will shave neither head nor beard till the independence is regained.

So Botha has bought a house here,[3] and a very nice one it is, and will bring Mrs. Botha to it this month. He must work his farm through an agent. So far he has not sold any of his land but tells me he must do so shortly. I gather he has raised money upon the land to buy this house. He will be very comfortable there, and I do not think the people will let him go and bury himself in Standerton.

Mr. Van Velden, with whom I am staying, has also a military receipt unpaid. It is a small amount, perhaps £30, but they are very poor and it would come in very handy. The Military resided in their house and destroyed most of their things and they have not claimed compensation for this but thought they would be satisfied with the receipt. It was sent in after "Joe's" speech about the "bank notes", but people have realized now that his speech was only intended "for the British Public".

There is a whole set of things classed as above. When Arthur Fichardt was arrested in Bloemfontein just after the occupation he said to the officer: "But you cannot arrest me, I am protected by Lord Roberts' Proclamation."[4]

"You d--d fool," was the officer's reply, "don't you know that was only for the English Public?"

In like manner it is said now that a "British officer's word is as good as a bank note" is for the English public.

In town today I met the Rev. Bosman in Church Square with a large number of black-coated, serious men assembled outside the church. They were all his elders and deacons come in from the districts to discuss the Education question, and how they are to checkmate the Government and have an education and teachers they can approve. To be allowed to elect their own school committees is all they desire. The rest would follow. Already in this Colony the Governemt has started farm schools in marquees with English teachers, and there is unrest and dissatisfaction. Private schools are springing up apace.[5]

General Smuts was telling me today much about the Settlements. The one at Potchefstroom is put by the Government in the hands of a Jew of the worst speculating character, Wolff Carlis by name. Part of the town commonage of Potchefstroom has been given him, besides other ground, and Andries Cronjé, the National Scout, has also been given land. The Government has supplied this Jew with all he wants and has handed the people entirely over to him. He takes half of whatever they produce, and they must buy at his stores and his prices, and in a thousand little ways they are at his mercy. He is making money out of his speculation (financed as he is by the Government) and the people are in a tight place out of which they cannot come and where they are so bled they cannot rise to their old independence. It is another form of submersion camp.

The Settlement at Vlakfontein near Heidelberg is in the hands of a syndicate and run in the same way. The Rev. Louw told me about it and equally bewailed it. Major Leggat, who used to have prominent work with the old Camps, is in some way overseeing these, but whether on behalf of the Government or the syndicate I cannot tell. As Smuts says, the people *must* be got out, but it may take years to do it unless money comes to set one family after another upon its legs. They are being pauperized.

In this colony also there is relief work in the form of road-making, and the families follow along with their husbands in a sort of moving camp. In this work the men get 5/- a day, bare food as prices are here.

Smuts is a very charming man, clear-headed and clever. His wife is, as he says, intensely bitter, but he is not – he is only absolutely indifferent, neither hopeless nor hopeful, he says, but feeling himself quite apart from and out of it, neither part nor parcel of the country as it now is. He does not wish to get rid of Milner, for, as he says, if the British Empire is satisfied, he is. If Milner is the best fitted for the post that England can produce, well, so be it. The Boers feel sorry for England's judgement that it should be so, but he does so ill that he does well enough for them.

Smuts is very busy in his profession and planting trees, etc. to undo the wreck the Military made of his garden, but he hardly cares even to criticise the Government policy, it is a thing on one side with which they, the Boers, have nothing whatever to do. General Lyttelton's tents are close to his house and he says the Lytteltons are very friendly and do not at all approve of Milner's goings-on, but Mrs. Smuts does not care to see much of Lady Lyttelton, nor does she accept her advances.

Such English as really tried now to make friends with the Dutch (like Lady Lyttelton) unfortunately go the wrong way to work and make the breach wider.[6] *First* they have not the slightest notion of what the Dutch women have suffered; *secondly* their continual attitude is *how* glad the Boers must be to have British rule at last!; *thirdly* these smart women out from England keep saying: "*We* can forgive and forget – why can't *you* forgive and forget?", forgetting entirely the difference. As the Dutch reply, "We never did them any harm; what have they got to forgive and forget?"

It is all too near the time for any sort of general mixture of the two sets – it will and must take years.

The Van Veldens are very poor but very hospitable. So they are obliged to take a boarder, and a Mr. MacDonald[7] is the individual. He is head of the Agricultural Department and edits the agricultural journal. He is nice and gentle, but his whole underlying attitude is that now everything is going to begin at last and he is going to teach farming, etc. Mr. Van Velden writhes under it, but wreathes with smiles when he learns that already some of the old laws have to be re-enforced.

Mrs. Van Velden is very delicate, but notwithstanding does all the work except what a black boy can do. I have decided to give her an easy chair out of my Refurnishing Fund; she has not one in the house and she gets so tired and fagged out and has lost so much.

This afternoon I am to spend at Harmony, the Van Warmelo's[8] place, and to-morrow the Reception they have prepared for me takes place in the form of a garden party to which a general invitation is issued. I think I told you they applied for the Burghers' Park for this affair, and it was refused because it was *in my honour*. Another nice little snub for me – and not the way to conciliate the Dutch or make them believe the English forgive and forget. A private garden was at once offered, in fact several, so it does not matter, and once more the Dutch go their own way with one more black mark registered against the Government.

I am busy trying to organize from here my various treks. It is *very* difficult. I start Middelburg way on Thursday, 9 July.

I paid a visit to the orphanage here today. There are 48, 25 being boys. It is decided to remove this orphanage shortly to join Mr. Kriel's at Langlaagte.

I was shown over it by a girl of about eighteen called Lindequist. She is herself an orphan and has a small brother and sister there as well. I happened to ask her from which camp she came and where her mother died, and she replied with that dead calm which is such a curious characteristic of the Boers, "My mother was shot dead, before we left home, by the English."

Not a muscle of her face moved. Then I questioned her and with Mr. Van Warmelo's help got the facts clear. Her father was *bijwoner* to Mr. Pretorius of the farm Luipaard's Vlei in Steenkampberg, Roos Senekal. Their house was about a hundred yards from the farmhouse. Her mother left the house at 3 p.m. to walk across to the farm. The English soldiers were near. As she did not come back at 6 p.m. they went to look for her and found her dead between the two houses shot through the body. Presently the Tommies came to their house and they asked them why they shot their mother. They acknowledged the deed and just said

226

women must not walk about. Then they burnt the house and carried off the family to Middelburg Camp. The old father of 73 was ill, but he too was carried away and died almost at once from the shock. "That is why we are orphans", she said with impassive face. I asked if she was sure it was not armed Kaffirs who had shot her mother, but she said, "No, white Tommies."

Lily Rautenbach, now Mrs. Boshoff,[9] has come from Vereeniging, and I have written down her whole history and sent it to Dorothy Bradby. I hope it will reach her safely and that compensation will be obtained for her.

8 July. I am just off for the Eastern Transvaal and must leave this for Mr. Van Velden to mail on Monday.

One of the committee who received me here is a Mrs. Smit, whose husband was formerly Railway Commissioner. A son of hers, Mr. J. S. Smit,[10] is studying at the Temple and she would be so thankful if you would ask him to call and stretch out the hand of fellowship to him. His address is: 43 Ryecroft Road, Lewisham, S.E.[b]

I am too tired after my Reception today to write, so must hope for a lucid interval at Middelburg. Mrs. Fawcett[11] is here, lecturing.

From the memoir

a) During our journey to Pretoria Botha told me he had sent a long letter to England describing the sad conditions in the old Republics, material and political. This letter lies before me now, Mr. Courtney having communicated it to *The Times* which published it in July. In it Botha had spoken of the "dismal failure" of Chamberlain's visit and how he had taunted them with ingratitude though the Government was spending fifteen million pounds upon the country.

"Everybody," wrote Botha, "has been asking how and on whom this vast sum of money has been spent, for there is certainly no public evidence of it . . .

"The work of Repatriation is a complete and dismal failure . . . The Repatriation Boards have been struck with a strange powerlessness, for which their composition in the teeth of our advice has been largely responsible. Lord Milner's despatches about the huge success of this Department are nothing more than a fairy tale . . . These Boards are still travelling over the country and wasting the public funds in order to apportion the 'free grant' of three millions. No wonder that the burghers have given up all hope of ever having anything given them out of this 'free grant'. Although this relief was in the Vereeniging conditions of surrender, I have not yet met a single burgher in the Transvaal who has received anything free or gratis . . . all relief having to be signed for or secured by sureties or promissory notes."

It was clear that his experience in the Transvaal was similar to mine in the Orange River Colony. [. . .] In the quiet of the Van Velden's house I set myself to study existing affairs in the Transvaal, and arrange for a trek in the country.

227

The first trek was eastwards and I went armed with a letter of introduction from General Botha.

b) How curious, dear Mrs. Steyn, to read these last words and to know that this same young law student is now, 22 years later, High Commissioner in London for the Union of South Africa and the husband of your niece!

68. TO LADY HOBHOUSE

Witpoort, near Roos Senekal
12 July 1903

I am writing tonight in the house of a Jew (converted), a wayside store-keeper, and though a good man and, I believe, glad to welcome me, one feels instantly the marked difference between him and the true Boer whose hospitality bursts out all over him and makes every inch and package of you feel welcome. I have a room, too, which is nice and makes me feel grateful, as the house is being put up again. There is a clay floor and windows without fastenings, etc., but still a room, and that is everything. I have so much to say, I feel I cannot write enough to put the right aspect of things out here before people at home. It would take reams, for in every district matters are so different, and only some statements are true of every part.

After my reception party at Pretoria I started for Middelburg. This reception was a great success. I told you Government had refused the Burghers' Park because it was in my honour, so we had a private garden and it was made to look very pretty with decorations, and a carpet and sofa were placed under some loquat trees, and there I stood, while a solemn address was read to me sealed with a big Transvaal seal and the *Vierkleur*.[1]

After I had replied to this in a very halting fashion, the young ladies "*Vereeniging*" presented me with a basket of flowers, and then all the Pretoria ladies were brought up by the committee one by one and introduced. It was a long and trying ordeal, but the day was so perfect and the people all so pleased that it was impossible not to enjoy it, which I did throughly. I told them I represented a large section of English people and received their attentions and honour the more gladly on behalf of all these.

There were speeches too from Generals Botha, Beyers, Smuts, etc. and the Rev. Bosman spoke very beautifully. He said there had been much talk of "conciliation" (*verzoening*) and Mr. Chamberlain had come to do it, but there was a kloof, wide and deep, and I alone, he said, had found the way to make the bridge which spanned it. Sandwiched between these speeches was continual photography.

Kruger's granddaughter, nice Mrs. Jacobz, lent me her carriage, which indeed has been at my disposal throughout my visit. I only wish it was the pretty time at Pretoria, but it is winter, and few flowers and much dust.

When I reached Middelburg in the afternoon another array of women was drawn up on the station to greet me and a good sprinkling of men. These as usual begged me not to trouble about my things, but, remembering my lost cloaks, I felt obliged to keep one eye on my various belongings and could only give one therefore to my hostesses and so lost half their names.

I was of course taken to the parsonage, and there, instead of being allowed to enjoy the lovely afternoon on the wide stoep, was forced into a terrible *sit-kamer*[2] where all the party flocked and sat round on stiff-backed chairs, and all conversation fled from you. Seeing hours of this in front of me, I proposed in desperation a visit to the camp burying-ground, and was driven there by Mrs. Theron, who used to visit the camp in its worst days till prohibited.

The memory of that camp will never fade from the people of this generation. The sun had dipped and the full moon was rising in splendour when we reached the spot. There are three burying-grounds, but this was the largest; rows upon rows of children's graves, most bearing the date of that fatal July written on a bit of paper and put in a glass bottle. As old Mrs. Van den Berg said to me today, the memory of those five months of 1901 and of that July in particular will haunt her to her dying day.

I was glad there was just light enough for me to make this rapid sketch[3] – the sky already purpling for night and the after-glow vying with the moon to gild the long dry grass of the Transvaal winter. It was dark when we returned to the parsonage.

Mrs. Burger, the minister's wife, is a dear little woman, with a face whitened by the trouble she has been through; a very typical parson's wife. The parsonage is large and was much envied by the Military who made every effort to oust her, but she clung to her home with tenacity. Seven times she was ordered to go, and seven times she faced the officers and, timid woman as she is, point-blank refused to leave, for her baby was coming and she could not face it in the unknown. But at last she *had* to go, because she would not consent to bring in her husband who was chaplain to the District Commando, and with her six children and her coming baby she was sent to Howick Camp, all seven being plumped down in a bell-tent bare of everything. Then her house was filled with Army nurses and rang with dancing and music night and day. It was left in a state so filthy she could hardly believe white people had lived in it.

Middelburg is much annoyed by the presence of a large garrison of some two or three thousand troops, and the iron sheds for the men and the smart villa-like houses put up for the officers form a town itself. But the Government, which consists largely of youths from England who neither know or enquire into the laws of the country or the rights of the people, have made the mistake of placing this garrison on the commonage or town lands which in Middelburg is really church property, and on which the townfolk who bought erven or lots have the inalienable right of grazing, etc. In consequence a meeting has been held and a protest sent up, and the elaborate garrison will have to remove itself farther away.

The same stupid thing has been done in planting settlers on the town lands without enquiry if there was the right, and these too will have to be removed and compensated for loss sustained in settling there. Another grievance is about the water. The owners of erven bought them with water rights, which water never failed from a good dam. Suddenly the water failed and they were told the Military were "improving" the dam. This was followed by a tax collector asking for 7/6 a month water-rate, but the water was gone! They had let the water run away at an important time, the gardens were ruined for lack of it, and a 7/6 rate imposed per month.

At Roos Senekal the people took their farms from Government *with the right* of cutting wood on the commonage, about twenty thousand acres. There is plenty, but now an order has been issued forbidding them to cut wood and at this moment of ruin when not a roof is to be seen in the village or district the people have to *buy* wood from neighbouring farms. These things and scores like them make dissatisfaction on all sides . . .

14 July, Belfast. I could write no more the other night from cold. Now I take up my parable in Belfast with what strength remains after a trying, tedious, painful but I hope useful trek. There are two things that never fail in this land – sunshine and kindness – all else lacks (off the railway line). The question for me is how long I can exist upon these immaterial things. At night, when the sunshine we live upon has faded, and the kindness, overflowing as it is, can perforce only take the form of accommodation so dreadful one shrinks from the thought of it, then my heart sinks and I feel I must give up and come away. With sunlight things seem more bearable again and so I go on. But now that I have reached Belfast I feel as if I could hug the railway line and will never go out of its sight again. Yet I must try to carry out my plan for Carolina and Ermelo.

Unfortunately the neuritis which began to trouble my right arm last winter and which the voyage had cured has been brought back this last week in acute form, and every jolt of the waggon (which is continual) makes the pain worse. Perhaps if I could get some rest it would be better, but there is, so to say, no comfortable moment in the whole twenty-four hours of these trekking days.

The Boers, partly by custom, partly, indeed largely now, by neccessity, eat so much less than we do, that I am underfed, and though I carry some food with me I am ashamed I have to confess I must supplement their meals. At night I chew a little biltong and crack up some bread which has dried in this air beyond cutting with a knife.

When I left Middelburg we stopped first at the house of Mr. Smit, who had been a blacksmith and owned sheep, horses, etc. His tools were all taken, besides everything else, so he could not begin work again; he and his wife were filling up the time with influenza. She I fear with lung trouble resulting from a bullet wound in the chest which she showed me. An armed Kaffir had shot her through the window. I resolved to talk to the minister about getting them some tools.

I had seen in Middelburg the orphanage with 54 children in it, about 18 of whom were total orphans. They were dreadfully in want of stockings, so I left money to buy them a pair apiece. The orphans in every place are alike, a set of boys and girls not at all downcast, but contrariwise holding up their little heads with pride because their fathers and mothers had died for their country. They enjoy a reflected heroism.

To visit an orphanage is a great handshaking business even in this handshaking country, for every orphan naturally expects to shake hands with one, even down to the tiniest mortal. So also in the farms from top to bottom you must shake hands, even babies of one and a half years will solemnly walk up and put out their wee hands to be shaken. I find it wise to keep my gloves on till I am well ensconced in a house.

Our outspanning that morning was at a beautiful farm, Wonderhoek, where the people who had been very rich were living in a shanty beautifully appointed (so to speak). Five-hundred fruit trees had been cut down *below* the graft. I roughly sketched the views and we went on passing equal ruins to right and left upon the way. This Transvaal District is well watered, beautiful streams here and there, so the face of things is far in advance of the Free State, but on the other hand not a sheep or goat is to be seen. It is more of an agricultural district and their first efforts must be in that direction. Consequently the people have no fresh meat, and few can afford the bully beef which is so dear and so unsatisfying.

It began also to be very hilly, and the dust thicker by inches than any I had seen and the four wretched mules could hardly get along and the old carriage (a victoria I suppose I must call it) which hung in ribbons was heavy to draw. Towards the end of the day after stopping for coffee at other farms we came to a mountain which had to be descended and they thought it would be safer for me to get out, for, as they said, as I had come so far it would be a pity if I had an accident. Gladly enough I consented and the vehicle tumbled itself down somehow, shaking things out as it went.

We were to sleep that night at the Haupts, everything having been arranged for me in advance by His Highness the *Predikant*. Mr. Haupt is a deacon, and woe betide the deacon who does not obey the minister. It seemed to me a large order to have given a poor man reduced to a stable, to house three guests – myself, an escort and a driver – and feed us and provide conveyance for me for two or three days. But the Haupts are the best of people and it was done. Their welcome was hearty and the stable and its effects wholly at my service. Their big stone house lay a wreck close by. I said a few words of sympathy, but Mr. Haupt said he was quite satisfied, he had given all for his country and done his duty and his conscience was clear; *he* had not burnt the house. He would leave regret for those who had. There was a large party at supper and my heart sank at the thought of the night. I said I had my bed and would sleep outside, but this produced great consternation. Mrs. Haupt is a delightful woman and she was greatly distressed. As near as I can give it in English she said, "I have no longer a large house and large rooms, but I still have a large heart and I cannot bear you to sleep outside." After that I felt it would be ill-mannered to press it, so to bed we went in the stable which was exquisitely clean and full of draughts.

Sleep was not possible, of course, and at 4 a.m. Mrs. Haupt got up and made coffee and woke us all up in her night-dress to drink it, then blew out the candle, and to bed again. Such a work of supererogation! I rushed out of the stable as early as I could and sat on the hillside to sketch the house, and when I came back they were singing hymns and giving thanks for food, clothing and shelter!

We visited widows and others round that morning, and in the afternoon started for Roos Senekal. The country grew more and more hilly and as we neared the village the sun was setting on the mountains of Mapoch's and Sekukuni's country, stretching range beyond range away to the North.

The Boers had assembled for *Nacht-maal*[4a)] and the scene was most picturesque. There is not a roof in Roos Senekal except that which shelters the Constabulary, so tents and waggons were the order of the day, grouped round about the ruined church. As these things are now scarce only about a fifth part of the usual congregation was assembled. The Rev. Burger of Middelburg came out to meet me, and his assistant, a young Mr. Krige.

They had a tent ready for me, and said furniture for it would come, and sure enough it did, for *Boers* don't put *English* people into empty tents! Bedstead, chair, table, washing things, candle, mirrors even, came tumbling in, all given from the things they bring for *Nacht-maal*, and all Boer-made but convenient. Everyone crowded round, but I found I was considered the guest of the Van den Bergs who fed me throughout my visit. Mrs. Van den Berg is looked upon as the "great lady" of the district, and a very striking personality she is. She retains grateful recollections of Mrs. Rendel Harris's visit to Middelburg Camp, and spoke of her several times. Afterwards she was sent, this stately old dame, to Merebank Camp. She has given me her diary.

The parsons, myself and Mr. Haupt were entertained by her in her tent, sharing their quaint meals. All round Kaffirs were busy cooking the evening meal, and the mules and oxen were busy munching mealies and grass.

It was a happy family-party kind of Concentration Camp, where everyone had brought what was necessary for comfort.

It was biting cold in the tent that night, and the Kaffirs chattered so one could not sleep. I had spent the previous evening seeing 'cases' and when at last the sun got up and got into my bones I went round with the clergyman to pay more visits. He was particularly anxious about a man called Schutte, whose wife and one child had died in Middelburg Camp and who was left with six children under fourteen. He himself had been badly wounded and reported dead, his wife having mourned for him four months. But he recovered, though his wounds (one in the arm) have left ill effects. He has struggled on since the peace thirteen months ago, but heart

232

and hope were failing at last and Mr. Burger feared he was one of the many who must sink without instant help. His house was in ruins, his flocks and herds all gone and no money. Repatriation has given him food twice since peace, *with the bill*, and he dare not run up more debt, even if it were possible to get it, but since 1 June cash has been demanded and he has none. The Repatriation also advanced him twenty zinc sheets and some beams to build his house, but his arm is too bad. Now and then he can get a day's work at 5/- equal to about 1/6 at home. Now this man is a deacon and respected in the district but quite helpless now *unless helped*.

His claims sent in for compensation were £400, a very moderate sum considering all he has lost, but not a penny has yet been paid to any farmer of these claims, and when it does come it may be 6d in the pound, not more. All hope about the claim is waning, not a single penny of the three millions has yet been given to the fighting burghers or prisoners-of-war. What little the Repatriation has dealt out has all to be repaid – it is not a gift. Where is the three millions? is the daily question. Who and what paid the salaries of the big Repatriation Boards with their travelling expenses and their train of Kaffir servants? It is all a mystery, but one thing is plain, men who had little have now large banking accounts, and the farmers are not helped.

Mr. Haupt told me men who bought animals from the Repatriation were not allowed by the custodian of the animals to choose which they would buy. Any sort of creature they were forced to take *unless* they gave large bribes of £2 to £5. He bought his six mules at £24 a head, but to escape having worthless animals foisted on him had to give £2 to the man who looked after them. That day that man so received £17 and the next £50.

The horses supplied frequently die shortly after purchase, and the Boers say it is because they are poisoned with the arsenic which our Military use to make them fat and sleek, but if it is not continued, feed them as you may, they die soon. The Madagascar cattle they have imported the Boer thinks nothing of. They are very small and have a hump and are little good for these roads. The stories of the time they take upon the road with comparatively light loads are numerous, and if they are slower than the ordinary Boer trek-oxen, then they must be slow indeed! Those worthy creatures go about two miles an hour.

But I have wandered from Mr. Schutte and his personal troubles to the universal grievance of the repatriation.

The Rev. Burger and I sat in solemn council over his case, and after elaborate calculations decided that hardly less than £50 would put him on his legs again. That is the amount in which the Phipps Fund[5] was paid out, and the result is successful. Every family that received it has been set up. On the contrary the Boer Generals' Fund[6] has been perhaps necessarily paid out in sums so small, £5 or £6, that it has no permanently useful effects. So I left this sum in Mr. Burger's hands for him, and if he gets £10 from the Compensation (6d in the pound), he will be repatriated. I have dwelt at some length upon his case because it is typical.

When such burghers as still had frock coats saved by their wives in the clothes' chests from the general conflagration had donned these and gone into church, I sat outside to sun myself and sketch some ruins. I preferred listening to the long tuneless hymns at a respectful distance. The church benches all being burnt, everyone carried in a chair or stool or box or what he could find to sit upon. The windows too are gone, and so had "unbleached" nailed over the openings, and the roof clung on here and there to the cracked walls. Afterwards I went in to see the place and found a table set at one end, so we all dined together in the empty ruined church as the bell-tent was so small. It has been very hard indeed upon the people of Roos Senekal, for they only began to settle there after the Kaffir war eighteen years ago, and had but just reached a period of prosperity when the war came and ruined them completely.

We left in the afternoon; all the people crowding round to kiss and cry over me. Mrs. Van den Berg was unhappy because I had made my own bed, and she wanted to do more for me, much more. She talked a great deal about the camps in her mystic Transvaal way, but ended by saying the "Man Above" had allowed it, so it must have been for the best.

That night we passed at Witpoort where I came upon the first Government farm school I have seen. It was a marquee and there had been two English teachers, but they could not stand the lonely life and had left. A Dutchman, Mr. Van den Poel, had come to take their place. People liked these girls, but they could not speak the language.

It is so beautiful to see the streams of water in the Transvaal, so different from the dry Free State, and at Witpoort there was a lovely stream and a big water-mill which we English had thoughtfully broken to pieces!

Next day we passed over break-neck roads through the mountains to Dullstroom. I called upon a National Scout as we passed, my escort saying, "Come away, come away", as if he were infectious. Further on I saw some ruins (in fact I get quite annoyed now whenever I see a roof, it seems so unnatural and well-to-do). I was passing them by when I spied a white garment, and thinking there must be some people I went and explored.

I found two dear little girls, the eldest about nine and able to talk a little English. She took me to the back of the ruins where a lean-to roof had been fixed, and in the dark, windowless place I found her mother just confined and not able to rise and greet me. Mr. Britz, her husband, had fought to the end and was penniless, but had gone to the ruins of Dullstroom to see if he could get work and food. I had some rice and flanelette in the waggon, which I left for herself and the baby. The nine-year-old was in charge. I heard afterwards that Mr. Britz had been very brave.

So with patience and pain we lumbered on. At the very top of the pass was a grave with a big white cross standing against the blue sky: Captain Angus Menzies of the 1st Battalion Manchester Regiment, who fell near the end of the war. We got out and visited it. We generally do to all the graves, and singly or in groups we pass very many. There was something about this one, lonely and aloft, that struck me as very pathetic.

Then we fell down upon Dullstroom, or what remains of it, among its green fir trees. First I had to confess to the Boers that I was too hungry to talk to anyone till I had refreshed, so we made some cocoa outside the ruined church. It was a pretty village, and is a pretty though desolate ruin, and there were some sad cases. The men who come and tell you all about their suffering neighbours are often as badly or worse off themselves, but they don't say so, and you find it out afterwards by chance.

Here in Dullstroom the people were full of the trials of an old man, Kroon, who lost his wife in camp and can't get over it, and returns broken-hearted to a deva-stated ruin, and is sick and penniless and no one to help him begin again. The neighbours out of their own penury were helping him with a meal here and there, but said they could not continue this and he must starve. I sent a bag of meal to him, and as he is a Hollander must try to see the Consul in Pretoria about his case. He was prosperous and had sent his son to Holland to study for the university.

But there is no room to dilate upon cases. We passed that night close by at the farm of Piet Taute, the Veld Cornet,[7] a fine Boer specimen. He had been very rich and prosperous. His house had been burnt down *three* times, and he had been trying, himself, to rebuild it. But cash for roof and fittings had failed, and it was, though large, in a terrible confusion, awful to sleep in, the holes in the roof blowing blasts on your head all night. His wife was stamped with the camp look, a look quite absent from her old mother who had kept in the hills all through the war, and looked hale. She was a Colonial woman and could speak English, and looked on my visit as a godsend. Her confinement is imminent, and no cash. There was a large party of us at supper and so little to eat. These meals are mostly long graces. She sat reading her Bible all the afternoon, she said, for she felt heavy and miserable, and she had stumbled on the words about the righteous never being forsaken nor his seed begging their bread, and it cheered her to see me come.

Evenings like this one in the farms, the entire family and workmen sit round in solemn parliament and discuss the situations, political and material. "Die toekomst is donker" (the future is dark) is the beginning and ending of it all.

The Boers are watching narrowly, wide awake now for every sign from England of hope for themselves. Recently there was a cable, probably false, of a joint ulti-matum delivered by England and Japan to China to oust Russia from Manchuria. You should have seen the light on Boer faces that day: would it bring deliverance for them?

But I am digressing from Piet Taute's home. It was a terrible night to me, but next day the sun came to cheer us. Mrs. Taute gave me some bread spread thick with lard to take with me, and I got her husband, Oom Pieter, to come outside with me and very shyly offered him some money to finish his house and help in his wife's illness. And then this huge Veld Cornet broke down and began to cry! He

235

was *so* glad, *so* thankful. Mind you, he was a man of position and had had large possessions once. I was not quite sure if he would be offended but was glad I summoned courage to offer him help. For the more I see the more certain I feel that the one necessary thing is to set the big landowners going and as life is arranged in this country all will then follow well and poverty will vanish.

I got at last to Belfast, the highest town in the Transvaal. As we jogged along I dozed a little in the waggon, and when I opened my eyes I thought I saw our Cornish Kit Hill with the chimney on the top, but it turned out to be the monument in memory of 1881, where Dingaan's Day is kept in this district. Now the rails and pedestals are broken and destroyed and the names of those who fell in that war defaced. It is situated seven thousand feet in altitude. Hence we dropped five hundred feet down upon Belfast and surprised that little community, upsetting its kind plan of receiving me at the station (as intended) with an address of welcome. But Mr. Coetzee, whose guest I was, called the town together next morning and then the address was read to me, and I spoke to them, and the children of the "Privaat" school came and sang. Tea was handed round and then everyone began to tell their respective stories.

It was a busy two days while I waited to see if I could go on to Carolina and Ermelo, but horses were not to be found, nor other beast to take me there. I was not sorry to come back to Pretoria and rest and digest my tour, for the pain in my arm grew more intense. I am not sure if it is the high altitude or the nervous strain or being underfed or what it is. Anyhow, I think it will be wiser to go north and leave the High Veld for a few weeks later.

It would be hard to sum up the total impression of ruin and devastation, of privation borne with pluck, of silent determination, which was made by the whole tour. Even in Belfast, an occupied town, forty houses are wrecked, twelve or fourteen of which were the property of my host, once a member of the Volksraad. Had he but those houses now, the rent would be something upon which he could live, and he is, in his poverty, trying to help the more helpless. It was sad to see his beautiful farm six miles from town, every tree on which he had planted himself, and he took me there to mourn with him over the ruin and the wreck of his life's work in laying out the place. His wife was in Middelburg, Merebank and Belfast Camps. Relations of hers on a farm near by, Frederic Maré, had their graveyard torn up by the soldiers and the coffins were left lying about and the bones of their little children. But this has occurred in many places.

I end this at last in rest and shelter in Pretoria in the house of General Smuts.[b] He was asking after his old Cambridge friends, Mr. Gooch,[8] Mr. Masterman,[9] and others.

From the memoir

a) I was recommended by the Rev. Burger, who had gone to Roos Senekal for

236

Nacht-maal, that it would be well for me to follow him there, as many burghers would be gathered. He had kindly made all arrangements for me, so I took his advice and journeyed thither.

b) The physical relief of leaving the High Veld was very great, for neuritis is like a hell-fire within you. I was welcomed at Pretoria by General and Mrs. Smuts and taken to their house in Sunnyside for the first of what proved a long series of visits. Their hospitality is too well known to require word from me. It was so simple and easy and so overflowing. Santa was the baby then – a "peace" baby – and now, as I write, she is touring England on her wedding trip! All my baby friends are grown up, and they were so charming I should have liked to keep them "as they were".

My arrival was saddened only by a telegram which I found awaiting me. It announced the death of my kind friend and hostess, Mrs. Fichardt of Bloemfontein, so recently left in apparent health and strength. The message was already ten days old, or I should have left at once to pay her the last respect and share the family sorrow.

It was a restful, quiet time and General Smuts was clever at "beating off the wasps" in the shape of people who only called on me as a curiosity. Thus I had time to shake the red dust out of my garments and prepare for the next journey.

It was during this visit that I first met Deneys Reitz, a son of the well-known ex-President, now Senator Reitz. Deneys had just returned from Madagascar, worn out with malaria and his clothes hanging loose upon him. He very kindly escorted me to the station when I left, ill as he was, and in after days I often saw him as he worked his way to professional life.

69. TO LEONARD HOBHOUSE

Sunnyside, Pretoria
[Undated]

I wish you could meet him [General Smuts]; he is so cultivated and clever and full of fun, though underneath of course he is broken-hearted at the loss of his country. Having been so long in Cambridge and London he is entirely like one of ourselves, and it is curious how the English folk with grievances come to him, and General Lyttelton and Sir Arthur Lawley and other officials ask his advice . . . Even Milner, as long as he stayed in Pretoria, constantly sent for him and they had the straightest talks . . .

I prophesy a great future for Smuts; hopeless as he now is I feel sure he is the man respected by all parties and *feared* by Milner, and one day English and all will look to him to get them out of the muddle into which the country is drifting. But Smuts will work, not only side by side with, but behind Botha loyally, till someday I think his superior education will force him to the front . . .

General Smuts learned on Commando to see the value of a simple life, and so they go in for "plain living and high thinking". The "high thinking" is most enjoyable, and the memory of it will last. They are unconventional and charming people, and I feel thoroughly at home with them.

70. TO LADY HOBHOUSE

Passing Nylstroom
21 July 1903

I have been having a long and deeply interesting talk with Commandant Swemmer, late Medical Officer in the Boer Commandos and before that an official of the Free State. He accepted the post of Assistant Chairman of the Compensation Claims Board, and he has told me much . . . He first refused the work until he was assured that none of the expenses and salaries of the Commission should be paid out of the three million, for he could not bear living in such comfort on money so sorely needed. He was assured that these running expenses would be met from a fund specially set aside in the Treasury.

His work is to assess all the claims of the faithful burghers. It is indeed a long business, and it must be nearly four months longer before all will be examined and assessed, he says, and the moment of distribution comes. A *fixed* tariff has been set them from high places, and on that they *must* work. For instance, a man has a small waggon, new – he had just given £180 for it – he moderately claims £100 for it, but £40 is the fixed tariff sum for all small waggons new or old. As a shilling in the pound is the utmost limit they are likely to receive, he might get £2 for his waggon. In like manner a cart (often worth £60) is assessed at £20, and £1 will be compensated. Slaughter sheep are assessed at 10/-, so 6d will be got for them, and so on. There are hundreds of cases where not only nothing will be received, but less than nothing, debt will be incurred. For instance, a man claimed £120, a very poor man. Under assessement it dropped to £18. His share may be 18/- and he has to pay the Law Agent three guineas for expenses!

Fortunately the better class have ceased to believe in or hope for compensation, but the poorer and more ignorant still look to it to make a start, and the long-deferred day when the claims are paid will be one of bitter wailing through the length and breadth of the land. It has been a cruel mockery to raise such false hopes, attended with an elaborate machinery, and publicly to ask men to send in detailed claims and summon them repeatedly at cost of time and money to give evidence, and all for a pittance, for nothing, or for worse than nothing. Fourteen months have they waited already.

With regard to military receipts, Mr. Swemmer tells me that five rules about their payment were issued. The chief of these was that if any relative (son or brother) of the *man* or *widow* holding the receipt continued on Commando it was to be disallowed. Some of the receipts given by the officers were merely jokes which those who could not read English were unaware of. For instance, from a widow was

238

taken her all, oxen, sheep, etc. and a receipt for some hundreds of pounds given, signed with no name but "Don't you wish you may get it". This paper she had treasured two years and brought it safely up at last to find it a hoax.

Another elaborate receipt was drawn up for a host of things of value, and the amount written 3/11¾d by the officer.

This work of considering claims has given Mr. Swemmer a wide insight into the comparative destitution of the districts. He and the other members of his board say 85 to 89 per cent of the High Veld districts are unable to help themselves, are destitute; in the West and North-West 50 per cent; and round about Pretoria and the railway 25 per cent.

The financial condition of the entire country he considers deplorable, and nothing can stop the general ruin but instant loans at 5 per cent. He tells me the Government loan was stopped on 7 March last, after only £150 000 was loaned. He thinks it was going too easily and quickly, and was too helpful. This sum was only in the Transvaal. Now men can only borrow from the Land Settlement and at far stiffer terms. I do not know what sum was loaned in the Orange River Colony, but judging from all I have seen and heard *less*.

I specially asked Mr. Swemmer if he considered the claims sent in immoderate, as it is often said, though those coming beneath my notice had seemed to me very low. He said their moderation was remarkable, 50 per cent were far below par, 25 per cent might be cost price, but at any rate out of 1 260 claims personally investigated by himself only two were immoderate.

One reason for this moderate charging is that many have been told that if they ask reasonably they are more likely to be paid, not knowing, poor things, that it will be divided so much in the pound, and so the more pounds, the more shillings.

Another thing pressing hard in most cases is the law that house rent and interest on bonds during the war must be paid. People will be summoned to do this in January, it is said.

Mr Swemmer thinks the financial condition deplorable, and says it is imperative that help should come at once in the form of cash to help the farmers.

The facts he gave me of the fraud and bribery connected with the repatriation work are most distressing. I cannot remember much of it, for I did not write it down at the moment. Only one striking instance of Captain Morgan, who was Director of Civil Supplies, a soldier who came out with Lord Roberts. On one occasion a speculator wanted to bring up 800 head of cattle from the Colony, and sought permission for trucks, etc. It was refused until he promised to give Morgan £1 a head. He had hoped to make £3 on each, viz. £2 400 profit, but £800 was handed over and he only kept the £1 600. This Morgan made over £70 000, but it became too notorious and he was at last dismissed. He does not stand alone. In so many centres trials have been held over Repatriation men for frauds.

Have I said anything to you about the families of the Irreconcilables still in India?[1] I have come across some in dire distress who have urged their husbands, but urged in vain, to come home. Could their case be brought forward at home, and the Government be urged to afford the unfortunate women and children support, or could they be sent to their menkind, and the same released to start afresh in some other land? Something should quickly be done; friends, poor themselves, have helped them along, but in the impoverished condition of everybody this cannot continue.

I am also wondering if pressure could be brought to allow rifles to those Boers who, like those at Pietersburg and Louis Trichardt and those at Roos Senekal, live on the borders of Kaffir countries. Recollect these blacks have recently been armed against them, the Boers have been at their mercy, and the Kaffirs are now living in luxury with flocks and herds, while the Boers are in penury around them. I found men at Roos Senekal who *had* (to earn cash for bare bread) to leave their wives alone on this frontier region often for six days together.

And now I am at Pietersburg. A desert devoid of water separates Louis Trichardt from its mother church.[a] The people there are living on vegetables only, no meat and no meal. And yet meat in abundance is round them had they but their rifles, or money to buy the shot guns which can be licensed. Hares, guinea fowls, pheasants, *bok* of different kinds are plentiful.

Mr. Du Toit[2] and I (he drove me about today) hit upon a plan for helping to secure food for the people in these parts. He suggests each ward should be presented with a gun and 500 cartridges. Each farmer should receive ten cartridges and the gun should be passed on from one to the other all round the ward. Each man would shoot a springbok or some birds, and that would keep him a month till the gun came round again. I think this might be tried in one ward to see how it worked. As this is *boschveld*,[3] springbok can be followed and killed with a shotgun, which they say cannot be done on the High Veld. Failing this plan, no meat will be eaten by the bulk of the people in these parts for two years to come.

I was delighted with the scenery all the way from Pretoria[b] – ranges less stiff in outline. Pietersburg, too, surprised me by its size and importance, and the number of its beautiful trees. If you could forget the sea was so far away it would be a delightful place to live in. The Boer, however, prefers that the sea should be far away, so it just suits him.

The clergyman kindly took me in. South African parsons are hospitable people, and as they keep open house their houses are usually roomy. The chief people of the town assembled and read me an address and I made a speech and we shook hands all round and drank coffee. On these occasions it is usual for the guests all to contribute a cake so that the hostess has not too heavy a burden. I shall have quite a collection of addresses when I have visited the whole country. Of course this neighbourhood is full of Kaffirs in a semi-barbarous condition, clothed largely in beads and copper wire, and their chiefs inhabit the very beautiful kopjes on all sides.

From the memoir

a) I was, indeed, a bit staggered by what I heard of the difficulty of reaching Louis Trichardt. It was seventy-two miles, two days' journey across a desert, and for two reasons I felt it unwise to attempt it. One was the acute pain in my arm always increased by driving, the other the cost of getting there – money which I felt would be better expended on meal to send to the people. Moreover as the Rev. Kriel had only returned thence the previous day, it seemed better to act on the information he brought.

b) A pleasant incident of that journey north was the halt at Warm Baths where Mr. and Mrs. Potgieter, with whom, you will remember, I had travelled home on the *Saxon* in 1901, came to greet me as I passed. She was bearing a large bag full of delicious *pad kos* for me – a fowl roasted and still warm from the fire, bread, butter, eggs, etc. and a dozen delicious oranges from their own trees gathered with the leaves upon them. All was packed as only those who live in hot climates know how to pack food, and tired and hungry I set to upon that fowl and never made a better meal. They wanted me to stay later with them and take baths for my bad arm.

I do not now recollect if I stopped at Nylstroom either on my way north or on returning, and I find no journal letter concerning it. Many have been lost, and I did not write very fully till I reached Pietersburg. . .

The great warmth of that lower and more northerly country was very grateful to me. I was surprised to find so considerable and thriving a town, indeed it was full of prospectors and miners and capitalists from Johannesburg running back and fro, for there were rumours of gold, etc. in the adjacent hills. There were beautiful gum trees and fair-sized villas and much building going on. The country after Nylstroom was very pretty with rocky tors, the rocks covered with brilliant lichens like a coat of many colours.

71. TO LEONARD HOBHOUSE

Pietersburg
23 July 1903

I sent today's letter in two halves to Berta and Barbara and now begin the continuation while waiting for an assemblage of Pietersburg folk who are to address me, or something of the kind. Rather a pity I think with the eight hundred graves so near by of those whom my representations failed to save!

During the war Colenbrander[1] was in command over this district. Some call him a half-breed, in any case he is an adventurer and bore a bad reputation from Rhodesia. There were also those officers Morant, Handcock,[2] and Captain Tailor, besides others. My information has come from several sources and is always the same, but I write down these stories as told me now by Mr. Du Toit, a resident

241

here, and before the war a man in authority under the Boers to be in command always against the Natives and to know and manage them. He knows the chiefs personally and can speak and understand Kaffir. Sintoumoula,[3] a very well-disposed Chief, brought in after peace the paper *containing his orders* to burn and destroy all the Boers had and to give no quarter, make no prisoners. He was promised money, etc. and especially his reward was to be a white girl for a wife. He came into Pietersburg and asked for the girl to be given him. Nothing was done about it and fortunately Sintoumoula is not the man to press it, for he is a good sort and reads the "Book". Other Chiefs around are not so pliable. These armed men with assegais and rifles swept the farms in this district and now enjoy a considerable number of the flocks and herds they looted. To the lonely women they were such a menace that numbers of husbands surrendered after the occupation of Pietersburg in order to protect their families, leaving their sons in the field. When at last the families were concentrated, entire black Commandos brought them into camp.

Last night I went to see Mrs. Vahrmeyer. Her husband, the schoolmaster of P. P. Rust (Piet Potgieters Rust: so called because he, the father of our Mr. Potgieter, was killed there long ago) was one of those murdered men on whose account the German missionary Mr. Heese protested and was in turn himself killed. Mrs. Vahrmeyer, a quiet, white-faced woman, told me all she knew of her husband's death; she had come into town for *Nacht-maal*. Mr. Vahrmeyer, a Hollander but naturalized burgher, was with a party of friends, eight in all. These were Mr. Boucamp and son, young Du Preez, Mr. Lochner, Mr. Wouters, Mr. Carl Smit and Mr. Westerhof, also a Hollander schoolmaster, of Pietersburg. They had surrendered, and their arms were given up, one of them was sick with malaria. It is said that Handcock, finding the sick man impeded progress, ordered him to be shot. A National Scout, one Botha, said if one was shot all must be lest the remainder tell. This was agreed to and the order was given to an English soldier (a corporal or sergeant) to despatch the eight. He refused and protested. Consequently the Scout Botha had to do it, and he carried out the order. One man, Carl Smit (he was a deacon of the church), begged to be shot with his eyes uncovered and with one bullet. The bullet only wounded him and seizing his penknife he rushed towards Captain Tailor to fight him. Tailor had a gun and discharged the whole full of grape shot in Smit's face. They had previously been made to dig their own graves. This National Scout Botha was afterwards killed near Heidelberg. This happened near Elim in Zoutpansberg.

It so happened that Mr. Heese, the German missionary, was coming from Dr. Lieghme's sanatorium not far off, just as the eight men were going to be shot. He was driving with a pair of mules and a Kaffir boy. He protested in vain against the deed and drove on saying he would make it known in Pietersburg. One of the officers thereupon rode after him and crossing the bush cut him off by the Dwars River and shot both him and the lad. A grown, friendly Kaffir, who had seen the

242

cart pass and heard shots, went to another missionary and told the tale, and people came and found the bodies dragged into the bush.

Mrs. Heese, a German subject, has had £5 000 given her, and a pension. I learn she is living now in the Orange River Colony.

Mrs. Vahrmeyer told me she had applied herself, direct, for help soon after she knew she was a widow. The murder took place on 23 August 1901, near Elim in the Spelonken. At that time she was in Van der Hoven's Camp near Pretoria, and she knew nothing of her husband's death till Mrs. Heese came and told her of it on 4 May 1902, eight months after. The Colonial Secretary, to whom she applied, gave Mrs. Vahrmeyer a pension of £50 a year, which began last October. She has no children now, but she is a weak, delicate woman, always sickly and quite unable to earn a living. In Pietersburg one cannot live on £50 a year. The most miserable hovel has a rental of £4 a month, so she lives out on a farm with a widowed sister, and the two struggle on together. A gentle, sweet-looking woman, neatly dressed in black.

Handcock and Morant have already suffered for this deed, but those who know and have all the documents in their hands believe them to have been made scape-goats.[4]

Mrs. Smit lives at Louis Trichardt, but I do not feel inclined to apply for a pension for her, because she has not conducted herself well since peace. The others were, I believe, unmarried. Young Du Preez was a cousin of Mr. Du Toit, who, as well as Mrs. Vahrmeyer and the *Predikant*, related this story to me.

Unfortunately the story does not stand alone. Only a few miles distant from that spot and much nearer Dr. Lieghme's sanatorium, another such murder was committed. Mrs. Kriel and Mrs. Hofmeyr were under treatment there at the time and heard the shots fired. Shortly after old Mr. Geyser's waggon with the Kaffir servant driving it came to the sanatorium where they were. He told them what had occurred. Old Mr. Geyser was in the waggon sick, his son, a lad of twelve, was with him, and Jan Greyling and Jan Verceuil, also two others. The whole party had surrendered and were unarmed. The boy begged and prayed them not to shoot him, but it was in vain, he was killed with the rest and the old man in his waggon bed.

A curious incident which happened to Mrs. Geyser adds interest to this story. She was at the time in Pietersburg Camp, and the evening of the murder her husband came to her tent with a wound above his right eye from which the blood was streaming. He told her he had been murdered. Next day Mrs. Geyser told the neighbours what she had seen and that her husband was murdered. She told also the Camp Superintendent, Mr. Tucker, and Major Bolton, who laughed at her. She told the *Predikant*, Mr. Kriel, who told me. About a fortnight afterwards the news came of the outrage. Since peace Mrs. Geyser got a permit to open her husband's grave, and neighbours who were with her bear witness that the wound on the brow was just where she told them she had seen it on the apparition. I hear

Mrs. Geyser, who lives rather further than I could get from Pietersburg, has applied for a pension through a lawyer in town, but has heard nothing in reply. Surely she ought to have it.

I much wanted also to see Mrs. Van den Berg. She lives at Magato Mountain near Louis Trichardt in the Zoutpansberg. Her husband had come home to visit his wife as was customary in that district after the Natives were armed and the women were in danger. While there, Captain Tailor and a few of his men came to the house, and Van den Berg, seizing his rifle, jumped out of the back window and hid in a thicket of young blue-gums. In a few minutes he heard screams from his wife and not being able to see what was happening he crept from the blue-gums and hid behind a rock whence he could watch. In a few moments his wife rushed from the house half naked with clothes torn and hair flying, and an English soldier in full pursuit. He fired and the soldier fell. Another then came out of the door and he fired again, wounding the man. Then as no more durst venture from the house Van den Berg crept from behind his rock to follow his wife. Then a National Scout, one Piet Vogel, followed them and called out in Dutch to them to surrender, promising they should not be hurt. The woman, fearing for her husband, one against several, urged him to come with her and surrender as safety was promised. This was done, he advanced and gave up his rifle and was then shot at his own doorstep before his wife and children.

But the story that seems to me so heart-rending is that of the Van Stadens. He and his two sons were coming in sick, having surrendered. The younger boy was fourteen. Morant, Handcock and Tailor with a white and black contingent shot the three and threw them all into a grave, but the boy was not dead, he was only disabled, shot through both knees. As the sand was thrown into the grave he raised himself to a sitting posture and wildly tried to shovel it away with his hands, crying for mercy. So he was left, the sand reaching to his chest, struggling to free himself. A Kaffir who passed that way on the third day heard faint cries from the spot, and going up to the grave found the lad, but he was just dead.

The people wanted me to visit all these graves, but this story haunts me and I simply cannot, someone must be found to do it, built of sterner stuff. The Van Stadens also are living at Louis Trichardt.

There were other victims more especially at the mercy of the armed Kaffirs. You will remember that these were mostly the half-savage men one sees about these parts almost unclothed, or only a blanket and beads, not those quiet and often reliable Kaffirs who had been in service with the people.

Mr. Max Meyer was a German, but a naturalized burgher. He was Secretary to the Native Commissioner of Spelonken. These Kaffirs came to his house, and, dragging him out to the doorstep, murdered him there in sight of his wife and children.

I cannot learn whether Mrs. Meyer has any pension. She is still at Spelonken.

They came also to the house of Mrs. Botha and her husband living at Woodbush. There were so many blacks that Mrs. Botha threw her arms round her husband's neck and begged him not to shoot lest he enrage them. The Kaffirs seized her by the hair and threw her back, and beat her husband to death with *knobkerries*[5] before her eyes.

But perhaps the worst butchery was that perpetrated upon Pieter Oelofse. His cousin, Mr. Du Toit, told me about it and showed me the farm where he lived and where his father still lives. He, his brother Marthinus, and another man were following the Commando with a waggon, and, being slow, had fallen behind. They were attacked by a large Kaffir Commando.[a] At first they saw it was hopeless to shoot, the numbers were so great and they dreaded enraging the Natives. But suddenly three mounted Kaffirs joined them, and hastily shooting these three, Pieter and the other two men rushed to take their horses and escape. Marthinus and his friend accomplished this, but unfortunately for Pieter as he mounted the girths slipped round and he fell. He was wounded and captured and dragged before the Chief Seripa. The Chief said to him "Your grandfather made my people cry and now I will make your people cry."

Clapping his hands together in the Kaffir mode of pleading, Oelofse begged for mercy. The Chief ordered his hands to be cut off and this was done. He cried aloud and the Chief ordered his lips to be cut off. This also was done and he died. Then they cut him up and mixing the pieces with an ox they were roasing, ate him up.

Near Heynesburg[6] again a horrible thing took place. Nicolas Grobbelaar and another man were coming in, sick with fever, on a spider. Two others were with them. Suddenly the English were seen coming and these two rode away, leaving the sick men in the spider. A contingent of black and white soldiers came up. The whites handed the two patients over to the blacks, and at a small distance they were brutally murdered with assegais under the eyes of the English who belonged to Colenbrander's command. Old Mr. Grobbelaar found his son's body pierced through in thirteen places by the assegais. Their two friends as they rode away could hear their cries for mercy.

But is it any use telling you these cruel deeds? There are many more, in this and other parts, but for any of these cases reference can be made to the clergyman of Pietersburg and others in that town. I think I told you of the murder of the Kidsons in Lydenburg District and of the narrow escape of Mr. Coetzee.

The Rev. Kriel, my host, is lame. He had the day of my arrival just returned from Louis Trichardt, where he had been for *Nacht-maal*. Though seventy-two miles distant it is part of his parish. He was very anxious, as indeed were very many, that I should go there to get a true idea of the poverty. The people there, with the exception of the Constabulary and a few "Joiners", viz. National Scouts, have neither meal, meat, nor clothes. It is a fertile spot and they live on a few vegetables from last summer. Like Roos Senekal, this district was made up of occupation farms, which may indeed be sold if a purchaser can be found, but money cannot be raised on such lands. Cash is not, and in this part, as in many others, the order to give no more repatriation food except for cash is resulting in this condition of semi-starvation. Considering that last summer's crops failed practically throughout the country, the repatriation food ought to have been continued over this winter. Could you not get it restarted at once? Of course, everyone would not need it, but countless families would be saved from privation really terrible.

I am sending out a waggon-load of meal at once to Louis Trichardt and another to the Low Country, but I felt obliged to give up the idea of going myself. It is two days' hard driving each way, and the pain in my arm quite knocks me up and driving brings it on quicker than anything. Also the expense would have been very great, at least £30, though at last they said I should be sent free if I would only go. I think the meal is better than myself.

In the immediate district I took a long drive and found some sad cases. The first farm I came to was called Grootdorst (Great Thirst), and a more applicable name could hardly be found. The dam was empty, the parched ground spread for miles around, and there stood two bell-tents wherein sat the owner, an asthmatic old man, and his anxious stirring wife. Outside the son was trying to rebuild the house with some water brought from afar in a bag. The armed Kaffirs had swept the place bare of everything. The old man had one thousand morgen[7] and on this had borrowed £200 from the Government. With this money he had bought six oxen at about £15 a head, and there goes £90 at once. Two of them died immediately. He had also bought a horse and waggon, two little pigs, and some fowls which would not lay, and wood for his house-building. These things and food for the family, which must be paid for in cash, have brought him to the end of his borrowed sum, and what can he do? He had no zinc for the roof and shrank from incurring further debt to get it, so I gave him the roof, which relieved him very much. I also gave the old woman some flannelette. Who is going to save these people when the time comes to pay up? And who is going to support them either with food or cash till the crops come again?

On the next farm I went to, the conditions were very similar. Only there were eight oxen directly loaned from the Government, and four of these had died. They were said to have died of the Rhodesian pest, the Tic Fever,[8] a new importation, and in consequence the other four beasts were quarantined and so could not leave the farm for transport. This farmer had a considerable military receipt which he could not get paid. Compensation he had abandoned all hope of, but he said if only his military receipt were paid in full he could see his way, make a plan and begin. In the devastation of his farm his hand-pump had been broken up and so he too was without water and could not make even a garden. In searching for a way in which to give him permanent help at a possible outlay I hit upon the pump as the best, so that he can have a vegetable garden again. The compensation we know will be next to nothing and unless that military receipt is paid, what is such a man to do? There are hundreds in a similar condition.

I am sorry to hear that the banks which have been in the habit of lending largely to Boer farmers, are calling in their money. This is very serious. It is done even in the case of men of substance able to give good and sure security. It is regarded merely as another of the many ways in which pressure is being put upon the people to make them good and obedient and say, "Yes, we will agree to Chinese labour."

Cash is so short in the country, the condition is so serious, the land must slip from their hands unless help comes, and comes speedily, in the shape of loans from friendly capitalists. The bank that is *not* calling in its money at this sore moment is the Netherlands Bank.

Everyone is anxious about the state of affairs in Johannesburg. The miners (white) and the English party are very angry and have been asking the Boers to help them. The Boers say if they help it would spoil all; these Johannesburgers must act for themselves. The papers reflect nothing of the true state of affairs.

I am now at Warm Baths enjoying the kindness of the Potgieters[b] and must close. You can publish what you like of these murders with all names, and the Rev. Kriel says he is willing to be referred to about it if necessary. And you can publish anything else you like about it, under my name in letter form, if you deem it wise.

From the memoir

a) The main difference between this northern district and others that I had seen was of course the large Kaffir element and the stories and evidences of their terrible work as English instruments during the war. Their prosperity, a thing in itself to be glad of, gave one an unhappy feeling by its contrast with the poverty and barrenness endured by the surrounding Boers. This came very forcibly before me as I drove about the district and visited the bare farms and penniless Boer families. Turning from these to a Kaffir village there was every token of well-being. Mealies in abundance hung drying; sheep, goats and oxen were on all sides; heaps of wood cut and stacked, and Kaffirs lounging about in their khaki uniforms. Much of this was looted from the Boers during the war. Kaffir prosperity was very unpopular in Johannesburg, I was told, where their labour was wanted in the mines. Every inducement was being tried to coerce them to this end. Over and over again, I learnt, the women and children had been brought into the concentration camps by Kaffir Commandos, with never a white officer amongst them. The district too was still thrilling with the horror of the murders committed not only by armed blacks during the war, and it was some relief to people to tell me these shameful things. I made a careful record of a considerable number of these horrible deeds told me by relatives or eyewitnesses. They were indeed matters of common knowledge.

b) When my work at Pietersburg was over I returned south halting at Warm Baths where I had promised myself a couple of days' rest with the Potgieters. He had been *burghermaster*[9] of Pretoria, so possibly you may have known him in former years. They live not far from the baths and took me there to enjoy one, which I did

247

immensely – a course might have done my arm good. The remembrance is still fresh of the repose of that visit and the charming kindness of my host and hostess and their family.

72. TO LADY HOBHOUSE

Warm Baths

[about 25 July 1903]

The Potgieters' fruit farm is very beautiful. I will not mention now how many hundred trees were cut down in the war, or other destruction, but only say that the orange, lemon, citron, naartje, *pampelmoes*, shaddock, etc. still left are fine and laden with fruit. There are old orange trees here, forty years old, and over fifty feet in height, with dense dark foliage most grateful to the eye, and their oranges beggar description. I saw one lofty tree laden from top to toe, the branches lying on the ground heavy with fruit, the most dazzling mass of gold I have ever seen. It had about six thousand oranges on it. I am glad these beautiful specimens were spared.[a] I never tasted such good oranges, all day we ate them and I carried off a boxful with me. The other fruits were not in season, except bananas, there were plenty of them. The soil is very fertile, the climate perfect, consequently favourable for the growth of first-class fruit.

Mr Potgieter drove me round to see the Settlers, Milner's especial pets.[1] There were about fifty at Warm Baths, but only six have survived the first twelve months' work in spite of the coddling they have received. Of these, four are English, one Canadian, and one Colonial.

The Government has supplied them with every requisite, including £100 put to their credit in the bank. Most of them have abused their opportunity, perhaps because no care seems to have been taken to select men of even honest character. Six are now doing three years for stealing cattle, twenty are sent away to distant turf lands to be out of reach of the hotel, for, as a Settler informed us with a wink, "We Settlers don't bear a good name". The remainder, except the six, have departed. Of the six the Boers think one may succeed, he shows energy and common sense.

The return just laid before the Legislative Council shows that the cost of this scheme figures out at upwards of £2 600 apiece, nearly a million of money in all, which sum divided equally among the neediest Boers would have set the entire country upon its legs.

The Settlers could not complain enough, however, of the Government's delay in helping them, and they have a cause for complaint in that they have mostly been settled upon town commonage, the people of the towns not being consulted, and now protests are sent in from all sides and it is not certain yet if they can remain. If they do, it is hard upon the Boers, who bought their town erven (or lots) with the inalienable right attached of grazing upon these commonages.

The said grumbles from Milner's Settlers are heard all over the two countries,

248

and money has been poured out like water for a very small result. The Settler who told me these things was a soldier in Compton's Horse, and was in a white heat of indignation with the Government. But everyone is that.

The state of feeling amongst the Uitlander population in Johannesburg and Pretoria runs very high. They sadly contrast the present with the past, and all know that freedom is gone for Englishman and Boer alike, and that a great gold combine is to rule them with a rod of iron. Already the pressure is being applied in every department of business – men are tied hand and foot, and in this helpless condition will have to see, not merely Chinese labour brought in (that is but one item), but their whole country and its vast stores of wealth and all its future pass into the complete control of the gold combine. Milner is a tool in the hand of the capitalists.

Will Liberals worthy of the name get into power, and by recalling him strike a blow at the policy which Briton and Boer alike watch closing mercilessly round them day by day?

There is to be a meeting at Krugersdorp on Saturday, organized by a society of which *Milner is patron*, and Botha and Smuts have been *implored* to come. But I think Botha will reserve himself.

In a short time De la Rey will hold a great meeting similar to the one Botha recently held at Heidelberg, as in spite of lying cables there is perfect unanimity between them.

These meetings of protest are all that they can do to help their country which is being driven upon the rocks. The trouble is in every department and it is impossible in a letter to give any idea of its scope.[2]

I am leaving to-morrow for Heilbron, thence to visit the worse districts of the Orange River Colony – Frankfort, Lindley, Reitz, and Vrede. I have sent a waggon-load of meal in advance. That came to £50 though Mr. Fichardt with his usual generosity let me have it at cost price.

From the memoir

a) Accustomed only, as I had been, to the toy-like orange trees of the Riviera and Italy, you can imagine how astounded I was at the height and luxuriance of these orange groves and the magnificence of their fruit. It was said that in his work of cutting down trees Lord Roberts (or his representative) had yielded here to the petition of the soldiers who found the fruit a wholesome and refreshing change to their diet.

[c/o Mr. and Mrs. Jasper Theron]
Lindley, Orange River Colony
2 August 1903

I write from the ruins of Lindley in the intervals of interviewing the inhabitants.

When I left Pretoria I went straight to Heilbron, a horrid night journey with a change at a siding, minus waiting-room or refreshments or even lamplight in the dead of night at 1 a.m. This night work ceases after a while to be either picturesque or amusing. But the care of the kind people of Heilbron made it easier for me, for young Mr. Steyn[1] was sent to meet me at Viljoen's Drift and guide me through the dark and the sand with all my paraphernalia to the Heilbron coach. In the morning when we woke up he told me all his story, for he was one of the five prisoners who swam from the transport in Ceylon harbour and escaped on board the Russian man-of-war. The Russians were very good to them, treating them as first-class passengers. In British waters at Aden the ship was searched, but the five sat in the funnel and were not found. It was a curious thing that they only affected their escape because the Russian ship had *three* funnels. All five men had escaped separately intending to swim to a French vessel, but in the dark and the confusion of lights in the harbour they lost their bearings; however, each separately recollected a passing remark that the Russian vessel had three funnels, and each guided himself by that and found the other four had done the same.

Mr. Steyn brought me to Heilbron, sleepy and hungry, at 8.30 a.m., and at that cold-blooded hour I found myself met by an array of Heilbron ladies and gentlemen. Moreover, they had on their best clothes, with a brilliant display of pink feather boas, and I was coated with red dust.

They crowd a good deal into these days. After breakfast I was handed over to the minister who walked with me to various poor cases in the town who needed instant relief; then after lunch Mr. Theron, my host, drove me out to a desolated farm through other desolated farms to visit the Widow Els, and on my return I found the Resident Magistrate and the Head of the Constabulary coming to call on me. Then tea and off to the parsonage, where a large reception awaited me, about a hundred ladies and gentlemen; a solemn address was read to me in Dutch, and I was expected to make a long speech.

Soon I shall rival Mr. Chamberlain with the number of my receptions and addresses in South Africa! They are all so simple, so spontaneous, and so thoroughly heart-felt. Perhaps they ought to be made known, because with my name is always connected the *friends unknown* in England. They add considerably to my work and my fatigue, and I can quite understand "Joe" losing his temper from sheer fatigue. To continue smiling on everyone in every town who crowd round you with their tales of sorrow is a tremendous strain. Horrors! As I now look out of the window, behold the town of Lindley is collecting, and an address threatens me . . .

It is over and I have had the address and made my speech through an interpreter as some could not understand. They assembled out of doors and I stood on the steps to address them, just the lovely half-hour before sunset. A Dutch audience is dreadful to speak to, for it makes neither sign nor sound to intimate its feeling – absolute silence and bared heads and then, when over, it melts silently away. A week later they may have something to say on the subject. Generally a spy gets in; today there were S.A.C.'s[2] in plain clothes. At the end today there was an incident worth remarking. I invited remarks from anyone who wished, and a man came forward and with lifted hat very politely pleaded for help for a neighbour plunged in poverty and recently struck by lightning. I cannot tell what made me feel uncomfortable about the man whose words and manner were irreproachable, but I noticed when he turned round to others for confirmation of his words a chill fell on all though all acknowledged that he had done well in putting this neighbour's case before me. He left and then they said: "*He is a National Scout.*" The horror those words inspire here you can't imagine!

But I have wandered from Heilbron. The day was a hard one, especially the visit to the Widow Els. This old lady is, by the way, the aunt of Marthinus Els, whose Bible Mr. Alexander has found,[3] and he is well known, and if the Bible is sent to the Rev. Minnaar, Parsonage, Heilbron, it will be all right.

I was taken to Mrs. Els' farm because it had been the most beautiful in the immediate neighbourhood. It is a sore sight – in fact there was nothing to see and in the midst in her patched-up room was the fine old woman who owned the land and had been in affluent circumstances all her life, never known what want was. She had fled, fled always before the columns, even her waggon taken and burnt at last, still hiding and fleeing, to the very end. Never a penny piece or an ounce of meal had she had from the Government, and now penniless on her ruined land she is brought so low that she has had to beg a garment from the minister.

Her case is worth telling because there are so many in similar plight. Her husband, one of the most respected men in the district, died, leaving his well-stocked, rich farm to her for her life, and then to be divided between the four children. Thus according to the law here she cannot bond the farm and they cannot bond it – no money can be raised. Her hope is only the help of her daughter's son, a penniless prisoner-of-war, whose father has stood security for him for £200, and on this he is beginning. As nearly all the sum has gone in the necessary animals and seed and plough, clothes are not possible, nor food. Day after day she has no bread even, and what food comes is her son-in-law's.

She shewed us a really beautiful coat she had made on the veld out of sheep skins tanned by herself, both cut and stitching were excellent. She was very spirited in her accounts of all her interviews with the officers who had ruined her husband's life's work, but this fire went out and she cried a little when I offered her a bag of meal and some flannelette, those two never-failing gifts welcomed by high and low. I have since sent her a short thick cloak as she suffers much from cold on the chest

251

and only had a thin print gown. They eat so very little for they have so little to eat, and yet at first it seems so impossible to offer help to people of this stamp.

I could not get her out of my head till she was pushed out by the next farm I called at, Mrs. Boshoff of Boshoff's Rust. Mr. Theron and I outspanned here, and visiting with Mrs. Boshoff was a woman who greeted me with effusion for she had known me in Springfontein Camp. She still had a nighgown I had given her there, and for her best she still wore the gown in which she was captured nearly four years ago.

Mr. Boshoff's farm was swept clean, a column had camped there for three weeks, so not a tree or bush was left to tell the tale. A hundred-and-fifty bags of her mealies burnt in the yard were still black upon the ground, a bit of her house was put up in a fashion, but windows are £1/14s apiece, and cannot be afforded; nearly everywhere they make small square holes and nail sacking over these. The roof – as most are – was made of old zinc full of holes as big as half-crowns through which at night the stars twinkle.

Mrs. Boshoff is a good-looking woman of thirty. She fled to the hills to escape Heilbron Camp. At one time one of her children fell ill and she was forced to creep into town to buy some medicine, leaving her children outside. She evaded the pickets, but was captured in town, and they would not let her go back to her children. She was detained so long that her confinement, which was nearing, took place and detained her yet longer. When the baby was a few weeks old, mad with anxiety about her children, she disguised herself as a Kaffir girl and with her baby bound on her back and a bundle on her head walked past the sentries with the Kaffirs to the place where they washed, and then leaving them quietly ran on to the hills and the Commandos.

She has suffered bitterly, but she says she has her husband and her children, and there is peace and rest, and no more flight, though everything else is gone she is satisfied. Her house was exquisitely clean and neat, her children also, her baby's shoes made by herself from cloth and bits of skin, very dainty, their little stockings had about two dozen darns in them mended with red, brown, white and grey – bits of mending given her by the minister's wife. Her bed was the charred and bent remains of a once nice iron bedstead, with corrugated iron laid across it and a cowhide on that, but – as she remarked – it was better than the ground.

This woman comes of a good family; she was very comfortably off; she expects another baby soon and she had the blue-white look of an underfed woman.

Mr. Theron's four nice horses took us on to Driefontein where I saw the wreck of a very beautiful place. The people owning it have no cash now to speak of but have large and valuable properties that are worth many thousands of pounds; they had had a fine house with water all laid on and bathrooms, etc. and a well laid-out flower garden – all swept bare.

Mr. Theron (the owner's name) with his wife and a neighbour, Mrs. Potgieter, took me to her kraal to see the wool and bones of four thousand sheep slaughtered

252

there. With great difficulty he has now procured a hundred sheep from the Colony, and we wondered as we stood there how long it would take before those four thousand sheep alone could be replaced.

Mrs. Theron, who during the war kept outside on the veld, had come back to visit her farm place when the troops had passed and found these carcasses decaying; the odour was so terrible that she was made ill by it with a fever. Mrs. Potgieter was turned out of her house but begged them to spare one room for her daughter-in-law just to be confined. They refused – all was burnt and the poor thing's baby was born in the remains of the verandah.

These are good-class people, but their children can get no education, the O.R.C. does not seem to have begun farm schools, and for farms twenty to fifty miles from towns or villages people can no longer afford to board their children away from home.

It was late when we got to Lindley itself and the moon was all we had to guide us. The road was bad and the drift across the river deep, with very steep cliffs on either side, but we came through and at last drove into the silent broken village white in the moonlight. A strange medley it was of ruins and tents with a few new roofs, brand-new, rising here and there from the refuse of the past. No one was about, and it was some time before we could find our way or anyone to guide us. Finally I was consigned to old Mr. Kok, and Mr. Theron got a bed on the floor of an office, our Kaffir boy in the stable.

The whole of Lindley is too sad and dejected outwardly and inwardly to write about. Everyone is ruined except a fourth-rate hotel-keeper who became a 'Captain' under the English in a fortnight and, from being penniless, has now his thousands, and a store-keeper, Oates, who is doing well by grinding the faces of the poor. He is piling on the agony in the shape of enormous interest on bills owed him before the war. One woman told me she owed £7 when they were all swept away to camp, and Oates says he must charge interest for the same and makes it £20. Men are working hard only to pay their swollen debts and more debts now owing to the repatriation and cannot buy food or clothes. It is cruel. A large poor class which never existed before is being created in the land.

The Koks are so poor I hardly dared to eat their food; their bed was corrugated iron, the floor would have been pliable by comparison. The ruins of their nice house stand before the door never alas! to be rebuilt, for they are old and can never earn the money again. He is 74, but the plucky old man saved the church registers and stuck to them through thick and thin. He is an educated man. From affluence they are brought in old age to dire poverty. But there was no word of complaint; he spent his time telling me of all the poor around while he said no word of his own condition. I had to learn that from others.

It is all lamentable in the town and district. I shall never forget the pathos of the meeting when they came to address me – I felt so utterly at a loss what to say to them. Even General Olivier could not speak, but turned away, and they silently melted off, each with his burden of want and debt and barrenness, in face of which one's sympathy seemed a mockery.

It is the hardest sort of speech to make, talking to people who are well-nigh starving, whose homes are in ruins, who have no money and no prospects. They have struggled bravely for over a year, but now all is closing in dark around them. I fear hope is waning at last, and I dread lest their self-respect should be lost.

Here and there one hears of a man going out of his mind, and why more are not so affected is a mystery to me. I see one of the deacons of Lindley did hang himself the other day, a man very highly respected, and as people say, there was "no reason" for it. To my mind the desperate condition of his people and his district was sufficient and would so act on many temperaments. I felt quite nervous about General Olivier, his depression was so terrible. In addition to his own losses, and they were great for he was a well-to-do man, he had £400 in his house belonging to another person, and this was burnt, together with all his own money and goods, and he knows not where to turn to pay it back.

I left a bag of meal for about thirty starving families in Lindley; that means £60.

Our trek from Lindley was a sad one; we drove away from the ruins early, trying to shake off the depression which hung upon the place. About fifteen miles out from town we met a man with a bundle under his arm walking towards Lindley. He had on the green trousers of the Ceylon prisoners-of-war, and there was purpose on his face. Shortly we came upon his little daughter, a child of twelve. She was neatly dressed in a blue print frock and kapje, and she was riding a creature which must by courtesy be called a horse. At least it had four legs and a tail and a sort of bone which supported the saddle. She was leading another such animal which had helped carry her father to town. We called to her to ask the way, and she rode close up to our cart.

She had the motionless face of the veld girl with the deep still eyes, and she sat on her horse with grace and self-possession. We had some talk with her.

"How goes it with you?" we said.

"It goes well," she replied.

"Have you then food?"

"No, we have no food."

"You mean that you have no meat?"

"No, we have no meat."

"But you have vegetables or potatoes?"

"No, we have no vegetables."

"But at least you have bread?"

"No, we have no bread."

"What, no bread nor meal?"

"No, we have no bread nor meal."

"Then what do you eat?"

"Just mealies."

"And have you many of those?"

Some moisture gathered in the child's eyes as she answered: "Very few left."

"But your father is gone to town, will he not work and bring you home some food?"

"Yes, my father has found some house-building work to do in town, but he cannot bring us home food; he owed money to the store before the war and he must work to pay that off."

"But these horses are your own?"

"No, we had them from the Government and in two years we must pay for them."

"And how are you off for clothes?"

"It goes scarce with clothes."

We gave the child half a loaf we had with us, and as she took it her lips trembled and a flicker like the shadow of a smile passed over her face as she said, "My mother will be very glad."

Then silently she turned and hugging the loaf trotted away over the veld, a solitary blue speck in the vast brown expanse.

Some miles further we came to a place called Plezier; a greater misnomer could not be imagined. A piece of house had been patched up, but there was no smoke or other sign of life. Not a tree or bush or plant or green blade of any sort could be seen near or far. We knocked, seeking permission to outspan. A deadness hung over the place; I felt anxious, I wondered what we should find. Remember the Boer custom when a cart drives up to the door is for the master or mistress to come out, introduce themselves, and with all heartiness invite you in and make you welcome.

After several knocks the door was opened, leave was given us to outspan, but still we were not invited in. I got out of the cart and went to the door. The house was poor but exquisitely neat; there were no chairs, just a table and box or two to sit upon. Upon the clay walls were fastened the few relics of better days. A good-looking woman and a number of girls neatly but poorly dressed were grouped round the room and an equal number of tidy boys in the kitchen at the back. There were eleven children. They sat very silent looking at me, and I introduced myself as coming from well-known men in their town.

Mr. Theron wanted to take our luncheon in the house, but some instinct told me there was great trouble there and I could not eat with all those eyes upon me. So I only asked permission to boil my kettle on their table out of the wind, and then when we had lunched I said I would come and hear their story. I hated myself afterwards to think I had made my tea at their table.

When I made them understand who I was, the woman told me all – the same sad tale of course as everywhere; that they had nothing left, nothing to eat but mealies, and so few of them that they must eke them out by one meal a day only. There was nowhere to turn for money or for help, the husband had tramped away some thirty miles to seek work on a railway, at best he would get 4/6 a day, and on that no family here can live, it would not much more than feed *him*. But it might be weeks before she would hear from him, they had been comfortably off, tenant farmers paying £50 a year rent. They had come to the bare land and every improvement on it had been done by themselves, the houses built and all, and all had been swept and done away, no single sheep remained of all their possessions, and now a letter had come from the owner's agent in Bloemfontein raising the rent from £50 to £70 a year.

She and her children sat there face to face with starvation, that terrible kind which is combined with perfect respectability. (I had been told about them in Lindley.) Even if there were neighbours the girls could get no work, for no one can afford to put out washing, ironing or needlework.

One of the girls took me into the bedroom and in a whisper told me they had nothing to eat. The woman kept her secret longer. It is so awful to people of this good class to say they are in want or even seem to beg. They pointed to a house about half a mile off, and said it was just the same there. There was a big lad, and hearing there was a wayside store not far off I took him there and bought food enough to last them about a week till the bag of meal which I had ordered for them in Lindley should arrive. That may last three weeks, and then they are in the same position again. Government must feed the people.

At the store stood a lamentable vehicle, drawn by animals which might be either horses, mules, donkeys or ponies. I can't say which. The lad asked the driver if he could take for him the half bag of meal I had given him and leave it at the farm. The man said he was sorry, the animals were borrowed and so was the cart and harness and they were so weak they could hardly crawl along and he dared not add to the weight.

This man was a very fine young Boer with well-cut features. His young wife was with him. Mr. Theron introduced me to them, they belong to a good family, as indeed was apparent in their dress and bearing. The woman put her arm through mine and whispered she wanted to speak to me. She drew me out of earshot of the men on the stoep. Then her courage failed her and she could not speak. Her face was very white with blue shadows round the lips and eyes. I said: "Are you hungry?"

I am getting experienced now and begin to understand. She said for months she had eaten *nothing* but mealies, not meal, nor meat, nor coffee, nor *anything* else. They had borrowed the cart and come to the store to fetch the last half bag they could buy. She put her hand on my arm again and said: "I have nothing, we have nothing, don't you understand?"

And then at last I did understand, her baby was coming, the first baby, and she had not even a shawl to wrap it in. I understood her Dutch perfectly, but she was too shy to speak openly. She said she had a frightful craving for a bit of fresh meat, but none was to be got in the shop. A baby's shawl and a bit of flannelette made heaven open for her again, and I gave her a tin of Australian mutton and a few

256

groceries. She had a good face. Six of her brothers and sisters had died in Kroonstad Camp.

But I shall weary you – all along the route, wherever we stopped, the condition of the people was the same – mealies only, and those at the last ebb; a famine of money everywhere.

We had a hearty welcome in the ruined parsonage of Reitz where the Viljoens are struggling with the sorrows of their people. Mrs. Viljoen is in very poor health now. She was turned out of her home very soon after her baby was born, and the terrible journey to camp and the great privations of camp life affected her internally, and she is never likely to recover. All day long from before breakfast till after supper the parishioners stream into the parsonage for help – food and clothing. The Viljoens themselves are so ruined, their house half down, and all their furniture and books destroyed, they simply cannot feed the people who turn to them in their dire need. That day she turned them over to me and it was indeed a hard day. People kept coming in from hours distant in the district.

There was one set, a man, his mother-in-law of 65, a little girl of 11, who *walked* in over ten miles without having had any food. The child was very tired and sat upon a stone outside the store. I sent the man for a loaf of bread, and got a twopenny loaf for a shilling. Then I bought a tin of sausages and fed them and several others in the same way. They all had only mealies and very little of those. The shopman knew them all well – very respectable people but with no money to buy anything.

There was a young girl of about nineteen came in, neatly and carefully dressed; I could not believe she was in such want and was asking her general questions. Her eyes kept filling with tears, still she kept her composure, but she was rather blue, and at last I thought she would faint, and then I found she had had no breakfast and only one meal of mealies the day before. I had to feed her before I could talk to her, and then some colour came back.

Two young women came, aged about 25 and 26. It was the same story – nothing to eat, only the mealies and they had run out; their father was 72 and their stepmother "was not right". No animals to plough, no food, no cash, no hope. And so on all day long.

At night they met me in the school; it was packed. An address of welcome was read and I had to speak to them. The silence was profound, many women wept quietly. They sang a hymn and the Dominie prayed and by the dim light of three or four guttering candles I could see the hopeless look on the seamed, wrinkled faces of the men.

They all filed out, shaking hands with me at the door, young and old – it was very impressive.

We can only give them hope by ploughing for them. The Government must feed them now. I sent thirty bags of meal there, the transport is heavy, it cost £55. Had I bought it on the spot the same quantity would have been nearly £65, but it was sold to me at cost price. But this only helps thirty families for a few weeks, and then? Who will give the next?

At Frankfort and all along the road there it was the same. No food left, no money to buy. One old woman I met where we outspanned. She was a sweet old thing but in great distress, for Mrs. Viljoen had sent her one of E. D. Bradby's petticoats from England, a brand-new one, and it would not fit, so I took it away and replaced it with stuff from the cart. She said she had told her husband when she woke that morning that she had a presentiment she should get a present that day, and it had come true.

In Frankfort there was a poor man and when I offered him some meal he said, "I shall be so glad that I shall laugh without feeling any inclination to laugh."

But I must stop. I could run on for hours and tell you of the meeting to receive me at Frankfort and all the kindly ruined people there.[a]

I am pressed with correspondence, so cannot by this mail write more.

From the memoir

a) I feel sorry that the letter describing my visit to Frankfort is lost. I well remember it – the kindness of all there and the hospitality of the De Kocks. I met there, as well as elsewhere on this journey, interesting women who gave me the journals they had kept of their war experiences. These are valuable records[4] and will, I hope, be published before this memoir sees the light.

The whole of that week's trek and the distress we had witnessed made a deep impression upon both Mr. Jasper Theron and myself. With me it was a culmination of the varying degrees of misery I had seen in other districts; with him a first realization of the need in the open country, off the railway line.

My funds were low and as he drove me back to Heilbron we discussed what could be done.[5] Only two paths seemed open – first, a cable to prominent Englishmen to urge the Home Government to instruct the Colonial Government to provide food again; second, an appeal to the never-failing generosity of the Cape. I determined on both and instantly, on reaching Heilbron, I cabled to Mr. Courtney to use his influence.

Experience had, however, taught me the lethargy of Governments and that publicity was needed to spur them to action. So I wrote the appeal to the Cape which was published in the *South African News* of August 16th.[6] First, I read it to Mr. Theron, asking if it coincided with his judgment. He endorsed every word. It was a relief to have taken these definite steps.

You will remember that within two weeks of that cable's arrival the Repatriation supplies were re-opened, without a demand for cash, and I knew that the utmost limit of suffering was thereby averted. Further, the Cape made wonderful response to my appeal and provided the means for the ploughing teams which gave heart and hope in the worst districts.

I cannot pass from this subject without speaking of my deep appreciation of Mr. Jasper Theron's efficient help. He had lent his time, his cart, his horses, and his Kaffir boy for a week's travel under most difficult circumstances – a costly and most generous contribution to the prevailing need. Later, when the storm of criticism burst over my head, Mr. Theron was one of those who bravely wrote a corroborative letter to the Press. I say *brave* because under Coercion Act any public criticism of the existing state of affairs exposed men to official displeasure and needed unusual courage.

74. TO LEONARD HOBHOUSE

Pretoria

3 August 1903

Rumour says you are in Cornwall, but whether renting Maud's house or Carrie's[1] I do not know. In any case I expect it is raining and you are struggling with picnics under umbrellas and catching colds by sitting on damp grass of a make-believe summer! Anyhow, I hope the air of Cornwall, than which there is none more excellent, will inspire you with fresh ardour to cope with "Joe" and his machinations. Here the sun continues to shine and there seems no hope of clouds or rain. General Smuts' time is consumed in watering – watering his trees and plants all day long.[a]

To-morrow I go to the Bothas quite nearby, and thence I go either south to the Orange River Colony or else to Lichtenburg to the De la Reys. I think I must see dear old Oom Koos, as he is called here. Moreover, accounts of that district are very bad; the people are more famished than in almost any part, living on *meercats* trapped in the veld and porcupines and finches, etc. After that I begin to trend southwards and by the beginning of October I ought to be in the North of the Cape Colony.

The Murrays[2] much want me to go home with them, starting the end of October and going by the East Coast route. As yet I cannot say what I shall do. It would be delightful to have their companionship, but I expect that route is more expensive. I must learn particulars.

I sat down meaning to write fully, but the more one gets *into* the atmosphere here the less possible it is to write about or define it. The Coercion Act rules over all. Mr. Duncan, Colonial Treasurer,[3] has, however, written to ask if he may come and see me and out of this, I hope, good may come.[b]

I must not write the things I want to and so I will end with love to Oliver.

From the memoir

a) It was a real rest to fall down upon the comparative warmth and repose of Pretoria, and I went first to General and Mrs. Smuts. I loved their beautiful hedge of pomegranates, the glossy dark leaves, the brilliant blossoms, and the great, gorgeous crimson fruit. Magnificent pomegranates, not the insignificant specimens one sees in Europe.

b) The needs of the country people had been made known by my appeal and by the Johannesburg meeting. It was therefore most encouraging, when I was resting these few days with Mrs. Louis Botha, to receive a friendly note from Mr. Patrick Duncan,[3] Colonial Treasurer, asking if we could meet. In connection with his work as Chief of the Repatriation Department he said he would be interested to discuss the matter which I had made public with me. I was very glad of this kindly offered opportunity and he arranged to call on me at the Bothas' house.

On this occasion I put before him Captain Madge's[4] misrepresentations in his articles in the Cape Press (and later in the London *Times*), and I especially laid stress on the forlorn condition of widows, invalids and aged persons, urging their relief under Chamberlain's promises. I supplied him with a list of some of these – typical cases. I ventured to put forward the view that to press men into Relief Works at 5/- a day was in itself defeating the work of Repatriation. A man could hardly do more than maintain himself on that wage, and meanwhile his land remained untilled and his house unbuilt. Also, as a matter of fact, applicants were already being refused such work, and even several turned off. I assured him relief would not be wanted permanently, but *must* be given till the next harvest brought sustenance. I begged that teams might be sent to help the ploughing or supplied cheaply, and mentioned that oxen in the open market were to be had at a lower figure than those from the Repatriation Boards and that these last were too often sickly. I asked him the crucial question whether the heavy bills, sent to the people with every item of repatriation help, were indeed to be called in for payment, and if *not* I implored him to give relief to their minds by letting the people *know*.

I spoke to him of the universally numerous tales (many evidently genuine) of scandals, thefts and rogueries in the Repatriation *Dépôts*, and begged him to reduce and change the personnel. I urged him to realize the bar of language, custom and character, and to take into account the fact that the Boers were the last people to tell their troubles to sub-officials and police, etc. I laid before him also the hard fate of the ex-policemen of the Transvaal, and finally the starving condition of large sections of the black people.

Mr. Duncan listened with sympathetic interest to these various pleas. My impression was that neither he nor his officials had made due allowance for the crushing effect of the Coercion Act, so euphemistically called "the Peace Preservation Act". So difficult is it to realize the weight of such laws if you do not yourself come under them!

Mr. Duncan at once looked into the question of the widows, and most kindly sent me next day a list of widows helped to date which he acknowledged showed "as regards certain districts very little has as yet been done". He added that "the work was being pushed on as fast as possible".

This list dealt with the Transvaal only and showed that 930 widows had made application under the promised grant in Circular 120.[5] Of these 930 only 205 had received assistance, and of that number only 86 had been given the full grant; 119 a partial grant. This raised the question what conditions and reservations were being made as to which widows should receive the promised grant. Mr. Chamberlain had made no reservations.

After studying this Schedule I at once wrote to some of the ministers in whose parishes certain widows were stated to have been given the full grant, but when investigated by them the grants did not appear to tally with the official list.

Mr. Duncan also allowed me to study the official estimate for ploughing expenses. This was severely criticized by farmers whom I consulted. The Colonial Treasurer thought my own scheme under-estimated, but by *trusting the Boers* and giving a team in charge of well-known men in each district it could be, and indeed was, done at far less cost. He was also most kind in asking me to let him have names of individual cases of distress and in offering help in any way.

In a letter dated 9 September I rejoiced to hear from him that instructions were being issued for the "renewal of rations in necessitous cases" and that "a notice will also be sent to the Dutch papers". Two days later Mr. Duncan wrote that a cable had been received from the Home Colonial Office in regard to my having stated to my friends at home that there was alarming distress in certain districts and that the Boer representations to the Pretoria authorities had failed.

> "I should be very much obliged," he wrote, "if you could let me know what facts or cases you have in mind or what suggestions you or any representatives of the Boer people wish to put forward with a view to improving the present method of assistance or rendering it more effective."

Unfortunately this letter, which was very kindly couched, took long in reaching me, and I was not able to answer it till the 26th of that month. It had, however, been partly answered, as in the meantime I had been sending Mr. Duncan a list of cases that needed investigation. I replied to his cordial invitation [suggesting]:

First: Reduction of the staff with a view to the expenditure being more used for repatriation or relief and less for administration. Is it necessary to keep these expenses going to issue supplies almost entirely to officials and public servants?

Second: Some change of personnel, eliminating all who do not speak both languages and substituting people really interested in the work.

Third: *The carrying out* of each Regulation as issued from the Central Office in lieu of the uneven administration of relief brought about by qualifications and exceptions not mentioned in the Regulation and apparently made by the individual Repatriation Officer.

Fourth: *Less delay* in providing relief applied for. There are cases of over three months' delay.

261

Fifth: *Communication of instructions*. The people have hitherto been in the dark concerning what help or relief they are entitled to by governmental order. An order merely hung on the door of the committee room of the *Dépôt* (and in English) can never reach the people.

Sixth: The addition of the minister and two church wardens or elders to the Relief Committee of every Board would ensure completer work and inspire confidence, for the work should be carried out as far as possible in consultation with local people who have knowledge in each ward of cases of distress.

Seventh: That relief should as far as possible take the form of putting a man into a self-supporting position rather than doling out rations.

Mr. Duncan, who was anxious to improve and hasten matters in repatriation work, himself now took occasional tours into the districts. On one of these he arrived in Wolmaransstad while I myself was there, and at once sent me a kind note proposing a meeting and discussion of affairs. He then proceeded on his way to the West and I crossed him returning east.

Meantime a Reuter despatch from Pretoria stated that soon after the publication of my appeal I had had "the opportunity of placing the facts before one of the ablest and most humane and sympathetic members of the Transvaal Administration". Mentioning that arrangements had been made for continuing assistance on credit and that the Department would plough for the people at low charge, the message ended:

> "The Administration is heartily to be commended for its prompt and sympathetic action and upon being strong enough to disregard the silly attacks made upon Miss Hobhouse by journalistic and other critics who are ignorant or worse."

Indeed, dear Mrs. Steyn, I do not think Mr. Duncan can be too highly commended for his wise and prompt action. Had his spirit and his energy and diligence permeated more of the local boards, much suffering could have been saved and much poverty averted. It made me wish that a Mr. Duncan could have been found in your Free State Administration also at that painful time.

During August and September a number of corroborative letters appeared in the Press from leading ministers and others in widely different districts.

To conclude the subject it may be clearer to mention here that the food *Dépôts* thus re-opened remained so till near the end of the year, and a couple of months later, after the rains, Mr. Duncan wrote me at Cape Town, kindly sending me Circular 149 just issued which contained orders for their final closing on 30 November in the districts and 31 December on the railway lines.

As he recognized that people could not get food from the next harvest till the end of March 1904, authority was given on this Circular to issue rations in the interim on terms of *credit*, and tenders called for from local tradesmen to supply. As Mr.

Duncan expressed to me his wish that ministers and others should co-operate with the magistrates in seeing that this authorized assistance was carried out, I wrote to every minister in the Transvaal directing his special attention to this and other helpful circulars.[6]

The Circular 149 further urged "getting forward with the grant to widows". This matter was still hanging fire.

Indeed it was for me, dear Mrs. Steyn, a most trying and puzzling time. On the one hand were the Ministerial promises like Chamberlain's and some pale reflections of these which were typed on reams of paper and issued by the Transvaal Government, and there was Mr. Duncan's sympathetic concern and evident good will. On the other hand I had the evidence of my own eyes and ears, supported by ministers and leading men in every district I had visited, and yet the chasm would not get bridged; help was dilatory, grants were not fulfilled. Here are extracts from several Dutch Reformed ministers' letters, showing the delays to be universal:

"Up to the present our meetings have ended in a farce and the Repatriation officers have not fulfilled their promises, nor up to the present given a' quarter of the grant in the Circular about the widows.

"On 29 September several came into the village having *no* food, and asked for some rations. The answer was, 'You can come again 20 October, and then we shall see if you can get some.' I suppose they must stay without food all that time and must live upon air! We have sent a petition to the Governor – no answer yet – it is no use asking or complaining. May God have mercy upon us!"

Another wrote:

"We have some time ago sent in a list of the names of such widows as require help to the magistrate here, but he returned it to our secretary. So far very little has been done for them."

Another:

"The District Inspector goes his round on the farms, brings out his report, and recommends to the Repatriation Committee some widows or invalids who need help. After some time the committee sends this to the Head Office for confirmation of what they propose to give to these parties. In some cases a reply comes after a month or six weeks, and sometimes not at all. Applications by the Repatriation were made in July for some widows, and up to now (October) no reply has come."

And your own father, dear Mrs. Steyn, wrote me the following from Philippolis. You know how careful and accurate he was.

> "You have no idea what trouble we have to obtain rations for those in distress – then there is no meal; then again they are told they must go and work in the Relief Camps; and this to men who are burdened with families that cannot go, or who have stock too poor to slaughter but which have to be cared for."

To try and get to the bottom of the trouble I had forwarded to certain districts the Official Schedule of widows relieved partially or fully under Circular 120. I had hoped my friends would be able locally to confirm this return.

The list each time came back to me stated as quite incorrect or so worded as to give a wrong impression, and in order to clear up the mystery I submitted extracts from one of my correspondents' letters to Mr. Duncan, in which the writer had expressed himself perhaps somewhat strongly, characterizing the official return about widows in his district as "a glaring untruth or misrepresentation". As a matter of fact it *did* prove to be the latter though of course inadvertently so. Perhaps a measure of misrepresentation can never be avoided when it is attempted to depict human distress in schedules and figures. The ministers and I were in touch with the living, suffering, human beings, the Repatriation Headquarters knew them only as "cases" in terms of figures. The tendency to misunderstanding could not fail to be specially strong at such a moment as that – with the worn-out nerves resulting from a long war and the natural suspicion of foreigners, which was increased by the long waiting for Chamberlain's promised relief to the widows and the aged.

75. TO LADY HOBHOUSE

[c/o Mr. and Mrs. J. D. Bosman]
Johannesburg
13 August 1903

I seem to have lived through so much and seen so many people this past week that I have wholly forgotten where or what I last wrote and don't seem able to pick up the thread of my story.

I have been in Johannesburg three days and so far as I have seen the town I am disappointed in it.[a] There is, of course, a great deal of it to have grown up in so short a time (since 1887), but the buildings are disappointing, the streets patchy, big houses and semi-shanties alternately, the streets ill-kept, the shops nothing particular, not a single imposing edifice such as Pretoria possesses, and over all a thick coat of dust, making it a completely red town with red trees and plants. The town cannot hold a candle to Chicago or any new American town I have seen. But it has wonderful, clear air and abundant trees – large plantations and groves of blue-gum and Australian wattle and black wattle. Just now the mimosa is in full bloom and would be beautiful if it were not painted red with dust. It is a place where your feet go all to pieces and your breath gives out and you wish it were not against your principles to take a rickshaw!

People are very kind and I have to refuse to see callers, for my time and strength both fail. I wish they would be content to leave cards, but they will want to shake hands and all ask the same questions till one is weary. They kindly prepared a reception for me which took place last night in the Masonic Hall; there were crowds of people and I haven't yet recovered, having to be civil to everybody. The hall was beautifully decorated, and I had to shake hands with every single person in it. Moreover, every single person had a story which they tried to tell me but never got beyond a few sentences before they were interrupted and pushed on by the next.

Mr. Meiring, the clergyman, an endlessly tall man, exactly like the picture of "Curiouser and curiouser" in *Alice*,[1] got on the platform and made a long oration at me. Then a lady read the address and presented me with a beautiful *karros* or carriage rug as we should call it, made from the costly skins of the silver jackal said to be peculiar to the Transvaal and given by the ladies of Johannesburg. I see no way of "living up" to this rug. I gave them a good long speech in reply, rubbing in well the conditions of the poor in the districts, and they collected £100 on the spot. Moreover, it was announced that I would address a public meeting "on behalf of the poor" in ten days' time, and I was promised that four figures would be forthcoming if I did. It is absolutely necessary to raise funds somehow; we cannot let the people starve, and perhaps publicity may coerce the Government into feeding them.

I feel all eager for the chase. I shall love to make Johannesburg feel ashamed by a very realistic description of the present state of the country districts. I got away at last, after enduring much cramp in my feet with standing, plus a rug and address, but minus strength and temper.

Today I spent at Langlaagte, inspecting the Rev. Kriel's orphanage,[2] the largest and most important of them all. He is an energetic man, and the two-hundred-and-fifty children seem very happy, and though they have a hospital room so called, no one is ever in it. Several of the lads had been on Commando, some wounded, a good many in overseas prisons, girls had been wounded, one child's mother had been murdered by Kaffirs, the rest either in camps or on the veld. He has them on the cottage system – about twenty in each house under a teacher, so the whole village seems populated by orphans. They meet in a large marquee for meals, and some way off is a large school, a private one of their own, to which also some town children come. They cannot agree with the imported English teachers,[3] who know no word of Dutch and whose manners and mode of thought and religion are alien to them. Consequently Government refuses a penny of help to the orphanage, but Milner and Mr. Sargant[3] promised pound for pound if they would hand them over to the Government for education. This they will not do.

Very few orphans are in governmental hands. It is said, though I cannot vouch for the fact, that they are planting out the governmental orphans from the Irene Institution into English families in Pretoria. This means they will be made drudges – not brought up in the customs of the country.

The imported teachers are very much disliked. The Boers had been accustomed to have teachers from their best families, people who were all round good, in manners and morals and breeding, even if their specialized knowledge fell short of the English standard.

The girls sent out are very few of them ladies, they have all sorts of religious opinions, they are untidy in dress, and their manners, fast and flirtatious, are abhorrent to the Boers. In Reitz there was a Miss Allen whose conduct was such that after the holiday every inhabitant refused her lodging. She had been at the hotel where people were not particular, but even the hotel-keeper said he could not admit her again. In varying degree this sort of thing is universal. It is dull for them no doubt, and not knowing the language they take up and flirt with the S.A.C.'s who also are dull, do not know the language, and so it goes on. Private schools are growing and increasing.

The immigration girls, viz. the servants sent out by Lady Jeune, Lady Malmesbury and that set, are here, as in Cape Town, the subject of much conversation, and many stories of them are told.[4] I am glad to say Lady Lyttelton did speak to them recently on so many "going wrong", but the fault lies principally with those who send them to towns of this character, far from their friends. "Madam," said a girl, who was lady's maid, to her mistress, "Madam, I have now been with you a month, and you have not yet introduced me to an eligible man."

She proceeded to explain that she felt aggrieved, for she had understood the chief object in coming to South Africa was to be married.

The well-to-do Boers don't care to employ these girls because they speak such bad English with no H's and they fear lest their children will catch the bad accent.

Everybody is dissatisfied here as well as in Pretoria. I do not mean merely Boers – they say little and only laugh – but all classes. Municipal taxation is far heavier. The Post Office is bad, slow and unreliable. The Railway is slow, unsure, [with] constant thefts, dirty – even the Johannesburg paper devotes a stinging leader to it today complaining that military men are put in places to carry on work they know nothing about. Shop-keepers complain they cannot get their goods till the season is past – and so on. One looks in vain for any department that is well or satisfactorily worked. It all sounds very big and imposing in blue-books and newspapers, but the reality is failure and dissatisfaction with great squandering of the public money. However, I see Bishop Wilkinson[5] has sailed to arrange a great mission for next year; perhaps he will convert all the silly immigrants and make them good – for they need it – and then perhaps things may go better. If he would preach tact and good breeding it would be most to the purpose.

Take the S.A.C.'s – they are a nuisance everywhere; almost daily you see in the papers one or more of them had up for some theft or assault somewhere. Mr. Potgieter's house, where I was staying last month, had just been attacked by three S.A.C.'s who got into the house (having plundered the garden of oranges) and into the Kaffir girl's rooms. The Kaffir boy roused Mr. Potgieter in the dead of night shouting, "Baas, the English are here!" and he ran out and fired with his revolver, frightening them away; he made complaint to the Governor and others about it, and in the end two Kaffir police were sent up every night to march up and down and protect the house from the English police!

I am planning a visit to the Cornish miners; I want to see how they prosper and hear their point of view.

From the memoir

a) It was a big jump from quiet little Heilbron and the barren spaces and terrible gnawing hunger I had seen in the further districts to the bustle and plenty of Johannesburg. Nor could I escape a thrill on first entering the town which had been the centre of such an upheaval as your two little Republics had experienced. Whatever it may now appear, Johannesburg just after the war did not present a very pleasing face to a newcomer.

In the process of getting fresh air I saw something of the residential suburbs of Johannesburg which were a relief from the town proper. Even at that date there were some good houses though nothing very remarkable. One or two perched on the summit of craggy ridges had magnificent views. The tree-clothed valley lay below, with dense plantation of blue-gum, wattle and fir; beyond stretched ridge behind ridge, leading the eye to the blue heights of the Magaliesberg.

Away from its dust Johannesburg could be beautiful. Man had made it vile. Yet, all said, it was a marvellous growth considering the few years of its existence as a town. Born in 1886–7 its influence at the tender age of thirteen years had been strong enough to cause a war! One wondered whether its future influence on South Africa, which from its size and population must be profound, would prove malign or benign.

I was the guest of Mr. and Mrs. J. D. Bosman and in their home I was better able to deal with the work entailed by my public appeal. That work was heavy; the correspondence enormous, and I was minus secretary, office or typewriter. Mrs. Bosman was most helpful in letting me have a room where I could write quietly. It enabled me to follow up my appeal to the Cape by one to the *Manchester Guardian* which paper, always sympathetic to distress, opened a fund for the suffering farmers which very materially helped in providing ploughing teams for several districts.

It was striking that, as the days went on, the papers did not sneer much at my appeal. They sneered a good deal at *me*, but that did not matter as I was indifferent to their opinions. As regards what I *said* they were hardly able to deny it because they had not visited the country outside the towns. The *Cape Times*, after a little splutter, actually opened a fund, and itself headed the list.

76. TO LADY HOBHOUSE

Hartebeestfontein
30 [23] August 1903

I don't know if you follow my peregrinations on the map, but if you do you will see I am now at a point a few hours north of Klerksdorp in the Western Transvaal, and all yesterday and today I have been driving, driving further north again. I wonder if this will reach you in time to wish you a very happy birthday and a healthy one free from bronchial troubles, and for all our sakes lots more of them. By 13 September I shall be in the Orange River Colony, working southwards if all goes well.

I am now in the districts where Methuen operated so long, and I am amused to find he is known amongst the Boers as "the Everlasting Sweep". They hate him very cordially for his work; and it certainly was well done. I do not think there was a house left standing in the whole of this great church district – outside the town live about 250 families in the parish. These families live all sorts of ways now, clinging to walls and sheltering under pieces of hole-pierced zinc, minus windows or perhaps doors, not one that I have seen has been able to rebuild the house; there is neither material nor means, and it will be several years before there will be means. Some of the houses were really fine ones, as can be seen by the ruins, and all had a size and comfort now wholly unattainable. I slept in a piece of a very large house last night, for my sins; the windows had no glass and there was no furniture except the bed. Your woolly slippers are my only joy in these places where there is no floor and no carpet or mats, only the bare earth. Tommy had all the wooden floorings to cook his rations withal. It is horrid to put one's feet out onto mud floors. Of course I carry all my bedding, as I never know where my lot will cast me, and it generally casts me on kindness and barrenness combined.

I enjoyed this farm; there was a grove, untouched, of lovely orange trees (the Boers were at hand, and before they could be cut down the English fled). Moreover, the almond trees were in full bloom and here the blossom is not pink as with us, but white and very large. It was pleasant to see some signs of spring, and pleasanter still when we left in the early morning to hear the cuckoo!¹ Is this where the cuckoo comes to enjoy a second spring? I can't say he had quite tuned up his bill to so good a note as he treats us to, but it was pretty, all the same, and the Boers say he goes in for a family here too, which is odd to have two breeding times. They tell me the swallows do the same. Do you think they are our birds emigrated? Anyhow, there is something prolific about this country – in various parts the sheep lamb twice, viz. April and September, and often have twins on each occasion! This is accommodating where one wants, as now, to restock farms quickly. They say the Kaffirs work the sheep hard in this respect, but Boers rest the unfortunate mothers a year in between. The animals are altogether curious here, I often cannot tell them apart, the sheep from the goats, and neither from dogs. Their tails all turn the wrong way, and their shapes and sizes differ wholly from ours. I never admire a flock of sheep, but I am told they are goats, and vice versa!

My guide and host[2] of today enquired tenderly after Methuen; he was one of those who captured that hero, fighting with De la Rey. He was also a member of the Vereeniging Conference. He had four fat mules, the plumpest and sleekest I have seen, no skinny Repatriation mules these, but his own, saved among the kopjes and driven about with the Commandos. With these creatures he drove me about today like the wind, up hill and down dale, over the bumpiest and stoniest roads imaginable, so that I shrieked aloud with pain or fright all the time. The cart was but a wreck of former days, tied together with thongs, and how it lasted or we endured I do not know. We drove from 9 a.m. till sunset without once outspanning and without Mr. Kirsteyn or his small Oliver-sized[3] son seeming to want to eat. I *did*, and with apologies and much shame munched bread and cheese in the back of the cart. Owing to the bumps, going as David said "up to the heaven and down again to the deep",[4] it was difficult not to choke. But except to interview families *en route* we never paused.

It was a curious day because it was grey, no sun at all, the first grey day I have seen in the Transvaal. The last three days a few small clouds have been shewing themselves and this morning these had accumulated and covered the entire sky, though somewhat thinly. It has raised many hopes. One spot where we passed it had actually rained, for we could distinctly see the wet spots upon the dust. It would be the best and greatest news I could send, next to Milner's recall, if it *really rained*.

My poor little lunch did duty for a good many people today. I had six slices of bread and some cheese. I ate two myself and then we came to a house with four ravenous-looking little boys who sat in a row with hunger in their eyes. Their father had tramped to Lichtenburg (4½ hours by horse) to see if he could squeeze rations out of the Repatriation which he has no chance of doing. He has literally no food, had existed the last few weeks only by borrowing a bucket of meal or mealies from neighbouring farmers who are themselves at the end of their resources. He is thirty miles from the Government Relief Road Works, and if he is there only earns 5/- a day, out of which he must feed himself and the balance will not find the family in meal. Moreover, the weakness of these Relief Works is that they take the men off the land, and their only chance for next year is to be on the ground to plough and sow the instant rain comes and meantime to get things in order and undo, where possible, the ravages caused by the war. To leave home is to kill the goose which alone can lay their golden eggs. The mother of these lads was dead, but they had an aunt who looked after them, and a more hungry-looking woman I never saw. She just sat and looked but never spoke beyond the usual greetings. I gave each lad a slice of bread and cheese.

The next house was the same. In fact, all day it was the same – why write details?

At one house I gave my loaf of Boer biscuit; she was a widow with five children still at home. She owned a small piece of ground which the English had swept bare of every mortal thing, but because she *had* this piece no help or food whatever was or would be given her. She sits starving on the bare ground – no food, no soap, no money. By the law she cannot raise money on the ground nor sell it, nor can her children who are to inherit a share of it. Feed her till next harvest, and all will go well with her afterwards. The loaf comforted her, and a few yards of flannelette to boot.

At another widow's it was equally sad. Her house was a picture of neatness and cleanliness – a most superior woman. From the ceiling was suspended one leg of a table, a relic – all that remained of her once well-furnished house. No food has she, and none can she get, for, say the board, your son of sixteen must work on the roads. To send him there would be to destroy her last hope, for the neighbours had ploughed winter corn for her, it was already up, but if the lad was not there to send water on to it constantly, that and all her crops must fail, and there would be no outlet. After harvest all will be well with her, and as she and all the others say: "We don't want to beg; only pay our claims or our receipts and we can look after ourselves."

She had had much stock and has claimed for £1 000. She may get £10, but it will come too late to save her from this privation. She was a nice woman. I gave her my tin of milk biscuits over which she wept with joy. She said the day before she had cried all day not knowing what to do, and at last said to herself, something must turn up, when things come to the worst they mend. I promised her a sack of meal.

Another woman had two pumpkins in the house, *nothing* else, and so I might go on, the hungry look in these people's eyes speaks for itself. They will *never* ask for anything, always having known plenty they never begged nor can they now learn to beg, and you could go in and be civilly entertained and come out again without so much as guessing the real state of affairs.

I walked out to a distant hamlet by myself the first day I was here, unable to get horses, they are so scarce. I passed through a *poort* or narrow opening through the hills, and as I went I saw numbers of cartridges and things lying about. I did not know that I was walking right over the battlefield of Hartebeestfontein Poort where Methuen lost so many hundred men and seventeen officers. The Boers held the ridges on either side, only a few of them, and did their best to protect their pretty little town, but numbers and guns overpowered them at last and they fell back and the town was won but at bitter cost of life. Old Mrs. Joubert of Paarde Plaats happened to be in the town that day, and after the English had got in she inspanned and tried to drive out in her cart to get home. But they shot at her as she drove and that was how she was wounded through her two legs and is so lame and helpless now. She is a widow.

Mr. Kirsteyn, who brought me back yesterday, described all the battle to me; he was himself among the defenders of the town.

When I got to the hamlet I found a group of starving people, and a widow who was not starving because the Board was still giving her rations. Now this woman had saved eight donkeys from her wreck and these had five foals, so her thirteen animals are her substance and she can, by loaning them, earn something. Her neighbours are *all* penniless and with nothing, yet because she is a widow she is helped and others are refused. I quite think she needs help, but I think the others needed it even more. They were very nice people, all so clean and neat.

One family clustered in a waggon-house with a large opening; they had no means to buy material for a door, and all through this bitter winter had been thus exposed with bare bedding and clothing, and next to no food. One of them was making coffee, merely a courtesy title, from a few burnt grains of corn, and they had meal enough left for one baking, and many mouths to feed.

The want of soap is terrible, they are put to all sorts of straits to get or make it. Every man and woman can make their own shoes, but now there are no animals to kill and no leather, so they cannot make them, and cannot buy, and the men must have shoes to be able to go to work.

The Kaffirs are in as sore straits as the people themselves, and with this extra taxation the already poverty-stricken farmer has to pay the tax for them if he wants, as he does, to keep them on his farm. All the Kaffirs who were true to the Boers and came back to the land are suffering just as the Boers suffer.

Talking of Kaffirs, I don't think I told you about Mr. Alexander Tschwangtwe. He is an Evangelist amongst his folk, a Zulu with a wonderful profile who came to call upon me at Reitz. The clergyman spoke very highly of him as a man of very devoted life. He called in the kitchen, as it appears a Kaffir should always use the back door. He said he had heard the English Missis had come to look at the ruins and the poverty of the land, and he came to ask if I would not come and see the ruined location, church, school and huts all gone, and how hard his people had it too. So I said I gladly would, and much to the surprise of the Boers I deserted them all and walked off with Mr. Tschwangtwe and enjoyed his society very much. He wore a long brown coat and carried a walking stick. He has a handsome young wife and a small person of three in a chemise of minute proportions and a baby of six months with fat black limbs, which was untied from someone else's back to be introduced to me. He had built his school again with his own hands and inside was an intelligent-looking pupil-teacher drumming knowledge into seven black woolly heads. They had a packing-case for a table, but all their benches were burnt, blackboards and everything. The Evangelist had painted a strip of the clay-wall black and on that chalked the tonic sol-fa, and they sang to me English songs

271

taught by this method. Their singing was very sweet. All the huts and gardens were destroyed and the church, and the poor man did not know how to set to work again. Coming home he told me how he had been deported to Natal, and of the great black camp near Harrismith, and how the superintendent thereof had sent for him because the people were dying so fast. They died from thirty to fifty a day he said, which also I have heard elsewhere. He said: "My heart is sore, is sore for my people."

Reaching the house I found he left me at the front door and going in at the back came through the kitchen to bid me goodbye. I liked him very much. But this is a digression.

I am staying here with Mrs. Thea Hesse. You will remember her as the woman whom the Committee helped to pay her journey back from Germany and who returned part of the money so loaned. She is a charming and well-educated woman, daughter of a German missionary, and speaks English, German, Dutch and Kaffir equally well. She was delighted to have the chance of returning the Committee's kindness by housing me. Her husband, also a German, is Government schoolmaster here now. He has told me a great deal about the Education Department, its extravagance, its pig-headedness, its staff of officials ignorant of their subject, and of its imported teachers. Two of these near here were English M.A.'s, I suppose breakdowns from home, and both have had to be dismissed for drink. However, there is no doubt that most of these imported teachers will vanish in good time; already in his district he has got rid of all and substituted Afrikander teachers who can understand the language and are not above living on the farms with the people. A teacher in this country *must* be an all-round person, otherwise they are useless. The Hesses had lost everything and have had to begin from the very beginning again; he is fortunate to have got this post and I hope will be able to retain it.

Mrs. Winter, the clergyman's wife, is a plucky and spirited little person. She has lost everything and they are now living in an old draughty building used as a church before that was built. Partitions of corrugated iron make dismal stable-like rooms of this place, and the wind just rushes through and the sun cannot penetrate. I dined with them the first day. Mr. Winter is delightful, like a German philosopher in a skull cap, quite oblivious to his surroundings, bewailing only the loss of his large and valuable library. The Quaker gift of books[5] (£10 worth) had just come and he was charmed to have a few volumes again. His letter describing the state of his parish I hope to enclose (at least a translation).

Mr. Winter's youngest is called De la Rey.[a)] He was born while they were exiled in the Colony in bitter poverty, and though holding Lord Roberts' permit to return, not allowed to do so. She had no nurse or doctor, was alone with only an old Kaffir woman, and when the baby was born washed him herself when an hour old, and attended to her own needs herself. Married women may be able to sympathize in full.

They are too poor now to keep a servant; she does everything, and the entire parish in its poverty looks to them for material help they cannot give. My reception in Johannesburg realized over £100 and that sum I brought to them for the use of the people here, and I am also giving a load of meal which will cost £55 and perhaps keep thirty families alive for a month.

Hartebeestfontein[b] must have been a pretty little village, indeed it is pretty now, for there are gardens and water and a few orange trees. But it is a strange medley of ruin and rubbish and rebuilding and a new house here and there. Everything was gone but the church, and that was much damaged.

The population of the village, however, is mostly hands-upper and Scout, and these all are difficult to deal with and intensely dissatisfied. They sacrificed principle and honour and fidelity to their country to save their properties, for they were rich, and now they find their goods also were destroyed or seized and the compensation promised by Lord Roberts, for which mess of pottage they sold their birthrights, comes out or is coming only a shadow of itself. They are furious and I hear they mean in a body to prosecute the Government (?) in order to state their grievances and get their rights promised by Lord Roberts. These people are furious everywhere and get no sympathy from friend or foe. They think if they can't get sympathy and can't get respect, at least they'll try for the money. I doubt if they will get that either. For saying this I am liable to fine or imprisonment, these punishments having been inflicted on men who have so expressed themselves.[6]

Please forgive such uncomfortable, disagreeable letters as I am obliged to write.

From the memoir

a) How strange it was when recently I was working amongst the Germans at Heidelberg in Baden[7] to meet De la Rey Winter, the baby of Hartebeestfontein, studying in that university.

b) I loved Hartebeestfontein; it was one of the prettiest little villages in the Transvaal, having trees and golden fruit, and a mild and beautiful climate. It was there too that I met Mrs. Badenhorst, the "Tant' Alie" whose diary I recently translated and pulished. She was suffering even then, but so brave, and she made an impression that has never faded. Her own description in that journal of the ruin and destruction in their village is better than mine could be.

77. TO LEONARD HOBHOUSE

Randfontein
23 [27] August 1903

The train is resting for luncheon which I do not want at the above spot. I have written to Aunt Mary from and about Hartebeestfontein, and now will tell you about Klerksdorp. I was in a great quandary, having no funds left and face to face

273

with a wide-spread state of famine. In Hartebeestfontein things may be represented in figures something like this:

The country part of parish about 250 families:

First: about 70 of these starving.

Second: about 50 earning 5/- a day on Government Road Work equal to 1/6 at home.

Third: about 110 shaving along.

Fourth: about 20 able to help themselves.

One, two or three are all turning to four to feed them, asking to borrow a bucket of meal or mealies or pumpkins, etc., but four, who has done this for some time, can do it no longer, having only bare sustenance for itself, purchased with money raised on the land by a loan.

So all turn to the wretched minister who himself has had no income for three years, whose house and furniture is nearly always destroyed and who has now a diminished income.

Of course these figures are only approximate but I think may be taken as a fairly correct statement of the position.

(Train starts, must wait for next station.)

I want to tell you about rifles. It is clear to me from what I see and hear that there is a movement to take away their rifles from those Boer officers who had the right to them by the Peace terms.[1] This is done in different ways:

Young Mr. Steyn's was taken on the ground that he had no gun licence (which by the terms was not required); he, however, had no objection if it was demanded and went three times to the office for the licence but found no one there. Then the rifle was demanded on the ground that he had no licence, and he broke it to pieces rather than give it up.

I believe De Wet's has been taken from him also on some such pretext, but I must get this confirmed. Mr. Kirsteyn, a member of the Vereeniging Conference, was told to bring in his to have it marked with some particular stamp. That was eight months ago and he cannot get it back. The farmers, a list of whom was made at the Peace, with permission to keep their rifles round Zoutpansberg, all had them taken away, and when General Beyers asked for them, the Lieutenant-Governor said they were lost. Beyers said other rifles would do in their place, but nothing was done. I fancy they are very nervous with the fear of guilty consciences, but never was fear more unnecessary.

I have had an unusually large reception at Klerksdorp. I was the guest of the Strasheims, minister and wife, and he is the most irritating form of D.R.C. minister I have yet met. I get on well with most and am very fond of some like Mr. and Mrs. Winter and Louw and Viljoen, but Mr. Strasheim seems to think he walks hand in hand with the Almighty, and his attitude is overbearing to a degree that is beyond endurance. He is autocratic and dogmatic and conceited and narrow, and after he had described to me his interview with Chamberlain I could not help siding with Chamberlain. His heart is in the right place, but he lays down the law to an extent that is beyond endurance.

He had all the town in the big church to meet me and had one of those odious affairs, half-service, half-laudatory of myself, which I loathe, and I had to speak, knowing that all the "enemy" were present. Then the address was read me *in church* – oh, I get so cross! Afterwards there was a big social evening which lasted late and I had to shake hands and speak again.

A very pretty girl asked me to accept a present made by her father who is now getting a living as a jeweller! It was a Kruger half-sovereign (which is rare) which he had set for me as a brooch, reversible.

Now I am back in Johannesburg and I find the papers all on fire with anger at me for saying there is distress – "hysterical female" – again, and so on.[2]

I am sending you the translation of a letter from the Rev. Winter of Hartebeestfontein which you may publish in the *Manchester Guardian* if you like.[a]

From the memoir

a) This letter, too long to include here, had been addressed some weeks previously to the Rev. Meiring of Johannesburg in answer to his enquiry in the *Vereeniging* as to the famine conditions in the various country districts. Writing 21 July, Ds. Winter says:

> "Concerning my congregation these reports are in no way exaggerated but contain the purest truth. The need and misery amongst the people in the open country is indescribably great . . .
>
> "The people simply have no food to eat . . . The sunken cheeks and tottering limbs speak to you of poverty and famine. 'Hunger' is plainly written on the pale, emaciated face, which is verified by what is said with a deep sigh and at times a tear in the eye but with wonderful calmness. 'Since yesterday noon I have tasted nothing,' or 'I do not know what I shall eat tomorrow'."

Ds. Winter ends his letter by saying that the Government demanded a heavy import tax on even the old clothes sent as a gift by the people of Cape Colony.

I, who saw his people a few weeks after the above was written, could endorse every word. In his long, closely argued letter, Ds. Winter shewed the causes of this distress and spoke of Mr. Chamberlain's meeting with the farmers at Lichtenburg in the previous January and the promises he had made and the glowing picture he painted. But promises don't sustain life.

Johannesburg

27 [30] August 1903

I have been so very, very busy of late I have not been able to write English letters at all this week. I sent you a very long letter descriptive of my Heilbron, Lindley, Reitz and Frankfort tour, and I sent it via Mrs. Murray of Cape Town that she might read it *en route*. I cannot hear it ever reached her and so I fear will never reach you. This is very disappointing if it is so, as I can never re-write so long a letter and it was specially interesting I think; I wanted to keep it.

It was the most distressed by far of the districts I have seen, and after that, being out of funds, I appealed to Cape Colony and have generally called public attention here to the matter, with the result that already over £2 000 is sent me from the Cape; collections are being made here in Johannesburg, and people, even the Government, are stirring round to send in lists of names to the magistrates, *prepared by the clergy* who alone know the people, with a view to supplies being recommenced for them. Meanwhile as Authorities are so long I am supplying meal to the worst districts, but hope to be able to keep a good sum of my new fund for the purchase of teams to go round and plough for those who have no trek animals; otherwise next year will be as bad as this one has been.

I had a very good and crowded meeting here,[a] I set out to make it as British as possible in order to get it on a broad basis, and asked the support of the Chambers of Mines and of Commerce, which was refused. But people were nervous and dropped it, which made me angry, and so I accepted the offer of Irene Hall at present leased by the Dutch, and this of course gave a Dutch tone to the meeting, which was unavoidable. However, a great many English were there, and I rubbed in the poverty as thoroughly as I could, and feel the chief object was attained of making the whole matter public, for it was quite unknown. No one goes into the country districts, the roads are too bad and the expense of hiring too great, consequently town and country do not know each other.

You will have seen that the Cape Parliament, acting upon my appeal, has almost unanimously passed a resolution to send a representative to investigate the needs up here, and render, if necessary, substantial aid. They chose Captain Jenner,[1] whose just administration of martial law won him the respect and even the love of Dutch and English alike, and he was, they wrote me, to start at once. But I see in the papers that his mission is considered an insult and that the Government here will not favour or allow him, so for the moment I know no more.

To-morrow I return to Pretoria for my farewell visit and to pick up my goods left there and shall work down towards the Orange River Colony and the Colony, unless I have to meet Captain Jenner and in any way determine my plans by his.

De La Rey and I have been playing hide-and-seek with one another, but hitherto we have not met. I was within three hours of Lichtenburg where I am told the congregation had put horses at my disposal, but I had to come back for this meeting and hardly think I can get so far again. But they may insist.

Did I tell you about Mr. Van Rensburg? He got into our cart when we drove from Hartebeestfontein to Klerksdorp, a dark-eyed, gentle man who had sat over two years in St. Helena, as P.O.W.

I asked him how he lived now, the usual question, and he said by finding water with a stick. Soon after, as we were driving along, he said suddenly: "Stop, there's water here", and jumping out he went and cut a forked stick from a thorn tree, and, trimming it, held it in both hands and walked across the spot we had driven past. The stick went so madly round and round he could hardly hold it with all his force, and it shewed also the direction in which the water flowed. Mr. Hesse got out and taking the stick began to walk, but the stick only moved feebly in his hands; then I must needs try, but for me it made no movement at all. Mr. Van Rensburg took it again and it became quite violent and excited. So we got in and drove on, the Boer holding the stick he had cut. Between that and the town in two other spots it began to waggle and twist as we drove, and he said: "There is water here". He tells me he has found sixteen good fountains for people since peace, earning a nice sum thereby, and six places he has told people they would *not* find water, but they would dig and found none. It was quite accidentally he discovered his power before the war. There was a certain spot on his farm which he often passed and he always noticed that any wood he might be carrying, such as a handle of an implement laid across his shoulder or in his hand, began to dip up and down as he passed the spot, quieting again when it was crossed. At last he dug there and found a beautiful spring, and now, ruined, he is turning his power to account to earn a livelihood. This might interest Lord Farrer, who, I remember, wrote an account about a water-finder in the *Speaker* last spring.

Old Piet Cronjé, General Cronjé of Paardeberg fame, came to see me yesterday, and attended my meeting in the evening. He is a curious, stubborn old rock of a man of the old school. I rather liked him – it is his brother Andries who became the National Scout and of whom "Joe" made so much.

At Klerksdorp live the old father and the sister of Mrs. Master of Flaxbourton, and I enquired about them, meaning, if I had leisure, to call, because Mrs. Master had asked me to look them up if I was in their neighbourhood. I had not, however, time to do so, but my presence there was mentioned to Miss Francken by a mutual friend. She would not come to call nor attend my reception for she has joined the Loyal Women's Guild and does not wish to know me. Mrs. Fawcett has recently been visiting Klerksdorp and reviving the Guild and lecturing to it on Queen Victoria, etc. Miss Francken is maintaining herself and her father by keeping a boarding-house and Mrs. Master allows her sister £40 a year to help pull them through.

I have been seeing something of the Editor of the *Tribune*.[2] He tells me that though on the surface everything looks as if Chinese labour were inevitable, yet in

277

his opinion it will not come. This is the first hopeful person I have met on this subject. He says they are working hard underground against it. They have just completed the formation of a National Democratic Federation or League,[3] and have hopes that the Dutch will join their party and keep off all suspicion of *racial* ideas by working together. The capitalists are forcing everything on to *racial lines*, and do what you will you are called racial. I hope the Dutch will join them, but at present they mostly say no, we will sit still and watch you do the fighting, if we join we shall be called seditious. This Democratic League, he hopes, will in a very short time begin to organize demonstrations which shall be heard of beyond the borders of the Transvaal. At first they had intended to wait till after the report of the Labour Commission was issued, but that is long, and in November the Legislative Council meets again and Chinese labour may be passed any moment by the Milnerian nominees. So there is no time to lose. This Editor says he came here with the fullest faith in British Administration, but is now disgusted by the incompetency and ignorance and insolence of all concerned.

Knowing a good deal about farming himself he had been civilly invited to meet and interchange ideas with the Heads of the Land Settlement Deparment. He had done so and says he never before met with such a combination of ignorance and extravagance. The head, he says, is a writer from the *Spectator* who knows nothing about farming, who is at present full of a scheme for growing sunflowers!

I shall be interested to watch his organized demonstrations and see if he succeeds in stopping Chinese immigration. I fear the monied class is too powerful – money is passing all round, the screw is being put on all objectors. The mining folk mean to have a boom, then to load off on the public, and then the boom will die down and the opposite will be done. It is all an affair of the market manoeuvred up and down to suit people who sit here all day long and speculate.

I have been sent reams by an irate Englishman, who wants to come and pour out his woes, poor "loyal" man, ruined by his devotion to Milner and Co., but 'tis useless his coming to me. He gives England five years more in this country! Perhaps I will send his papers home, not because they are well written or very refined, but because they faithfully picture the prevailing feeling amonst British subjects out here. These complain all day and every day and about everything.

29 August, Pretoria. I am back here for my farewell visit, and am waiting to hear if the Cape Colony Emissary, Captain Jenner, is coming or not. If not, I must go to Lichtenburg as De la Rey brings a very sad account of the state of affairs in that town and neighbourhood.

From the memoir

a) I remember vividly my meeting in the Irene Hall, Johannesburg. It was crowded. I had to do two things – the easy one of describing the distress I had seen and could vouch for, and the difficult one of replying to accusations made against me. That is always difficult when your accusers are not face to face with you, but hit in the dark and with such little knowledge of the subject that they make assertions wholly foreign to the truth.

As I have told you before, I always feel it better to ignore Press attacks and should on this occasion have done so, but for the sake of my cause I was forced to reply to these critics. I challenged the *Transvaal Leader* to bring forward a single statement of mine about the Concentration Camps which had ever been disproved, and asked why their writers were allowed to rush into print without investigation. The *Leader* had published an article the previous day called "Humanity and Hysterics", which I found helpful because I could answer it point by point. In these modern days of women's work and women's influence in all public matters the adjective "hysterical" has nearly if not quite dropped out of use, but in those far-off days Victorian views still predominated, and "hysterical" figured frequently in the male vocabulary. I had always noticed that when a women held an opinion opposite to the men she had to do with, and they had no arguments with which to confront her, they invariably turned round and dubbed her "hysterical". I told the meeting in Irene Hall that to call a woman "hysterical" because you have not the knowledge necessary to deny her facts is the last refuge of the unmanly and the coward, and that I always felt when termed "hysterical" that I had triumphed because it meant my arguments cannot be met nor my statements denied.

After that I heard no more of that adjective in the Transvaal, but a few weeks later Sir Hamilton Goold-Adams, Governor of the Orange River Colony, found it useful in an attempt to decry my statements on a public occasion. Poor man! I appreciated the difficulty he was in and realized the word was too precious as a hiding-place to be lightly abandoned by men of that generation. No man would be tolerated who used it now.

79. TO LEONARD HOBHOUSE

Pretoria
2 September 1903

I feel very glad today. I have just had an interview with Mr. Duncan, the Colonial Treasurer and Head of the Repatriation Department.[1] He wrote to ask me if I would care to talk to him about my work in the country, and would I come to his office or appoint a place. I said I should much like to talk to him and would he call on me at General Botha's house where I am now staying. Yes, he would, and he has been, and we talked for two hours. Poor young man! I dealt gently with him, for he is inexperienced and so evidently means very well and is so wholly ignorant of the working of his boards.

It so happened that yesterday Mr. Van Gass, a very nice fellow, who has started a farm about ten miles from Pretoria, took me out to his district to visit the people.

There, so close under the nose of the Central Board, I found case after case of widows, wholly neglected, sick men, infirm and old, all practically starving, existing on the charity of most impoverished neighbours. I found also men of health and energy with that strained look of anxiety so common here, straining every nerve on empty stomachs to try and get on to their legs again. Helping these is a real joy, and their gratitude for the ploughing of a few acres or a bag of seed, etc. is most deep and touching. Well, I made careful notes of all these cases and they came in most handy to set before Mr. Duncan.

Poor young man! He made desparate efforts to defend himself and his boards, but case after case typical of the different needs bowled him over, and he fell back on the difficulties of the country, and the style of man he had been obliged to employ on the commissions – ex-Volunteers[2] and the like. He was very meek on the whole, only making one or two spasmodic efforts to defend himself, but the fact remains, Smuts and Botha have repeatedly put these things before the Governor and himself and they would not believe or act; now I have upset their apple-cart by my letter to the *South African News*, making it all public, and they want to stop my mouth and appease me. He has made me great promises, and asked me to send to him every distressed case I meet with. He is going at this eleventh hour to whip his boards into shape. Better late than never. He will take the men back from the Relief Works and put them on the land again, so that they can plough and sow and have hopes of a harvest, and he will feed them till the reaping comes. All this and much more he meekly promises, but of course Botha says "Of what value are promises? Chamberlain stopped our collection by promises never performed, and now they are stopping yours." Well, we shall see. It may be so.

Meanwhile my collection increases daily. It is now £2 700 and I can go ahead and buy teams of oxen and begin ploughing. Mr. Duncan says the Repatriation will plough too, and no doubt they will begin when our teams have concluded the work. The last subscribers have been Oom Paul himself, £50, and his son-in-law Mr. Eloff, £50, with a very nice message from the old gentleman brought me by his charming granddaughter Mrs. Jacobsz and his great-granddaughter.

Before I forget it – and I can only write this letter in scraps – let me say that the statement put about in the papers here, and I believe also at home, that Botha is leaning towards or favouring Chinese labour is a whole and complete lie. He has several times been obliged to publish a disclaimer of these falsified opinions said to be his. I tell you this in case you should find opportunity to refute. They are working up Chinese labour for all they are worth, putting the screw on everywhere, and holding meetings and getting petitions, and all the well-known plans are being tried. I have mailed you a *Tribune* and a *Critic* which say something of these things on opposite sides and have also some remarks on my meeting.

I think I told you that I met Mr. Outhwaite, the Editor of the *Tribune*, and his hopefulness that even yet the Chinese may be averted. Feeling in Johannesburg is very tense. Milner is hissed and groaned at by the British and Uitlander alike; the

Dutch keep quiet and say "It is your business, fight it out." The British say: "Only join and lead us and we'll rise in a body."

And so it goes on. Botha and Smuts are frequently warned that it is intended to deport them, but I do not think this will be done.

Dorothy Bradby and others say that the effect of Botha's letter to you in *The Times* was to make people think all was going well with the country folk. But he particularly said the work of Repatriation is *a failure*. Think what those few words involve. It is true he said that everywhere they are building their houses and I own this is calculated to mislead: he should have said *parts* of their houses or waggon-houses or stables. Of the large farmhouses I have only seen two or three rebuilt or habitable, and those without windows, with about one exception. For the most part the ruined house stands aside untouched waiting for compensation to be rebuilt. Or a back room is fitted up with old zinc. In the Ermelo District I believe this is better, farmers there having more cash laid by to rebuild, but I speak of what I have seen. He speaks too of ploughing, but only the winter ploughing of corn, mostly done by large farmers and not in all districts – the ploughing for mealies, the great staple crop of the country, has yet to come, and this affects all the small farmers and *bijwoners*. The prevention of famine next year all depends on this crop.

General Botha – with whom I am now staying[a)] – takes just the same view of the country and its wants as I do. At the time that letter was written he was conducting negotiations with the Governor upon the very subject of the distressed people. They dare not now write openly and support me lest it should be thought they were using me as their political agent. As a matter of fact they knew nothing of my doings. My appeal, which I fondly thought a very simple and innocent one, was written away in the Orange River Colony, at a moment of despair in the face of starvation I had no funds left to relieve, and I never thought it would have created so great a stir as it has done here, or so upset the apple-cart again. However, South Africa is down upon me now with a vengeance, and fear of the Coercion Act keeps those silent who wish to endorse my statements. I care not, understanding all the ropes now, and have netted near £3 000 thereby, and what is more important, far, opened the eye of the public, which causes instant activity in the Government, which sends the Colonial Secretary to me, who stirs up the Repatriation Boards, which feeds the people, and it all reminds me of the old woman whose pig would not get over the stile. I am the old woman, but I think now my pig will get over the stile and so I think I shall get home at last!

You would be amused if you could see and hear the madness of the British subject here. They come now and then and pour out to me. The last was a Dr. Kay who wants his articles published, but now that he writes against Milner no one that he can find will publish his writings. He has supplied the *Western Morning News* throughout the war, so you can imagine the sort of man. "Pugnacious" is written all over his countenance and stamped upon a nose which has been turned on to one side. He may go shortly to England, and if so I shall give him an introduction to

281

you because you may find it useful if not amusing to see the type that worked up the war – a man who will give you opinions of the present, typical of the Britishers and their sentiments.

I am off on Monday to Potchefstroom and I know a reception awaits me there. Oh! to be received no more! Thence to dear old Oom Koos at Lichtenburg and to do that famine-stricken region. I guess that spells yet another reception. On Sunday I am to stand godmother to the granddaughter of old General Joubert, Commandant Malan's daughter, another "peace" baby who is to receive my name.[3]

The other day an old lady came up to me and said: "My dear, you are not the only Emily Hobhouse."

I said: "Oh?"

She said: "My son has got a little girl and it is christened Emily Hobhouse, so *you* are not the only one."

Triumph of the old lady! – So you see, I am multiplying in this uninteresting way, and wretched babies are being saddled with my very ugly name.

I am staying this week with the Bothas. He has bonded his farm and done some successful speculation with cattle brought into the country, buying in herds and importing and selling, and has bought a very nice house, and Mrs. Botha and the children have come and they have at last a happy home again. Here people pour in to see him all day long and he has to fight every point inch by inch with the Governor, Milner, etc. They all speak well of Lawley as a man well disposed, and if let alone likely to do well for the country, for farmers as well as mine-owners.

This letter is dull, but the fact is I have had loads of South African correspondence this week, which has tired me out and I have left unsaid all I ought to have said and perhaps said what I had better not have said, anyhow, there is at the moment no health in me, so I must stop.[. . .]

From the memoir

a) During those quiet days in General Botha's house in Pretoria I was closely tied by the correspondence resulting from my appeal to the Cape. The response was most generous, and further involved much writing in regard to its distribution, the purchase of meal, of ploughs and of oxen, etc. When cramp threatened my hand I found change and delight in Mrs. Botha's music. Her voice, a clear ringing soprano, gave me great pleasure, and her songs carried me back to old days of my youth when music filled our lives.

80. TO LADY HOBHOUSE

Pretoria

4 September 1903

I am so saddened by your letter of 14 August saying you and Uncle Arthur are still cooped up in London and that owing to the accident to his knee he is actually in his bedroom. I am so very sorry you should be missing the usual summer delights and the pure air of Somersetshire. And I am afraid my letters are not calculated to cheer or enliven you, being all about sad and desolated things. So this week my long letter is going Leonard-wards.

Now that September has come I do hope you will have picked up enough to go to Banwell. Cables speak now of a heat wave, and that will do you both good I hope. Anyhow, please do not bother about the horrid things I write about. After having seen a large number of people with absolutely nothing to eat, and having exhausted my English fund, I sat down in despair and wrote a very simple little appeal (as I thought) to the *South African News* of Cape Town, asking if people there would help again. To my astonishment this appeal has brought the whole of South Africa down upon my head. At first even the Jingo papers supported me and the *Cape Times* opened a fund, then suddenly turning round they stopped their fund and have belaboured me for all they are worth.[1] At this moment they are still sending reporters from one to another *asking* men to *deny* my statements.

However, I care not, for nearly £3 000 has come in, enabling me to send loads of meal hither and thither and to provide ox teams for immediate ploughing in several of the worst districts. But better even than that, the publicity has aroused (the anger, perhaps, but also) the activity of the Government. This week the Colonial Secretary wrote, asking if he might call to talk over my views and information as he was Head of the Repatriation. And of course I was only too glad. He came and had an evil two hours. I was able to give him full details of case after case, and told him of the deplorable doings of some if not most of his Repatriation Boards. I think he was beginning to doubt the success of his Boards, and well he may. If his promises to me are fulfilled, then all will go well and the present tension be relieved. He was very "whipped" and begged me as I went about the country to send to him at once every case I found in need and unattended to, so I shall be in pretty continual correspondence with him! A great deal of what I told him was an eye-opener to him. The people *have* no money and *can* have none till harvest, so I said if he would feed the people till then, I could attend to their clothes. Then they can plough.

But will he keep his promises? If he does, all will go well and I can consider my work ended and wend my way southwards and so home. The Murrays are sailing in early November and much want me to go with them, but they are going by the East Coast route, very interesting but too costly I fear. However, I shall see. At this moment I am due in Potchefstroom and go thence to Lichtenburg to the De la Reys, all that district being proverty-stricken in the extreme. They are eating *mier-cats* and roots.

Pretoria
6 September 1903

Dearest Nora,

It is long since I have written to you, but hand and brain refuse to write more letters. My correspondence in *this* country has become so very large, so that when I come to a town ostensibly to rest, I find a huge pile of letters awaiting me which have to be attended to, and so I get no rest. But I think progress has been made, that I have considerable grip of the subject now, that relief is being poured into the right channels, and above all that the Government *here* in Transvaal at any rate is amenable and is listening to my ideas and taking my advice!!!

Today I have been godmother to Commandant Malan's "peace" baby, and it has received my name. The mother is the only child of old General Joubert and a very nice woman. Mrs. Widow Joubert is rather dour, but her daughter is very sweet. The baby is No. 9, and though not yet 18 days old, the mother has journeyed with it all the way up from Standerton, a night journey, and well and radiant attended the ceremony this morning. It was a very funny one.

The old church, which stands in the centre of the great square at Pretoria, was crowded. *Dominus* Louw conducted the service. He stood aloft in his elevated pulpit with a deacon sitting on the steps to keep guard. The font was just below. At a given signal we all got up and stood around the rostrum, a great party of some fifty godparents. Not all for one baby though. No, it appears that a large number were to be christened and though no babies were in evidence at this juncture, they were all secreted in the vestry, whence a combined howl issued, and a door at the back opening, I saw the vestry converted pro tem into a nursery, the coloured girls with the babies, and the table littered with hoods, cloaks and bottles!

We godparents were harangued, and at a given point we all bowed our heads in acquiescence I suppose, but I did not, not having had it explained. And then the mothers departed, returning from the vestry with a variety of screaming babies. Fortunately for the minister the father presented him in every case with the name written on paper, for most babies had three names. One was called Lemmer Gravitt [*sic*] Spruyt after the three Generals killed in the war,[1] and one was called Cordua after the innocent man who was executed here,[2] and Christians and Jacobuses of course abounded. Talking of names, both sides vie with each other. I heard of one called Belmontia Graspania Modderrivieria Methuen.[3]

Rev. Louw read the 42nd Genesis about Joseph's brethren going to buy corn, and preached on the subject, taking as the text verse 30 – the lord of the land spoke roughly to them, etc. He drew obvious morals. He prayed a long extempore prayer, and prayed for poor me.

7 September. I am now on my way to Potchefstroom and go thence by motor car to Lichtenburg. It is the postal service. May I survive!

I have enjoyed staying with the Bothas. They have a roomy and delightful house and the children are nice. Louis is being gradually transformed from a Commando burgher to a schoolboy. I notice he shares Oliver's liking for disappearing suddenly and being lost, and then there is a hue and cry for hours or days as the case may be. Mrs. Botha sings beautifully. I had no idea she had such a fine voice, and well trained too. She is singing chiefly Saint-Saëns' songs and I found it very hard to manage the accompaniments. Her old father, Mr. Emmett,[4] a very courtly old gentleman of 81, has come to live with them, and an orphan niece. They are, like everyone else, most hospitable, and all day long people pour in to talk to Botha and have a meal. General Cherry Emmett spent a day and I found him charming. He is on the Repatriation at Vryheid and said it had been very hard work to keep it right, but they had succeeded better than most, only spending £5 000 in the outlay of £100 000, and he would not have let it run so high, only the salary of the Head was fixed beyond their control, which was hard as they had to account for the money. Most of the boards have been prosecuted for embezzlement, theft or bigamy, and a few such high qualities and noble deeds. Such an Augean stable!

Today I travelled with Rev. Louw to Boksburg, such a nice fellow, one of the nicest ministers I have met. To my surprise he told me he was a brother of Willie Louw, who you remember was executed at Colesberg, and whose story I published. He wants me to come to Boksburg, but everyone wants me to go everywhere, and flesh and blood won't and can't do it. I am beginning to feel quite fagged out.

Pretoria looks lovely now in spring garb. Weeping willows are a great feature of the country, and they weep very long tears of pale spring green, and mingled with them on all sides are the peach trees in full blossom, veils of purplish pink drawn over the trees and gardens. The combination is lovely. Peaches are very common, almost wild, a stone dropped anywhere grows and bears fruit, even among bare rocks by the railway side. A fine country is the Transvaal – full of possibilities, more water and more beauty than the Free State, and the people far more go ahead. Moreover the people are not *nearly* so bitter as the Free State, but more ready to accept and make the best of the new state of things.

8 September. I am writing this in Potchefstroom and am conscious that it is Leonard's birthday. Many happy returns to him. Last night there was a big reception in the hall for me, but though they *made* me an address, they did not *give* me one as usual. But the youngest orphan, a small charmer clad in white china silk, came and presented me with a large bouquet of flowers. A very nice man was Commandant Douthwaite, which, you will perceive, is a North-Country name.

Can't finish this, so no more.

From E. H.

Holfontein, Biesjesvlei, Lichtenburg
12 September 1903

I have been thinking much of you and Uncle Arthur and wondering if August dealt more gently with you and if you escaped from the imprisonment of bedrooms to Somersetshire gardens. I hope the next letter will tell me so, but this week and probably next I shall have a famine of letters, for it is hopeless to have them sent after me, they must accumulate in Pretoria.

I left Pretoria a week ago, and it will be more than a week before I can get back, for this district (I write between Lichtenburg and Schweizer Reneke) is in a terrible condition of heart-rending poverty and I have to take notes of case after case, and hardly one can be passed by. Food is so scarce and vegetables do not exist, indeed no green blade. The Harts River I have crossed and recrossed today without knowing it was ever a river. There is nothing to shew that it was ever such. The drought is terrible. All day the wind has blown and the dust driven us mad, and they say the wind brings the rain, but this year it does not do so. Hereabouts it has not rained since last January, and then not the usual amount. If it does not come, the present serious state of things will become terrible indeed.

You will have heard from my other letters that the Transvaal Government in the person of the Colonial Treasurer, Mr. Duncan, has had the sense to make use of me and work with me, instead of insulting me as the Free State Government has now twice done. Mr. Duncan as a *man* is, I think, nice and trustworthy, but as an *official* I do not yet know what to think. But I do think he is awakening to the fact that his Repatriation is a fraud and a failure. Take this *one* point. I told him I could as yet find no case helped under the Widow Scheme. He replied uncomfortably that was very odd, for already £70 000 had been spent on that department alone. He said he would send me a list of those thus helped. The list shewed only 86 under the *full* grant and 105 under the partial grant.

I have been hunting for these and after travelling 250 miles found two or three, but though returned under the full grant not one of them *had* the full. Taking the fullest of the market prices of the goods supplied I find the total for the 86 widows would only come to £3 096 and the 105 *partial* grants to about £200. Say in all £3 300 as against the £70 000 he says has been spent. The money vanishes in salaries and frauds. I have put this before him, and am also carrying out his request to send him the details of every destitute case I meet with. This is satisfactory, but adds immensely to my work.

Of course I see the other side of this, namely the partial shutting up of my mouth, if not an entire stopping of my collection.

It is dreadful to see how hungry the people are in these districts. There are here too many Griqualanders who are regarded as rebels,[1] and these the Government flatly refuses to feed or help, so they are wholly dependent upon charity.

I have much to write about, but I am so tired after a very long day and no nice meal that I cannot write more but must go to a very unattractive room and get what sleep I can. I feel this is the last trek I can stand.

17 September. Schweizer Reneke. It is actually raining!!! Or more truly trying to do so while the sun scoffingly shines on, scornful of the attempt. But as all the roofs are zinc and all the houses one-storied, a very little rain makes a great deal of noise. Still it is hopeful, and after driving as yesterday 35 miles without finding a drop of water for the mules it is refreshing even to see a drop. Schweizer Reneke seems to stand in a little Sahara all its own, and is feebly trying to rise from its ruins and pronounce itself a village once more. It has not got very far yet, only the parsonage was finished four weeks ago, and I am the first guest therein. For the rest it is mostly tents, ruins, and a few shanties put together anyhow without windows and not always doors. It was a rich farming region and now all is swept away and the community further impoverished by the influx of Griqualanders. These unfortunate families had all their property in Griqualand confiscated and cannot return there. They must try to get a living here, but the Government refuses all help. There must be full five hundred of such families in the West Transvaal.

The poverty is very great in this huge parish. The minister tells me he has about 420 families, all of course desperately poor, and, to put it moderately, half that number are in need of food. For six months they have been living on charity; for the widows here Mr. Chamberlain has as yet done nothing whatever except the stopping of their rations last February. The Generals' Fund has kept the wolf from the door during this cruel, cold, dry winter, and collections from ourselves and the Colony. I have seen case after case today and am sending full details up to Pretoria. Without windows and even doors, in a loaned waggon-house or a shanty, these poor women – clean, neat, respectable people – are struggling along with several children, and Chamberlain I suppose has never given them another thought, and Botha's collection for them might have been twice as great if it had not been stopped by him.

Now the Government is behaving like an angel towards me just to stop my mouth too, and it is amusing that they send wires down to wake up the Repatriation where I go. The magistrate has been sent to call upon me here, and has had to call a meeting this afternoon to consider the list of the poor. I do not think they will dare to let things slide again, for I think Mr. Duncan is now fully alive to the awful state of things which will be next year should the harvest again fail. They muddled the ploughing then; to do so again would be fatal. So you can understand, with the ploughing of the Transvaal upon my mind, my anxiety about the rain is very great.

The magistrate is an ex-Volunteer and a Scotch barrister, so what is he likely to know about Boer farming? You may say and what can *I* know? The difference is this: I live with the Boers and adopt their views and plans; he lives apart and expects them to adopt his.

We hope to have a splendid team here at £16.10s each (Repatriation oxen are £22) and in this parish we have decided to plough large tracts in two or three good centres and pool the harvest rather than risk delay in sending the span from farm to farm where the land might not be so good.

The drive from Lichtenburg here has been tremendous and I barely came out alive. I started from Lichtenburg, not knowing how or to whom I was going, and as usual had to go in faith. When I asked, General De la Rey said he would arrange everything and I need do nothing but obey. The Boers are curious people, one never knows what they are about, and they never tell you even the plans relating to yourself. The *only* way is to trust them implicitly and then it all works out right. I am always treated as a precious bundle to be handed about the country, and so now I left Lichtenburg in the dark but find myself here today – a chain formed for me right across the great stretch of country. Everywhere the best attainable was given me, but in such a poor neighbourhood it was, of course, very rough. In future I shall always look upon a face towel as one of the great luxuries of life. I sometimes wonder whether there is a point at which hospitality becomes a vice!

Did I tell you of De la Rey's farm – just a few acres of rubble? We poked aside the rubbish with my parasol and found the outline of the foundations – 75 by 45 feet. They feel it so dreadfully; Mrs. De la Rey cannot speak of it yet, much less look at it without tears, for there is no probability that they can rebuild it again.[a] And the dreary rows of hundreds of stumps of fruit trees that both there and elsewhere I have to help weep over! They are endless. Now the De la Reys live in their Sunday house in the village, just two bedrooms opening off a dining-room, all very rough and temporary. Here all day long the General sits and the men and women file in at the open door with their tales of desperation and distress. Three or four weeping widows round him always and a cluster of hungry and desperate men. Here too he sits and writes his book[2] which bids fair to be the most interesting of all the three[3] if only he gets a good translator. So he is very busy; he does *not* talk of "my friend Mr. Chamberlain", quite the contrary, entertains a poor opinion of him in every way.

I was taken about the district by Mrs. De la Rey's brother, a young Mr. Greeff, and we dined at his house, a dreadful ruin, with the floors all rooted up and the doors gone and the wall broken. It was a fine big house and remained intact until 19 May 1902, when ten days before Peace and during negotiations the troops took it into their heads to wreck it utterly. So they live in terrible discomfort in a couple of rooms and wonder if they will ever have the money to rebuild it, seeing Compensation is a fraud, and they have no cash properly to restock the farm. The last paragraph of Botha's famous letter saying the Boers were busy rebuilding their houses, etc., etc. has, I fear, misled the English people. Smuts told him it would and that it was liable to misapprehension, but Botha would add it. It makes you all think of peace, contentment, and returning prosperity, a state of things far from the truth. As a matter of fact it is a rare sight to see any of the good houses rebuilt. *Some* of the *bijwoners'* small cottages are renewed, but the big houses will be

288

many years unbuilt; what Botha should have said was that they were busy putting up shelters in waggon-houses and stables. In Ermelo District I hear the houses have been more freely rebuilt, because in that part the farmers were possessed of more cash in banks.

Botha also drew a long bow about the amount of winter ploughing. In this district the drought has almost wholly prevented it. I came for instance through Rietfontein, which farm formerly yielded up to seven hundred bags of wheat. Last year only *one* bag, and this year there has been no sowing at all.

I was driven by Mr. Greeff and Mr. Malan, and found the entire population of the hamlet assembled in the marquee school to receive me, from the grand-dame of 82 to the babies at the breast. The children struck up the Old Hundredth[4] as I arrived and when that torture was over there was a great handshaking and all the family histories.

They are all existing on the earnings of the man on the Road Works, no clothes at all, ruined and windowless homes, and food not enough to go round – of dry bread alone. Brave but wretched little community made supremely happy by a bag of meal apiece and an assurance that the Government *shall* indeed plough for it.

We could not talk because of the dust-storm which raged, so drove away to Biesjesvlei where misery and starvation reign supreme.

It is no good going into all the cases, 'twould weary you, but in this place I made two blacksmiths radiant by a pair of bellows each, for Lord Methuen had destroyed theirs, and they could not work. Consequently farmers must go to the expense of sending their work all the way to Klerksdorp forty miles away, when if the Repatriation had thought more of repatriating and less of embezzling, these two village blacksmiths might now be comfortable instead of starving. These bellows come out of Distress Fund money.

Here at Biesjesvlei I picked up two or three of Lord Methuen's good deeds, which are duly remembered and talked of by the ever-grateful Boer. The blacksmith's wife had three pigs which she dearly loved and clung to the more closely since everything she loved was being taken and destroyed. So she summoned her courage and went boldly to Methuen himself and "spoke prettily"[5] to him and took him to the sty and begged for her pigs. And he listened to her request and ordered that the pigs should be left, and they are there to this day, bearing witness to Methuen's softer heart. Moveover, two houses in the village were spared, one because an old couple in it were ill and so they remained and were fed by the Commandos. Biesjesvlei has therefore tender recollections of Methuen, but I must say, comparing it with the whole of his work, his "good deeds" remind me very much of the frail figure of Good-deeds in the play *Everyman*[6] – a figure too weak to make its voice heard far.

Afterwards we passed the battlefield of Klipdrift where De la Rey captured Methuen[7] and saw the kraal where a number of the English defended themselves and then threw up the white flag, and the bones of the three hundred oxen killed that cruel day and the white line in the distance, too far for me to walk in the heat, where the soldiers and officers are buried. One of our mules had been in Methuen's column and was given to my host's son as his share of the capture. The place appeared to me as a complete flat, nothing whatever to hide anybody right to the horizon line, no tree or shrub, ant-hill or rock, so *how* anybody *could* have been surprised by anybody else is a miracle to me!

I must have driven full thirty or forty miles across this absolutely flat veld, *so* flat that it seemed you were on the deck of a ship and looked at the horizon all round clear and unbroken against the sky just like the ocean.

That night we got lost; dark came on and there was no moon, and the stars, glorious as they were, could not shew us the road, and we had to get out and creep about in the bush of the veld searching for the road. We found it at last, but got in late to the farm where, nevertheless, the Boeress opened her hospitable doors and took in five utter strangers to eat and sleep that night! For we were three, a ruined schoolmaster who was driving me, his little sister and myself, and to meet me had come up from the South De la Rey's sister and her little boy of fifteen, hardly bigger than Oliver.[8] The way that child outspanned and inspanned and drove four-in-hand (mules) for forty miles next day was wonderful. A real little trump is Petertje.

It has been good to reach the kind Faustmans (whom I knew were people of private means), so I do not feel I am taking the bread out of their mouths, and I can enjoy the relief of being in their renewed parsonage.

Mr. Faustman has a dear old Kaffir boy of eighty, who was taken by the Military and left at De Aar and thence *walked* all the way back to find his old master. Of course Mr. Faustman has had to pay the new £2 tax[9] for him; very few of the country Kaffirs can pay it and from here and elsewhere large numbers have trekked away to Basutoland to avoid the obligation. Of those who remain, few can pay, so it falls as an extra tax on the farmer who must pay to return his labourer. The Kaffirs on the farms are suffering greatly from the scarcity of food and money, and many are starving. The times are bitter hard indeed and no one can see the end unless it rains.

I told you the other day that the banks were all calling in their money, the Netherlands Bank only excepted. Now this one too has followed suit. I suppose it cannot stand alone against the others. The few who have cash are holding tight to it; no one knows what turn affairs may take and so dare not begin any enterprise. Only if Chinese labour comes they say there will be a boom, however short, and a chance will come to sell out without complete ruin and clear out from a country so accursed. This is the feeling, in the towns.

Here in Schweizer Reneke the most picturesque figure is old Mrs. De la Rey, mother of the General. She is quite a character and holds everyone now by her charms though in her eighty-sixth year. A sweeter old lady I never saw. She has been spending the day here, dressed in a short black velvet skirt, a lace mantle, and an old-fashioned black bonnet tied round her chin. She wore black mittens studded with steel beads. She has a wonderful hooked nose and the bearing of a Duchess. Always wealthy and respected she has through life been one of the great ladies of her land. She had never known want, but from the moment her house and goods were burnt she has not possessed a penny. She told me all about it and how her coffin (*doodskist*) which she had all ready for herself, was burnt too, and how she fled a year or more before the troops, but was captured at last and sent to Klerksdorp and Pretoria. She is a fascinating companion, as merry as a girl, with the appetite of a man, sound and healthy, eating any amount of sweets and cakes between her meals. In her youth they say she was a great dancer and she still pirouettes about the room in youthful fashion. Altogether a great contrast to the run of Boer women, for she loves pretty things and likes to wear them now, silks and laces and so on, and she uses scent and is altogether dainty in her ways. Coming across the village square today I heard a voice singing loud and clear, and getting nearer I saw it was Mrs. De la Rey sitting alone on the stoep and singing to herself in sweet piping notes. I think she is too old to feel her losses really and everyone is too fond of her to let her actually want (though she has to live with a whole family in two rooms), but now and then she recalls it all and weeps. Her compensation is the thought of her son's fame. "Koos was always," she said, "a sweet and obedient boy, his heart was always good, there is no ill in him."

It grows late and I must close if this is to catch the mail. I cannot stay to tell you all about how the Repatriation is waking up and all its repentance and confession and *promised* amendment, but I believe it is *real* and if that is so, my work here is done.

From the memoir

a) It was several years before they did so.

83. TO LADY HOBHOUSE

Wolmaransstad
20 September 1903

Dearest Aunt Mary,

I am spending Sunday in this small town, rising like many others from the ruins of its past. Some Scotch folk, the Leasks, are putting me up, for the parsonage is not yet rebuilt and moreover the parson has just lost his wife. It is a curious thing but go where I will, the ministers' wives are all sick or dead. I have only seen one with any measure of strength. It has tried them too severely, the camp life, and those terrible open-truck or cattle-truck journeys lasting four or five days, when these well-nurtured women were *locked* into cattle-trucks with some fifty others, so that even to *sit* down was impossible, much less to lie down. The suffering they have endured has been so great that we may consider we have either killed or reduced to invalidism nearly every minister's wife in the land.

If the ministers' wives alone were to write their stories, it would horrify you.

The Leasks have a large house which they have had to rebuild and refurnish. Mr. Leask came out as a young man for his health, and finding it suit him, set up in business and has done well. He could not fight his own people, nor the country where he has lived and done well, so he took the oath of neutrality and remained at home, serving both sides with his medical knowledge. Then at last came the evacuation. After having been told in the morning that the sick would all be left in her charge, Mrs. Leask was given a half-hour in the afternoon to clear out, and as she hastily packed the one box allowed, the troops filled the house and opened her drawers and robbed her right and left before her eyes. A few miles out from the village they had to sleep out in midwinter, and then making a great turn the column was back at the village next morning. She begged leave to go to her house to get a few more of the things she valued. It was granted but the doors and windows were smashed and all her valuables stolen and gone, while all the large things were destroyed. She felt it so much being thus robbed by her own people, and they were wealthy with handsome things about them. Mr. Leask, of course, comes under the "Protected Burghers" for he took the oath of neutrality under Lord Roberts and thus had the promise of protection and compensation for all losses sustained.

The payment of compensation claims to this class of men under the £2 000 000[1] has been going on the past fortnight, causing in every community what you might describe as very dull excitement. Lord Roberts' "full compensation" waited for since February 1900 has come at last and is very far from "full". They had already found out that his "protection" was farce and now "compensation" is little better. Mr. Leask has received not quite a fourth part of his claim and that by no means represented his losses. And before being given this they are bound to sign a paper saying they are satisfied and exonerating the Government from further payment. Or if they will not do this, then they must wait another two years, with the chance of receiving more but the probability of receiving less. A couple of minutes and the decision must be made.

Mr. Faustman told me the same story. He got £300 for the total loss of everything, not a fourth of his claim, and so on all sides. Many, however, have returned their cheques saying they will have their rights or nothing, and I hear some of these intend prosecuting the Government, but I doubt if many can face the great expense this would entail. Money is so scarce in the land that the majority are forced by bare need to take the fraction offered them in order to begin life again. But the dissatisfaction deepens.

So you can see if Protected Burghers come thus badly off that when the fighting burghers come to be paid it is not likely to be 6d in the pound even when lowered *after* assessment. It is supremely ridiculous, for the work has been made so complicated and has lasted so long, and cost in salaries such a huge sum, and in the end they will have to say: all this trouble and expense it has taken to inform you that there is nothing for you.

They try every plan they can to make the sum look less ridiculous. The last thing I hear is that *sheep* are struck off the claim. They had previously assessed slaughter sheep at the low figure of 10/- each, now they are struck off and yet they formed almost the staple wealth of the country. Hardly a *bijwoner* but had his flock of sheep.

On all sides I can assure you that dissatisfaction deepens daily. Hungry, despairing men cannot well feel content. A great deal will depend upon the ploughing prospects and the help either I can or the Government will give this season.

Fortunately Cape Colony has been so generous. I hope to be able now to plough for all the most distressed districts, and that softens their feelings and gives them a measure of hope.

Last night the *kerkraad* met me here in the vestry and we discussed the situation thoroughly. They tell me there are about 300 families in this district, and while all are desperately poor, about 150 families, moderately estimated, are in need of food.

One farmer, with wide lands, stated that his earnings this year have been £2.9.0. They can no longer feed their *bijwoners*, many of whom are their near relatives, which hitherto they have been doing, and outside help must come. The men here warmly welcome a team and the scheme of ploughing for the entire parish.

27 September. For many days I have had no time to write, and now can only end this rapidly in Pretoria. My cable home has succeeded and the Government there has wired all I said to the Government here. Consequently hurry-scurry to do better. Within *three* days an order was issued, re-opening the Repatriation supplies on credit, and they are beginning to put the Widow Scheme in force and extend it to aged, infirm and sick.

Mr. Duncan, Colonial Secretary, has been round the Western Transvaal following on my trail, and we knocked against each other in Wolmaransstad. This is also partly the effect of the publicity I have given to it and the action of the Cape Colony. As with the *camps* they have asked for my "suggestions" which I have handed in to Mr. Duncan and I fancy he will act on them more or less thoroughly. In the Free State things are different and as yet I cannot say what will happen.

But I feel matters are now on a better basis, the two parties brought into closer touch and made to work together, thus the people should no longer, between two stools, fall to the ground. In that hope I leave them, much tired out, and give my last month to the Free State.

As at present arranged, to get company home, I have promised to sail with a tribe of Murrays and Moltenos by the East Coast route to Naples, leaving 4 November and going *second class* on a German boat.

If the Government is true to its promises, and with the help England and the Cape have sent, the present acute moment may be tided over; and we must prepare ourselves in body and purse for what we *dread*, namely a much worse condition of things next year. Famine for black and white is threatening, the young wheat is withering and full of blight, and the drought continues so that mealie crops cannot yet be put in. Everything depends on *rain* and that tarries – will it come or won't it?

I am sending food to some blacks; they need it sorely. I enclose an article from the *Rand Daily Mail*, which paper has attacked me strongly for daring to say there is distress!!!

The heat is upon us and I must fly from Pretoria, for it reduces me to helplessness.

Many, many thanks to Uncle Arthur for his extra gift to the people. His name is held in great veneration, and there certainly will be a whole crop of little Hobhouses scattered about this land.

I am *so* glad you are at Banwell and hope it may be drier and warmer.

Yours, E. H. Hobhouse.

84. TO LADY HOBHOUSE

Kroonstad
30 September 1903

Dear Aunt Mary,

I am back in the Free State again and very glad to be in cooler air, for Pretoria had become suffocating indeed. The summer heat came in so suddenly and without the usual thunderstorms to clear and cool the air, so we all collapsed. Botha got a relaxed throat and so did I. He left yesterday for a visit to his farm and the Vryheid and Utrecht districts.

The Government is at last agreeing to send him and the other Generals to India to persuade the irreconcileables to sign and return, and they will probably have to start in about ten or twelve days. It is very inconvenient for them and they have begged the Government in vain to have the prisoners brought to Durban or some port and let them run down there to harangue them. No one has the least sympathy for these tiresome men, certainly not their own countrymen, and least of all the majority of their wives, who, poor things, are the sufferers from their obstinacy and who have repeatedly written, urging their return. But it appears that it is largely a religious mania which has wrought upon minds affected by the monotony of prison life, while some few are really a lazy class of good-for-noughts who don't care to come home and work for their families.

I had a lovely moonlight night to start from Pretoria, and Mr. Michaelson,[1] a Jew capitalist of Liberal tendencies and a great admirer of mine, drove me down to the station and despatched me very comfortably. Mrs. Botha, General Smuts and

294

a crowd of other friends all came too, and my carriage was filled with bouquets of lovely flowers – roses and great Transvaal lilies. Pretoria is a bower of roses now, and the people are very warm-hearted.

Mr. Michaelson is going to send me a new sort of chair for steamer lounging and the first diamond from his new mine, Kaalfontein, near Pretoria he has set aside for me. So I shall have a Transvaal as well as a Free State diamond.

I was very, very sorry to leave the Transvaal; it is a much more loveable country than the Free State and the people in the towns much further advanced. There is some stir in the air which the Free State wholly lacks.

Financial affairs are in a dreadful state – most men think a crisis is imminent. The Government has been reckless in its expenditure upon officials, etc. who do nothing, not knowing the country or their work; three have been occupying the place of one. As for the Repatriation, its administrative expenses are a matter of common talk and common knowledge. Most of their money seems to go to keep up a supply of food at cost prices to S.A.C.'s and J.P.'s and other public servants, and all this is counted in as if it were repatriating the Boers!

In Johannesburg money matters are in a desparate situation and some half dozen of the great houses are, it is said, in a most shaky position. Not a bank in the country will lend money or allow any overdraft, but they are calling in their money on all sides. They are trying in every way to force Chinese labour on an unwilling public. It is too bad the way the Jingo papers all misrepresented Botha's evidence before the Labour Commission[2] and cabled it over the world. The fact is he had *written down* his complete view on the labour question and handed this to the Commission who *refused* to take it because it was so unflinchingly hostile to their views on the subject. So they put him in the box and simply asked him such questions as they chose and before he had received and corrected the minutes, false reports were wired to Cape Town and probably to England. Before long he will publish his paper which they refused, probably directly *after* the Commission have pronouced in favour of Chinese labour. He hopes then also to hold meetings of protest.

Every sort of pressure has been put upon him, but he will not budge an inch.

I got here (Kroonstad) at 5.30 a.m. today and found several early risers at the station to meet me, and I had to hold a sort of *conversazione* at 6 a.m. after a bad night in the train. Since then I furnished myself with a list from the clergyman and have been all the morning visiting the people.

Nothing at all seems done here for the widows, and I must try and make this Government do what the Transvaal has it *on paper* to do. Mr. Chamberlain's promised care of widows and orphans is delightfully airy. So easy to make promises of that kind and forget the carrying out. The Natives are perplexing me much; many of them are starving all over the country. Missionaries implore me for some food for them, the old and the young. Eleven thousand have crowded into Kroonstad to find work as they can get no food upon the farms.

1 October, Ventersburg. I left Kroonstad at 5 a.m. and got here at 9.30 a.m. in the early hours of a very hot day. I have lost my voice entirely, which is a drawback in my work. The drought is awful. The Government has proclaimed next Sunday a Day of Humiliation and Intercession for rain. It is one of the saddest things to see the wheat and oats, sown with such hope and such expense when last I was in this Colony, now withered and dead in the veld as it stands. In some parts this is due to drought alone, in others to wheat-lice also, a scourge which however is brought about by drought. This failure spells ruin to scores of families and even greater scarcity next year for hundreds more. I thought the Transvaal dry, but it is nothing to this.

Mr. Snijman is minister here and he tells me a box was sent to him, as I arranged, of the seeds sent out recently by the Committee at home. People say (and both Sutton[3] and the Committee may be pleased to hear it) that the *seed* was splendid. *Every single seed* came up. But alas! this refers only to those fortunate few who had *water*, others sowed but all in vain. One man told me today the whole of his died in the ground with the drought.

That man's is a sad case, and yet only typical of this parish and of most others. He is a fine man and very hard-working and industrious, by name Barnard. He is not a Scout but was one of those who surrendered under Roberts' Proclamation which promised protection of property and full compensation for losses sustained. That was years ago, in 1900, and now in October 1903 not a penny compensation has he yet received. He returned to his home and rebuilt it to some extent but was driven by the lack of water to move further on. The ground is fertile but all the wheat and oats he put in at the winter's sowing now lie dead and withered, and the seed alone had cost him upwards of £10. He put in our vegetable seeds and these likewise were killed by drought. The farm has now changed hands and he has the offer either of leaving on 1 January – or of farming it entirely, paying rent in half produce. Gladly would he accept, but he has not an animal with which to plough, and nothing on which to give security. Some months ago he sent his son to Cape Colony to seek help. He was given a few goats and I think the money which bought the seed which has failed. He lives on dry bread and coffee, barely getting that by his own handwork and two sons'. These lads are gone to the Relief Camp and these earn 3/- and 3/6 a day, being but 15 and 17 years old. Out of this they must feed themselves and the balance comes home procuring hardly meal for the family. The father got some work in town to repair and almost remake 27 000 bricks for £5. He had to hire a man to get it done in the time, which cost him £1, so four pounds have been his earnings during the last few months.

They will take no more men at the Relief Works, and I fear will soon be turning off large numbers. For the Governments are in sore lack of money. They have been so foolish and extravagant, pouring out money on useless things, and employing huge numbers of incompetent people who know nothing of the country and must be paid.

I hope I have made clear Mr. Barnard's position. From Repatriation he has had no help at all since last January, and before that only rations for a month or two, not regularly.

Barnard's claims which he put in very moderately are £400; he *may* get £90 being a Roberts' man; but when?

It is the story of hundreds of families and the anxious look on the men's faces tells its own tale. To buy clothing is of course out of the question. The Rev. Snijman says he has 400 families in his parish and thinks it would be well within limits to say 300 cannot support themselves. The remaining 100 can *just* support themselves, but *cannot* go on giving food to their neighbours. It is the terrible waste of money that makes one so mad. The imported teachers for instance. Think what they cost, their journeys and their salaries. And nearly everywhere they have to be sent away. And recently the Government issued a notice asking all the *old teachers* under the *late* Government to send in their names and qualifications for positions! So they have to come back to them after all and if this is done it will save the education question better than anything else. In the Free State they are too poor to start so many private schools as exist now in the Transvaal.

Ventersburg you recollect was burnt by Bruce Hamilton. It is quite a big little place struggling up out of its ruins, though a good many of the roofs are bogus roofs with nothing under them, only just fixed over the walls to prevent them being washed away by the rain which never comes. One gets very tired of the gaping mouths and staring, lidless eyes of scalped and ruined houses all over the land. Did I tell you the other day I was in a farm that was rebuilt on the old lines? – the first I had seen – *really put right*, and it was a treat. It gave me a better idea than anything else of how the Boers used to live, and the contrast was striking. Also at Biesjesvlei I was in two houses quite different to the rest. Papered walls, table cloths, and many such etceteras. What, I asked, does this mean? And the answer came: "These two men have had their military receipts paid." We wondered and wondered why these two were singled out for this blessing and came to the conclusion it might have been begun alphabetically and as these were De Bruyns their initial came early in the A.B.C.

I gather that immediately after "Joe's" speech there was hurry-scurry to pay out receipts, but very soon it was found the money fell short and then they stopped and haggled and qualified and excepted and dwindled it away to almost nothing.[a] So the first few were in luck as the Repatriation officials say, and the rest must do without.

I am visiting in the village this morning and again in the country this afternoon; to-morrow I meet the *kerkraad* in the morning and then start for Bloemfontein. I am going to my old friends the Fichardts, which will be rather sad, for my earliest Free State friend, Mrs. Fichardt, has died since I was there in July. Her daughter is, however, a great help.

So I must end this scrappy letter, written a sentence now and then, with many

many thanks for the extra sums cabled to the bank by the Committee and for Uncle Arthur's donation of £100, all of which will help relieve much patiently borne suffering now, and if the rain comes, help towards greater prosperity next year. If it does *not* come, the state of affairs will be grievous beyond description.

Yours with much love, E. H.

From the memoir

a) Amongst English M.P.'s to whom I had appealed to bring forward in Parliament the facts about these unpaid military receipts was Mr. Thomas Shaw (now Lord Shaw of Dunfermline). He replied that he had spoken in the House of Commons on the question of the dishonouring of military receipts, and he added:

> "I told Mr. Chamberlain privately beforehand that *you* were my authority, that you were on the spot and *knew*, and that I believed absolutely your testimony. He was quite civil, and I think rather staggered; but fell back on the hackneyed complaint that the information should have come to him more directly – say by the Courtneys sending all the letters – and the hackneyed promise that he would send to Africa and enquire. My opinion was that he was in the grip of forces which he could not control and that he was unhappy over it."

I felt that there must be some serious breach in the information sent to the Home Government. Would Mr. Chamberlain's unhappiness, for which indeed there was good cause, result in his insisting upon the keeping of a public promise which had pledged the faith of the Army and upon which a large number of people were depending for their very livelihood? For in the meantime, as Mr. Shaw wrote, he had started the fiscal question[4] and the public were off on the new scent. Often, indeed, as I laboured in South Africa I had feared this was the case, and the general public, tired of your country, wanted a fresh field of interest.

Mr. Shaw also mentioned the Ministerial changes then taking place, the best of which he thought was Mr. Alfred Lyttelton's appointment to the Colonial Office; in his opinion this augured well for the cause of justice and good government in South Africa.

Personally I was chewing the bitter cud of disappointment in governmental promises generally. Brittle things evidently. I had been brought up to gaze with awe on all those in high places and never to question the wisdom of those in authority. My experience, first about the camps, secondly regarding the injustice meted out to me in my illegal deportation, now thirdly in respect to the broken pledges to the people of the old Republics, was of a nature to disillusion me completely. Never since have I believed Ministerial promises. They may serve some momentary purpose, affording credit to the Minister, giving popularity in his constituency, or

298

silencing agitators. Also in the last resort they can be used as weapons to enforce betterment if public opinion can be raised in support. But for *me* faith in Ministers and their promises was broken by all I had lived through. These experiences were mainly responsible for my ardent support of the Suffragist movement. I hoped that women might bring higher and purer standards into public life, less personal ambition and more thorough attention to the detail and economy of administration. Will this belief be justified or will Governments never achieve more than a bad second-best?

85. TO BARBARA HAMMOND [NÉE BRADBY], DOROTHY BRADBY AND LEONARD HOBHOUSE

Bloemfontein
4 October 1903

Dear Barbara, Dorothy and Leonard,
Forgive a triple letter, also a stupid one this week, written to Aunt Mary from Kroonstad and Ventersburg, but the truth is I am too worn out and too pre-occupied to write home as much as I did.

I thank (1) and (2) for their letters; (3) never writes, so I can economize gratitude.

I am so sorry (1) has had such a bother editing my badly written hasty letters for the papers. I hoped she improved grammar and style. I confess to being a little curious to know what has been printed. Keep the papers for me, please. I do hope (1) and her half will get their week's holiday at Bruges; it sounds delightful. How horribly wet your summer has sounded. Today all the Orange River Colony is on its knees praying for rain and keeping a Day of Humiliation.

(2) sounds very below par from her letters and I fear her wrist is not in better writing condition. She will like to know that the bale of clothes that came to Ventersburg's share was *greatly* admired and appreciated, and really went to the *right* people. I mean to those who are the best people, but have not money now to buy a yard of material. For instance, Sarah van Zyl, intimate friend of the parson's child, came in clad in one of your scarlet blouses, and *nice* clothes had gone to Mrs. Louis Wessels (sister of Ellie Cronjé[1]), and so forth. These English clothes were considered superior to any other cases sent, which is a feather in the cap of (1) and (2)'s sister.

Many thanks also for information about donations, etc. England is stupid and stingy. My one little letter to the *South African News* brought me £5 000 without further effort, and heaps of help in clothes, animals, foodstuffs, etc., etc. In fact I have now choked them off a little because if the drought continues, everything will be much worse next year and we must economize charitable feelings, and *make* Government do its part. Government has now done it *on paper* and I am leaving instructions with the entire Dutch Reformed ministry how to act in getting these

299

regulations solidified into actions. Thus I can leave, confident that if they fight in the way I tell them things will be better and no one suffer so much. I have arranged the ploughing in the worst districts and provided oxen, ploughs, yokes and seeds. So we sit and watch the skies. If rain falls, all will go well; if *not*, next year will be terrible indeed and all hands must to the rescue.

For all these reasons I regret Mr. Richardson's hasty journey; it would have been better had he held back to learn the issue of the harvest and learn Dutch (without which he is useless)[2] in the interim. Moreover, he is not a good man to send. He and Mr. A. created gentle amusement from Pretoria to Cape Town on their last trip.[3] They kept to the railway, believed officials implicitly, and the Boer folk they saw in towns thought they were Intelligence spies and talked to them accordingly!!! But it was too late to stop him, he lands on Tuesday and will be here in a few days. Moreover, it will cost him hundreds and hundreds of pounds to go where I have been, for no one but myself could or would at this trying period have been taken about as I have been. But when he comes Arthur Fichardt and I mean to talk to him together *for his good* and put him into stays.

I feel as if I had lived through ten years, the work and experience have been tremendous. I like best meeting the *kerkraads* – the very pith and backbone of the country – fine men who get up and sing the Old Hundredth over me, and make wonderful and eloquent Dutch speeches, and nod their heads in grave acquiescence when I discourse to them about ploughs and teams.

(3) may like to know that I hope to leave Cape Town on 4 November by East Coast, reaching England about Christmas and cutting the Bay[4] by landing at Naples. This will give me time for my last trek in the south-west Orange River Colony and some promised visits in the Colony, Paarl and Stellenbosch, and then I have to be "received" and "addressed" in Cape Town, which will be the finale.

So (1) and (2) need not write again. It is unnecessary to tell (3) not to do so.

Yours, E. Hobhouse

86. TO LADY HOBHOUSE

Bloemfontein
11 October 1903

Dear Aunt Mary,

I have failed to write anything of interest this week owing to pressure of work, and today I am just off to the south-west Free State.

The Quakers have arrived and I talked to them fully,[1] but I fear they mean to do as before, haunt the line and the officials, and go on "asking information" instead of finding it for themselves. Last time Mr. Richardson came with Mr. Alexander the pair were thought to be "Intelligence spies", and consequently no Boer would speak plainly to them. I fear the same thing will happen now. They are kind and good, but don't inspire confidence in a people who have been under espionage for four years or more. But I hope they'll get on.

Many thanks for your letter of September 17th and for enclosing kind old Colonel Williams' note which is as illegible as usual.

I do not quite know when or by what route I shall return as the plan made seems to have fallen through.

Ever yours affectionately, E. Hobhouse

87. TO LADY HOBHOUSE

[No address]
23 October 1903

Your last letters are from Banwell Abbey. It is so very, very kind of you to write to me so regularly every week without missing, and I am afraid sometimes when you are very tired. But I have been very grateful for your letters, not otherwise owning a regular correspondent.

I was so interested to have the little cuttings with your letter to the *W.G.*[1] and Uncle Arthur's to the Liberals in Somersetshire. There is, however, one point in which I must correct the *W.G.*'s printing, or else my own bad writing misled you. I said the Boers were eating '*miercats* and roots' not '*mice*, cats and roots'. I don't know if it makes much difference, for *miercats* are no more considered articles of food than are mice and cats.

I have just seen the first of the Repatriation articles in *The Times*[2] and had a good laugh over it. I hope I shall see the others.

I was at Jacobsdal when I last wrote and must take up the thread from there. I was staying in the minister's house; he still keeps the parlour windows with the round bullet holes in them through which the soldiers thought fit to fire with women in the house. The church too has its bullet marks, for it was used as a hospital and fifty sick lay therein and two Red Cross flags floated from the roof, and they just stood and fired in at the big end-doors. Fortunately an inside partition broke the force of the bullets, some of which, however, pierced the wall just above the beds.

I found many old friends from Kimberley Camp in Jacobsdal.

The magistrate's report from this district in the *Government Gazette* was to the effect that there was no distress and that he had offered work at 4/6 a day and everyone was too lazy to do it. I found that no one in the district knew of this offer of work, not even the other members of the Repatriation Board themselves!! People are very poor there and living at the lowest ebb, but just saved from starvation by the drought in Cape Colony, which has forced farmers there to trek over the border with their sheep to find water and pasture. These pay, if in cash, from 3/- to 5/- per 100 (hundred) sheep per month, so you see it is not a fortune that is earned but just

301

the few shillings that make the difference and stand between a family and utter destitution. Sometimes they pay in stock.

A few "Protected Burghers" were paid out in Jacobsdal. One man, Lombard, came to me; he was very sorry for himself. He had surrendered under Roberts; life and property were thus to be protected. After this his flocks were all taken, his house burnt, and his wife taken to Kimberley Camp. He was used to drive our Army waggons and broke his leg. Now he claims £1 300 and he has been told £300 is his share with £20 deducted for rations since leaving camp. So he has £280, laywer's fees to pay, his living for the past year as well, and has £130 left to begin life upon. Into the bargain his military receipts worth another £300 are disallowed, because the man who signed them is "not known". Evidently only an irregular, though he wore a British regimental uniform and so took in the poor Mr. Lombard. I could not pity him very much, because having £130 to begin upon he is in clover compared to most Boers; but I mention his case to shew you exactly how Lord Roberts' promises worked out, and consequently you can easily deduce what is thought of him and the country he represents. And if these things are done in the green tree ("Protected Burghers"), what will be done in the dry?

When I got to Petrusburg, which I did after a very fatiguing day's drive, I stayed with Mrs. Van Breda (the woman who ran away from Kimberley Camp).[2] She is a really fine woman, and her husband a dear old gentleman, of a Cape family and so speaking English properly.

How you would dislike it in this country that you never get your potatoes served without nutmeg grated all over them! Very often too the potatoes are served *cola* with the nutmeg, which is beyond my powers entirely. At this moment, too, I am drinking tea with boiled milk, half and half as if it were coffee, *so* nasty and so ˙nnecessary, but almost universal.

At Petrusburg I stumbled across the old Dopper[3] clergyman, Du Plessis, whom I had known at Kimberley. His wife is now quite an invalid and they are desparately poor. Their congregation is too poor to help them and their beautiful parsonage in ruins. If he could only have been allowed to save his documents, private and church, he would have been less sore, but they refused him permission to step back into his house to save even these.

The neighbourhood is one much given to potato-growing, and these were watered by means of *Bakkie's pumps*.[4] But our troops broke all these pumps, thus striking a blow at the entire industry for many years. Why did not the Repatriation Board replace these pumps? That would have been a solid service to the district. A *Bakkie's pump* costs about £42 and then you must have a horse or mule to turn it – say another £20. And where, without compensation, is the money to come from to start this initial need again?

I spent the Sunday morning by walking out to a group of houses some two miles on the veld and talking very fully with the farmers there. They were holding service when I got there so I went in to see the wife of one, who lay in bed with a new-born baby, and she told me her experiences of Bethulie Camp. And now they have had to sell their land, the beautiful farm where they have always lived. The farmer came in and told me the whole story, too long to repeat, but which would shew you exactly how far and in what way the Repatriation had helped or perhaps rather hindered him. It is very pathetic, the parting with their land.

I found in this district that the widows were already being made to repay the little help they had had – such as seed potatoes (though not a potato had resulted owing to the drought), and building material, etc. – for that is Mr. Chamberlain's way of looking after widows.

I am trying hard to get the Orange River Colony on the same footing as the Transvaal with regard to widows and ploughing, at least on paper: I can hardly say the Transvaal is any better in *action*; but if you have a rule on paper it is at least a weapon to fight withal.[a]

Paarl. Now I am down here and have seen rain again, a wonderful sight, and everything is green and fresh, a different world when you drop down from the Karoo through the Hex River Pass, and find youself in the verdant and flowery Cape Peninsula.[b]

I am with Mr. Moorrees,[5][c] whom you will recollect as lunching at Charlton, in his beautiful oak-bowered parsonage under the shadow of the great Paarl mountains, a village nine miles long with very lovely scenery. Coming so suddenly down from mountain heights I feel utterly collapsed, for I was tired out up above; the cart-driving for five months has nearly done me up and I could go on no longer. I feel, however, as regards walking as if leaden weights where knocked off my feet and I can use them again without weariness and pain. Perhaps as the change is so great it would have been better if I had arranged to rest a month down here and then return to the scene of work, but as matters now stand I have arranged to come home.

Mrs. Murray tells me we are obliged to give up the East Coast route because of the plague in East London which has caused passengers to be prohibited from landing at any port after that, so it would be impossible. I am disappointed, especially too as you so kindly offered me help as a Christmas present towards it. Now we propose taking an extra-intermediate, the *Goth*, which is far cheaper even than an intermediate, and we can do it first class, for twenty-seven guineas. But they are slow and go round by Ascension, St. Helena, Las Palmas and Teneriffe. The *Goth* leaves 14 November, and so if I go thereby I shall get back just before Christmas. But I shan't believe I am gone before I have actually sailed. Many, many thanks for your kind thought, however.

I am so glad to hear Banwell has been a quiet retreat and less fatiguing than big Charlton, also that the autumn somewhat redeemed the summer.

The great news is that in some parts of the Transvaal rains have fallen and advices reach me that my teams have begun ploughing. This, however, is by no

303

means universal and in the Orange River Colony the rain has been much less and not been what they call "land rains".

Now if the rain continues (blessing No. 1) and you will keep Milner in England[6] (blessing No. 2) we would relinquish compensation, which won't be worth much anyhow, and fight with hope through further difficulties.

But the rain is *not* really come and Milner *is* sailing soon, so improvement will be slow uphill work.

The money that has come in from England has been *very* helpful, besides the £5 000 Cape Colony poured into my lap. It is just *now* that it has all been needed to take the place of the compensation that never comes, and our aim in distribution had been always to *repatriate* and *not* to drive into the Relief Camps which are simply creating a large pauper class which never before existed.

But I must close. I am writing now in Mrs. Sauer's beautiful home, an old house they have bought in the country with a beautiful wine farm and magnificent Scotch-like views.[7] Yesterday we paddled out in the pools and rain to gather flowers, and I picked armfuls of arum lilies which ornament every ditch and meadow now. The more it rains here, the less it rains up-country.

From the memoir

a) I think it was on this occasion, on my final trek, that I also visited Fauresmith and Philippolis. Unfortunately the letters describing these places are lost. I so well remember my first visit to Philippolis and meeting your dear father and mother there. As you know, the parsonage was in ruins, burnt with all that was in it, and Mr. and Mrs. Fraser were living in part of one of the few village houses left in decent order. I marvelled at their pluck and patience as they faced that difficult moment and helped to inspire their ruined and largely houseless congregation with similar courage and persistence.

I talked over the ploughing scheme with your father, whose opinion was that a team of donkeys would best suit their local conditions, and you know how well he and his *kerkraad* worked the scheme for some years, during which the donkeys multiplied and were finally sold and the money distributed at his discretion.

b) You, dear Mrs. Steyn, on your occasional visits to the Cape must have experienced the pleasure afforded by its contrast. You know, too, the trial of prolonged drought – the parched and barren veld, the suffering for man and beast, the tense nerve strain as you wait and watch for the early or the later rains. Thus you can enter largely into the relief that was mine when I stepped out of the train at the Paarl. But even you cannot wholly gauge the awful and depressing influence of drought as I had seen it: its deadening hand stretched across the wide regions I had visited where on all sides it had followed on the heels of a destructive war. The country behind me lay like a corpse and here one found life, growth and verdure.

And the mental joy was equalled by the physical relief – the moisture in the atmosphere more native to me and the lower altitude combined in soothing influences. Worn out as I knew myself to be, I had not, till the strain was over, realized the extent of my exhaustion.

Still my heart was with the people of the North and I had left Bloemfontein with very deep regret. The family at Kaya Lami had shown me such abundant and unvarying kindness. Though Death had claimed its head and my first Bloemfontein friend and hostess had left us, the young members of the family came forward to fill the void. It was then I noticed Ella's thoughful and independent mind, singular in one so young, and formed with her the friendship which has lasted so many years. Her wide sympathies were early developed. Mr. Charles Fichardt, too, helped me much by superintending the care of a number of distressed families, and for a couple of years he kept me informed of their condition. His brother Arthur had shown frequent generosity, supplying me with meal and such things at cost price for the people.

But goodbye it had had to be.

At the Paarl I stayed with the Rev. Moorrees and his wife in the parsonage, thus renewing the friendship begun in England in the summer of 1900. The memory of that characteristic and lovely village in its early summer garb has never left me. It was delightfully renewed last year when at Gwelo Goodman's[8] exhibition in London I saw his exquisite painting of the church at the Paarl depicted by moonlight.

Excessive fatigue made me stupid at the time, and my brain non-receptive. I could take in no more facts. Instead, I fell under the healing moral and physical influences of that lovely and lovable place, the uplift of Mr. Moorrees' society, the calm atmosphere pervading his home, the mountains, trees and flowers. Particularly did the tender, deep, moist blue of the Cape sky with its grand cloud masses attract me after months of the hard, cruel sky in the arid North, where the heavens were as brass. There was mercy in it.

I owed much to the Paarl, and so did your people. Such generous donors had supported my fund and often anonymously. In particular Mrs. Hauman of Draaihoogte led the way by the gift of a fine milch-cow, and set herself to collect a team of animals from her neighbours, and despatched these to the North with the necessary adjuncts. It was a noble gift. Such practical gifts are rare as the will and energy to organize them.

88. TO LADY HOBHOUSE

Wynberg House, Wynberg
8 November 1903

My dear Aunt Mary,
After all my wanderings you will see where I am again – with the Chief Justice and Lady De Villiers.

All things considered, I have decided to stay here a little longer, at any rate till a mass of correspondence and organizing work is completed. For this I am going into retreat again at the Sauers' beautiful place, because there one has not the constant interruptions of callers. The Merrimans and Dr. Beck[1] invite me also to their lovely country homes, but I think I shall stick fast to the Sauers.

But I do not think that even after a month's bodily stillness I could return to the work in the North. It is the Cape-cart travelling which tries me so sorely; there is no other mode of getting about the country and I have Cape-cart-travelled for five months on end and my nervous system won't do it any more. They say few could have stood it for so long.

Here in the Colony, as in the North, I might stay and pay visits for ever, but I doubt the utility of that, so as far as I can see at present I should sail either the end of November (24th) or end of December (22nd). These dates are those of German vessels, which are cheaper than the Donald Currie line[2] and are highly recommended. They would be pleasanter for me as an escape from the disagreeable English passengers who think it loyal to be rude. But I do not see my way clear yet.

I have been much interested in your Repatriation articles from *The Times* and intend this week drawing up the reverse side for the English use. Meantime another Repatriation official was safely clapped into gaol the week I left the Orange River Colony. He got eighteen months, also another S.A.C.

My one appeal to the Colony brought me over £7 000, and the *Manchester Guardian* wired me £1 000, irrespective of all the D.F.[3] has sent. This money has gone a long way; it would hardly be possible to describe how much it has done indirectly as well as directly.

My teams are ploughing busily in places where the drought has broken, but the rain so far has been only partial. In one parish I had two teams at work and after they had ploughed for a week the Government *sent five teams* to plough also.

9 November. Today Sir Henry has gone in to the levee for the King's birthday, and it reminds me that to-morrow is Uncle Arthur's birthday. Many congratulations and much love to him and congratulations to ourselves also for having so long had the privilege of his uncle-ship. I hope fogs and east winds will deal gently with him and you, because the summer does not seem to have had for anyone the healing effect it usually has.

In some parts of the North the drought has broken, but the rain is very partial, and in Bloemfontein and south of that there has been no rain. They first officially ordered a Day of Prayer for Rain, and waited a week. Receiving no answer, they issued another order, this time trying military rather than clerical means. Twelve-pounder guns were called out and marched up the hill at Bloemfontein whence they attacked the heavens, firing at the clouds till they had all retreated and the skies were clearer than ever! This continues still at intervals, jarring the overtaxed nerves of the inhabitants, worn with the incessant dryness, but now I think they are going to try the civil arm and make plans for boring more wells, etc.

Best love, Yours,

E. Hobhouse

89. TO LEONARD HOBHOUSE

Wynberg House, Wynberg

9 November 1903

Dear Leonard,

I am sending a few clippings which may be of interest to you. To-morrow I return to Mrs. Sauer's in the country[a] to get through a mass of correspondence which may keep me some time in the land. Thus I have given up hope of going with Mrs. Murray on the 14th and hardly know if I shall even get off on the next opportunity, viz. the 24th. Time will show.

Sir Henry has just gone off to the levee, for they keep the King's birthday here, as well as the Queen's birthday in May, and it is a real solemn keeping, not a mere form as in England.

Here in Cape Colony no one will talk of anything except the elections now imminent.[1] It is altogether such a different and I think duller world than the northern Republics, the mental atmosphere of which I greatly prefer.

Yesterday afternoon I spent at Professor Fremantle's (now Editor of *South African News*). He was very angry with the *Manchester Guardian* which has just informed Mr. Cartwright that they no longer require a South African correspondent. I should advise the *Guardian* to seek a correspondent in both Bloemfontein and Pretoria or Johannesburg if they want to know anything at all that is true, but perhaps they don't.

Mr. James Molteno lunched with us yesterday, characteristically optimistic[2] on the outlook, but others less hopeful think the South African Party chances for the Upper House *very* doubtful, though all agree that the Assembly is sure of a small majority.

The Council Elections are now taking place and may have great influence on those of the Assembly, which are not until January.

My Cape Colony fund has been over £7 000, the product of one letter.

Love to Nora and thanks for her letter.

Yours, E. H.

From the memoir

a) . . . there for weeks I worked uninterruptedly with the sense of perfect rest about me. Mr. Sauer was full of fun; his jokes kept us alive, and he laughed at me unmercifully. I was a veritable target for his ironic wit and I enjoyed it. He was specially down upon my unfortunate luggage which, when he met me at the station, did indeed present a curious assemblage of bags, baskets and parcels. In vain I protested that a year's supply of things took space and had to be of a kind that would tuck into any cart or vehicle; that I had to carry a folding-bed, a sleeping bag, provender for myself and as much food for others as possible. No good – he teased my about it all the time. And teasing is very refreshing. I am sure he thought it good for me.

If he had the gift of humour, Mrs. Sauer had that of creating a reposeful atmosphere. She lived amongst her flowers, tending them with her own hands, and she seemed to imbibe their nature. Whenever, cramped by writing, I sought my hostess, she was always to be found in her garden, which she and Miss Cloete cultivated with the skill and knowledge which comes from sheer love of flowers. It was a garden of healing for soul and body, a riot of colour, and afar, over a bank of lilies and above the garden wall, rose Table Mountain blue in the distance.

90. TO LADY HOBHOUSE

Cape Town
17 November 1903

Dearest Aunt Mary,

Mrs. Murray has sailed and I am still here, unable for various reasons to get off with her. From the point of view of letters home it is useless my remaining, for I am no longer on the scene of distress; from the point of view of being useful this side, to continue organizing and finish distributing my funds, and prepare an account of the Cape fund for publication, it was necessary to remain a few weeks longer.

Now that I am thoroughly, or nearly thoroughly, rested, I *might* return north again, but that would involve breaking in on the £60 sent for my expenses by the D.F. which I have not touched and do not wish to if possible. I did not use it because I soon found that sixty pounds would not have paid my way about the country for more than a fortnight, if that; and I was obliged to accept all the help so generously offered me and give up payments except for railway journeys.

You will see what an expensive world it is when I tell you that though I have not had to pay for board or lodging anywhere since I landed, and have bought no clothes, my expenses have run to £112 in the six months. That and the Cape-cart travelling prevented my doing more. It prevented my going to Bothaville, seven hours' drive from Kroonstad, bad as I knew things there to be, but I sent a load of meal. When the Quakers came I begged them to go there and mentioned also other places I could not reach and where I knew distress was great. But they are instead chiefly going where I told them we had got things well in hand and the relief organized, and keeping mainly to the railway line.[1]

Now the Government, after gazetting the fact (acquired by the telegraph) that

308

there was no distress, has been sending out to investigate more thoroughly and the report of the official sent to Bothaville is: "The poverty is appalling, the people are half naked and starving, the majority existing only on a little mealies."

The Government is, however, here and there doing more than it was to relieve, but its delays are so terribly long that people must be fed by charity in the interim.

Where rain has fallen the tension has relaxed, people *feel* more hopeful and can get a green shoot from the ground. I have nearly thirty ploughs at work in as many districts, and on Thursday I am going to a sale near here to buy another span or two. The truckage hence is £10.10.0 for eight oxen, and yet the oxen work out much more cheaply a head bought here. Immense interest is taken in these spans, and, barring disease, the oxen will make money by transport after harvest and be there to plough again next season, for it will be long before the country is stocked again. They all say it is worth more than a £1 000 to a parish.

Meantime affairs in Johannesburg grow worse and worse, the town is simmering with anger, and revolution is in the air.[2] Only a leader is wanted, but the Boers won't be those leaders, though they have been asked. So possibly they will continue only to complain in underground ways. Great demonstrations (a) against Chinese labour (b) in favour of Representative Government are mooted but always seem stopped just when coming to a head. Spies abound, trade is at a standstill, money is almost unobtainable, and the unemployed increase. Oh, for the old days! is the cry on all sides. The administration is wretched, the officials corrupt; it is all common knowledge and common talk among all sections of society, and all races feel alike.

It was all like this a month ago when I was there; now a gentleman has been visiting us from Johannesburg who endorses all this and more, and says daily it is growing worse, only a match is needed, but none dare strike it, for the Boers won't. They laugh and look on.

Send Sir William Butler to us, say the leading Boers, and all will go well. An individual English man or woman whom they trust can do anything with them, Milner never can nor will. He is the root of the evil. Better Kitchener with all his brutalities than Milner with his duplicity.

Here in Cape Colony it is another world, and they are wrapped up in their elections. Dr. Petersen's[3] return for Cape Town, the centre of Jingoism, was a great triumph for the South African Party and shows the turn of the tide. It may be a drawn game in the Upper House, but the Assembly is sure of a majority.

I am still with the Sauers, a very lovely spot. Their land joins Mr. Merriman's on one side and the Chief Justice's on the other, a really lovely old Dutch house, the flowers glorious.

I sent you by Mrs. Murray a box of *ornithogalums* – "Chin-Chêrin-Chees"[4] – which keep weeks without water. If still in bud, put them in a *dark* room till they blossom. They often keep for two months.

I hope you are keeping well and having a dry autumn. I was hoping for a little summer here this month, but the south-eastern is very icy. Still, the roses seem to like it.

Best love to all,

Yours ever, E. H.

P.S. No time to write to anyone else this week.

91. TO MRS. LEONARD COURTNEY

De Oude Drostdy, Tulbagh
23 November 1903

My dear Kate,

I send enclosed crumpled sheet to show you that I really did my best to write to you long since, and got no further. As it gives you a breath of Free State air, I send it, with apologies for delay.

This week I am staying with Dr. Beck who infuriates me, and has made me a Jingo and supporter of "Joe". I must go back to the Sauers who are delightful to stay with and where I feel quite at home. A most delectable spot is their home, with flowers which beggar description.

Poor Mr. Sauer – they all went up sky-high over Dr. Petersen's election at the top of the poll for Cape Town, but for a whole day spirits were at zero when Owen Lewis got in for Worcester Circle and made the Progressive majority of *one* in the Council. This is as it stood before (numerically), but the South African Party vote was tremendously increased in spite of disfranchisement[1] and Rhodes money. I believe they (the South African Party) are sure of a majority in the Assembly.

I have had some talks with Professor Fremantle, now co-Editor of the *South African News*. He is nice; weakly and neurotic-looking with an unsympathetic (politically) wife. He is not considered a great success as an Editor, and certainly his articles are very dull. Altogether I think the *South African News* takes a line too weak to be respected or to be of much use.

I wonder how you are getting along with West Edinburgh.[2] Does Mr. Courtney think there will be a General Election in 1904?

It is no use writing a long letter because I suppose I shall meet you face to face in January and can enlarge on any point you would find most interesting.

I hope you are both well, also Shirra. I feel anxious about Aunt Mary who has not written at all like herself since I left.

With much love,
Yours ever affectionately, E. Hobhouse

Bloemfontein

8 October 1903

My dear Kate,

I am here with only one more trek before me and almost too done up for that.

I am sorry I have had no time to write in answer to your last. My correspondence has got so large on this side.

I am back in the wholly different atmosphere of this state – unflinching aloofness, standoffishness, won't-have-anything-to-do-with, delighted-to-see-Government-making-a-mess-of-it attitude of the young and vigorous Free Staters. They will correct no lies in newspapers, for, say they, the more the better, the more lies the more misunderstanding; misunderstanding brings more misgovernment, and *that* at last always ends one way.

As for England and the English Cabinet, what matter to them who is in it? Let it all go to the dogs, they have no interest in the British Empire, they think it rotten to the heart's core; to see Chamberlain ruin it would be a pleasant amusement for them.

92. TO LADY HOBHOUSE

[De Oude Drostdy, Tulbagh]

23 November 1903

Dearest Aunt Mary,

This mail day finds me staying at Dr. Beck's house, De Oude Drostdy,[1] near the town of Tulbagh.[a] It's a wonderful old house, built by the first Landdrost over a hundred years ago, with a great broad flight of steps leading up to double cedar-wood doors, a hall some forty feet long and very lofty, and great double doors leading into all the rooms. The house is raised upon cellars where the slaves were kept when in disgrace, but the slave houses, long rows of which cluster about these old farms, are as good as and very like our thatched labourers' cottages, and their quarters infinitely superior to what the modern slaves enjoy in the compounds of Kimberley and the mines. The windows of this house are still glazed with the Rosa glass, very old and full of opalesque tints. These are pretty outside, but inside not very clear for looking through. The house, which is of great length with pure white walls, is thatched; behind is a thick orange grove, and in front the vineyards, some 90 000 vines sloping down the hills. Like the Sauers' and others about here this is a wine farm, and the wine cellar is a feature of the place, a very long thatched building with vats of immense size. I do wish it were grape time, one could feast, and vintage, so that I could see the wine-making process and the Natives treading the wine press.

A feature of Cape life now is the exit from Cape Town of one good old family

311

after another, disgusted by the change that society there has undergone and the vulgarising advent of the Johannesburg element. Consequently people are buying up these beautiful old places that were falling into decay owing to the bad times brought about by the phylloxera,[2] and after restoring them to their old condition are forming a regular landed gentry element in the country.

Country life in South Africa is perfect, barring a cobra or two in your rose garden; the scenery is exquisite; the flowers simply love to grow, and you have only to make up your mind to devote yourself to your hose and your watering pot. After all, the main business of life from one end of South Africa to another is to "lead water", and it's only when you have none to "lead" that you begin to be really unhappy. It is the work of life and you can't expect people thus engaged to write letters, keep accounts, give receipts, or make "returns". Take a man like General Smuts. No sooner is he out of court, or out of office, than he rushes home and begins to lead water. He leads it all Saturday afternoon and all Sundays too. Spasmodically he will say, "I ought to write to Mackarness",[3] but you know quite well the water will be more important and he won't. Three weeks ago I sent him a cheque of £200 and half hoped for a receipt, but I know full well he is leading water and won't send it. So with Botha; so with Mrs. Sauer; so with everyone. The time *we* save by having the sky for a hose is now quite plain to me.

We drove to a farm sale last week as I wanted some oxen for the North. It was a beautiful day and a beautiful drive. We took our lunch and bought some strawberries on the way. It was curiously unlike our sales, for the Auctioneer did not stand on a table or cry up the articles sold, and the Dutch farmers stood about in groups as if they had no interest in the sale. The Auctioneer moved from group to group and the slow and cautious farmer usually told him in a whisper what he could give; then the Auctioneer shouted it out, and then again would be privately pushed a little higher.

Old Mr. De Waal said he would bid for me, so I sat and looked on. Of course there were no other women there, so they soon found out who I was, and the oxen which had advanced upon £15 dropped again to that figure when they knew I was bidding and for what purpose. Then as the price was being entered in the Auctioneer's book a farmer went up and said I was not to be charged the entire sum, he wished to pay 10/- upon each ox. Then another farmer came and said he would see to the oxen and send them home for me, and so I got a lovely team cheap. The farmers congratulated me on my oxen – they said they were in first-class condition and *geleerde goed* (learned goods), what we should call *trained*. Then I bought six more off Mr. Sauer cheap, and sent them all up North in two trucks. Mr. Sauer gave me the forage for their journey, and his own man to go with them to feed and water till their journey's end. This means a week's work and wages. The generosity of the Dutch is extraordinary and it's all over the same. Now the trucks cost £10.10.0 apiece, but with this expense thrown in we still save some £50 on the team.

In this part of South Africa particularly the arum lilies abound. It was quite a new sensation standing in a bog and gathering them by handfuls; in every dell and gorge and by every stream they grow thick, hundreds and thousands of white blossoms. But to begin on the wild flowers would be a never-ending theme.

My drive to the sale knocked me up for a couple of days, because driving is the one thing I cannot do. It is sheerest misery, but I had to pull together to come here to the Becks and then I return to the Sauers where I feel completely at home.

I have not much time to enjoy the scenery or anything else because my correspondence is so very large, but soon I hope things will be arranged.

It looks serious though; the little rain that came up-country, and on the strength of which we began our ploughing, has stopped (it was only partial at best). From Reitz I hear we had ploughed for 23 families and then the ground hardened, so we could not go on, and the season is so advanced. After December it will be too late to sow mealies. This means a serious business next year.

Now I must close. The Council Elections are over and the Jameson Party still have a majority of one, though the South African Party votes were immensely increased in spite of the number disfranchised. Still it was a disappointment, and Mr. Sauer did not speak a word all day – quite glum. The Rhodes money has been hard at work for months past amongst railway men and Natives.

Yours ever, with love E. H.

From the memoir

a) In this village one met with a fresh series of beauty. The memory of the sky-blue morning-glory which adorned the houses as if the heavens were reflected below has never left me. Over and over again since that sight of Tulbagh I have bought seed and endeavoured to grow the *Ipomoea*, but hitherto in no place have I succeeded in getting it to flower. The Tulbagh morning-glories must remain a fairy dream.

93. TO NORA HOBHOUSE

De Oude Drostdy, Tulbagh
23 November 1903

Dearest Nora,

A line with the enclosure which may interest Leonard. Not enough Native labour is a trumped-up cry. However, they are doubtless preparing the Chinese to come and then they expect their boom. But it will most likely be a short-lived one.

I am staying with Dr. Beck, but have described that in my letter to Aunt Mary, so will not repeat. How is Leo's fight with "Joe" getting on? All the week I have been standing up for "Joe", for the war, for Milner, for everything, perfectly infuriated by Dr. Beck. I am now a fully developed Jingo!

If the *Manchester Guardian* had a fund for me, why doesn't it send it? This is, as

Maud would say, the very identical moment. But it only sent me £1 000. I have sent a statement of my Cape Colony account to the *South African News* this week and hope to forward the same by next mail. As things stand I expect to sail on 22 December and begin in January the weary search for a dwelling. I hope your rain is nearly over. I am glad to have missed that at least, and by January the days will begin to lengthen. Is there going to be a General Election?

How is Oliver and the little ones? Fortunately I shall escape Christmas.

Much love, E.H.

94. TO LADY HOBHOUSE

Uitkijk[a)]
Mulders Vlei Junction, Stellenbosch
30 November 1903

Dearest Aunt Mary,

People say that this is the Christmas mail so I must send a line to wish you and Uncle Arthur a happy and cold-less Christmas and I wish I could have sent you a nice dish of apricots such as are now just ripening in the Sauers' orchards. The last few days have been real summer with no cold winds just round the corner, so I have been able to do some of my work of incessant writing out of doors, where the flowers scent the air.

I am still organizing relief which necessitates correspondence all over the Transvaal and Free State, always bearing in mind the different governmental methods in the two Colonies. I have been buying and despatching oxen for the Free State, and milk cows.

I have had no English letters for three weeks; I suppose you all thought I was leaving before now.

Mr. Duncan acted on my suggestion and the Repatriation Department is being swept away, while arrangements, all admirable on paper, are being made to provide food for people till reaping time. The worst is these admirable plans never get off the paper on which they are issued. I have, however, sent a copy to every minister urging that he should write direct to the Government and say if the regulations are not fulfilled, and I have told Mr. Duncan that I have done so. Some districts like Lichtenburg we have provisioned with sacks of meal, for these are far from railway lines and we have no longer any trust in Government promises. There the drought has set in again and it is feared the seed sown after the recent rains will not come up.

I have been trying hard to get the Widow Scheme adopted in the Free State as well as in the Transvaal, but the reasons why *not*, are outlined in the Blue-Book of last April on "Transvaal Finance", where Milner proposes to stint the Free State because, as I therein see, the relief given after all comes out of the country itself! No wonder the Boers ask: Where does Article 10 of the Peace Convention[1] come in?

314

People – penniless widows and ruined ministers – are already being made to pay back material aid had from the Repatriation, though they have large claims against the Government, not a penny of which has been paid.

I sat down and tried to write a reply to *The Times* articles you sent me written by Captain Madge; but on dissection I found them such a mountain of lies that I really did not see how or where to begin.

As at present arranged, I have reserved myself a cabin on the German line S.S. *Herzog* sailing on 22 December. Dreadful to leave when the grapes are ripening! And *such* grapes!

With best love, Yours affectionately, E. Hobhouse

From the memoir

a) It was hard to leave Tulbagh but delightful to return to Uitkijk, which its hostess made like home to me.

The fruit was ripening and I saw the apricots brought in large baskets from the orchards, and at long tables set under the trees shared a little in the novel work of sorting and packing them for the market, laying them carefully in rows in their clean flat boxes. I stayed long enough, too – into December – to see the beginning of the vintage – the men treading out the grapes in the vats of the long wine-cellar.

Before I left the farm, a disagreeable but amusing insident happened, which might have been serious. Mr. Sauer had told me much of his "dry" farming, and one evening Mrs. Sauer proposed a stroll to show me their new orchards. The word "orchard" brings to our English minds the vision of a green field with apple trees under which you stand and pluck the fruit or sit down and gather up the windfalls. As we approached the Uitkijk orchard I saw no blade of grass, but small stiff trees grew out of an apparently dry brown field. At that moment Mrs. Sauer was recalled to the house by the arrival of the doctor to see a sick servant. It was several minutes' walk to the house but we could see afar the trap before the front door. Promising to rejoin me quickly she hurried away while I walked innocently into the orchard to look at the trees.

All at once I found myself sinking. At first I got my feet out and jumped to a spot that looked very hard and dry. On the contrary, it was even softer and I sank quickly to my knees. Still trying to get free I found myself sucked in yet deeper. Plainly it was safer not to struggle. I was planted like a tree and immensely tickled at the humour of the situation. At the same time the possible danger of the position was clear enough, the more so as the sun had set and dusk had fallen. Mrs. Sauer was detained, so I felt rescue depended upon my voice. The doctor's trap was still faintly distinguishable at the front door, so I hoped to make his "boy" hear. It seemed a long time that I called and shouted, varying my notes to find the one that would carry furthest, and pausing at times to economize strength. When one is held in such a prison times seems long, but that is imagination; in reality it could only have been about twenty minutes.

At last they heard, and most thankful I was, not wanting to be planted all night in your Cape soil. A "boy" came running down, but I warned him off from coming near me lest he too should sink in. Seeing my plight he ran back for the manager who wisely brought a spade and some "boys" carring corrugated iron sheets. With these lying flat a path was made by which to approach me, and in the dim light they dug me out. In this way I learnt exactly what "dry" farming is. To my annoyance a garbled account of this incident got into the Comic Press, but by whose indiscretion, was never disclosed.

Something of the same sort had happened to me in 1901 at Bloemfontein. Walking back to the town one evening after a long day's work in the camp I was deceived by the look of the veld and found myself a prisoner. On that occasion I did not sink much below the ankles, for fortunately someone came along in a Cape-cart, and, helping me out, drove me home. In the Northern States of America I had been warned of such danger spots and taught to recognize them by a certain bright green surface growth, but in your country the uninitiated lack natural warnings and must suffer the consequences.

Those weeks at Uitkijk have proved, as I then knew they would, unforgettable. At times I tried to sketch, wanting to carry away some concrete souvenir of its charm – the flower masses, the mountains, the white pedimented house, the old carved door. It was not necessary; the vision has never faded.

95. TO LADY HOBHOUSE

Uitkijk
8 December 1903

Dearest Aunt Mary,
It seems little use writing much as I shall be coming back so soon.[a] It is dreadful to sit here amid sunshine and flowers and ripening fruit and read of your intense and early cold and bad fogs. I shudder at the thought of going back to such.

I hope the weather has not affected you or Uncle Arthur at all, but I am afraid it will keep you indoors very early in the winter – hard lines when the summer did the same.

My correspondence and organizing work is nearly ended, likewise my funds, so I shall be quite ready to start by the *Herzog* on the 22nd. They land us at Flushing, but one takes one's ticket to London, so I suppose there is some vessel to transfer to us.

I am still at the Sauers. It is a perfectly beautiful spot, and so quiet, where I could work uninterruptedly six hours a day. On Thursday I leave it and spend

316

some days with Professor Marais at Stellenbosch,[1] then go to Lady De Villiers again for the remaining days[b)] to pack up.

Now I must go and help pack apricots. The orchards are full of them.

They are trying to agitate in every way and protest against Chinese labour. Petitions are being signed and yesterday a mass meeting held at the Paarl, which will be followed by others.

Yours with much love, E. Hobhouse

From the memoir

a) The Merrimans and others had most kindly welcomed me, but I dared not accept. I knew I must hurry home.

Only one more visit in the neighbourhood did I pay – a long-promised one with Professor and Mrs. Marais, at Stellenbosch. Thither I went for a couple of days. It gave a pleasurable opportunity of renewing old friendships like those of Professor De Vos, the Neethlings and others. Still, I realized that I was still too mentally exhausted to be a pleasant guest anywhere, and time was pressing – I had to hurry on and be in Cape Town during the remaining days.

It was hard to tear myself away and not be able to stay longer and enjoy the surrounding beauty, but my Aunt was putting pressure upon me. For many weeks my Aunt's letters had given me uneasiness. Without wishing to injure my work, she too evidently felt her failing powers and wished to have me near her. My Uncle's health was causing her great anxiety. I felt bound to return as soon as was possible, but could not leave the Cape till I had quite fully carried out my duty in distributing and accounting for the funds so generously entrusted to me. It meant several weeks of hard work at my desk and I did not shake myself free till Christmas week.

b) Before the day of sailing (I think it was 5 November) there came the long-desired chance of climbing Table Mountain. Mr. and Mrs. Purcell[2] took me. We started before sunrise and were well towards the summit before the intense heat. The climb was more difficult than I anticipated, the heat near the top terrific, and indeed I was in no state of health to have attempted it. But I did not then know it. If the climb was a tax on the *heart*, it seemed to me the descent after we crossed the summit and came down the further side was even more painful. The declivity was so steep that it shook one painfully, and any attempt to steady oneself by clinging to the rock and boulders was only to scorch one's hands with their burning heat. Nevertheless the grandeur of mountain, sea and sky and the exquisite beauty of foliage and flowers repaid fatigue, while Mr. Purcell's knowledge of plants and insects added immensely to the interest.

It had been during these weeks, after my return from the North, that the Synod of the Dutch Reformed Church was sitting, and the moment was chosen to hold a reception at which I could meet representatives from all Cape Colony. It was indeed a brilliant and a hearty welcome that awaited me. Mr. Moorrees, Assessor to the Synod, conducted me to the hall which was crowded. He took the Chair and introduced me in Dutch. It was a memorable gathering fraught with deep underlying emotion.[3] The ovation given me that night was overwhelming in its simple heartfelt sincerity. I found some difficulty in gaining sufficient calm to speak. After a fairly comprehensive account of all I had seen in the North, I concluded my speech with the following words, in a silence that was tense:

"Most especially do I feel grateful for your warm welcome to me here, in Cape Town, the scene of the great insult practised on me by my own countrymen. The wheels of Time are turning. I thought so as I approached your town yesterday and fell once more under the spell of your majestic mountain which looked down upon me like some benign strong friend in those distressful days and which has been the silent witness of so many changes. I remembered that it was two years ago, this very week, that I was arrested at your shores, kept prisoner there and finally forced upon the long voyage for which I was physically unfit. Yet today I stand amongst you all, perhaps knowing you more deeply and intimately for that very event.

"That occurred two years ago, but I have never forgotten it and I shall never forgive it. For I was brought up on simple principles, and one of them was that forgiveness to be obtained must first be asked for. Yet here it would seem a different doctrine prevails. I hear on all sides that people are told to forgive, are expected to forgive when neither reparation or apology has been offered. Are people then but worms to have their natural feelings thus trampled upon?

"Something more is due to self-respect. For myself, the time to forgive will come when public apology has been made me by the authors of the deed – the three men whose positions made them responsible: Lord Milner, whose sinister policy has brought grief and ruin to your land; Mr. Brodrick, Minister of War, who had not the courage to face me in a Court of Law, is today, I notice, acknowledged as the most incompetent Minister of an incompetent Government; and Lord Kitchener, who, unable to subdue the enemy in the field, attacked them through their wives and children, and even arming thousands of savages, turned them too against these helpless people.

"I learn that recently in London a meeting has been held to protest against the atrocities of the Turks.[4] To my mind that savours of hypocrisy. Are our hands clean?

"It is true the Turks have burnt villages: but I have just come from seeing village after village that *we* have burnt.

"It is true the Turks have laid waste homes and lands, but over vast areas

318

I have passed where *every* house – if it stands at all – is but a group of blackened walls, roofless and empty.

"It is true that women and children have fled before the Turkish troops, but so also Boer women and children in their hundreds and thousands have fled month after month and year after year before the British troops. They too have been torn from their homes, yea, even from their very beds, with infants newly born, in sickness, infirmity and age. Their babes have been brought to birth in crowded railway trucks, in open wagons, amid ruins and in mountain fastnesses. They have seen their children perish in the camps from starvation and disease, and have so died themselves.

"Our nation allowed these deeds to pass unnoticed or but glossed them over as 'military necessities'. To point out, object or denounce was to have the unscrupulous and libellous parts of the Press turned upon you. But facts remain and as a nation we then lost our right to criticize similar deeds, whether committed by the Turks or others; and here and now I earnestly protest against the hypocrisy of doing so. All honour to Mrs. Ramsay Mac-Donald who after that meeting in St. James' Hall wrote an indignant protest to the *Daily News*. She had seen with her own eyes in South Africa and found there a parallel for all such deeds of the Turks as were condemned from the platform in London.[5]

"With her noble protest I associate myself. Can public injustices and crimes be glossed over and pardoned? Must they not rather be remembered so as to be rectified and so as to ensure that they never should happen again?

"To you, here assembled, I say these things because you have so much to forgive. You are of one blood with the peoples of the North. Many, perhaps most of you, have there kith and kin who have undergone indignities, sufferings and death, or who are now enduring an extremity of privation. For their sakes you have protested and protested in vain. You have passed through agonies of suspense and pain on their behalf. You have watched us dealing harshly and cruelly towards your helpless friends, and now you are expected, without a word of penitence or regret on our part, to forgive. So far as I know our deeds against your kinsfolk have never even been confessed to by us as a people. Rather, they have been condoned under high-sounding words, while the national indignation is reserved for the Turks.

"Yet I *do* know, and use this opportunity to assure you, that thousands in England are desirous of expressing their sorrow and of asking your forgiveness. These are people who have first striven by their gifts to alleviate suffering and given token of goodwill. In the presence of these representatives here gathered from the whole Colony I now assure you that we – viz. large sections of the British people – deplore the past and have worked our hardest to limit the evils and to ameliorate them. In their name and my

319

own I crave your forgiveness. No adequate reparation can we make; only –
we should be humbly grateful if you could accept as token of our sorrow
and our shame such small sacrifices as we have here and there made.

"'Forgive and forget' is the constant refrain of thoughtless writers in the
Official Press.

"Forget you never can. These things are laid by as sacred memories in
your hearts. But – I ask it of you here and now –

"Forgive us if you can."

Boer home industries
1904–1908

Introduction

There followed restful months in Bruton Street.[1] My Aunt and Uncle were much aged, but life went on in ordinary channels though limited in scope and degree. Letters from South Africa kept me well informed as to the work of the ox teams, the continued neglect of widows and ever-deferred payment of claims and military receipts.

I had leisure to study the question of suitable house or cottage industries for the girls on your farms. I had seen so many sitting in their ruined homes where every means of occupation had been destroyed. I knew they had skill with the needle and I had detected here and there a latent sense of art. They appeared to cling to home and family life, and time was theirs in abundance. This tranquil existence combined with brilliant skies all helped to suggest lace-making and particularly needle-point as a most suitable occupation.

Obviously the first step was to inform myself and I set to work to study the various methods and systems throughout England, Ireland and the Continent. I became a plague to every lady I knew who possessed old lace, and many exquisite collections were shewn me. I studied exhibits in the museums and haunted antique lace-shops. I procured introductions to the principal lace-shops, asking advice upon my scheme. To recount all that was said by the "Trade" would be too technical for these pages.

When I had learnt all I could in London, my mind turned to Venice as the cradle of European lace, and the best starting-point. An introduction to Lady Layard, whose long residence in Venice had brought her in close touch with the lace industry, opened the way. I felt able to leave my Aunt for a few weeks. She did not mind such absences so long as I kept in northern spheres, and her interest in my work was unfailing.

You will remember, dear Mrs. Steyn, wintering at Cannes that year, and you had given me a very hearty welcome to pay you a visit and be introduced to President Steyn. The objects combined and I left for France in the last days of March. I remember so well your brother Gordon and Miss Hannie coming to meet me at the station and the very sweet welcome you had prepared for me in your villa. Tibbie and Emmie were at their most fascinating age, and, clad in white, held baskets of flowers for me, while behind them, rising from his chair to the fullness of his great height, towered your President to greet me. The honour of

323

meeting him was mixed with emotion. You know too well how peculiarly moving was the combination of that unbroken moral and mental vigour with the sad bodily incapability – a physical weakness only lessened by your watchful tenderness through those years. No words can depict that; it belongs to the hidden things of your life.

At that time President Kruger was at Mentone and after a couple of sunny days with you – which, I recollect, included a visit to Grasse to see the preparation of flowers and fruits – I went there for a couple of nights. Oom Paul's Secretary, Mr. Bredell, called at my hotel and took me to the little villa where I had my first and last view of that remarkable man. It impressed me deeply.

As we stood in the hall the door of the parlour was wide open, and there, clothed in sombre black, was the old man, solitary and absorbed. He sat before a table on which rested a high brass reading-stand which in its turn supported a heavy folio Bible. Paul Kruger was reading and was evidently so withdrawn that he was impervious to sight or sound. I stood in the hall and gazed at this unusual sight framed like a picture by the doorway.

I did not want him disturbed, but Mr. Bredell insisted on taking me into the room and arousing his President to greet me. Our talk was not long; I saw that already his mind was elsewhere and the world ended for him. Indeed in less than four months he was in his grave. He wanted so much to know if I had seen his wife, and when told I had not been allowed to visit Pretoria before her death, he seemed too disappointed to make further effort. I stole out of the room and looking back saw he had turned again to the Bible and was once more absorbed in its pages. He belonged so clearly to another age – the little modern French villa was a cheap, incongruous setting to that medieval and puritanical figure.[2]

I was thoughtless enough to choose Easter Eve for leaving Mentone on my journey across North Italy to Venice. The train was slow and crowded with very questionable people. At Alassio I left the train a few minutes to try and find a niece who was wintering there and had hoped to see me *en passant*. In those few minutes my bag must have been rifled, for shortly after I found my purse missing. It was so awkward. I had no loose money left. I carried notes in a bag round my neck and those were the days when we wore our blouses fastened at the back, a stupid fashion. I could not get at the notes or move in the throng that filled the corridors. Yet cash I must have for the change at Milan. It was midnight when we got there and when at last I got at my money they cheated me horribly in the exchange given. But at such a moment one is grateful for small mercies. The journey was a nightmare but wholly atoned for by the singular beauty of my arrival in Venice. It was just before dawn on Easter morning, an hour of magical beauty. In the western sky the moon hung silver while the glow of coming day was brightening in the East.

A single gondolier awaited the train and we glided on between the two soft lights in a silence broken only by the bells as they announced the first Mass of the great festival.

My Brother joined me in a few days and we had some beautiful weeks in Venice. I worked very hard at the study of lace; that was my primary purpose there and took precedence of sightseeing. Lady Layard's introductions opened many doors, and information was readily given me at Burano and elsewhere. I noted the defects in the organization there established and felt these need not be reproduced in South Africa. The whole subject in its many branches is wider than generally realized and needs long and close study. Moreover, the story of lace and its various developments is bound up with the history of Western Europe of the last four centuries. I took lessons myself, conquering the principles of the work, and I was strongly recommended to go to Bologna and study the work of the Amelia Ars, but that had to be left to a later date [. . .]

During that April you had moved your husband and your family to the Black Forest where Dr. and Mrs. Berne[3] welcomed you to their charming abode. I was much delighted at their invitation to me to visit them for a day and meet you once more. So I travelled by the Brenner Pass and Innsbruck to Freiburg im Breisgau, where Mrs. Berne met me and drove me through miles of forest to her home. The trees were in their daintiest dress of early spring green. It was cheering to see how well the President had borne the journey and benefited by the bracing air. Later in Rome I was to see much of Dr. and Mrs. Berne and again in Holland in 1915 when she was left a widow, and yet once again in Freiburg itself in 1920 when I was travelling in Germany on relief work.

I next broke my journey at Wiesbaden where Count and Countess Bothmer entertained me. Count Bothmer afterwards gave me much help with my industries. Thence I went to Brussels to study lace and lace-making, a very different kind in that vicinity, and at Malines, Ghent and Bruges. What I learnt is too long, complicated and technical for these pages. Kind friends put me at once into the right circles for my purpose. I remember the sad plaint of the old woman in Malines, who alone was left of those who could make that exquisite pillow lace – her grief that modern girls lacked the patience to learn and the taste to appreciate.

I took ample notes of all I had seen and learnt. I felt and always have believed that it was a cottage industry admirably adapted to your people; to girls on quiet farms where there was little dairy work to occupy, where the light was excellent, the life tranquil, where little material was needed, and that easily obtainable by post; and the finished article could easily be sent away by post.

I have never thought it a suitable industry for a woman's whole livelihood. Lace-work, whether needle-point or pillow, is of a nature to accord with other avocations; it can be taken or left at will in intervals of leisure. It is refining and educative, for it demands patience, extreme cleanliness, absolute thoroughness, delicacy of workmanship and an appreciation of outline and design. Completest command of the needle is a matter of course. A girl gains in moral qualities as well as skill, and she could produce in hours that are otherwise often only idle a work of art which, though not a livelihood, will bring pocket-money. And that is the idea of cottage industries – occupations suitable to the home, where they can be woven in with the ordinary routine work of a farm and by which a little money can be added to the family purse.

There was much in the Continental lace centres that I disliked – an attempt on the part of the employers to exploit the workers and on the part of the workers to make it the sole source of living instead of an additional occupation for leisure hours. In parts of Belgium there was a disposition on the part of the women to work at fine lace only in the winter when farm or garden work was slack. In the grey northern winter the light was not sufficient, the cottages dark, and lamp or candle light poor, and fine work done under such conditions strained the eyes. This was not the work but the circumstances under which it was done. It seemed to me that in the wholly different conditions prevailing in your country these and other drawbacks would not or need not appear.

I reached London just in time to join my Uncle and Aunt at Crowsley Park, where during May we enjoyed the perfect garden and the nightingales. It was a restful time, and the old couple revived in the peace and the open-air life. But they were indeed older and feebler. I sat much on the lawn practising lace stitches and wished I had begun younger. I took long walks in the bluebell-carpeted woods with my Uncle and the little dog, and sometimes, to get further afield, my Aunt would meet us in the carriage at an agreed point and drive us home. It was a great relief to me when she did so, as my overtaxed strength, not by any means renewed, made these long walks a serious strain.

After my return from South Africa many encouraging letters reached me, either sending donations for your people or expressive of joy or relief that we were helping them. I mention these that you may know how people felt about it all and that I was but a sample, so to say, of the many who sympathized. To give you an idea I will quote one or two.

A well-known Harley Street doctor in sending a cheque wrote:

> "I have a fancy that the money should go direct to the recipients from one who would have them believe that England still loves justice and tries to live by the same faith that upholds those we have wronged in their sufferings . . . I, with millions of others, am responsible for putting a Government in office which had no real sense of the honour of England. That this is the case is more clearly manifested every day. And I would have just one wronged man and wife, or one wife and children, understand that those who have wrecked them do not really represent this England of ours, and that many of us, her children, would do much to undo the wrong we have not willed and yet are responsible for. I honour and thank you so deeply for your work that I send my thoughts with a little bit of my money."

Many similar things were written by a number of people who that year joined with

Mrs. Courtney and Lady Ripon in making me a little presentation. This took place on 11 May in the Courtneys' house in Chelsea. Lord Ripon and the Bishop of Hereford, two of the finest men of that day, were the speakers. The presentation could not have been more kindly done and yet I rather shared the view of one friend who refused to join the movement. She wrote:

> "Is it a crank in my composition which makes me jib at the idea of admiration, love and esteem for noble work done, taking the form of a joint presentation? I have always known that to sacrifice yourself in every way – health, wealth and reputation – for the sake of the Boers, was the natural outcome of your character, and I hold you blessed among women because God had given you the power to perform as well as the heart to feel; and I felt it was a matter of 'how otherwise' with you. I should as soon have thought of getting up a presentation to Queen Eleanor for sucking her husband's wound or the Lady Godiva for riding naked round Coventry! It seems too small to bring acts wrought for love on to the level of the doings of a popular mayor and to lose sight of the spiritual joy of service, so to *me* it seems a profanation of the feeling I have for you to join in a round-robin gift."

Lady Ripon was herself too ill to be present but the message she sent through Lord Ripon touched me very deeply:

> "She bids me say that as she lies on her bed of suffering, the thought of all Miss Hobhouse has faced and done gives her courage to bear her pain."

The lovely summer days passed tranquilly at Crowsley Park and by the time the bluebells had faded in the woods we were back in Bruton Street. The lease of my Chelsea flat had ended the previous year and my furniture then stored, so that Bruton Street was my sole resting place from that date. Indeed, my Aunt used to say as long as she lived it would be always home for me. And very grateful I was, and much I loved them and valued the privilege of being with them. Still – given a couple who, however old, were yet singularly self-reliant and independent, added to a houseful of competent servants – there was nothing for an active person to do, no outlet for one's energies. It was difficult to see on what ground they wanted me. *Now*, with personal experience of old age, I understand the truth of what Lady Farrer[4] suggested, viz. that not wishing to make use of any personal services did not affect the question of how needful one's mere presence may be.

It is a lesson to me, for people of my nature often forget that "being" is more important than "doing", or to put it another way, what you *are* has more influence that what you *do*. My Uncle and Aunt, though I did not know it, were both in the last year of their lives and must have been feeling all the weakness attendant upon

327

that fact. Outwardly it was concealed with great calm and dignity. I see it far more plainly now as I read old letters. They wrote more than they spoke.

Just then my attention was turned more definitely to spinning and weaving, and a visit to Ireland was the result. Mrs. J. R. Green,[5] always interested in your country, asked me to lunch shortly after our return to town and we discussed the possibility of cottage industries. I found her opposed to lace, but very strongly in favour of spinning and weaving. Her opposition was based on the fact that lace was a "luxury" and that only wealthy Johannesburgers would be able to purchase it. Spinning and weaving appealed to her historically; she pointed out that the women of every nation in the Old World had spun and had woven, they had been through the educative processes entailed in producing all the textile necessities of their peoples till within the comparatively short period that machinery had replaced them. She felt, perhaps rather romantically, that such handicrafts would help the formation of your national life, while making use of your staple product – wool. It would add interest to solitary farm life, and articles made would not necessarily be sold but in the first place provide the workers' homes with blankets, rugs, tweeds, coatings, and so forth. On these lines solid benefit must result. If, on the other hand, the industry took the shape of articles made by girls at high wages, living the dearer life of towns and with various overhead expenses, I knew the products could only be costly and end by ranking as "luxuries" also. Hand-made products, made under such circumstances, cannot compete in price with machine-made goods. Useful it might be, but by no means in the degree intended. Still, I yielded to Mrs. Green, as she urged a study of these industries and others in Ireland where much could be seen doing in the cottages. With this in view I went shortly after to Ireland under the wing of Mrs. Green herself who could give me the best introductions. Meanwhile my suggestions about home industries were laid before the Committee of the Distress Fund.[6] They approved and were willing to send out circulars to test the feeling of their supporters. Whether or not the scheme could evolve depended upon sufficient supplies being assured for at least the first three years.

I do not remember in which month I ran over to Paris to see you and the President once more,[7] and I know I felt uncertain about final decisions pending a detailed talk with him as to the chances of success.[. . .] But most clearly do I remember the trip to Ireland in July, its delightful people, its interest and enjoyment; so beautiful, too! It was a revelation also to hear the opinions there openly expressed about England, so near home. Here, thought I, is a country with the climate of my own Cornwall and the sentiments of South Africa. I imagine all is different *now* that Ireland is a "Free State". I am always so sorry it has taken your name. I constantly find myself plodding through a paragraph in *The Times* headed "Free State" thinking it is about you, and then find it is Ireland. Why not "Free Erin" and "Free Orangia"? We saw much under the escort of Mr. Walker of the Congested Districts' Board. There is a fascinating spirit in the people. Such humour, buoyancy and poetic idealism combined with unpractical don't-care habits, really astonishing. We went long drives on uncomfortable vehicles called outside cars, and I have seldom laughed so much as at the anecdotes and stories which followed each other in unfailing supply replete with Irish wit and humour.

I need not enter into all I learnt and thought about Ireland. What alone interests you is that I visited all important centres of spinning, weaving and lace-work. I bought home-made flannel straight off the looms which take so much space in their tiny cottages, and it seems to me that such flannel alone would be a most valuable product for family use on your farms.

Sir Horace Plunkett[8] kindly asked me to lunch and gave me valuable advice and information. Lace had been introduced into Ireland during the potato famine in 1848 as a means of helping the impoverished, and during the fifty odd years it had spread and had done much to bring money into the country. The system was not altogether good; the convents and others, while maintaining a standard in the work, in many cases exploited the workers. Some Irish laces have great beauty and excellent workmanship – truly "painting with the needle" – such as the needle-point of Youghal and Kenmare, and the "run" lace of Limerick. But like all modern laces they often fail in design. Reacting from the over-conventionalism of Venice, modern designers in North Europe have lost the dignity, restraint and balance which characterize their forerunners. This, however, is not the case with the lace-makers of Normandy centering about Bayeux; here the French genius has known how to break from the shackles of the Renaissance conventionalism and has succeeded in adding grace without loss of dignity and restraint. Modern lace also loses in not having the hand-spun flax thread of olden days. Wonderful as are the smooth fine threads which machinery produces, they have often an admixture of cotton and can in no case compete with the beauty of the hand-spun product. But perhaps I am getting too technical.

As regards spinning and weaving I thought it was probable that early Dutch and French emigrants had taken their spinning wheels and looms to the Cape, and that some remnants of such handicrafts might still exist. It might have been so, and the wheels and looms had been left idle for want of raw material, for from a careful reading of Theal's *History*[9] I do not gather that flax was produced under the Dutch East India Company; and the native fat-tailed sheep not giving a good wool for spinning it was long before a better strain was produced by sheep imported from Europe.

Theal does hint that the art of weaving was known to some, at least, of the settlers; he describes the attempt to organize such needed industries and the quaint reason for its failure – a reason not without its counterpart in modern times.[10]

From Ireland I went straight to Somersetshire by sea, joining my Aunt and Uncle at Banwell Abbey and only left them once more when, in the break of our move to London I ran down to Devonshire for a couple of days. Miss Audrey Trevelyan, who had done so much to revive and raise the standard of the once famous Honiton lace in Devon, had most kindly invited me to visit them at Seaton and see the collection made in earlier days by her relatives. In early Victorian times priceless laces could be and often were picked up in Italy for a song. Miss Trevelyan also took me into the cottages where I saw the old people making the delicate Honiton sprays ready to be appliquéd on fine net. At her suggestion I visited the lace *Dépôt* in Exeter on my return journey.

During those quiet weeks at Banwell Abbey I worked hard all the mornings at South African correspondence, at lace-work, at the collection of funds and the further investigation of industries. Writer's cramp and acute neuritis seized my right hand and it ended by going to Bristol and buying a typewriter. In the beautiful Somersetshire churches of that part I found rare carvings and sketched the designs for future use. In the afternoons we drove and walked lionizing one point after another. In an adjacent combe or valley full of rocks and trees an overhanging rock is shown as the one under which Mr. Toplady[11] sheltered from a storm, and which inspired him to write the well-known hymn *Rock of Ages, cleft for me*.

We made great use of bicycles in those days, the dear days before motor cars ruined our country roads, and mine gave me an independence which I have much missed since. On one occasion my Brother, who was spending August further down the coast, proposed a meeting at an interesting historic spot, and I rode some 25 miles west while he and his little boy came a similar distance east. I intended returning by rail, not having strength or time for the return ride. After lionizing we had tea and a substantial one it was, for they had a long ride back. When we had finished it appeared that my Brother, with this usual superiority to everyday practical things, had forgotten to bring any money, and I had only a very few shillings. So when I had paid for our three teas, behold there was not enough left to buy my ticket home! Consternation ensued when my little nephew confessed that he had a small fortune. It came out that he had recently been making a collection of halfpennies and on rifling his pockets we found 37 of these upon him. Promising to repay the sum in halfpennies we hurried to the station only to find that we were still three halfpence short of the required sum. My Brother nobly offered to pawn his watch, but there was no time, so I bethought me of my brooch and appealing to the Station Master to advance me the ticket on that security just managed to catch the train. We often laughed over that incident and Oliver's fortune in halfpennies. It was memorable to me as my last long ride through our beautiful country lanes, for it was a year of many "last things"! The last too of a long series of beautiful holidays in fair country places with the old people.

When years later I came back to Europe to live it was with wrecked health and permanent disability of the heart and no home.

Soon after, another "last thing" occurred which stays in my memory. My Uncle within a few weeks of his 85th birthday maintained considerable walking powers, and, attended always by his little blind dog, put me to shame. He was passionately attached to his native county of Somerset and his pleasure never failed in getting to high points whence he could see large stretches of it. As a boy he had climbed to the highest point of the range of hills called the Mendips and his heart was set on going there once more. My Aunt begged me to go with him. She drove us several miles to the foot of the range; there my Uncle and I and the little dog got out and began our climb while the carriage took her home. Exhausted by the work of the past three years I found the climb worse even than Table Mountain simply because I was so much less able to face it, in addition I had every few minutes to rescue the dog who in her blindness repeatedly plunged into clumps of gorse which pricked her nose and entangled her long hair. It ended by having to carry her. To crown all I was filled with anxiety lest my Uncle should collapse, his breathing grew laboured, and every few minutes we had to rest, but plucky to the last he refused all suggestions to be content with anything less than the summit. Miserable trio, physically, as we were, the top was reached at last, though he was really too exhausted at the time to enjoy the panorama which rewarded us. He enjoyed it more in retrospect and in the satisfaction of having accomplished the ascent. I carried the little Meg down the hill till we reached the roads where she could safely run, and then came our long tramp home. I noticed from that moment that my Uncle's breathing was permanently more laboured and I always believe it hastened the end which followed so soon.

Lady Farrer paid us a visit before we left. She has wide sympathies and encouraged me to discuss my difficulties with her. She held the strong opinion that as long as the old are well cared for it is the duty of those who are still active to work for the good of society, and she saw no reason why our old couple should not yet enjoy many tranquil years. In a word her advice was to continue my preparations and go.

On our return to town in early October I halted a night at Street. The Clarks[12] had asked me to speak at a meeting. I had met the older members of the family before, but it was on this occasion I first saw Margaret. How much arose from that meeting! To you I need not describe one whom you all came to love and who loves South Africa as her second country. Her university career ended, Margaret was at a pause in life when my good fortune brought us together and she offered to help me in any way. I remember so well; she had driven me to the station to see me off. The train was already moving when she repeated this offer more emphatically. "Even in South Africa?" I asked through the window.

"Even South Africa," echoed the answer as I lost sight of her. It was a noble offer and opened up fresh vistas and lightened dark places in my plan. I wrote to her fully the next day and received in reply a repetition of her offer, combined with a most modest estimate of her capabilities. Well, we have long since sampled those capabilities, haven't we? Mr. and Mrs. Clark gave willing consent even though tinged with anxiety as regards health. Even you can never know what a companion she proved, an ardent worker, good organizer and wise counsellor. She entered not only into the practical work but wholly shared the idealism of the

331

scheme – our attempt to work out William Morris's view of art as things "made by the people for the people as a joy for the maker and the user". In fact the little we were able to achieve was due to her unfailing efficiency and endurance.

All this year I received a steady stream of information shewing how severely your people were still suffering. Of course the renewed governmental supplies, coupled with the extra ploughing and a fairish harvest, had relieved the most acute stage, but there was privation of every other sort. Among others Lady De Villiers wrote me some description of what she and Lord De Villiers saw in the neighbourhood of Kroonstad.[13] They had sought change from the damp of the Cape, and Lord De Villiers had benefited by the frosty keen air of your high altitudes.

The time had become ripe for winding up the South African Women and Children Distress Fund and at a meeting at Mrs. Courtney's house in November this was done and instead it was proposed to form the Boer Home Industries and Aid Society.

During these autumn weeks I had been working hard at spinning and weaving, going daily to a school, but early in November my Uncle's condition caused us alarm, and my time and strength were wholly taken up. I hardly know which needed most care, he in his weakness or my Aunt in her utter desolation. It was soon over, and on 6 December he left us. He was 85. The memorial service was held in St. Margaret's, Westminster, a very noble service, but my dear Aunt was too broken; I represented her, instead, as chief mourner, with my cousin. [. . .]

Those were sad weeks. My whole being was absorbed in helping my Aunt to bear her loss. For 56 years they had been man and wife, rarely apart, and with the special possession in each other of those who have no children. She had never faced the world or faced anything alone. Letters appreciative of his life helped her now.

Mr. J. X. Merriman wrote me from Stellenbosch:

> "I beg that you will say to Lady Hobhouse how sincerely I mourn the loss of a brave and good man. I shall never forget the kindness that he showed to me at a very trying time nor the noble stand that he always made on behalf of truth, justice and right. England is the poorer when such citizens are taken from us, for their number is not large. I am glad to see that the Press seems to have recognized the high and unselfish ideals that Lord Hobhouse set before him. Like Cato 'the beaten cause was dear to him', but the fact that men of that stamp are still to be found is the salt that prevents our race from being overwhelmed in the slough of stockjobbing Imperialism.
>
> "There are many homes here who will sympathize with you in your trouble and in which the name brings the recollection of sympathy bestowed which can never be forgotten."

Lord De Villiers, who had often sat with him in the Privy Council, wrote me from the Cape of "the consolation that must arise from the universal testimony paid to his worth as a man and his eminence as a Judge".

I dwell much upon this loss, for I never felt any death so deeply. Since I was six years old I had been closely linked to my Uncle, and I always looked on him and my Aunt as my mental parents. It was hard to creep into her room that dark winter morn and break to her that the end was near, and together we stayed with him till all was over and I led her back to rest.

When she and I had settled down to our quiet life the question confronting me was hard. Some months earlier I had seen you in Paris, and the President had encouraged the initiation of my plan. I had accepted funds for it; and Margaret Clark was anxiously waiting to start. Our berths, with a third helper engaged,[14] were secured on the ship in which you also were sailing from Rotterdam, January 25th. On the further side preparations had also been made and your father had all in readiness at Philippolis and a schoolroom prepared.[15] My furniture had been sent as well as looms and wheels, etc. Difficult as it was, I told my Aunt she had only to express the wish and I would stay with her, and sorely I felt she needed me. She would not consent. It is easy to be wise after the event; it is clear enough now that I ought not to have laid on her the onus of asking me to stay; I ought to have simply assured her that I would not leave her. But one cannot see the future and I little thought she would go so soon. Finally I determined the wisest thing was to go as arranged, set the work going under Margaret Clark and return to spend the summer with her in England. Meantime her sister, Lady Iddesleigh, and other nieces would be constantly with her. But it cut me deeply to leave her so forlorn. I never saw her again. [. . .]

The old year had ended and the New Year opened in a period of grief, anxiety and uncertainty. Usually some kindly alleviation comes when one is depressed. This time it took the shape of a New Year's letter form William Watson, a poet I have always admired. I had written to thank him for his new volume of poems. He replied:

"Your letter reaches me here and will remain with me as one of my lasting treasures. Any beauty which words of mine may possibly have is pale beside the beauty and splendour of your deeds, which will outlast and outlive many words.

"To you chiefly our country owes it that the most lamentable and most tragic phase of the late war was arrested ere its full consummation, and the English people of the future will be as grateful to you as the Boer people of the present have reason to be. Now that you are going among them once again, your great influence will I am sure make for the reconcilement, if such a thing be possible. It is a pity that they and we realise so imperfectly how near akin we are. Our very word 'neighbour' is but nigh 'Boer', near countryman, and the dialects and place-names of our eastern countryside are full of the evidences of our community of origin with all the folk of Frisian stock; yet we and these dwellers on the South African veld stand apart 'like cliffs that have been rent asunder'.

"May your work be the beneficent one of healing the scars of that cleavage."

Prince Kropotkin[16] wrote me a farewell from his bed, where he lay very ill largely, he said, because, alluding to Russian affairs, he could not be in the thick of that great awakening of a nation and was not able to bring his "little unit of energy to *deepen* that movement . . ." You will remember the stir in Russia at that time.[17] He went on:

"You go to South Africa . . . my heartiest good wishes will accompany you and be with all those who will help you there in returning hope and life and new ideals too, broader and wider – (this is what makes the force of a nation) – to the unfortunate Republics."

Mr. James Bryce wrote from the country, expressing regret at being unable to see me before I left on this "beneficent mission . . .

"Let me wish you all speed in it. No better work can be done than to help the Boer women, whose lot has in many ways been the hardest, to learn or relearn household industries. And apart from that result, it has always seemed to me a thing of inestimable value that when so many bitter and foolish voices here were denouncing the South African Dutch, and the country was behaving as it did, you should have shewn them by your presence and example that there was another spirit and feeling in England, and a sense of justice and humanity in a large section of our people. I am sure your going now will do immense further good . . ."

Mr. Courtney came up from Chelsea the last day to say goodbye to me in person. That touched me very deeply. We all loved and honoured him so much. He brought me a copy of the book he had published anonymously, letting me into the (then) secret of the authorship of the *Diary of a Church-goer*.[18] He came, he said, to throw some "cold water" on my schemes in the shape of warnings of different kinds; of discouragements I must expect, of failures and disappointments galore, which would certainly dog my path. It was a dear, kind, prudent warning, and I loved him for it; unfortunately, our talk was broken into and I could only write him my assurances that I was prepared for "cart-loads" of difficulties, also that General Smuts had assured me that "discouragement" was not for such as us,[19] and had laughed my fears away. I said I hoped that one at least of all my plans might succeed, and that all along I had asked myself what harm would result if I failed. I could not see that any great harm could result, whereas much good *might* do so.

334

My Brother came and little Oliver, and took me to the station where were gathered Margaret Clark with a sister and friends in attendance. The wrench of parting was over at last, we had an easy crossing, but my head ached with unshed tears for my dear old Aunt, that had to be repressed.

At Antwerp we drove to the *Kronprinz* in a cab, finding the ship decked with bunting from stem to stern in honour of Mr. Steyn. We were there several hours before you came, bringing him and your party on board, and accompanied by a large circle of friends and sympathizers.[. . .]

Philippolis

MISS HOBHOUSE'S BOER INDUSTRIES
(Lines written by Mr. C. E. Maurice[1])

"From the silent depths of a deep-felt wrong
We wake the notes of a nobler song;
From ruined farmstead and wasted grain
We rise to the hopes of a purer gain.
To the sound of a wheel with blessings rife
We spin new hopes for our country's life.
The voices of those who died to save
Have called new life from a nation's grave;
And the ills that grew 'neath the soldiers' blades
Shall be crushed by the wheel of the spinning maids.

96. DIARY, 27 JANUARY 1905 TO 6 APRIL 1905

Friday, 27 January 1905. A glorious day and the ship sped down the Channel calm and steady, everyone enjoying the voyage. So calm was it that I got out my spinning wheel and gave Margaret Clark a lesson. She spun or carded all the morning while I read to Mr. Steyn. The French coast was in sight all day and very pretty. After lunch I read poetry to my two companions and then William Watson's *For England* to the President. At tea where we all gathered we had a lively discussion on Women's Suffrage and women's position and rights in general, Mr. Steyn proving himself a splendid champion for our cause, and all the women supporting him against two Hollanders, a Dutch Consul and a certain young Baron. They seemed to advance no arguments. It grew cold as we rounded Ushant, and instead of keeping the Emperor William's birthday with a ball as intended, most of the ladies retreated to bed.

Saturday, 28 January. Most people affected by the Bay. I was not ill. Nursed Margaret.

Sunday, 29 January. Again glorious weather. Out of the Bay and everyone cheerful. Being Sunday we all attended the German service at which my friend the Rev.

Arndt, of former Bloemfontein memories, officiated. Then a great sleep overcame us all which lasted till tea-time. A merry tea and then on deck where Mrs. Jacobsz[2] herself offered to teach me Boer Dutch and did so for an hour. She herself speaks it very sweetly. Her little girl wins all our hearts.[a] The young people became uproarious over a game of French tig and I talked quietly with Mr. Steyn. He is indeed a good and great man. To my joy I find he takes a liberal view on the question of British Indians in South Africa. He thinks the first step should be to carry out the law (never heeded) and send home the Natal Coolies, and then do the same with the Chinese; and allow such Indians as care to come *naturally* to do so – not prevent them.

Monday, 30 January. A disappointing day, for we had expected to be able to read and work, but we met a trade wind which upset the whole ship more or less. I could not read to Mr. Steyn nor could he listen. But the ship's company and servants are pleasant and all is simple and kindly.

Tuesday, 31 January. A lovely day enabled us to be busy. Read Mr. Steyn More's *Utopia*, and Boswell's *Johnson*. The Peak of Teneriffe in sight and land promised to-morrow.

Wednesday, 1 February. Early roused, for we were anchored at Las Palmas. Glorious day and all looking beautiful. Directly after breakfast we joined Mr. Jacobsz's party for the shore. Having formerly seen the town I should have preferred a drive into the hills, but we could not separate. All excited by the brilliance of sun and air. We bought things we did not want, and much fruit, and after lionizing the town finally lunched in Hotel Catalina. The scarlet hibiscus was very fine; I drew it and other flowers, both whole and in section, wondering if they would not work into good designs. My mind leaps across the long interval that must intervene between now and the moment when such may be needed. Shall we succeed or fail? That question arises and looks me in the face rather closely now. From such talk as I have had with Boer friends on board I fancy they all think us doomed to fail, but perhaps they do not quite realize our schemes or understand the kinds of work it is proposed to produce.

Thursday, 2 February. Very busy.

Friday, 3 February. Yesterday having passed in the same round of occupations I did not write but spent the time designing. Today the lovely weather continuing we were as busy as ever . . . A talk today with my second helper occasioned great perturbation of mind . . . The surprising information obtained must have very serious effects upon our work. It weighs heavily on my mind, but I am powerless. Talked it over with Margaret Clark who felt as I did.[3]

   Dr. Malan gave us an interesting lesson in Dutch today.[4]

337

Sunday, 5 February. Took a real rest today; one can't stand much application on board ship. The girls are all indefatigable in their games – never once do they sit down except for meals. A stout man on board has had a silly bet with the doctor that he would fast a day for £5. Friends tempted him in vain. At 7 this morning his time was up, or so he believed, but not until 11 o'clock (sandwich time) did he break his fast. Then the doctor said the bet was his, for he meant it must last, not the twenty-four hours, but till noon of the next day. The Captain was made umpire and decided, unfairly as we thought, for the doctor, who won the £5. He then treated his combatant to a lunch with iced champagne. Read *Utopia* to the President. Began *Erewhon* by Samuel Butler. The sea continues perfectly calm, and today for the first time we have felt the warmth oppressive; but the thermometer is only 82° Fahrenheit. Last night we practised Dutch with Mrs. Jacobsz.

Tuesday, 7 February. Yesterday and today we worked hard again. Margaret improves with her spinning. It was hot but not unbearable as we were blessed by a strong head breeze, which after dinner increased suddenly and before we knew it we were in the midst of a heavy thunderstorm, rain lashing, and lightning, almost incessant, illuming the entire sea. It was grand and lasted about three hours, somewhat relieving the oppression. Margaret and I, unable to breathe in our unventilated cabins, stood outside in the dark watching the storm. This morning passengers report having seen a waterspout not far off, but this I did not see and luckily our ship escaped. Today the order of things is upset by a fancy ball which will keep us up late and makes me half wish for a cabin below. Rather hard to have two balls in one voyage, and stupid to try and dance where we now are – exactly *on* the equator . . .

Wednesday, 8 February. Little Ellie Jabobsz's birthday. I gave her a toy I had bought at Las Palmas. All day I, like the rest, was '*paap*'[5] owing to the bad night caused by the dance, joined to the heat. The ball had been kept up till very late and degenerated into rowdyism at 4 a.m. in the smoking-room . . . I lay in my hot bunk and listened to the noise next door . . . At 3.30, unable to endure the combined heat and noise any more, I left my cabin and fled to the ladies' saloon; at 4 a.m. the smoke-room emptied and the tipsy men went noisily round and round the deck, making sleep impossible. So we were disorganized all day. I finished reading *Utopia* to Mr. Steyn, and his masseur[6] kindly massaged my neuritic arm while Mrs. Steyn made me lie down in her cool cabin. Here I should have slept had not people talked loudly outside all the morning. The after-lunch rest brought no sleep. I read *David Copperfield* to the President and translated some Dutch with Dr. Malan.

Thursday, 9 February. A good night partly set us up again, but it seems a general complaint that our heads feel somewhat turnippy! Carried on our usual avocations. Margaret and I called on Mrs. Arndt who shewed us their premises and we sat some time at the stern. Afterwards the Captain kindly gave me leave to sit on the boat deck, his sanctum, during the sports which are filling the ship with noise this afternoon. It was perfectly quiet and peaceful there and I read my Brother's difficult philosophical book for three hours undisturbed.[7]

Friday, 10 February. Wrote nothing being very poorly.

Saturday, 11 February. Yesterday was a perturbed day because not only were Margaret and I very poorly but our companion[8] was also laid up with a bad knee ... having cracked her knee-cap by a fall in racing with another passenger. The doctor hopes fourteen days may see the end of it. I must get Dr. Murray's opinion in Cape Town. We are making bad runs and not likely to get in till the 18th.

Yesterday was Margaret's birthday, a rather dreary day for her as she was poorly. I gave her *Marco Polo* which pleased her very much.

Sunday, 12 February. The month slips by. We now feel sure we shall not land till the 18th. Today I had considerable giddiness and felt shaky. The President too had a headache, and several of the others were poorly. We do not know why, unless it is some new movement of the ship occasioned by a fresh swell ... Read and walked the deck. Head still bad. At dinner Mr. B. entertained us by talk of his experiences in China where he dwelt seven years. He told us how he got into trouble and disrepute in England by "shewing up" the falsity of the sensational *Daily Mail* telegrams about the people said to be murdered in China in 1900, which proved, as he had said, wholly untrue. Had a long talk with President Steyn about South Africa and the prospect of our Liberal Party. The invalid's knee still painful; it must yet remain in splints. Margaret most kind and attentive.

Wednesday, 15 February. Last night we anchored near the wreck off Swakopmund,[b)] unable to get in until the mist lifted. But this morning we found ourselves arrived, the vessel having crawled in at half speed in the night. Good, after fourteen days, to see land and life again, though the "land" be but a sandbank and the "life" three or four officials in a tug and three or four negroes in a lighter. Owing to the war (with the Hereros)[9] some half dozen German ships are in the bay. There seems no dock or even mole or pier and we have to lie two miles out with no chance of going ashore. The delay is considerable as the majority of our passengers and a good deal of cargo is to be discharged here. We shall have to do our own packing today ... I agreed with our invalid to keep all her things and send nothing up-country till we had Dr. Murray's advice about her knee.

Monday night they had a farewell dance and next morning the girls all appeared with black ribbons worn as mourning for the ship-companions who were to get off at Swakopmund. I finished *Erewhon Revisited*, ingenious but not so amusing as *Erewhon*, and all my other books and am half through Sidney's *Arcadia* and Boswell's *Johnson*,

339

also various books on co-operation, banks and co-partnership. I have read to Mr. Steyn two hours daily and we continue our Dutch lessons. Writing, designing or anything that involves stooping have been a difficulty. Today's long entry is due to our pause at this little place.

Thursday, 16 February. A very dreary day, the trade wind almost due ahead, causing a most dismal pitching.

Friday, 17 February. Ship still pitching though somewhat abated. All of us affected in our heads and unable to pack except in short stages. Margaret much upset by packing. The Chief Officer promises to call us at 4 a.m. to see the approach to Table Bay at dawn. He told us it was true about the two black spots seen by some of the passengers in the tropics, but that they were only visible in some latitudes. They had seen them last voyage and had reported them at Hamburg but had heard nothing in the way of explanation. To bed early.

Saturday, 18 February. Rose at dawn and there was the grand still beauty of the Bay, the mountains outlined against the already glowing sky. The Blaauwberg range[10] was sharp-cut against the gold, the Table Mountain group more tenderly. Soon we passed into the dock (the old familiar dock where my weary imprisonment was spent), and there news and letters came on board. The President calm and grand as usual. We had time for breakfast before various friends began to arrive – Van Broekhuizen,[11] Mr. Bredell,[12] Onze Jan,[13] Mr. Chiappini,[14] Mr. Malan,[15] Mr. Fischer,[16] the Transvaal delegates Ewald Esselen[17] and Mr. De Villiers.[18] Mr. Schultz was there, kind and helpful as ever, and General Smuts. There were many more, a rare and delightful gathering to meet and honour their great invalid on his return to South Africa after two and a half years in Europe.[c]

Soon they all left with the President, leaving General Smuts to look after us. It transpired that the carriage good Mr. Schultz had brought down for me had broken down *en route*, and as he would not let me take a cab I was to wait till he brought another. So we sat on the dock with General Smuts and enjoyed his talk, and watched our looms unloaded onto African soil. It was good to see him look so well. Suddenly, radiant and flower-like as usual, Mrs. Sauer appeared and together we all drove off, Mr. Schultz and Smuts in a cab behind us. At the Customs gates a rough-looking man stopped our carriage saying: "Which of you four ladies is Miss Hobhouse?" A momentary shudder went through me, but he added: "Because I want to shake hands with her. I have read her book and admire her!" This was easy and we proceeded on our way, he shouting after us: "I'm Irish, that's what I am!"

To the bank for our mail, where we found two letters for me, thirteen for Margaret! What a difference having a family! Aunt Mary's was *very* short ... Then we went up to "Avignon" to greet Mrs. C. De Villiers and left Mrs. Sauer with the

President there. At 11.30 we started for Kenilworth, Margaret going on to Wynberg in charge of Mr. Melius de Villiers,[19] while I got out at Kenilworth with my limping companion who was helped up to the house by Mr. James Molteno, who also jumped out of the train. Mrs. Murray gave us a warm greeting and we lunched and had a quiet afternoon, Margaret coming over later to do some writing for me.

Sunday, 19 February. I did not sleep much; I was excited and missed the rocking of the waves. I lay all night thinking of the past and of the future and interwoven with my thoughts were the inspiriting words spoken to us by several that day . . . I talked to Dr. Murray about the bad knee which he thinks will take some time to cure, and at 10 a.m. came Margaret from her friends in Wynberg, and she wrote for me. Mr. James Molteno kept us all alive with his jokes. After lunch Margaret came back . . . Then came Mr. Abraham Fischer. He told us much news . . . When he left I went with Mrs. Murray to look at a Swedish stove much recommended to me, and thence to call on Mrs. Koopmans in Wynberg . . . The days here are full, my thoughts various and it disappoints me to find how impossible it is to write all in one's journal, how little of one's true inner feeling one writes; one is shy even of one's own journal.

Monday, 20 February. Early up and to town with Jarvis Murray[20] who was very attentive and took me to the north express to see my friends off. Mr. De Villiers, Mr. Esselen, Helen Botha[21] and the Rissiks were the party leaving. I was impressed with their courage and hope for the future of the country. They thought the future held more hope than before the war, the people had been tried and tested and were now consolidated as never before. The issues were clear . . .

Then Margaret and I turned to our hot day's work. This consisted in the usual weary round of offices and clerks. We succeeded, however, in at last getting the promise of a rebate on the duties charged. They had put a 10 per cent duty on all our hand machines, etc. as if *foreign* goods, whereas *British* should only be $7\frac{1}{2}$ per cent. I had written careful instructions from London that this was to be seen to, as our things were almost wholly British; but they sprung upon us the rule that *private assertion* was not enough, it was necessary to have certificated assurance from the *head* of English firms. I pleaded ignorance of this rule, and eventually the Comptroller of Customs consented to take my word for it.[d]

We bought a stove and saw to other matters, lunched with Jarvis Murray and on the way back got out at Rondebosch to call on Mrs. Philip Botha at Ivydene. She was out and we only saw the girls . . .

Tuesday, 21 February. Wrote for the mail all the morning and in the afternoon to drive with my two companions, up Wynberg Park, through Newlands Avenue, and into Groote Schuur. They, overwhelmed with the beauty, I, missing the *green* of other seasons. Moreover, the blue hydrangeas were over.

Wednesday, 22 February. Early to town where joined by Margaret; meeting Mr. Fischer we went to see him and the Jacobsz family off by the express. Said goodbye to sweet little Ellie. Went round to the bank, Mr. Schultz and agents, to find out if all our goods, looms and cases, etc. were gone. All *had* gone, so we hope to find them north on our arrival. Met Lady De Villiers, Mrs. Marais and others, all difficult to tear ourselves away from. The day previous Margaret and I drove to call on the Purcells at Bergvliet, Diep River, their charming home in the old picturesque farm.[22]

Thursday, 23 February. Up early to catch the 7.40 train for the Sauers. Took, in our English fashion, 2nd-class tickets, but at Salt River met the Sauer trio and had to get in 1st with them. Met Mrs. van der Post in the train. At Mulders Vlei I drove with Mr. Sauer in the buggy and ponies, the others with Constance Cloete in the Cape-cart. Coolness and fruit met us on arrival in the well-remembered beautiful place. Delicious to be among such sweet and friendly people once more! How impossible to put down a tithe of what passes daily in one's life, leave alone in one's thoughts! Constance came and sat on my bed telling me much of her wishes to go north and help in the up-bringing of the Dutch girls. But she dreads leaving her sister . . .

Friday, 24 February. Delightful to be at Uitkijk once more. Yesterday we saw them bringing in the grapes and treading out the wine in the press. Wonderful to see the juice pouring out in a great stream! Little Paul with his bare feet newly washed trod merrily with Africa, the Kaffir. Today up early at 6 a.m. and down in the orchard to gather figs and eat them ice-cold off the trees. For the first time, too, I wandered in a vineyard and gathered my own bunches of grapes in what quantity I would. Mrs. Sauer watered her garden and at 8 we assembled for breakfast. A delicious morning sitting on the stoep reading and writing, while Margaret rode with Mr. Sauer for the post. The papers annouce that the Paris enquiry exonerates the Russian Admiral (Dogger Bank),[23] which in my own mind I always thought it would; but we know no details yet.

After lunch Constance drove us to Stellenbosch to Mrs. Marais who assembled the De Vos's. Professor Hofmeyr and Mrs. Neethling to meet us and they made me tell my plans and ideas. I called on Ella Neethling in her bedroom and talked about my troubles with regard to the translation of my book . . .[24] Home rather late and to dinner, after which we talked about lace and Mrs. Sauer showed me what she had.

Saturday, 25 February. I slept badly and lay listening to the crickets and the night birds and thinking much of what the future has in store. Margaret walked up the mountain to see the sunrise and at 9.30 the Sauers departed, leaving us to follow by the next train. A delightful visit, a memory to carry with us. We got away easily and had a quarter of an hour to wait at the station where the station-master talked to us of the bad times and of the docking of wages. £25 knocked off his salary now. We tried 2nd class and found it very uncomfortable, much worse than English 3rd class. At Cape Town came Mr. Schultz and Mr. Van Zyl to meet and escort us to luncheon. I talked the whole time to Mr. Schultz, being very glad of the opportunity, and evidently Mr. Van Zyl had much to say to Margaret. Mr. Schultz's many-sided kindness to all and sundry impressed me more than ever, even sending fruit once a week to Visser, the convict on the breakwater. He has hopes of helping Lily Boshoff-Rautenbach through the fund for the wounded, of which he still has a reserve. He showed me a copy of the letter written by Scheepers[25] the day before his execution, a farewell to Steyn and De Wet, very brave and manly. He has the original in his possession which has recently reached him by a circuitous route. In the letter Scheepers asked to be buried in Bloemfontein Cemetery, but, said Mr. Schultz, the body can never be removed for it was covered with lime to burn it to ashes. Mr. Schultz took us to the train for Kenilworth and helped us book our seats for the coming journey north. After tea we wrote six letters and went to Wynberg to call on Mrs. Koopmans. She talked much of the rival societies for women formed and especially of Mrs. Solomon's,[26] and I was glad to hear she disapproved of refuge for such Boer women as had fallen through the past unusual events. I agreed with her that it *stamps* them. She also fancies people have exaggerated the situation. She talked long and then we walked to Plumstead to the Etienne de Villiers'[27] who pressed me to stay to dinner. They put me into the train and so home where I found the Murray family assembled to enjoy music and joined them. Dr. Murray sings well.

Sunday, 26 February. Very hot. I wrote and packed all the morning; in the afternoon came Margaret and we walked to the Chief Justice's and had an hour's chat with him and Lady De Villiers. Meeting there Mr. and Miss Philipson Stowe. From there to the De Bruyns, apologising for an untimely call on clerical folk. She was nursing a big baby. Much talk of Brandfort.

Monday, 27 February. Up early and to town for final arrangements. Happened on the Chief Justice and went with him and Mrs. Charlie Molteno. He told me of the Preservation Society[28] recently started and how they hoped to protect the Castle.[29] I spoke of the ruined cottage near Stellenbosch where Piet Retief was born,[30] and this he thought should be purchased. He said *two* farms at Colesberg claimed to be Paul Kruger's birthplace. Our business done, Margaret and I went to Avond Rust[31] to call on Onze Jan. His wife busy canning tomatoes, he at leisure in a cool library. He told me £200 had been given as compensation for the misappropriated Lydenburg goods.[32] Not adequate indeed and only got after endless procrastination and when he had repeatedly spoken to the Governor. Back to lunch having first purchased a green veil (to avoid glare and dust), and finished packing and registering our boxes. The Murrays were all dressing to attend Lady De Villiers's garden party, while I sought a good bath and prepared our luncheon baskets. Dr. and Mrs. Murray came to town with us to see President Steyn, and the faithful Mr. Schultz and many others were in attendance.[e]

Sunday, 5 March. Philippolis. All this week I could not write; two days in the train and the rest sheer fatigue from overwork. More or less we *are* settled in, though every night I am possessed by fears that I have attempted a task wholly beyond my powers and my means. The history of our journey up and the warmth of the welcome to Mr. Steyn and also to myself I have somewhat fully described in my letters home, which, after being typed, I shall hope to get again, and this set of letters will form a kind of journal.[f] Starting the Monday night it was Tuesday 28 February when we crossed the Karoo which was wonderfully cooler than usual, and in one place rain was falling. The welcome given the President at each station but specially at Beaufort West was very heartfelt and so simple. Mr. Weeber, the M.L.A., and Dr. Neethling headed the crowd and talked much to me. Indeed, there was hardly a station but people came to see the President and brought me gifts of flowers and fruit, making a bower of our train. But the next morning was the most moving surprise when some twenty prominent Free Staters appeared at Norvals Pont having crossed the river to welcome their Chief and escort him across the border. The feeling was silent but intense.

We, joined by the Frasers,[g] left them at Springfontein, and came here to Philippolis. Moses, to be our "boy", was at the station to meet us. I learned he had just come out of prison (for no great offence).[h] A spider took Mr. and Mrs. Fraser, Margaret and myself, with much changing and chopping of steeds, and our companion and the two little Steyn girls went in the Cape-cart. We crossed the veld for nine weary and jolting miles on a lovely day with clouds flecking the sky and not too much sun. Emeline Fraser[33] had dinner ready for us and nice cool rooms and there for two days we rested in comfort as far as bed and board went, but working every moment between whiles to unpack and get our house ready. Such a work! Fifty cases or more to be opened and unpacked and the house to be cleaned, and new, untrained servants. We toiled till Saturday night more dead than alive and on Sunday were but fit to lie on the sofa. That rested us and we started with fresh strength and hope today (Monday). But at moments and in the heart of the novelty, and the pressure of work, everyone wanting direction at once, my heart nearly failed me and weakened my belief in my own scheme; the mass of detail temporarily obliterating the ideal in my mind. Now it dawns again and if my plan of getting Constance Cloete to come and keep house for us succeeds, I think we may yet prosper.

Nothing can exceed the goodness and hospitality of the Frasers and of other people here, or the eccentricities of black Moses![i]

Tuesday, 7 March. A week in Philippolis, and we have done nothing yet but struggle in the heat with our unpacking, our servants, and our settling of the workroom. The work has been severe and at times I felt as if I must break down. I had to be everywhere at every moment, and my feet ache unmercifully. Today Margaret, who has been invaluable, was laid up, and nursing her has been on the top of all else. She looks better tonight and I hope it will pass off, for I need her much. People in the village are tired of waiting for us to shew ourselves, but we hope to be able to begin by the end of this week. That is, if all goes well with our various *bodies* and with our various looms and machines. The idea occurred to me yesterday to implore Constance Cloete to come to our rescue – to take the entire housekeeping off my hands and give us her sunny presence. We have written and now also I shall telegraph, for daily it is plain I cannot hold out long at this rate. We long to begin teaching and see how it "takes" and in what directions we most need to develop the work . . . Each night I am too tired to write, so a journal fails after all to be the companion and confidante I had hoped to make it.

Wednesday, 8 March. A somewhat lighter day. Rose at 5.45 and called the others and made early tea. Drew my bath water from the tap in the yard before sunrise, and was dressed just as Moses arrived at 6.20 a.m. Set him to light the stove and sweep the parlour, etc. and hurried round to help Widow Boshoff[34j)] get breakfast. After a struggle this was ready at 7.45.

Set Davel[35] to work. Superintended Cook in flooring the new room and worked at unpacking in the workroom. Things getting on. Mr. Fraser and General Nieuwoudt called. Wired to *beg* C. Cloete to come and schemed to make her comfortable. Rested two hours and worked hard till 6 p.m. Large cupboard made and therein packed our various work materials. Altogether felt more sanguine about the future. After supper Emeline Fraser called.

Thursday, 9 March. Very hot, fatiguing and busy day, but the workroom begins to look shipshape and that consoles. Early my soul was refreshed by a glorious cactus flower sent in by Mr. Liefman[36] as a gift. The scent was powerful, the petals feather-like and purest white; the bloom full six inches across. It blossoms at night and closes with the coming of the sun upon it. I have seen one almost like it in Mexico. Later he gave one to Margaret . . .

In the evening I left the house, the first time for a whole week, and went to congratulate Mrs. Fraser on her birthday. Mr. F. very poorly and ordered to bed.

Poorly myself and very hot. All day wondering if Constance Cloete will come to our rescue.

Friday, 10 March. Too tired to write.

Saturday, 11 March. Yesterday I was poorly and it was so hot and we so busy I

345

could not write. Today it was cooler and I set the convicts to wash the school and had a hard day myself as Mr. Davel did not turn up and I had to nail down C. Cloete's carpet and do much work myself . . .

By 4 o'clock all was clean and tidy and we had our first batch of girls[k) headed by Emeline Fraser who interpreted. We explained and they listened intelligently and all are to come and begin on Monday at 8 a.m.

I am so far relieved but full of qualms at our expert's too evident inefficiency.

Sunday, 12 March. Up early, and at 6 a.m. found to my horror my fresh one lb. of butter put outside to keep cool *wholly gone*, milk untouched. Too evidently the work of fowls, as dish, butterpaper and cloth were all left behind. Vexing. Went to church with Margaret. Mr. Fraser was ill, so an elder read interminably in Dutch. Nearly fell asleep. Home and wrote for the mail. Finished preparing our wheels for the next day, and after tea called on Mrs. Van Heerden.[37] She in bed. She told me of the Governor's (Goold-Adams') visit and his fear of the word "compensation"; and how she told him she hoped it would follow and haunt him day and night. After supper wrote.

Monday, 13 March. A red-letter day. At 8 a.m. began our teaching. The six girls came punctually and proved most nimble and intelligent. Kept Davel and Moses also at work. At 4 p.m. they came again and Hester Strauss began with the knitting-machine. When school was over at 6 p.m. I went down to the parsonage to tell Mr. Fraser how it had gone off. Found him in bed with bronchitis but determined to see me. He told me Mr. Van Heerden, the resident magistrate, had asked the Government what (as an official) his attitude was to be towards me and the reply had been to "help the enterprise". Hence the convicts.

After supper walked with Margaret over the veld in the moonlight.

Tuesday, 14 March. Second day of teaching. The four morning hours very hard as the weather was unusually oppressive. Busy also trying to get the little outside room in order for the arrival of Constance Cloete. I was up at 5.30 a.m., not having slept after 3 a.m., and made tea before six. Dressed and out to work before 6.30. Made Moses sweep the school.

Mr. Lubbe called and brought me a basket of tomatoes. Hoped we would remain here twenty years!!! After lunch so dead beat I went to lie down when thunder began, and hearing the rain I had to rush out and shut doors and windows and take in curtains, etc. It *poured*, filling the tanks and washing the court clean. School at 4 to 6 p.m. Girls busy and interested. Weaving began. After school to the parsonage were Emeline found with neuralgia and unable to go and meet Constance to-morrow.

Saw Mr. Fraser, in bed still, very bad, says he is besieged by applications of girls wanting to learn of me. Had some grapes and come back, found a small snake in

346

the front passage which Margaret tried to kill by throwing the *Manchester Guardian* upon it and then stamping wildly. I removed this and killed it with Uncle Arthur's heavy umbrella. Moses says he killed two today.

Mrs. Bezuidenhout sent in a present of freshly baked Boer biscuits, a sort of bread-cake flavoured with caraway seeds . . .[38]

Cannot make up my mind where best to put C. C. to sleep, and whether I ought to take the new room and give her mine.

Wednesday, 15 March. Joy! Constance Cloete's arrival.

Thursday, 16 March. Delightful rest, for she took the household in hand. Fresh hope for all!

Friday, 17 March. Glad to end our week's schooling. Much fatigued but on the whole feel progress has been made and the last half hour we collected the girls and talked over the work and its prospects. We are a little uncertain as to their feeling on the subject. After school Mr. Liefman and Mr. Van Heerden came in to see the school and expressed much interest. Called on Mr. Fraser who was on the sofa, somewhat better but coughing much, and asked him about housing Winifred de Villiers and the girl from Wolmaransstad (also a De Villiers) . . . Sat in the moonlight after supper and planned work, also play for Saturday.

Saturday, 18 March. Very busy all day preparing our week's work, doing accounts and so on. Not till after tea did we go out, I to sit on the nearer kopje where I watched the sunset and wrote letters. In the evening we each chose and read poetry aloud.

Sunday, 19 March. All enjoying the pleasant meals and the order which C. Cloete had brought into the house. Moses with bare feet waits table in a clean apron and Mrs. Boshoff is made happy by getting away early to bed. We worked or wrote mail letters all Sunday. I decided to write and ask if Miss Jones[39] could come.

After tea a delicious walk with C. C. when we looked for cactus flowers and sat on a boulder and read William Watson aloud.

Monday, 20 March. The new girls arrived, but to our dismay Susie Siebert, one of the most promising old ones, sent word she was not coming and later came to excuse herself from further attendance. A blow! Jealousy, I am sure, because there was no knitting-machine for her use. A hard day but fairly satisfactory. Saw Mr. Fraser in the evening and discussed pros and cons of Winifred de Villiers and the Wolmaransstad girl coming.

Tuesday, 21 March. Hard work. Teaching new girls . . . Very hard day . . . Thought of cabling for Miss Jones . . .

Wednesday, 22 March. Cooler day, grey and showery. Steady work with twelve girls regular and eager . . . Spent siesta-time tying headles[40] which my helper could not tie. Cabled to England for Miss Jones, cost £1.17.6. Hopeless to go on without someone who knows perfectly the elements of the work. Wrote yesterday to Winifred de Villiers and her mother, asking her to come here for a month as my guest and to remain if it suits her. Walked with Margaret after school and enjoyed the damp air and wet soil. Moses quite another boy under Constance's management and training.

Thursday, 23 March. Full day. Up by 6 a.m., not having slept much from colder air and paucity of blankets. Spun angora before breakfast. Hard school.

Mail day and brighter letter from Aunt Mary who wrote from Sandhurst Lodge. After dinner washed wool, Constance helping me. Dyed fleece and to school. A new girl, deaf, came, making thirteen. Gift of a loaf in the afternoon and flowers and eggs in the forenoon. Hardly a day passes without these gifts in kind. Walked with Margaret on the kopje and rejoiced to hear her say she has never been so happy in her life! . . .

Friday, 24 March. Last day of second week's teaching, a thirty-hour week. Odd so short a sum of hours should exhaust us so. Girls very good; thirteen of them. Cannot take more at present. Four presents today: Mrs. Lubbe – milk; Mr. Van Schalkwijk – mealies and melon; Mrs. Snijman – plants; Mrs. Van Heerden – springbok. Very tired. Emeline Fraser visited school and seemed pleased . . . Very tired. Gave Moses a comb, he much pleased. Ups and downs of mind about our enterprise, one day all hope, the next all despair. All depends on plenty of ardent spinners.

Saturday, 25 March. Lady Day. Found that C. Cloete had never heard of Lady Day. Curious. No teaching but much work. Experimented all the morning with dyes and washing and found the walnut husks answer best. Afterwards I tested this dyed fleece in the spinning and found it excellent. After lunch the others to walk on the kopje with intent to choose a spot for us all to go and sleep out tonight. However, thunder came on and this plan fell through. I stayed at home and took opportunity to sort my papers and try to arrange my books, a heart-rending affair as so many are missing. In the evening we read Paracelsus[41] aloud, and Nellie van Heerden[42] came in and listened. A great bunch of flowers was sent to me.

Sunday, 26 March. Lovely morning after the thunder. I stayed in bed till 6.30 and drank my milk there. After breakfast took writing things and Margaret and I to the top of the kopje, where she wrote an article for the *Manchester Guardian* and I my circular and other mail letters . . . Suggested to Dorothy Bradby to send not only Miss Jones but also my lace teacher from Venice, Signora Moratti.

348

Walked home at noon, very hot, dined and to sleep. Then I wrote again and after tea spun my dyed samples and at dusk had a run with Constance . . .

Monday, 27 March. Busy day. All up early. Girls showed more grip of work. Cloudy afternoon and heavy rain, which lasted all night. Sore throat and chill, dosed by the two homeopathists with arsenicum. Read Shelley aloud, *Euganean Hills* and *Sensitive Plant*. Mrs. Bezuidenhout sent a great loaf of bread. Delicious. Feeling poorly and unhappy about Margaret who undoubtedly feels the close air of her bedroom and must be moved. Hard to arrange. Lay awake all night planning. Decided to hire a room in the village for our weaving teacher. Overslept myself and told Constance my plan when she called me. She agreed to enquire. The *Friend*[43] still tarries; ordered it twenty-two days ago.

Tuesday, 28 March. Up late. Breakfast 7.15. Very wet, steady rain all day. Much doctored by all the kind of friends and got through school wrapped in a shawl and Margaret's woollen waistcoat. Much happier about the work. Girls grasping the sequence of processes and worked well. Steady heavy rain.

Wednesday, 29 March. Still steady rain. Will fill dams and soften ground for ploughing, but alas! is too late for many of the crops. Slept late and by much kind nursing from Margaret and Constance felt better and able to work. Girls improved, all except one. Flax-spinners promoted to wool. In the afternoon dyed with walnut husks and pomegranates . . . No *Friend* yet come. Tiresome to miss so many weeks' daily news.

I hear Mrs. Van Heerden will very kindly let us have a stoep room, and insists on taking nothing at all, much as I wish to pay. So I hope to arrange for the weaving teacher to go across there and sleep and Margaret to have her room. I feel sure Margaret feels the damp close air of her room in the court.

Moses has taken French leave and disappeared all the afternoon. Margaret overdone and poorly. We made her lie in C.'s room, she very, very angry thereat, and Constance took the parlour sofa. Boxing and Coxing as regards their clothes. All to bed at 8 p.m.

Thursday, 30 March. Pouring rain in the night awakened us all. Did not sleep till after 3 a.m. Fortunate that we had kept Margaret out of her room as the wet streamed through the ceiling and all was damp. I kept her on the sofa all the morning and sent her for a walk when the sun came out. Moses arrived saying he had been very sick the previous day. I dosed him with success.

One month in Philippolis is over and I have as yet hardly realised that I am here. In fact, I am not living in Philippolis but in an Idea. This seems to be taking solid and permanent shape and there is much to encourage us in the aptitude and intelligence and eagerness of the first thirteen scholars. A new one joins us to-morrow.

Our dyeing of yesterday seems a success – a delicate green (pomegranate) and a brown (walnut husks). Two gifts of flowers today. Continued and heavy showers. Margaret in school in the afternoon. Constance an angel.

Friday, 31 March. Lovely day, bright and cool. My voice gone . . . Difficulties with my staff shook me much. Mr. Fraser came and talked awhile before school. Sarie Bezuidenhout, the new girl, very pretty, sweet and clever. Spun, as if by nature, on a difficult wheel: extraordinary. Found Hester van Schalwijk had attempted home dyeing. *Very* encouraging.

Walked out with Constance, sunset delicious. All tired and very glad 'tis Friday. Only gift today walnut leaves and a tin of rusks. Useful.

Saturday, 1 April. Voice bad. Stayed in bed to breakfast. Pulled wool in the court with Margaret and began to spin it. Mrs. Van Heerden called and told me the room was ready. Weaving teacher moved into it. She very willing. After dinner we helped her to settle in. Busy preparing for some guests; laid out tea in the dining room, but only a few came. Mr. Marais, Commandant Du Toit, Mrs. Lubbe, old Mr. Lubbe and wife, Mrs. Tarr, Miss De Villiers, Mrs. Louw, Mrs. Snijman, Miss Young and Bultermann. My voice departed. Mrs. Marais the most interesting of the party. Later Mrs. Snijman sent a lovely dish of figs. Had a long talk with Emeline Fraser about the girls and the work. She most helpful . . .

Sunday, 2 April. Very low physically. No voice all day. In bed to breakfast. Kept quiet, wrote mail letters . . . About 11 arrived a cable from E. D. Bradby saying Miss Jones could not come till autumn, possibly not then. I proposed others. Constance and Margaret busy arranging their rooms after the change. Went a short walk rather late and sat under the aloe shade as I had neither strength nor voice. To bed early, rubbed with Elliman.[44]

Monday, 3 April. Breakfast in bed. Voice a wee bit better. Very little in school. Sat in the "green room" and prepared a lace sampler for Constance, also in the afternoon gave her a first lesson. Long visit from Emeline Fraser who kindly found a Kaffir girl for us in room of Mrs. Boshoff. Margaret read aloud *Persuasion* in the evening.

Tuesday, 4 April. Lovely weather. Still in bed for breakfast but I felt stronger and was more in school. Dialina Rensburg in school, a new girl. Began angora spinning. Finished brown wool. After dinner slept. Very tired. Mr. Steytler came to see me about the wools and offered to take back the lambs' wool – too short.[1] Lace lesson. Dr. and Mrs. Strachan called. After lesson walked with Margaret to the cemetery. Jacoba Enslin began knitting-machine.

Cabled to England, cost £2.17.6.

Wednesday, 5 April. Constance away to the Gertenbachs' farm[45] with Emeline to spend the day. Brought home flowers, plants and mealies . . . The fifteen girls were good and interested, but the day was oppressive and we teachers found the time long. Margaret and I half swept the school at six as Moses did not appear and the light begins to fade early. Working with angora, and Margaret has produced a baby's sock with this wool. No *Friend* arrived yet and it becomes tiresome to have no daily paper. In the evening we are reading *Persuasion,* but my voice has failed and now Margaret is reader. I fancy it tries her a little. We go to bed at 9 p.m. and glad to get there. Mr. Fraser has gone to Bloemfontein.

Thursday, 6 April. Mail day. I felt very poorly, and, staying in bed for breakfast, was a trifle late for school. A new girl, making sixteen. The black girl, Marie, arrived and looks promising. Mrs. Boshoff departed and Moses delighted. Margaret was saddened by the news of the death of her great-aunt aged 88. Davel brought the pipe and put up the stove, so now we can wash and dye. Corded the stoep to prevent impudent prying at the windows. Work full of interest but anxious. My one home letter from Aunt Mary short and rather shaky, obviously written with effort. But if she were gone I should have no regular correspondent, none to whom I *ought* to write or from whom I am *sure* of an answer. The last days of my year are passing and on Sunday I shall be 45! . . .

FROM THE MEMOIR AND FROM OTHER LETTERS BY E. H.

That ends the longest diary I have ever kept, and bare enough it is, but at least it gives the outline of our first months in Philippolis and the ups and downs we experienced in starting the industries. It took us some time to get acclimatized. It would have been more prudent to have gone slower until fitted to conditions. Again, I am wise after the event.

a) *To Lady Hobhouse. Las Palmas, 30 January 1905*: . . . Mr. and Mrs. Jacobsz, *very* charming and their child, Kruger's great-granddaughter, a fascinating little creature of 6, who speaks French and Dutch and is beginning to learn English.

b) *To Lady Hobhouse. Las Palmas, 30 January*: We find that at the last moment the ship has been ordered to put in at Walfish Bay at a place called Swakopmund and here we have to put off a dozen passengers and a lot of railway material, for a company is going to exploit a mine there and is building a railway thereto.

c) *To Lady Hobhouse. Cape Town, 21 February 1905*: The pick of the three colonies were on the docks to meet and welcome Mr. Steyn and me too, they kindly said – Delegates from Pretoria and the Free State – amongst them General Smuts, Advocate De Villiers and Mr. Fischer. The crowd had been kept away and we had just this pleasant sort of family party – some 20 or 30 real and trusty friends. [. . .]

d) The promised rebate remained a promise. We wrote many reminders of it, but never to my knowledge received it. O officialdom!

e) [. . .] thus we left on our northern journey in the same train as the President and yourself, and well I remember the remarkable scenes of that soul-stirring journey.

To Lady Charlotte Graham Toler of the B.H.I. Committee, 5 March 1905: . . . unpremeditated groups to meet the President . . . Wellington not before 11 p.m. so he was made to go to bed and Mr. Du Preez and I did the handshaking business by starlight and received the lovely baskets of fruit, chiefly grapes. Peaches were ready for us at Worcester, but we got there at 2.30 a.m. and they spared us.

At Beaufort West Margaret's friend the Somersetshire railway foreman[46] brought us a great quantity of fruit. Mr. Steyn stood at the window, too tall for the people to see much of him beyond his flowing beard, and the endless handshaking went on. Hardly a word spoken on either side. Boers don't say much and the feeling was too deep.

At Norvals Pont were all the men who had worked in his old Government, who had followed him through the war and had done so much to help him since. General Hertzog, General Brand, Dr. Ramsbottom[47] stood there trying to speak, but could not. It was an indescribably moving scene, not that there was anything said or done, but everyone was overflowing with an intensity of feeling which words cannot convey. He belonged to them, and they to him, absolutely, and they had come to escort him over the border into what all feel is his own by right of birth and love and sacrifice and everything else.

At Springfontein we had to leave the train, not without many invitations to Bloemfontein and other parts and words of encouragement from all the leading men.

I am longing to begin and yet I am half afraid for fear of failure, but all the up-country Boers are so encouraging that I think we shall get along. All the gentlemen say they will come to us for socks, etc.

To Lady Hobhouse. Cape Town, February 1905: I was so sorry to finish the Presidential journey, for De Wet was to appear at Edenburg and a special train of Bloemfontein folk at Kaalspruit.

f) *From the memoir.* Alas! I never saw them again.

g) *From the memoir.* As I look back the extraordinary kindness and untiring help I received from your family stands out in strong relief. I find many long letters from Mr. Fraser written the previous year (1904), which make clear the trouble he took and the time he gave to prepare the way for our coming and experiment. And all this at a time when he was rebuilding his own burnt parsonage and encouraging and sustaining his ruined and half homeless congregation. Without the preparatory help he gave me, we could have done nothing. Then, when we actually arrived, his house was open to us, his carriage at our disposal, and always, throughout our difficult weeks, he was ready to listen, advise and help. My gratitude to him was and is unbounded.

Your father, dear Mrs. Steyn, belonged to that type of clergyman, rare nowadays in England and elsewhere, distinguished by a beautiful Old World courtesy which was most endearing. This and his high-minded devotion to duty recalled my own Father in many ways. He gave us a good start and Philippolis proved a suitable nursery for our scheme.

To Lady Hobhouse. Cape Town, 26 February 1905: Mr. Fraser tells me he has secured as housekeeper a Mrs. Boshoff, widow of a once rich farmer, now penniless, and under her a Kaffir for the heaving of wood and carrying of water, and I do so wonder how we shall get on with this pair.

h) *To Lady Charlotte. Philippolis, 5 March 1905*: Moses [. . .] to gaol for helping himself to raisins and sugar in his master's shop, and his defence is that his master had given him leave to do so.

i) *To Lady Charlotte. Philippolis [Undated]*: Moses is everything to me. He has adopted a plan of ringing for me whenever he wants me. Rather upside-down according to English notions, but it works fairly well, for it saves his dusty feet from coming into the parlour, and the moment I hear the bell I run. There being none inside the house I can't retaliate.

j) *To Lady Charlotte. Philippolis [Undated]*: The Widow Boshoff is improving. She says she could cook far better if the English had not burnt her recipe book in their destruction of all her goods. Poor soul! She was in that dreadful Bethulie Camp where her six younger children died and where she said they starved, and since her return she has never been able to buy more than bread . . . Eating our ampler food has already brought colour to her cheeks and I hope she will soon lose the "camp look" which is so unmistakeable.

k) *To Lady Charlotte, 9 March 1905*: The difficulty has been to choke off our too numerous applicants and to appease their impatience to begin. I am determined to begin small and with very few; and so six girls are to come on Saturday afternoon to have everything explained to them, and to choose their special vocation. In a few days we shall be able to double the number, and so proceed.

To Lady Charlotte, 19 March 1905: They took to the work like ducks to water, and quite ashamed us (remembering our own efforts) by the rapidity with which they learnt to spin, and sat at the loom as if they had never done anything else. A seventh girl, whose mother called on me *three* times, to beg permission, came on Friday. [. . .]

Miss Clark is training one girl, Hester Strauss, on the knitting-machine, and we have so many orders for socks from gentlemen in Johannesburg and Pretoria, etc. that we could do well with those if we had but more machines . . . Hester has made rapid strides with the machine in this week's teaching and triumphantly carried home her work to show her father last night. She is the daughter of one of the elders of the church, and her mother died in Bethulie Camp. In order to come to us she gets up at 2.30 a.m. to wash, bake and iron, to be free at 8 o'clock. She has her little brothers and sisters to be-mother, so six hours at the machine in addition to her home work is pretty hard for a delicate girl; but she won't give in.

To Lady Charlotte, 2 April 1905: You would be pleased, I know, if you could see the seventeen of us all at work; almost perfect silence and intense application and resolute determination to conquer every branch of the work. This week they have spun several pounds of wool, and we mean to dye it this week and weave a carpet.

l) *To Lady Charlotte, 19 March 1905*: My great interest and anxiety at this juncture is how best to deal with the wool of this country. We want to use what is here, and not import, if possible, and for this purpose I am training *all* to spin. But the wool is very different to our English wool and so at first I have myself to try endless experiments with it to see for what purposes it is most suitable and how to prepare it.

First, there is the merino of exquisite quality, very soft but rather short and not of staying power for hard (warp) wear. I can spin very fine with it, like Shetland, and I think it will make excellent soft flannel. Next there is a coarse mixed wool and this, I hope, will make strong rugs and carpets and perhaps a little mixed with merino will strengthen that and make it useful for stockings. Then there is black (brown) wool and lastly, the lovely angora goats abound which yield the soft mohair and I am looking forward to experimenting upon that. Once we have learnt the merits and demerits of our raw material we shall know better how to shape our plans.

From the memoir: Indeed we found ourselves confronted with several difficulties for which our English training had not prepared us. It seemed as if no recipe – no ordinary process – turned out the same as at home. Whether it was the action of the sun, or of different qualities in the water, or atmospheric influences – extreme heat, extreme dryness alternating with extreme moisture at times – something or other acted adversely and often made us despair of producing the same effect from the same processes of dyeing wool, washing, etc. as in England. Then too the abundant red dust of the veld and the dense harvest of grass seeds that stuck in the fleeces filled us with dismay. We soon learnt to try and buy only the spring clipping as less likely to contain such seeds. There is a kind which seemed to have a wee hook that fastened on to the wool in a most determined method. Added to all was the scarcity of water. Since reading Theal's *History* and his account of the occasional abortive attempts to create a woollen industry I have wondered if those pioneers shared our difficulties. The settler Bradshaw's effort in the early nineteenth century was abandoned in 1834 because it did not pay. Probably the expense of these processes contributed to make the finished article of prohibitive price.

Langlaagte and after

By the end of April we ourselves had learnt much and realised our chief needs, also our personal drawbacks and ignorance. Often, as the difficulty of importing a supply of cumbersome plant faced me, I regretted having abandoned my cherished scheme for a lace-school and its comparative simplicity. Nor had I duly estimated climatic effects on imported teachers or wooden machines. We ailed a good deal and were indeed long in learning that to attempt such hard physical work as is customary in England was to court breakdown.

We soon understood that Philippolis, though admirably suited for a nursery or preparatory school, was not well situated for a centre of influence. We lacked space and accommodation to expand or to welcome pupils; above all, we needed water, so essential to wool and dyeing industries.

Determining to take advice from Boer leaders in the North, I packed a bale of our first, naturally rough, products, and set off for Pretoria[a] to discuss possibilities with General Smuts and others.

Our chief *immediate* need was for a fully expert spinner and weaver. That post was to be filled by Miss Picard who was already on her way to join us. I was under promise to my Aunt to return and spend the summer with her, and was due to start in a few weeks, Margaret Clark having kindly promised to take control during my absence. I was the more anxious to have a settled policy to work towards, which on my return to South Africa could be speedily developed while I still had Margaret's incomparable help before the time came for her departure.

In Pretoria and Johannesburg I found many ladies stirring in the effort to find suitable employment for young women. The number in need of work had of course been vastly increased by the general ruin of the war. Slum districts were forming or increasing in the towns. And there were the orphanages with scores of girls rapidly approaching womanhood.

Generals Botha and Smuts and others felt assured that the work had a too great future value for the country to be kept in a remote corner,[1] and that to give it a chance it must radiate from a large centre, – while ministers of the church urged that we should come to the help of the orphanages or do something to raise the conditions in the slums of the big towns.

I looked over the ground, studied maps, interviewed house agents and questioned ministers and mission-workers in contact with the people. I saw then and see more clearly now that there was danger of mixing two big and rather contradictory schemes: viz. our primary plan of a national industry for home and farm occupation, and the attempt to lift a rapidly degenerating class by wage-paid work. I had hardly been aware how the war-ruin, plus the impoverished conditions succeeding it, had pressed the *bijwoner* class into the towns in such increased proportion. Yet it was but the natural outcome of the misery I had seen in 1903. The natural desire to help these unfortunates, urged, too, as I was by the clergy, caused me to swerve from my main object in some degree, but I soon realize that we could only help this town class indirectly and in but a few individual cases. A more promising field for our work were the orphanages.

Just then, when these matters were under consideration, the blow fell which caused a fundamental change in my outlook. It was while I was staying with General and Mrs. Smuts in Pretoria that the cable reached me announcing Lady Hobhouse's death.

That very day I had been writing to secure my berth for England, and I had to realize to the full the cruel words "too late". I had promised to be with her before June. No one had written to me that her condition was so serious, and probably her own letters had made the best of it. The blow was heavy indeed, though somewhat lightened by the letters that for three weeks continued to come from her, in which she assured me, with delicate comprehension, that whatever might happen I was to remember she would rather think of me as useful in Philippolis than present at her bedside. For me, her death left a blank nothing could fill, it was the loss of one who always understood.

The full realization of my great loss came upon me. I knew then I was absolutely alone for the remainder of my life.

I will not dwell further on this grief except to explain that it profoundly modified my plans. From the first she had shewn an ardent interest in our industries; she had undertaken to be my own main financial support in doing it besides making her home my own. We had lived simply, even roughly, but already it was plain that life in your country, dear Mrs. Steyn, was more costly even than I had anticipated. I felt assured also that the work could not be securely established in three years, yet now, beyond that limit, I should not be able to pay my way. It was clear that to attain any measure of success in that short time we must work harder and accelerate our plans. The expected quiet months in England must now be devoted with Margaret's help to establish the Transvaal Centre so strongly urged.

Leaving Pretoria with this changed outlook I returned to Johannesburg to consider openings in good earnest. I knew that go where we would we should never find another Mr. Fraser, our counsellor and friend.

The choice of houses was small, and rents really prohibitive. Workrooms of any size conspicuous by absence. The position seemed hopeless when Mr. Kriel[2] of Langlaagte came forward and urged me to consider his orphanage. He had then 250 children and expected more. He proposed we should teach those of over twelve years. Some Philippolis pupils could come and help teach these children. Mr. Kriel was prepared to offer a house belonging to the orphanage at Langlaagte. The village was but a quarter of an hour from Johannesburg by rail, and in spite of adjacent mines and gangs of Chinese it was quiet. Mr. Kriel also offered us a free supply of water, one of the greatest inducements. The work-room was bad, being but a worn-out zinc shed with mud floor, but might serve temporarily. The orphanage had a resident carpenter whom Mr. Kriel wisely thought would be helpful to us. There was no suggestion that we should confine ourselves to the orphans, we should be free to take girls from elsewhere if convenient. Nor was it proposed we should become part and parcel of the institution in any way. It seemed possible, and indeed it was the only feasible plan which offered itself.

I hurried back to Philippolis where we discussed pros and cons. My companions shewed true sympathy with my own loss and they agreed broadly with my view of the position, minor considerations being also taken into account. We felt that so long as we maintained the absolute independence of our little industry, Mr. Kriel's kind offer afforded advantages which it would be folly to ignore. We decided to divide our staff as soon as Miss Picard was fully established and to lose no time in organizing this Transvaal Centre. We knew there were drawbacks. One of these would be the fatigue involved in making a second start within the year. The work was, in fact, too hard. We wore ourselves out and the exhaustion of over-work at a high altitude inflated and injured my heart to an extent that it has ever since been enlarged and permanently disabled. However, happily unaware at the time of the coming penalty for over-work, I forced the pace, hoping to bring the industries to a point where, when the three years were up, they would be securely rooted and in no need of fostering care.

Our decision was shelved till Miss Picard's arrival, as everything depended on her competency. In a few days she came. We took her through the school, and noted with deep satisfaction how instantly her practised eye detected the faults and how apt were her criticisms. Her thoroughness delighted us. Miss Picard proved most stimulating to the work and we all gladly took lessons from her. She was an exceptionally good spinner, having a different method to that in which we had been trained, and certainly a better one. Few pupils if any attained to her standard in spinning. Certainly the South African type of wool had much to answer for in that. The short staple made a fine, drawn thread difficult, the girls tended to put too much wool into the thread, and then, twisting it very tight, made a thick clumsy yarn. The woven material thus became double the weight it should have been. Probably the wools are now greatly improved, but at that date, so soon after the war, wool was bad, hairy and short-stapled.

About that time the preparation of wool, its cleaning, picking and carding, had become a serious question. The looms demanded an increasing supply of yarn. In the school, time and space both failed. So we hit on the plan of getting the old people and young children in the village to prepare the wool, offering so much per pound. A number came forward to do this work, and when more cards came from England that process was also done in the village. My object was to get the spinning also done at home and the hanks of yarn brought to the school. The lack of wheels retarded this step.[b] Davel had already made four, and copies had been made by fathers and brothers of some of our pupils, but many more were needed. The dearth of wood and its high cost when brought from the coast was a bar.

In despair I had written to Europe of the need for a "ship-load of wheels". That wish floating away like a winged seed fell into the hearts of the Swiss people. There, fostered and nurtured by Mme Degli Asinelli of Geneva and Mme d'Orelli of Basel and others, my audacious wish bore fruit in a veritable ship-load! These precious wheels, many of beautiful workmanship, were heirlooms, and I could not forget that under the skilful handling of the Swiss women had for centuries provided the yarn which their winter weaving turned into the clothing of a people. Mme Degli Asinelli was an indefatigable and devoted worker. Her pen was always busy, and kept the Swiss people and many French also informed of every development of the work, as well as collecting wheels, winders and accessories. Boer girls owe much to the generosity of the Swiss. I can never forget the day when I saw the great waggons coming in procession down the road, piled high with cases containing spinning-wheels, and knew that my wish had been fulfilled.[c]

Count Bothmer also sent us a most valuable consignment of wheels of the German type, and the old Grand Duchess of Baden sent us a special gift of three which I gave to as many picked spinners. It was long years after – in 1920 when doing relief work in Germany – that I reminded her of that gift and thanked her personally for it.

When all was arranged, Miss Picard duly established in Philippolis, and Margaret Clark had assumed superintendence there,[d] Constance Cloete and I went to Langlaagte to prepare the house.[e]

Langlaagte at that time had unfortunately many pigsties and was also thick with flies.[f] I resolved never to take a house again without counting the piggeries in the vicinity. It destroyed the pleasure of our life upon the stoep. We *had* to get away for fresh air now and again, and on Sundays would usually take sandwiches and seek fresh air on the veld in one or other direction.

In August all was ready to begin teaching in Langlaagte. The corrugated iron shed[g] with its mud floor was dark and ill-ventilated, most unsuitable for a work-room. The new knitting-machines were sent to a small work-room in Vrededorp, for we had learnt the mistake of combining machine-work and hand-work under one roof. Miss Hester Krugel of Braamfontein, who had gone to Philippolis to be trained, was to return and teach in that place, and meantime a Philippolis girl came up with us and took charge. Anna Muller also, one of the best spinners, began teaching Mr. Kriel's orphans. [. . .]

An event of first-class importance was finding Mrs. Goetzsche.[h] This lady and her husband, and architect, had come from Denmark after the Boer war. Receiving an introduction I called upon her and found her with her looms. She was at work on a great piece of Gobelin tapestry, very fine. I at once recognized a first-class expert and an enthusiast. Particularly I was pleased with her blankets, a branch I very much desired to develop, as the duty was 20 per cent on those imported. She gave me most valuable hints and information about getting a supply of wheels and looms. Indeed, through her, I was able to get wheels from Scandinavia at £1 apiece. From that time Mrs. Goetzche became our standby and for three years our competent and resourceful head teacher. We felt that on different lines we had now really good teachers both at Langlaagte and Philippolis.

Do you remember, dear Mrs. Steyn, bringing the President to Johannesburg that October?[3] I recall the reception in the Wanderer's Hall and how some 1 500 people assembled there and filed past him to shake hands. That was a great drain on his strength. Yet weak as he was and greatly in request, he found time and strength to come to us at Langlaagte and there lunched with us and saw our school and work. You have no idea how our resources were strained to entertain your party of five or six extra people!! However, as the shopman in the village said everything in his store was at my disposal, I took him at his word and borrowed cutlery and crockery ad lib. The main difficulty was chairs, but that, too, was managed at last.

I remember how interested and encouraging the President was about the school. He walked through that shed, in spite of the heat, and saw all.

Soon after, the springtime calling to us, we took a party of our girls to Kaalfontein to collect dyes on the veld. There were rumours of dyeing having been practised up to recent dates. We urged the girls to collect the names of plants so used before this knowledge died with the old people. (In Pretoria Mrs. Eloff had told me that her mother, Mrs. Kruger, did much dyeing in early days, while Oom Paul himself made his buttons and combs!) We provided each pupil with a dye-book in which to enter all the facts they collect of this old knowledge; they were also to copy each recipe we taught them, attaching a sample of the coloured yarn produced. But this is a digression.

[It was] a picnic we all thoroughly enjoyed. We took many trowels and garden tools, but only one pickaxe. Unfortunately the ground was still so hard and the roots so deep, we broke that one axe, and the smaller tools were useless. We came home wiser, but not much richer in dyes! These veld flowers have by long experience found it advisable to provide themselves with very large roots, and very deeply set in the ground, so that they manage to sprout fresh and green in such droughts as we were then experiencing.

I wished I had known the names of all the flowers. There were brilliant patches of wild sweet peas, some deep blue thing like a glorified lobelia, great pink heads of lilies, perhaps agapanthus, and everywhere the waving green and delicate yellow of the *elandswortel*, the root of which we particularly sought. There was a little scabious too.

In early November the rain came at last, and that filled our minds beyond all else. It came at last to lay the dust, soften the air, improve our tempers, give us water enough for good baths, and set going dyeing and scouring once more. The tension was relieved, everybody looked and felt differently when the exasperating drought was broken.

The new work-room was finished, the looms moved in, Mrs. Goetzsche in command, and the old shed was given over to dye-vats and scouring tubs.

The time was drawing near for Margaret Clark's departure. Only the great help of Mrs. Goetzsche, joined to the hope that Marion Rowntree[4] might replace her, enabled me to face the thought of that loss. Compensation lay in the thought that her presence at home would evoke fresh interest and more funds, as indeed events proved.

I shall never forget the blank pain of Margaret's departure. I had little hope of her return. It seemed hardly possible we could hold on without her. I took her into Johannesburg and saw her off. My house seemed very empty when she had left it, and the work arduous, especially in the hot December weather.

My staff dispersed for Christmas and left alone with Black Joanna, I packed her, a box of groceries and some tinned beef into a trolley, and off we went to a friend's farm which we had permission to use for holidays. By a chapter of accidents my tent did not arrive, so I ensconced myself in a summer-house open to the four winds, and there Joanna and I spent that lonely Christmas on a fare of corned beef and boiled rice. Fortunately there were no thunderstorms and the nights were quite perfect in their beauty, the air sweet and pure after Langlaagte and its pigs.

Those open-air nights did much to restore my strength and I spent the three days writing and taking stock of our position. Looking back on the year, I could feel a fairly satisfactory start had been made. It had, of course, been largely experimental. During the coming year we might hope to see clearer the best lines of development.

Encouragement had not been lacking. Besides that so kindly given by the friendly people around me, the year had brought letters from England[5] of a very helpful nature, and often containing welcome glimpses of political affairs. We felt so starved for news that these were eagerly read. The fall of the Tory Government had been pending, and in the Transvaal we hoped that might mean a change of personnel, which would ease the galling position of the Boers. In our own small sphere of work we thought new officials might give us more facilities, such as freedom from rates and dues and even free railway passes for our staff of teachers, who perforce must come and go. We heard that journalists had free passes, and we made bold to think we did not do more if as much harm as they did!

Miss Picard was due at Langlaagte with the New Year, coming to meet both Marion Rowntree, whose arrival was imminent, and make acquaintance with Mrs. Goetzsche. It seemed well that we four should know each other and lay our heads together.

Marion Rowntree arrived the 28th, having come straight up by the mail. I went early to Park Station to meet her and had to practise patience for two hours, the mail having been delayed by locusts on the line.

"We have sent you," wrote Joshua Rowntree to me, "our best." And indeed, she resembled some tower of strength as she stepped from the train, bringing hope for the coming year.

Marion Rowntree soon took general control at Philippolis, Miss Picard remaining head teacher in the school. She soon shewed special capability for making friends with the Boer girls and their families – visiting home-spinners, and weighing, judging and paying for their yarn. In English fashion she first paid these visits on foot, but after a breakdown in health a bicycle was insisted upon. In your country the strain of long walks, such as we in England love, is too great. I wanted to avoid working her too hard as I had done with Margaret, but I did not succeed. She worked too hard in all directions, keeping the accounts, house-managing, and above all dyeing – a difficult matter where water is scarce.

At Langlaagte Mrs. Goetzsche and Constance Cloete were in charge, while I gave all the time left over from correspondence and general management and the frequent journeys to Johannesburg goods station, including fatiguing interviews with Customs officials and agents. Countless hours were thus consumed and endless patience was required.

Before Margaret left, she and I had discussed the advisability of a gradual withdrawal of my own personality from the regular school work. In view of the fast-dwindling period that I could stay in the country this withdrawal, necessarily developing local independence, seemed wisest. I was sorry, for it was the actual creative work[6] and the contact with the girls which so delighted me. But I knew too that my room at Langlaagte was needed for girls from a distance. So, finding no suitable house in Johannesburg, I arranged to build a cottage such as would house me and my various helpers who came and went.[7] This place, though fruitful of trouble at the time, was economical and proved a good investment which was never regretted.[i)] In any case failing strength was rapidly obliging me to abandon physical work such as weaving and dyeing. I could not stoop, was constantly giddy and a martyr to nosebleeding. Indeed I felt very ill, and undoubtedly I was. But our family has never run quickly to doctors, and it never occurred to me to seek advice. Had I done so, no doubt I should have been saved future breakdown and these long years of recumbent life.

A glorious view of the Magaliesberg range decided my choice of a site, but in going so high (nearly 6 000 feet) I unconsciously increased my physical disability. The purity of the air, most refreshing after Langlaagte, was a relief, and early in the year I moved, regretting the companionship left behind. From Johannesburg I would go three times a week to Langlaagte to give lessons in design, and listen to Mrs. Goetzsche's excellent lectures on the theory of weaving. The rest of the week was filled with a heavy correspondence, reports for Europe, drawing designs for workers of both schools, and countless duties connected with them. [. . .]

There were foreshadowings that Langlaagte would not long remain suitable. The orphanage authorities had pressing uses for the house we rented and as they did not at that time deem our teaching of special value for the orphans (in fact, shortly after, all were withdrawn) there was no object in remaining in such depressing surroundings after our year's tenancy was concluded. I felt Constance Cloete, accustomed to the rare beauty of Uitkijk, shewed real self-sacrifice in staying so long with us. The better water-supply anticipated at Langlaagte had proved delusive; the one tap was sadly inadequate and even uncertain.

Perplexed by the trend of affairs in Langlaagte I visited Pretoria to consult General Smuts. He strongly advised, should the lack of water and other more imponderable disabilities at Langlaagte prove insurmountable, that we should seek temporary premises in a Johannesburg suburb rather than spend our money on building, an idea which had been proposed. He urged that we should train girls, as many as our means would allow, arranging to keep on till Responsible Government was in power. He held out hopes that were almost assurances that there was every likelihood that Government would support industrial schools with a grant.

Acting on his advice I searched in Johannesburg, and with the kind help of Mr. Poulteney[8] found premises a few minutes' walk from my cottage. These offered accommodation far superior to any hitherto found, and the water-supply seemed really adequate for it came from three sources – the earth, the skies, and the municipality! We took the place for twelve months. The elections which would settle the colour of the Government were not due till February of the ensuing year.

Marion Rowntree and I exchanged several visits during the year. She could now always be sure of a bed in my cottage, while I in Philippolis was, as ever, allowed by your hospitable parents to use the comfortable stoep room in their house. I loved that room; it spoke of coolness and rest. It became a necessity not easy of attainment to try and equalize the standard of work in the two schools.

It was on one of those trips to Philippolis – in July 1906 – that I spent that lovely fortnight with you at Onze Rust. The rest was so grateful to me. I remember your sympathetic interest, and the quiet stoep talks with the President. And night after night that pageant of the skies, the red-gold sunsets, making a glory of your veld! The physical relief of a fall from Rand altitude was in itself a rest, and your excellent housekeeping and knowledge of cookery added to nature's restoratives.

I returned to Johannesburg invigorated to superintend the removal of girls and looms and the inauguration of our better work-room. Alas! we found the premises inhabited by an army of mice overjoyed at having our woollen goods to nibble. Many hanks of yarn were destroyed, fleeces marred and fouled by nests, and even finished goods, pile rugs and blankets, etc. were eaten into holes. We fought this plague by every procurable means, but with little avail. They withdrew from the scene only when they were surfeited.

Though Margaret Clark was absent she was rarely out of mind and still filled the chief place in our undertaking. In defiance of ill-health and considerable suffering she worked for us unceasingly. Her success was manifest in the solid form of ample material aid as well as in many a spontaneous tribute written to me. I had asked her very specially to visit Switzerland and in person convey the thanks which seemed so inadequate on paper. [. . .]

Our devoted helper and friend Madame Asinelli wrote:

> "You will better understand the feelings she aroused in us all if I here repeat the words her host pronounced as he shook hands with her at the station: '*Votre venue au milieu de nous crée un nouveau lien de sympathie entre Miss Hobhouse et nous, entre votre oeuvre et nous, entre tous les Boers et nous.*'"[9]

And Lady Farrer summed it up in these words:

> "*November 2, 1906.* I went to Manchester to hear Miss Clark. She spoke beautifully and as I looked at her pure expressive, enthusiastic face I felt, as you said, that a *schöne Seele*[10] dwelt therein."

After leaving Langlaagte we saw fewer Chinese, but we did not cease to hear of them. I often recalled my talk with Mr. Lyttelton and wondered if he had, as I prophesied, lived to regret his scheme; if he ever realized the failure of the Chinese labour he had so unwisely backed in Parliament. The poor Chinese themselves were doubtless unhappy enough; they made frequent efforts to escape, and these starving men, terrified lest they be trapped again, roamed about the veld and were a menace to the farms. Few of the outrages reached English ears. On the other hand there were disquieting rumours of ill-treatment and flogging within the compounds. Soon after I settled in Johannesburg one such case became well known. A Lancashire miner named Ratcliffe stated boldly that he had witnessed the flogging. He was accused of perjury and of course lost his work. His trial was continually postponed and he soon became penniless. Mr. Outhwaite, at that time occupied with journalistic work in Johannesburg, told me these facts and I offered Ratcliffe work in my garden and in this way became interested in his case. When eventually he was tried the Public Prosecutor found he could not support a case against him, so he was discharged free but penniless. Meanwhile the Compound Manager was *not* arrested for perjury nor for illegal flogging, and such was justice under Crown Government rule!

Writing this story to Lord Ripon, I was greatly chilled by his reply:

> "What you tell me about Ratcliffe is bad – but we must look to the establishment of Responsible Government to put a stop to such things."

I was astonished that the Liberals who had opposed Chinese labour and had denounced it, perhaps chiefly from the point of view of the Chinese themselves, would not now intervene to protect these Coolies from illegality. Yet it was still nearly a year before Responsible Government could be established.

In fact the hard work of that year had many compensating interludes of interest or pleasure. I have always found truth in Goldsmith's words:

"Still to ourselves in every place consign'd
Our own felicity we make or find."[11]

One great pleasure early in the year had been the visit of Sir William Butler[12] to Johannesburg. He wrote, asking to see me and was soon spending an afternoon with us at Langlaagte. He was charming and won our hearts by his interest in our work of which he bought various samples, admiring even the faults; which we honestly pointed out. Any visitor from home was a delight, and in his case unusually so. He had much to tell us of interest. We had mutual sympathies on South African affairs. I wrote home:

"I was very glad to find General Butler so strong upon the desirability of clearing out all men connected with the Raid from administrative positions here, and he of course includes Selborne also in that category and is strong in a desire to sweep him off – but he thinks Selborne will be forced to resign. I *don't* think so, unless the Colonial Office is changed and strengthened. Do not let Liberals grow shaky on this vital point."

Sir William was writing a series of articles for the English Press,[13] and one of these dwelt chiefly on Raiders in high positions. As you will remember the Liberal Cabinet shewed itself disappointingly weak, and we in South Africa who, with you, had expected so much from it were bitterly disillusioned.

I recall a long talk with Sir William as we sat on the bench at Langlaagte Station. It was in the after-glow of a brilliant sunset and we were awaiting the tardy train. Discussing the events of the previous years I asked him how he explained the South African War. "The Devil," he replied, "just the Devil". And, noting my surprise, he continued: "I know it's out of fashion to believe in the Devil and few do so now, but I do. There is much in this world we can't explain without the Devil, and I think he was at the bottom of that war." This at any rate exonerated Chamberlain and others!

Sir William invited me to lunch and we had many pleasant meetings before his departure which seemed to snap my last link with England. He was not too hopeful about the Liberal Government. Campbell-Bannerman was oppressed by ill health and domestic anxiety and overweighted by the Imperialist element in his Cabinet. We in South Africa were, however, bidden to look forward to the promised Commission which was to advise on a constitution. General Butler wrote me from Cape Town and the Courtneys from London asking me to see Sir West Ridgeway[14]

365

and urging I should do what was possible to bring the Commissioners in touch with Boer circles. Already it was thought that they were being roped in and railed off from the real leaders of the country.

The personnel of the Commission had disappointed people. Except Sir West Ridgeway their very names were unknown in South Africa. Ex-Governors, titles and military men predominated, whereas competent civilians of national repute had been hoped for.[k] I was of course in no position to proffer help to strangers, and when later Sir West called upon me he told me he thought they had already arrived at a settlement. His own remarks struck me as fair, but I fancy he was overweighted and had encountered strong influences. Boer points of view[l] cannot be learnt without time and preparation, and this had been incomplete. President Steyn told me the arrival of the Commissioners at Kroonstad was announced by telegraph *only two hours* beforehand, consequently it was impossible to summon the important men to meet them.

Disappointed beforehand we did not feel particularly so when in August the Constitution was at length published[15] [. . .] My ruffled feelings found vent in an outpouring to my old friend, Lord Courtney, of the bitter disappointment felt in the New Colonies with the Liberal Government so long looked for. Downing Street did not seem to understand the South African atmosphere, so we thought. To this Lord Courtney replied, taking, as was his wont, that large, long view which so often rebuked the impatience of us smaller folk who expect to build Rome in a day:

> "I do not quarrel with what you write about the Government; but I think and believe that things will go better, and are indeed moving towards a better condition in spite of everything and everybody. We may be vexed with delays, we may be irritated by the incompetence of one man and the stupidity of another, but larger causes are at work and if we have a little patience we shall see the end. The new Constitution will open the mouths of the real leaders in the Transvaal and will reduce to comparative unimportance both the Governor and the Secretary of State. [. . .]"

I find a letter from Lord Loreburn, the Lord Chancellor, of this date, saying no Government ever had a more difficult task than to decide how to act after the events of the past seven years in South Africa, but he averred that they were honestly trying to do justly by all classes. Was it only the physical strain arising from that year of terrible drought that made us in South Africa feel they ought to have gone back in thought more than seven years – even to the Raid itself?

In the course of a letter Lord Ripon wrote:

> "28 August 1906. The framing of a constitution for the Transvaal was a difficult task; but our proposals seem on the whole to have been well

accepted except by the so-called 'Progressives', whom we never expected to please.

"Sir P. Fitzpatrick[16] and his companions did their best to add to our difficulties and to frighten us, but I think that it may be fairly said that they made little impression on public opinion in this country even with the strong backing which they of course received from *The Times*."

A few weeks later in early December I was present at a Het Volk meeting in Pretoria[m)] when the new Constitution was accepted – certainly *faute de mieux* – by the people's delegates.

I wrote to Margaret:

"It was like the burial of the dead. A pathetic scene, crowded and silent."

Looking back, we can see Lord Courtney was right – matters were moving in the right direction, however slow, larger causes were at work than appeared on the surface, the Constitution, though imperfect, *did* open the mouths of the Transvaal leaders, and the way was paved to full Responsible Government. Yet, even at this distance of time, I still feel the Liberal Ministry lost a precious opportunity by the methods they adopted, and by what they left undone as well as what they did and the way in which they did it. They shewed no appreciation of how the iron had entered into souls, seemed to forget what they had said in Opposition, appeared more anxious to save the prestige of their pre-runners in Office than to add to the prestige of the nobler England whom they had been so enthusiastically called to represent. Being often in the society of the leading Boers of both Colonies and deeply concerned for the honour of my country, I had watched with dismay throughout the year the effect the new Government's weak methods on the Boer mind.

As the months passed and no prompt action was taken by the Liberal Government, disillusionment spread. I found myself losing hope and beginning to adopt the Boer view that no English Government, be it Tory or Liberal, could be trusted. Perhaps we were all too impatient, but we had all suffered much under the Tory Government, and that suffering was the measure of our hope in the Liberals.

It was not till February 1907 that the elections took place which resulted in the triumph for Het Volk and brought about a more settled and hopeful outlook. Though in no way connected with politics or parties and maintaining always an independent standpoint, I followed them with deep interest and liked to attend meetings when possible, and often heard Generals Botha and Smuts speak when they visited the Rand.

As Het Volk gained influence, you will remember there was much speculation as to the future Ministry and especially who should be Prime Minister. Amongst others Sir Richard Solomon[17] was suggested. Just at that time in returning from Philippolis I paid you a flying visit. The President was eager to discuss affairs and shewed great anxiety as to the choice of the Premier. He would not hear of Sir Richard Solomon. He insisted that Botha, and Botha alone, must fill the post. Then and there he solemnly charged me with a message to General Botha. He said I must make opportunity to see him without delay and must tell him from himself, President Steyn, that he must take the Premiership, putting aside every personal disinclination. I promised to bear the message and in a few days found a chance in Johannesburg. It was at the close of a crowded Het Volk meeting. As the platform was emptying I drew General Botha aside to deliver my message. I can see it now, the confusion and stir as people were leaving, the dim corner to which we had retreated, and Botha's perturbation as I unfolded my message. He was very much put about. I had not anticipated such strong opposition. He refused even to consider the idea. Again and again he asseverated: "I will not be Prime Minister, Miss Hobhouse; I cannot and I will not."

"But, General Botha, President Steyn says you must be."

"Nothing will induce me, you must not ask me; I would rather go over the border."

"But the President says there is no one else. He says Sir Richard Solomon is not strong enough; he says you must put personal disinclination aside and you must be Premier."

"Miss Hobhouse, you must tell the President that he must not ask it; that I cannot and will not."

I replied: "I can't take him that message; if you think it over you will see there is no one else."

But Botha ended as he began by asseverations that he could not and would not. I followed up my words by a letter to confirm what had been said and beg that he would think it over quietly.

It was not long after, that, happening to be in Pretoria, I met General Botha alone when walking from Arcadia to Sunnyside. His acceptance of the Premiership had been announced the day previous. Perhaps, knowing his feeling, it was ill taste of me to congratulate him. It was too soon; he could not speak and, breaking down entirely, burst into tears.

Later Mrs. Botha told me how hard he had found it, how at first he had refused to think of it, how he sat for hours on the stoep fighting with himself before he would answer Lord Selborne's[18] summons, and with what reluctance he went at last.

To most this incident will read like a fairy tale. But it is true, and years after I reminded him of the incident.

Whatever views may be held of Botha's policy as Premier in the after years, there can be no doubt that his consent to take the Office was an act of supreme self-sacrifice, for he saw clearly ahead and knew all that it must and did involve.

Amid all difficulties and anxieties, to which indeed they often contributed, our

Natives, boys and girls,[19] supplied continual interest and often amusement. Like children they were often troublesome, and the explanations and arguments they required were irritating if you were in a hurry. They served us on the whole with devotion, and were, I think, quite happy.

The Natives brought a new and to me an attractive atmosphere. They shewed humour and imagination. Capable, where they trust, of great fidelity, they have that instinctive sense of justice common to sensitive children, to whom it is often a source of misery till tempered by a greater knowlede of life. This groping after justice is surely the root cause of Native troubles while at the same time the main lever, under wise handling, for their education and general advancement.

When leaving Langlaagte I asked little Joanna to come with me, but her anxious mother opposed the plan. Finally the black Mamma came to talk to me about her daughter, and sermonized me at great length on the way I was to treat her and the care I was to take. No white servant's mother has ever spoken to me so seriously. She was rightly apprehensive knowing the character of Johannesburg. She insisted on coming to see to what sort of place I was taking her daughter, so it ended in our all going together. It was well for me she came if only to help work, for little Joanna was so awed by the appointments of a town house that she could do nothing but sit in a corner ejaculating "Yah! yah!". And when she saw a sink with two taps for hot and cold water she was like the Queen of Sheba, and there was no spirit left in her![20]

Joanna was small and I was weak, so the need of strong arms caused me to succumb to the proposals of Jeremiah, one of many who passed along the street and offered themselves. The times were bad and many people were discharging their "boys". His persistence overcame my hesitation and I engaged him. He knew everything about Johannesburg housekeeping and led me gently but firmly in the way I should go. He said he should stay with me six months – twelve months – long, long months. He went off to fetch his luggage which consisted of two blankets and three books, viz. a Kaffir Bible, a Lutheran Catechism, and a French Grammar. He said he spoke German and was learning French, which he studied with the book upside-down. But the intention was there. Jeremiah would follow me about like a child all day, taking the entire house as his own and looking after my things with great care. He loved cleaning silver and did it incomparably well. He would say: "I take you as my mother, but Missis must never scold me, for it makes my heart go pit-a-pat."

Jeremiah had a room at the bottom of the court where, if a scolding had been administered, he would sit for hours with tears streaming down his face and, as he said, "trembling too much to work". After some months Joanna went home ill. Plain as my meals were the food was too rich for one used to Kaffir food. Obliged to have a woman in the house owing to the uncertain state of my health, I engaged a white woman, and she objected to the presence of Jeremiah. He was sacrificed and great were the lamentations. It proved a mistake, for Jeremiah was scrupulously

369

honest, whereas the white widow turned out a thief and departed in a few weeks, taking many things with her.

I was so thankful when Zimba came to help me, a Zulu, calm, grave, majestic and courteous. I think he was the best servant I ever had in my life. Such shining cleanliness is rare. Zimba was very firm in his opinions, but he did listen to reason and seemed to me less argumentative than the other Kaffirs. It was heart-breaking when he announced his time was up and he must return to his kraal. While with me Zimba had been much troubled about a hat. He did not need one and looked ridiculous in the one in question, a battered straw with brim half off. The hat was lost and for some reason which I fully acknowledged and do not now remember, it was lost through my fault. Zimba was inconsolable. He so desired to go home to his people with this token of civilization. In vain I tried to explain to him how much handsomer he looked without it – he was not to be comforted till I bought him a brand-new hat which quite spoilt his dignified appearance. When Jeremiah had visited his kraal he had insisted upon a pair of boots. He had never worn boots and had a long tramp of some seventy miles before him, but no matter, boots he must have. When he started I was relieved to see that he only carried them slung to his shoulder.

My mind had been in a see-saw of anxiety all the year as to the chances of Margaret's return. Her health was poor and I dared not put pressure. Still, I felt that I could now offer her a fairly comfortable home in my cottage. For she, too, came from a beautiful home and had found our previous surroundings trying. The relief was great when she finally decided to come. As Constance Cloete now felt bound to return to the Cape and Marion Rowntree was going to be married,[21] Margaret's return was all-important.

She had succeeded in engaging for us a professional weaver and dyer in Mr. Milroy,[22] and he arrived early in the new year. [. . .] He arrived by post-cart, bringing with him that breath of super-abundant European energy which we were rapidly losing.[n] He was soon settled and introduced to his pupils. He was lenient in his criticisms of our work as a whole, rightly pitching upon the dyeing as our weakest spot. (It is, however, fair to say that imported yarn, dyed by the best European firms, lost its colour quickly when exposed to your air, sun and red dust.) Mr. Milroy soon plunged into dyeing experiments and it interested me not a little to find that a professional fared at first no better than we amateurs. Things would not turn out according to receipt, or as they did in Europe. I saw that like ourselves he would have to serve some apprenticeship to the country and learn that in South Africa things are apt to turn out contrary to expectation. He possessed, however, the knowledge and resource to apply modifications and soon conquered difficulties. In the school cupboards I was ashamed to find many rolls of woven cloth, supposed to be ready for sale, but full of grease and harsh with sand. With these Mr. Milroy gave a useful demonstration in the scouring of cloth. Suds were boiled,

370

all available baths put in the court, and Mr. Milroy, with trousers turned up to the knees, trod out the cloth in the baths. The girls, grouped to watch, were astounded to see what came out of the cloth they had supposed clean. One must admit the excuse that scarcity of water made all scouring processes a difficulty.

It was arranged that Mr. Milroy should shortly follow me to Johannesburg to give dyeing demonstrations at Bellevue and put up the large intricate loom sent us by the Friends at Bradford. Stacks of yarn were waiting for him to dye.

Alas! the very day after he came he fell ill of a fever and I had him to nurse in bed with a temperature of 105°Fahr. With Maria's help I hoped to pull through, but the following night, when exhausted by nursing I had fallen into a heavy sleep, I was aroused after midnight by a call of "Missis!" to see Isaac, Maria's husband, standing in the moonlight at the open stoep window. Maria, he said, was very ill and would I please write him a pass to go for the doctor. I did so, waiting up till the doctor came, in order to get all that was necessary for her relief. It was a long and serious illness.

And troubles never come singly, for at the same moment a new pupil from Ermelo developed measles at the school and in spite of all precautions others, including Miss Aucamp, the matron, succumbed to the infection. It was a terrible strain to cook and clean and nurse two invalids, to superintend affairs at the boarding-house and find a deputy matron. Boys passed along the street, but none of them were cooks. At last, in despair, I engaged a Zulu who knew neither Dutch nor English and had to be directed by signs. He made long speeches in his beautiful language which fell uselessly on my ignorant ear. As soon as Milroy's fever abated I hurried to Pretoria, hoping my friend Mrs. Ewald Esselen could help me find a servant. Mrs. Esselen, always a most helpful friend, found me a coloured girl, really a trained servant, quite a gem.

Her presence in my home taught me the intricacies of etiquette amongst the varying degrees of colour. When after some weeks Maria became better, the questions of precedence were curious and very serious. This "Cape girl" was as dark as Maria, but her hair was *long*, while Maria's was only wool! "Oh! the little more and how much it is"[23] – for as Maria slowly recovered, it transpired that she was on a social level so different that the kitchen could not be shared. Maria might not ride in a tram unless she wore a hat. In this she looked ridiculous. If she wore her becoming kerchief bound round her head, she could not go. Kate might ride in the tram but refused to do so except with me as protector, for she feared rebuff on the ground of her colour.

The day I spent in Pretoria General Smuts had told me of General Botha's approaching visit to England with his daughter and threw out a suggestion that I should take the opportunity of companionship for the voyage and go too. Margaret, who was just due, would carry on in my absence. The idea was attractive, but I had to consider if I could rightfully leave all to her and if I could justify the expense. There was no longer the great attraction of my Aunt's welcome nor her home to go to. London would seem empty. As I try to recall Margaret's return I find I cannot do so. It is curious that the event to which I had looked forward for sixteen months should have vanished from all recollection. The actions of people at that time who were indifferent to me are vivid, while the long-wished-for coming of Margaret, in which feeling was so closely concerned, took place at a moment of brain fatigue, and memory could not register it.[24]

Margaret came [. . .] and was my guest. We had over ten days together of which I recollect nothing except a conversation about arrangements. She must, however, have approved of my visit or I should not have gone. [. . .]

It was nearly mid-April when we landed.

Staying with my Brother at Wimbledon and paying several other visits made time pass quickly. Mr. and Mrs. J. E. Ellis, whose daughter (now Lady Parmoor) was acting as Honorary Secretary to the Committee, at once offered their drawing-room for a gathering. They felt the subscribers would like to meet the Miss Bothas. Lord Courtney was in the Chair. The scene came back to me very vividly lately when reading the *Life* of Mr. Ellis. He describes the meeting in his diary. Helen Botha had been asked to speak, but, instead, she read a letter from her father. After thanking the subscribers for their support General Botha went on to say:

> "I have to thank Miss Hobhouse for starting this industry, and I feel sure when I look at all the difficulties she has had to contend with that I cannot sufficiently thank her for her noble work, and my earnest hope is that this industry will prove as profitable to South Africa as the old Huguenot industries did to England . . . In starting this industry in South Africa, Miss Hobhouse has done as much as anybody for the co-operation of Briton and Boer, and I feel sure that as the industry grows, so will the good feeling between the English and Dutch spread throughout the whole country."

[. . .] The Committee wished me to pay a visit to the Swiss people and thank them in person for their support. In this I heartily concurred. Unequal to details of travel in addition to the public work, the delightful plan was proposed of sending me under the wing of Miss Marian Ellis, a most accomplished courier.

Perhaps it was the Swiss love of freedom which evoked lively sympathy with the Boers and from which had sprung the ardent desire to support any movement for your country's good. I have told you of their great and untiring help. The gift of over a thousand spinning-wheels from as many homes is in itself unique. And that was but one item. Frau d'Orelli of Basel, Frau Syfrig, Frl. Anna Roth and Frl. S. Hafter of Frauenfeld, Madame A. de Salis of Grisons, Madame Wegmann-Schoch of Zürich, and Herr Ineichen of Lucerne were amongst those who organized this collection which was guided and centralized from Geneva by Madame Degli Asinelli. Everywhere I was received with warmth and was careful to explain that I had not come to beg for more but simply to bring them my own thanks and those of the Boer women.[25]

I still maintain friendship with many of those whom I then first met, and some of these generous people, like the Kochers of Bern and Herr Ineichen of Lucerne, have helped me more recently in feeding German children and others after the European war.

Switzerland looked lovely in her May garb, and everything, as well as everybody, seemed perfect in the kindness of their words and welcome. But I felt ill, spoke lamely and with effort, and seemed unable to be adequate to the occasion. I know now that the altitude was affecting me.

During this visit I was welcomed by some peasants or small farmers to their chalets and saw the products of their toil. They shewed me stuffs spun and woven by different members of their families during three generations. During summer, work was chiefly in the open, and for those months the bulky loom was taken to pieces and stored in the loft. Spinning could be done at any leisure time, and the yarn or thread thus accumulated till winter came. Then the loom re-appeared, and it was woven into woollen stuffs or house linen. It was rarely necessary to put out money for clothing or for house or bed linen. Here indeed, though just expiring under the increasing factory system, was my dream for the Boer people. Industry carrying with it the joy of creation gave occupation and interest to home life. From the sheep they tended on the mountain-side and the flax they sowed, cut and retted, every process was done by themselves, and great skill resulted, and pride in their handiwork.

South Africa was still blessed by an absence of factories and the crowding of the people into towns. Perhaps for generations to come her women could make all that was needed in their own homes and have a superfluity for sale at a moderate figure. It was with this aim that we worked. Already at Philippolis and elsewhere spinning was getting into the homes. Would the more complicated weaving follow? All depended upon the policy of those who guided the initial stages.

Physical relief followed on leaving Switzerland, and feeling stronger in London I was able to join my Brother in a short trip to Normandy. I had only a week to dispose of, for my berth was already booked by the *Saxon* which left before midsummer. We had a pleasant week visiting Caen, Bayeux and the coast villages. I was troubled to find myself quite unfit to share the long walks he loved. I did not know they were the last country walks I should ever even attempt.

At Bayeux I saw, of course, the famous Norman needlework, called tapestry. It appeared to me to be worked in coloured threads on a bare linen background, and historically most interesting. The skill of Normandy women with the needle and their power of design persists. This was manifest in a room hard by where the marvellous needle-point lace made in the vicinity was shewn. In this dépôt I saw the "point de Paris", as it is called, which excelled all modern laces I had seen.

373

Here the problem had been solved of giving variety and enlightenment to the cold, monotonous Renaissance designs. French grace and charm were introduced without loss of Venetian dignity and restraint. The workmanship too was perfect; but it was too costly to buy even a sample. It is a lace for royal personages and royal fortunes only.

I can't pass over this period without telling you about my St. Bernard.[26] I became possessed of this dog (or it might be truer to say possessed *by* him) in London. He was a beautiful creature and won all hearts. We English make close companions and friends of our dogs in a way not very usual, I found, in your country. I wanted a watch-dog for my cottage in Bellevue, but I little knew how delicate a pure-bred St. Bernard can be, nor how much time and attention his proper feeding and training would involve. Nor did I dream that Fate would take me to live in Pretoria where the heat would try him so severely. During the next twelve months he was my constant joy. His intelligence was remarkable, in some things almost human. He was quick to understand and respond to my various moods. He would carry my basket or parasol when shopping, and strangers often stopped in the street to ask what I would take for my dog. One man said: "I'll give you £1 000 for your dog."

But never would I have sold him.

As he grew he became so powerful that in any tussle he conquered by sheer strength. It followed that out walking he led me by a chain rather than the other way. One day in Johannesburg a passing man watched a struggle which ended in Caro's dragging me where I did not want to go. The man said: "If you don't master that dog, he will master you."

I replied that he did so already, but how could I prevent it? The man then kindly gave me a few simple rules on discipline needed for big dogs unless they are to become a nuisance to society, and it proved a complete success. He soon became a well-mannered, obedient dog. Sometimes in playing he would unknowingly throw me down, but that was from sheer exuberance of spirits. Later, when full-grown, he developed the embarrassing habit of welcoming me or anyone who came to the door by standing on his hind legs and throwing his arms round your neck. This was alarming for strangers and disastrous to clean summer muslins. Mr. Ewald Esselen told me how to cure this habit, and a couple of lessons sufficed. In the school he was adored, the girls loving to play at hide-and-seek with him round the looms – a sad disturbance of discipline which Mrs. Goetzsche had to forbid. Having taught him to enter water in the stream behind the school (which he was loath to do, suspecting it might be another bath which he disliked immensely) I took him to a deep pool on a neighbouring kopje to learn to swim and to fetch out a huge doll I threw into the water. This he accomplished with ease, bringing out the baby again and again and laying it at my feet, swimming with delight. I was confident that he could or would save a drowning child with ease.

Only dog-lovers can understand what I felt when the billiary fever took him. The vet warned me he must be nursed like a human being. He was. I spared no pains or strength. Night after night I sat up with him and every two hours gave beef-tea, eggs or brandy. The fifth night I brought a chair-bed into the room and, unable to keep up any longer, fell asleep. I must have slept a bit over the time for his beef-tea, for I awoke with a start, feeling something was wrong. Caro had raised his head and was looking at me with reproachful eyes. The effort was too great, and before I could reach him he fell back dead.

His death made a great difference; I missed his welcome, and having someone to speak to; it was the blank left by an intelligent and devoted companionship. I never cared to fill his place, so his collar, chain and the whistle he so faithfully responded to have been preserved unused. In after years I never saw a St. Bernard in the streets in London or Switzerland without stopping to speak to him. But I never saw one the equal of Caro in beauty or with an eye so intelligent. It is quite an experience to have entered so deeply into the dog-mind, and it is a curious fact that while before I had this experience the average dog had ignored, if it had not actually avoided me, yet afterwards he had singled me out for attention. Probably, like children, dogs instinctively feel if they are understood.

To resume. Those holiday weeks flew past. I had much to do and settle on behalf of our industries. I remember some of our things were exhibited (I believe it was that spring) in an Albert Hall handicraft's exhibition. The Princess Christiane was present and was graciously pleased to shew much interest and to receive and welcome my explanations.

A slight incident of those days remains in my mind because of a warning it brought me. An old friend who had been impressed by the cleverness of a woman who read character from the hand (not the palm but the back) insisted on taking me to her. We had some difficulty in finding her and sent in no name. She required merely the hands placed, backs upwards, on a cushion. Without even a glance at me she sat down and for a long half-hour gave an astonishingly accurate sketch of my past life, my character and doings. I remarked that she did not even look at my face. "Faces," she said, "mean nothing to me; I do not understand them."

I felt as if she had turned me inside-out and shewn me to myself. She ended with the warning: "You will have to take care of your heart; it is going to give you trouble."

I laughed, being even then one of those happy beings, such as I see around me now, who do not even realize they possess such an organ. I had never associated my feelings of illness with any special function of the body, deeming it merely over-work which would pass. Six weeks later her words came back to me, for returning to the Cape and hastening north to relieve Margaret at her post, that sudden elevation to 6,000 feet brought the trouble to the fore. I felt as I had done on the Swiss mountains.

375

During my absence Margaret had been active. Amongst other things she had arranged to open the school weekly to visitors after school-hours. People were shewing interest, and it was right to give the public opportunity to see what was shortly to be supported by public money. It meant extra work for the staff, and we often took it in turns.

From Philippolis she wrote me the sad news that your father, dear Mrs. Steyn, was resigning his charge after some forty-three years of incumbency. He was so much part of Philippolis one could not visualize the village without him. He had baptized and married a whole generation. He was as their honoured father. As to ourselves he had made us feel the parsonage a home to which we might turn, assured of sympathy and advice. His enthusiasm and patience alone had ensured such success as we attained. None, however, can know better than yourself his devotion as a minister and the high honour in which he was held.

On my return from England in early July I found the new Ministry firm in the saddle and General Smuts (as Colonial Secretary) prepared to discuss industrial education in detail. Mr. Adamson,[27] Head of the Education Department, was also in consultation about it. It was considered advisable the school should move to Pretoria to be under the Administrative Eye. In spite of obvious advantages I was somewhat fearful on climatic grounds, the heat being so much greater. But I was adamant on the point that such a move must depend upon Mrs. Goetzsche's consent. She was everything to the still infant industry. Better small premises with her than superior ones without her. Her knowledge and power of imparting it were unrivalled. Anxiety on this point was, however, set at rest, for notwithstanding inconvenience Mrs. Goetzsche finally decided to accept the Government's offer to teach in Pretoria, arranging to return to her husband in Johannesburg for week-ends.

My own removal followed suit. Though sorry to leave my cottage there was compensation in the lower altitude of Pretoria, which gave physical relief. I was conscious I was near the end of my tether physically, and in any case the three years planned for were fast running out. I intended to hold on as long as health and means permitted. I knew the work was approaching a critical stage when most careful organization would be needed, and fresh controllers could not in the nature of things have the judgement born of experience. I felt in honour bound to the Government also to continue to guide and help the work as long as I was able.

By August I was free to report progress to the London Committee. The estimates had been before the House and the vote for industrial schools, of which there were also some under missionary guidance in the North, was passed without question. It was a moment of great relief for me and for Margaret. We were very grateful to the Transvaal Government for their confidence in our undertaking and gratified that in spite of many imperfections it had received this token of appreciation.

Yet beneath this contentment a little worm of doubt gnawed at my heart. The release from financial responsibility might, probably would carry with it loss of power to initiate, guide or restrain. I believed that the work, after many experimental vicissitudes, was finding at last a sure footing and was on the right road to a realization of its aims. But the moment was critical. It was a child that must still be led by the hand of an experienced nurse. To become a firmly planted national industry it needed still the fostering care of one who had studied the matter for years and was conversant with every detail of the interdependent processes. There was fear lest, taken under the control of strangers who, however interested and well-meaning, did not and could not know anything about it, its guidance should be unwise and the effort be marred or ruined.

I unburdened these fears to General Smuts who quite grasped and even, I think, shared my anxiety. He wished the work to develop on the lines laid down. He told me he must appoint a board to whose care the public funds would be assigned, and of this I felt very glad. He said that he wished me to be in a position of authority on that board when formed and suggested I should take the position of "Adviser" to that body of persons. Taking this word "Adviser" at its face value, my natural fears were set at rest, and I accepted the office with a light heart.[o]

At the first meeting of the board when formed, premises were decided upon and as Mrs. Goetzsche had promised to continue as Principal we arranged to move the school bag and baggage by 1 October when our lease expired. Margaret was to remain Organizing Secretary as long as she stayed in the country, but her six months' visit was fast nearing its end. I had seen disappointingly little of her – for after my return from Europe she was much occupied in visiting Free State schools and only joined me in Pretoria in October.[28] I think it was that very month that you and the President came north and stayed a few days in Pretoria. I understood one of his objects was to discuss with the Transvaal leaders the fuller organization of the fund for the Memorial to the women and children.[29]

We were soon in full swing at the new Weverij in President Street. It had been good practice for the girls to learn to take down and put up their looms. The heat became intensely trying. I note that writing home on 27 October I mentioned the thermometer was 94° in the shade.

As all was going well, I was able to escape from this heat to Philippolis to meet Milroy on his return from Europe and discuss the fresh arrangements which were to follow Responsible Government so soon to take Office in the Orange River Colony also.[p]

I paid, also, my long-deferred visit to Olive Schreiner at De Aar where she and her husband were then living. This visit stands out as one of my chief pleasures of those years.

The Schreiners had built a wee house on the open veld about a mile from the ugly junction. It consisted at that time of one room. In a later year I believe a couple of rooms were added to it. It was very charming and there was a box at the side for Olive's pet *meercats*. The air was pure (apart from dust-storms) and the plain was ringed with distant kopjes that took gorgeous colours at sunset. I made a

377

pen and ink sketch of the tiny place. Olive and Mr. Cronwright-Schreiner took their meals at the inn in the dusty village where also I had a room. He was, of course, occupied all day professionally, and Olive and I spent the day together roaming the veld, playing with her *meercats* or sitting at the foot of some kopje. Her walking powers exceeded mine. The week passed like a flash. Olive did all the talking and I asked nothing better. Her large mind and fertile imagination seemed inexhaustible. She refreshed one like bathing in a sea.

On her side I gained the impression that she craved a receptive ear just to enjoy the relief of pouring out pent-up thoughts. She was alone all day and not well enough to find her natural vent in writing. Often in after years of solitary life I experienced a similar craving for the relief of speech. It is common to most spinster women who, debarred from the contacts arising from work or pleasure owing to ill health and small means, pass their days and weeks in a silence which becomes oppressive. I would, however, be the last to disparage solitude. I was fond of it from a child, and at last, though not without painful initiation, have accepted it as the most abiding factor of my life. I could not, now, exist without long spells of it. There is, too, much truth in the French saying: "*Tout notre mal vient de ne pouvoir pas être seul.*" Still, everything in reason, and there are periods in life and certain conditions of health that demand sympathetic companionship.

There was Olive Schreiner, hidden from the world, like a diamond in the desert, cut off from her intellectual peers, her very gifts oppressing her by their fulness. Olive was a child of the veld, and few understood her who had not seen her in that peculiar setting. To me she herself has always seemed greater than anything she wrote.

Enlivened by this precious contact with a rare mind I returned to the Free State.[q] Your elections and their outcome occupied all minds. When all was over to your satisfaction you invited me to spend Christmas with you, and I saw you trying to fit our winter festival customs to your midsummer heat!

The President talked much with me of his treasured scheme of a worthy Memorial to the women and children who perished in the camps. I felt it a right thing not merely as a matter of your history, of a tribute to their fortitude, but as an undying remembrance to the horror of *War*, and its crushing weight upon those innocent of it. The President had already formed a committee and was considering the selection of a competent sculptor. I remember Mr. Abraham Fischer saying to me that when the work was completed I must come and unveil the monument.

a) *To Leonard Hobhouse, 9 July 1905*: ... I went to Pretoria whither I had been invited to attend the Het Volk Congress ... Of course you know the greatest subject under discussion was the Constitution, and this occupied a whole day.[30] Every man wanted to speak and all *can* speak in an astonishing way. In a few moments 50 names were handed to Botha of men desirous to speak. They were a grand set of men – serious and thoughtful, with a deep sense of responsibility and entire absence of self-consciousness. One after another, during that whole day, these men got up and solemnly denounced the Constitution and said their districts had instructed them to reject it. Only two were for a qualified acceptance. The leaders who in previous consultations had determined to guide the congress into *acceptance with a strong protest* were, I think, carried away by the strong feeling of the delegates, and Botha burst out in a strong speech which wholly surprised those with whom he had parleyed. Then came Beyers,[31] a man whom we all respect and like but who loses all balance when he gets on his legs, and made a wild speech; and finally De la Rey said the more he thought about it the less he felt any conviction of what was his duty to do. These speeches so terrified Smuts that he put on a patch in the shape of an extra pacific speech, while Advocate De Villiers who was to have made *the* speech which could have been the wisest and most thoughtful by far, remained altogether silent, feeling that his words could then only be a criticism of Botha and the others. Thus in this terrible muddle he could only urge postponement of the decision to a later congress and meanwhile the appointment of a committee to draw up a resolution to send to the King stating the objections all felt.

He and others drafted this and next day it was carried unanimously. It has many points, but I suppose you have read them all. He, Mr. De Villiers, was dreadfully cut up about the way it all fell out and quite failed to understand Botha's sudden change. The head committee consult him about everything though he is not actually on it and undoubtedly he is the man with ballast, uncommon brains and force of character. Like Smuts he has had a European education and is a more thoughtful and much stronger man. He fears the *Takhaar*[32] element within Het Volk which can play upon Wolmarans,[33] and it will be all that he and Smuts and Esselen can do to keep that Party in a good temper but subordinate.

You have no idea how pathetic it was to sit there and listen to these men with their unconquered spirit struggling against the humbling conditions imposed upon them, as unconquered people. Now with this resolution the King will have a chance of making himself beloved in South Africa.

One reason for desiring to postpone the decision to accept the Constitution was that it will depend greatly upon how registration is carried out and also the carving out of the electoral districts. On these points they expect nothing but gerrymandering. The country districts are so immense and so thinly populated, and transport so difficult and costly – the people so poor – it would take vast sums which they have not got to see to the registration. The Jingoes have enormous wealth and are hard at it in the easily managed towns.

They have been made extra suspicious on account of an incident connected with the military vote. Nothing was known about it till one day a man (a Tommy I think) brought them a set of private instructions which had been issued, saying every soldier was to have a vote. This would have meant 15 000 in the Transvaal. Most indignant, off they went to Lawley[34] and Selborne with this document and I think roused some shame in them, and the promise was exacted that fresh instruc-

379

tions should be issued (I was *not* told this was a secret, but perhaps it ought not to be made public property).

I was the only woman the first day present at the congress; the Boers were *very* proud to have me there and very pleased that I could follow Dutch and took trouble to do so. The second day a few ladies came in for a short time (among them Miss Stead who is staying with the Bothas). The third day I was alone again, but Boers never let you feel alone or in the way. I saw such lots of men whom I knew or whose wives I had known and who came to hold my hand and thank me.

Lord Selborne invited all the congress to a garden party at Sir A. Lawley's and they went *en bloc*, all in their ordinary clothes and broad felt hats. Not even Botha or the other leaders would dress, determining to be all alike. My path lay the same way, so I walked with my 200 Boers so far as the gate of Government House and felt rather like a shepherdess with a flock of sheep and there delivered them to the wolves inside. Lord Selborne and Lady Mabel (whom they call Miss Selborne) made a fair impression of friendliness, but certain smart ladies walked about with cameras and took snapshots of them, which they thought most ill-bred.

I left Friday night and came straight down to the Steyns on my way to Philippolis [. . .]. Mr. Steyn thinks English Liberals ought to know that there are both diamonds and gold in Basutoland and that the Basutos are aware of this (as was also Rhodes who, had he lived, would long since have had a finger in that pie); that a railway is being made to Maseru much against the will of the Basutos who have taken up the surveyors' pegs, etc; the Basutos have for some time been flocking back to Basutoland. They have a great number of rifles which they never gave up after the war.

By the way, the Chinese troubles wax hotter on the Rand. You have no idea of the daily troubles and how the terror of the white miners grows and grows. They sent a deputation to Selborne to ask him for protection and he talked to them like a Sunday-school teacher and told them they must be white inside. They were very angry and re-iterated the absolute need of protection. Now whole columns of the S.A.C. have been at a half-hour's notice placed along the Rand, and people wonder who is to pay. Another trouble followed hard upon the deputation's demands so perhaps this is Selborne's more practical answer. The Kaffirs on the farms around the Rand dread them (the Chinese) for they have a rooted belief that the Chinese will kill and eat their babies, and flee at their approach and huddle together at the nearest farm while the Chinese enter the kraals and help themselves to the food left about. Several men at the congress have described this sort of thing.

b) *To Lady Charlotte.* [No address; undated]: We are getting more and more puzzled how to get enough spinning-wheels. Everything depends upon a good and regular supply of yarn. We must supply our own yarn and we cannot without wheels. I tried having one copied in Johannesburg with this success: it is a beauty but the charge made is prohibitive.

"I thought I would stagger you," said the man as he handed me the bill, and I *was* staggered. I had never tried to get an estimate from him, but he said he had never made one before and assured me he would be very moderate and would not overcharge. So that door is closed and I am now trying a Boer at Philippolis who says with a turning lathe he would make them. I have agreed to supply the lathe and the wood, getting both from the coast, if he will pay back in wheels, which he will gladly do.

c) *To Lady Charlotte*. [No address], *16 September 1905*: The great excitement of the week has been the news of the great and welcome gift of spinning-wheels from Switzerland. I hear hundreds of these are upon the way. I remember writing that I wanted "a ship-load of wheels" and launched that wish in faith that some result would issue, but it seems almost incredible that the wish is fulfilled! We cannot be grateful enough to the Swiss ladies whose interest in the work has led them to organize this splendid "trek" of wheels from the old world to the new.

To Margaret Clark. [No address], *18 January 1906*: I am in woe over the Swiss wheels. The cases block the street. The stoep is a mass of mangled wheels and winders. The old school is a forest of the same, and yesterday, as the trolley came with load after load of broken, bulging cases, limbs of spinning-wheels and etceteras strewed the way. Oh! It is pitiful! The packing is execrable. So far I have not found one intact . . . I fear but a few can emerge from such a haystack of ruined and broken bits.

d) *To Lady Charlotte*. [No address; undated]: Margaret Clark writes from Philippolis cheering accounts of the progress and general tone of the school, as well as the improvement of the work under Miss Picard who is an excellent teacher. My hope is that she will be too interested, when her time expires, to leave us.

e) *To Lady Charlotte*. [No address; undated]: This is my first letter from our new house. It is rather eerie; rats scuttle overhead at night and strange people make a thoroughfare of the garden. There are any amount of Chinese about and Kaffirs in blankets, and these as well as the white loafers who infest the outskirts of Johannesburg make it undesirable to walk alone in the veld, especially at dusk.

Langlaagte is quite a wee place, mostly orphanage now. Indeed I find myself suddenly the "aunt" of 250 orphan nephews and nieces who surround me in batches when I go out, all shouting "Auntie, Auntie Hobhouse!"

I wish they would keep to the Dutch form *tante*, prettier to our ears, especially as the custom of calling old people "aunt" belongs peculiarly to this country.

Our house is bitterly cold, for a verandah excludes the sun without which one cannot live in this country, and fireplaces there are none.

f) The house is surrounded by stables, and flies are as bad as the plague of Egypt.

They swarm in myriads over the food and table and walls, and although we sweep them up in their thousands many times a day, they do not diminish but increase.

g) *August 1905*: Our "cowshed" school is a sore trial. There are holes and cracks everywhere; the dust and wind come pouring in, and all the forenoon we have to work in our fur coats. It is *very* low and ill-ventilated, in the afternoon it is so smelly we can hardly stand it. They whitewashed it with carbide left over from making acetylene gas, and this has an odious smell. I have sent for lime and intend to rewash it myself. Worse is in store, for as soon as the rains set in the whole school must be flooded, as it appears to be a drain and watershed for the entire road above . . .

Our cowshed is greatly against us . . . We had a shower of rain, the first for about six months. It ran all through the school in a stream and discharged itself under the door. The sloping corrugated iron roof is full of holes and does not attempt to join; the wind and dust are insufferable. The temperature in it alternates from extreme cold to exhausting heat, and the floor is so uphill and uneven that our looms will not stand. So, in despair, I spoke to Mr. Kriel; he told me he had a large lined and floored school, but it was at Klerksdorp and he had no money to bring it here. I offered at once to pay the railage if it could be set up in our garden, and at this moment his carpenters are taking it to pieces for conveyance here; I live in hopes of seeing the work of putting up begun next week. I do not think this will cost much over £100, and to build would be three or four times as much. It is large and I shall be able at once to increase my pupils and my rug-looms and take in girls from the district who have hitherto applied in vain.

h) *To Lady Charlotte*. [No address], *16 September 1905*: I think I have struck "oil" here, in the discovery of a Danish lady whose heart is set on helping to establish these industries in South Africa. She is really a Swede but taught spinning and weaving six years in Denmark. She married a Danish architect . . . no children . . . They came out to South Africa thinking that there would be much building after the war . . . He is now working for Eckstein. I found her in a wee room, her looms quite filling the little front room. She wore clothes entirely woven by herself and shewed me her work. She speaks English easily and is herself a simple, direct, sweet little woman. Her work is so first-class and even and thorough that I feel ashamed that she should see our rough early attempts, but after all, her people have been at it for centuries.

i) *To Leonard Hobhouse. Langlaagte, 18 February 1906*: . . . the expenses have run up and I need £500 at least.

It seems a very purgatorial place to me, but folk say it is a *very* nice little house and will sell well. At any rate I am more likely to be able to hold out another year if

I am removed from active contact with either school and I can give undivided mind to the supervision and organization of the work.

I do not *want* to live a day longer[35] but if I *have* to, I *must* have a house – and if it came out rather more than the experts anticipated I cannot help it and have no choice but to pay.

To Leonard Hobhouse. Langlaagte, 15 April 1906: . . . I cannot get the stand railed in under £20, and the builder chose to alter the plan without leave and ran me into an extra basement room in consequence, which cost about £30 . . .

All houses about this size and character are valued at about £2 000 here, but as I built at a cheap time mine will be about £1 500 I believe (inclusive of stand) . . . As the view can't be built out it has the chance of always selling well.

j) To Margaret Clark [then in England]. *Langlaagte, 5 January 1905*: Marion Rowntree and I wrote to Mr. Kriel a sort of epitome of five months' experience, and I said at the close of the week I should send him a list of the girls I felt I could continue to teach and those I felt I must dismiss. For reply, instead of wanting to hear the names, he forbade all the girls to come. And has not let them since. High words for two hours.

To Margaret Clark. Langlaagte, 25 May 1906: We all consider the institution a very bad one and think, in common with all sensible Afrikaners, that Mr. Kriel is doing very badly by these children, giving them no technical training whatever. We alone offered this to some two dozen girls, and it was not appreciated. The spirit of the Authorities is adverse and the girls feel pulled in two ways. It is distressing that these penniless girls, some of whom are now doing good work and are really interested, should be taken away and our work for them probably wasted. I've spent six months and more in a vain struggle with Mr. Kriel. We have girls with us from other orphanages, well-run ones, from Winburg, Heidelberg and Middelburg, and the difference in the children is most marked. What a continual regret that 300 children are being brought up so badly at Langlaagte. Consequently we have no further reason for remaining at Langlaagte, a very dirty and depressing village, except that I have the lease of the school building.

k) To Leonard Hobhouse. Langlaagte, 18 February 1906: But is a Commission coming out here and are you going to be on it?

l) To Leonard Hobhouse. President Steyn's farm, 8 February 1906: . . . President Steyn is of course in deepest anxiety to know what the Libs will do. But the prominence of the Imps causes great fear in all Boer minds, and distrust that the Libs will act as they have talked. They have nothing to bring against Selborne personally, but they feel it would be better to wipe the slate clean – and have someone who was not (like Lord Selborne) in the Colonial Office at the time of the Raid. And if only you could give up sending peers and peeresses. Mr. Steyn would like a Labour man very much – a John Burns – or some very simple, plain untitled gentleman. They feel, amongst other advantages, this would break up the toadyism which is increasing here.

And remember always the Transvaal issue is "Chamber of Mines versus the rest of the Colony" – not Boer versus Briton.

[*Postscript.*] Mr. Steyn thinks it would be a very good thing to amalgamate the Transvaal and O.R.C. and have one Governor and one House of Assembly. It would lessen expenses and equalize, or tend to, town and country voters.

To an unidentified correspondent. Onze Rust, 9 February 1906: I write from the President's stoep[36] where I am sitting for a couple of days with its big patient master. It is pathetic to see how he watches for the issue of the meeting of Parliament and yearns to know how the Liberals will act. He feels it would be so much wiser and better to take away Selborne and begin fresh with someone else, best of all, he says, a good Labour man.

To Leonard Hobhouse. Mara, Becker Street, Bellevue, Jo'burg, Whitsunday 1906: I hesitated about writing to C.-B. as you urge;[37] and so sent for Mr. De Villiers to give me his advice. He favoured it and gave me pointers and is to read it when written. I have just written it in the intervals of stewing my dinner, for Jeremiah was eating out his black heart with longing to go a-visiting this Whitsunday, so I hope the letter will not savour of the kitchen. I shall not send it unless Mr. De Villiers approves. It is 7 sheets and feminine.

I had a letter this mail from Lord Ripon and in reply have given him a dose of our views.

Nothing will be done till Selborne and all that crew depart. It's an open secret that he has backed up the Progressives in the obstructions they have offered to Sir West Ridgeway's efforts to make a compromise fit. And Sir West made no secret of his scorn for them. Their game was to obstruct as to make a settlement impossible with the hope of delay to see if the Education Bill[38] would not help them by forcing an appeal to the country and so a possible return of Toryism.

Besides, Selborne talks such rubbish. [. . .]

Why on earth don't you publish Sir William Butler's letters? We wait in vain for his voice, the first that understands, from here.

[*Postscript.*] Repatriation of the Chinese must be *compulsory*, not voluntary, and *gradual*. Say 1 000 every month and at the mines' expense. From the point of view of good of the country, not the happiness of Chinaman. Sir P. Fitzpatrick is just off to England to make more mischief there.

To an unidentified correspondent. Onze Rust, 7 July 1906: I met De Wet in the train coming here. He was proudly wearing Mimi Burger's stockings.[39] He would rather have Milner than Selborne – too much Bible and too much talk altogether. In his broken English he said: "If you take my land or any ting from me, you must not come with the Bible under your arm."

384

m) *To Lady Charlotte. Pretoria, 6 December 1906*: Het Volk was sitting and at 11.30 adjourned purposely to come and see our work as an object lesson. They came headed by Generals Botha and De la Rey, Mr. Schalk Botha and all the well-known names. I explained everything to them and their astonishment was delightful.

An old Boer bought a pair of baby socks, knitted from our angora, for 1s 8d. He said he had neither children nor grandchildren but he wanted a "remembrance" and evidently could afford nothing else.

n) *To Margaret Clark.* [No address], *22 December* [1906]: How to squeeze out his brains before he leaves in six months, and who best to squeeze them into!

To Margaret Clark. [No address], *January 1907*: Milroy is charming in everything connected with his work, but outside that I find him second rate and a bore. Perfectly nice, you know, but a real old maid and a bore. Then he goes to work and becomes a man, alert, interesting and delightful.

o) *To Margaret Clark.* [No address], *15 August*: I have had to decide upon my resignation of my post as Adviser to the board. That body has never shewn the least inclination either to seek my advice nor to take it when offered and at the meetings my remarks were waved aside as though a fly buzzed. The only link of usefulness was with Mrs. Hofmeyr and she left some months ago.

It has become more and more impossible for me to work at the school, having the knowledge from intimate contact with the work and yet no authority.

p) *To Leonard Hobhouse.* [As from] *305 Wessels Street, Arcadia, Pretoria, 23 December 1907*: I am in the Free State for a fortnight to see the New Ministry – Hertzog called on me early and we had a preliminary canter over the industries and agreed I should draft a scheme with Mr. Gunn,[40] Director of Education, and he would send him to me. This he did and next day I went to Gunn's Department in Government Buildings and we worked for 2 hours in sweltering heat. Then we had in Mr. Meiring, Chairman of the Industrial Board, and catechized him as to what he had done with the £5 500 given him annually for industries. He said all but £50 for a secretary was given in bonusses to a jam factory!!!, and this was promised to them for three years longer!

It was a strange feeling to me, walking into Government Buildings after a lapse of 6½ years, and the terror of Martial Law was upon me, and the awful way I was bullied there long ago. Now all was bowing and scraping.

Mr. Fischer, looking radiant, came to see me off at the train and we made plans for future meetings this week.

They are very keen about the work and ten towns in the Free State have begun or wish to begin, and on this basis we are estimating.

They invited me to the Distinguished Strangers' Gallery for the opening of Parliament, but I was not down in time.

385

To Lady Charlotte. [No address], *21 October 1908*: [Reprinted in the final report of the Boer home industries, December 1908]:. . . The schools I have handed over to the Orange Free State Colony are now ten in all, as follows:

Weaving and spinning: Bloemfontein (Lappiesdorp), Philippolis, Winburg (three schools), Ficksburg, Bethlehem, Smithfield.

Spinning only: Boshof, Brandfort, Heilbron, Bultfontein.

[. . .]

Turning to the Transvaal, the schools there are as follows:

Weaving schools: Pretoria, Ermelo, Schweizer Renecke, Belfast, Lichtenburg.

Spinning centres: Vrededorp, Roseville, Irene, Heidelberg, Roodepoort (E. Transvaal), Bloemhof farms, Standerton farms, Lydenburg and Rustenburg (just beginning) Honingsnestkranz.

In addition, the work is spreading into many farms and groups of houses. [. . .] It is this purely country side of the work which I now rely on chiefly for the future. Whatever becomes of the central school, I am confident the principles of weaving have taken root in the land and will flourish there, no matter how many mistakes may be made.

The requests that reach me from the Cape Colony, Rhodesia and even Central Africa for weaving schools are very numerous, but I have to turn a deaf ear.

I trust the Committee and subscribers will be satisfied with the expenditure of their money and its results during this five-years' work. Three and a half of these I have spent *in* South Africa, and, hard as the work has been, it often seems wonderful to myself the progress that has been made, both in the quality of the work and the extent that it covers. [. . .]

Vrouwen-Dag

1913

Letters

97. TO J. C. SMUTS

c/o Sebasti e Reali
20 Piazza di Spagna, Roma
6 March 1913

. . . You will think I am really mercilessly bombarding a busy man with letters, writing again so soon – but the fact is I want to consult you about the Unveiling of the Bloemfontein Monument,[1] which is to take place on 16 December next. Though when I say "consult" I use that word in the rather feminine way – merely meaning that I want to know your various points of view about it, not binding myself to follow your advice, but certainly using it to help me make up my own mind.

For I have received an invitation from President Steyn to come and unveil the Monument and must ere long send a reply. In *many* ways of course I should like to do this – but on *this* side naturally the difficulties facing me are considerable, the chief being my strength. At present I cannot possibly judge of that and in any case should need my doctor's opinion.

On your side I want to know if this really *is* a National Monument provided by a *National* movement or if it has settled down to be only a Free State and local affair. *Who* are on the committee, and what on the whole is the general attitude of the country towards it and of the Government in particular? Will it be treated as a National dedication and the Prime Minister, etc. be officially present?

In fact, I want to know these points and all you think about it, for I seem to remember when I left Pretoria you and Botha were not very much inclined towards it. Personally I *cannot* think it either *should* or *could* arouse racial animosity; should it do so in anyone, that person must be of a type of mind so mean as to be best disregarded. Certainly – if I am ever to visit South Africa again it would be only for this reason that I could pull myself together for such an effort – and not *very* probable even for this.

Forgive awkward grammar and answer me soon.

Yours ever afftly, Emily Hobhouse

98. TO J. C. SMUTS

c/o Sebasti e Reali
20 Piazza di Spagna, Roma
12 May 1913

Dear Oom Janie
Your letter with its warm welcome came last mail, and many, many thanks for it. But you have gone ahead of me in mind – I have not got so far as *thinking* I will come

389

Africa, only to collecting other people's views on the subject and reckon-
e many difficulties (of health and others) which stand involved. When all
ts are before me and I have had some complete repose this summer, if I can
hen and then only shall I begin seriously to consider if it lies within the
limits of possibility. In my present condition it would *not* be possible, but I count
much on the effect of a quiet summer. So please don't *expect* me and in any case I
fear the Transvaal with that altitude would be impossible – and the welcome to
Doornkloof must remain a *dream*.

Besides, it seems to me now very unlikely that the Monument can be ready in
December. Van Wouw[1] told me the central group was to leave Rome before the
end of April, but it is still being cast at the foundry and hardly likely to get off before
June. With regard to the bas-reliefs, one is only *just* begun in the clay, and it seems
to me impossible it can be finished. Between you and me strictly – it required real
artistic genius for this job, and the poor man is only an inferior though painstaking
artist and quite devoid of genius. I wish they had not done it in such a hurry and
with so little money . . .

99. TO MRS. CHARLES MURRAY[1]

c/o Sebasti e Reali
Piazza di Spagna, Roma
9 June 1913

Dearest Mrs. Murray
Your letter was a great help and as usual a great inspiration to me. By believing in
people, as you do, you call out the best that is in them in response.

Olive has also written, though she offers no advice, she wished to prepare me for
the general atmosphere which she deems would pain me to plunge into unawares. I
fancy that her state of health plus the lonely life she leads to some extent biases her
outlook on public affairs; on the other hand, my experiences personal and otherwise, before I left Pretoria $4\frac{1}{2}$ years ago, make me aware that much of what she
describes is true. Probably, however, it is mostly in the big towns where people are
living a smart, restless, rushing, unthinking life that the atmosphere she deplores
chiefly exists among those who rapidly forgot the past in the excitement of the
present. I'm thinking of a *whole* nation. We must beware of thinking only of those
who after all are more than balanced by the real stern stuff of the country, living in
many a quiet corner.

Anyhow, I do not think that a cold, callous, forgetful and even adverse attitude
to those who stood by them in trouble either will or ought to influence my present
decision. Thinking over my action in the past, I know that I was impelled by three
leading motives so strong and deep that I think I could more rightfully call them
"emotions", and these were:

1. A sense of justice towards the innocent victims of a great injustice.

390

2. An overwhelming pity for suffering childhood which could not understand but must suffer.

3. A determination to uphold those higher standards of human feeling and action which England holds in sane and sober moments.

All other considerations, and they were many, were secondary to the above.

Certainly I never paused a moment to consider what would be *said* or *thought* of the course I took.

The thing itself filled me too full to leave room for any such ideas, indeed I little thought that the, to me, perfectly simple act of going to help the homeless and starving people would ever bring me into publicity. Hence, as I have never looked for nor wished for anything of the sort from the Dutch, I do not think this change she indicated need or should affect me *now*.

But naturally, to all us humans gratitude is very pleasant and from the Free State people I have always received much of that. Even so recently as two years ago in the worst moment of my illness, the Free State women sent me that most beautiful and touching address which is perhaps my greatest treasure. And it seems to me the invitation to unveil their monument is in itself a token (official if not general) that they deem gratitude and appreciation are due to me. And due to me not as an individual, but as a type standing for *all* who felt with me, and worked thro' me. Don't you agree?

I feel it so and I feel it a Sacred Duty with a big D to respond to their feelings by accepting, if it be in my power to do so. It seems to me it would be a Seal upon the Past. Ingratitude and forgetfulness are very common failings and South Africans are but human – but perhaps Olive in her passionate idealism demands an impossible standard from her people. I have lived in so many lands and amongst so many races and comparing one with the other I often marvel at the fineness of the South African character. So large an average emerges in proportion to the very small white population. Out of our 40 odd millions in England, or 24 millions in Italy, the 70 millions in the USA, does anything like the same proportion of really noble spirits arise as from your tiny 1¼ million? I may be wrong, but I think not.

Here in Rome it oppresses me, the low average spirit. It is like being shut into some dirty room where the windows are never opened to sun and air, and at last I am wrenching myself from it to save my soul alive, and I am going out into the country to live in a lovely but lonely spot, where at least one has Nature and one's own highest thoughts for companionship . . . I clearly see at last, I have no doubt but that it is my highest duty to accept the official invitation – if it can be done without absolute madness.

I have asked for a month in which to decide. During which month I can test my strength (and collect more) in this quiet country place in the hills near Rome.

I know, of course, that I can only do it taking *every bodily help* that can be obtained and keeping strictly to my doctor's rule of life – and among these is the necessity of travelling with my little maid, which I fear may make me an unwelcome guest in many houses, but on the other hand she could help not only me but in general ways; or perhaps I could get a room for her.

I am now able to *consider* the scheme because during the past month I have made extraordinary progress. I feel Vitality the first time in four years, instead of feeling dying all the time – a feeling that has never left me. I can do one flight of stairs once a day or at most twice. I can walk a few hundred yards on the level and even breast a slight incline, always with my stool on my arm. I can talk for a good half hour. I can listen (much more useful) for hours together. I can sit up to meals that are not too long and I can walk about a room in quite my natural manner – in fact there is no end to my accomplishments and I am an astonishment to myself and all who see me.

What I cannot stand is Vibration, and I can only bear it lying down or sitting well thrown back.

Now you have the outline of me. I eat, and must eat only very little; and I go to bed like Cinderella when the clock strikes nine. I only hope *you* are as wise as I have learnt to be.

I plan to ship on 9 October, stay a month with Cape friends and a week or so with the Steyns and escape from South Africa before the heat is too great.

Of course I want to see everybody and I hope to be far better than I am now, by that time.

There is always a thing that is delight to my mind to dwell upon and I should like to experience it again, and that is the welcome at Cape Town after that ghastly voyage, people coming with smiles and flowers to greet one. It is like a Resurrection then. I try thus to rub out the recollection of that one awful arrival at your docks.

But my foolish pen runs on. Don't trouble to wade through what I have written. Only recollect that I should, if I may, like to stay with you once more and particularly to consult you and Mrs. Brown[2] and Olive and Mrs. Sauer and others before I go north. And I want once more to see the flowers of South Africa and to give a nice greeting and say a long farewell to all my friends.

Last time I came back – via the East Coast – an Arab soothsayer at Port Said begged to tell my fortune. He said I should go back to South Africa once again. And last week a friend here given to occult studies outlined my future and told me I was soon to take a journey. I asked what the journey was about and was told it would be connected with "affections and affairs" and I thought it sounded like South Africa.

. . . But I must stop, for if I write like this, you will think I am really coming before the decision is made. Indeed I have *not* decided but I feel . . . a feeling.

[Letter not signed]

392

100. TO J. C. SMUTS

c/o Barclay & Co. Ltd
137 Brompton Road
South Kensington, London
25 June 1913

... But I am filling my sheet with things I did not mean to say and leaving out what I sat down to write, which is this: that I have yielded to pressure and have at last accepted the Bloemfontein Committee's Official invitation to unveil their Monument. Three months ago I should not have dared, but the spring weather, plus what the doctor said, that my big illness this winter would, if I survived it, probably clear away certain poisons from the systems and leave me better – have together brought about this marvel and I can thankfully say I have now more vitality than I have known for 4 long years. However, even this improvement could not make me decide to go, because I cannot afford the journey, doubled as it must be by taking a maid – then came the Official letter with the generous offer of defraying my expenses, which alone enables me to accept their invitation and meet their wishes. It seemed churlish not to do so. So I am preparing to start and next week I leave for London where the above address will find me. My plan is to reach the Cape in the spring and see something of my friends there before going to Bloemfontein for 16 December. I *dare* not stay many days at the high altitude so I hope you and yours will be at Muizenburg or thereabouts in order that we may meet without the risk from the Transvaal altitudes . . .

But it would disappoint me much if on arrival at Bloemfontein I found this function *not* National in character. I do hope you and Botha and Sauer, as well as Hertzog, Fischer and Co.[1] and all will be there, officially, to give it that character – if not, I shall regret my decision and wish I had stayed away . . .

P.S. "Birds in their little nests agree," and to give this function its really solemn and representative character *all* must sink their differences, personal or political, that day, and meet to do honour to the dead heroines.

You must all be there as men if not as Ministers; there can be no quarrels round the grave.

101. TO J. C. SMUTS

London
20 August 1913

Dear Oom Janie

Things are very criss-cross in this life – this worst of all possible worlds – and now my carefully made plans have suffered change at the eleventh hour and I have to postpone my voyage a fortnight, taking the *Garth Castle* instead of the *Galway* and not leaving Southampton till 13 September, and I think not reaching the Cape till one of the early days of October. However, by that ship I shall have the advantage of the companionship of the Moltenos, and so some good comes out if this evil; still, a whole 2 weeks of my short visit to the Cape is thus cut off. Such is Life . . .

Will you please tell Mrs. Smuts of this change in my plans – and oh! do send her and the children down to the sea early this year before Christmas – it would be *too* aggravating not to see her at all . . .

I am very sorry to read of all the political unrest in South Africa, but even unrest is better than stagnation. I only beg of you all to kiss and be friends for my visit to Bloemfontein and bury the hatchet beneath the *Vrouwen*-Monument!

Yours ever, Emily Hobhouse

102. TO MRS. STEYN

Bergvliet

12 October 1912 [1913]

[. . .] How I wish I could put a feather-bed into an ox-waggon and in that old historic way start to-morrow on that long climb. You know the doctor forbids me to rush up to your heights in a day. Or I wish I had a travelling van to stay a few days here and there at the different levels. How much less fatiguing than getting in and out of the train at so many points. I shall probably have to leave here the third week in November or earlier. I must shorten as much as possible my stay at a high altitude. [. . .]

103. TO MRS. STEYN

Bergvliet

29 October 1913

Dearest Mrs. Steyn

I am horrified to think you should have imagined from my joke about the ox-waggon attached to the train that I was "asking for a saloon". Indeed, no. I was thinking of the joy of travelling stretched out on a mattress as in olden days, but brought up to date by being quicker and obviating the necessity of finding hotels upon the way. I assure you nothing would have induced me to *ask* any favour of *any Public Authority*, and *certainly* not from this Government from whom I have never received the slightest recognition or even civility. I feel dreadfully hot and unhappy about it and hope at least that such a request did *not emanate from me*. – If they had wished to *show* me civility they would certainly have offered it, especially as they must be aware that I am an invalid. Now it will very probably be refused and I shall feel horribly ashamed and unhappy. I feel sorry I wrote so as to have caused misapprehension. Forgive me.

P.S. In writing I think I said a "van". In England that is a small hooded waggon –

a travelling house like a "gypsy van" – and I should like to travel up to you as a gypsy. Still, a saloon is next-best and would be a solace. [. . .]

It is good to know that the three Generals have accepted and are to be present. No doubt all will go well. In that faith and the underlying justice of things I go calmly on, and so, I know, does the President.

Best love from Emily Hobhouse

104. TO MRS. STEYN

Bergvliet
30 October 1913

Dear Mrs. Steyn

I feel I *must* write to you on a subject that is much on my mind, but which I know is not my business – but I do so privately to you, trusting to your judgement to communicate my thought to the President or not, as you deem fit.

It is about Olive Schreiner. She and I are much in touch by correspondence now – nothing, not one direct word has been written by her – but – things have come to my knowledge and I gather that she has not been specially invited to the unveiling. Of course it would seem to me and others that she was marked out to be one of the *chief* speakers and her eloquence and right feeling would have raised the occasion – but even if her health prevented her that effort, has she been offered a prominent seat as an honoured guest? When I hear she is *planning* to leave South Africa on 6 December I fear the reason is plain – that her feelings are hurt. But I know she has engaged an *alternative* cabin on 27 December, which makes me think she still hoped an invitation might come. Do you think she has been asked? Had anyone more right? She is the one South African woman of European – more – of world-wide fame and she suffered beside the Boers throughout the war. She championed you with her pen. She therefore got into trouble. She was practically a prisoner in Hanover throughout the war. Her house was burnt to the ground in Kimberley. Her life's work – a book in manuscript – was burnt in Johannesburg and her books destroyed. She was penniless when the war ended. Her sympathies were all with you.

It is *possible* that she has been overlooked? Pray forgive me for even thinking it, but if it *is* so, do consider suggesting it to the committee.

Olive's address is De Aar. She is planning to come down to the Cape on 20 November but in any case the invitation should be wired now and without delay of a moment. It seems to me it would be a dreadful thing not to have her present.

I do so well understand her probable feeling and if I had been in her place and had not especially been asked, I too should try to be out of the country. Ah! do have her offered a place of *honour*, if not to *speak*.

And a smaller thing. I suppose the committee will have remembered that *down*

395

here many prominent women worked themselves *to the bone* for the camps and naturally feel they should be specially invited.

Forgive me if I intrude, but I do trust I have not done wrong in just telling. You know committees of *men* often forget these little but important amenities.

Much love, E. H.

105. TO J. C. SMUTS

Bergvliet
Diep River, Cape Town
Wednesday [undated]

Dear Oom Janie

. . . It was good to see you. Mrs. Purcell came back just after you left, having heard from Mr. Burton[1] that if I paid my maid's fare, I could have the coach up to Bloemfontein. But as I must then send it away and return by ordinary train, you must not expect me to go further afield to visit the Transvaal. My *looks* are the best part of me, you know.

Besides, now I shan't be able to take a lady companion with me to Bloemfontein. Do you know Mr. Burton is afraid of adverse criticism in affording me this help and I assure you, if I were not so weak I certainly would not accept what he tells Mrs. Purcell is so difficult and so unusual to give.

How much I look forward to seeing the children and Mrs. Smuts at the seaside. Forgive this scrawl.

Yours, Emily Hobhouse

106. TO MRS. STEYN

Bergvliet
5 November 1913

Dearest Mrs. Steyn

. . . I *quite* understand now about the *saloon* idea. Certainly, if granted, it will be an immense physical relief to me. I ought to leave the Cape on the 24th at the very latest. I think that's a Monday.

On the other point, I now understand the committee's standpoint generally – but for us, outside Africa, it is almost impossible to conceive such a day, such a memorial, such a gathering and yet that Olive Schreiner should not be a speaker, if not the foremost speaker. I suppose South Africans have *no* idea of the position she holds in the world at large – America, Australia, Europe – and all that she stands for in the World of Womanhood, leave alone that of Literature and Politics. Her position is so striking and so singular, her genius so marked, that it is and will be a puzzle to our minds that she should be absent.

But please do not think she has said *one word* – she has not. Only the fact dawned on me that she would not be there and speaking and I thought I saw underneath what she was feeling and the reason of her departure before the day. She would be Furious if she guessed I had written to you, so please forget it and burn these two letters . . .

Will you send me a postcard to tell me if I am to wait for a definite personal invitation from Mrs. Charlie Fichardt or write to thank her for the intimation received from you that I am to be her guest, about the 13th?

Tell Gladys I will bring the Montessori pamphlet for her.[1]

With love, Yours ever effectionately, Emily Hobhouse

P.S. I have felt much stronger the last week and think I have now quite recovered from the voyage and am nearly up to my Italian standard!

107. TO MRS. STEYN

c/o Rev. Steytler
Parsonage, Beaufort West
Sunday 30 November 1913

Dearest Mrs. Steyn

As you have a telephone to Bloemfontein I think it wisest to write you as fully as I can and when you have communicated with others, get your reply. I have been here two days, close on 3 000 feet and, in addition, for the first time since landing I have experienced *heat*, though so far only in the afternoon.

Last evening the great rapidity of my pulse made me send for the doctor. He said the only thing for me to do was to *turn round* and go back. I replied I was bound to go on and only needed his advice how to do it with the least danger. Also if it was chiefly the altitude or chiefly the heat which brought about this danger. He thought both, but said that if I left the coach and went into the cooler town for a few days I could thus eliminate the heat factor and see what effect the altitude produced. Also, he strongly advises staying here at 3 000 feet to see if I can get used to the height, for the difference between this and sea level is far more important in its effects on the heart than the difference between here and Bloemfontein's 4 500 feet.

So he counsels what I was beginning to feel: best that I should stay here till the last moment possible, then dash up to Bloemfontein in time to stay in bed or sofa unseen for one or two clear days before the function and come straight away again.

This would mean giving up my visit to you – also I have leave to keep my saloon till 6 or 7 December at the latest though I *might* through Botha get an extension for a day or so.

Now supposing I do not in the meantime collapse, could you find out, explaining the circumstances, if the Fichardts could have me a few days earlier and if I might feel free to arrive when I found it possible and go to bed? Secondly, will you let the committee know the difficulties and risk? I have known since I made quite a small effort those weeks ago at Bergvliet that I was taking my life in my hands by making this greater effort – known it, I mean, as one knows things for oneself apart from what the doctors tell one; but I had been pleased with myself as far as Laingsburg.

Believe me, if my body will do it, I shall come on – but there is a point at which the body *won't* and *can't* and if I reach this point, please assure the committee I shall repay the journey money sent to me in due time.

It would be a great help if you would wire me the degree of *heat* usual daily at Bloemfontein now, also at Onze Rust – but as I say, I think I had better definitely give up Onze Rust, alas! as that means more driving and more talking. I *feel* so well in between these attacks that it seems incredible heart failure is always hanging about so near.

You ought to know that I left direction with the Purcells in case of my complete collapse. You see what a quandary I am in. Still, a few days may clear the outlook. When I hear from you about going direct to the Fichardts I will wire to General Botha who told me to do so – to know if I can keep the coach a bit longer and try to reach Bloemfontein direct from here by the 9th or 10th.

But it is *most* important to know the degree Fahrenheit of temperature at Bloemfontein.

Forgive me being such a plague, but hearts are troublesome things as I know to my cost.

Yours ever effectionately, Emily Hobhouse

P.S. I think it best to send *shade* temperature.

108. TO MRS. STEYN

c/o Rev. Steytler
Parsonage
30 November 1913

... The doctor came and motored me to the cool shady parsonage house and at once I felt relieved and different. Mrs. Steytler with wondrous hospitality is begging me to stay here with her and I am also coming to the conclusion that I can judge better of what my powers are to bear both the altitude and the heat in a *private* house than in a hot, exposed railway car. For instance the thermometer in this room stands now, at 1 o'clock, only at 68 degrees Fahrenheit. I mean to watch it these coming days and find out to what degree I can bear without an attack dangerous to the heart. I believe the coach yesterday afternoon was about 100.

Thus, if I stay here in a private house and get accustomed to the altitude and escape further serious attacks I think I can easily run right through to Bloemfontein in a week's time for I know Kaya Lami can be kept very cool. So now let's be cheerful. I feel so much relieved by the thought. Really I did not want to present myself at your door as a corpse nor repay the Fichardts' hospitality by being ill in their house.

I shall look forward to your wire telling me the temperatures of Onze Rust and of Kaya Lami in the shade of an afternoon when it is highest.

Tell the committee to rest assured, I will not fail them unless I *know my presence will be worse than my absence.*

'Tis a year of deaths, is it not? Mr. Sauer, Mr. Fischer, Sir Richard Solomon and many others. My eldest sister who has been suffering from heart fell down dead in church a month ago. Prince Venosa, a Roman aquaintance who has my disease, has also died suddenly this month. Thus you see, it is always in my mind and I try to have everything arranged and ready.

By the way, a very skillful artist, William Arnold Foster, son of the Tory Cabinet Minister of that name, made clever drawings of me which were exhibited in London and pronounced very good and I have brought one out for Bloemfontein Museum, as I promised, for the £15 sent me. The first done, an oil portrait, was a failure.

E. H.

109. TO MRS. STEYN

Beaufort West
1 December 1913

Dearest Mrs. Steyn

. . . The committee have sent me a long and very kindly worded telegram setting me free, but of course I still must feel the moral obligation. Also there is my strong personal desire to be present. Dr. Williams examined me today and will every two days during my stay. My heart has again enlarged but *not much* so far. Considering the state of the organ and its past history a *sudden* dilation or a considerable one even if gradual must be fatal.

Remember I feel quite content to have tried to come, whatever happens. Alone, exiled and invalided as I am I always feel there need be

"no sadness of farewell
when I have crossed the bar"[1]

and I am ready, almost anxious, to go.

Still, I shall try my best, my very best to get to you that day. Leave alone other aspects, I can't bear to disappoint the President.

My regretful love to him, please, for giving him even this amount of extra worry.

I will try each day to send you a bulletin of my condition and progress.

With greetings to Gladys and Mrs. Fraser.

Yours most lovingly, Emily Hobhouse.

P.S. Between whiles I feel so absolutely well, tho' always imprisoned by my body –

for the doctor said at once, like my own doctor, that I am in an advanced state of senile decay and can only do what a person of 85 or 90 can do. Such old folk should not go a-voyaging.

110. TO J. C. SMUTS

Bergvliet
Diep River
Sunday 7 December 1913

My dear Oom Janie

Not even all the luxuries or comfort so generously afforded me could carry me through. The old horse fell exhausted (though I think I may say in harness) at the very last stage of the journey, and I write to tell you how sorry and in a way how humiliated I feel.

I have told you already of the serious attacks I had at Beaufort West – that the doctor had, as far as he could, forbidden me to proceed, but that I had definitely decided to take my life in my hands and go on and abide by the consequences. So it stood, but each day, each hour at Beaufort I grew weaker till at last the moment came when the decision was taken out of my hands and I became too weak to whip my body into obedience.

I knew my heart could only last three of four days more at that altitude (under 3 000 feet). I was already in a dying condition and even if I reached Bloemfontein could not live till the 16th.

If the ceremony had been on the 6th I should have risked it . . .

Words can't say how sorry I am to have thus disappointed the people; but Fate decided, I did not.

It will be a very impressive scene and I hope you will all be there.

They brought me here and put me to bed where I must bide awhile to see if my heart regains what it has lost or is, as the doctor half fears is, permanently injured and enfeebled by this great strain. I can just whisper.

Goodbye and love to Mrs. Smuts.

From yours ever, Emily Hobhouse

111. TO MRS. STEYN

Bergvliet
9 December 1913

Dearest Mrs. Steyn

Please tell the President the moment I had the committee's telegram I communicated with Mr. Merriman and am now awaiting his reply which in its turn I will not delay to wire back. He may very likely reply that it will depend on whether he approves of my address and wish to have time to read it. I sent him a written copy

400

at once. I shall be most thankful if he consents. If he refuses I should prefer that the address be scattered amongst the people as my gift and no one should read it. I will send the President a telegram message for him kindly to read.

I am ordering about 4 000 copies in each language. Miss Metelerkamp[1] has translated it for me and I am asking her, if possible, to go herself as she longs to do, and take the parcels up under her own care and see them delivered to Charlie Fichardt who will, I am sure, guide her to arrange about disseminating them to the people and later to the newspapers. If she arrives, as I hope, would the committee arrange some accommodation for her? She is Dutch and most sympathetic, but earns her living on the staff of *The Argus* writing on women's topics.

I have hardly spoken since my return here. I cannot, the pain is so great around my heart, and I am entirely in my bedroom, can hardly crawl across it without the pulse racing. But relief came the moment I got south and perhaps with time and completest cessation of effort, of voice in particular, I may pick up a bit once more.

Do take care that the President does not overtax himself. I am much touched at all your many careful considerate plans for my care and comfort.

Love, best wishes, from Emily Hobhouse

P.S. If Miss Metelerkamp cannot go in the end, I must have the parcels sent by passenger train direct to Kaya Lami.

112. [PAMPHLET]

Commemoration speech by Miss Hobhouse
(Undelivered through illness,[1] but distributed amongst the crowd in pamphlet form)[2]

VROUWEN-DAG,
16 December 1913.

In Memoriam, 26 370 Women and Children,[3]
And with them 1 421 old men

"Would ye be wise, ye cities, fly from war!
Yet if war come, there is a crown in death
For her that striveth well and perisheth
Unstained."

EURIPIDES, "TROJAN WOMEN"
Translated by Prof. Gilbert Murray.

Friends,
From far and near we are gathered today to commemorate those who suffered bravely and died nobly in the past.

401

Of old a great man said: "Acts deserve acts, and not words in their honour," and this is true. Yet having come so far at your request to share in this solemn dedication, and having been most closely bound with the last hours of their lives, I feel constrained to offer my tribute to the memory of those women and those little children who perished in the Concentration Camps.

Many of them it was my privilege to know. How strange a thought that from their memory today flows a more vital influence for good than can be found amongst those who have lived and prospered. In this way, perhaps, is the prophetic vision fulfilled: "Refrain thy voice from weeping and thine eyes from tears; they shall come again from the land of the enemy; thy children shall come again to their own border."[4]

Do we not in a very real sense meet them again this day?

Yet another thought urges me to offer this tribute of words.

From ancient times men have pronounced eulogies over the graves of their fellow-men who had fallen for their country. Today, I think for the first time, a woman is chosen to make the commemorative speech over the National Dead – not soldiers – but *women* – who gave their lives for their country.

My Friends, this day, this *Vrouwen-Dag* is good. Like the Sabbath in the week, it breaks into the hurrying years, and in the pause, the past can calmly be recalled, its inspiration breathed afresh, its lessons conned once more.

Let us take this moment to consider, where we now stand and what these lessons are.

You are gathered here from all parts to consecrate this spot to women and children who were stripped of all – I say it advisedly – of *all*. Husbands and sons, houses and lands, flocks and herds, household goods and even clothing. Denuded, it was good to watch how yet they "possessed their souls". "It is tragic," says a writer, "how few people ever possess their souls before they die."

That these did I know, because I saw. I bridge in mind the years, the thirteen years, and move once more amid the tents that whitened the hillsides. Torn from familiar simple life, plunged into sickness and destitution, surrounded by strangers, were those poor souls – stripped bare. The sight was one to call forth pity, yet pity did not predominate. Quite other feelings swallowed that. Even throughout the deepest misery the greater pity was needed elsewhere. "Christ," I have read, "had pity for the poor, the lowly, the imprisoned, the suffering, and so have we, but remember that He had far more pity for the rich, the hard, those who are slaves to their goods, who wear soft raiment, and live in kings' houses. To Him riches and pleasures seemed greater tragedies than poverty and sorrow."

So, as we turn our minds back thirteen years to dwell on the stormy past, pity enters in, but whom is it that we pity? Surely, had you watched the inward and spiritual graces that shone forth from that outward and visible squalor you yourselves might have felt that it was not the captives in those foul camps that were most in need and pity. The rich and highly placed, the financiers who wanted war, the incompetent Statesmen who were their tools, the men who sat in the seats of the mighty, the blundering politicians of that dark story – all the miserable Authorities incapable of dealing with the terrible conditions they themselves had brought about – these needed and still need our deeper pity. That vast tragedy as it rolled through your land upon its bloody way, came at length face to face with the great array of the women and children – the weak and the young. Wholly innocent of the war, yet called upon to bear its brunt, nobly rose to meet the trial that awaited them. Sympathy indeed they craved and did receive, but they towered above our pity.

And so today. What gave the impetus to this movement? What stirred you to gather pence for this monument? What brought you here from far and wide? It was not pity; it was Honour.

Yet if you have pity and to spare, give it even now to those, who, still alive, must ever carry in their hearts the heavy memories of the blundering wrong by which they wrought that war. You and I are here today filled only with Honour for those, their heroic and innocent victims, who passed through the fire.

For this monument is a symbol.

Far away in Rome I have been privileged to watch its creation. I noted its conception in the Sculptor's thought. I saw it first issue in the common clay; moulded by his hand it passed into the pure white plaster; at length chastened to his mind and meet for the supreme ordeal it was cast into the pit of burning metal whence issued the perfected work.

Even so did Destiny, the mighty Sculptor, like clay in his hands take those simple women and children from their quiet homes, mould and chasten them through the successive stages of their suffering, till at length, purified and perfected to the Master-mind by the fierce fire of their trial, they passed from human sight to live forever a sacred memory in your land.

Their spirit which we feel so near to us today warns ever: "Beware lest you forget what caused that struggle in the past. We died without a murmur to bear our part in saving our country from those who loved her not but only desired her riches. Do not confuse the issues and join hands with those who look on her with eyes of greed and not with eyes of love."

Is it not the glory of those weak sufferers to have laid down this principle: In this South Africa of ours, true patriotism lies in the unity of those who live *in* her and *love* her as opposed to those who live *on* her but *out* of her. The Patriots and the Parasites.

This issue though fought out of old is ever with you, it is alive today; voices of the dead call to you, their spirits lay a restraining hold upon you as they plead: "Here is the true division beside which all other cleavages are meaningless. There can be no permanent separation betwixt those who *love* our country, live *in* her and are bound up *with* her. At bottom such are one."

Alongside of the honour we pay the Sainted Dead, forgiveness must find a place.

403

I have read that when Christ said, "Forgive your enemies," it is not only for the sake of the enemy He say so, but for one's own sake, "because love is more beautiful than hate."

Surely your Dead, with the wisdom that now is theirs, know this. To harbour hate is fatal to your own self-development, it makes a flaw; for hatred, like rust, eats into the soul of a nation as of an individual.

As your tribute to the Dead, bury unforgiveness and bitterness at the foot of this Monument forever. Instead, for you can afford it, the rich who were greedy of more riches, the statesmen who could not guide affairs, the bad generalship that warred on weaklings and babes – forgive – because so only can you rise to full nobility of character and a broad and noble national life.

For what really matters is *character*. History clearly teaches this.

In the present day, minds are strangely confused, eyes are blinded, and it is the almost universal idea that the all-important thing for a country is Material Prosperity. It is false.

Noble Character forms a great nation. Statesmen who aim at material prosperity as if it were an end in itself, forget or have not recognised that too often great national prosperity is accompanied by deterioration of national character and the highest well-being of the people.

For it is not the rich and prosperous who matter most, but you who live the simplest lives, and upon whom in the last resort, if trial comes, falls the test of the national character.

This thought ennobles the humblest life. The Dead we now honour met that test and did not shrink. They died for freedom; they clung to it with unfaltering trust that God would make it the heritage of their children. The years have brought changes they little dreamed; but South Africa is one and it is free. Its freedom is based on all they did; they suffered; they died; they could do no more. The supreme offering was made, the supreme price paid. Their sacrifice still bears fruit. Even could the graves open and give up their Dead, we would not wish those women back, nor have them relinquish the great position they have won. Not even the children would we recall, the children, who – counting the vanished years – would stand before us now, some 20 000 youths and maidens, fair and comely – a noble array – peopling the too solitary veld. For who does not feel their spirit move amongst us here today? Who fails to recognise the noble example by which they still live?

In this vast throng can there be found one unresponsive soul? One heart that will not go hence filled with high resolve to live more worhty of the Dead?

My Friends, memories and emotions throng.

Thirteen years have passed since under the burning January sun I trudged daily forth from your wire-girt town to that kopje of many tears. Daily in that camp, as later in others, I moved from tent to tent, witness of untold sufferings, yet marvelling ever at the lofty spirit which animated the Childhood as well as the

Motherhood of your land. So quickly does suffering educate, that even children of quite tender years shared the spirit of the struggle, and sick, hungry, naked or dying prayed ever for "no surrender".

Think what it meant for an Englishwoman to watch such things.

Did you ever ask yourselves why I came to your aid in those dark days of strife? I had never seen your country nor ever known anyone of you. Hence it was no personal link that brought me hither. Neither did political sympathy of any kind prompt my journey.

I came – quite simply – in obedience to the solidarity of our Womanhood and to those nobler traditions of English life in which I was nurtured, and which by long inheritance are mine.

For when Society is shaken to its foundations, then deep calleth unto deep,[5] the underlying oneness of our nature appears, we learn that "all the world is kin".

And surely, the honour of a country is not determined by the blundering acts of some passing administration or weak generalship, but lies in the sum-total of her best traditions which the people at large will rise up to maintain.

Even as the noblest men are ever ready to admit and remedy an error, so England as soon as she was convinced of the wrong being done in her name to the weak and defenceless confessed it in *very deed*, and by thorough reformation of those camps, rendered them fit for human habitation.

Thus she atoned.

I stand here as an Englishwoman, and I am confident that all that is best and most humane in England is with you also in heart today. Reverent sympathy is felt with you in this Commemoration and in your desire to accord full honour to your Dead.

You and I were linked together by the strange decrees of fate at the dark hour; we stand now face to face for the last time.

One thing I would ask of you:

When you remember the ill done, remember also the atonement made.

Dwell also upon all you have gained through this great episode, in the legacy left you by the Dead.

Let me explain: It is not mainly sorrow that fills your heart today; time has already softened personal grief. Therefore many may and do say it is useless to perpetuate as we do today memories so drear. But these very memories are needful because they embody that precious legacy from the past. My own face now is turned towards the West, and soon each one of us who witnessed the sufferings of the Concentration Camps will have passed to our own rest; but so long as we who saw those things still live, they will live within us *not* as memories of sorrow, but of *heroic inspiration*. For what never dies and never should die is a great example. True is it of your Dead that which Pericles said of his countrymen:

405

"The grandest of all sepulchres they have, not that in which mortal bones are laid, but a home in the minds of men; their story lives on far away, without visible symbol, woven into the stuff of other men's lives."

Your visible monument will serve to this great end – becoming an inspiration to all South Africans and to the women in particular. Generation after generation it will stand here, pressing home in silent eloquence these great thoughts: In your hands and those of your children lie the power and freedom won; you must not merely maintain but increase the sacred gift. Be merciful towards the weak, the down-trodden, the stranger. Do not open your gates to those worst foes of freedom – tyranny and selfishness.[6] Are not these the withholding from others in your control, the very liberties and rights which you have valued and won for yourselves? So will the monument speak to you.

Many nations have foundered on this rock.[7] We in England are ourselves still but dunces in the great world-school, our leaders still struggling with the unlearned lesson, that liberty is the equal right and heritage of every child of man, without distinction of race, colour or sex. A community that lacks the courage to found its citizenship on this broad base becomes "a city divided against itself, which cannot stand".

Lay hold of and cherish this ideal of liberty then – should your statesmen be hostile or coldly neutral, should your rich men be corrupt, should your press which ought to instruct and defend the liberties of all sections of the people, only betray – never mind – they do not constitute the nation. "The nation," said John Bright, "is in the cottage."

You are the nation, you whom I see here today, you, most of whom live in remote villages and silent farms leading simple hard-working lives. You are your nation's very soul and on whom lies the responsibility of maintaining her ideals by the perfecting of your own character.

The old old watchword "Liberty, Fraternity, Equality" cries from the tomb; what these women, so simple that they did not know that they were heroines, valued and died for *all other human beings desire with equal fervour*. Should not the justice and liberties you love so well, extend to all within your borders? The old Greeks taught that not until power was given to men could it be known what was in them.

This testing time now has come to you.

For ponder a moment.

We meet on Dingaan's Day, your memorial of victory over a barbarous race.[8] We too, the great civilised nations of the world, are still but barbarians in our degree, so long as we continue to spend vast sums in killing or planning to kill each other for greed of land and gold. Does not justice bid us remember today how many thousands of the dark race perished also in Concentration Camps in a quarrel that was not theirs? Did they not thus redeem the past? Was it not an instance of

406

that community of interest, which binding all in one, roots out racial animosity? And may it not come about that the associations linked with this day will change, merging into nobler thoughts as year by year you celebrate the more inspiring *Vrouwen-Dag* we now inaugurate? The plea of Abraham Lincoln for the black comes echoing back to me: "They will probably help you in some trying time to come to keep the jewel of liberty in the family of freedom."

Still more intimately will this Monument speak to the Womanhood of South Africa and beyond to a yet wider range.

To you, women, it should cry ever: "Go back, go back, to simpler lives, to nobler principles; from these martyrs learn the grandeur of character that chooses rather to suffer to the uttermost than to win life by weakness."

Women, high or low, rich or poor, who have met in your thousands today; do not go empty away. You cannot be as if these Dead had not died. Your country demands your lives and your powers in another way. As the national life broadens, difficulties appear little dreamed of in a simpler state. Complicated problems arise which seriously affect the well-being of your sons and daughters. It is for you to think out these problems in your homes, for you to be the purifying element in the body politic, for you to help guide the helm of state.

The Dead have won for you a lofty place in the life of your nation, and the right to a voice in her counsels. From this sacred duty you surely dare not flinch. No one is too humble or unknown; each one counts.

For remember, these dead women were not great as the world counts greatness; some of them were quite poor women who had laboured much. Yet they have become a moral force in your land. They will enrich your history. As the diamonds and the gold glitter in the bedrock of your soil, so their stories, written or handed down, will shine like jewels in the dark annals of that time.

And their influence will travel further. They have shown *the world* that never again can it be said that woman deserves no rights as Citizen because she takes no part in war. This statue stands as a denial of that assertion. Women in equal numbers to the men earned the right to such words as the famous Athenian uttered at the grave of his soldiers: "They gave their bodies to the commonwealth, receiving each for her own memory praise that will never die."

Nay, more – for they gave themselves, not borne on by the excitement and joy of active battle, as men do; but passively, with open eyes, in the long-drawn agony of painful mouths and days.

My Friends: Throughout the world the Woman's day approaches; her era dawns. Proudly I unveil this Monument to the brave South African Women, who, sharing the danger that beset their land and dying for it, affirmed for all times and for all peoples the power of Woman to sacrifice life and more than life for the common weal.

This is your South African Monument; but it is more; for "their story is not graven only on stone, over their native earth".

We claim it as a WORLD MONUMENT, of which all the World's Women should be proud: for your Dead by their brave simplicity have spoken to Universal Womanhood, and henceforth they are "woven into the stuff" of every woman's life.

Bergvliet, December 1913

Emily Hobhouse.

Appendices

I ON E. H.'S ARREST AND DEPORTATION

(i) *Statement* re *Miss Hobhouse's forcible removal from the* Avondale Castle *on Thursday, 31 October 1901, by Betty Molteno.*

I went to the Castle today about half past ten o'clock, to ask for a permit to go on board the *Avondale Castle* to see Miss Hobhouse. After waiting a long time I saw Commandant Cooper. I told him I had seen Miss Hobhouse yesterday and asked if I might arrange to get her a laundress. He replied that there was no necessity as Miss Hobhouse would leave today in the *Roslin Castle*. I asked for a permit to go and say goodbye to her. He said: "Yes, but only one permit will be granted."

I asked if it would not be possible to grant one to Mrs. Murray as well, as she was Miss Hobhouse's greatest friend, and asked if I might telegraph to her. He hesitated and then said he would telegraph to her himself. He then checked himself, saying, "Mrs. Murray saw Miss Hobhouse yesterday; there is no need for her to see her again. No, I will not grant more than one permit." He then asked some questions about Miss Hobhouse and her relationship to Lord Hobhouse. He said he could quite understand that she was unwell and much upset.

I asked if I might stay to lunch. He consented and arranged about a permit. I reached the ship somewhere after 12 o'clock and found Miss Hobhouse leaning back with closed eyes in her deck chair, apparently asleep. I quietly seated myself near her. After a while she opened her eyes, and gave a great start, not expecting to see me. A large official envelope lay on her lap which she asked me to read. It was a notification from the Dock Authorities that a free passage was granted her in the *Roslin Castle*, requesting her to embark that afternoon. She looked very tired and exhausted and whispered, "they were at me last night after you left and again this morning to persuade me to go on board the *Roslin Castle* which is a military transport taking back invalid soldiers." She seemed very exhausted. I sat quietly beside her until the luncheon bell rang when she roused herself and said: "You must go down to lunch."

On my return I found she had taken a little broth and seemed less drowsy but was getting anxious about Nurse who had had leave to go ashore and was long in returning.

Nurse returned about 2.30 p.m. and was still kneeling beside her telling her

411

about Cape Town when Lieutenant Lingham approached. Miss Hobhouse did not see him until he was beside her, and was startled and shaken when she did see him.

Captain Lingham said: "Miss Hobhouse, will you order your maid to pack your boxes and prepare to embark on board the *Roslin Castle* at once."

Miss Hobhouse spoke with restraint but under great excitement, saying, "I have told you, sir, that I cannot think of undertaking another sea-voyage so soon; I am not well enough, I want time to recover strength."

Captain Lingham said: "My orders are that you must embark this afternoon."

Miss Hobhouse said: "No man in his senses could press such a request upon me under these circumstances. I must repeat I have not yet recovered from my last sea-voyage and the shock I have undergone, sufficiently to be able so soon to undertake another voyage."

Captain Lingham abruptly turned away and left her. Nurse was called away, and returned to say she was ordered to pack Miss Hobhouse's boxes. Miss Hobhouse said: "Nurse, I forbid you to touch my boxes."

Nurse left and shortly returned saying the stewardesses had been sent for and were to be ordered to pack Miss Hobhouse's boxes.

The Chief Officer of the *Avondale Castle* came and apologized to Miss Hobhouse for what was being done and asked Miss Hobhouse to permit her maid to be present in the cabin while the packing was done. Miss Hobhouse said she forbade Nurse to have anything whatsoever to do with the packing. The Chief Officer said he desired Nurse's presence as a protection to the stewardesses. To protect them Miss Hobhouse consented to Nurse standing in the doorway while the packing was done.

After a while Nurse returned to say that the packing was finished. Not long after, a visiting-card with the name of Colonel Williamson was brought to Miss Hobhouse and a request that he might see her. Miss Hobhouse asked Nurse to say that she was quite unequal to seeing a stranger and must ask Colonel Williamson to excuse her. Nurse returned with a message that Colonel Williamson was a medical man and wished to see Miss Hobhouse professionally. Miss Hobhouse told Nurse to say that she did not wish to see a strange medical man and must beg to be excused. Colonel W. then approached, himself, and said: "Miss Hobhouse, I am the Chief of the medical staff and am ordered to see you professionally."

Miss Hobhouse replied: "I am exhausted by the voyage I have made and by the shock I have had, but a strange medical man with whom I am totally unacquainted cannot help me in any way. What I need is rest and quiet."

Colonel Williamson moved away and sent for Nurse. They returned together after a few minutes' consultation when Nurse knelt beside Miss Hobhouse and told her that the Doctor said he must examine her. Colonel W. came nearer and said soothingly: "Miss Hobhouse, will you not allow me to assist you to the smoking-room, it is quite near and I must examine you."

412

Miss H. again repeated that a strange medical man could not be of any use to her. Colonel W. continued to insist but remarked: "I may find you too unwell to sail at present."

Miss H. finally asked Nurse to help her to rise and with Colonel W.'s assistance entered the smoking-room. He examined her heart, told Nurse to take her temperature, also looked at her tongue. He then said: "Miss Hobhouse, I understand you do not take stimulants."

Miss H. replied: "I do not, except under Doctor's orders."

Colonel W. said she needed some stimulant and he could prescribe for her. He then left the smoking-room and Miss H. concluded he would not press her further. Nurse had gone with Colonel W. When she returned, Miss H. asked: "What does he say, Nurse, am I to stay?"

Nurse replied that he said her heart was all right, that she must have some champagne or brandy and that she was well enough to go. Miss Hobhouse burst out indignantly: "I never supposed I had a diseased heart! What did he expect to find? It is my nerves and the exhaustion and shock I have had that I am suffering from."

Nurse helped to make her comfortable on one of the seats in the smoking-room and went out. Presently she returned and said that Miss Hobhouse's baggage and bicycle had been removed from the hold and that a cab had come. Soon after the Chief Officer asked to see Miss Hobhouse. He came in and his face and manner were very kind and sympathetic. He again said: "Miss Hobhouse, I am in no way responsible for this, but I cannot prevent it. I am ordered to give up your luggage but have asked for a written order. I will do nothing unless it is put down in writing, but Captain Lingham is now writing the order. I want to suggest that there may be some small things that had better remain with you as your luggage is now to go on board the *Roslin Castle*."

Miss Hobhouse thanked him for his thoughtful kindness said: "I had better have my handbag, I had forgotten that it contains my cheque-book."

The Chief Officer brought the bag and two more small parcels which he placed on a seat. Miss Hobhouse said: "They may take my luggage but they will not take me."

Lieutenant-Colonel Williamson returned and said: "Miss Hobhouse, everything is arranged; will you kindly prepare to come."

Miss Hobhouse re-iterated that it was out of the question, that she could not make another voyage so soon. Colonel Williamson replied: "I am acting under orders and if you will not come voluntarily, force will be employed."

Miss Hobhouse said: "I do not believe that any English gentleman will carry out such an order."

Colonel W. interrupted her by saying: "Miss Hobhouse, I cannot argue the matter, but it will be done. If you will not come voluntarily, two Army nurses will be sent for and they will forcibly remove you."

413

Miss Hobhouse broke in: "I do not believe it. Women will not do the dirty work that men refuse to do themselves. I shall appeal to their sex and their womanhood; I know they will not touch me."

Colonel W. went out. Miss Hobhouse sent for the Chief Officer and asked whether the Captain had returned. He had not. She then repeated to the Chief Officer what Colonel W. had said and begged of him to be present when the Army nurses came. He said: "I am powerless to assist you, Miss Hobhouse, I can do nothing, I am under orders myself."

Miss Hobhouse said: "I only ask of you to remain here to give me the protection of your presence when they come."

The Chief Officer promised to do as she wished.

During the interval when I was alone with Miss Hobhouse she lay back closing her eyes, evidently trying to husband her strength. She said to me: "I do not believe the women will do it. I am sure they will not."

Suddenly Colonel W. re-appeared and two women burst into the smoking-room. They were not Army nurses but wore what looked like an attempt at a uniform. They were large, stout women but did not give the impression of having undergone any regular training. They approached and took up a position on either side of Miss Hobhouse. I was ordered to move from beside her and crossed to the other side of the room. Miss Hobhouse appealed to their womanhood, to their sense of responsibility to a Higher Power, addressing them as Sisters whose mission was to succour, aid and bless, not to use violence. She said she was sure they would not touch her – that they would not disgrace their womanhood by doing work that men were ashamed to do themselves. After listening silently for a while the women who had placed themselves in a resolute attitude – with bodies stiffened and arms akimbo – gradually relaxed their faces; their arms dropped and finally they turned and quietly went out. Miss Hobhouse said as they moved away: "Thank you both, Sisters, I was sure you would not do it, I knew that women would not so disgrace their womanhood."

Miss Hobhouse was calm and collected, speaking quietly but with penetrating intensity and resolution which the women seemed wholly unable to resist. Nurse went to fetch some tea. The steward came also with some biscuits, etc. Miss Hobhouse took a little tea. Nurse went away. Later she returned and said: "They say they are going to send for a stretcher and bearers and that they will carry you away as a lunatic."

Miss Hobhouse made no comment but asked Nurse to fetch the Chief Officer. He came at once and Miss Hobhouse said to him: "I hear they are going to send for a stretcher and bearers to carry me away as a lunatic. I beg of you to come here if they come and to remain all the while. I want the protection of your presence." The Chief Officer promised to do as she wished. Later when the Captain returned she sent for him and also requested him to be present should an attempt be made for forcibly remove her. She also asked whether he had no power to protect her.

414

Captain Brown replied: "Miss Hobhouse, I am quite helpless. I have absolutely no power. I could not punish one of my own men."

She begged of him, as she had done of the Chief Officer, to be present if the stretcher-bearers tried to remove her and added: "I should be glad if more of the ship's officers would be present", and again added: "But I do not believe the men will touch me."

She then asked Captain Brown about the *Roslin Castle* and said she wished to go in a mail-boat, not in a troop-ship. Captain Brown said the *Roslin Castle* was a good ship and would not be very slow.

Later the two nurses came back and one of them came close to Miss Hobhouse and tried very kindly and gently to persuade her to go with them. She said: "It will be so horrible for men to touch you. We are volunteer nurses. We are free. We can refuse to touch you, but the stretcher-bearers dare not. They cannot help themselves. They will have to do as they are told. They will take hold of you if they are ordered to do it."

Miss Hobhouse asked what kind of men they were. She replied: "Army service men" and continued to persuade. Miss Hobhouse shook her head and said: "Do not ask me, Sister – I cannot do as you wish, it would not be right."

The volunteer nurse turned to Nurse P. and said: "Do try to persuade her, Nurse, it will be so horrid for men to touch her."

Nurse Phillips continued what she was doing – not seeming to hear. Presently she asked the women who saw that further persuasion was useless, about themselves. One of them replied: "We are Colonial volunteer nurses. I am going to England in the *Roslin Castle*. I have never been to England before."

The women left.

Miss Hobhouse said: "I will speak to the men. I do not believe they will touch me." After a while Colonel W. re-entered with the nurses and said: "Now, Miss Hobhouse, come quietly with these sisters and do not give us so much trouble." Miss Hobhouse, much nettled, broke in: "It is I who am being troubled by what you are doing! I have said that I cannot make the voyage so soon. I ask for time. I ask to see my own medical man from the shore – Dr. Charles Murray."

Colonel W. broke in shortly: "You shall not see him. He will not get a pass."

She continued: "I will undertake to do my best to be well enough to go by the *Kinfauns* next week. When I go I will go in a mail-steamer. I will not go in a troop-ship."

Colonel W. said: "I am acting under instructions – you will have to go today."

The scene was inexpressibly painful. Colonel W. went out. I asked Miss Hobhouse: "Shall I ask him to let you remain till next week?"

She said: "You can try."

I went out on deck to where Colonel W. stood, looking very perplexed. I said: "You see the condition Miss Hobhouse is in. It is not possible to grant her request? She has offered to go by the *Kinfauns* next week."

He said: "Impossible. We are acting on orders direct from Lord Kitchener."

I said: "But do communicate with Commandant Cooper, put it to him."

He replied: "I am now in telephonic communication with Commandant Cooper."

I returned to Miss Hobhouse. The steward brought us both some broth. Miss Hobhouse drank hers and lay back to rest. She was very fatigued and scarcely spoke at all to me. When it was nearly 7 o'clock she said she thought she would go to bed. Shortly after, Nurse came in and said: "The stretcher-bearers are come, they are coming now. They say they are going to touch you on the shoulder", and she used a word I did not catch. I had urged on Nurse more than once that she must return with Miss Hobhouse to England should she be forced on board the *Roslin Castle*. Miss Hobhouse did not want to interfere with Nurse's plans as she knew she was desirous of remaining in South Africa. Nurse said she was quite willing to return with Miss Hobhouse. Miss Hobhouse seemed unable to give her attention to the matter.

At this point Colonel Williamson entered; I am not sure about the nurses but the smoking-room seemed full. I noticed the two stretcher-bearers who took up a position near the door. They were square-looking men – not tall, but heavy and stolid, their faces absolutely expressionless as though they wore masks. Colonel W. came close to Miss Hobhouse and said: "Now, Miss Hobhouse, you have had your will, you have had the scene you wanted. I will touch you on the shoulder, that will be sufficient for your purpose, you had better come quietly."

Miss Hobhouse tried to say as she had attempted to do many times previously: "This is not martial law. You have no right to do this. Martial law has reference to taking steps against the enemy. You have no right to interfere with private individuals."

Colonel W. broke in coldly: "I am not here to argue. I cannot listen. I say, will you come quietly?"

Miss Hobhouse tried to address the men: "You will not do this thing you are asked to do. You would not treat your mothers or wives or sisters so. There is a Higher Law – you cannot, you dare not obey these orders."

Colonel W. signalled to the men. Miss Hobhouse broke out: "You are disgracing your uniforms by obeying such an order. A Higher Law forbids you. The laws of God and Humanity forbid you. Colonel Williamson, you will rue this to your dying day. You all will rue it. You are untrue to the Highest Law – Martial Law does not give you the power to do this."

The men on either side seized and lifted her. She freed herself and planted her feet on the cabin floor. Colonel W. seemed to me to deftly slip out a long black band and slip it round her waist as he helped the men to seize her again. With his help they succeeded in lifting her off her feet and she lay all her length like a baby, helpless in their arms.

While they were seizing her and struggling with her, she burst out: "You brutes, you brutes, you touch me."

As they were trying to lift her through the doorway, Colonel W. saying, "Be careful, be careful, don't hurt the lady", she gave a great terrible heartbroken cry. They placed her, still struggling, in a madeira chair on the deck and quickly lifted it. While they began to carry her she struggled free of the chair and succeeded in planting her feet on the deck. Again Colonel W. placed his arm round her from behind and the three men seized her to the steps leading to the lower deck. I heard Colonel W. say repeatedly: "Be careful, don't hurt the lady."

As she was carried off the ship, she called back, "Goodbye Captain, goodbye officers, goodbye stewards. Thank you all for your kindness."

I ran down the steps opposite those down which she was being carried, and got to the gangway when she was already across it. To my surprise I heard sullen horrid hisses and hootings and low growls as from savage wild beasts and looked up to see whence they came. Then I saw they came from a crowd of ill-looking men standing so close to the forepart of the ship that they seemed to mingle with the crew. A high shrill voice cried: "Canting old hypocrite – serves her right! A sousing in the salt-water would do her good!"

Then a fresh horrid growl – a kind of wild-beast sound I have never before heard except from wild beasts – went up from the ill-looking little crowd near the gangway.

I ran to the carriage. Miss Hobhouse was already being placed in it. One nurse springing in put her arm round her. The other seated herself opposite. I was thankful to see Nurse Phillips seat herself opposite Miss Hobhouse. I placed a basket of fruit belonging to Miss Hobhouse in the carriage and passed on. Two men seated themselves beside the coachman. I think one was Colonel W. Another carriage followed. As the carriage passed, Miss Hobhouse saw me and called: "Goodbye!"

Miss Hobhouse was extremely dignified and mentally collected throughout. She scarcely spoke to me throughout the day, seeming exhausted and under great strain, [and to] reserve her strength to combat the attempt to remove her forcibly. The struggle seemed to me interminably protracted.

The arguments Miss Hobhouse used were:
>   That martial law gave no power to effect her forcible removal;
>   that she protested against being placed on a troop-ship;
>   that she wished to consult her medical adviser, Dr. Chas. Murray;
>   finally, that she would undertake to do her best to be well enough to leave by the *Kinfauns Castle* the next week.

417

One of the milder sensations of the week has been the removal of Miss Hobhouse. She arrived by the *Avondale*, an intermediate steamer, on Monday, and Lord Kitchener had sent express orders to the Military here that she was not to be allowed to land. I should have thought the wise course would have been to let her land and not to have let her go up-country, where *everything possible* is now being done for the people in the Concentration Camps. However, thank goodness, we, the Civil Authorities, have no responsibility in regard to people who don't leave their ships. She was therefore told she must stay on the *Avondale*. She wrote an indignant letter to the Governor, saying she had come out to look after the *British* refugees this time! The Governor said he could do nothing, as the matter was in the hands of the Military, but that meanwhile she need have no anxiety in regard to the refugees, for whom all possible efforts were being made. She was asked to go back by the mail on Wednesday, but she refused and said she was too ill. At the same time she could not remain on the *Avondale*, which while discharging cargo in the docks was no place for a lady. So orders were given to put her on board the *Roslin*, a hospital ship and transport, which sailed on Friday morning. Of course a Doctor had to see her, as she said she was ill, and the whole job of seeing her and superintending her removal fell on Colonel Williamson, R.A.M.C. . . . He is an awfully good fellow, a thorough gentleman and with great war experience – he was with Roberts at Candahar – but very reserved and shy with women; he is about fifty-six, I should say, and a bachelor!

It took more than four hours to get Miss Hobhouse from the *Avondale* at the South-Arm, to put her in a carriage, and then to drive her round to the coaling jetty! She made a series of speeches to Williamson, which began in this way: "If in addition to being an Officer, you also happen to be a gentleman", etc.! A couple of Civil nurses were got from the *Roslin*, but she harangued them also and fixed herself in a corner of the saloon behind an immovable table, from which retreat she defied everybody. In vain poor Williamson tried to explain that he was only doing his duty and was obliged to carry out his orders. She only rated him the more. He asked her to go under protest and make her complaints afterwards; she refused. "Well," he said then, "I have no alternative but to send for a stretcher party!" Soon a party of hospital orderlies were on the spot. These Miss Hobhouse also passionately harangued; told them they had a higher duty to perform than to obey their Officers, etc., etc. In the middle of it all old Williamson quietly said: "Take the lady out"; and the orderlies, joining hands in the way in which sick or wounded people are carried, lifted her up, bore her down the gangway and placed her in the carriage. A small crowd had assembled and the poor woman, beside herself with excitement and anger, shouted and screamed to them also. The only result was loud laughter and coarse remarks; and thus amid the jeers of the dock loafers the unfortunate lady made her exit. Whatever may be thought about the wisdom of sending her back, there can be no two opinions about the want of self-restraint and dignity on her part. Old Williamson is much put out about the whole affair, and takes it *very seriously*. To hear his account next morning at breakfast to me was simply excruciating; I laughed till I was tired. In the middle of it when he was telling how the orderlies were obliged to carry her out I said, "Williamson, I hope what Elizabeth calls her 'frillies' were all right." Without a smile, and very earnestly, Williamson said: "I am an old hand; I had thought of that; and when she was picked up I threw a shawl over her feet."!! I had not breath to say a word, but I thought Harry Piers who was sitting opposite would have a fit.

You will be tired at this long history of the Hobhouse incident, but I thought it would interest both you and Dolly; there will be a great deal about it in the English papers in a few weeks.

(Sir James Rose Innes: *Selected Correspondence 1884–1902*, ed. Harrison M. Write, pp. 312–314.)

(iii) *Reaction of English friends and admirers of E. H.*

Sir Henry Campbell-Bannerman had heard with indignation of my arrest, and speaking at Bath on 20 November 1901, before I reached England, he said, after alluding to the recently published Blue-Book on the camp:

> ". . . That noble lady, Miss Hobhouse, who has the credit of having first called the attention of the British Public to this matter in which the Honour of the British Public is so much involved, has now, if all we read is true, been further honoured by being expelled from South Africa (shame) and shipped back to England, as if forsooth the power of this great Empire was too weak to stand the presence of a woman." ("Good" and cheers.)

As a matter of fact, when he paid me this tribute the whole audience rose to its feet and cheered. I have a note which Sir Henry wrote to Lady Courtney describing this scene and the strength of the feeling exhibited, ladies and gentlemen rising and cheering. "And," added Sir Henry, "it was a champagne audience."

My Uncle and I received many kind letters of indignation and sympathy. I will select a few passages from people whose opinion I valued to shew you the sort of thing.

Professor Sully wrote:

> "I think it may cheer you a little to know that you did me lots of good yesterday. I have been overworked and there is always this hideous war to seize on the first thoughts after waking. But seeing you so calmly brave had

manned me. You are right to be calm. Your work cannot be lost: in the worst case your example will shine like a bit of illuminated work on this soiled and blotted page of our history."

Lort Ripon wrote:

"You have undergone much in the Cause of Mercy, but you have won the admiration of all who are not blinded by the passion of the moment. May God bless you."

I was very touched with the letter of another veteran – a woman – *Mrs. Wolstenholme Elmy* who long years past had laboured with Lord Hobhouse in the Cause of Womanhood and in the passage of the Married Women's Property Act to which women owe so much.

She wrote from Congleton to Lord Hobhouse:

"Dear Lord Hobhouse

All women ought to feel profoundly grateful to Miss Hobhouse, not merely for the noble work she has done in the interests of humanity, but for her dignified resistance to unconstitutional proceedings. Many women, of whom I am one, thank her with all their hearts.

"It is a pitiful sight to see the self-styled 'Constitutional' party busied in tearing to pieces the British Constitution; and what must the end be? Revolution or utter destruction.

"I could not help wishing that you had been still a member of the Judicial Committee of the Privy Council, in view of Lord Halsbury's proceedings in the 'Marais' case. I only hope it is true, as currently reported, that Lord Davey said in the committee that they might as well tear up the 'Bill of Rights' as issue such a judgment.

"Will our so-called Statesmen recover from the mad delirium of the war fever before *all is lost* that made Britain truly great? . . ."

Another woman's greeting gave me great pleasure. "*Edna Lyall*", Miss Bayly, asked my friend Mr. C. E. Maurice to forward her letter to me, saying she found it impossible to resist the impulse to write:

"In these sad times, when in so many ways we seem as a nation to be taking steps back, it cheers one to see such an instance of the courageous upholding of justice and of our national liberties as you have given us. How wonderfully the brave endurance of even one human being can work for good! If I say little of the indignation that so many of us feel at the way in which you were treated, it is not because I am not indignant, but because above that feeling there is always in a greater degree the thankfulness and the

420

glow of genuine admiration which conduct such as yours calls forth. It will surely stimulate millions of men and women to aim high."

Joshua Rowntree from Scarborough wrote:

"You may rest assured our thoughts have been with you day by day. At first we were greatly puzzled as to what actually occurred on your arrival in Table Bay, but the Reuter paragraph, presumably official, made your (illegal) arrest and deportation clear, and on its testimony, which can hardly be friendly, we feel thankful to know that in a time of great tension and difficulty, alone and unfriended, you acted just as one could wish an Englishwoman to act, standing simply, fearlessly, unflinchingly for duty in the face of danger. We knew you to be capable of such a stand; we never thought countrymen of our own would force you into it.

"The last few days my chief hope for you has been that we might none of us shew ourselves to be little men in the presence of great events. I was glad of the committee's request against any demonstration until all was known. The boiling over of small vessels often stands in the way of the development of greater forces. Your arrest is too grave for sectional protests until at any rate the greatness of the issue has been properly put before the country.

"My message after the manner of our Dutch friends would be this:

"'They looked unto Him and were lightened, and their faces were not ashamed.'"

That champion of public liberty, *Mr. H. F. Wilson*, M.P., was deeply stirred. He wrote from Sheffield:

"I have only today got two or three copies of your little pamphlet. It is an amazing story.

"I am full of sympathy with you in those most trying and difficult moments. I am full of admiration of your courage, self-possession and persistence in throwing the whole burden of responsibility on the Authorities.

"But I am more full – you will, I am sure, not misunderstand me in saying it – of alarm for my country whose rulers have sunk so low as to practise such actions of pure, unmitigated despotism.

"If you had suffered this at the hands of Turks, or Chinese, it would have been natural perhaps, and our rulers would have demanded apologies and reparations.

"But it is done by England! In no case of emergency even!

"It is *awful, horrible*.

"I'm so glad to have seen your uncle's letter, so glad to know proceedings will be taken, so glad that in addition to ordinary legal advisers you have Lord Hobhouse at your side.

"All we can do is to thank you from the bottom of our hearts for the stand you made; and to beg that we may be allowed the privilege of sharing the costs of the steps to be taken to vindicate your action at the Cape, and to retrieve the tarnished Honour of our country."

Mrs. [*Jane M.*] *Style*, wife of the Leader of the Positivist Church in Liverpool, very kindly wrote me the view of that group of women:

"As one who greatly rejoices that a woman so devoted as yourself has been found amongst English women to uphold the cause of the oppressed, I venture to put before you the views of our little group of women, which has followed every movement of yours with the deepest interest and sympathy. We feel that with regard to the treatment that you have yourself received at the Cape – it is now fully before the Public – and that the whole effect on the Public of your noble championship will be a little marred by any appeal to the Law to vindicate your own personal rights.

"We feel that you are a woman engaging in public work not because you desired to go outside woman's sphere but because of the great need and suffering of others, and we are sure you were prepared to endure hardship and even death without murmuring, had it fallen to your lot.

"Therefore we should regret that your name – now become a pride to womanhood – should be connected with anything smaller . . ."

I hope Mrs. Style and her friends realized later, as indeed I hastened to explain, that the proposed appeal to Law was not a personal matter but to safeguard Public Right and Constitutional Liberty.

II E. H.'S COMMENTS ON THE REPORT OF THE LADIES' COMMISSION ON THE CAMPS

An event of public interest was the publication early in 1902 of the Blue-Book Cd. 893, containing the report of the Ladies' Commission on the Camps. Many in England had been watching for this issue, withholding full sympathy pending this official confirmation. One would have thought the figures issued monthly in a White Paper with approximate correctness would have sufficed to shew the terrible state of affairs. At any rate many leading medical and diet experts expressed themselves publicly on these facts. The main body of educated people seemed unable to grasp the significance of those figures, and the report was useful in impressing this type of mind. It did not excite me personally, because I knew full well what it *must* contain if issued by honest women, and I knew that it *must*, as indeed it *did*, confirm my statements. I knew, too, that its recommendations must, as indeed they did, follow the lines I had laid down.

But I own I was not prepared for the disagreeable innuendoes and ill-natured remarks which mar the pages of a serious report, nor for the acceptance of occasional trashy information which a little care in verification or more converse with those who knew the country and people better would have prevented. Such are unworthy of space in an official document.

Conning this Blue-Book again after 23 years, I am struck by the "war neurosis" which was too evidently affecting the commission. It accords oddly with the practical common sense of their recommendations. The embittered outlook of Dr. Jane Waterston was too well known; it was disclosed by herself in a long letter published in July of 1901 in the *Cape Times*. [See Letter 15, note] This unfortunate document lies before me as I write. Mrs. Fawcett had given evidence of very similar warfever, notably in her article in the *Westminster Gazette* on my report, in her strange statement that she could get no help from the Distress Fund Committee in London, in her treatment of the Cape Town Ladies' Committee, and later in her unverified tales at sundry meetings. Statements then made were refuted by myself and others in the Press. Yet, incredible as it may seem, Mrs. Fawcett actually repeats such statements 24 years later in a book she has recently issued, entitled *What I Remember*. She devotes a chapter to South Africa, boldly starting out with the blatant inaccuracy that the Boers declared war on Dingaan's Day, 16 December 1899. Thus even her dates are not reliable. I have seldom read a more unfair or misleading chapter. She closes it with a bit of ship gossip designed to support her

423

theory that the Boers were bad mothers and that their children died as much outside as within the camps.

Ship stories are, as you know, proverbially unreliable; yet, on the strength of one, Mrs. Fawcett affirmed publicly at the time and now repeats in print that out of six of her grandchildren living with old Mrs. Kruger in her house in Pretoria four died of measles notwithstanding the care received from the outset of their illness. Why did not Mrs. Fawcett verify this story? In 23 years there has been ample time. Through Mrs. Louis Botha, to whom I appealed for verification, these qualifying facts were disclosed: Mrs. Kruger lived in her own private house which was known as the Presidency. Mrs. Eloff and Mrs. Malan and their children were living with her when the old lady died. Some of the children were ill with pneumonia. After Mrs. Kruger's death the Military Authorities wanted to seize this private house for their own use, and sent to say the family must leave. The two mothers replied that their children were too ill to be moved. Their doctor, Dr. Reinhard, testified to this fact. Unsatisfied, the Military sent their own doctor to examine the children with the result that he also said they could not be moved without danger to life. Nevertheless the soldiers were moved into the house and the mothers had no choice but to wrap the sick children in blankets and remove them. As a result *two* (not four) died.

[Boer] children caught prevailing illnesses. The proportion that recovered was higher than in the camps. We have Mrs. De la Reys' full account of her life on the veld from which with all her children she issued in perfect health. And Mrs. Badenhorst (*Tant' Alie*) gives similar information. Many other statements there are written at the time which support this fact.

No, the exhaustion of the families entering the Camps was due to – first, the shock experienced by the sight of the complete destruction of their houses and all they possessed; secondly, by the long journeys with military convoys, without shelter and frequently (as many of their accounts and diaries show) without food being given – these convoys took often a fortnight or three weeks to reach a Camp; thirdly, in the case of families sent from the North to the Colony Camps, there was the terrible journey, usually five days travel in open coal trucks, 34 in a truck, without shelter from sun or storm. Many a pen has described the suffering of these cruelly organised compulsory journeys.

Mrs. Charles Murray and others refuted Mrs. Fawcett's statements in regard to her interview with them, and I was able to deny the story that she "could get no help from the London Committee". My Aunt, Lady Hobhouse, a leading member, knew Mrs. Fawcett, and wrote, herself, inviting Mrs. Fawcett to meet me at her house. She read aloud to me the quite definite and, it must be owned, rather curt refusal she received from that lady. It was so couched as to give the impression of a closed door. I myself have never met Mrs. Fawcett, at least to my knowledge, but years after the war I was told that a lady to whom I was unexpectedly introduced and whose name I did not catch was Mrs. Fawcett.

Her commission did not enter the camps till four and a half months after I left them. It was an interval of rapid whitewashing. They did not see the camps as I had seen them, but nevertheless found a grave condition of things: two-thirds of the people still lying on the bare ground, water supplies still needed, overcrowding. They had to cable for scores of nurses, had to dismiss several superintendents, to order an increase of fuel, and urge upon Kitchener the service of another weekly truck from the coast to provide rice, etc. for the children.

Knowing how matters stood and hearing direct of the vast sums needed in specific camps such as Middelburg to supply the most *pressing* necessaries, it is lamentable to read in Mrs. Fawcett's recollections that Miss Hogg of Dublin had actually (so she writes) "cabled to their committee at home to cease sending out cases of condensed milk, because everything of that sort was already being amply supplied by the Government Authorities". Even if the children had received an *"ample"* supply, which they did not, how many sick and frail adults would have been saved if they could have had some such extras to the desperately bare ration allowed. War neurosis was evidently at work here.

The South African Conciliation Committee at once issued an admirable "Comment" on the report of the Ladies' Commission. This pointed out that the country had "waited from June to February only to hear a re-iteration of the facts then stated". The interval had supplied a tragedy unprecedented in history. It shewed our essential agreement on all practical points.

III E. H. AND EVIDENCE ON THE "KRUGER MILLIONS"

I made no mention of a point which emerged in my conversation with the Colonial Secretary [Lord Alfred Lyttelton, in 1904] and which occupied my mind for some months.

In pleading the lack of money to provide the promised relief for widows, orphans, sick and destitute, Mr. Lyttelton mentioned that there existed Boer funds which were available, and as long as these funds were withheld the English Government would give no more. He affirmed that the Generals – in particular Botha – knew of this money and had control of it. It was the old story of the fabulous gold which President Kruger was accused of carrying off. It was an obscure mix-up of gold sent to Europe before the war and gold sent during the war. I assured Mr. Lyttelton that I had seen much of General Botha and talked intimately with him and I was personally convinced that if such reserves existed, which was doubtful, that he had no knowledge of them and no control. The Minister refused to believe me and said they had official information to the contrary. I could not, of course, contradict him, but I shewed myself unconvinced.

You can understand that I felt this affair should be cleared up, both for the sake of the widows and the removal of a blot on Botha's character. So I told Mr. Lyttelton that I was expecting very shortly to see President Steyn and other leading Boers, that I would speak to them and let him know the result. For I had been planning a visit to Italy, and as you and President Steyn were then at Cannes I had accepted, as you will remember, your invitation to stay a few days with you there. It was after talking to the President, and to Dr. Leyds whom I encountered by accident at Mentone, and Mr. Bredell, President Kruger's Secretary, that I wrote to Mr. Lyttelton, and find the rough draft of the letter still amongst my documents. It ran as follows:

To Rt. Hon. Alfred Lyttelton
I am anxious to refer to remarks you made about certain monies supposed to have been sent from Transvaal to Europe
(*a*) before the war, or
(*b*) during the war.
  I have two reasons for doing so:
First: The supposed existence of this money paralyzes the Government in giving

426

adequate support (as promised) to widows, etc., it having been again and again brought up when that subject is discussed,

(a) between the Boer Generals and Mr. Joseph Chamberlain;

(b) a few months later between Mr. Chamberlain and the Burghers at their meeting in Pretoria;

(c) six months later between Generals Botha and Smuts and Sir Arthur Lawley;

(d) nine months later between the Colonial Secretary (Mr. Lyttelton) and myself, on 15 March 1904 in London.

Secondly: Responsibility for this money is held to rest on the present Boer leaders, especially Botha, and as the Government refuses to accept as final their statement that they know nothing of such monies, a web of suspicion has woven itself about these men which seems an unfair burden for them to bear. My personal friendship and respect for them make me desirous to remove this if possible.

If it were clear that this money either has *never* existed or does not now exist, then

(a) there would be no further excuse for withholding relief from widows and others;

(b) the character of brave men would be cleared.

A. Monies sent *before the war*:

Certain sums naturally left the Transvaal for Europe, viz.

1. For payment of munitions of war.

2. For secret service. With this the Generals had no concern.

B. Monies sent *during the war*:

On this point all the information attainable is negative.

1. General Botha has stated again and again to me and others that he knows of *no* money sent away during the war.

2. General De la Rey said the same.

3. Ex-President Steyn, though unable to speak with so much certainty of Transvaal matters, tells me he is *sure* in his own mind that there was no money to send away – all being needed on the spot. His Government had in all £750 000 from the Transvaal Exchequer – £500 000 when the war began, for initial outlay, and later £250 000. Of this sum the last £25 000 was with great difficulty forthcoming when he went to say farewell to President Kruger on the Portuguese border. A portion of it had to be given in Transvaal bluebacks.

4. Mr. Abraham Fischer has written to the Colonial Office a full letter, which, if referred to by Mr. Lyttelton, will inform him that no gold was sent in the ship suspected by Mr. Chamberlain and that he, Mr. Fischer, never went to Naples to meet it as supposed.

5. Dr. Leyds agrees with Mr. Fischer and states to me that he received *no* monies during the war (rather, he had to send money to the Transvaal) and as Mr.

Chamberlain had every ship well searched that left Delagoa Bay, gold must have been found if it existed.

Mr. H. C. Bredell, acting as private Secretary to the President, agreed with the foregoing statements.

He further wrote me from Mentone, 14 April 1904:

"No money or gold whatsoever – to my knowledge – was ever sent or taken to Europe or elsewhere by His Honour or anyone else for the Government. It is all a myth. The presumption alone is too absurd to believe. I solemnly declare the foregoing to be in strict accordance with my knowledge and contains nothing but the truth. Considering that I have been living with the President since the outbreak of the war and having been every day with him I ought to know something and be able to state the foregoing facts without reserve. It is an absolute falsehood that His Honour ever appropriated Government monies to himself. Our late Government owes the President £40 000."

Thus all are agreed. I added:

If the Colonial Office has *reliable* papers asserting the contrary, why not publish the same? So that Botha and others implicated may meet the charges in detail and have the chance of clearing themselves publicly. So far they have been accused and have given denial. Does not the onus of proof now lie with the Colonial Office?

So much for the supposed monies sent away *during* the war.

Shortly after, I continued my journey to Venice and there my Brother joined me. We discussed the above and his view was that though Mr. Joseph Chamberlain may only have enquired about the distribution of money *during* the war, yet the public mind was confused and it became mixed up with the money admittedly sent to Europe *before* the war. Of this sum it was believed a considerable amount remained unspent. It seemed therefore that what would best clear Botha and his colleagues would be a statement by those concerned with that pre-war fund of the amount of, broadly, the purposes on which it was expended and what balance remains, together with a declaration that the Generals never had control over that money and, if any remains, have not now; consequently they could not produce it for the widows.

I thought that, if not convenient to publish, such a statement might be embodied in a private letter to me or some other person, with the avowed idea of sending it to the Colonial Office so that it could be docketed with the other papers and the affair finally cleared.

I embodied this suggestion in a letter to Dr. Leyds, asking if he would do as suggested. Mr. Kruger himself was obviously too old and weak to be troubled; he was indeed within a few months of his death, otherwise I would have asked him.

428

I ended my letter to Dr. Leyds:

"As it is I turn to you as the one knowing most about it to help set the matter right and in this simple way to promote the two objects in view."

It was a great disappointment to me that, after consideration, Dr. Leyds finally excused himself from doing this. In the first place, he wrote that he could not act without the consent of others across the water, and in addition he felt such profound distrust of the English Government, such certainty that they would never be satisfied, never exonerate their former enemies and not give a penny more for the widows and orphans, that he thought, on the whole, silence was preferable in a matter that after all did not concern the English Government and into which they had no right to enquire.

Thus failure was written on my efforts to remove this bar to adequate relief for your widows. I never heard the end of the matter, or how General Botha succeeded in clearing himself and his colleagues in the eyes of the Colonial Office. As he was so highly esteemed in later days he must somehow have removed the unfortunate suspicions.

IV. E. H.'S APPEAL TO THE *SOUTH AFRICAN NEWS*, 16 AUGUST 1903

Widespread distress – Urgent appeal to Cape Colonists.

Miss Hobhouse's inquiries
Miss Emily Hobhouse writes to the South African News *from Pretoria:*

Sir,

I am constrained to appeal for the distressed in the late republics, and I ask leave to do it through your pages.

I am aware that Cape Colony has been already drained to help her kinsfolk in the North, and yet I feel there is no choice but to write, with the hope that my words may meet the eye of some who have not yet given or who can afford to give again. For the people are famished.

I have travelled from district to district, farm to farm, stable to stable, ruin to ruin, passing in and out among the people sheltering in their broken homes, sharing bed and board. At first, as I travelled in the Western Orange River Colony, and found people in want, I hoped that it was but a stray case here and there, for which some special reason might account, but proceeding, I found it even worse, the poverty deeper, the distress more widely spread. Far north in the Zoutpansberg, at Louis Trichardt, the Low Country, and around Pietersburg, are people who are starving. About Roos Senekal, Dullstroom, and Belfast families also are starving. Throughout Frankfort, Reitz, Lindley, Heilbron and other parts people are starving indeed.

How can it be otherwise? Lord Kitchener's work was done so well that the land was swept bare as the seashore. To their ruined heaps and blackened walls the people came, and strove to begin afresh. Oxen were scarce, so in many places women and children were yoked to the plough. The harvest failed, a drought has supervened. Except in the North Transvaal, there are no vegetables. The few bags of mealies reaped could not be sold, but had to be kept for food, thus no money was earned. On 1 June the Repatriation Boards closed their food supplies, except for cash payments. The people have no cash. They have lived on the remainder of the mealies, watching them lessen in the bags, eking them out with one meal only a day. These are finished now, and whole families sit face to face with starvation.

Many instances rise before me as I write. A man, his mother-in-law of 65, and his little girl of 11, walked over 10 miles into town for help. They had eaten nothing that morning, and only one meal the day before. For months they had had nothing but mealies, and the end of these had now come. A young girl of 19 came to me; the minister and his wife could do nothing for her, the strain of their resources had been too great. At home were 10 children and a sickly father. The girl was blue round the mouth and eyes, and nearly fainted. She had eaten nothing that day, one meal the day previous, and nothing but mealies since the last of May. Now none were left. Before she could talk I had to buy food and feed her; then some colour returned to her face. Two young women called; they had come from far – had eaten nothing – their father was 72 – nothing was left them. A young wife came and begged to speak to me. Laying her hand on my arm, she drew me aside. Then she could not speak; her face and lips were very white. More by a look than words she told me a woman's greatest secret – her first-born was coming, and there was not even a shawl to wrap it in. She and her husband had nothing. For months they had lived on mealies alone – only half a bag remained. She craved for a bit of fresh meat. I could not get it for her.

I visited a family – there were 11 children in the house; the father had tramped 30 miles away to try and find work. The mother was left with the ebbing bags of mealies and her hungry brood. One meal a day, and the end very near. Two old people came into town. They were in a similar condition. The minister's wife gave them a joint of salt meat. Going home, such was their craving, they ate half of it raw. All these people and hundreds of kindred instances are clean, neat, industrious folk, many of them of superior class, well known to their ministers, once possessing abundant flocks and herds, and solid comforts.

It is the starvation of perfect respectability which is most heart-rending to witness. Not *bijwoners* and tenant farmers only are today in need for food, but many a landowner also.

Large numbers have been pressed by want into the towns, already filled with the impoverished. The women hope thus to earn cash by washing, ironing, or needlework, but everyone wants to earn, and few can afford to employ. Men tramp hither and thither in search of work, which is rarely to be found. The relief works employ some, but at a wage which can only procure bare food, and no clothes or other necessaries. In any case the employment of a large number of men at these places is to be deprecated. It takes them off the land, thus retarding its cultivation, and tends to create a population of navvies and paupers. The very existence of these camps is an outward and visible sign of the failure to "repatriate" the people. If the country is to prosper they must be helped on the land not off it.

I have done my best to feed the people, spending most of my funds in bags of meal. I can at present neither repeat the gift, nor make it go all round. Individual ministers have collected large sums in the Colony, but these are expended, though they have supported the people thus far. There is a famine of money in the land, and half a famine of food, and it is yet six months to the harvest.

Who is going to help?

There is no doubt that Government must feed the people, and feed them freely.

So far every morsel thence received was accompanied by a bill, and the people shrink from incurring further debt, which they cannot pay. Only in rare instances have military receipts been paid, and "compensation" is but a ghostly shadow in a future which never draws near. Thus money they cannot get.

The people are very quiet; the hungrier they are the more restrained they seem. The women retain their composure, though the moisture is in their eyes when they describe their condition, and I have seen tears well up in the face of many a stalwart Boer at the mere prospect of a bag of meal. A great depression is setting upon them, which, one fears, as one door after another closes, may result in the loss of hope.

There are two ways in which to give help: Money for a sufficient supply of meal to maintain life until the Government undertakes the duty, and further help devoted to a plan for rekindling hope. It is proposed, and we hope to work it in some places, to purchase a team of mules or oxen, a "charity" team, which shall go in turn from farm to farm, ploughing for all, and there are many who have no animals.

The rains should soon be here, and that will be the moment to carry out this scheme. From £100 to £120 will be required to purchase the teams for each district, and it should be provided without delay. Farmers and ministers agree that could this plan be carried out, and men could see a chance of a summer crop, hope would revive.

I have not touched on all the other things – clothing, house material, furniture, etc. which are lacking everywhere. A Boer can do with very little, and I would be the last to destroy the power of endurance and proud spirit of independence which characterise the race. I only ask that his wife and children may be kept alive and he himself be kept in hope, till he can see the fruits of his labour and joy with the joy of harvest.

Any subscriptions can be sent to me, care of the Standard Bank, Pretoria.

c/o Standard Bank
Cape Town

Private

To the Minister and kerkraad *of* ....

Dear Sirs,

I am leaving South Africa shortly and for the moment shall be unable to do more in the matter of assisting your people. But I leave with the hope that the machinery is in better working order whereby relief shall be attainable for those in need of actual food and that both by the aid of the Government, and through the teams of oxen provided here and there by the bounty of the Cape Colony, ploughing may be possible on a large scale.

The order of 1 June, to stop Repatriation supplies except for cash payments, which has resulted in so much misery, has now been reversed, and a fresh order issued early in September, that food be again supplied on credit as before. Thus no one need be without *some* food.

I think it would be a great help if you kindly see that your people know this, lest the regulation remain on paper only. This opportunity being open for all I feel we have no longer any right as far as food is concerned to appeal at this moment to charity.

Besides this I would call you attention to the "Widow Scheme" detailed in Circular 120 probably now in your hands, also the recent Circular 139 which is of great importance. Please secure copies.

Circular 120 speaks of the free gifts for widows, and *I understood in conversation with the Government* that in cases of widows living in towns or for whom for any reason the gifts mentioned are not suitable, an equal value should be given in another form, if the minister or other friend took the trouble to probe individual cases and find out what would help them best. I also asked if the scheme was not equally applicable to those numerous cases where the bread-winner is incapable, from age, sickness or infirmity. I received the assurance that it should also cover their cases.

I think it rests with the clergy and *kerkraads* to see that in their respective parishes these circulars are fully known to the people concerned and acted upon. There is every right to *insist* as they must be looked upon as the tardy fulfilment of Mr. Joseph Chamberlain's public promise that he would care for the widows and orphans and destitute. This announcement of his last year made it impossible for the Boer Generals to collect more funds in Europe on their behalf.

433

It seems to me if this large class of the needy is thus relieved, and if the able-bodied at present without cash are able to obtain food on credit, there should not be much further need of charity in that line, excepting where the Repatriation occasions great delay in the fulfilment of the Government promises.

I think that where the delay is undue the minister should at once advise the Head Office at Pretoria. Charitable help where still available can then be devoted to clothing, house material (windows and doors), and furniture or stock.

In districts where a charity team has been given, care should be taken that this in no way supplants or stands in *lieu* of the Government work in that direction, for it is intended to supplement and make more plentiful the food supplies of the parish.

To sum up, the position I think is this: The Government has made promises and made them on paper. Through bad administration or through careless sub-offi-cials these may not be carried out. Still, holding them in our hands, printed and officially issued, they are powerful instruments with which to fight for the well-being of the people. A policy of gentle but firm insistence and persistence may bring about much improvement.

My thanks are due to numbers of the ministers who, with their wives, have given me such generous and warm-hearted assistance in my otherwise impossible work. I earnestly beg that if the promises alluded to are not fulfilled, if the drought con-tinues and therefore if great distress ensues, the ministers will be so good as to write full details of the trouble to me.

I am with many thanks
Yours very sincerely
Emily Hobhouse.

Notes

PREFACE

1. Towards the end of her second visit to South Africa she was, however, confessing to her brother: "I owe such lots of letters – but I fear the Afrikaner powerlessness to write letters is falling upon me, and it seems a greater and ever greater effort. Life here is on a different pattern."
2. Edmund Waller (1606–1687), in *On the foregoing divine poems*.
3. Maurice Maeterlinck (1862–1949), in *L'Oiseau Bleu*.

OUTLINE OF E.H.'S LIFE

1. Trelawny, Trelawney – the spelling of the family name appears somewhat arbitrary. The famous bishop of the 17th century, whom E. H. claimed as an ancestor, was Trelawny, and so was her mother. Her brother Leonard however is sometimes credited with Trelawney as a second name.

THE CAMPS

INTRODUCTION

1. Sir Alfred Milner (1854–1926) had in 1897 become governor of the Cape and British high commissioner in South Africa. An ardent imperialist, he was largely responsible for the British Government's war policy towards the republics.
2. Founded on 1 November 1899, three weeks after war was declared, the South African Conciliation Committee (SACC) publicly stated its aims on 15 January 1900:
    (i) To watch South African affairs with a view to issuing accurate intelligence and taking such other steps as may be necessary for enabling the public to form a just estimate of the political questions affecting the colonies and states of South Africa.
    (ii) To advocate the paramount importance of a policy, the object of which

437

shall be to re-establish goodwill between the British and Dutch races in South Africa by a full recognition of the just claims of both, and the urgency of a pacific settlement upon these principles of the deplorable conflict between this country and the two republics at the earliest moment when such a settlement is practicable.

3. It was more moderate in tone than W. T. Stead's Stop-the-War movement.

4. She still helped, however, with the election campaign of John Burns who, as one of the radical Liberals, retained the hotly contested seat Battersea in the khaki election of 1900.

5. E. H.'s flat in Rossetti Mansions, Chelsea, was within walking distance of the Courtney house in Cheyne Walk.

6. Frederic Harrison (1831–1923), historian and philosopher, was a founder-member of the South African Conciliation Committee.

7. E. H. was in America, doing social and church missionary work in Minnesota, when the Cuban insurrection broke out in 1895 and the new USA "yellow press" whipped up American sentiment against Spain, resulting in the Spanish-American War of 1898.

8. The siege of Mafeking, 13 October 1899 to 18 May 1900.

9. Derived from Mafeking as a supposed present participle, the verb "to maffick" came to mean "to indulge in extravagant demonstrations of exultation on occasions of national rejoicing" – *The Oxford English Dictionary*.

10. Joseph Chamberlain's Conservative Party was opposed by the Liberals, themselves divided between Liberal Imperialists (Limps), led by Sir Edward Grey, and the anti-Imperialist "Little Englanders".

11. Samuel Cronwright-Schreiner – husband of the writer Olive Schreiner – was in England as the first one-man mission to enlighten the British public on South Africa, from the Boer perspective. Well-spoken, well-educated, he had been invited by J. A. Hobson, then Johannesburg correspondent of the *Manchester Guardian*. Most of his tour was arranged by the SACC and W. T. Stead's Stop-the-War Movement and his expenses were paid largely by well-wishers in Britain, among whom was Percy Alport Molteno. In the prevailing war hysteria a York paper put out the poster: "Britons! A Boer is among you!" (Arthur Davey, *The British Pro-Boers, 1877–1902*, pp. 93–6.)

12. A. P. Cartwright.

13. *A Greeting*, William Watson's poem – no sonnet – was printed as a leaflet and distributed at the Queen's Hall meeting.

14. A protest meeting against the war by Cape women held at Paarl on 27 June 1900 in a fourth and final resolution thanked the women of London "voor hunne hulp en sympathie met de zaak van vrede in Zuid-Afrika" (for their help and sympathy with the cause of peace in South Africa). (*Ons Land*, 28 June 1900, p. 3).

15. Notably Mrs. C. P. Scott, whose husband was editor of the *Manchester Guardian*.

16. Mainly on Mrs. Steyn's initiative, a fund was started for a house for E. H. and £2 300 was collected in small sums such as half-crowns. It enabled her to buy Warren House, a cottage in St. Ives on the Cornish coast. She lived there from 1921–3, when she sold it to move to Tor Gardens on Campden Hill in London, in order to be within better reach of her friends.

17. One year, for example, an iced birthday cake, more than fifty pots of jam and forty pounds of dried fruit were among the gifts, each contribution bearing the name of and often an appreciative and affectionate little note from the sender. Orange Free State towns took turns to make up these annual "Wonder Boxes".

18. E. H. was born in the rectory of St. Ive, where her father, archdeacon Reginald Hobhouse, was the Anglican rector from 1844 to his death in January 1895. She thereupon left the village where she had spent the better part of her first 35 years, and never returned to it.

19. He gained the seat as a Liberal Unionist.

20. Kipling's *Recessional* begins:

> "God of our fathers, known of old,
> Lord of our far-flung battle line,
> Beneath whose awful Hand we hold
> Dominion over palm and pine –
> Lord of Hosts, be with us yet,
> Lest we forget – lest we forget."

21. The deputation consisted of Professor P. J. G. de Vos of the Dutch Reformed theological seminary at Stellenbosch, the Reverend R. P. Botha of Richmond and the Reverend P. L. du Plessis of Cradock, with D. J. de Wet of Prins Albert as secretary. In England they were joined by the Reverend Adriaan Moorrees of Paarl (a cousin of Mrs. Koopmans-De Wet). They were the first Afrikaners E. H. met, and the Reverend Moorrees remained a friend, whom she later visited at Paarl, (see Arthur Davey, *The British Pro-Boers 1877–1902*, pp. 98–103, for an account and evaluation of their mission).

22. On 1 September 1900 E. H. wrote to her friend Mrs. Charles Murray of Cape Town:

"I am now in a great grief at the decision of the Deputation to return to South Africa. Fearing that their work was too desultory and their meetings sprung too suddenly on the large towns, I drew up a scheme of work for them and offered to organize them entirely. Beginning 15 September and plodding steadily on and working on the pioneer system, I calculated we should have made a fairly comprehensive tour of England by Christmas . . ."

The offer was not accepted.

23. John Morley (1838–1930), barrister and editor of, successively, the *Literary Gazette*, the *Fortnightly Review* and the *Pall Mall Gazette*, entered the House of Commons as a Liberal in 1883. He was the first British politician of stature to

439

warn against the coming war, and many now looked to him to vigorously lead the anti-war movement. (See also p. 463.)

24. In the Afghan War, 1879–81.

25. E. H. quotes extensively from them in her book *The Brunt of the War and where it fell* (chapter 1).

26. Miss E. D. (Dorothy) Bradby, p. 520.

27. Henry Scott-Holland (1847–1918), canon of St. Paul's Cathedral in London, editor of *Commonwealth* (1895–1917), a paper devoted to "the study of various elements of social life in the light of Christianity".

28. Mrs. Charles Murray, p. 532. E. H. asked particularly for the opinion of Mrs. Marie Koopmans-De Wet, Mrs. Anna Purcell and Lady De Villiers, wife of the chief justice. In Britain she found that "those who have grasped the facts feel it deeply and are keen to help. On the other hand, some say it is the duty and business of the Government to supply them with all the necessaries of life and that a fund collected specially would only make the Government shirk its duties. I want so much to know by return post what you all think, and any facts you can send me as to the probable number of sufferers in the two States. And whether clothing will be acceptable even if money be considered undesirable . . ."

29. On Hofmeyr, the Afrikaner statesman, see p. 475; on De Vos, note 21, above.

30. Joshua Rowntree (1836–1925), chocolate and cocoa manufacturer, was a prominent member of the Society of Friends (Quakers). A former MP, he was a member of the Distress Fund Committee and chairman of the Scarborough branch of the S.A. Conciliation Committee. The broader aim of his visit was to "aid in restoring the lost vision of brotherhood between two peoples." But his brother-in-law and fellow-Quaker, J. E. Ellis, an MP closely associated with the Liberal leader, Sir Henry Campbell-Bannerman, had apparently also encouraged him to go to obtain first-hand information on the treason trials of Cape rebels, censorship and the extent of civilian distress and suggestions how this might be alleviated. (Arthur Davey, *The British Pro-Boers, 1877–1902*, p. 169.) His wife and his nephew, Harold Ellis, accompanied him.

31. The following paragraph on Afrikaans has been transposed here from elsewhere in the memoir, as a fitting follow-up on the foregoing.

LETTERS

I

1. Probably the Hottentot Holland range to the east of Table Mountain.

2. A common Cape pronunciation of *meerkat* (Afrikaans), an inquisitive, cat-sized rodent, which makes a charming pet.

3. Among the English-speaking Cape people who sympathized with the Boer

cause and were in touch with British pro-Boers (to whom some of them were also connected by marriage) were the J. W. Sauers, the Curreys and the Merrimans, all of whom were to become E. H.'s firm friends.

4. For the Sauers, see p. 536.

2

1. He was John Henry de Villiers (p. 525).
2. C. P. Schultz – "a kind of Archangel always helping everyone connected with the Afrikaner cause," as Margaret Clark wrote years later – was at the time secretary of the Cape Town printing-firm Van de Sandt & De Villiers which he had joined as an accountant in 1895. A member of the Afrikaner Bond, he became secretary of the "werkend comité" which the Afrikaner parliamentary group and Bondsmen formed immediately upon the outbreak of the war to collect funds for widows, orphans and wounded, so that "the overwhelming desire that fills the hearts of our People to do something for relatives and friends across the Orange and Vaal should be given an opportunity to express itself legitimately." It was at the time greatly feared that there would be an uprising in the Cape. Onze Jan (J. H.) Hofmeyr was the Cape Town chairman of the committee.
  Schultz also acted as secretary for the women's committee which met every week at the Strand Street home of Mrs. Marie Koopmans-De Wet and in which the wives of prominent Dutch Reformed clergymen such as Mrs. Elizabeth Roos, wife of the church administrator Johannes Roos, Mrs. Steytler, wife of the Groote Kerk minister, the Reverend A. I. Steytler, and Mrs. Bernard Marchand served, together with other Cape women, both English- and Afrikaans-speaking.
3. Adrian (Vollie) van der Byl was a brother-in-law of Mrs. Agnes Merriman, John X. Merriman's wife.
4. The motherly, childless Mrs. Roos, who was to be a founder of the Afrikaansche Christelijke Vrouwen Vereeniging, was one of Cape Town's most influential women.

3

1. E. H.'s aunt, Lady Hobhouse, and her cousin Henry Hobhouse, Unionist MP for Somerset East, had given her introductions to Sir Alfred Milner – "well known to our family".
2. Miss Nellie Hauptfleisch (d. 1916) of Stellenbosch, a teacher, was at this stage matron at the Port Elizabeth women's camp. She later became head of the Oranje school for girls which President Steyn founded in Bloemfontein and head of girls' hostels in Cape Town and Stellenbosch (Harmonie). For her work in the Port Elizabeth camp she received great appreciation, both from the inmates and the administrators.
3. Ellie Cronjé, daughter of General Piet Cronjé, and her mother had been sent

to Wellington by the military authorities. From there she wrote to her former teacher Miss Hauptfleisch (see above), and described how their farm Welgelegen in the Winburg district had been burnt by the military:

". . . that night we slept among the furniture standing on the *werf*, the wind carrying sparks over our heads."

John Morley sent a copy of the letter, dated 6 November, to *The Times*, where it was published on 17 November 1900. (For the full letter, see Emily Hobhouse, *The Brunt of the War*, pp. 53–7.)

4. A useful contact: Dr. Murray (1848–1917) had extensive Orange Free State connections and experience. From 1849–60 he had ministered to the whole of the sovereignty. He was then called to Worcester, in 1860, and to Cape Town, in 1864, and from 1871 until his death worked at Wellington. He founded the Wellington Huguenot Seminary for Girls, modelled on Mount Holyoke Ladies' Seminary in Massachusetts.

5. Miss Kitty Murray had been head of the Dames Instituut (Girls' Seminary – later called Eunice) which the Reverend Andrew Murray had founded at Bloemfontein. She was deposed by the English authorities in 1900 but later invited back (pp. 63–4).

6. Edward Thring (1821–87) as headmaster of the famous English country school Uppingham insisted on a broader educational basis than the classics, and introduced also practical courses, musical education, etc. He was the first headmaster to support the idea of a liberal education for girls. His educational approach, like that of Dr. Murray, was marked by "a deep sense of moral and religious purpose".

7. For the story of the sisters' experiences, see Emily Hobhouse, *The Brunt of the War*, pp. 83–9. They were the daughters of C. M. Neethling of Stellenbosch. Mijnie (Wilhelmina Jacomina) was married to the former Free State judge General J. B. M. Hertzog, and her sister to James Hertzog. The frail baby was Albert Hertzog, who lived to become a cabinet minister in the Republic of South Africa and a controversial figure in South African politics. He died in 1982.

8. On 31 December 1900 Milner was writing in his diary:

"I managed by a gigantic effort to galvanize people into activity today. Prolonged interviews with Sprigg, the General and Rose Innes, finally resulting in a call-to-arms to all loyal citizens by the military. I am also pressing for martial law."

These stern measures were precipitated by republican troops penetrating into the Cape Colony. (C. Headlam (ed.), *The Milner Papers*, vol II, p. 178.)

9. Schoongezicht – the name means just that: beautiful sight/view – was bought by Merriman in 1892. It was a phylloxera-free wine-farm.

10. For her case, see Emily Hobhouse, *The Brunt of the War*, pp. 47–9.

4

1. In a letter to Chamberlain on 31 October 1900 Milner had expressed himself less mildly, saying that he objected to the indiscriminate burning and found it "(1) barbarous and (2) ineffectual", and that he would set his "face against the wholesale destruction" as soon as he took over the civil administration. (*Chamberlain Papers*, 13/1378, quoted by S. B. Spies in *Methods of Barbarism?*, but omitted from Headlam's version of the letter in the *Milner Papers*, vol. II, pp. 166–9.)

2. Lord Kitchener (1850–1916), known as "Kitchener of Khartoum" for his role in the successful Sudanese campaign, became Lord Roberts' chief-of-staff in the early months of the war and succeeded him as commander-in-chief on 2 November 1900. He vigorously pursued the former's "scorched-earth" policy and greatly extended the scope of what were started as refugee camps for burghers loyal to Britain, and their families.

3. "Thousands of Joans of Arc" probably echoes a phrase in a letter which Betty Molteno wrote to her brother Percy in England on 22 October 1900 and which may well have circulated, as did many Cape letters of the time, in E. H.'s pro-Boer circles. Miss Molteno wrote:

"The women are magnificent. Numbers of them are literally Joan of Arcs, exulting in the thought of death and the most agonizing suffering, if it can benefit their country."

4. A reply came only on 17 January 1901. Milner had promised to telegraph to Kitchener but wrote instead, to avoid, he said, misunderstandings which were always arising from telegraphic communications, and in view of the "fearful block on the telegraph wires owing to the military use of them".

5. E. H.'s cousin Henry Hobhouse (See 3 n. 1.)

6. Confidence could well be expected in a committee consisting of, respectively, the moderator of the Cape Synod of the Dutch Reformed Church, the chief justice of the Cape Colony, and the speaker of the Cape legislative assembly.

7. On Leonard and Kate Courtney, see p. 523.

Kate Courtney, E. H. says, cheered her with her account: "I must tell you what your old aunt said when I lunched with them. Talking of you, I expressed a slight fear (forgive me) that you might be imprudent, and Lord Hobhouse said 'Oh well, we've tried prudence and we've tried caution – perhaps a little imprudence may do better!'"

5

1. The Loyal Ladies' League/Guild of Loyal Women thought of themselves as non-partisan – "they belong to no party, only demand that those that join must recognize that they are daughters of the British Empire," the *Bloemfontein Post* summed up in its leader on 4 February 1901. Lord Milner considered them "quite sensible and not at all anti-Dutch" (C. Headlam, *The Milner Papers*, p.

232). According to their delegate in Britain, Mrs. K. H. R. Stuart, "they felt that a crisis had come which called on all women true to Queen and Country to bestir themselves and to throw their womanhood's loving gentle influence upon the right side." (John Fisher, *That Miss Hobhouse*, p. 136.)

2. Harry and Ethel Currey lived at Pinewood in Rondebosch. Harry Latham Currey (1863–1945), a former secretary of Cecil John Rhodes, Consolidated Goldfields and the British South Africa Company, was a member of the Cape house of assembly from 1902–10.

6

1. As a member of the Cape committee for the Distress Fund. (Letter 4.)
2. Within weeks of this Sir Henry collapsed on the voyage to England, having followed Sauer and Merriman on their peace mission. Carried off the boat, he spent six weeks in hospital.
3. After the second invasion of the Cape Colony by generals J. B. M. Hertzog and P. H. Kritzinger, which increased fears of a Cape uprising, martial law was on 7 January 1901 proclaimed in the districts of Stellenbosch, Paarl, Malmesbury, Piquetberg, Tulbagh, Clanwilliam and Calvinia.
4. P. A. M. Cloete.
5. The South African Party met in Cape Town on 7 January and appointed J. W. Sauer, John X. Merriman and J. H. (Onze Jan) Hofmeyr – the latter already in Europe for reasons of health and his honeymoon – as a delegation to bring the state of affairs in South Africa and their possible consequences to the notice of the British public and parliament.
6. Since martial law had been proclaimed in the Stellenbosch district that very day, there was a real danger that Merriman would be prevented from returning to Cape Town if he were to go to his farm in the Stellenbosch district. Dr. Andrew Murray was at this time refused a pass to go to Cape Town from Wellington.

7

1. The Van der Merwe farm Mooihoek was two hours on horseback from Bethlehem. (Emily Hobhouse, *The Brunt of the War*, pp. 62–8.)
2. Under the heading "Vrouwen Beschoten" ("Women fired upon") *Ons Land* on 24 November 1900 carried the following paragraph:

"Op eene plaats liet Genl. French vijf kanonnen op een huis richten waar verscheidene families in gevlucht waaren. Een soldaat zeide 'but General, there are women and children in the house too' . . . Vloekende zeide hij 'I don't care. Shoot the beggars. Afrikanerdom must be wiped of [*sic*] the Earth'. Met de vijf kanonnen schoten zij het huis aan stuk zoodat de bommen de vrouwen en kinderen uit de huis dreven en lieten hen zoo liggen zonder te zien of er een bij was die nog leefde . . ." (On one farm General French had five cannon directed at a homestead into which several families had fled. A soldier said "But General, there are women and children in the house, too." He cursed and said "I don't care. Shoot the beggars. Afrikanerdom must be wiped off the Earth." With the five cannon they shot the house to pieces, the bombs driving the women and children out of the house, and [they] let them lie without ascertaining whether there was one left alive among them.)

This was a transcript from a letter that had been forwarded to *Ons Land*'s editor, F. S. Malan, by Joel Krige of Caledon. Malan, on the point of leaving on holiday, had given instructions that the letter be published but all names deleted. General J. D. P. French's name was apparently overlooked and Malan was, on his return to office, arrested and sentenced to one year's imprisonment for criminal libel of General French.

J. de Jong, editor of the *Worcester Advertizer*, and J. A. Vosloo, editor of *Het Oosten* in Somerset East, who had both taken over the *Ons Land* report, were also sentenced. While Malan was in prison, C. P. Schultz, secretary of *Ons Land*'s publishers Van de Sandt & De Villiers, was acting-editor.

3. P. 442, note 10.

4. Kitchener's telegraph to Milner on 17 January read:

"I was asked from home whether I would distribute funds among the Boer refugees kept out of their homes by the Boers. I willingly agreed to do so, but no funds arrived. Probably Miss Hobhouse is the bearer. I have no objection to her coming as far as Bloemfontein, but I cannot allow her further north at present. I hope this will be clearly understood. I should also prefer that she were not accompanied by a Dutch lady. There are numbers of ladies in Bloemfontein who will give her every assistance.

"If she has any funds that she could pass to me I would have them distributed in camps north of Bloemfontein by the military governors and Colonel Flint, the controller of refugee camps, and receipts sent her. £1 000 would be very acceptable."

E. H. carried this letter with her everywhere, as well as a letter of authorization from Milner, dated 21 January 1901, saying that he was "quite willing that she should visit any refugee camp either in T.V. or the O.R.C. if the Military will allow it". Since Kitchener approved of her going as far as Bloemfontein Milner said he did not think there could be any difficulty about her visiting camps anywhere on the railway line south of Bloemfontein. "In any case," he wrote, "you can show this letter as evidence that as far as I am concerned such visits are authorized and approved of."

5. Backed by her impressive credentials, E. H. was assigned a bogie truck capable of holding twelve tons of goods by Colonel C. T. Cowie.

6. Adriaan van der Byl, head of customs.

7. Leonard Hobhouse's wife (p. 528–9).

8. On 1 December 1834.

1. Beside clothing, E. H. took food and bedding to the value of "only about £300, the sum I had myself collected before leaving England".
2. At Nooitgedacht, on 15 December 1900, General R. A. P. Clement's troops were surprised by Generals Botha, Smuts and De la Rey while encamped in a narrow Magaliesberg ravine and forced to retreat with a loss of 600 men. The memorial stones were packed the next day, Dingaan's Day.
3. Charles Fichardt, the eldest of the six children of Gustav A. Fichardt of Bloemfontein and his wife Caroline (p. 526). Paardeberg was the first major British victory of the war, Lord Roberts capturing 4 049 Transvaal and Free State burghers.
4. Negotiations between President Kruger and Sir Alfred Milner (31 May – 5 June 1899), in a final effort to prevent war between Britain and the Boer Republics.
5. The first bulletin that "the Queen has not lately been in her usual health" went out on 19 January 1901. She died three days later.

1. E. H.'s own footnote to the letter says "these were daily added to, till the camp contained some 6 000 souls".

1. Vasili Vasilieviech Verestchagin (1824–1904), Russian genre and battle painter.
2. Mrs. Caroline Fichardt (p. 525–6).
3. Major-General G. T. Pretyman, military governor of Bloemfontein, also had general control over the civil administration of the occupied parts of the Free State.
4. Kaya Lami, across the street from Bloemfontein's old Dutch Reformed *Tweetoringkerk* – historic double-steepled church – and next to G. A. Fichardt's general store. For Ella Fichardt, later Mrs. Percy Fischer, the scent of loquat trees would always bring back memories of the Kaya Lami garden and she would remember the sweet scent of freshly cut flowers, turpentine and beeswax as characteristic of the house itself. Mrs. Steyn, the president's wife, would in old age recall how one could smell the violets in the *voorhuis* of Kaya Lami right across the street on the market-place. (Karel Schoeman, *Bloemfontein*, p. 144.)
5. Psalm xvi:6.
6. Ella, then ill, and Maude (p. 48).
7. Major R. B. Cray.
8. Mrs. Philip Botha, born Stegmann. Her sister Hester lived in Cape Town. Philip Botha had been landdrost (magistrate) at Philippolis and became assistant-commandant-in-chief with De Wet's forces. Later, when Mrs. Botha was in Cape Town, Agnes Merriman, writing to E. H., said:

"They tell me that when your name is mentioned, her whole face lights up."

9. British Intelligence in London conceived the plan of employing educated Boers who knew the country to go among the commandos and induce them to surrender by "dissipating lies spread among them about the character and intention of the British" and by convincing them of the futility of their hopes of foreign intervention on the side of the Boers.

10. Mrs. Herbert Chitty was, with Dorothy Bradby, E. H.'s chief helper in England with the Distress Fund and clothing for the camps. Her house was for many years crammed with clothing to be sent off to the camps. (Arthur Davey, *The British pro-Boers, 1877–1902*.)

11. These, as they existed before 16 January 1901, are given by E. H. in an Appendix to *The Brunt of the War*. There were, she showed, two categories, the Refugees and the Undesirables.

(a) "Refugees"		*(b) "Undesirables"* (families who had some member with the Boer forces)
Flour/meal	1 lb. daily each	3 lbs. daily each
Meat	¾ lb. daily	1 lb. twice a week
Coffee	1 oz. daily	1 oz. daily
Sugar	2 oz. daily	2 oz. daily
Salt	½ oz. daily	½ oz. daily

Children under six, each		*"Undesirables"*
Flour/meal	½ lb. daily	½ lb. daily
Meat	½ lb. daily	½ lb. twice weekly
Milk	¼ tin con. milk daily	¼ tin daily
Sugar	1 oz. daily	1 oz. daily
Salt	½ oz. daily	½ oz. daily

12. Sir John Hamilton Goold-Adams (1858–1920), an Irish-born professional soldier, had served in Southern Africa since 1884; he was in charge of the town guard in the siege of Mafeking and mentioned in despatches. He resigned from the army in December 1900 and soon after took over the civilian administration in the Orange River Colony. In this capacity he was liked and respected by the Boers for his approachable, sympathetic and just if stern administration.

13. The official residence of the lord mayor of London is known as Mansion House. A mayoral collection had been made for the British refugees from the war zone, who were then in coastal camps. The assumption here is that another such collection would meet the needs of the Boer "refugee" camps.

14. Black farm labourers and their families were brought in from the farms in large

numbers, having been made destitute by the destruction of crops and stock animals. The Black "refugee" camps were started at about the same time as those for the Boers. By the end of 1900, when E. H. arrived in South Africa, the authorities had placed some 400 Blacks in the so-called Kaffir Camp at Bloemfontein. By the end of May 1902, 115 700 Africans had been settled temporarily in 66 refugee camps, and 14 154 Black refugees are recorded as having lost their lives in the camps: in December 1901 the annual death rate reached 380 per thousand (436 in the ORC camps), a rate of mortality more severe than that of all the "white" camps in any one month. (Peter Warwick, *Black People and the South African War*, pp. 145–53.)

E. H. drew repeated attention to these camps and e.g. in Bloemfontein suggested that the Guild of Loyal Women look into them, since she herself could not do that as well.

15. W. Burdett-Couts was sent out by *The Times* to inspect army hospitals, following shocking reports on their conditions. His articles resulted in the appointment of a royal commission which not only led to considerable immediate improvement but also to important reforms after the war. The members of the commission were created Knights Commander of the Bath (KCB).

16. Bishop Alan Blecher Webb had been in Bloemfontein since 1871.

17. Bishop Edmund Hobhouse (1817–1904) of New Zealand, was an elder brother of E. H.'s father.

18. Mrs. Fichardt, of English-speaking Grahamstown stock, was an Anglican and thus in his diocese.

19. The writer, a passionate protagonist of the Boer cause (pp. 537–8).

20. Nurse Kennedy, daughter of a clergyman near Salcombe in England – "small, delicate and full of pluck". (Letter 17.)

21. Mrs. Fawcett's Ladies Committee investigating the concentration camps in South Africa in the latter half of 1901 comment:

"The heavy part of the death-rate in the camps is that of children under five. It is not because they are in the camp, but because war has exposed them to poisonous conditions of water and atmosphere, and has deprived them of food suitable to their tender age. More is being done for them in camp, ten times more in the way of skilful doctors and feeding and nursing than could have been done for them had they remained on their fathers' farms." (*Report of the Ladies Committee*, Imperial Blue Books, CD 893, p. 15.)

22. The Reverend J. G. Grosskopf of the Berlin Missionary Society, stationed at Bethany near Edenburg, distributed a great deal of relief in the burgher camps as well as to farmers with money sent to him from Munich and elsewhere in Germany. (Lawrence Richardson's *Selected Correspondence*, p. 130.) He was the father of the early Afrikaans authors E. B. and J. F. W. Grosskopf, the Stellenbosch economist and amateur dramatist.

23. Adriaan Hofmeyr, former minister of the Dutch Reformed Church in Wynberg,

was suspended by his church circuit for alleged immoral conduct with a music teacher from the congregation and subsequently resigned from the ministry. He became Rhodes' agent in Bechuanaland. When Boer commandos entered Lobatsi he was captured and held as a prisoner-of-war in Pretoria until he was put over the Portuguese border on 12 May 1900. Invited to a lecture tour of England, he was much in demand as a speaker during the khaki elections of that year. Back in South-Africa, he worked for the British in the war and incurred considerable opprobrium in circles sympathetic to the Boer cause. "That hypocritical sneak", John X. Merriman's outspoken mother called him, while J. H. (Onze Jan) Hofmeyr, in a letter to E. H., referred to him as "that scapegrace of a cousin of mine".

24. Probably C. Pienaar, a civilian tried at Bloemfontein on 25 September 1900 for murder or accessory to murder, and hanged on 5 November 1900.

25. After President Steyn joined De Wet's commando, Mrs. Steyn and her four young children fled from the Free State presidency three days before Bloemfontein was taken by Lord Roberts. She spent the next three months trekking across the Free State and the Transvaal to escape capture, and joined up with her husband whenever possible. In July 1900, however, she was arrested at Fouriesburg and taken to Bloemfontein where she lived under strict military surveillance for seven months.

26. The Reverend Colin MacKenzie Fraser, his 21-year old daughter Emeline and "a number of other Dutch partisans" (as Reuter reported on 13 October 1900) were arrested in Philippolis and brought to Bloemfontein. The Reverend Fraser was taken to goal while Emeline had to trudge to the concentration camp. John (later Sir John) Fraser, the Reverend Fraser's elder brother (who was opposed to the Orange Free State's participation in the war and who, as a member of the committee for public security, had handed Bloemfontein over to Roberts) intervened and they were allowed to join Mrs. Steyn in the Zastron Street house allocated to her by the authorities and later to return to Philippolis.

27. Mark vi:7.

12

1. It was a week of commotion and rail disorder. De Wet was expected to break into the Cape Colony across the Orange River but British army headquarters had no idea where. While horses, fodder, ammunition, etc. were hurriedly entrained at Bloemfontein and headquarters were telegraphing Lyttelton that they believed "crossing would be between Bethulie and Aliwal", De Wet had already on 9 February crossed at Zanddrift. Meanwhile train traffic was seriously disrupted by Assistant Chief Commandant C. C. Froneman who near Naauwpoort blew up the railway line in front of and behind the Hoopstad train.

2. The Reverend Carl Christoph Sandrock of the Berlin Mission Society. He

came to South Africa as a young man of about 25 in c. 1857 and worked first at Bethany and then Springfontein. He married Albertina Clara Rossman. They had nine children.

3. Eventually there were three tennis courts. According to Mrs. Johanna Christina von Moltke (born Boshoff) there was "one for the higher classes, one for the hospital, and one for the mixture classes – you must remember there were all classes of people in such a camp." (In a personal interview with the editor.)

4. E. B. Sargant. (Letter 75, note 3.)

5. Johanna Christina (see 3 above) and her sister. With them was their little brother, the later Professor S. P. E. Boshoff, distinguished Afrikaans language scholar.

6. Major J. K. Apthorpe.

7. Dr. C. H. Bidwell, who later married Maude Fichardt.

8. The sanitary situation was such that E. H. said the memory of it would never leave her:

"... after I had visited the other camps and came back [to Bloemfontein] to find the people being brought in by the hundreds and the population rapidly doubling, I called repeated attention to the insufficient sanitary accommodation, and still more to the negligence of camp authorities in attending to latrines. I had seen in other camps that under proper administrative organization all could be kept sweet and clean. But week after week went by, and daily unempted pails stood till a late hour in the boiling sun and the tent homes of those near the sanitary section of the camp were rendered unbearable by the resulting effluvia." (Emily Hobhouse, *The Brunt of the War*, p. 119.)

Heinrich Dahms, a prisoner-of-war brought to the Bethulie camp from Green Point, gives a horrifying description of the primitive latrine trenches into which small children sometimes fell so that they had to be hauled out with great difficulty, and which the aged and weak avoided, especially at night, for fear of a similar fate.

He speaks of the "billions of flies" surrounding these places. (Emily Hobhouse, *Die Smarte van die oorlog*, pp. 310–7).

Dahms also, however, makes the point that "sometimes there were those who had not had included in their upbringing so much love of cleanliness ..." This aspect is stressed by Mrs. Fawcett's Ladies Committee, who found the "pestilential atmosphere of the camps" such that " the Saxon word 'stinking' is the only word appropriate". In estimating the causes of bad health, they said:

"It is necessary to put on record the insanitary habits of the people ... their inability to see what may be comparatively harmless on their farms becomes criminally dangerous in a camp ..."

One camp superintendent who dealt firmly with this vital matter was Springfontein's Captain Gostling. His camp, the ladies found, was very clean and the veld less fouled than in many places. He had "put up a strongly worded notice, in Dutch, in the most central part of the camp, threatening severe punishment for the offence of fouling the ground". (*Report of the Ladies' Committee*, Imperial Blue Books, CD 893.)

9. Former Boer Commandant-General Piet de Wet (1861–1929) was a younger brother of General Christiaan de Wet. Orange Free State-born, he farmed in the Transvaal for some time and fought in the first Transvaal war of independence, taking part in the battle of Majuba. He then returned to the Orange Free State, became a successful farmer and member of the Volksraad. He distinguished himself early in the war, becoming the first general among the younger Free State men.

By July 1900, however, when Bloemfontein and Pretoria had surrendered, he was like many others questioning the advisability of continuing the war against the tremendous odds of numbers and finances. When he suggested surrender to his brother, General De Wet snapped at him "Is jy gek?" (Are you mad?), thereby probably precipitating his subsequent surrender to Lord Methuen. As a "protected burgher" he became the Orange River Colony chairman of the burgher peace committee and was used by Kitchener to try and undermine Boer morale.

The Orange River Colony Volunteers, the ORC equivalent of the Transvaal's National Scouts who were enlisted to fight on the side of the British, was formed under his command in August 1901.

14

1. Mrs. Hannie Blignaut, a sister of President Steyn, was married to P. J. Blignaut, formerly government secretary and in 1896 acting president of the Orange Free State. At the time of the camps she was a power in the Bloemfontein committee. Although she herself was no longer allowed in the camps because she was reported to have talked politics, the camp women were allowed passes to visit her at her house – challengingly called Villa De Wet – and she was a great hand at organizing bazaars and collecting clothing for the camps. On one such occasion, Miss Maynie Fleck remembered, Sir Hamilton Goold-Adams sent her word that he would donate £10 if she sent her girls to collect it. She replied "thank you very much", but she would "not dream of insulting the girls by sending them to ask a favour from you."

As E. H. remembered in a letter to Mrs. Steyn after Mrs. Blignaut's death, "she was a fine woman with a large heart and a great natural ability. Her sense of humour always delighted me. It showed both knowledge and sympathy with Human Nature . . ."

2. Miss Maynie Fleck, daughter of the former surveyor-general of the Free State, was to become secretary of the Boer home industries' weaving schools which E. H. founded after the war.

At this time she was followed everywhere by a trooper if on foot and by a

451

soldier on horseback if on her bicycle rounds to the camps – a saucy and fearless Free State patriot.

3. Mrs. Marie Krause.

4. See p. 77.

5. See 1. on previous page.

6. See Letter 10, note 9.

7. Porfirio Diaz (1830–1915), five times President of Mexico, and Benito Pablo Juarez, Mexican guerilla leader (1806–72). E. H. was a guest at Diaz's presidency in the company of delegates to a medical convention in Mexico City with whom she became friendly when she first visited Mexico with a view to settling there with J. C. Jackson.

8. President Steyn's gold cuff-links were captured some time earlier. Steyn and De Wet's commando were surprised by General Knox just after dawn on 6 November 1900. In the pandemonium that followed Steyn got away on a horse which his adjutant Cornelis du Preez had in readiness tied to a food-waggon and the British captured only his cuff-links. (Thomas Pakenham, *The Boer War*, p. 474.)

9. See Letter 3, note 5.

10. Marlborough College was Leonard Hobhouse's old school; Captain Hume could have been a contemporary of his, to whom he apparently alluded in a letter to E. H.

15

1. Dr. Jane Waterston (1843–1932), Scots-born medical missionary and social worker, was South Africa's first woman doctor. She started practice in Cape Town in 1883 and was much involved in philanthropic work, at this stage especially with British refugees from the war zone who were flocking to Cape Town and for whom she tried to find employment. Her sympathies with the Boer camps were scant, as proved by her letter in the *Cape Times*, of 24 July 1901:

"We ordinary Colonial women who have been through the stress and strain of these last two years are not very favourably impressed by the hysterical whining going on in England at the present time. It would seem as if we might neglect or half starve our faithful soldiers, and keep our civilian population eating their hearts out here as long as we fed and pampered people who have not even the grace to say thank you for the care bestowed upon them. This war has been remarkable for two things – first the small regard that the Boers from the highest to the lowest have had for their womenkind, and secondly the great care and consideration the victors have had for the same, very often, ungrateful women. Let this be well ground into the minds of our English pro-Boers . . . At present there is the danger that the Boers will waken up to have a care for their womenfolk, and will go on fighting for some time, so as to keep them in comfortable winter quarters at our expense, and thus our women and children will lose a few more of their husbands and fathers . . .''

E. H. comments:

"Did ever a woman pen such nonsense? Did she not even know that it had been laid down at the Hague Convention that a belligerent consists of combatants and non-combatants – that in case of capture both have a right to be treated as prisoners-of-war – that they must be humanely treated – that all personal belongings except arms, houses and military papers remain their property – that pillage is prohibited and that a Government is *bound* to maintain its prisoners-of-war? It is further ruled that such maintenance must be on a par with that of the soldiers of the said Government (and this for many months it certainly was *not*; moreover child and infant prisoners-of-war need a different kind of maintenance).

Nothing was asked for in England from the Government beyond the scope of these acknowledged rules, except the privilege of sending volunteer nurses to distribute a few other necessaries of clothes and medicines such as the unusual sex and age of their prisoners needed to preserve life.''

See also Appendix II, p. 423.

Dr. Waterston was appointed a member of the Ladies' Committee investigating the concentration camps in the latter half of 1901 and, whatever her political views, tackled issues like sanitation and hygiene in the camps with impressive dedication and drive.

16

1. Bubonic or oriental plague broke out in the Cape Colony early in 1901. The first official reference to it appears in the *Government Gazette* of 26 February 1901 (p. 470), giving symptoms of the plague.

17

1. *The Bloemfontein Post* of 21 February 1901 carried the following story under the heading "A Lady Missioner":

"Miss Hobhouse who is at present honouring Bloemfontein with a visit is one of these intense beings – a lady missionary. We have only the vaguest idea what Miss Hobhouse's mission is . . . Miss Hobhouse was kind enough to afford to a meeting of ladies, mostly members of the newly founded Women's Guild, an explanation of the precise nature and scope of her mission in Bloemfontein. We understand that the ladies were not convinced and some of them left the meeting very indignant. At Miss Hobhouse's request the meeting was regarded as a private one, therefore no official or authentic account is available to us. We regret this for many reasons. Miss Hobhouse's activities in Bloemfontein have roused curiosity in the male as well as the female breast and there is considerable disappointment that the male public is not to be allowed to participate in the confidence yesterday reposed in its wives and sisters. Curiosity, however, stimulates enquiry, and we have no doubt that in the course of time we shall learn all we are anxious to know about Miss Hobhouse's mission in Bloemfontein and the Bloemfontein Refugee Camp. From one or two stray words which reached our ears concerning yesterday's proceedings – such words as 'soap' and 'filthy English slums' – and a vague digest of Miss Hobhouse's oration of one hour's duration, we imagine that that lady has not been fortunate in the sources of her information, or her choice of mentors and guides since her residence here. We should say rather she has been singularly unfortunate.

... South Africa has suffered enough from impressionists and we do hope Miss Hobhouse is not of their number. The manner, however, according to rumour, in which she set herself yesterday to instruct and correct ladies who have spent their lives in this town, or in South Africa, argues that she is not altogether free from the failings of this pernicious class of historian. But be that as it may, we must certainly, by way of conclusion, express the earnest hope that Miss Hobhouse will not, as part of her mission, teach the refugees at the Refugee Camp, who have so much to be grateful for, to believe that they have grievances – grievances quite unimagined hitherto."

2. Lucy Barbara Bradby. However, she married J. L. Hammond (p. 520) and Misses Mellor and Monkhouse eventually came.

3. In connection with the distribution of clothing in the camps.

4. *Bywoners* were akin to share-croppers i.e. not owners of landed property though living on the land.

5. Several appear in *The Brunt of the War*.

6. The Hague Convention of 1899 laid down international rules for the treatment of non-combatants in war. Article XLVI, for example, said that "family honour and rights, individual lives and property as well as religious convictions and liberty must be respected. Private property cannot be confiscated". Article XLVII read that pillage was "formally prohibited."

7. Samuel Pepys in his *Diary* (1660–9).

8. E. H. quotes "ladies sent out by the Society of Friends" writing on their "religious work at Volksrust", as published in *The Friend* of 30 August 1901:

"This Sunday morning we all went to the Concentration Camp at 10.30 and found a crowd of about 3 000 persons assembled for the service . . . Then Mrs. [Rendel] Harris spoke to them most beautifully and tenderly of the great love which broke down all divisions; in which, as the Apostle said, there was neither Jew nor Greek, and, she might say to them, neither British nor Boer, we were all one in Christ. And down those rugged cheeks the tears simply poured as she spoke to them of the great love of Christ which had constrained Him to leave His throne in heaven . . . It was one of the most touching scenes I have ever witnessed . . . the Benediction was pronounced and then that vast crowd came up and shook hands with each of us, murmuring 'God bless you', 'Thank you'.

Some were completely broken down. One woman said to me 'I have been living for myself, now I will live for God.'

"I never witnessed anything to compare with this, and feel quite unable to describe it. Mr. Knoble told me afterwards that a man had said to him 'I never thought there was anyone in England cared for us as these ladies do'." (*The Brunt of the War*, pp. 198–9.)

The writer was Anna Hogg. (*Southern Africa Quaker Newsletter*, Johannesburg series, No. 117, pp. 3–4.)

For Mrs. Charles Murray's views on Mrs. Harris, the camps and Boer religion, see Letter 35, note 3.

18

1. See the Appendix to E. H.'s *Report of a Visit to the Camps of the Women and Children in the Cape and Orange River Colonies, London 1901.*

2. Afrikaans: *velskoene.*

3. This description prompted the "little gift from my Aunt's old maid for the camp of Springfontein on hearing of the lack there of all such necessaries". (See postscript to letter 29.)

4. On recrossing the Orange River at Bothasdrift on 1 March 1901. Excessive rains had caused them to abandon their second, disastrous, invasion of the Cape Colony.

5. City Imperial Volunteers. In the upsurge of patriotism after the "Black Week" of Stormberg, Magersfontein and Colenso early in the war the Lord Mayor of the City of London raised an amateur battalion of a thousand volunteers as " a gift to the nation". By the end of October 1900 – Lord Roberts having said that the war was "practically over" – they returned to London; their march from the docks was "a kind of victory parade". The Canadian contingent had also sailed for home and the Imperial Yeomanry were about to leave South Africa. (Thomas Pakenham, *The Boer War*, p. 469.)

6. Gostling died of septic pneumonia caught from children in the hospital. His funeral was attended by a great concourse of camp people who said of him "He has been a father to us." (Millicent Fawcett, *What I remember*, ch. XVII.) One of the camp people said to the Ladies' committee that he wished to speak with thankfulness of the kindness and goodness of Captain Gostling, from the beginning of the camp and all along. "Everything he could do for us he has done." (*Report of the Ladies' committee on the concentration camps in South Africa*, Imperial Blue Books, Cd 893, p. 161.)

19

1. Two well-to-do Kroonstad farmers Andries Bernardus Wessels (60), a former member of the Free State Volksraad, and his influential son-in-law Johannes Jacobus Morgendaal were among those burghers of the former republics who

came to believe that there was no hope of victory for the Boers, and that a continuation of the war could only mean senseless death and destruction for their people and their country. They were the first volunteer peace envoys Kitchener sent out to the farms and commandos after he took over command from Lord Roberts. They carried a circular explaining the new treatment promised to burghers who surrendered. Boer officers encountered and took them to De Wet, who promptly had them up before a military court. Their case was however referred to a higher court. Pending that, they were taken along by his commando. Three days later, on 9 January 1901, the Boer camp at Nobelsfontein was disrupted by a dawn report – as it happened, erroneous – that the British were advancing. In the scurry to get away, general Froneman sjambokked Morgendaal for refusing to help with the inspanning of the waggons. Morgendaal seized the sjambok and was shot and fatally wounded. The next day Wessels appeared before a military court presided over by De Wet, was found guilty of treason and sentenced to be shot. On a petition from the old man's friends, President Steyn did not confirm the sentence. At the time of E. H.'s letter, Mrs. Steyn may well have been aware of this. Wessels was freed by British troops on 7 August 1900 (A. M. Grundlingh, *Die 'Hensoppers' en 'Joiners'*, pp. 101–4).

2. SACC pamphlet No. 75 gives the details. On 31 January 1901 a spurious death-notice appeared in *The Times* about one John MacLachlan alledgedly shot on Christmas Day 1899 in the market-place of Harrismith "for refusing to fight against his own countrymen". *The Evening News* of 2 February followed it up with a report calling for vengeance on the "murderers" of MacLachlan and "two comrades".

These three men subsequently showed up in Durban, alive and well.

3. Lord Roberts' 25-day march from the ORC to the Rand with an army of 43 000 men.

4. E. H.'s "pet nephew", the son of Leonard and Nora Hobhouse (p. 528).

5. She had spent some time in Mexico (1896–9) with a view to settling there with her fiancé, J. C. Jackson, a businessman, onetime mayor of Virginia, Minnesota, where she had been doing church and social work.

6. Belmont, 23 November 1899; Modder River, 28 November 1899; and Magersfontein, 11 December 1899.

7. The South African Constabulary, formed by Baden-Powell to police the new colonies and take over the work of the military garrisons once Bloemfontein and Pretoria surrendered, was subsequently put to wider military use (p. 491).

8. Emily Hobhouse, *Die Smarte van die Oorlog*, p. 273 ff.

9. Emily Hobhouse, *The Brunt of the War*, p. 122:

"All through March and part of April 1901 fresh sweeping movements had resulted in the advent of crowds of families to the camps. In all directions I had witnessed this, and read of it as happening elsewhere. I had seen families swept close to the railway line at Warrenton and Fourteen Streams; I had seen a crowded train crawl the whole day into Kimberley – the people, young and old, packed in open trucks beneath a cruel sun, kept in the station without food until late at night, brought up at midnight to bare tents where, groping in the dark, they sought their bundles and lay down, finding no preparation, no food, no drink.

"I had seen them in crowds by railway sidings in bitter cold, in streaming rain, hungry, sick, dying, dead.

"I had seen these patient people packed in train-loads for Bethulie and elsewhere and I never doubted but that every countrywoman of mine, had they seen and known, would have felt as I did, a great sympathy with their forlorn condition and a desire to alleviate it. I believe most of the soldiers round me shared the same thoughts."

See also Letter 25, From the Memoir, pp. 103–4.

10. For Mrs. Hurdus' war-time experiences, see Emily Hobhouse, *The Brunt of the War*, p. 98.

11. Anna Hogg of Dublin and Annie Frances Taylor of London. They belonged to the Society of Friends (the Quakers), and Miss Taylor was a sister-in-law of the Quaker manufacturer George Cadbury, of chocolate and cocoa fame.

Miss Taylor in 1903, when she met Mrs. Fawcett on the latter's second visit to South Africa, urged her to tell her brother-in-law Mr. Cadbury that "the concentration camps were not in the least what we expected them to be".

12. 25 March: Lady Day commemorates the Annunciation.

13. The reference is to employees of De Beers Consolidated Mining Company, formed by Cecil John Rhodes in 1888, and to date still one of South Africa's most prestigious companies.

14. J. B. Robinson, pioneer mining magnate, started life as a travelling wool buyer and made his first fortune on the early Kimberley diggings.

15. E. H. must have mistaken his rank (her letters reveal her to be rather shaky on rank), for Commandant-General Piet Joubert, who disastrously conducted the Natal campaign of the Boers, died in Pretoria on 27 March 1900, aged 69.

16. General F. W. Forestier-Walker succeeded Sir William Butler as general officer commanding the Cape Colony.

17. Nicholas Culpepper (1616–59), astrologer and unconventional physician, was well known for his herbal remedies.

As to the "Boer domestic pharmacopeia", the Ladies' Committee comment, "no doubt parallel horrors could be found in old-fashioned English receipt books of 150–200 years ago." (*Report of the Ladies Committee*, Imperial Blue Books, CD 893, pp. 16–7.)

18. Alida M. Badenhorst whose *Diary* (1880–1903) E. H. translated and had published. See also Introduction to Visit to the ruined districts, note 13.

19. In the *Report of the Ladies Committee*, p. 173 – an incident related by Edwards, the camp doctor at the Orange River camp, who was training ten Boer girls from the camp as probationer nurses and found that he had to insist on personal cleanliness. Incidentally, the ladies found that this camp had no bath-houses at the time "but cement for making them has been promised". The committee's overall view on Boer cleanliness is probably best expressed in their comment on the situation at Mafeking camp: ". . . our own observation showed that there was as much variety in the degree of personal cleanliness as there would be in an English working-class population . . . some were exquisitely clean and neat, others, with the same resources, equally dirty and untidy."

21

1. E. H. was once again staying with Mrs. Charles Murray.
2. Among these was a meeting with Joshua Rowntree (pp. 93, 95), which she remembered as one of the highlights of this Cape Town visit. However, some of her "own doings" which she had "confided to Mr. Rowntree" subsequently appeared in the *Daily News*, in extracts from Rowntree's letters which J. E. Ellis made available to that paper. E. H. believed that these "gossippy paragraphs", cabled back to South Africa, together with the report in the *Bloemfontein Post* (letter 17, note 1) were responsible for a change in the official attitude towards her, which up to that time had been helpful. British papers also carried news of E. H.'s own letters read out at a private subscribers' meeting of the Distress Fund at the house of Lord and Lady Hobhouse in Bruton Street.
3. Letter 19, under 18 March 1901.

22

1. The management, although officially supposed to be civilian, was still partly in military hands until Chamberlain, in November 1901, insisted on full civilian control of the camps. See also Introduction to Work in England, note 13.

25

1. The Hobhouse estate in Castle Carey, Somersetshire.
2. Mafeking, falling at the time under Bechuanaland, for convenience was administered from the Transvaal. So also Aliwal-North, in the North of the Cape Colony, was administered by the authorities of the Orange River Colony.

26

1. His Excellency Sir Alfred Milner.

28

1. The fourth of the nine Sandrock children. She married a British soldier, Captain Fred Fulton, who captured her brother Christoph Theodor when he was with Danie Theron's scouts.

2. General F. W. Maxwell.

3. See pp. 28–9.

30

1. See letter 17, note 2, and p. 520.

2. The Dutch-born South African sculptor Anton van Wouw (1869–1945) had by then made his mark with the Kruger statue, now on Church square, Pretoria. Together with the architect Frans Soff he was commissioned to design a memorial for the women, children and old men who perished in the concentration camps. E. H. drew his attention to Michelangelo's Pieta in St. Peters (see also Letter 98 and note 1).

3. Dahms says the camp people were treated with friendliness at the camp office "ja wij hadden ten latzte met eenen Edelman te doen" (we had at last to do with an aristocrat). Cole-Bowen had the tents taken down and erected at a greater distance from each other, he saw to a better water supply and brought "meer en beetere beschaving ender de menschen, zlechte reden, [h]arden en vloekwoorden durfte niet meer geuiter worden, de Inspector was overal zoo te zeggen, met opgerolde mouwen zonder baaidtje werkte hy zelve mede maar het moeste ook een eider zijn eigen plicht doen" (he brought more and better civilization among the people, bad talk, hard words and swear words dared not be uttered, the inspector was, in a manner of speaking, everywhere, working with his sleeves rolled up and without jacket himself, but everyone (else) had to do his duty too).

Dahms, however, thought that disease had gained such a foothold in the camp that "de verbederingen waren byna te laat gekomen" (the improvements came almost too late).

This passage from the Afrikaans version of *The Brunt of the War* does not occur in the original. (Emily Hobhouse, *Die Smarte van die Oorlog*, p. 316.)

31

1. P. J. Potgieter (1855–1911). Appointed by the South African Republic as the first full-time mayor of Pretoria, he handed over the keys of the capital to the British on 5 June 1900, as instructed by acting president S. W. Burger. He refused to stay on as mayor of the occupied city, and Roberts forced him to leave. With his large family he settled in Dresden for the duration of the war. E. H. kept up the friendship and visited the Potgieters on their farm near Warm Baths in 1903. (pp. 247–8.)

2. The Bay of Biscay, notoriously stormy.

3. The former Reverend Adriaan Hofmeyr. (See Letter 10, note 23.)

32

1. When Mrs. Koopmans-De Wet heard that Sir Alfred and E. H. were both

travelling on the *Saxon*, she anxiously turned to Mrs. Charles Murray and said: "Don't you think that Sir Alfred may talk Miss Hobhouse over?"

Mrs. Murray replied that she, too, might have feared it if she did not know E. H. as well as she did. (Letter of Mrs. Murray to E. H. on 11 May 1901, among the Hobhouse papers in the Steyn collection.)

2. At the Versailles peace talks Milner was, according to Smuts, "all for a fair and generous peace, a peace of understanding which might be lasting and which could heal the dreadful wounds war has caused". (J. E. Wrench, *Alfred Lord Milner*, p. 357.) Milner was himself born in Germany, of British parents, and partly educated there.

3. He assumed the title Lord Milner of St. James and of Cape Town, since he had no estate . . . the first person to "take his title from his lodgings" (J. E. Wrench, *Alfred Lord Milner*, p. 227).

WORK IN ENGLAND

INTRODUCTION

1. See Letter 21, note 2.
2. St. John Brodrick, secretary for war; A. J. Balfour, prime minister.
3. See note 9, below; also Appendix II, pp. 423 ff.
4. They appeared on about 18 June as a penny pamphlet entitled: *To the Committee of the S.A. Distress Fund, Report of a visit to the camps of women and children in the Cape and Orange River Colonies, by Emily Hobhouse.*
5. See p. 534.
6. The Victorian novelist Mrs. Humphry Ward (Mary Augusta, a niece of the poet Matthew Arnold), was best known for her "spiritual romance", *Robert Elsmere* (1888). She believed in a "vigorous Christianity divested of the miraculous element and fulfilling a social gospel" (*Dictionary of National Biography*). She opposed women's suffrage.
7. Because of the pro-Boer sentiments attributed to the controllers of the Distress Fund another relief fund for Boer women and children was started in June 1901, under the auspices of the "loyal" Victoria League. This body had the support of the British Government, and the wives of prominent public men served on it, e.g. Mrs. Margaret Asquith, wife of the later prime minister, Mrs. Alfred Lyttelton, wife of the later colonial secretary, Mrs. Neville Lyttelton, wife of the general. Their fund was to be administered by Mrs. Millicent Fawcett's Ladies' Committee, whose members the government shortly afterwards appointed.
8. A disreputable old body, an unqualified, drunken midwife in Dickens's *Martin Chuzzlewit*, whose large untidy cotton umbrella made her name a household word in England.

9. E. H. had in her interview with Brodrick on 4 June raised the matter of her own return to the camps, which Lord Milner had promised to consider. On the publication of the Government's concessions on the camps shortly after the publication of her pamphlet, she wrote to Brodrick to express her "relief and thankfulness" that women in certain categories she had suggested (see Letter 34, note 3) would be allowed to leave the camps. She pointed out, however, that the "successful carrying out of the instructions of the Government, and the desires of the English charitable Public, will practically depend upon full facilities being accorded to a sufficient number of voluntary but accredited workers."

Early in July Lord Ripon, as acting Chairman of the Distress Fund, approached the Government with a suggestion that ladies should at once be sent to the camps and put forward E. H.'s name as "one prepared to go on this mission". Brodrick replied that there were two more proposals to this effect before the Government. The Government, however, would "shortly send certain ladies to visit the camps and co-operate with the local committees in the distribution of comforts or gifts of money which may be entrusted to them".

"The long delay before sending workers and the rise of the death-rate" combined to make E. H. seek and obtain another meeting with Brodrick, on 18 July. She again urged that she be allowed to return to the camps. Brodrick, on refusing, promised to make his reasons for the refusal clear in a letter.

In the meantime, towards the middle of July, Mrs. Millicent Garret Fawcett, widow of Professor Henry Fawcett, and author, public speaker and ardent feminist, was approached to chair a Government commission of six ladies to visit the camps. They would be Mrs. Fawcett, Lady Ann Knox, wife of General George Knox then serving under Kitchener, Miss Lucy Deane, Government inspector of factories and an expert on infant-welfare; trained nurse and former Guy's Hospital sister Katherine Brereton who had been in charge of a Yeomanry hospital in South Africa; and two medical doctors, Dr. Jane Waterston and Dr. the Hon. Emma Scarlett.

They were to go, E. H. notes in *The Brunt of the War*, "not themselves to work but to make more inquiry".

On 26 July E. H. once again wrote to Brodrick, asking for his reasons for refusing to let her go out too.

"I am continually asked on all sides when I am going out again. It is generally expected that I shall start soon, which is indeed my own desire." If she could not go "it was due to myself to convey to all interested that the failure to do so was due to the Government".

Brodrick replied the next day:

"The only consideration in the selection of ladies to visit the Concentration

461

Camps, beyond their special capacity for such work, was that they should be, so far as is possible, removed from the suspicion of partiality to the system adopted or the reverse."

Her own reports and speeches, he wrote, had "been made the subject of much controversy".

It was amusing to learn, E. H. noted, that "two of the ladies selected, Mrs. Fawcett and Dr. Jane Waterston, had very openly published views in favour of the camps". She referred to "Dr. Waterston's effusion in the *Cape Times*" (see Letter 15, note 1) and Mrs. F.'s review of her report in the *Westminster Gazette* "Penned by great and shining lights in the feminine world, they make one rather despair of the 'new womanhood' – so utterly wanting are they in common sense, sympathy and equilibrium. The Blue-Books they subsequently issued were better than themselves; they moved somewhat to the influence of facts."

Lord Ripon, in a letter to E. H. at the time, said:

"I expect nothing from the mission of Mrs. Fawcett and the rest – but the work is really done and done by you alone. Everything may not be as we wish in the camps but the principal evils have been checked."

For E. H.'s stringent comment on the report of Mrs. Fawcett's Ladies' Committee, see Appendix II, pp. 423–50.

10. The death-rate of children in the Transvaal camps for whites rose from 449 per thousand in July to 544 in August; in the Orange River Colony camps for whites the death-rate rose from 281 per thousand in July to 484 in August. (Emily Hobhouse, *The Brunt of the War*, Appendix B.)

11. See note 9, above. With some obvious envy E. H. commented:

"She and her commission travelled *en luxe* – each had a private compartment, their house for their sole use, a cook and saloon-servant, friends to help, a position of authority; no need for beleaguering offices and waiting for hours for permits and passes, no need to scramble for a seat or a meal – her almost royal train could go from one camp to another with ease and the minimum of fatigue to her party."

12. E. H. wrote this on 29 September, after publication of the August mortality figures. The tenor of the letter is shown by paragraphs like:

". . . Will you now, with the thought before you of those 3 245 children who have closed their eyes for ever since I last saw you, on their behalf, will you not now take instant action, and endeavour thus to avert the evil results of facts patent to all and suspend further enquiry into the truth of what the whole world knows? . . .

"The children must die, die where we have placed them, in their hundreds and thousands, unless war ends and sets them free . . . Will not your own and every parent's heart in England respond to their cry, and beat in sympathy with those mothers who have bravely borne the loss of home and possessions but stand aghast and enduringly resentful as they witness their children swept away? Do we want 'unconditional surrender' at the cost of so much child-life?" (For the full text, see *The Brunt of the War*, pp. 137–40.)

13. After a period of partly civilian and partly military control of the camps since early 1901, Chamberlain insisted that the civil authorities assume full control by 15 November 1901. It was widely believed by contemporaries that this led to radical improvements. Chamberlain demanded satisfaction that "all possible steps are being taken to reduce the rate of mortality especially among children".

The death-rate did indeed drop, from 344 per thousand in October to 313 in November, to 261 in December, to 160 in January, and 69 in February. (Emily Hobhouse, *The Brunt of the War*, Appendix B.)

The readiness with which the recommendations of the Ladies' Committee were implemented under the new dispensation doubtless also contributed to this. By the time their formal report was drafted in December 1901, ten substantial recommendations of the committee had already been carried out.

LETTERS

33

1. P. A. Molteno (p. 531.)
2. See Introduction, note 4.
3. Vigorous as John Morley's condemnation of the war in South Africa had been, he did not, as his friends had hoped, emerge as a strong leader of the anti-war peace party among the Liberals. More a man of letters than an active politician, Sir Henry Campbell's nickname for him was, tellingly, "Priscilla". E. H., Leonard Hobhouse and others made an effort to mobilize him.
4. Mrs. Murray wrote to E. H. on 12 June 1901:

"When Miss Monkhouse and Miss Mellor arrived yesterday I was a little taken aback to find they had some scruples about staying here for fear of too much identifying with our part! Of course I said I would not like to advise anything that would be contrary to their instructions but honestly I could not think it would make the smallest difference to their work whether they stayed here or at a boarding-house in Cape Town for they could only work with one set of people, and those were all sympathizers. So it was finally decided they should remain."

1. Brodrick's own information had apparently been far from up to date or even accurate. On 24 May 1901 he had spoken in the House of "20 000, 30 000 or 40 000 women who had placed themselves in our charge"; of "women coming for food and protection against the Kaffirs" and of "no occasion on which in these camps food ran short". He also mentioned "immense improvements" which had been effected. (*The Times*, 25 May 1901, quoted by E. H. in *The Brunt of the War*, p. 126.)

Following the notes she and her brother had drawn up on her return from South Africa E. H. outlined the condition of the camps – "so far as could be done in one short hour". She told of "the insufficient supplies, attempted improvements swamped by increased numbers; the great sickness and heavy mortality; that the great majority were there by compulsion and were prisoners not allowed to leave though health and life itself were endangered". (Emily Hobhouse, *The Brunt of the War*, p. 127.)

2. See Letters 19 and 50.
3. E. H's suggestions are reproduced in her report to the committee, p. 14:
"In view of the hardening effect of imprisonment upon the hearts and resolution of the women, of the imperfect supply of tents and other shelter, of the scarcity of food, the difficulty of transport and the appalling effect of camp life upon the life and health of the people, and in support of recent statements made in the House of Commons, I urge:

"(i) That all who still can, should at once be allowed to go, viz.
(*a*) those who, themselves penniless, yet have friends and relatives in the Cape Colony;
(*b*) those who have means and could support themselves in the Cape Colony or in towns on the line;
(*c*) those who have houses in towns to which they could go;
(*d*) those divided from their children who wish to find and rejoin them.
"(ii) Free passes into towns for all equally wishing to find work there.
"(iii) Equality of treatment, whether the men of the family are fighting, imprisoned, dead, or [have] surrendered.
"(iv) In view of the size of the camps, the sickness and mortality, a resident minister in every camp, or free access to any one living close by.
"(v) That, considering the countless difficulties ahead, and the already overcrowded state of the camps, no further women and children be brought in.
"(vi) That, considering the mass of the people are women, and seeing the success in organization of the matron at Port Elizabeth, a matron conversant with both languages be appointed in every camp. Many would undertake this voluntarily. I do not consider this so necessary in the case of Norvals Pont.

"(vii) That, considering the congested state of the [railway] line, and the great lack of fuel, any new camp formed should be in a healthy spot in the Cape Colony, nearer supplies and charitable aid.

"(viii) That, because all the above and much more (including economical distribution of clothing) demands much careful organization, detailed work and devoted attention, free access should be given to a band of at least six accredited representatives of English philanthropic societies, who should be provided with permanent passes, have the authority of the High Commissioner for their work, be absolutely above suspicion, and be fully responsible to the Government as well as to those they represent for their work. Their mother wit and womanly resource would set right many existing ills.

"(ix) That the doctor's report on the state of the health of the children in Bloemfontein Camp be called for and acted upon. [Dr. Henry A. Becker's report CD 819, p. 94.]

"(x) That the women whose applications are appended be at once allowed to leave. Their health is failing under the long strain. All three are good, respectable women." [According to a version of E. H.'s notes for action, Mrs. Botha, Mrs. Brink and Mrs. Viljoen.]

The report had another recommendation "unfortunately omitted from those sent to Mr. Brodrick", viz.:

"(xi) That, considering the growing impertinence of the Kaffirs seeing the white women thus humiliated, every care shall be taken not to put them in places of authority."

On Milner's recommendation these suggestions were forwarded to Kitchener.

Reading the suggestions a quarter of a century later, E. H. says they "seem to me very inadequate, making no urgent mention of the increase of food, clothing, water, fuel, tents, etc. But those urgent necessities had been dwelt on in conversation when imploring extra supplies."

4. See p. 123 for the subsequent cancellation of the meeting.

35

1. See note 4, above.

2. Anna Hogg, who had come out with Annie Frances Taylor to follow up the visit of Joshua Rowntree for the Society of Friends, had procured a permit to visit the Volksrust camp.

3. Mrs. Helen Harris, a Quaker – a cousin of Lawrence Richardson and the wife of professor J. Rendel Harris of Cambridge – visited South Africa on her own initiative in 1901. She had Kitchener's permission, with the proviso that "she took some help with her beyond good words".

E. H's Cape Town friends were not entirely at ease about her and their concern throws into relief E. H.'s markedly different attitude in her work with the Boers.

Mrs. Murray, with whom Mrs. Harris stayed before going north, wrote to E. H. on 26 June 1901 that they were much interested in her "but we all feel some anxiety as to her aims. While saying she is non-political she yet says that in her opinion the Boers should give in from a religious point of view. To me it seems that from that point of view the appeal should rather be to her own countrymen who are the strong power trying to rob the weaker of their country. I think that with that want of appreciation of the feeling of the Dutch People her mission will, to say the least of it, do no good . . . I shall be very curious to know the results of her visit, but what I think she does *not* understand is that the physical sufferings the people are enduring are ennobled by lofty ideals that inspire them and that those who cannot recognize that will only seem to degrade them by any help they may bring."

Betty Molteno on 18 August 1901 wrote to her brother Percy Molteno:
"I understood Mrs. Harris that she had given a pledge to the Authorities that she would not speak of what she saw. [Miss Molteno had questioned her about scurvy in the Potchefstroom Camp.] We found her very shaky and ill and very unwilling to tell anything to the discredit of the Authorities . . ."

Mrs. Murray, again writing to E. H. on the subject of Mrs. Harris on 20 August says:
"I feel sure that she is an earnest good woman with the deepest, tenderest heart for all suffering of mind and body and which she has had the insight to know and to set about finding in the camps; but what she cannot enter into or in any way appreciate in people is the sense of suffering in a noble cause which is closely intertwined with their religion and is the great ideal of a life with few intellectual resources. It is this sense of self-sacrifice which has uplifted them and given them courage and strength to bear the loss of all they hold dearest in the world – therefore to throw doubt upon what is to them a real religious belief and their one source of comfort in their darkness seems to many of their friends an injury more cruel than any material aid can counter-balance. I gather that that has been felt by some in the camps, for, in two letters received by Mr. Schultz the judgement expressed was: 'She has done more harm than good.' On the other hand, Mrs. Harris speaks of prayer meetings she held as being full of reward to her and warmest appreciation on the part of hundreds who crowded round them and pressed around her afterwards for a word and a handshake . . . Mrs. Harris and I have discussed our differences of view and remained friends notwithstanding . . ." (See also Letter 17, note 8.)

36

1. Miss Wessels had been in the Aliwal North camp and was on her way to Germany with a sick friend. Mrs. Murray reported:

"Miss Monkhouse (representing the Distress Fund) thinks she might be of great use as she can give her actual experiences to British audiences and I don't find they attempt to colour the statements they make. She is so much afraid of in any way bringing trouble upon her father and sister who are still in camp."

2. Foremost of these was that women in E. H.'s suggested four categories would be allowed to leave the camps "unless there is some military objections" (Letter 34, note 3).

3. Mrs. Murray's youngest sister, Maria, married Thomas Anderson.

4. Barbara Bradby married J. L. Hammond (p. 520).

5. This meeting was organized for the Boer peace mission of Sauer and Merriman by the National Reform Union. It was addressed by Sauer, but Merriman "heeded a strong warning to stay away", according to Percy Molteno in a letter to Charles Molteno in June 1901. (Vivian Solomon (ed.) *Selections from the Correspondence of Percy Alport Molteno, 1892–1914*, p. 181).

6. Mrs. K. H. R. Stuart, who was born in Fraserburg, Cape, was the Guild of Loyal Women's delegate in Britain and was collecting money for the graves of Boers and Britons alike. In a letter to *The Times* of 2 July 1901 she said:
"If the women in the camps are not very comfortable, they ought to be."

7. At Newcastle-on-Tyne Dr. Spence Watson had suggested that "a prominent man" should write to *The Times* to ask why Miss Hobhouse was not sent out to the camps as the most obvious person to go; he also suggested that a question to that effect be put in the House of Commons.

37

1. It was the only one of her forty public meetings that summer at which she was completely silenced. Two others were disturbed by serious rowdyism: the sticks and stones hurled at her at Bristol she "kept for a long time", and the meeting at New Southgate was attended by "a good many rowdies".

Most meetings were at venues arranged for her by the Quakers.

38

1. On 7 July Mrs. Murray had written:
"Since the cable appeared in which Mrs. Brodrick said Lord Kitchener was giving permits to those who had friends to support them to leave the camps, I hear some applications were made and refused. However, I thought I would have a try. Mr. Schultz asked me to try and get a Mrs. Theron and her children from Bloemfontein Camp to her parents in Tulbagh, so I wrote to Lord Kitchener for a permit for her and for Mrs. Philip Botha and their children. I wonder if he will deign to reply. I wrote as a member of our committee here."

Mrs. Botha did eventually get permission to come to Cape Town; by 2 August she was in the Volks Hospital with typhoid fever. She subsequently started a boarding-house at Ivydene in Rondebosch.

On 24 September Alice M. Greene wrote to E. H.:

"At the meeting last Friday at the Ladies' Central Committee in Cape Town no one seemed to know any instance of any one released in answer to Mr. Brodrick's concessions."

On 25 September Anna Purcell wrote to E. H. about the two Hertzog wives whose release could not be procured although their father "was a wealthy man and could pay for them."

2. It eventually appeared in the *Contemporary Review*, October 1901, the *Nineteenth Century* having apparently rejected it at proof stage as "too strong". (Arthur Davey, *The British Pro-Boers, 1877–1902*, p. 59.)

Actually it was written with considerable if ironic restraint, E. H. saying *inter alia*: "I have never, and do not now, put forward any criticism on the policy (be it military or civil) which led to the formation of these camps. Seeing, however, that it is a new departure in our own history to have placed 93 000 white women and children (besides 24 000 natives) in camps after total destruction of their homes, it is also for us a new and a difficult problem to learn how to carry out so serious an undertaking without undue suffering and loss of life."

39

1. Miss Monkhouse and Miss Mellor, recruited by the Distress Committee to nurse in the camps, had to wait three weeks in Cape Town before getting permission to proceed to the camps. Miss Mellor was in November 1901 appointed matron of the Kimberley camp. Miss Monkhouse was in charge of Tweespruit Relief Camp after the war. See Letter 57.

2. After the proclamation of martial law in the Stellenbosch district, John X. Merriman, recently back from the Cape parliamentary mission to Britain, was on Sunday 25 August confined to his farm and deprived of his travel permit to Cape Town to attend the weekly meeting of the Old Mutual board of directors on which he served. Armed guards were stationed at the farm. Merriman wrote to Sir Henry Campbell-Bannerman, amongst others, and the affair caused concern among his friends in England. (Phyllis Lewsen, *John X. Merriman*, pp. 247–8.)

40

1. The Cape Town committee had cabled the British government asking if three of their number could accompany the Ladies' Committee to the camps, but, Mrs. De Villiers wrote, "we found we were talking at a stone wall". Mrs. Murray found them "quite polite, but one could not touch heart or sympathy anywhere". She adds this comment on the ladies themselves:

"Mrs. Fawcett is of course an able woman but cold and hard I should think, by nature as well as now by intention. Lady Knox is quite commonplace. Dr. Murray was much amused when I described her by telling him how she said she had seen a good deal of people in the various camps before she last went to England and how she gave the children sweets making a condition that their 'hands should be washed and they should touch their caps'. Still, I daresay she meant to be kind in a very superior way. Miss Deane said very little but took some notes of the things we said about various camps."

Mrs. Fawcett acknowledged that her committee held the power to add to their number in Cape Town, "but she did not think they would exercise it – that only Dr. Waterston was to accompany them".

The Cape Town committee thereupon notified the Ladies' Committee:

"Since no representative of the committee had been added to the commission . . . the committee desires no connections with the aforesaid commission."

2. Sir Neville Chamberlain, a retired field marshal, wrote to the *Daily News*, which delayed publication of the letter, but it was published in the *Manchester Guardian* on 5 August 1901. It read, *inter alia*:

". . . The necessity has never been made clear to this nation to justify a departure from the recognized laws of international warfare. I mean the frequent injudicious if not reckless burning or sacking of farmsteads or houses of the Boers . . . as also the forcible removal into camps of all women and children, and there being kept in bondage . . .

"What would be the indignation in the United Kingdom if anything approaching to such miseries were enacted by an invading army in our own country where even the nests of birds are under protection of the law?"

A letter in similar vein followed a few weeks later.

ARREST AND DEPORTATION

INTRODUCTION

1. In a letter to the committee of the South African Women and Children Distress Fund published immediately after her return, E. H. again emphasized that she "naturally had no expectation of revisiting the Concentration Camps, but I knew a great need was arising among the deported women of all nationalities scattered in the coast towns, and I thought the Committee might be willing to extend help in this direction after full investigation. It was my desire to above all find out what real need still existed among Uitlander refugees, whose sufferings I had been accused of neglecting, and to help them from some other funds if necessary".

She also pointed out that she had undertaken this journey, like her former one a year before, on her own initiative and, incidentally, at her own expense.

41

1. See Letter 42. The letters are incorporated in the report E. H. sent her committeee on her arrest and deportation.
2. Elizabeth Phillips (p. 137). Mrs. Charles Murray, in a letter to her brother Percy Molteno describing the incident, says she was "a nice, bright girl who was evidently a general favourite on board". Nurse Phillip's lively letter to Canon Barnett's wife from the RMS *Avondale Castle* bears out this impression. Both letters are among the Hobhouse papers in the Steyn collection.
3. Sir Jonathan Trelawny (1650–1721), bishop of Bristol – "who happens to be an ancestor of mine", E. H. wrote to her committee – was one of the seven bishops of the Church of England who petitioned against James II's declaration of indulgence exempting Catholics and Dissenters from penal statutes. The bishops were eventually acquitted of a charge of criminal libel and released from the Tower of London where they had been imprisoned. The episode gave rise to a popular song with the refrain: "And twenty thousand Englishmen will know the reason why".
4. Amy L. Aldis.
5. A Congregationalist minister who in 1901 emerged as a strong critic of the concentration camps and martial-law arrogance. (See also pp. 180, 476.)
6. E. H. came to believe that her arrest and deportation was at least in part due to a mistaken view of her attitude towards the camps.

   Lady Hobhouse wrote to Chamberlain in this regard on 22 January 1902, shortly after her deportation. She enclosed a copy of E. H.'s report to show that "Miss Hobhouse does recognize the efforts of those in charge and does not write anything against them and in fact has never done so in any public utterance or writing". Chamberlain replied:

   "I think I am also justified in saying that such expressions as 'the murdered 11 000' and 'a smoky hecatomb of slaughtered babes' are founded on what I hope may be a misconception of Miss Hobhouse's real opinions."

   In a pencilled marginal note to his letter E. H. pointed out that these expressions were "not mine" but those of Augustine Birrell, a pro-Boer Liberal MP who lost his seat in the khaki election of 1900.

   Both letters are among the Hobhouse papers in the Steyn collection in the state archives, Bloemfontein.

42

1. Back in England E. H. reported the details of the episode to her committee, incorporating most of her correspondence with the authorities in Cape Town. The extensive extracts from the report given here take up the story where her letter to her brother leaves off.

2. In her letter to Sir Walter she says, *inter alia*:

"This summary arrest of an Englishwoman bound on a charitable errand appears to me so astonishing that I cannot believe you are cognizant of it.

"If for any reason you or the local military authorities object to my doing the work indicated I will of course desist from it but I must beg you to allow me to land if only for a few weeks in order to obtain rest and change . . . I hope to send to Lady Hely-Hutchinson a letter entrusted to me for her from Lady Ripon – Lord Ripon with whom I was staying just before sailing sent you his remembrances I believe.

"It amuses me *now* to think Lord Ripon said that in *his* opinion I had done a great public service and ought to be received wherever I went with "a cannonade". Consequently his surprise at my present treatment will surpass my own.

"I trust however that our older notions of justice and common sense will prevail . . . (John Fisher, *That Miss Hobhouse*, pp. 176–7).

3. Miss Betty Molteno (p. 532) was allowed on board on the strength of this request and spent most of Thursday 31 October with E. H. (see Appendix I, pp. 411–7 for Miss Molteno's account to her brother Percy Molteno.)

4. According to Mrs. Murray, describing the incident to her brother Percy Molteno (a copy of the letter is among the Hobhouse papers in the Steyn collection), Dr. Williamson for his part found E. H. "a very charming woman he could not but admire". He also wrily remarked that she "has the face of a madonna but she fights like the devil".

5. Sir James Rose Innes, in a letter to his wife, with huge amusement tells the story from the angle of Dr. Williamson. (Appendix I, pp. 418–9.)

6. Mrs. Murray's husband, Dr. Charles Frederick Kennan Murray (p. 532).

7. E. H.'s suspicion that the permit was withheld "until they knew it was too late" is not borne out by Mrs. Murray's description of the event to her brother . . . (Note 4, above.)

43

1. This "spirited parting shot to Sir Walter in her best 'melo style' " was unearthed in the public records office by a recent biographer (John Fisher, *That Miss Hobhouse*, p. 184). To his knowledge it had never been published before. E. H. probably lacked strength or energy to make a copy, as she did of her other letters to the authorities in Cape Town.

45

1. A marginal note to this letter in E. H.'s hand says it was "copied from memory". Like the letter to Kitchener, it is roughly written in pencil. Both letters are among the Hobhouse papers in the Steyn collection.

2. See also Letter 32 and note 2, and pp. 163–4.

47

1. E. H. says in her memoir that Miss Molteno wrote the best account of her days of imprisonement, having "a rare gift for understanding the spiritual forces underlying such moments", but adds that the document "seems to have disappeared". Possibly this is the letter Miss Molteno wrote to her brother Percy in England, a copy of which is among her papers in the Jagger library of the University of Cape Town. (Appendix I, pp. 411–7.)

2. A prominent solicitor of the firm Lewis & Lewis.

3. Brodrick in the end did refuse service of the writ. After considerable public ferment and – to E. H.'s "disgust" – an offer of money to settle the matter out of court, the case was dropped. Five senior counsel found that "in view of the certain passage of an act of indemnity covering the proceedings complained of by Miss Hobhouse, not only would the action be defeated, but the attempt to obtain an authoritative or useful decision on martial law would prove abortive".

   "Anyhow", E. H. concludes, "the chief men responsible for the outrage on public liberty shewed themselves afraid to face the music and the action could not be brought."

4. As officer commanding the troop ship *Roslin Castle*.

1. The anonymous writer was Alice M. Greene, no "Afrikander" in fact but an Englishwoman living in South Africa (p. 426).

2. On a copy she made of the poem E. H. explain this as "alluding to my description of children in the camp 'like faded flowers thrown away' ". This was in a letter to Lady Hobhouse (p. 55).

A VISIT TO THE RUINED DISTRICTS

INTRODUCTION

1. In the south-east of the High Savoye mountains in France. E. H. was at the resort Talloires.

2. Originally the old Benedictine monastery.

3. Mrs. Louis Botha had been allowed by Kitchener to visit Europe on a peace mission. Her "chief hope", according to E. H., was "to weld together the two parties among the Boers – those, like Mr. Potgieter, who would accept the British flag and those stern old dappers [*sic*] who would not at any price".

4. The situation created by roaming bands of blacks in the two former republics

constituted one of the reasons why British peace proposals were accepted in 1902. In the preliminary Boer proposals on peace that year this episode was cited as a recent example of "murders and all kinds of atrocities" perpetrated in "many districts of both republics":

"Zoals nog onlangs gebeurd is in het district Vryheid alwaar 56 burghers op gruwelijke wijze by dezelfde gelegenheid vermoord en verminkt werden." (Facsimile of the Boer proposals in J. D. Kestell and D. E. van Velden, *Die Vredesonderhandelinge*, following p. 112.)

5. Lord Milner died of sleeping sickness (*encephalitis lethargica*) probably contracted on a visit to South Africa with his wife in 1924. (J. E. Wrench, *Alfred Lord Milner*, p. 366.)

6. Madame Degli Asinelli was instrumental in getting the Swiss to contribute spinning-wheels for the Boer home industries. (pp. 359, 381.)

7. The Dutch offer to the British government to mediate between the Boers and the British was forwarded to the Boers, and this started the final peace discussions. (J. D. Kestell, *Through Shot and Flame*, pp. 273–5.)

8. The Dutch shipping magnate A. G. K. Kröller.

9. *De Strijd tusschen Boer en Brit/Three Years War*, published simultaneously in Amsterdam and London in 1902.

10. Antoon van Welie (1866–1957). His striking portraits of E. H. and the Boer generals, formerly in the C. J. K. van Aalst collection in Amersfoort in the Netherlands, are now housed in the national war museum at Bloemfontein.

11. *The Brunt of the War and where it fell*, by Emily Hobhouse, published by Methuen & Co., London in 1902.

12. See p. 180.

13. In September 1922 she wrote to Mrs. Steyn from Warren House, St. Ives, about her work translating *Tant' Alie*, then more than half-way:

"The work is very hard and at times I turn sick and faint, but then I take a few minutes in the garden among my plants and so go back refreshed. I am anxious it should be well done for I feel certain it will take a place in the history and literature of your own country and even amongst the diaries of the world . . . so disarming in its simplicity, so natural in its presentment of life in the Transvaal, it is unique and its human interest quite intense. I've tried to put it into very simple English that suits her very simple Taal . . ."

14. Joseph Chamberlain and his party, including his wife, landed at Durban on 26 December 1902 and left from Cape Town on 25 February 1903. In two hectic months he visited 29 towns, delivered 67 major speeches, received 87 deputations and gave some 250 interviews. The object of his journey was inter alia recuperation from his serious illness after falling from a cab.

15. Loyson wrote *Deux Ans Après* (Two Years After) on reading E. H.'s appeal for the ruined Orange River Colony in 1903. She quotes two verses at the head of her memoir chapter on her visit to Lindley, Reitz and Frankfort:

"Les femmes, cependant, orphelines et veuves,
Surprises de connaître une nouvelle épreuve,
Vers Faim qui s'approche ouvrent des yeux grandes;

"Et c'est ainsi que, jour après jour, elles restent
Le long des murs brûlés, assises sur un rang,
Sans plus d'espoir, sans nulle plainte, sans une geste"

(The women, however, the orphans and widows,
Surprised to know a new trial
Open their great eyes to the approaching Hunger.

And it is thus, day after day, that they sit
Alongside the burnt walls, in a row,
With no hope, with no complaint, without any gesture)

16. *Commonwealth* (p. 440 n. 27).
17. Henry J. Phipps of the Carnegie Steel Corporation placed 100 000 dollars to the credit of General Louis Botha in a London bank, to be used at once for widows and orphans, not for education. He himself undertook to audit expenditure. (For Botha's letter on this to Smuts see W. K. Hancock and Jean van der Poel (ed.), *Selection from the Smuts Papers*, vol. II, p. 32).

LETTERS

49
1. Lord Shaftesbury, Anthony Ashley Cooper (1801–85), the social reformer, who introduced legislation prohibiting the employment of women and children in coal mines, providing care for the insane, and establishing a 10-hour day for factory workers. He also promoted the building of model tenements.

50
1. Mrs. Charles Murray.
2. Mrs. C. C. ("Charlie Avignon") de Villiers.
3. C. P. Schultz.
4. J. G. P. van der Horst (1876–1950). One of the first Afrikaners to make a successs of a business career, his name was to be associated with the Imperial Cold Storage Co. and Fletcher and Cartwright's department store. He later played a prominent part in activities leading to the founding of the Nationalist party.
5. Act 47 of 1902, passed on 22 December, and implemented on 3 January 1903.

6. Called "Avignon".

7. *The Brunt of the War and where it fell*, published in 1902. See p. 180, however, for E. H.'s claims that the authorities tried to suppress the book.

8. At Miller's Point.

9. Mrs. Hermina van Breda.

10. Presidents Paul Kruger and Marthinus Theunis Steyn and, presumably, General Christiaan de Wet, for good measure.

11. Burghers of the Transvaal forces who had laid down their arms and were from August 1901 recruited to enlist in the British army, notably by ex-Commandant A. P. J. Cronjé after the surrender of Potchefstroom (A. M. Grundlingh, *Die "Hensoppers" en "Joiners"*, ch. 6).

12. J. H. ("Onze Jan") (1845–1909). A powerful figure in the Afrikaner Bond, he was now back in Cape Town having left for Europe in September 1900, after the outbreak of the war he fought so hard to avert. Hofmeyr was a former editor of *De Volksvriend*, then of *De Zuid-Afrikaan* (which became *Ons Land*) and became a member of the Cape house of assembly in 1879. In 1880 he founded the Boeren Beschermingsvereeniging which in 1884 fused with S. J. du Toit's Afrikaner Bond. Although Hofmeyr had by 1903 resigned from parliament, he continued to exercise a very strong influence in South African politics. (For his work behind the scenes John X. Merriman knicknamed him "the mole"). His was a moderate nationalism and he encouraged at the same time the revival of the Dutch language and culture and a reconciliation between Afrikaners and the English.

13. Called Welgelegen.

14. Chamberlain's guiding aims on this visit was to reconcile the Dutch (Afrikaners) and British in South Africa, as a prerequisite for the development of the country, and to obtain from each colony some contribution towards "the financial burden of Empire". These considerations figured prominently in his first meeting with Hofmeyr. On Hofmeyr's side there was particular concern about amnesty for captured men from the Cape Colony and Natal who, although British subjects, had fought with the Boers. Almost all of them, 380 in all, were set at liberty by 21 March 1903.

15. The death penalty of Visser, "one of the rebels who had been sentenced for shooting a Kaffir on commando", was commuted by the Governor of the Cape, Sir Walter Hely-Hutchinson, chiefly owing to a desire to avoid anything that might hamper Hofmeyr's efforts at reconciliation. (J. H. Hofmeyr, *Life of Onze Jan*, p. 585.)

16 and 17. The two Nieuwoudts, Frederik and Hermias, of Hanover, Cape, were among the party of five employed on A. J. Pienaar's farm De Bad who were brought to military trial in March 1901 after the derailment of a train near Taaibosch siding, close by, on 18 February of that year. Some of its passengers were robbed and killed. Jan van den Berg of the party turned crown witness.

Frederik Nieuwoudt was sentenced to five years' imprisonment, with a further five years' police surveillance, while Hermias and Jan Andries Nieuwoudt and Jan Petrus Nienaber were sentenced to be shot. Kitchener commuted Hermias Nieuwoudt's sentence and remitted Frederik Nieuwoudt's five years' police surveillance; the others were shot, leaving Mrs. Nienaber destitute at Hanover with seven children – much to Olive Schreiner's concern. See Letter 55 and p. 188.

The Taaibosch siding affair was re-opened with the trial, on 14 January 1902, of A. J. Pienaar's brother, P. A. Pienaar. On the night of the derailment he had left with the Boer commando but was subsequently caught. At his trial commandant Wynand Malan testified that he himself had derailed the train as an act of war. (J. H. Snyman, *Rebelleverhore in Kaapland* in *South African Archives Yearbook*, 1962.) Snyman makes the point that the Nieuwoudts and Nienaber were tried before a court that trespassed on the preserves of the special courts set up under the Indemnity Act.

51

1. At Miller's Point beyond Simonstown.
2. *The Friend* was to be a revival of *The Friend of the Free State*, founded in 1854 by the Barlows. Young Arthur Barlow, left in charge when the war broke out, refused to co-operate with Roberts's occupation forces and from 16 March to 16 April 1900 the paper was run by a group of war correspondents under Rudyard Kipling. In 1903 it was bought by "a power syndicate of irreconcileable and disaffected boers" among whom were Abraham Fischer, Jack Brebner, Charlie Fichardt and Dr. A. E. W. Ramsbottom. According to Milner it was managed "with an ability as conspicuous as its unfairness". In imperialist quarters it was thought that it "bids fair to outstrip even its journalistic fellows at the Cape in the malignancy of its attacks on British rule and British administration generally". (See, for these quotations, Karel Schoeman, *Bloemfontein*, p. 214.) Arthur Barlow resigned as editor to go into politics – apparently finding the paper's new line rather strident – and the Reverend Dewdney Drew succeeded him as editor.
3. That section of the press representing the interests of the big mining houses, of which Hermann Eckstein & Co was one of the most powerful.

52

1. Joseph Chamberlain met the Afrikaner Deputation – members of the Afrikaner Bond/South African Party – at Government House on 21 February 1903. He made such a conciliatory impression that the Cape Town deputation told him their "history would have taken an entirely different course" had he visited South Africa three years earlier. (T. H. R. Davenport, *The Afrikaner Bond*, p. 243.)
   Elsewhere in South Africa he had considerably more critical audiences.

2. The first consignment of *The Brunt of the War* must have been quite considerable, however. See Letter 50 and Letter 58 for evidence that the book was apparently being widely read.

3. J. Ramsay MacDonald, *What I saw in South Africa, September and October 1902*.

4. J. D. Kestell, *Met de Boeren Commando's: mijne ervaringen als Veldpredikant*. This was originally confiscated by the customs because of the verses worked into the design of the front and back covers of the first edition. On the front: Syn goedheid is seer groot/Hoop op die Heer jul vrome/Is Afrika in nood/daar sal verlossing kome (His goodness is very great/put your hope in the Lord, you devout/ If Africa is in distress/deliverance is at hand); on the back page: Hy maak op ons gebede/heel Afrika eens vry/Hoe die ons vertrede/dan leef ons vry en bly (In answer to our prayers/He will liberate all Africa one day/however much these oppress us/we shall then be happy and free).

5. *Songs of the Veld*, by various authors, reprinted from *The New Age*, 1902. It contained verse by Alice M. Greene, Anna Purcell, and others.

6. Probably W. van Everdingen's *De Oorlog in Zuid-Afrika*, 1902.

7. E. H. started a diary on arrival in Cape Town and kept it up for some pages, to which she refers here.

8. Miss Emmie Murray, long active in volunteer social work, founded a home for unmarried mothers on finding that many girls from good homes were falling pregnant as a result of the presence at the Cape of large numbers of soldiers. This became the Magdalena Home about which Miss Murray and matron Lulu de Villiers wrote a book, *Geknakte Lelies*.

53

1. The immigration of British women was planned to play an important role in post-war reconstruction. Already in August 1901 Milner, writing to Roberts, foresaw "they are going to be of great assistance to us in the settlement of the country". In June 1902 the S.A. Expansion Society and the British Women's Emigration Society started a widely publicized scheme to send 100 women per month to South Africa with a view to finding work for them in the new colonies, and Milner started a special women's immigration department. The scheme had the patronage of leaders of both sides in parliament and the backing of "ladies of title and leaders of fashion".

Ramsay MacDonald saw it as representing to the "trustful British female" that there were many employment opportunities for her in South Africa and that, in addition, "it is her duty to throw herself at the heart of the lonely Britisher who, without her, will marry into some Boer family". "The Jingoes," he added, "regard the immigration of women not as an employment but as a marriage matter. They deliberately propose to apply the methods of the stud to South African political problems." (J. Ramsay MacDonald, *What I saw in South Africa*, p. 77.)

1. F. S. Malan, editor of *Ons Land*. (See letter 7, note 2 for details of his libel case.)
2. A. P. Cartwright, editor of the *South African News*. South African Conciliation
   Committee pamphlets 74 and 96 give the curious particulars. On 15 January
   1901 the Dublin *Freeman's Journal* published an authenticated letter from "a
   British officer now serving at the front". It described military manoeuvres
   ordered by Kitchener in 1900 to surround De Wet. *The Times* published the
   letter on 18 January 1901. W. T. Stead sent Cartwright a copy of *The Times* of
   18 January and also of 19 January in which it was reported that the South
   African Conciliation Committee had drawn Roberts' attention to the letter and
   the importance of having it immediately contradicted. No such contradiction
   came.

   On 6 February Cartwright published the main body of the letter under the
   heading: "How we are waging war/A dreadful disclosure/by a British officer in
   command/Lord Kitchener's secret instruction as conveyed by a leading general./
   Are prisoners being shot?"

   The Cape attorney-general Rose Innes telegraphed Kitchener for the truth
   of the charges. They were promptly denied and Cartwright published the denial
   prominently. He was none the less charged and condemned, like Malan, to one
   year's imprisonment. The gravamen of the libel was:

   "Lord Kitchener, having as he thought caged his enemy, sent secret instructions to the troops to take no prisoners; that is, if the Boers surrounded on all
   sides found themselves unable to resist and hoist the white flag as a token of
   surrender , they are to be shot down to the last man."

   In the meantime copies of *The Times* and also of W. T. Stead's *Review of
   Reviews* and *Reynold's News* with the original letter were circulating freely at the
   Cape, and the Port Elizabeth *Cape Daily* had also taken over the letter with
   impunity.

   The severe sentences of the two leading Cape Town editors were at the time
   seen as part of a clamping down on a "violent campaign of calumny against
   British men and generals" as details of army policy filtered through to a shocked
   public.
3. After the war M. J. Pretorius petitioned that the conduct be examined of the
   military authorities who took action against him during the war, causing him to
   be deported to the military camp at De Aar. Pretorius had been forced to
   witness, in the prison-yard of his home town, Middelburg, the execution of the
   young Cape rebel F. A. Marais. General French had instructed that civilians of
   all degrees be mustered to attend the execution of rebels.

   The theme of forced witnessing of the execution of a rebel by local inhabitants
   is vividly treated by C. Louis Leipoldt, the Afrikaans poet, in his classic poem
   Oom Gert Vertel (1916), and also in his posthumously published novel *Stormwrack*.
4. T. P. Theron (1839–1908), a man of little formal education, but according to

J. H. Hofmeyr capable of expressing himself "fluently, correctly and forcefully in both English and Dutch".

5. For an eyewitness account of the ceremony, which however makes no mention of field cornet Louw, see Thomas Pakenham, *The Boer War*, pp. 428–9.

6. Hofmeyr's conciliatory letter reflected his speech at the meeting of the Afrikaner deputation with Chamberlain on 21 February 1903 in Cape Town, where he said:

"We beg with you, sir, that no member of the Town Guards or District Mounted Troops should be ostracised or cold-shouldered in society, be injured in his calling or ordinary avocation, be made to feel that he is in any way the worse off in either a social or business point of view merely because he fought for his country.

"We reprobate all acts of an offensive character, irritation of loyal subjects by the sporting of colours of the late republics, the wearing of the distinguishing badges of rebel forces or chiefs, or the singing of songs of a character to bring misunderstanding and suspicion . . .

"We are prepared to address our People in the spirit of this statement and to co-operate to the fullest of our power to promote good understanding between and the happiness and prosperity of both the great European sections of our population under the flag which waves over us all."

7. Prof. H. E. S. Fremantle was appointed to the chair of English and philosophy at the South African College, Cape Town in 1899, but soon branched out into political science and eventually resigned to enter politics. He represented Uitenhage in parliament and co-edited the *South African News* with Cartwright (1903–8).

55

1. The Reverend John Murray, son of Dr. Andrew Murray of Wellington, was on 16 August 1901 sentenced to three months' hard labour and then deportation as a prisoner-of-war. While a missionary at Waterberg he had gone to Delagoa Bay for supplies and on his return found his house burnt down and his wife – a niece of General Louis Botha – deported. He surrendered to the British at Pretoria and was allowed to go on parole to Wellington, where his wife was undergoing medical treatment and staying with his father. From there he wrote the postcard that, in his family's view, led to his arrest: he had expressed the opinion that Britain had, quoting a Dutch proverb, bitten off more than she could chew in South Africa.

2. See letter 50, notes 16 and 17.

3. *The Story of an African Farm*, 1883.

4. A collection of allegories – or *dreams*, as she called them – were published in 1890; *Dreams and real life* in 1893, *Stories, dreams and allegories* in 1923. She also wrote an allegorical novel, *Trooper Peter Halket of Mashonaland*, published in 1897.

5. For E. H.'s impressions on Olive Schreiner on visiting her at De Aar in 1908, see pp. 377–8
6. But see p. 179, Letter 50.

56

1. About 10 000 children were estimated to have lost either one or both parents during the war. Most orphans were cared for by relatives, but if the relatives were in no position to do so the children were handed over to the orphanages of the Dutch Reformed Church which they preferred to government orphanages. (Lawrence Richardson, *Selected Correspondence*, p. 197.)
2. In the Afrikaans idiom " 'n soet druppel in 'n bitter beker", the "sweet drop" is a metaphor for any small solace in a bitter time of trouble or suffering.
3. The Reverend H. J. Neethling was a son of the highly respected Reverend J. H. Neethling of Stellenbosch, one of the founding fathers of the Stellenbosch theological seminary. His wife died in the Balmoral concentration camp after many unsuccessful attempts to secure her release – it was apparently impossible to convince the authorities that her husband was not *on* commando, but *with* the Boer commandos, as chaplain. (Emily Hobhouse, *War without glamour*, pp. 152–8.)

57

1. The Reverend Carl Christoph Sandrock and his wife. (Letter 12, note 2.)
2. The Peace of Vereeniging included a clause setting up committees, later known as repatriation boards, in each district of the Transvaal and Orange River Colony to apportion relief from a fund of £3 000 000 to be made available by the British Government. The boards were regarded by the applicants for relief as dilatory and incompetent, and recipients were required to provide securities for repayment on receipt of what they had understood to be a "free grant". The amount spent by the government on repatriation and relief was, in the end, over £16 000 000. Some of this went as additional aid to "protected burghers" i.e. "hands-uppers", and about £2 000 000 to blacks; but nearly £3 000 000 was issued in short-term loans, of which only about half was recovered.
3. See note 2, above.
4. Widespread distrust of military receipts for property seized during the war made Chamberlain realise "that nothing less was at stake than the confidence in South Africa of the good faith of the British Government". On 3 January 1903, within a week of his arrival in South Africa, he spoke in the town hall of Ladysmith and said he had heard much about military receipts being disallowed . . .

   "I say nothing of the kind is permitted. Those who hold these receipts and who can show they are the legitimate owners of them and who have not . . . acted against us in the field or elsewhere may rely on it that the receipt of a British officer must be, and always will be, as good as a bank-note."
5. Probably Zacharias Enslin, of Heilbron. But he had been sent to Bermuda, not Ceylon.

6. General George A. Brand.

7. See letter 39, note 1.

8. This "stormy interview" as the newspapers called it, took place in the ballroom of Government House in Bloemfontein on 3 February 1903. The Boer population – represented by De Wet, Hertzog and some fifty others – had sent Chamberlain a list of the matters they wished to discuss, among others the alleged violation of the peace treaty by Britain. This latter so incensed Chamberlain that he, immediately upon entering, ordered all the delegates to sit down, including De Wet who was standing to give the address of welcome. Two and a half hours of " a most animated discussion" – as Mrs. Chamberlain called it – ensued between Chamberlain and Hertzog. While "loyal" reports were that Chamberlain had "rolled over and flattened" Hertzog, the Afrikaner view of the exchange was very different – as E. H. found in Bloemfontein.

9. The legislative council of the Transvaal colony at first consisted of officials only, but from May 1903 it included 16 officials and 14 nominated members who were not officials. Among the latter were four Afrikaners, of whom one, former Commandant A. P. J. Cronjé, brother of General Piet Cronjé, took a leading role in the recruitment of the National Scouts so loathed by the Boers.

58

1. Afrikaans, lit. food for the road.

2. From the Afrikaans word with a similar sound: *mielies*, i.e. maize.

59

1. Ezekiel, 37:1.

2. In the ballad *Widdicombe Fiar* "Uncle Tom Cobbleigh 'n all" borrow Tom's old gray mare to go to the fair, but "her took sick and died". So –
"When the wind whistles cold on the moor of a night . . .
Tom Pearse's old mare doth appear gashly white . . .
And all night long can be heard skirling and groans . . .
From Tom Pearse's old mare in her rattling bones . . ."
(*Oxford Book of Ballads*, p. 845–6.)

3. Afrikaans, lit. red neck – nickname for the English who, coming from a less harsh climate, often suffered grievously from sunburn in South Africa.

4. Afrikaans: kappie – a bonnet (often of calico), shading the face and neck.

5. The Peace Preservation Act, popularly known as the Coercion Act, imposed peace-time censorship, blocked criticism of the executive and enabled the authorities to banish without trail, or imprison for 21 days, without warrant or cause shown, whomsoever they pleased. – "A monstrous act," said P. A. Molteno. A "disgrace to our statute book," said Abraham Fischer. (V. Solomon (ed.) *Selections from the Correspondence of Percy Alport Molteno*, pp. 210, 224.)

60

1. Letter 59, note 5.
2. Andrew Carnegie (1835–1919), Scottish industrialist who made a steel fortune in the USA, retired in 1901 and devoted the rest of his life to the distribution of his great wealth for the benefit of society; this included the establishment of numerous public libraries all over the world, also in South Africa. He endowed the Carnegie Corporation in New York with $125 million to continue this work after his death.

61

1. See letter 19, under 18 March.

62

1. General De Wet captured General Broadwood's convoy at Sannaspos near the Bloemfontein waterworks at Thaba'Nchu on 31 March 1900.

63

1. E. H. replied, expressing "considerable surprise both at the contents and the tone" of the letter. She explained the purpose of her visit and strongly objected to the "very discourteous treatment" and the "unnecessarily insolent manner" she and General Brand encountered from the camp superintendent. (Letter in the Hobhouse papers in the Steyn collection.)

64

1. On his farm Roodepoort in the Koppies district.
2. The famous Fleur.
3. A character in George Eliot's Adam Bede, renowned for "having her say out". Mrs. Cornelia (Tant Nelie) de Wet's account of her gruelling war-time experiences – given verbatim by Eric Strockenstrom in Die Afrikaanse Vrou, pp. 208–11 –shows her own mettle e.g. she refused to send her children to fetch rations when in the Krugersdorp camp, saying "Ek het gereken dat ek, met Gods hulp, sonder 'n Engelsman sou kon klaarkom". (I reckoned that I would, with God's help, manage to cope without an Englishman.)
4. Military buildings of a temporary nature were sold for civilian use after the war. For example General Smuts's permanent home at Doornkloof, near Irene, with its weatherboard walls and corrugated iron roof, had been erected as a recreation centre for British officers and was after the war transported to Doornkloof.
5. Chamberlain advocated imperial trade preference – with a defensive tariff system against other countries – as a means of strengthening the economic and so also political coherence of the British empire. This not only went counter to

the long-accepted British Liberal tradition of free trade but had highly dangerous side-effects for a British politician: his opponents were quick to point out it meant dearer food. After his first public plea for the policy at Birmingham in June 1903 (he had already privately expounded it on his visit to South Africa) Chamberlain wrote to J. H. Hofmeyr:

". . . many of my friends think I am mad to undertake it, and all my enemies are predicting my political extinction."

In September he resigned as colonial secretary to devote his energies to this campaign.

6. This was the first of a number of country-wide meetings to discuss matters with which the enlarged and government-appointed legislative council would shortly be dealing "without any mandate from the People of the country". (See W. K. Hancock and Jean van der Poel (ed.), *Selections from the Smuts Papers*, vol. II, p. 97 for Botha's letter to Milner advising him of these meetings on 1 June 1903.)

Het Volk as a political party was formed in 1905.

7. The council was set up by Milner in June 1903 to advise the high commissioner on matters common to the Transvaal and Orange River Colonies, particularly the control of a joint police force, the South African Constabulary, and the combined railway systems of the former republics. Ten of its members were appointed by the high commissioner and four elected by the non-official members of the two legislative councils. The council met for the first time on 2 June 1903. It was regarded with contempt by the Boer leaders but seen by Milner's supporters as a step towards a South African federation.

8. After the war the railway systems of the Transvaal and Orange River colonies were combined by Milner and named the Central South African Railways. This was done partly to lessen the sharp competition for railway revenue which had previously existed between the Cape/Free State/Rand line and the Delagoa Bay/Rand route, but also to feed an intercolonial fund formed by Milner to meet the expenses of the war loans imposed upon the two new colonies and to finance the South African Constabulary.

65

1. E. H. from time to time sent her brother refused receipts and claims, or copies of claims alleged to have been lost in the offices.

2. See letter 67, note 1.

3. The Military Manoeuvres Bill, No. 28 of 1903, was passed in December against the strong opposition from especially the farmers for it gave the military the power *inter alia* to "pass over, encamp or construct military works not of a permanent character and to execute military manoeuvres on any land whether under cultivation or not", with the proviso only that the military "shall cause all land used under the powers conferred by the ordinance to be restored as soon as and as far as practicable to the previous condition or pay compensation".

66

1. D. E. van Velden (1869–1923) and J. D. Kestell (1854–1941) were joint secretaries of the Vereeniging peace conference and published an account of the proceedings. Van Velden had been acting auditor-general of the South African Republic, secretary of the second Volksraad, and general Botha's adjutant and secretary during the war. He accompanied the Boer generals to Europe.

2. A pastoral letter issued by the Nederduitsch Hervormde of Gereformeerde Kerk of the Transvaal exhorted National Scouts to make a public confession of their guilt in order that they could again enjoy Holy Communion: "Zij hebben zich bezondigd tegen God en mensch, en tensij zij tot waar berouw en betering des levens komen . . . kunnen zij onmogelijk met een goed geweten de Sacramenten gebruiken." (A. M. Grundlingh, *Die "Hensopper's" en "Joiners"*, ch. 9.) Some National Scouts stoutly refused to do so and this led to the formation of a separate, though short-lived *Scoutkerk* (Scouts church) in several Transvaal communities. Others did confess their guilt and moral transgression – sometimes in the most abject terms, as the following letter of Hans Grady illustrates. Writing from Hartebeestfontein, District Heidelberg, to the bimonthly Hervormde Church magazine the *Vereeniging* in October 1904 he says:

"Het is tamelijck algemeen bekend dat ik mij tijdens den jongsten oorlog ook zoo zwak heb gedragen, dat ik het wapen tegen mijn ouden vader, mijn medebroeders en mijn volk heb opgenomen. Ja, ik heb het zelfs zoo ver gebragt, dat ik tot kapitein onder de 'National Scouts' werd aangesteld.

"Wat aanleiding gegeven heeft tot die treurige daad moet hier liefst verzwegen worden want het strekt niet tot eer, noch van mij, noch van hen, die mij daartoe aanvoerden.

"Ik heb reeds aan den Kerkeraad al hier geschreven, vragende om vergiffenis van mijn verkeerdheid, en ik heb zulks ook verkregen. Ook bij den Heere ben ik nog steeds bezig te roepen om genade over mijn groote zonde.

"Maar ik gevoel mij toch zoo onwaardig en schuldig, dat ik geen rust voor mijn gemoed kan vinden. Want het is mij nog altijd of mijn broeders bloed aan mijn handen kleeft. Ofschoon ik zelf ernstig gewond werd, toen ik trachtte mijn volk te helpen uitroeien en daardoor nu ook levenslang met een mankement zal moeten gaan, zoo wil ik niettemin als in het stof mij neerleggen en het gansche Afrikaander volk om vergiffenis smeeken. Zoo er nog iemand is, die tegen mij iets gevoeld, weet dan, mijn broeder, dat ik gereed ben tot u te komen en u om vergiffenis te vragen. God zal mij vergeven. Wilt gij allen, mannen, vrouwen en kinderen, die ik zooveel kwaad en smart heb aangedaan, zulks toch doen, opdat ik rust voor mijn gemoed mag vinden!

"Dit is de smeekbede van uw bedroefden en beschaamden mede-Afrikaander.

"P.S. Hierbij geef ik ook verlof aan eenige ander couranten om deze mijn brief over te nemen. Ja, ik zal zelf dankbaar zijn, zoo mijn dierbaar volk over geheel Zuid Afrika deze mijn schuldbelijdenis mogen zien en hooren."

(It is fairly well known that I, during the recent war, behaved so badly that I took up arms against my aged father, my fellow-brothers and my people. Yes, I even brought it so far that I was made a captain in the National Scouts.

What occasioned this sad deed, is best left unsaid for it does not reflect honourably either on me or those that led me to do it.

I have already written to the church council here, asking forgiveness for my wrongs and I have received it. The Lord, also, I am still beseeching for mercy over my great sin.

But I feel myself so unworthy and guilty that I can find no peace of mind. Because it is as if the blood of my brothers still cleaves to my hands. Although I was myself seriously wounded while I was trying to help destroy my people and as a result will suffer from a lifelong disability, I nevertheless want to prostrate myself as if in the dust before the whole of the Afrikaander people, to beg their forgiveness. If there still is anyone who harbours anything against me, know then, my brother, that I am prepared to come to you to ask your forgiveness. God will forgive me. May all of you, men, women and children, whom I have caused so much ill and suffering, do likewise, that I may find peace of mind!

This is the supplication of your sorrowful and shamed fellow-Afrikaander.

P.S. I herewith give permission that any other newspaper may take over my letter. I would even be grateful if my beloved people all over the whole of South Africa could see and hear my confession of guilt.)

3. Suggested peace terms in preliminary discussions between Kitchener and Botha (7 March 1901) and Kitchener and Smuts (4 May 1902) in both cases included amnesty for the rebels, with a loss of franchise. The Peace of Vereeniging made no amnesty provision, the Boer leaders being informed by Milner that this would be dealt with by the colonial governments. In the Cape Colony, which had produced far the largest number of rebels, they all stood trial, but most of them received a nominal sentence. They were, however, disenfranchised, in effect for five years. By the time of the Heidelberg meeting on 2 July 1903 almost all the rebels in South Africa had been released, as Botha admitted, but the fact that no general amnesty had been granted still prevented the return home of those who had gone to Europe, among them the Boer envoys Fischer, Wolmarans and Wessels.

4. Article 4 of the peace treaty required that Dutch should be taught in the public schools where parents desired it. But by the Education Ordinance of 1903 English was the only medium of instruction and Dutch was to be taught as a subject for not more than five hours a week. At Heidelberg one of the three resolutions unanimously passed expressed "profound disappointment" at the treatment of Dutch both in the administration and the schools, and asked for

485

equal rights with English and also for local school committees elected by parents. Some 124 private fee-paying schools attended by about 4 000 children had already been set up in the Transvaal to meet the needs of the Afrikaners. These Christelijk-Nationale Onderwys (C.N.O.) schools played a significant part in the preservation of the Dutch language and Afrikaner national feelings.

5. At a meeting with Boer delegates of the Transvaal at Pretoria on 8 January 1903 Chamberlain made much of the "missing millions" which the British authorities believed had been secretly sent to Europe during the war by the South African Republican government, for an unidentified purpose. At the Heidelberg meeting Botha had categorically denied the existence of such a fund. See W. K. Hancock and Jean van der Poel (ed.), *Selections from the Smuts Papers*, vol. I, pp. 544–6) for Smuts' memoirs of the Boer war, in which he tells of the origin of this "spook", not yet laid. He recounts how, at the surrender of Pretoria, he removed the government gold and money from the National Bank and the mint and despatched it to the Transvaal government in exile, then at Waterval Boven (see also Appendix III, p. 426 for E. H.'s efforts to lay the "spook".)

6. A £30 000 000-contribution to the cost of the war had been imposed on the Transvaal, the loan to be issued in three instalments, the first of which was to be generated by certain mining houses and banks. A further loan of £35 000 000 was to be raised to buy the Transvaal railways from the Netherlands South African Railway Company, to pay war compensation to the Cape Colony and Natal, to finance new public works, etc. The resolution passed at the Heidelberg meeting declared the £65 000 000 debt to be "the largest national debt in the world in proportion to the population" and a flagrant contradiction of the British tradition of no taxation of a colony without consent of the colonists. It asked that the question of war debt await the decision of the people of the Transvaal "in a constitutional manner", i.e. under self-government. The debt was cancelled by the Liberal Government in 1907.

7. The labour issue raised at Heidelberg concerned the proposal of the Transvaal Colonial government to recruit Chinese as workers in the gold mines in view of the serious shortage of black miners and the need for the fullest possible gold production to revive the economy of the Transvaal. The Boer leaders fought the importation of "Asiatics" on every possible occasion, chiefly on the grounds of its threat to the future of South Africa as "a white man's country". Nevertheless the first group of indentured Chinese arrived in June 1904. They were presently regarded, not always without cause, as a criminal element. The conditions under which they lived and worked was an issue in the British general election of 1906. The new Liberal cabinet paved the way for their repatriation by the self-governing Transvaal in 1908.

8. The *Transvaal Leader* of 3 July 1903 reported E. H's speech, heading the relevant paragraph in their report of the Heidelberg meeting *Miss Hobhouse redivivus*:

486

"... her address was in English, being translated into Dutch by the Rev. A. J. Louw.

"She spoke of the pleasure it gave her to be present. She had often been among large numbers of Boer women before, but this was, she said, the first time she had been at a gathering of Boer men. She would like to say to them that she greatly admired their treatment of their wives and children. Their sufferings during the war invoked the sympathy of the whole world. Women who went through what the Boer women had gone through were women to be proud of (cheers). Those present had been kind enough to meet her today with great kindness, and they might be sure that she would not forget this day as long as she lived, although it had been her lot to visit Africa before. It would be unfair of her to allow them to suppose that she was alone in her sympathy with them. She was merely a representative of a large section of the English People, and she was quite sure that if the remainder of English people knew what she knew they would be equally interested and sympathetic. She wished them particularly to remember this, so that they might judge her People fairly. She would close with sincere thanks to them for their kind reception."

For all her indignation with newspaper reporting, E. H.'s own account of her speech tallies pretty closely with this.

9. The weather of the first Monday in August was a matter of popular concern in Britain – it was bank holiday and a traditional occasion for outings.

10. The Prince of Wales visited South Africa in 1925.

67

1. Written by Smuts and signed by Botha, the letter was sent to Leonard Hobhouse. It was published in *The Times* on 15 July, together with a covering letter by Lord Courtney. (W. K. Hancock and Jean van der Poel (ed.), *The Smuts Papers*: vol. II pp. 106–7.)

2. Under the terms of the peace treaty the repatriation of prisoners-of-war was made conditional on their signing a declaration of allegiance to the king, thus becoming a British subject.

3. In Cilliers Street, Sunnyside.

4. Lord Roberts, in the first of his many proclamations aimed at inducing the Boers to surrender, in February 1900 promised that "those that desist from any further hostility towards His Majesty's Government ... will not be made to suffer in their persons or property." – Arthur Fichardt had so desisted.

5. See p. 485, note 4.

6. An instance: anxious to bring Dutch and English together, Lady Lyttelton "began with a children's dance, which many of the Dutch would feel to be wrong". (Lawrence Richardson's *Selected Correspondence*, p. 59.)

7. Dr. William MacDonald. He was the Government expert on dry-land farming.

8. The Reverend N. J. van Warmelo, a former secretary of the Hervormde Kerk,

died in 1892, but his Pretoria home remained a centre of Afrikaans culture and activity. His daughter Johanna (later Brandt) was a nurse in the Irene camp during the war and wrote a book, *Die Kappiekommando/The Petticoat Commando*, about Boer women's secret war work.

9. Lily Rautenbach was head nurse at the Bezuidenhouts Drift Red Cross Hospital near Harrismith when it was fired upon by men of Rimington's column. She was taken to a Cape Town hospital with multiple wounds. E. H.'s committee in England collected £15 for her, which was used for batteries for electric treatment of her permanently impaired arm. At the time of this letter she had married Louis Boshoff of Vereeniging (a brother of the Misses Boshoff E. H. knew in the Aliwal North camp) and she was applying for a lump-sum pension.

10. J. S. Smit (1878–1960) was high commissioner for the Union of South Africa in Britain in 1925–9. He was admitted as an advocate to the Transvaal bar in 1905 and served as private secretary to Smuts and J. A. J. de Villiers. He later became administrator of the Transvaal.

11. Mrs. Millicent Fawcett, chairman of the Ladies' Committee appointed in 1901 to investigate the camps, returned to South Africa in 1903 to visit her daughter Philippa, then teaching there. Miss Fawcett had accompanied her mother at the time of the committee's visit and was so inspired by E. B. Sargant's educational work in the camps that she returned to work under him in his new post as director of education in the new colonies. She had had a brilliant career in mathematics at Cambridge.

68

1. The old Republican flag of the Transvaal consisted of three parallel horisontal panels of red, white and blue, and a vertical panel of green – thence the name *vierkleur*, lit. four colour.

2. Afrikaans for parlour, lit. sit-room.

3. Twenty-one of these sketches from the ruined colonies were published in 1927 in E. H.'s book of Boer women's war recollections, *War without Glamour*. She had had the sketches reproduced in colour in Leipzig in 1922 – "at considerable cost" – originally with a view to using them in a personal memoir which she envisaged as a sequel to *The Brunt of the War*.

4. The big quarterly Holy Communion services, a great occasion in the life of the Afrikaans community, for which families from far outlying districts would come to town, camping on the church lands for the extended week-end.

5. See p. 474.

6. The Boer Generals' Fund (pp. 167 ff.) had by July 1903 brought in about £103 819, of which £70 000 went to war widows and the rest to Christian National Education schools.

7. Field-cornet.

8. Dr. G. P. Gooch (1873–1968), the historian.
9. C. F. G. Masterman (1847–1929), politician, author and journalist. He studied at Christ Church, Cambridge.

70

1. These were about 800 deported burghers who refused to sign the declaration of allegiance to the British king, causing some impatience at home. Botha, speaking at the Heidelberg volksvergadering on 2 July 1903 said:
   "With reference to the men still in Bermuda who refuse to sign the declaration of allegiance, there appears to be an obstinate spirit among them. I and others tried our best to induce them to sign, but in vain."
   The Boer leaders asked the government that they be brought to a South African port where they could possibly be talked over, the irreconcilables having refused to listen to anybody but their generals. The request was refused. However, general J. H. (Koos) de la Rey was sent to India in 1903 and had considerable success.
2. Du Toit also drove Richardson and Butler, the Quaker representatives, on their trek to the northern districts in November 1903 and Richardson found him "a man of high character, though with the Afrikaner fault of sometimes lapsing into gross exaggeration". (Lawrence Richardson, *Selected Correspondence*, p. 175.)
3. Afrikaans: *bosveld*, lit. bushveld, with scattered trees.

71

1. J. W. Colenbrander (1856–1918), a flamboyant frontiersman nicknamed "*die Wit Gésel*", (the White Scourge), commanded Kitchener's Fighting Scouts after 1900. Short, thickset, with an adventurous and opportunistic spirit, his career started as a bugler in the 1879 Zulu war and ended with his death by drowning in the Klip River while impersonating Lord Chelmsford in a film made of that same war. In the years between he was *inter alia* a trader in Zululand, secretary of the white Zulu chieftain Dunn and Rhodes' agent in Rhodesia.
2. Lieutenants H. H. Morant, P. J. Handcock and G. R. Witton (Australians), and H. Picton (British), members of the irregular corps the Bushveld Carribineers, which was formed as an answer to the Boer guerillas, were court-martialled for shooting some Boer prisoners-of-war in the remote Spelonken district of Northern Transvaal, and also the Reverend Daniel Heese, a German-born missionary of Makapanspoort, who had witnessed the shooting of the prisoners.
3. Sinthemule was a son of the Venda chief Magato/Machado. In the succession battles and intrigues after his father's death Sinthemule and his equally rebellious half-brother Katuma were defeated by another half-brother, Mphephu.

Mphephu was eventually defeated with the help of a burgher force, which probably explains Sinthemule's favourable disposition towards the Boers. Mphephu fought on the British side in the war.

4. The rumour that Morant and Handcock had been made "scapegoats" was supported by Swift MacNeill's charge in the House of Commons (16 May 1902):

"Unless these men had had the misfortune to come into contact with this German missionary they would have enjoyed immunity. But . . . the Government, well aware that the German authorities would press the matter further, found it necessary to bring the men to trial." (Spies, *Methods of Barbarism?*, p. 276.)

The secretary for war, St. John Brodrick, had in November 1901 also spoken of how easily "a torch might be put to the German powder magazine". How substantial this fear of German intervention was, is another matter.

Breaker Morant, Beresford's Australian film of 1980, makes much of the question whether the officers were not merely acting in accordance with Kitchener's orders that no further Boer prisoners were to be taken.

5. Afrikaans: *knopkierie* – club.
6. Probably Haenertsburg.
7. Land-measure: One morgen equals 100 by 100 yards.
8. On 19 November 1902 a consignment of cattle imported from German East Africa had brought into South Africa the dreaded Rhodesian/East Coast/redwater fever which is carried by the brown tick *rhibicephalus appendiculatus*. Since a peculiar form of the disease had broken out there early in 1902, the fever had devastated Rhodesia. Early in August 1903 the South African veterinarians Theiler and Turner visited the Pietersburg area to do post-mortems on Spelonken oxen that had died from this rapid, virulent and then "absolutely mystifying" disease. By then "not a beast remained in Barberton" and more than half had died in Lydenburg. Repatriation oxen were greatly affected. (Thelma Gutsche, *There was a man*, p. 89.)
9. Afrikaans burgemeester, English burgomaster/mayor. E. H. had her etymology slightly mixed-up.

72

1. The objects of Milner's plan to put English-speaking settlers on the land were to blunt the division between the predominantly rural Afrikaners and the urban British and to ensure an "English" majority in the new colonies. It was also hoped that such settlers would be more amenable to new agricultural ideas and so act as a kind of leaven in the rural areas. The plan did not succeed. Whereas Milner had hoped for some 10 000 immigrants a year, lack of money to buy land and lack of support for the scheme from the British government resulted in the settlement of only about 1 300 English-speaking heads of families. Many of

them were ruined by the particularly hard drought conditions of the post-war years.

2. See E. H.'s paper on repatriation prepared for her brother, among the Hobhouse papers in the Steyn collection, state archives, Bloemfontein.

73

1. Willie Steyn, whose war-time adventures were described by P. Visagie in *Terug na Kommando : die ervaringen van Willie Steyn en vier ander*. Steyn called his eldest son Vladimir, in remembrance of the captain of the Russian boat which took them on board after their escape.

2. The South African Constabulary under General Robert Baden-Powell, established on 22 October 1900 to police Pretoria, Johannesburg and Bloemfontein after their surrender, were now also used to protect and help the resettlement on their farms of 'hands-uppers' Boers, to assess compensation claims and to disband black troops. (See also Letter 19, note 7.)

3. W. H. F. Alexander, clerk of the relief committee of the Society of Friends (the Quakers) and Lawrence Richardson, a Quaker emissary, on their South African visit of 1902 became aware that a number of bibles had been removed from Boer farm-houses as war souvenirs. On their return to England they tried to trace the bibles and return them to their original owners. Their efforts had the support of Lord Roberts who issued an appeal that these relics should be returned, pointing out also that in view of the "unavoidable destruction" of some church registers during the war the family records kept in the bibles were often the only source of that kind of information. There was an extensive response. However, well into the second half of the twentieth century some Boer bibles still surfaced in Britain. (See Lawrence Richardson's *Selected Correspondence* for Arthur M. Davey's editorial comment, pp. 8–9.)

4. They were published in *War without Glamour* (a title originally intended for the Diary of *Tant' Alie*), the reminiscences of Boer women collected and translated by E. H.

5. "Burdened with a sense of responsibility", E. H. had already written to private people at the Cape, among them Sir Henry de Villiers. She found his reply, dated 25 July 1903, awaiting her in Pretoria. He had sent her letter to "Mr. D. Graaff, a wealthy gentleman who takes great interest in the well-being of the former burghers of the republics". David Graaff replied that he and his brother Jacobus (who were to expand their meat business into the Imperial Cold Storage Company and one of the largest commercial concerns in the country) were placing Thomas Theron as their representative in Pretoria. He was "well acquainted with the farming population of the Transvaal" and enjoyed their confidence. He would "assist in a quiet and judicious way any worthy soul who may wish for a mortgage on his property" and further "assist and re-instate such people as may be in need of it" – as far as possible "in concert with General Smuts".

Sir Henry promised to enlist other help as the opportunity offered. In the meantime he asked his son-in-law P. A. M. Cloete in Cape Town to handle applications for loans free of charge.

6. Appendix IV, p. 430 ff.

74

1. Caroline Thornton and Maud Hebblethwaite were the two eldest surviving Hobhouse sisters.

2. Dr. and Mrs. Charles Murray.

3. Patrick Duncan (1870–1943), later to become governor-general of the Union of South Africa, had been Milner's private secretary when he was chairman of inland revenue in England, and was asked by him to undertake the work of colonial treasurer at this critical time of reconstruction in the new colonies.

4. Captain C. A. Madge, who had for thirteen months been an inspector of the repatriation department of Transvaal, on 19 August 1903 wrote a letter which was published in the *Cape Times* on 20 August and in the London *Times* on 6 October, refuting allegations that the repatriation boards were incompetent or dilatory. He said the "machinery for relief in cases of destitution are in full order". The British Government was notorious for "its almost foolish benevolence". If E. H. "in her very limited experience has discovered such appalling cases of destitution . . . the proper course for Miss Hobhouse and her friends is to put the matter exclusively and definitely before the representatives of the Imperial Government. Miss Hobhouse and her friends can rest assured that England will not allow the terrible state of affairs to exist for one moment longer." They would find far greater relief in going direct to Great Britain "than they would get from funds collected by and through the instrumentality of those who are blind, either wilfully or ignorantly, to the advantages of being an English subject". Captain Madge was on his way back home.

The *Cape Times* in a leading article on 31 August, referring to a similar letter from one Eros of Bethlehem elsewhere in the paper of the same date, said: ". . . to use charity as a cloak for politics is so despicable a thing that we prefer to believe that Miss Hobhouse in making her rash and random charges was simply a victim of hallucinations born of hysterical philanthrophy". (See also p. 495.)

5. The items of the grant for war widows as agreed upon by Generals Botha and Smuts and ordered to be issued in circular 120 of the repatriation department were: "one cow and calf; three months' ration free; £10 worth of wood and iron for house; £5 worth of fowls or cash for same; ten acres ploughed free and seed for same" – E. H., in a note.

6. Appendix V, p. 433.

75

1. Lewis Carroll: *Alice in Wonderland*, chapter 2.

2. See also Langlaagte, note 2, on p. 507.

3. E. B. Sargant, entrusted with education in all concentration camps as a result of the enthusiasm and originality with which he tackled the task, realized the overwhelming need for trained teachers to meet the Boer craving for learning. A fiery imperialist and admirer of Canadian educational methods, he canvassed the whole of the British empire for young women to come to South Africa and teach – which they did in often wretched circumstances and for a pittance. The imported teachers faced considerable Boer distrust and dissatisfaction, as this letter shows.

E. H. pays the following tribute to Sargant:

"To Mr. E. B. Sargant the country owes its gratitude for creating what has been the redeeming feature of camp life – the schools – where already many children have learnt a higher side of English character and thought than that which the war seemed to have taught them. Much, very much, may develop from the beginning made in these camp schools." (Emily Hobhouse, *The Brunt of the War*, p. 317.)

4. See Letter 53, note 1.

5. Bishop G. W. Wilkinson (1833–1907), known for his evangelical open-air preaching, was a zealous advocate of foreign missions, especially in South Africa. He combined "deep spirituality with practical sagacity, courage in dealing with others and intense humility". (See *Dictionary of National Biography*.)

76

1. Roberts' authoritative *Birds of South Africa* does not show the Western Transvaal as the habitat of any of the cuckoo species.

2. Probably commandant J. F. Kirsten.

3. Oliver (p. 528) was no more than ten years old at the time.

4. Ps. 107:26.

5. From the Reverend D. J. Viljoen of Reitz, whom he had met in Cape Town, Lawrence Richardson heard how many ministers had lost all their books during the war. A Quaker appeal was launched and 37 ministers benefited from the response. (Lawrence Richardson, *Selected Correspondence*, p. 29 and pp. 206–7.)

6. Under the Peace Preservation Act (Letter 59, note 5).

7. E. H. was actively involved in combating starvation in Germany after World War I.

77

1. The relevant clause provided for the retainment, under license, of rifles necessary for protection.

2. The *Transvaal Leader* of the 24th of August 1903 had an editorial under the heading "Humanity in Hysterics". E. H. was reproached for not mentioning in her appeal what was in fact being done for the Boers, and for the anti-British

tone which the *Leader* perceived in her letter. (Appendix IV, p. 430.) The editorial said:

".... It is always distasteful to write anything that can be construed into carelessness of suffering, or into doubt of the motives that underlie charitable appeals. But ... Miss Hobhouse's past record, the manifest absurdities of her statements about ploughing, the anti-British suggestions and omissions of her letter drive us reluctantly to the conclusion that mischief, not mercy, is the motive of her action."

Against the *Leader's* assessment of E. H. as "hysterical" – and a similar innuendo of the *Bloemfontein Post* on her first visit (p. 453) – there is the evaluation of that level-headed Quaker, Lawrence Richardson. On 14 October he wrote in his diary:

"He (Goold-Adams) gave great offence the other day by referring to Miss Hobhouse as an "hysterical lady" (he afterwards withdrew the expression); I do not approve altogether of Miss Hobhouse's attitude; she is too one-sided, but she is not hysterical but remarkably calm and business-like; she has accomplished a very great deal ..." (Lawrence Richardson, *Selected Correspondence*, p. 130; see also Letter 78, From the memoir, for E. H.'s reaction.)

78

1. The proposal that Captain Jenner should investigate the position in the former republics was made by John X. Merriman, on 18 August 1903, and the House was apparently unanimous that "that distinguished civil servant" would bring out an objective and impartial report.

   The *Cape Times'* Johannesburg correspondent reported on 21 August that the Cape Government's proposal to send Captain Jenner ... "has been received here with the utmost indignation. It is regarded as a piece of bumptiousness unequalled in South Africa ... Dutch and English resent the interference in Transvaal affairs."

2. R. L. Outhwaite.

3. By the end of June Dale Lace and the editor of the *Transvaal Leader*, R. J. Pakenham, had started a movement to form the Transvaal Political Association. Overtures were made to some Boer leaders, but they refused to become involved.

79

1. For further comment on the interview, see Letter 80.

2. The ORC Volunteers were the Free State equivalents of the National Scouts, in whose formation Piet de Wet, general C. R. de Wet's brother, took a prominent part. (A. M. Grundlingh, *Die "Hensoppers" en "Joiners"*, ch. 9.)

3. Commandant A. H. Malan. For E. H.'s full and graphic description of this ceremony, see p. 284.

80

1. On 19 August 1903 the *Cape Times* leader commented on E. H.'s letter, saying *inter alia*:

     "We know how Miss Hobhouse's tendency to run riot in tear-compelling phrases betrayed her into sad, mischievous misrepresentations and exaggerations in the case of the camps. Such a style of writing is to be distrusted as much as the Brussels cartoons which the Attorney General very properly detained ...

     "It is necessary to warn the public against the sensational utterances of Miss Hobhouse because they follow on a deliberate attempt in more than one quarter to misrepresent the work of the Repatriation Department."

     The writer of *Notes from the House*, in discussing the debate on "distressed neighbours" in the former republics, on the same day referred to "the Hobhouse version" of the facts as "coloured in characteristically startling hues".

     See also p. 492.

81

1. After the Boer generals G. H. Gravett, H. R. Lemmer and C. J. Spruyt.
2. Lieutenant Hans Cordua, a German Uitlander, was executed for his role in an abortive bid to kidnap Lord Roberts in Pretoria. It is widely accepted that he was the victim of a British *agent provocateur*.
3. After early British victories in 1899 – at Belmont on 23 November, at Graspan on 25 November and at Modderrivier on 28 November.
4. John Cheere Emmett, one-time auctioneer at Harrismith who claimed that he was a close relative of "the famous Irish patriot".

82

1. Griqualand West – disputed territory after the discovery of diamonds in 1867 – was proclaimed British in 1871 and incorporated into the Cape Colony in 1879. Griqualanders thus became British subjects and those who, still considering themselves Free Staters, fought on the Boer side were branded as rebels.
2. General de la Rey published no book on the war, but his wife's war-time experiences, told to Lucy Hotz, was published in 1903.
3. E. H. probably had in mind De Wet's *De Strijd tusschen Boer en Brit/Three Years War* and J. D. Kestell's *Met de Boeren Commando's: mijne ervaringen als Veldpredikant* as the other two notable contemporary war books from the Boer perspective.
4. To the tune of the Old Hundredth – "Praise God from whom all blessings flow" – the Boers sang "Dat 's Heeren zegen op u daal/zijn gunst uit Zion u bestraal", a hymn invoking divine blessings upon the person in question.
5. A literal translation of the idiomatic Afrikaans *mooipraat*, meaning to coax or cajole.
6. In the anonymous English morality play Everyman (c. 1500) Everyman, sum-

moned on his last journey by Death, in vain seeks help and companionship from friends such as Beauty, Knowledge and Five Wits. It is only Good Deeds, feeble at first but growing ever stronger, who stays and supports him to the end.

7. Methuen was captured at Tweebosch on 7 March 1902, the only British general taken during the war. It is on record that Mrs De la Rey gave him boerbeskuit and killed her last chicken for him.

8. See p. 493, note 3.

9. The £2 poll tax.

83

1. Of the money made available by the British government (see Letter 57, note 2) £1 900 000 was earmarked for the relief of "protected burghers".

84

1. Probably Michelson.

2. The labour commission was appointed in July 1903 by the governor of Transvaal, Sir Arthur Lawley, to enquire into possible means of supplying the labour needs of the country (and specifically the mines). Botha's written evidence was drawn up by Smuts but not accepted by the commission, which declared it to be mainly concerned with the question of Chinese labour, a matter not specifically before the commission. A closer reading would have shown that the greater part of the memorandum dealt with ways of making better use of Native labour. Botha was questioned by the commission and had to give unprepared answers. (See W. K. Hancock and Jean van der Poel (ed.) *Selections from the Smuts Papers*, vol. II, pp. 123–33, for the memorandum.)

3. The British seed merchants.

4. See Letter 64, note 5.

85

1. See Letter 3, note 3.

2. On his second visit, in 1903, Lawrence Richardson had the benefit of the company of a fellow-Quaker who did speak Dutch. He was James Butler of Cradock, editor of the *Midland News*.

3. Richardson, having volunteered to undertake inspection on the spot, first visited South Africa from 24 September to 3 December 1902, accompanied by W. H. F. Alexander, clerk of S.A. Relief Committee of the Society of Friends. Their aims: "to renew links with Friends already in South Africa, investigate conditions afresh, provide relief on the spot on a modest scale and make recommendations to the Society for the continuance of its humanitarian work." (Lawrence Richardson, *Selected Correspondence*, p. 4.)

4. The notoriously stormy Bay of Biscay – the wide inlet of the Atlantic Ocean between the West coast of France and the North coast of Spain.

86

1. Richardson gave this account of the meeting:
   "We had a long talk with Miss Hobhouse – two and a half hours on Friday and two hours more on Saturday morning . . . She has seen much of people on the verge of starvation, but the re-opening of the repatriation stores on credit should relieve the immediate necessity in the matter of food. I have always had a high opinion of Miss Hobhouse, but am *very much impressed* with the amount of trekking she has done and what she has accomplished in distributing relief; also with her judgement and business ability and absence of anything hysterical. Where she seems open to criticism is that she has been moving among one set of people and consequently has only seen one side in some questions; e.g. she stated that the Britishers had lost all faith in Milner. Bullen (who must know much better) [a former resident of Johannesburg whom Richardson had met on the voyage out in 1902 and then again in Bloemfontein, where he now lived] says they still believe in him thoroughly in Jo'burg. Also, she has a strong anti-official bias and seems to have needlessly and foolishly got into conflict with the Authorities on one little point. On the other hand, she has seen a good deal of Duncan, colonial secretary in the Transvaal, and thinks highly of him as trying to do his best in spite of inefficient subordinates . . ." (Arthur Davey (ed.), *Selected Correspondence of Lawrence Richardson*, 1902–3, p. 126.)

87

1. The Westminster Gazette.
2. Captain Madge's. See Letter 74, note 4, and Letter 94.
3. Nickname for members of the Gereformeerde Kerk.
4. Afrikaans *bakkiespomp*, i.e. bucket-pump or Persian wheel.
5. She had met the Reverend Adriaan Moorrees in England, where he came as adviser to the Cape delegation led by Professor P. J. G. de Vos.
6. On Chamberlain's resignation as colonial secretary, prime minister Balfour offered the post to Milner. He refused, on the grounds that "in a situation which, though improving, is still full of difficulty, my personal influence on the spot has a somewhat special value . . ." (G. Headlam (ed.) *The Milner Papers*, p. 473.)
7. Uitkijk.
8. Robert Gwelo Goodman (1871–1939), British-born South African painter, exhibited in London in 1924.

88

1. Dr. Johannes Meiring Beck (1855–1919), a medical doctor, amateur composer and politician, was MLA for Worcester from 1878. He was a prominent Bonds-man and at one stage chairman of the South African National Society for the

Preservation of Objects of Beauty and History. In 1903 he bought the historic Oude Drostdy farm at Tulbagh as a home for his family.

2. The Donald Currie Line (Percy Alport Molteno succeeded his father-in-law after whom it was named as chairman) was the forerunner of the Union Castle Line.

3. The South African Women and Children Distress Fund, which supported E. H.'s work.

89

1. Elections for the Cape legislative council were held in November 1903, and those for the Cape assembly in January 1904.

2. See, for James Molteno's temperament, p. 531.

90

1. The difficulty of reaching places away from the railway line late in 1902 is described by J. Ramsay MacDonald:

"... tried to get from Mafeking to Johannesburg but no horses to be had ... and from Kimberley to Bloemfontein, but it cost £30 per cart and two horses per day instead of £4 because fodder is so scarce ... tried to drive from Barberton to Standerton ... reports no transport to be got ... tried to leave train at Standerton and drive back to Ermelo: we failed ... impossible to get horses ..." (J. Ramsay MacDonald *What I saw in South Africa*, p. 49.)

Chamberlain, on his visit some months later, for short distances such as from Lichtenburg to Ottoshoop and from Kimberley to Bloemfontein had the benefit of "a sprung waggon drawn by a grand team of grey mules".

2. On Milner's return to South Africa early in December 1903 after his holiday he found "the Rand still suffering from slump and there was little hope of a speedy recovery. Grumblers abounded, for the large towns, and above all Johannesburg, were thronged with unemployed whites, while every week further immigrants seeking work arrived. At the beginning of the year 1904 the revenue of Transvaal was falling at the rate of £10 000 a month ..." (J. E. Wrensch, *Alfred Lord Milner*, p. 249.)

3. Dr. A. H. Petersen, a member of the Cape Town ward committee of the Afrikaner Bond, stood as an independent candidate. He was, however, backed by the Bond as well as by Dr. A. Abdurahman's African People's Organization and Isaac Purcell's Working Men's Union in District Six. He headed the polls in the western circuit. The South African Party (the Afrikaner Bond) won 11 seats in all, the Progressives 12.

4. Chincherinchee, named for the sound made by its fleshy stems when rubbed together.

91

1. It was agreed at the peace negotiations that leaders among the Cape rebels would be tried for high treason, but that the punishment for the rank and file, having acknowledged that they were guilty of high treason, would be loss of franchise in any parliamentary, divisional council or municipal elections. In effect, the disenfranchisement was for five years.
2. The 74-year old Leonard Courtney contested the West Edinburgh seat for the Liberals in January 1906. He brought the Conservative majority down from 1 500 to 300 votes, but could not oust the sitting member, Sir Lewis McIver. (G. P. Gooch, *Life of Lord Courtney*, p. 491 ff.)

92

1. The old drostdy (magistrate's dwelling), was built in 1803.
2. The dreaded insect-borne disease in vines, which had all but ruined the vineyards of France, had, in the 1880s, also attacked Cape vineyards, with disastrous results and serious political side-effects. The commission on phylloxera appointed in September 1890 recommended that the culture of European vines be grafted on stocks of certain American varieties which were resistant to the disease.
3. F. C. Mackarness (1854–1920), barrister and former member of the Cape bar, had played a major role in the founding of the S.A. Conciliation Committee.

94

1. The relevant part of article 10 read:
   "As soon as conditions permit, a Commission, on which local inhabitants will be represented, will be appointed in each district of the Transvaal and Orange River Colony, under the Presidency of a Magistrate or other Official, for the purpose of assisting the restoration of the people to their homes and supplying those who, owing to war losses, are unable to provide for themselves, with food, shelter, and the necessary amount of seed, stock, implements, etc. indispensable to the resumption of their normal occupations.
   "His Majesty's Government will place at the disposal of these Commissions a sum of three million pounds sterling for the above purposes . . ." (J. D. Kestell and D. E. van Velden, *The Peace Negotiations*, p. 345.)

95

1. Professor J. I. Marais (1845–1919) of the Stellenbosch theological seminary, a man of wide learning, eloquence and open mind.
2. For the Purcells, see p. 533–4.
3. See report on the meeting in *De Zuid-Afrikaan*, 5 November 1901.
4. The reference is probably to the Macedonian insurrection of 1903.
5. Mrs. MacDonald accompanied her husband, J. Ramsay MacDonald, on the visit to South Africa he described in *What I saw in South Africa*.

BOER HOME INDUSTRIES

INTRODUCTION, 1904

1. This followed on a great deal of activity reminiscent of her work in England after her visit to the camps. The draft memoir contains fuller details.

On her return to England she had found the question of Chinese labour "universally discussed" and she did all she could to put before the country and its leaders the Boer leaders' objections to the scheme.

She wrote to the *Manchester Guardian* and, also, to Smuts' chagrin, published in it a forceful private letter he had written to her on the subject (W. K. Hancock and Jean van der Poel (ed.) *Selections from the Smuts Papers*, vol. II, pp. 156–162).

She addressed a public meeting at Manchester and had interviews with prominent public men such as John Morley, Lord Spence and the colonial secretary, Alfred Lyttelton.

She told Lyttelton he would "rue the day" the ordinance admitting Chinese labour was passed.

She also took up with him the matter of destitute war widows; the plight of former Transvaal policemen now unemployed; the question of unpaid military receipts; and individual cases of hardship for whom all possible steps had been taken in South Africa and whose only hope now lay with the colonial office: Lily Rautenbach-Boshoff, Mrs. Vahrmeyer of Zoutpansberg, T. Webster, the Kimberley blacksmith whose smithy had been shut down during the war; the widow Nienaber at Beaufort West whose husband had been shot by the British after the Taaibosch siding affair, etc. She was aggrieved when Lyttelton in the end merely referred these cases back to the South African authorities.

She also took pains to lay before Lyttelton evidence to refute the persistent allegations that the Boers had during the war secretly sent "the Kruger millions" abroad – which money, Chamberlain and others had suggested, could now well be used for their own needy countrymen (Appendix III, p. 426).

2. On 2 May 1904 H. C. Bredell wrote to E. H. from Mentone:

"I am directed by His Hon. S. J. P. Kruger to convey to you his grateful thanks for that great work executed by you during the late Transvaal war – in reference to your unparallelled sympathy and undisguised interest shown towards the poor, unfortunate women and children in the now abolished Concentration Camps.

"His Honour gladly appreciated and ever will appreciate your continued interest on behalf of his countrymen in South Africa and directs me further to forward you his autograph [sic] photograph as a small token of his gratitude."

3. Dr. and Mrs. Berne of Güntherstal, near Freiburg.

500

4. Widow of Lord Thomas Henry Farrer, English lawyer, economist and statistician, the brother of E. H.'s aunt Mary, Lady Hobhouse. He died in 1892.
5. Alice Stopforth Green (1847–1929), Anglo-Irish widow of the historian J. R. Green and herself an historian of Irish affairs, was very active in the Irish Nationalist movement and in humanitarian work. She sympathised with the Boer cause and, with the blessing of the War Office, took gifts, made possible by the generosity of Percy Alport Molteno, to Boer prisoners-of-war on St. Helena.
6. Her "Scheme for establishing certain Home Industries among the Boer Women and Girls" confidentially discussed by the committee of the S.A. Distress Fund on 22 June 1902, still saw lace-making as a priority. But, the committee noted, "to some extent Miss Hobhouse also recommends spinning and weaving . . . although the almost total extermination of sheep has made wool scarce".

   E. H. in the end never herself established lace-making in South Africa. However, when she left South Africa in October 1908 she took with her to Europe Johanna Rood (her sister Sarah, later Niemeyer, had been at the Philippolis school for seven months) and introduced her to lace-making. Miss Rood then established the first lace-making school at Koppies in the Orange Free State in 1909, helped by Lucia Starace from Italy.
7. For E. H.'s letter to Smuts on her visit to the Steyns in Paris, see W. K. Hancock and Jean van der Poel (ed.) *Selections from the Smuts Papers*, vol. II, p. 183.)
8. Sir Horace Plunkett (1854–1932), Irish agricultural reformer and political leader, founded the modern co-operative movement in Irish agriculture.
9. G. M. Theal: *History of South Africa*.
10. "During the war [at the end of the eighteenth century] there was such a scarcity of blankets and rough cloth in the Colony that the slaves were almost naked. Thereupon several enterprising persons formed the idea of manufacturing blankets and cloth at the Cape, and a company was got together, prepared to risk the necessary capital. There was coarse wool to be had in plenty, and a burgher named Frederick Heyneman, who was living in the village of Stellenbosch and who had been a weaver before he came to this country, was engaged to begin the work. All was in readiness and only permission was needed from the Government . . . All the members (of the Council) were willing except Mr. Broers [the fiscal], who denounced the project of establishing manufactures in the Colony as little short of treason and succeeded in thwarting the plan." (G. M. Theal, *History of South Africa*, vol. II, p. 257.)
11. The clergyman Augustus Montague Toplady.
12. The Quaker family from Street, Somersetshire. They were well-known shoe manufacturers. For Margaret Clark, see p. 521.
13. Lady de Villiers wrote:
    "I often thought of you when I saw the ruined homesteads and heard the tales of woe in every little home I went to – it is so depressing and I marvel how you

stood it for so many months." (Her letter is among the Hobhouse papers in the Steyn collection.)

14. Sister Adeline Darby, daughter of the clergyman Dr. Charles Darby, was a social worker whom E. H. had engaged under the erroneous impression that she had taken lessons that would equip her to be their expert on spinning and particularly weaving.

15. See p. 352. But an earlier plan had been to start at Wolmaransstad. On 11 December 1904 General Smuts wrote to E. H. from Pretoria:

"I received your letter in reference to your plans of work for the future last week. You had provisionally determined to make Wolmaransstad the centre of your beneficent activities. In reference to your ideas I may say that I heartily endorse them as I feel certain that you could do lots of good; you will see your way more clearly once you start; and as for discouragements – they are not meant for such as you. But Wolmaransstad District is sparsely populated and the result of your starting there would be that a certain amount of effort will have less educative effect than in a more populous district. I therefore took the liberty to wire to you to make Klerksdorp your point of departure. The Schoonspruit valley is one of the most fertile and populous parts of the Transvaal, and the good effects of your work will reach such a bigger population. I would therefore – without in any way seeming to interfere with your plans – suggest Schoonspruit as the best locality in which to start your work. Of course you and your helpers will come to stay with us at Pretoria before you start; and the details could be discussed fully."

16. Prince Peter Alexeivich Kropotkin (1842–1921), Russian geographer, author and anarchist revolutionary. His political activities and writings brought him into conflict with the governments first of Russia and then of France, where he had fled. After three years' imprisonment in Lyons he went to England and lived there from 1896 to 1914. He returned to Russia in 1917 but remained critical of the Bolshevik dictatorship.

17. Russian liberals, opposing the repressive Tsarist regime, formed an illegal underground party, the Union of Liberation. In 1904, at a combined conference in Paris, they joined the Socialist Revolutionaries in demanding parliamentary government. The co-operation of the two groups did not last.

18. *The Diary of a Church-goer*, by Lord Courtney of Penwith (first published anonymously), was, according to the *Christian Times* "a modest, sincere, and at times striking commentary on the questions raised in the mind of an intelligent layman who has ceased to believe in orthodox Anglicanism, but does not want to give up church-going, and remains at heart a Christian . . . Specially a book to be read by all preachers who would understand their congregations".

19. See note 15, above.

1. C. E. Maurice had been honorary secretary of the Distress Fund.
2. President Kruger's daughter, Mrs. Louis Jacobsz, who had her husband and little daughter Ellie with her.
3. "Miss Hobhouse told me with much agitation that she had just discovered Sister Adeline had not after all had the training in wool spinning and weaving she'd engaged her to have, it seems ... What explanation there can be is dark to me but it will be a great calamity if our expert turns out to be none such.". ... Margaret Clark, in a shipboard letter home.
4. Dr. D. F. Malan (1874–1959), later prime minister of the union of South Africa, was returning home after acquiring a doctorate in divinity at Utrecht. Margaret Clark wrote of him that he appeared to be "of great ability" and that she found his Dutch lessons "very satisfactory". She commented on his "sharp mind".

   "He has been writing a thesis on Berkely – which he pronounces Burkely – and so we talked of Sidgwick and Berkely's power to inspire".

   In her diary she noted that he was "very learned and a regular pedant, much better able to narrate the story of the Zimbabwe ruins than to describe home life on a farm ... awfully funny to see him staring out under knitted brows while he puts easy sentences extraordinarily slowly together. He has knots in his bootlaces and very dirty shirt-cuffs, but he is very clever and interesting and a good fellow."
5. Afrikaans: *pap*, weak, exhausted.
6. This was Cornelis du Preez, President Steyn's former adjutant and devoted *aide*. Margaret Clark described him as "the son of a blacksmith, who had been with the President on commando, and had tended him all through his illness ... always ready to do anything for anybody".
7. Apart from a history of the labour movement, L. T. Hobhouse had by then published *A Theory of Knowledge (1896)* and *Mind in Evolution* (1901). *Morals in Evolution* was to follow in 1906 and E. H. may have been reading the manuscript.
8. Sister Adeline Darby.
9. The Herero, a powerful pastoralist tribe of South West Africa, had revolted against German rule in January 1904; their rebellion was now all but quelled although mopping up operations were to continue well into 1907. In the course of the campaign German ships brought re-inforcements from Germany.
10. Evidently the Stellenbosch and Hottentot Holland ranges. (See also Letter 1, p. 32, Letter 2, p. 33.)
11. The Reverend H. D. van Broekhuizen was at the time Dutch Reformed Church minister at Kuils River near Cape Town. He had been refused permission to return to his parish in Pretoria by the British authorities who, not

altogether without reason, considered him a firebrand. He was married to president Kruger's granddaughter and had spent some time in the household of the exiled president in Switzerland.

12. H. C. Bredell, formerly President Kruger's bodyguard, became the president's private secretary until Kruger's death in July 1904.

13. J. H. (Onze Jan) Hofmeyr was a leading Afrikaner stateman (p. 475).

14. C. du P. Chiappini – one-armed since a hunting accident in the Transvaal in the 1890's – was a well-known Cape businessman involved in agricultural co-operatives and other farming interests he would have shared with many members of the Afrikaner Bond.

15. F. S. Malan was the editor of *Ons Land* (Letter 7 and note 2).

16. Abraham Fischer, a former member of the Orange Free State executive council, was now practising as an advocate in Bloemfontein.

17. Ewald Esselen, former state attorney of the Transvaal, was legal adviser to Commandant-General Piet Joubert during the war. He was to become a member of the executive of Het Volk.

18. J. A. J. (Jaap) de Villiers, former state advocate of the Orange Free State, was now one of Johannesburg's foremost advocates. He had been on commando with the Free Staters and banished to Bermuda. (See p. 524.)

19. A younger brother of Sir Henry, Melius de Villiers had been chief justice of the Orange Free State up to the British occupation in 1900.

20. Jarvis was the second-eldest son of Dr. Charles and Mrs. Caroline Murray. He became a farmer.

21. General Louis Botha's daughter Helen had been in Brussels for four years, for her education, and had returned on the *Kronprinz* – "a real beauty who rules the ship," E. H. wrote to Lady Hobhouse.

22. Dr. and Mrs. F. W. Purcell (p. 533). Margaret Clark in her diary described the "house in the Groote Schuur style, standing in a *Werf*, with stables and an [illegible] to one side of it, a round flower garden with a posted white fence in front, all pure white, with views up to Constantia and the mountains".

Of the interior she recorded the "exquisite natural taste and many books, some Bartolozzi engravings and Holbein drawings, and two portraits, Van Riebeeck and his wife, and bowls of blue water-lilies – very pleasant, cool and quiet feeling". The Van Riebeeck portraits are free copies, by Jan Veth, of contemporary portraits attributed to Dirk Craey, and were commissioned by Willem Frederik Hertzog, previous owner of the farm (See Jocelyn Purcell on The Van Riebeeck Portraits in *The Quarterly Bulletin of the South African Library*, June 1974, vol. 28, No. 4.)

23. The Russian admiral had fired on a British fishing trawler off the Dogger Bank mistaking it, he said, for a Japanese submarine. Russia was at war with Japan and the Russian fleet was steaming through the North Sea to the Pacific war zone via the Cape of Good Hope.

24. Although E. H., according to a letter to Mrs. Steyn in 1922, would have liked a woman to translate it and did in fact approach Gladys Steyn, *The Brunt of the War* was eventually translated by Dr. N. J. van der Merwe, President Steyn's son-in-law. It was published in Afrikaans as *Die Smarte van die Oorlog en wie dit gely het*, by Nasionale Pers in 1924.

25. Gideon Scheepers, famour Boer scout and commandant, was tried by a British military tribunal and executed outside Graaff-Reinet on 18 January 1902. He was reported to be buried under lime in the grave beside which he was shot, but rumours long persisted that he had been exhumed on the night of his execution and secretly buried elsewhere because the British feared the Boers might claim his body for a martyr's grave.

26. Both societies were founded in 1904 by Cape women who had been involved in helping the victims of the concentration and prisoner-of-war camps; Mrs. Saul Solomon's Zuid-Afrikaansche Vrouwen Federatie was to be open to white women of all denominations, while the Afrikaansche Christelijke Vrouwen Vereeniging, whose founding Mrs. Marie Koopmans-De Wet had at first backed, wanted to confine their membership to Protestant women, and was committed to the Dutch/Afrikaans language. On their failing to come to an agreement on these issues, the Cape was left to the A.C.V.V. while Mrs. Solomon, with the support of Mrs. Louis Botha, concentrated on starting branches of the Federatie in the Transvaal.

27. Jean Etienne Reenen (Oefie) de Villiers, son of a well-known DRC minister from Carnarvon, was called to the bar in London in 1900 after an exceptionally brilliant academic career in law at Cambridge. He returned to South Africa in the same year, to practise in Cape Town. In 1903 he had just married Minnie, daughter of Sir James Drummond, who was, in 1915, to be the first woman in South Africa to obtain the LL.B. degree.

28. The South African National Society for the Preservation of Objects of Beauty and Historic Interest was established on 18 February 1905, with Sir Henry de Villiers as its first president.

29. The Castle of Good Hope, South Africa's oldest and most historic building, (1666–79), was three times in the nineteenth century in imminent danger of demolition. It was declared an historical monument in 1936.

30. Piet Retief, the Great Trek leader (1750–1838), was born on the farm Soetendal in the Wellington district. He lived on his father's farm Welvanpas in the same district until about 1807 when he moved to Kromme Rhee near Stellenbosch where he farmed until he left for the eastern Cape.

31. In 1904 Hofmeyr and his second wife (whom he had married in 1900) moved back to Avondrust, the house he built in Stephens Street. It was not far from Welgemeend, the old Hofmeyr homestead where he had spent his youth with his grandparents and where he had returned after the death of his first wife.

32. Some sixty cases of clothing which the Cape Town relief committee had forwarded to Lydenburg had not reached their destination and were feared to have been appropriated by the much distrusted local repatriation board.

33. Mrs. Steyn's youngest sister, who shortly after married a Philippolis shopkeeper and businessman, John Steytler.

34. The widow Boshoff is described by Margaret Clark in her diary as a "an old quaddle, very well-meaning and anxious to please but quite incompetent. She wears a sweeping black dress and is a most untidy sight . . . poor old thing . . . she babbles softly to herself all the time and comes every few minutes to Miss Hobhouse to ask which egg to boil and what pan to use and when to take it out."

35. The carpenter.

36. Moritz Liefman, Jewish shop-keeper much beloved in the town, whose unused house and shop E. H. and company were allowed to occupy – they set up their looms in the shop. (Petronella van Heerden, *Kerssnuitsels*, p. 144.)

37. The wife of the resident magistrate and former member of the Orange Free State Government F. W. van Heerden, and mother of Nellie (Petronella) van Heerden.

38. In Afrikaans *boerbeskuit*, i.e. rusks.

39. As a replacement for the disappointingly inexpert Sister Adeline who was succeeded, in the end, by Miss Picard.

40. Or *heddles*: the cords or wires through which the warp is passed and which separate it, allowing the passage of the shuttle with the weft.

41. Robert Browning's long dramatic poem on this bold-thinking and controversial sixteenth-century physician and alchemist.

42. Petronella van Heerden, 18 years old at the time, was to become the first Afrikaans woman doctor and a champion of women's rights in South Africa. Much of this she traced back to that Philippolis encounter with E. H. and Margaret Clark who, fresh from Cambridge, was the first university woman she had ever met. E. H. introduced her to J. S. Mill's *Subjection of Women*, which she greatly enjoyed. She confessed, though, that she had found E. H.'s first book for her hard going. It was Aristoteles' *Ethics* (Petronella van Heerden, *Kerssnuitsels*, p. 145).

    E. H. obviously enjoyed the young Boer girl's ready response and enthusiasm. "She delights me hugely," she wrote to Margaret Clark, when the latter was later in England.

43. The Bloemfontein newspaper (see Letter 51, note 2).

44. Popular medication for rheumatism etc.

45. Grootfontein – "an hour and a half of a glorious drive with fine bounding horses through this great spreading country bristling with kopjes", wrote Margaret Clark.

46. Hembury, former station foreman at Glastonbury in Somersetshire (the nearest

railway station to Street, where the Clarks lived). When he came to South Africa, he left his aged cat, Peter, with Mrs. Clark.

47. Dr. A. E. W. Ramsbottom, a Bloemfontein doctor with strong republican sentiments. He served with the Free State ambulance during the war and after the war was one of the syndicate of "disaffected Boers" who in 1903 bought the *Friend* in order to counterbalance the influence of the imperialist *Bloemfontein Post*.

LANGLAAGTE AND AFTER

1. This had from the outset been Smuts' advice on the best site for starting the industries. (See Boer Home Industries: Introduction, 1904, note 15.)
2. The Reverend Abraham Paul Kriel (1850–1926). As the first minister of Lang-laagte, and because of his long-standing concern about destitute children, he founded an orphanage for children whose parents had died in the war. He had been chaplain of the Boer forces. It is characteristic that he and his wife had, in addition to their own three children, adopted an English child left behind as a baby of three weeks when its parents fled from Johannesburg just before the war (Lawrence Richardson, *Selected Correspondence*, p. 81).

   The Langlaagte orphanage opened on 4 September 1902, and within a year there were 254 children. Eventually there were some 600. The institution was remarkable in that it had no fixed source of income but depended – often on a day-to-day basis – on the prayers of the Reverend Kriel and his staff.
3. They came for the wedding of H. C. Bredell and President Kruger's grand-daughter Nettie Eloff.
4. Marion Rowntree (p. 535–6).
5. Notably from Lady Fry, the Dowager Lady Farrer and the Bishop of Here-ford (Hobhouse papers in the Steyn collection).
6. E. H.'s design for a rug for Advocate Jaap de Villiers is described by Margaret Clark in a letter to her sister Hilda:

   "It is a deep green blue and the field is plain. In the border there is a lighter band with the letters in the natural white wool on it: *Alles sal reg kom* [All will be well] which is the favourite Afrikaans motto, first spoken by President Brand of the Orange Free State when that piece of the Free State containing diamond mines was taken by the British, a motto with which they always try and comfort themselves. At each corner there is an orange tree representing the tree of liberty and life and therefore connecting every nation's imagination with the Free State, and the Eastern rug-makers and us. The tree is in a soft green and there are oranges in it. I had endless trouble to get these colours right, but in the end they are a great success".

   She thought De Villiers had "no possession more beautiful than the rug".

Marion Rowntree in a letter to Margaret Clark speaks of "a gorgeous design of the Missis [E. H.] worked out from a sketch of Italian columns". E. H.'s *wacht-'n-bietjie* (acacia) design became almost synonymous with the industry and she soon determined that "no design shall be worked in either school unless I have passed it", remarking that "Mrs. Goetzsche would like to harp back to Irish plants and much exploded naturalism". (E. H. in a letter to Margaret Clark, 15 March 1906.)

7. The cottage was in Becker Street, Bellevue. She bought the ground with her legacy from her aunt and calculated that a pro-Boer gift of £400 and £100 she had herself saved would pay for the bulk of the building. In the end her brother and cousin Edmund arranged a further loan of £500. She called the house Mara(h), meaning "bitterness" (*Ruth* 1:20) in a mood probably created by her sense of loneliness after her beloved aunt Mary's death and the end of all hope of marriage.

8. Probably W. H. Poultney (1860–1913), a Johannesburg businessman, formerly interpreter to the high court of the Orange Free State and joint chief of the commissariat during the war.

9. Your arrival in our midst has created new ties of sympathy between Miss Hobhouse and us, between your work and us, between all the Boers and us.

   (M. Ernst Faure, writing to E. H. from Paris, expressed the opinion that if England sent to the Transvaal such a group of young women as represented by the one they had just seen and heard, the hearts of the Boers would soon be conquered and the work of reconciliation well done.)

10. Beautiful soul.

11. Samuel Johnson in *Lines added to Goldsmith's Traveller*.

12. Sir William Butler (1839–1910), former general officer commanding the British forces in South Africa and acting high commissioner in South Africa while Milner was on leave, was recalled in 1899 on account of his conciliatory attitude towards the Boer republics.

13. Sir William's articles were sent to the *Tribune* whose staff Leonard Hobhouse had joined. When they did not appear promptly Leonard was roundly berated by E. H. (Letter to him on Whitsunday 1906, p. 384).

14. Sir West Ridgeway (1884–1930) was chairman of the commission on the constitution of the Transvaal and Orange River Colonies in 1906. This was not his first difficult assignment. He had formerly been under-secretary of the government of India, special commissioner to determine the Russian-Afghan frontier (1886–7), under-secretary for Ireland, and governor of Ceylon.

15. The Transvaal constitution, promulgated by letters patent on 6 December 1906, granted self-government to the colony. In the Orange River Colony self-government became operative in June 1907.

16. Sir Percy Fitzpatrick (1862–1931), born near King William's Town as the son of a supreme court judge, was at this time member of the legislative council of

the Transvaal colony. He was a partner in the gold-mining firm of Eckstein & Co. and had been secretary of the Reform Committee urging franchise and citizen status for Uitlanders at the time of the Jameson Raid (although like other members of the committee unprepared for Jameson's "precipitate action"). Now he was one of the Progressives and opposed the granting of early responsible government to the colonies.

17. Sir Richard Solomon (1850–1913), a lawyer, had been a member of the Cape parliament and attorney-general in Schreiner's cabinet (1898–1900). He was attorney-general in the Transvaal (1902–7). After defeat in the Transvaal elections by Sir Percy Fitzpatrick he became the colony's agent-general in London.

18. Lord Selborne (1859–1942), succeeded Milner as governor of the two new colonies and British high commissioner in South Africa. His appointment was highly unpopular in the former republics, for he had been under-secretary for colonies under Chamberlain at the time of the Jameson raid, and, as later research was to reveal, in fact in favour of the raid. (His father-in-law, the Conservative British prime minister Lord Salisbury, had appointed him as under-secretary). Milner, when following the intransigent policy that made war inevitable, had spoken of Selborne as his "great standby". When the Liberals came to power in 1906 his position was difficult and he was widely distrusted for his close links with the preceding government. He was reprimanded for his active support of the Progressive South African viewpoint at the time of the Ridgeway commission, and there was talk of his either resigning or being removed. In 1907, after responsible government had been granted to the former republics, both he and Milner's kindergarten worked for closer union of the various South African colonies and much of the old distrust of him in the former republics disappeared.

As a man he was likeable, easy of approach and had a sense of humour. He was keenly interested in farming himself and in this found common ground with the Boers.

19. The phrase has nothing to do with age but designates that they were servants – revealing the paternalistic white attitude of the time.

20. 2 Chron. 9:4.

21. To Kenneth Wilkinson, a York lawyer.

22. R. P. Milroy, author of *A Handbook on Dyeing*, came from North Berwick in Scotland.

23. "Oh the little more, and how much it is!
And the little less, and what worlds away!" – Robert Browning, in *By the Fireside*.

24. See Preface, pp. 7–8.

25. The Boer girls, in their own "Address to the Swiss Nation", which Marion Rowntree sent to E. H. for forwarding, addressed the Countess Degli Asinelli

as follows: "Eedele vriendin, wij de ondergeteekende jonge dochters, leden van het Bond al hier gesticht door de eedele Mej. Hobhouse, het Comitee en nevens al de leden van het Bond gevoelen ons gedrongen bij deze aan u over te brengen onze innige en hartelijke dank voor de onverdiende, ja onverwachte Gift van de spinwielen aan ons gezonden. Voorwaar een Gift, dat ons laat gevoelen dat in Switzerland ook warme harten voor ons arme geruineerde Afrikaansche volk klopt. U, Eedele, zal ons moeten gelooven en aan nemen dat wij deze Gift door u aan ons zeer hoog waardeeren en hoog op prijs stellen. Neem aan, Edele vriendinnen, bij deze noch mals onze hartelijke dank en erkentlijkheid en geloof U Eedele voortaan een plaats heeft ingenomen in de harte van het Afrikaansche volk. Nu sluiten wij met hoogachting en dank-baarheid en heb de eer ons te noemen

"U dankbaren Dienaressen

Mimie Burger, Chrissie Enslin, Martha Lubbe, Hester van Schalkwyk, Susara Bezuidenhout."

Marion Rowntree added:

"The committee sat on it with due solemnity on Friday and decided to reserve for their five selves the privilege of signing in the name of *het volk* [the Afrikaner people].

"In spite of my efforts to explain the rank of countess and the deferential mode of address demanded by European society, the letter began boldly to Miss Asinelli. Mrs. Leopold [the housekeeper] thought other slips in grammar and orthography called for a re-copy, but I hope the countess will prefer the original with the full flavour of the veld. There can be no mistake about their gratitude."

26. At the head of this part of her memoir E. H. put some verses of Rudyard Kipling's poem *The Power of the Dog*, containing such lines as:

"Brothers and sisters, I bid you beware
Of giving your heart to a dog to tear . . ."

27. J. E. Adamson, English educationist, came to South Africa as principal of the Normal College in Pretoria and was director of education for Transvaal from 1905 to 1924.

28. In October 1908 in Pretoria, just before she left for Europe via Lourenço Marques, the Transvaal Huisvlytraad (council for homecrafts) presented E. H. with her more than life-size portrait of herself by Hugo Naudé. In their address they said:

"You did your best to mitigate the miseries of war, and thereafter you did your best to repair its ravages by introducing into the homes of the people those manual industries which have been practised in other countries with such benificent results. The success of your efforts has been so great that the work has been taken up by several South African governments and gives fair promise of becoming in the best sense national."

General Smuts, then colonial secretary of the Transvaal, said in his speech on this occasion that he thought "Miss Hobhouse had become, from her work in the country, in a manner part of the history of South Africa . . . [remembered for] not only the work – and the work was a great work – but the spirit in which the work was done".

29. See Letter 97, p. 389.

30. The Lyttelton constitution envisaged a predominantly elective legislature but an executive of British officials. It was dropped when the Liberals came to power in 1906.

31. General C. F. Beyers, who had been chairman of the Vereeniging peace conference, was now an executive member of Het Volk.

32. Afrikaans word for backvelder, indicating someone from the outlying country districts lacking in sophistication.

33. A. D. W. Wolmarans, a Transvaal farmer, was an executive member of Het Volk but not fully in accord with the conciliatory politics of Botha and Smuts. With Abraham Fischer and C. J. Wessels he had been sent to Europe on a Boer mission to seek the intervention of European powers in the war against Britain. He and Wessels went on to America, where they were when the peace was signed in May 1902. Only in January 1903, however, did the British authorities give him permission to return to the Transvaal.

34. Sir Arthur Lawley was lieutenant-governor of the Transvaal from 1902–5.

35. From her new house "Mara" [Bitter] in Becker Street, Bellevue, E. H. wrote to Margaret Clark on 17 November 1905:
    "With no interest in the present and no hope for the future I find thoughts turn backward very much during the solitude and I again live through the long succession of sorrows that have gone to make up the story of my days. I can honestly say that not one single day of it would I care to have again . . ."

36. E. H. comments in her memoir: "The house is moderate but quite nice and his study is a pleasant room though he sits mostly on the wide stoep. Mrs. Steyn has tried hard to get back her own furniture from the Presidency but has had a lot of trouble about it. What they have given up has been disgracefully handled and she has put in a claim for about £250, which does not at all represent the original value. But of course she will never get it, and one does think that Goold-Adams who has used the furniture all these years might pay her that sum."
    She remembers the quiet Sunday she spent with the Steyns at Onze Rust, "walking about with Mr. Steyn to see his bees and poultry and fruit trees and dams," and records that "one family has given him 150 ewes and another 25 and so one way and another he has got together a flock of sheep and they have six cows in milk."

37. Leonard Hobhouse had obviously written to E. H. asking her to put the Boer perspective on Chinese labour, Lord Selborne, etc. cogently to Campbell-

Bannerman. According to Margaret Clark, writing to Smuts on 31 May 1906, Hobhouse was at this stage "gloomy over the Government and South Africa ... he thinks much is lost because you have no one here who sees people and keeps your side vivid with the Government. He considers the Missis [E. H.] has the Premier's trust and if she would come here at once, could influence ... As you know, 'Methods of Barbarism' made the personality which now is Premier; and it was the Missis who created the situation in which C.–B.'s native worth could not but choose to commit himself". (W. K. Hancock and Jean van der Poel (ed.), *Selections from the Smuts Papers*, vol. II, p. 280.) There is no record in the letters or the memoir that E. H. saw Campbell-Bannerman on her subsequent visit to England.

38. The education bill of 1906, which came up in the first session of the new Liberal parliament, was an attempt to remedy the injustices imposed upon the Nonconformists by the education act of 1902 (G. P. Gooch, *Life of Lord Courtney*, p. 520.) The more conservative house of lords, however, blocked the bill, and it was thought in some circles that an appeal to the country could provide a way out of the impasse.

39. It became quite the thing to wear products of the home industries. After a three-day exhibition in the old Good Hope Hall in Cape Town in April 1908, E. H. in a letter describes "Members of Parliament, hurrying home to distant provinces, bought rolls of tweed, and were seen wending their way to the station like black ants, each carrying a role of tweed under his arm. The Premier bought an ulster length, and so did the Governor; the Speaker, Mr. James Molteno, bought a suit and his tailor tells him it will *never* wear out, and maybe this is its merit and its drawback." General Smuts, too, wore a suit of it, but was reported to say that he felt like a female ostrich in it. E. H. considered the men-folk very feeble who found it scratchy and uncomfortable, and adds: "So it is worn in the Transvaal as a patriotic duty with a very bad grace, far different from the Cape where even the Editor of the *Cape Times* walks proudly about preening himself and saying 'I'm dressed in Boer-tweed.'" (Ruth Fry, *Emily Hobhouse*, p. 256–7.)

40. Dr. Hugh Gunn, coming from the Hebrides, had tried to get weaving started in the camps but these were by now being broken up. The Orange River colony therefore watched E. H.'s efforts with particular interest. Marion Rowntree found Gunn a man of "good sense, generosity and pleasantry, and with a thorough grasp of education, too.".

VROUWEN-DAG

97

1. See pp. 377, 378. The idea of the monument was first mooted in July 1906 at a

meeting of prominent Free Staters chaired by President Steyn's brother, J. W. G. Steyn. Feeling that this was an issue for the whole *volk* they called a big conference at Bloemfontein on 7 February 1907 with President Steyn in the chair and attended by representatives of all the Afrikaans churches and Afrikaans cultural organizations.

98

1. E. H. had been following Van Wouw's work on the monument closely in Rome. Already on *5 August 1911* she was writing to Mrs. Steyn:

"I look forward to seeing Mr. Van Wouw and giving him all the hints and help I can in his efforts to visualize the camps and symbolize all . . ."

On 12 January 1912:

"I am in touch with him and went to criticize his first clay model at his desire. I did not like it and had to tell him so. He is too easily satisfied and will have, I think, to rub shoulders a bit with the sculptors here who are capable of expressing their ideas in stone and bronze – and of composition – and are not content with mere portrait work such as Mr. Van Wouw has chiefly done.

"It is a great subject – a grand opportunity – and since he has appealed to me for help I shall do my utmost to keep him up to the pitch and not let him be satisfied too easily. But of course he may not have *greatness* in him. I do not yet know. I always thought only Rodin could treat that subject worthily."

Auguste Rodin (1840–1917) was at the time, in spite of his age, still doing impressive work.

On 21 March 1912:

"Mr. van Wouw is finding the full difficulty of his task. He sent for me this week to come and criticize the clay model, three feet high – in which size he is trying to work out his first idea. It certainly is an improvement on the small model I saw a couple of months ago, yet very far indeed from what it should be and must be. However, there was *some* feeling in the woman's face who is standing behind the grief-stricken mother – some hint of tragedy – a look as of calling upon heaven to witness the suffering endured. But the mother seated with the child on her knee is soulless and expresses nothing, and the child is comfortably asleep and neither sick nor dead in appearance. Hence the group in its present stage is meaningless. I ventured to point out these things and Mr. Van Wouw accepted the suggestions gratefully. I particularly suggested he should ask Pander to come and give him professional hints. He promised to do so. I think Mr. van Wouw shuts himself up too much instead of rubbing shoulders with other sculptors and gaining from their knowledge and experience."

On 5 April 1912:

"Saw Van Wouw's work this week again and thought his group very much improved. The standing woman seems to me very good, full of feeling, and the sitting mother is better, though still far from satisfactory. The child on her knee is nicely modelled though still only appears to me a *sleeping* child and neither sick nor dead. I suggested he should get leave to go to a hospital and study one or two dead figures. However, on the whole he has now more grip of his subject ... he is sending you a photograph but I daresay it will be hard to judge from that."

On *12 July, from England*:

"Mr. Van Wouw has sent me photos of his proposed bas-reliefs ... I think I shall prefer them to the central group. I do not suppose, do you, that the monument will be ready 16 December 1913? I think you had better say 1914."

99
1. From the May Murray Parker collection in the Jagger Library of the University of Cape Town.
2. Mrs. Mary Brown (1847–1935), wife of Dr. John Brown and close friend of Olive Schreiner, whose high ideals for women and the moral upliftment of the nation she shared. That was why she fought to get women the vote. She was particularly active in temperance work and social reform, and her profound spiritual quality drew people to her even when, later in life, she became completely crippled by arthritis as well as blind and all but deaf. The remarkable Solomon family into which she was born – Saul Solomon was a great-uncle – came originally from St. Helena and were of Jewish descent, but Mary's father, Henry Solomon, became a devout Christian and greatly influenced his daughter. Dr. Brown earlier practised at Fraserburg in the Cape and at Burnley in Lancashire, but the Browns had by this time settled in Cape Town. Their daughter Julie married Hugo Naudé, the Cape artist, in 1915.

100
1. The rift between the Botha government and the movement led by Hertzog was widening. The breach was precipitated by another anti-conciliation speech by Hertzog, then minister of justice in Botha's cabinet, at De Wildt on 7 December 1912. In order to remove him from the cabinet, Botha resigned on 19 December, reformed the ministry and excluded Hertzog.

105
1. Henry Burton, minister of railways and harbours (1913–20).

106
1. Gladys Steyn, daughter of the president, was the first headmistress of the Oranje girls' school founded by her father in 1907. E. H. had in Rome met Maria Montessori (1870–1952), pioneer educationalist and physician, who lectured in pedagogy at the university of Rome (1900–07) and opened the first Montessori school for slum children.

514

109

1. From Alfred Lord Tennyson's *Crossing the Bar*:
   "And may there be no sadness of farewell
      when I embark."
2. Sannie Metelerkamp, veteran Afrikaans woman journalist.

112

1. Steyn, in the name of the entire Afrikaner people, expressed his deep disappointment that E. H. could not be present, saying:

   "Wij weten dat van de aanvang zij, als het ware, haar leven in haar hand had genomen om die laatste eer aan de vrouwen en kinderen van ons volk, voor wie zij in het verleden zoveel heeft gedaan en gelede, te bewijzen. De moeite en zelfopoffering die zij zich voor ons volk getroost heeft, wekken by ons een gevoel van diepe eerbied en innige dankbaarheid op. Onze bede is dat zij nog lang gespaard moge blijven.

   "De naam Emily Hobhouse is een van de geliefde namen in Zuid Afrika en uit menig moederhart gaat nog gedurig de bede op 'God zegen haar'."

   (We know that she from the outset virtually risked her life to pay her last respects to the women and children of our people for whom she did and suffered so much in the past. The effort and self-sacrifice she took upon herself for our people awaken in us feelings of profound respect and heart-felt gratitude. Our prayer is that she may long be spared.

   The name Emily Hobhouse is one of the names loved in South Africa, and from the heart of many a mother there still unceasingly rises the prayer 'God bless her'.)
2. E. H. approached Mrs. Steyn and John X. Merriman respectively to read the speech, but in the end this was done by Charlie Fichardt who had played a prominent part in organizing the unveiling ceremony and was one of the first people E. H. came to know in South Africa.
3. In a footnote E. H. contrasts this number with the number of combatants who died in the war:

   "The total number of burghers who fell in battle, died of wounds or from sickness under confinement as prisoners-of-war during a war that lasted two years and eight months was 6 189; of these 1 118 died under British guardianship in the war prison camps".
4. Jer. 31:16.
5. Ps. 42:7.
6, 7 and 8. In the translated and somewhat condensed version of the Vrouwen-Dag speech in *Die Volksblad's* commemorative issue of 13 December 1963 there were some notable ommissions that were not indicated: after 6 the sentence "Are not these the withholding from others in your control, the very liberties and rights you have valued and won for yourselves?"; after 7: "We in England are ourselves but dunces in the great world-school, our leaders still struggling

515

with the unlearned lesson, that liberty is the equal right and heritage of every child of man, without distinction of race, colour or sex. A community that lacks the courage to found its citizenship on this broad base becomes 'a city divided against itself, which cannot stand' "; and, after 8 "We, too, the great civilised nations of the world, are still but barbarians in our degree, so long as we continue to spend vast sums in killing or planning to kill each other for greed of land and gold. Does not justice bid us remember how many thousands of the dark race perished also in Concentration Camps in a quarrel that was not theirs? Was it not an instance of that community of interest, which binding all in one, roots out racial animosity? and may it not come about that the associations linked with this day will change, merging into nobler thoughts as year by year you celebrate the *more* inspiring Vrouwen-Dag we now inaugurate?"

Family and friends

BOTHA, General Louis (1862–1914) and Annie (1864–1937), born Emmett, in Swellendam, of Irish parents.

She married Botha in 1886 when he was sheep-farming in Natal, having met him when her father was auctioneer at Harrismith and his parents were farming in the north-eastern Free State, near Vrede. According to F. V. Engelenburg there was no-one with whom the girls rather danced at the time! Although he had had less than three years at school – and that at little farm schools – he was a born leader. When he was one of the youngest members of the First Volksraad of the Transvaal, Frederik Rompel of *De Volksstem* wrote that he was a calm speaker who considered everything he said carefully . . . and that he soon shone because of his clear judgement. "Hij is de minzaamheid in persoon, staat ieder vriendelijk te woord, maar is meestal te zwak iemand rondweg een verzoek te weigeren. In het dagelijksch leven is hij een alleraangenaamst mensch die zich overal thuis gevoelt en over bijna elk onderwerp kan mee praten. Wie Louis Botha eenmaal heeft ontmoet, houdt van hem." (He is loveableness personified, lends a friendly ear to everybody but is usually too soft to refuse anybody a request outright. In daily life he is a most charming person who feels at home wherever he goes. Whoever has met Louis Botha, likes him.)

E. H. first stayed with the Bothas in Sunnyside, Pretoria, when she visited the ruined former republics in 1903. She recorded her enjoyment of Mrs. Botha's singing. Apart from an *Ode to Table Mountain*, written at the same time, E. H.'s only other known poem was written for Mrs. Botha after staying at the prime minister's residence Groote Schuur in Cape Town on her way back from her thwarted attempt to take part in the unveiling ceremony of the women's memorial at Bloemfontein.

Dated 28 January to 14 March 1914, these verses are addressed to:

> *My Hostess*
> *Gentle Annie*

Forget-me-nots from Irish streams
  Still linger in thine eyes;
The face reflects the clouds and gleams
  That sweep o'er Erin's skies;
Bloom her wild roses, pink and white,
  On cheek and neck and brow.

519

Through thy clear notes old griefs vibrate,
        Her sweetest melody thou.

As flowers transplanted richer bloom
        So it befell with thee;
Set in this southern, wider home
        With life unfettered, free,
Thy Irish charms 'neath Afric's sun
        To perfect ripeness grew;
The veld its web of mystery spun
        And o'er thy spirit threw.

He found thee blooming in the veld,
        That Shepherd young, unknown,
Divin'd in thy sweet nature dwelt
        Fulfillment of his own;
Through weal, through woe, thy love burnt bright,
        Thy grace filled hall or farm;
Proud hero he of many a fight,
        Yet proudest of thy charm.

At Groote Schuur, sweet chatelaine,
        All wait upon thy word;
Vast granary hast thou formed again,
        From roof to cellar stored
With healing balm and sweet heart's-ease
        Alike for all to share.
Thy prowess gained in arts of peace
        Excells thy man's in war.

BRADBY, E. Dorothy and L. Barbara

These two sisters were warm sympathizers with the Boer cause. Barbara was a former student of Leonard Hobhouse. E. H. thought of her as a possible successor to herself when she returned to England in 1901 and was looking for someone to follow up her work in South Africa for the S.A. Women and Children Distress Fund. However, Barbara married J. L. Hammond, editor of the *Speaker*, and together they wrote several books on labour history and sociology.

Dorothy Bradby was – in E. H.'s words – a "tower of strength" in the women's branch of the South African Conciliation Committee. She also became Secretary of the South African Women and Children Clothing Fund started by E. H. after the war. The spirit in which she and her co-workers undertook this work is reflected in a letter she wrote to Betty Molteno on 21 August 1902:

"... Her (England's) name and honour is lost forever. [...] I told you that we had no hope, and we have none, now, that England will *repent* because it is right. But there is always the sad hope left of a reaction set up by disaster and loss of prosperity ... And it is partly because one still hopes for this that it seems these funds and work for the Boers are of more importance than the very little material help we can give [...] If one could do nothing, one would have to *try to* drown thought, or one's heart would break; but while there are petticoats to be made, one can go on ... I do not think the Africanders can have any idea what it meant to us English (guiltless but most miserable) that our help was *not* rejected. God has been very merciful to us, that we have been allowed to help at all; and that, I know from many letters, is the feeling of the Clothing Fund helpers." (Letter among the papers of E. M. Molteno in the Jagger Library of the University of Cape Town.)

CLARK, Margaret (1878–1962)
Born of Quaker parents in Street, Somersetshire, where they were shoe-manu-facturers, Margaret Clark was the leader of the Liberal Party when at Newnham College, Cambridge, and active in the Society of Friends and women's enfranchise-ment work. She was the granddaughter of John Bright, and her great-aunt Margaret had already worked for women's suffrage. Home from Cambridge she on the spur of the moment agreed to help E. H. with the Boer home industries in South Africa (p. 331) – seeing E. H.'s spontaneous invitation as typical of her "vitality, enter-prise and courage". E. H. followed up the invitation with a letter in which she explained that she needed Margaret as a factotum, but would never ask her to do anything she herself would not do ... a promise Margaret later often smiled at as she added urine to indigo to settle the dye in the dyeing vats at Philippolis. Before going to South Africa she prepared herself in a small way by taking lessons in handling a knitting-machine, which lessons were given in an Oxford shop-window, so that a former teacher of hers remarked on passing the shop: "Whatever is Margaret Clark coming to?"

Margaret Clark shared E. H.'s broader idealism and saw the home industries venture as at the same time an exercise in the moral rehabilitation of the Boer girls and a gesture of reconciliation born of a fierce loyalty to the England she, too, believed in. She always passionately defended E. H. from an interpretation of history that claimed her as a heroine on the side of the Boers over against her own people. "I couldn't bear to have my Missis misrepresented," she said, and told how E. H. had warned her: "Don't you come with any idolizing of the Boers – a very great mistake."

Of the period of their co-operation Margaret Clark wrote:

"I never before had work to do in which there was a person and it had been

521

a new world of delight to be at work with a person that stimulated and interested me, whom my whole nature recognized as a leader (in spite of some differences) and found nothing but honour in serving, whom I loved and gave everything I had."

E. H. said of Margaret Clark to Lady Charlotte Graham Toler, chairman of the Boer Home Industries Committee: "Of her own work it is scarcely possible to speak too highly. She has been head and hand and mouthpiece and correspondent all in one, I do not know what I shall do without her. The Boer girls will miss her very much and everyone hopes she will return before long."

After working in South Africa in 1905, Margaret Clark returned to England in 1906 and did public relations work for the industries there and in Europe. She again came out in 1907 and was eventually appointed organizer of the industries under the new responsible governments in the former republics. In 1909 she married Arthur Gillett, a banker, and they settled in Oxford, where E. H. was a frequent guest. The Gilletts' great friendship with General Smuts, whom Margaret learnt to know in her South African years, is vividly illustrated by their correspondence in the *Smuts Papers*.

CLOETE, Constance Annie Mathilda (1868–1958), "Aunt Con".
She was a daughter of Hendrik, the last of the Constantia Cloetes, and a sister of Mrs. Mary Sauer. She looked after her Aunt Bonna for many years and was one of South Africa's first professional typists, working for her brother-in-law, J. W. Sauer.

To the early pioneers of the Boer home industries she was a godsend. She came to Philippolis in reply to an SOS from E. H. to rescue them from the housekeeping strains in which they were immersed upon their arrival – came with "a breath of strength and vigour and cheerfulness that at once set us all going easily", Margaret Clark wrote. Coming back from a walk on the evening of her arrival, they found her in evening dress, "and so we celebrated our return to civilized life by dressing too". Warm and impulsive, she gardened vigorously (like her sister at Uitkijk) and found solace in it. She came provided with her aunt's now famous cookery book, Hildagonda Duckitt's *Where is it?*, and a collection of homeopathic medicines.

Margaret Clark described her as a "delightful and hearty and interesting person . . . very friendly and cuddly and we are very happy in mind and body under her reign"; Marion Rowntree wrote to her fiancé: "Our matron is a perfectly delightful Miss Cloete from the Cape."

After some months there was a little less of the first fine enthusiasm on E. H.'s part. Writing from Langlaagte, where Con Cloete had followed to help with the housekeeping in very primitive circumstances, she says:

"Con means so well; however, her lack of method and judgement makes me very anxious over many things . . . she does not keep control of the house and the girls and the servants as she should . . . lets everything slide so dreadfully and everything go filthy . . ."

It also worried E. H. that Constance, used to the beauty of the Cape and particularly of Uitkijk, should be living in their Langlaagte squalor.

Miss Cloete returned to the Cape for family reasons but was in 1909 again inspanned to run the housekeeping, this time for the lace-making project at Koppies, started by Hannah Rood and Lucia Starace. She formed a particular friendship with the latter and into her seventies regularly visited her at her home in Italy.

COURTNEY, Leonard (1832–1918) and Kate – Lord and Lady Courtney after he was created a peer when the Liberals came to power.
Leonard Courtney, born from a humble background, had a legal education and became professor in politics and economics at the University College, London – one of the few professors at that time who invited women into their classes. In 1896 he became a Liberal MP but his opposition to Home Rule for Ireland cost him his seat in Liskeard, the Cornwall constituency in which E. H.'s home village St. Ive fell. As a recognized specialist of long standing on South Africa, he became president of the South African Conciliation Committee when it was founded in November 1899. Two months earlier, at Manchester, he had regretfully described his former friend Milner as a "lost mind".

His contemporary biographer G. P. Gooch saw him as one who "dedicated his life to and found occupation and happiness in the formation of public opinion". As leader writer of *The Times* Leonard Courtney was admired for the "Euclidean precision of his writing". C. P. Scott, editor of the *Manchester Guardian*, said he was "one of the rare men whose motives are never doubted", while Gladstone, on recommending him as financial secretary to the treasury, described him to Queen Victoria as "a gentleman of great talent, great mental ability and assiduity, and, I should add to complete my portrait, considerable self-assertion". Towards the end of his life he went blind – from October 1896 he knew that he would never be able to read again – but maintained his public life. George Unwin, L. S. Amery and Lionel Curtis were among his private secretaries in these years, Unwin characterizing him as "undoubtedly one of the greatest men I have known but also the most lovable".

His wife supported him to the end with touching devotion. She was the eldest of the nine Potter sisters among whom was Beatrice, Mrs. Sidney Webb. Kate Potter worked for eight years at the Octavia Hill reformatory, collecting rent, and then became chairman of the women's industrial committee, for which E. H. came to work after her return from Mexico and a broken romance in 1898.

The Courtneys first met at a party where T. E. Huxley attacked a leading article in *The Times*. "A pity," said Leonard Courtney, "for I wrote it." Overhearing Kate Potter's hearty laughter at this, he and she became friends and subsequently married when he was 51, in 1883. Theirs was "a happy hospitable house where people of every creed, colour, race and country with sincerity and intelligence were welcome – so, too, many South Africans".

His friends liked to remember Courtney at the head of his table in Cheyne Walk, dressed in his "famous buff waistcoat and blue coat with brass buttons", a "sturdy, joyous personality, with curiously bright eyes under thick eyebrows and a whimsical smile", and a great favourite with all children.

The Courtneys showed E. H. particular friendship and theirs was probably the circle of friends which she found most congenial.

DE VILLIERS, Jacob (Jaap) A. J. (1868–1932)
A later chief justice of the Union of South Africa, Jaap de Villiers was born in Fauresmith in the Orange Free State, educated at Grey College, Bloemfontein, Victoria College, Stellenbosch, and in Amsterdam. He became a barrister of the Middle Temple and was state attorney of the Free State (1896–8) in between periods of practising as an advocate in Johannesburg. During the war he fought for the Free State and again became its state attorney before he was seriously wounded and sent to Bermuda as a prisoner-of-war. On his return he resumed practice in Johannesburg and he came with "the pick of the three colonies" to welcome President Steyn returning on the *Kronprinz* (pp. 340, 351). E. H., meeting him then, wrote to Lady Charlotte Graham Toler: "This last name (De Villiers) is not so well known in England, but out here it is a power", and described him as "the leading advocate in Johannesburg".

Later in 1905, when she attended the Het Volk congress in Pretoria, she wrote to her brother about Advocate De Villiers "who was to have made *the* speech which could have been the wisest and most thoughtful by far [. . .] the head committee consult him about everything [. . .] and undoubtedly he is the man with the ballast [. . .] uncommon brains and force of character."

When Leonard Hobhouse urged her to write to Campbell-Bannerman on Chinese labour and related issues (p. 384), De Villiers was the one she asked to give her "pointers" and to read over what she had written.

In intimate letters in the E. H. circle he was at this time referred to as H. M. (evidently "His Majesty"), and there are references to his riding over on horseback to Langlaagte to visit and see to the pruning of the fruit trees; to dinner parties at his house in Bellevue, where this eligible bachelor lived with his brother and his family; to picnics and camping on his farm Mabulani. Margaret Clark says E. H. spoke of his "thoughtful and kind actions such as you would find oftener in a woman than a man". Miss Clark herself found that he had "the wonderful gift of listening and counselling. Yet it isn't so much what he says as the atmosphere he makes for composing your views . . . It is the unimpassioned way in which such a man speaks of his war experiences that impresses one so. There is no lack of passion at the back, but it is controlled in an extraordinary way in expression."

By the middle of 1906, however, E. H. was writing that he had "good judgement but he was rather lazy by nature and good judgement stopped somewhere in the machinery and didn't come to good use." In 1907 when he married fashionable young Mietjie Meintjies, aged twenty, many of his friends – and certainly his more intellectual women friends – were disappointed that he hadn't chosen someone more "worthy" of himself, Olive Schreiner referring to Mietjie as "that ninny".

DE VILLIERS, John Henry (1840–1914) and Lady De Villiers
The chief justice and his wife were among E. H.'s most influential friends at the Cape and she often stayed with them at Wynberg. He was a brother of, among others, Melius de Villiers, the Free State judge, and Charlie "Avignon" de Villiers, the Cape Town lawyer and MLA. He was born at Rosenfontein, Paarl. Because of education – he qualified as a barrister at the Inner Temple – he was, however, very English in his ways and introduced aspects of English law to the Roman Dutch legal system at the Cape. His political aspirations were whetted by offers of high office: Rhodes approached him to be prime minister of the Cape, the Orange Free State wanted him for president (after Jan Brand) and at one stage there was also talk that he would be a presidential candidate in the Transvaal. These options he all turned down but he played a role as mediator between Kruger and Milner by arranging their abortive Bloemfontein meeting that failed to avert the war. In forty years as chief justice he gained the reputation of an impartial judge capable of getting at the gist of a complicated case, and of quick – some said brusque – decisions.

Margaret Clark met him in 1905 and said he "had a dignity that has never thought of dignity and a look of quietness and gentleness which is repeated in his voice".

He married Anna Aletta Jordaan, daughter of a wine-farmer and MLA from Worcester. She was described as "an ideal partner who helped him in his career".

Chief Justice De Villiers was chairman of the national convention that led to the union of South Africa. He was knighted in 1910.

FICHARDT, Caroline and family, especially Charles, Ella, Maude and Arthur.
The Fichardts were one of the Orange Free State's most influential and moneyed families, close friends of the Steyns. *Mrs. Caroline Fichardt* was E. H.'s Bloemfontein friend and hostess. She was born Beck (her mother was an Enlishwoman who had come to South Africa to teach) and married Gustav A. Fichardt, in whose large firm her father had become an accountant when they came to Bloemfontein from Grahamstown. She was widowed in 1900. She braved military disapproval by taking E. H. in on her first arrival in Bloemfontein (p. 48). She was at the time already suspected of "signalling to the enemy" when she drove out to her husband's grave on their farm Brandkop outside Bloemfontein, and when her son Charlie wrote from Cape Town to suggest that E. H. stay with them, she said "that's the end of us," but did it none the less. Her large and comfortable double-storeyed

house Kaya Lami with its spacious garden became E. H.'s headquarters, to which she returned again and again during her camp months. In the draft of her *Vrouwen-Dag* speech in 1913 she said, with evident reference to Mrs. Fichardt: "The moral strain added to the physical fatigue was so overpowering that I must have failed if it had not been for the unfailing sympathy and succour of one motherly South African woman."

Ella Fichardt remembered E. H. as "the sweetest guest" who sat with her on the hearthrug and sang "the Cornish songs she loved so much". *Maude Fichardt* played the piano very well and E. H. "used to lie down on the sofa when she came home from the camps and close her eyes and say: 'Play to me, don't stop, go on playing . . .'."

Ella married Percy Fischer, son of the former prime minister of the Orange Free State. She was the mother of advocate Abraham (Bram) Fischer. *Maude* married Dr. C. H. Bidwell, a Bloemfontein doctor. Her brother *Everard* married President Steyn's daughter Hanna. *Arthur*, who succeeded to the family business, married Violet Borckenhagen of the prominent Bloemfontein family of that name. Arthur did not oppose the British occupation forces but helped E. H. throughout her South African years – by offering her storage for her camp provisions when she arrived in Bloemfontein, providing her with foodstuffs at cost price when she came to the aid of the ruined districts of the former republics after the war, and by selling (albeit not too enthusiastically) the produce of the Boer home industries in his shop.

Charles Fichardt (1870–1923) was the first member of the Fichardt family whom E. H. met, soon after her arrival in Cape Town where he was then on parole with his wife and son. He had served as captain of the Boer scouts in the southern OFS commandos, escaped from Paardeberg, but was wounded at Poplar Grove and taken prisoner. Educated at Grey College, Bloemfontein, and further trained in commerce and administration in Scotland and Hamburg (from where the Fichardts originally came), Charles Fichardt had as a boy had an English governess who had a great influence on his life and manners. He was nevertheless a staunch Free State patriot. He was popular and sport-loving (at one stage OFS's cricket captain) and had briefly been mayor of Bloemfontein in 1898. After the war he was one of the group who bought the *Friend* as a mouthpiece for the Orangia-Unie (the OFS equivalent of Het Volk) which he helped to found.

GREENE, Alice M., d. 1920

Alice Greene came of a distinguished family near Cambridge – one of her uncles was Sir Graham Greene, who was for many years head of the admiralty; Graham Greene, the novelist, was the son of another uncle.

She was one of the well-educated English girls recruited for teaching in private schools in South Africa by Miss Hall and was vice-principal of the Collegiate Girls' School in Port Elizabeth when E. M. (Betty) Molteno was headmistress (1899–1900).

These two were inseparable and their names were always coupled. They left South Africa for England in 1913, settling at Trevone in Cornwall. They are buried in a dual grave at St. Merryn's on the Cornish moors. It is marked with the inscription: "They loved and served South Africa."

Miss Molteno (p. 532) and Miss Greene were both passionately engaged in the Boer cause during the war, sharing this dedication with their great friends Olive Schreiner and Anna Purcell, as they did a concern about women's rights.

When they lived in Cape Town after leaving Port Elizabeth, Alice Greene taught the daughters of Betty's brother Charles Molteno. Mrs. Carrol Williamson recalls the pair of them, with their sandals and unconventional dress, wearing sometimes "one dress over another to save carrying more than a string bag when going to stay with anyone".

Former pupils at the Girls' Collegiate described them as "women of strong character and high principle".

Like many educated women of her class and time, Miss Greene was an enthusiastic writer of poetry (she composed the school song for the Collegiate, to the tune of the Harrow Football Song) which was published in periodicals like the *New Age* and collected, with others, in *Songs of the Veld*, 1902.

HOBHOUSE, Lord Arthur (1819–1904) and Lady Mary (d. 1905)
Arthur Hobhouse was the youngest brother of E. H.'s father. In August 1848 he married Mary Farrer, daughter of a solicitor and sister of a great college friend, and towards the end of his life he wrote: "I set down influences for the good of my life firstly, secondly and thirdly my marriage with a clever, good and right-minded affectionate woman and to the family of like-minded character which indeed I came to know intimately before I fell in love with her."

The couple had, as he said, a "joint dislike of displays, rites and ceremonies".

E. H. loved them both dearly. The young Hobhouse children often stayed with their Uncle Arthur and Aunt Mary when their parents were ill or abroad, and Lady Hobhouse's letters to their mother give a charming picture of their doings – and an early insight into E. H.'s character. When E. H. was seven and the little Hobhouse girls were with their aunt and uncle, Lady Hobhouse described how "Valentine Day brought them four Valentines each, greatly to their satisfaction, though Emily is rather dubious as to one containing a strutting hen and the motto 'Wherever I am, I will always be missis'. Her sisters and Miss Turnor think it highly suitable, which makes Emily a little SHY over it." (A. Ruth Fry, *Emily Hobhouse*, p. 25.)

Arthur Hobhouse played a prominent part in bringing about the acts which gave married women control over their own property and earnings, and was much concerned about middle-class education. His term on the Charity Commission consolidated his interest in welfare. Lady Hobhouse was particularly interested in female education. Lord Hobhouse became a legal member of the council of India, in which capacity he supported the then novel system whereby Indians could in certain cases try white men. He warned the British that they would "commit the greatest mistake" if they despised the people over whom they ruled and omitted to consult them when they might usefully do so or snub them when unpalatable advice was given. He opposed the Afghan and Boer wars on the score that it was immoral of Britain to seize territory to improve her own position, and he set Leonard Hobhouse to collect instances from history to show that "a nation which throws itself into the business of conquest loses its own liberties and with them its power of initiative and general health". The same survey, he said, "should show how conquest is habitually disguised under the name of Liberty, Religion, Peace". He wrote:

> "To withstand one's countrymen to their face because they are wrong is the hardest duty that can fall to any public man, yet there are occasions when it is the first and most sacred duty of every private citizen."

Such lofty ideas were often discussed at mealtimes at the Hobhouse table and probably helped to mould E. H.'s views.

Lord and Lady Hobhouse gave their support to the South African Conciliation Committee and E. H.'s Distress Fund; Lady Hobhouse helped to procure Chamberlain's approval for such a fund and gave E. H. an introduction to Sir Alfred Milner so as to obtain permission for her to visit the war zone. She regularly made her house at 15 Bruton Street, London, available for meetings in the pro-Boer cause.

Lord Hobhouse was a member of the judicial committee of the Privy Council in 1899–1902. He was created a baron in 1885.

HOBHOUSE, Leonard Trelawny (1864–1929) and Nora (b. Hadwen, d. 1925) E. H.'s junior by four years, her youngest brother Leonard was her intellectual and moral mainstay throughout her life. She again and again turned to him for help, encouragement and advice on the best line of action to take, as well as the presentation of her ideas.

As a tutor at Christ Church, Oxford, his former student Barbara Bradby remembered him as "a tall, energetic figure striding through Oxford [very reactionary at the time] in home-spun and a red tie". He was, she said, a "brilliant talker whose good sayings tumbled out with a laugh, and his impetuous interest in a topic would make others interested too . . ."

"He was extraordinarily happy in his home life with his wife and [three] small children" who, as Oliver, his eldest, described, found him an hilarious and fun-loving father. Oliver was E. H.'s "pet nephew": Once as a baby he was left in her care when his parents went abroad and were subsequently detained by ill-health, and she thought of him as almost her own, maintaining a particular friendship with him till her death.

Nora Hobhouse was described by Barbara Bradby as "frail in body but indomitable in spirit" and shared all her husband's social enthusiasms. Married in 1891, their marriage lasted till her death in 1925. She was the daughter of a mill-owner from Halifax and they met, tellingly, while "stirring up the village workers" near Oxford.

Nora who clearly shared her husband's sense of humour as well as his humanitarian commitment, used to recount an amusing incident. When, after the war, the Boer generals Botha, De Wet and De la Rey were in England, she took them to a livery stable to get a mount.

"But can the gentlemen ride?" asked the attendant.

Leonard throughout his life combined his intellectual interests with active humanitarian work, in the family tradition of an "intense desire to serve mankind" – in his case by "bringing to bear upon the problems of human life the methods and principles of rational thought". As J. A. Hobson showed, "his deepest instinct and belief was hope in human progress. He saw evolution of the mind as the central process of history", and Morris Ginsberg saw his particular contribution as helping to "transfer earlier mid-Victorian liberalism with its *laissez-faire* and individualistic concepts into the newer liberalism . . . in which concern for human values was brought into the political sphere".

L. T. Hobhouse left Oxford to join the *Manchester Guardian* as political correspondent (1887–1902) and in the war years, in the face of the prevailing tide of imperialism, E. H. co-operated closely with him to bring the situation in South Africa before the British public.

During these years he would work on his philosophical and sociological subjects in the morning, in the evening turning his attention to "the innumberable topics with which a daily newspaper is concerned" – a double life he in the end would find too strenuous.

His editor, C. P. Scott, drew a picture of him "sitting with his eyes three inches from the table – he never wore spectacles – and pen coursing rapidly over paper. Then, in less than half the time most men would take, his tall figure would stalk into my room and deliver the goods . . . For me his figure stands as an imposing expression of intellectual power allied to an almost childlike friendliness. No one, surely, better earned the title Friend of Man".

After a short and less happy spell as editor of the *Sociology Review*, L. T. Hobhouse became political editor of the *Tribune* until, in 1907, he was installed as first professor in sociology at the University of London, a position he held till his death, during which time he continued to write prolifically on sociology and philosophy.

MERRIMAN, John X. (1841–1926) and Agnes (b. Vintcent)

John Xavier was the son of an English bishop who came to Grahamstown as an archdeacon. After an English education young Merriman returned to South Africa to make a living as a land surveyor, diamond dealer and eventually wine merchant and farmer, with a pioneer crayfish-canning project as a sideline. From 1869 he was a distinguished member of the Cape legislative assembly (he was the Cape's last premier). He corresponded with well-known British pro-Boers of the conciliation circles in which E. H. moved in London.

Mrs. Merriman was the daughter of the Dutch-born Cape parliamentarian, J. Vintcent, from the Eastern Cape. There were no children of the Merriman marriage. They were an incongruous-looking couple. Paul Sauer remembered them coming down Government Avenue in Cape Town – he, tall, striding ahead in his number twelve boots, the tiny Mrs. Merriman trying to keep up at a trot, about four paces behind, with Merriman talking non-stop to her over his shoulder. (Dirk and Johanna de Villiers, *Paul Sauer*, p. 22.)

A mid-Victorian in outlook, opposed to newer imperial trends and devoted to parliamentary freedoms, Merriman's strong views and refusal to bow to events made him a storm centre in Cape politics.

The following excerpts from letters preserved by E. H. among her papers now in the Steyn collection give an indication of their relationship:

> *Mrs. Merriman to E. H. Roodebloem. Salt River, 8 August 1901*: "Just got your letter but so grieved to see how depressed you are. I cannot, however, wonder at it, but I am *so* sorry to think you despair about your noble work. You *have* already done wonders and achieved what you are aiming at, viz. the better condition of the camps. As to your name being hated in England – that may be by only a section, and have not all true reformers and workers in the Cause of Right and Truth been rejected by men? We must look higher and your work *must* meet with the rewards it merits. You have given more than the 'cup of cold water to one of my little ones' ... I *always* have a text hanging over my bed which greatly helps me:
>
> > "In Earthly races Winners only
> > do the heralds call.
> > But oh! in yonder high and holy place
> > *Success* is nothing but the work is all."

> *John X. Merriman to E. H., Stellenbosch, 31 December 1902*: ". . . You at any rate, whatever the humiliations and sad disillusions you may have had, have nothing to regret. In the retrospect you will be able to look back always on the great work you were the means of doing in the reform of those dreadful camps. I am afraid your reward has too often been that of the monk Telemachus who sacrificed himself to stop the gladiatorial shows and who was no doubt rejected by smart Roman society as a most inconvenient fanatic. But never mind; in South Africa there are thousands of Boer farms where your name will be a household word and where what you have done and suffered in their cause will be held in grateful remembrance . . . One

can only hope that some day before one dies the authors of this tragedy may come by their just rewards, but it is long to wait, and the mills of God grind very slowly."

MOLTENO/MURRAY

"My friends of the Molteno and Murray clan" E. H. called them: the ramifications of the large Molteno family and their in-laws, with some of whom E. H. was acquainted and corresponded even before she came to the Cape. Her Molteno friends were born of the second marriage of Sir John Molteno, first prime minister of the Cape Colony. They were descended from an Italian family that settled in England in the 18th century.

Percy Alport (1861–1937) lived in England, having married Elizabeth Currie, daughter of the shipping magnate Donald Currie in whose firm he served as a director. He was a friend of the Transvaal consul in London, Montagu White, and, through close correspondence with his brothers John Charles and James Tennant and other Cape politicians like Sauer and Merriman, he was well informed on South African affairs and considered to be the pro-Boers' "resident specialist" on the subject. He encouraged his contacts in Cape politics to take a firm stand on the war issue and was one of the leading men in the foundation of the South African Conciliation Committee. He gave generously if quietly to Boer causes, helping to sponsor S. Cronwright-Schreiner's information mission to England in 1900, enabling Mrs. J. R. Green to take gifts to Boer prisoners-of-war on St. Helena, and supporting a Boer education fund after the war. E. H. considered him one of her "inner circle" whose advice she valued on the best line to take after she returned from her visit to the camps.

J. Charles Molteno (1860–1924) was the chairman of the conciliation committee founded in Cape Town in May 1900. He was secretary to his father when the latter was prime minister and then managed the family's farming interests at Nelspoort. Considered an agricultural expert, he was offered the ministry of agriculture by his friend Merriman but declined on grounds of poor health. He was married to an American – Lucy Lindley Mitchell, the granddaughter of the pioneer Wesleyan missionary Daniel Lindley and sister of Bryant Mitchell, American consul in South Africa during the war years. E. H. upon occasion stayed with them at their seaside house at Miller's Point beyond Simonstown.

James Tennant Molteno (1865–1936), known in parliament as 'Baby' Molteno for his jolly round face and playful wit, was trained as a barrister and became MLA for Namaqualand at the age of 26, later representing Somerset East. After at first supporting Rhodes he became a staunch supporter of the Afrikander Bond and opponent of Milner. He was the last speaker of the Cape Parliament (April 1908 to May 1910) and was knighted in 1911.

It was J. T. Molteno whose interview with Milner, recording the latter's vow that he would "break Afrikanerdom", created such consternation in anti-war circles in England and South Africa when published in the *Daily Chronicle* in September 1899. Milner denied this statement but did not withdraw his view that there had been a Dutch "conspiracy" to evict the British from South Africa.

Elizabeth M. (Betty) Molteno, (d. 1927), was the eldest of the three Molteno sisters. Tired of the moneyed leisure that gave no purpose to her life, and in spite of considerable family opposition, she took up teaching at thirty. She studied at Newnham college, Cambridge, but came to teach at her revered Miss Hall's Seminary for Young Ladies at Graaff-Reinet before she completed her course. She became headmistress (drawing no salary) at the private Girls' Collegiate school in Port Elizabeth (1899–1900) until that school's financial position caused it to be taken over by the Government. During this time her bosom friend Alice M. Greene (p. 526–7) was the vice-principal. A former pupil, Mabel Smith (Mrs. Preston Thomas), described her as "a woman whom to know was to respect", and one who "preached the great Ruskin to us by the yard".

She fervently, if uncritically, supported the Boer cause and idolized the Boer women (her phrase that they were all "Joan of Arcs" did the rounds of pro-Boer circles). On the same ship with the Boer generals Botha, De Wet and De la Rey when they went to England and Europe after the war, she gave them the same whole-hearted devotion that she would give Gandhi and his cause a few years later. Her niece, Carrol Williamson (a daughter of Charles Molteno), remembers her Aunt Betty as an "inspired orator" who would "recite speeches from Shakespeare if she had no special cause at the moment to talk about"; a friend of all who were in need or whose cause she thought worthy. Not surprisingly, she spoke up with particular force and conviction at the Paarl women's meeting protesting against the war, in 1900.

Her letters – describing the great *volksvergadering* against the war at Graaff-Reinet in 1900, the climate of Cape English thought at the time, E. H.'s arrest and deportation, die Boer generals' arrival in England in 1902, the unveiling of the women's memorial at Bloemfontein in 1913 – made E. H. comment:

"Your gift of seeing into the heart of things is so great and you have control of such exquisite language for expressing moral and spiritual aspects . . ."

In her turn Betty Molteno told E. H.:

"You lie warm in the hearts of all people connected with the camps, as no outsider, but as part of their being."

Caroline, the second Molteno sister, was, as she described herself, E. H.'s "greatest friend in Cape Town". She was a renowned beauty and in 1886 married *Dr. Charles Frederick Kennan Murray,* a former naval surgeon who practised at Kenilworth with her brother *Vincent,* became the first president of the SA Medical Association, and was much loved and respected. He was E. H.'s medical adviser in Cape Town. The

Murrays had eight children and an open, hospitable house. E. H. wrote to Percy Molteno:

"Words fail to express Mrs. Murray's kindness to me all the time, allowing me to make her house so comfortably my headquarters."

She and Mrs. Murray corresponded regularly and E. H., on re-reading Mrs. Murray's letters, was, as she wrote to Betty Molteno on 1 April 1923, struck by "the excellence of the grasp and the fine feeling and perfect expression. I often think what a great Prime Minister she would have made. She has the mind of a Statesman" – a compliment which, incidentally, W. T. Stead also paid to Mrs. Marie Koopmans-De Wet.

Caroline Murray showed solicitous concern that E. H. should not over-tire herself, and assured her that whatever good was done to improve the camps "will always be rightly attributed to the battle you have fought against such odds and won".

She added:

"We small party of English in South Africa owe you perhaps the greatest debt of gratitude of all, for you have helped, more than you can ever estimate, to restore the old ideals of the English character which it has been such a pain to see shattered."

PURCELL, William Frederick (1866–1919) and Anna (1870–1943)

Dr. W. F. Purcell was one of South Africa's first academically trained natural scientists, qualifying for his doctorate in philosophy in Germany with a thesis on a section of a spider's eye. He became well known for his work on the genus *Peripatus* and on scorpions, spiders and solifuges, and was assistant-director in the department for land invertebrates at the South African Museum until 1905 when he retired for reasons of health. He then devoted himself, with his wife's keen help, to the collection of Cape flowers in the Constantia valley. The plaque above his worktable at the South African Museum reads:

"He had the true scientific spirit, modestly but devotedly searching out after truth regardless of the word of praise or payment. He was also a lover of nature in all its aspects and a lovable man himself."

Added to this, he was a noted collector of porcelain, antiques and books and was instrumental in the founding of the Koopmans–De Wet-Museum in Strand Street, Cape Town, of which he was the first honorary curator.

Purcell and his Jeffcoat cousin inherited the Bergvliet estate from his bachelor uncle W. F. Hertzog in 1904, after a famous court case in which a will leaving the

533

estate to Michael Hidding was successfully contested. Since the Jeffcoats lived in England, the Purcells moved to Bergvliet.

Anna Purcell, whom he married in 1898, was the granddaughter of Dr. P. E. Faure, minister of the Wynberg Dutch Reformed Church, and the daughter of J. Cambier Faure, a Cape magistrate. (The well-known Reverend Abraham Faure was an uncle.) Before they moved to Bergvliet, they lived at 70 Kloof Street at Vergeziend, next door to F. S. Malan's house Schoongezicht. Mrs. Purcell, beautiful, high-minded and gifted, wrote occasional poems which were sometimes published in periodicals and newspapers; several of her contributions to *The New Age* – among them her poems to De Wet and President Steyn, "an uncrowned king" – were published in the collection *Songs of the Veld* in 1902. A devoted friend of Olive Schreiner, sympathetic to, and in E. H.'s view deeply influenced by, Olive's views on politics and women's rights, Anna Purcell was honorary secretary of the Women's Enfranchisement League at the Cape and a member of the committee for aid to Boer prisoners-of-war at Green Point. In July 1900 she, though retiring by nature, spoke at the great Cape women's protest meeting against the war. When Botha, De La Rey and later De Wet passed through Cape Town after the war on their mission to collect money in England and Europe she was the "Africander Lady" reporting the event over three full pages in *The South African News*:

> ". . . We seemed to see them all pass before us as we gazed on the two leaders before us – the living and the dead . . . and above all that great silent army of innocent white-souled children who had perished in the camps . . ."

E. H. saw her as one of "those whose politics rest upon emotions and not upon principles", when in later years they differed about World War I. In September 1901 Anna Purcell wrote to her from 70 Kloof Street:

> "May your noble efforts to bring the truth home to your people bear some fruit at last. I feel sure that such self-sacrificing, untiring work as yours has been, *cannot* be in vain."

In May 1901 she had written:

> "England must still have a claim on our love for the sake of men and women like you who deprecate the awful misery inflicted by your countrymen . . ."

RIPON, Lord (1827–1909) and Lady Ripon
The marquis and marchioness of Ripon both served on the South African Women and Children Distress Fund committee. Lord Ripon, as an elder statesman, was one of E. H.'s staunchest supporters and most trusted advisers. He backed the fund from the outset and was for some part of 1901 its acting chairman. A former Liberal

MP, he served successively as secretary of state for India and first lord of the admirality and was Chamberlain's predecessor as secretary of state for the colonies, during which time Tongaland with Kosi Bay was annexed by the British, and the Transvaal thus finally cut off from the sea.

When E. H. returned to England from her visit to the camps, Lord Ripon was among those who gave full credence to her report. He called the camp system "cruel in the present and inconceivably foolish in regard to the future". In December 1901, after her arrest and deportation, he reassured E. H. that she had won "the admiration of all who are not blinded by the passion of the moment" (Arthur Davey, *The British Pro-Boers*, p. 59). E. H.'s decision to return to South Africa to visit the British refugees in the coastal towns, which had prompted this second visit, was taken in conjunction with the Ripons, when she was staying with them at their estate Studley Royal in the autumn of 1901.

Lord Ripon served in the cabinet when the Liberals came to power in December 1905.

ROWNTREE, Marion (c. 1878–1963).

A fellow-Quaker and Cambridge contemporary of Margaret Clark (she majored in English and German), Marion Rowntree came to take the latter's place in the Boer home industries venture when Margaret returned to England in 1906. Marion Rowntree later married Kenneth Wilkinson, a York sollicitor, to whom she became engaged while in South Africa. E. H., she told Margaret, "was rather pleased – there is a touch of the romantic about her – and wanted to know the colour of his hair and I couldn't remember."

Marion's technical knowledge of the industries was scant when she came to South Africa. She had briefly been to Mortons', the carpet merchants in Carlisle, to study their handwoven carpets and their government-susidized scheme for training peasant girls. In South Africa she proved very useful, however, establishing good relations with the Boer girls and their families and getting them to do home spinning for the weaving schools. She would bicycle out to the farms, and got along fine with her "German spoken with a Yorkshire accent".

At the end of 1906 E. H. wrote to Margaret Clark:

> "Marion takes a long time to know. But I begin to understand her – the reserved, hard-headed north country type so different from us Celts – and we fitted very well together. I shall miss her strength of body and mind very much."

She did find, however, that Marion had "very little eye for colour and none for design . . .".

Down-to-earth and less of a romantic idealist than either E. H. or Margaret Clark, her feelings for E. H. differed from Margaret's unbounded devotion. After a

535

few months at Philippolis she wrote to Margaret Clark:

> "My admiration grows almost in proportion to the nearer experience of her failings. Her character and unfailing range is a study more absorbing every day and the zeal of her work and masterly treatment of detail in relation to perfect organization is a stimulus that intoxicates. I can pledge you giving her this year my wonder and respect, and hearty devotion to her purpose, mingled with pity for the rough handling that has left ugly bruises on her sensitive skin. But personal love is a different thing . . . I love her character at a distance as it were and agree with her in all things that matter, but in the things that don't matter – the little everyday ways you like your bread buttered – that seems to me to call for love or aversion, and somehow our instincts about the punctillious are different."

However, at the end of her South African year she wrote to Margaret: "It's been a great year, *Geselle*, and I owe it all to you." (She called Margaret "Gretchen Geselle" – fellow-worker.)

SAUER, J. W. (1850–1903) and Mary (b. Cloete, 1863–1937)
The Sauers often had E. H. as guest at their farm Uitkijk in the Stellenbosch district. E. H. was especially drawn to the beautiful, generous, garden-loving Mrs. Sauer, but also much enjoyed the wide reading, and the teasing and sometimes caustic wit of Mr. Sauer. Sauer was a good parliamentarian and an eloquent if sometimes sharp and sarcastic speaker. He served successively in the cabinets of Scanlen, Rhodes, W. P. Schreiner and Botha and for 40 years almost continuously represented the constituency of Aliwal North where he, like his father, had practised as a lawyer.

Mary Sauer was a daughter of Hendrik Cloete of the historic wine-farm Groot Constantia, whose vineyard was so disastrously stricken by phylloxera in the late nineteenth century.

Of the Sauers, Smuts wrote to his wife:

"Zij zijn lieve menschen en vooral zij is een voorbeeldige Afrikanerin (kan echter niet Hollands spreken)". (They are dear people and she especially is an exemplary Afrikaner woman (but can speak no Dutch)). (*The Smuts Papers*, vol. II, p. 208.) At the time of Sauer's death Merriman said that though he had no drop of English blood in his veins, "his views on just government were more English than often the English themselves" and that he was "steeped in the highest traditions of English public life."

Paul Oliver Sauer (the Sauers' son named for their close friend Olive Schreiner) became a cabinet minister when the Nationalist Party took power in 1948.

SCHREINER, Olive (1855–1920)

Olive Schreiner, daughter of a German-born Wesleyan missionary who later turned businessman, and of an English mother, was the ninth of twelve children of whom a younger brother, W. P. Schreiner, became prime minister of the Cape in 1898. Olive had little formal education but was widely read and able to make a living as a governess on remote Karoo farms before breaking into fame with *The Story of an African Farm* (1883) which she took to Britain and published under the pseudonym Ralph Iron, and which led to a memorable friendship with Havelock Ellis, pioneer writer on sexual psychology. In 1884 Olive married Samuel Cronwright, a Cradock farmer who became a member of the Cape legislative assembly (he changed his name to Cronwright-Schreiner in deference to Olive's views on equal rights for women). Her passionate championship of the Boer cause in speeches and pamphlets, her fight for equal rights for women and her high-minded idealism struck a chord in E. H.

E. H. first met Olive Schreiner when the latter came with mutual friends to greet her at Beaufort West, on her way to the ruined districts of the former republics in 1903. Before she left South Africa in 1908 E. H. visited the Cronwright-Schreiners at De Aar, where they were then living.

Among E. H.'s papers are several letters from Olive Schreiner, mercifully copied in E. H.'s more legible hand.

On 7 July 1903 she wrote to E. H. from the Sauer farm Uitkijk:

> "... It was a great pleasure to me to meet you: not only as one who has done so much for our women, but for yourself even more. It seemed like a bit of my old past coming back to me. I hope it has not tired you very much to travel about. I never forget how pale you got suddenly that evening you were sitting by the window; but I know you will have met loving friends everywhere, I hope I shall see you again sometime . . ."

On 8 October 1903 she wrote from Hanover, where she then lived:

> "I am afraid you must be very, very tired. No one who does not know the country can realize all the simple hard labour you have gone through. I sympathized greatly with your letter in *The South African News* [of 16 August 1903] about the Difficulty and Complexity of distributing to the needy wisely and rightly and justly ... It is wonderful how to give the least bit of effective and wise help takes time and thought. I don't know how you got through all you have done. I do so wish I could see you, if only for a day before you go."

The preface to *Die Smarte van die Oorlog* (1924), the Afrikaans version of *The Brunt of the War*, is a translation of a letter Olive Schreiner wrote to E. H. on reading the *Brunt* which appeared in late 1902:

"Ek het u boek gelees. Onder die omstandighede moet ek oordeel dat u die onderwerp op bewonderenswaardige wyse behandel het. Dit is onverbeterlik. Baie Hollands-sprekende mense het my versoek om die boek vir hulle in Hollands te bestel.

"Ek beskou dat u meer doeltreffende en nuttige werk in Suid-Afrika gedoen het vir die saak van algemene menslikheid en reg as enige ander persoon in staat was om te doen. U het nie honderde nie, maar ongetwyfeld duisende lewens gered. Ek vrees u werk sal nadelige en blywende merktekens op u gestel laat. So 'n tyd van worsteling en onreg gaan nie in 'n mens se klere sit nie. [. . .]

"Hierdie is net om 'n woord van bewondering vir u boek uit te spreek, u boek met sy kragtige selfbeheer en diep gevoel."

(Re-translated: "I have read your book. In the circumstances I think you have treated the subject admirably. It can't be bettered. Many Dutch-speaking people have asked me to order the Dutch edition for them.

"In my view you have done more effective and useful work in South Afrca in the cause of common humanity than anyone else could have done. You have saved not hundreds but doubtlessly thousands of lives. I fear the work will leave injurious and lasting scars upon your system. Such a time of struggle and injustice leaves its mark. [. . .]

"This is only to express a word of admiration for your book with its powerful self-control and deep feeling.")

As the *Vrouwen-Dag* section of letters shows, E. H. was in 1913 much concerned that Olive Schreiner should be given her rightful place at the unveiling ceremony of the women's memorial at Bloemfontein. They became estranged, however, when E. H., at the time of World War I, refused to break with Smuts, who had confounded his pacifist friends by joining the British war cabinet. (Letter to May Murray Parker, 18 September 1918, Hammersmith – in the collection of Mrs. Parker's papers at the Jagger Library, University of Cape Town.)

Mutual friends were Anna Purcell, Betty Molteno and Alice M. Greene.

SMUTS, J. C. (1870–1950), and S. M. (Isie b. Krige, 1870–1954)
Judging from the voluminous correspondence preserved in the Smuts collection in the state archives in Pretoria, Smuts was the Boer leader to whom E. H. felt closest. Her letters to him are often playful and teasing and sometimes severely reprimanding on various public issues. He was, to her, soon no longer the general but affectionately "Oom Janie" or "Dear Oom" – significantly, for Mrs. Steyn, with whom she corresponded even more regularly, was to the end "Dearest Mrs. Steyn", with that touch of formality that apparently, in her view, was fitting for the wife of the former president of the Orange Free State.

Smuts had a gift for friendship with women of intelligence and indepent mind, although E. H.'s rather obsessive tendencies once made him describe her to his wife as "natuurlijk, zooals altijd, een klein beetje gek" (of course, as always, a little mad) and, on another occasion "een beetje lastig en natuurlijk, zooals altoos, tactloos" (a little troublesome and, of course, as always, tactless). At the same time he found her "heel lief" (very sweet) (*The Smuts Papers*, vol. III, pp. 473, 469 and 473, respectively). She, in turn, described him to Mrs. Steyn as a "dear, affectionate creature" (letter to Mrs. Steyn, 21 July 1921, in the Steyn collection).

Jan Christiaan Smuts, a farmer's son from Riebeek-West in the Cape, had had a brilliant academic career at Victoria college, Stellenbosch, which took him to Cambridge for even more striking academic distinctions. He qualified in law and became state-attorney of the South African Republic at the age of twenty-eight. Trusted by Kruger, he played a decisive role in the negotiations with Britain which led to the Anglo-Boer war. In that war he took a significant part, operating with general J. H. (Koos) de la Rey in the Western Transvaal and later leading his commando in a deep thrust into the Cape Colony. After the war he was the intellectual power behind the charismatic general Louis Botha in their policy of reconciliation and responsible government that lead to the union of South Africa and dominion status in the British commonwealth.

Isie Smuts was a woman of marked intelligence, though at this time primarily a homebody and devoted to her large family. E. H. was from 1903 a welcome guest in the Smuts house, first in Pretoria and later at their farm Doornkloof near Irene.

Margaret Clark, who became an even closer friend of the Smuts family, said theirs was "a funny household, not the most comfortable, but the people are delightful, invigorating and responsive and altogether satisfactory . . ."

Smuts found time to give E. H. advice on her business affairs and he spoke with feeling at the internment of her ashes at the women's memorial at Bloemfontein in 1926. "It was a great occasion," he wrote then to Oliver Hobhouse, "we buried her like a princess".

She, on her part, left him a small legacy.

STEYN, President Marthinus Theunis (1857–1916), and Rachel Isabella (Tibby, b. Fraser, 1865–1955).
E. H. set great store by her warm and lasting friendship with the former presidential couple of the Orange Free State. It evidently afforded her deep satisfaction to be so honoured and accepted in the highest Boer circles. She met many influential Boers – among them General J. B. M. Hertzog – when staying with them on their farm Onze Rust after the war.

President Steyn had enjoyed a legal education in the Netherlands and in England. He became President when he was thirty-nine. He had a breadth of vision which set him apart and enabled him to exercise great influence in public affairs, such as the making of the Union and the moderating of the rebellion in 1916, although he could then not, as an invalid, hold office.

His wife's parents, the Reverend and Mrs. Colin MacKenzie Fraser of Philippolis, were Scots. The loyalty Mrs. Steyn showed her husband and the dignity with which she bore the hardships of war and of his long illness earned her the high regard and gratitude of the Free State people. E. H. met Mrs. Steyn in January 1901 in Bloemfontein and kept close contact with her after leaving South Africa. They wrote to each other regularly – E. H.'s last letter to Mrs. Steyn was written a week before her death in 1926.

President Steyn's message to E. H. from Scheveningen (see p. 65) and his words about her at the unveiling of the women's memorial in 1913 (see p. 515) reflect his profound gratitude for the role she played in and after the war.

Alice M. Greene was on the *Carisbrooke Castle* on which the all but completely paralysed Steyn left South Africa for medical treatment in Europe in 1902. She was admitted to the Steyn cabin, and describes Mrs. Steyn "tenderly stroking his beard" as he said, referring to Miss Greene, " 'I should like to see one who has so loved our cause' or words to that effect. [. . .] For long afterwards I could only sit and feel what the actual meeting in the flesh had been with one of the noblest, if not the noblest, spirits of the age . . . I seem less and less able to resign myself to what these good people call 'the inevitable', and my great consolation – that Steyn himself said 'The end is not yet'. . ."

Of Mrs. Steyn's and E. H.'s friendship Margaret Clark remarked:

> "For Mrs. Steyn she had real affection. She would do anything for Mrs. Steyn and Mrs. Steyn for her."

It was through Mrs. Steyn that a Boer fund was started, enabling E. H. to buy a house of her own in St. Ives in Cornwall in 1921, and Mrs. Steyn was instrumental in having her ashes interred at the women's memorial at Bloemfontein.

References

Reference

Books

Amery, L.C.M.S., *The Times History of the war in South Africa*, 7 vols., Sampson Low, Marston & Co., London, 1900–05.

Barnard, C. J., *Louis Botha op die Natalse front, 1899–1900*, A. A. Balkema, Cape Town, 1970.

Davenport, R. J., *The Afrikaner Bond, the history of a South African political party, 1880–1911*, Oxford University Press, Cape Town, 1966.

Davey, Arthur M., *The British pro-Boers, 1877–1902*, Tafelberg Publishers, Cape Town, 1978.

–, (ed.) *Selected Correspondence of Lawrence Richardson 1902–1903*, Van Riebeeck Society, Second Series no. 8, Cape Town, 1977.

De Villiers, Dirk en Johanna, *Paul Sauer*, Tafelberg Publishers, Cape Town, 1977.

De Wet, C. R., *De Strijd tusschen Boer en Brit*, Höveker & Wormser, Amsterdam, 1902. *Three Years War, October 1899–June 1902*, Archibald Constable & Co., London, 1902.

Fawcett, Millicent Garrett, J. P., LL D, *What I remember*, T. Fischer Unwin Ltd., London, 1924.

Fisher, John, *That Miss Hobhouse. The life of a great feminist*, Secker & Warburg, London, 1971.

Fry, A. Ruth, *Emily Hobhouse. A memoir*, with a foreword by General J. C. Smuts, Jonathan Cape, London, 1929.

Gooch, G. P., *Life of Lord Courtney*, MacMillan & Co., London, 1920.

Grundlingh, A. M., *Die "hensoppers" en "joiners". Die rasionaal van verraad*, HAUM, Pretoria, 1979.

Gutsche, Thelma, *There was a man. The life and times of Sir Arnold Theiler, K.C.M.G., of Onderstepoort*, Howard Timmins, Cape Town, 1979.

Hancock, W. K., and Jean van der Poel (ed.), *Selections from the Smuts papers*, vols. I, II and III, Cambridge University Press, London, 1966.

Headlam, C. (ed.) *The Milner papers*, 2 vols., Cassell & Co., London, 1933.

Emily Hobhouse, *The Brunt of the War and where it fell*, Methuen & Co., London, 1902.

–, *War without glamour. Women's war experiences written by themselves, 1899–1902. Historical records collected and translated by Emily Hobhouse*, Nasionale Pers, Bloemfontein [1927].

–, *Die smarte van die oorlog en wie dit gely het* (translated by N. J. van der Merwe), Nasionale Pers, Cape Town (Die Burger leeskring, vol. 3, no. 6), 1923.

Hofmeyr, J. H., in collaboration with F. W. Reitz, *Onze Jan Hofmeyr*, Van de Sandt de Villiers, Cape Town, 1913.

Hobson, J. A., and Morris Ginsberg, *L. T. Hobhouse. His life and work. With selected essays and articles*, George Allen & Unwin, London, 1931.

James, Angela, and Nina Hills, *Mrs John Brown, 1847–1935. An account of her social work in Lancashire and South Africa, of her memories of Lancashire folk and of her friendship with Olive Schreiner*, John Murray, London, 1937.

Kestell, J. D., *Through Shot and Flame. The adventures and experiences of J. D. Kestell, chaplain to President Steyn and General Christiaan de Wet*, Methuen & Co., London, 1903.

Kestell, J. D., and D. E. van Velden, *The Peace negotiations between the Government of the South African Republic and the Orange Free State and the Representatives of the British Government which terminated in the Peace concluded at Vereeniging on the 31st May 1902*, Richard Clay & Son, London, 1908.

–, *Die Vredesonderhandelinge* (translated by F. J. le Roux in collaboration with D. J. van Zyl), Human & Rousseau Publishers, Cape Town, 1982.

Lewsen, Phyllis, *John X. Merriman*, Ad Donker, Johannesburg, and Yale University Press, 1982.

MacDonald, J. Ramsay, *What I saw in South Africa, September and October 1903*, The Echo, London, 1903.

Owen, John, *L. T. Hobhouse, sociologist*, in the series *Sociology in the making*, Thomas Nelson & Sons, London, 1974.

Pakenham, Thomas, *The Boer War*, Jonathan Ball Publishers, Johannesburg, and Wiedenfeld & Nicholson, London, 1979.

Quiller-Couch, Sir Arthur (ed.), *The Oxford book of ballads* (1963 edition), Oxford, 1910.

Roberts, Austin, *Birds of South Africa* (revised by G. R. MacLachlan & R. Liversage), Central News Agency for the trustees of the South African Bird Book Fund, Johannesburg, 1957.

Wright, Harrison M. (ed.), *Sir James Rose Innes. Selected Correspondence, 1884–1902*, Van Riebeeck Society, second series, no. 3, Cape Town, 1982.

Schoeman, Karel, *Bloemfontein*, Human & Rousseau Publishers, Cape Town, 1981.

Solomon, Vivian (ed.), *Selections from the correspondence of Percy Alport Molteno, 1892–1914*, Van Riebeeck Society, second series, no. 12, Cape Town, 1981.

Spies, S. B., *Methods of Barbarism? Roberts and Kitchener and civilians in the Boer republics: January 1900–May 1902*, Human & Rousseau Publishers, 1977.

Stockenström, Eric E., *Die Afrikaanse vrou. Die vrou in die geskiedenis van die Hollands-Afrikaanse volk. 'n Beknopte oorsig van die rol wat die vrou gespeel het in die 350 jaar tussen 1658 en 1915*, Pro Ecclesia, Stellenbosch, 1921.

Theal, G. M., *The history of South Africa from the founding of the European settlement to our own times*, 7 vols., London, 1888–1900.

Visagie, L. A., *Terug na Kommando. Avonture van Willie Steyn en vier ander krygsgevangenes*, Nasionale Pers, Cape Town, 1932.

Van Heerden Petronella, *Kerssnuitsels*, Tafelberg Publishers, Cape Town, 1963.

Warwick, Peter, *Black People and the South African War, 1899–1902*, Ravan Press, Johannesburg, 1983.

Wrench, J. E., *Alfred Lord Milner. The man of no illusions*, Eyre & Spottiswoode, London, 1958.

Dictionary of National Biography.
South African Biographical Dictionary.
Standard Encyclopaedia of Southern Africa.

Unpublished material

Emily Hobhouse, First draft of a memoir in the President M. T. Steyn collection, A 156, state archives, Bloemfontein.

–, Letters and documents not incorporated in the memoir, Steyn Collection, state archives, Bloemfontein.

–, Material collected for *War without glamour*, state archives, Bloemfontein.

Clark (Gillett) Margaret, Letters in the C. Smuts–Clark collection, A 357, state archives, Bloemfontein; diary personally made available to the editor in 1960.

Molteno, E. M., Papers in the Jagger Library, University of Cape Town.

Murray Parker, May, Papers in the Jagger Library, University of Cape Town.

Rowntree (Wilkinson), Marion, Letters to Ken Wilkinson, personally made available to the editor in 1961.

Pamphlets and periodicals

Government Gazette of the Cape Colony, 1901.

Government Gazette of the Orange River Colony, 1903.

Hobhouse, Emily, To the committee of the South African Distress Fund. *Report* of a visit to the camps of women and children in the Cape and Orange River Colonies, printed and published by the Friars Printing Association, Ltd., London [1901].

–, A letter [on her arrest and deportation] to the committee of the South African Women and Children's Fund, to be obtained from the The Argus Printing Co., Ltd., London [1901].

–, *Vrouwen-Dag*, 16 December 1913, Atlas Drukkerij, Cape Town, 1913.

–, *Reports* of the committee of the Boer Home Industries and Aid Society – January, 1905 to March 1906; May, 1907; Dec., 1908.

Imperial Blue Books, Cd 893, Report on the concentration camps in South Africa by the Ladies' Commission.

South African Conciliation Committee leaflets and pamphlets. National Press Agency, London, 1899–1902.

Southern Africa Quaker Newsletter, Johannesburg series, no. 117, July/August 1981.

Newspapers

The Bloemfontein Post, 1901.
The Cape Times, 1903.
Ons Land.
The Transvaal Leader, 1903.
De Zuid-Afrikaan Vereenigd met *Ons Land*, 1901.
S. A. News, 1903.

Illustrations

Africana Museum, Johannesburg: 28, 47
Archives, state:
  Cape 5 (VA 784), 6 (VA 328), 23 (VA 4556), 41 (VA 3183), 42 (VA 3186), 43 (VA 3187), 44 (VA 3182), 51 (VA 4971)
  Pretoria 21, 27, 54
Dreyer, Kas: 56
Family collections: 2, 7, 8, 10, 17, 19, 20, 22, 24, 25, 29
Independent Film Centre: 45, 46, 50, 52, 53
Museum of cultural history, Pretoria: 11, 49
National Museum, Bloemfontein: 16
Oranje Girls' High School, Bloemfontein: 12
Pretoria City Council: 4, 48
War Museum of the Boer Republics, Bloemfontein: 1, 3, 9, 13, 14, 15, 18, 26, 30, 31, 32, 33, 34, 35, 36, 37, 38, 39, 40, 55

Index